Global Perspectives on Social Media Usage Within Governments

Chandan Chavadi
Presidency Business School, Presidency College, Bengaluru, India

Dhanabalan Thangam
Presidency Business School, Presidency College, Bengaluru, India

A volume in the Advances in Social Networking
and Online Communities (ASNOC) Book Series

Published in the United States of America by
    IGI Global
    Information Science Reference (an imprint of IGI Global)
    701 E. Chocolate Avenue
    Hershey PA, USA 17033
    Tel: 717-533-8845
    Fax: 717-533-8661
    E-mail: cust@igi-global.com
    Web site: http://www.igi-global.com

Library of Congress Cataloging-in-Publication Data

Title: Global perspectives on social media usage within governments /
    edited by Chandan Chavadi, and Dhanabalan Thangam.
Description: Hershey, PA : Information Science Reference, [2023] | Includes
    bibliographical references and index. | Summary: "Global Perspectives on
    Social Media Usage Within Governments reveals the best practices of
    various countries regarding the use of social media by central and local
    governments according to public administration models. The book presents
    various case studies on the impact of public administration models on
    social media use in order to contribute to public administration and
    social media use. Covering topics such as climate action, knowledge
    behaviors, and citizen participation, this premier reference source is
    an essential resource for government officials, public administrators,
    public policy scholars, social media experts, public affairs scholars,
    students and educators of higher education, librarians, researchers, and
    academicians"-- Provided by publisher.
Identifiers: LCCN 2023017290 (print) | LCCN 2023017291 (ebook) | ISBN
    9781668474501 (h/c) | ISBN 9781668474549 (s/c) | ISBN 9781668474518
    (ebk)
Subjects: LCSH: Internet in public administration--Cross-cultural studies.
    | Social media--Political aspects. | Mass media--Political aspects.
Classification: LCC JF1525.A8 G563 2023 (print) | LCC JF1525.A8 (ebook) |
    DDC 351.0285/4678--dc23/eng/20230520
LC record available at https://lccn.loc.gov/2023017290
LC ebook record available at https://lccn.loc.gov/2023017291

This book is published in the IGI Global book series Advances in Social Networking and Online Communities (ASNOC)
(ISSN: 2328-1405; eISSN: 2328-1413)

British Cataloguing in Publication Data
A Cataloguing in Publication record for this book is available from the British Library.

All work contributed to this book is new, previously-unpublished material. The views expressed in this book are those of the
authors, but not necessarily of the publisher.

For electronic access to this publication, please contact: eresources@igi-global.com.

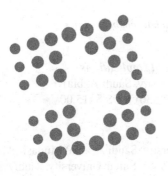

Advances in Social Networking and Online Communities (ASNOC) Book Series

Hakikur Rahman

Ansted University Sustainability Research Institute, Malaysia

ISSN:2328-1405
EISSN:2328-1413

MISSION

The advancements of internet technologies and the creation of various social networks provide a new channel of knowledge development processes that's dependent on social networking and online communities. This emerging concept of social innovation is comprised of ideas and strategies designed to improve society.

The **Advances in Social Networking and Online Communities** book series serves as a forum for scholars and practitioners to present comprehensive research on the social, cultural, organizational, and human issues related to the use of virtual communities and social networking. This series will provide an analytical approach to the holistic and newly emerging concepts of online knowledge communities and social networks.

COVERAGE

- Knowledge Communication and the Role of Communities and Social Networks
- Challenges of Knowledge Management
- Networks and Knowledge Communication in R&D Environments
- Organizational Knowledge Communication
- Networks as Institutionalized Intermediaries of KC
- Epistemology of Knowledge Society
- General Importance and Role of Knowledge Communities
- Importance and Role of Knowledge Communities in R&D and Innovative Knowledge Creation
- Leveraging Knowledge Communication Networks – Approaches to Interpretations and Interventions
- Learning Utilities

IGI Global is currently accepting manuscripts for publication within this series. To submit a proposal for a volume in this series, please contact our Acquisition Editors at Acquisitions@igi-global.com or visit: http://www.igi-global.com/publish/.

Titles in this Series

For a list of additional titles in this series, please visit: www.igi-global.com/book-series

701 East Chocolate Avenue, Hershey, PA 17033, USA
Tel: 717-533-8845 x100 • Fax: 717-533-8661
E-Mail: cust@igi-global.com • www.igi-global.com

Table of Contents

Chapter 18
>   *Ravishankar Krishnan, Vel Tech Rangarajan Dr. Sagunthala R&D Institute of Science and
>   Technology, India*
>   *Logasakthi Kandasamy, Universal Business School, Universal AI University, India*
>   *Elantheraiyan Perumal, Vel Tech Rangarajan Dr. Sagunthala R&D Institute of Science and
>   Technology, India*
>   *M. S. R. Mariyappan, VelTech Rangarajan Dr. Sagunthala R&D Institute of Science and
>   Technology, India*
>   *K. Sankar Ganesh, Sharda University, Uzbekistan*
>   *Manoj Govindaraj, VelTech Rangarajan Dr. Sagunthala R&D Institute of Science and
>   Technology, India*
>   *Anil B. Malali, Department of Commerce and Management, Acharya Institutes, India*

Detailed Table of Contents

Chapter 1
    Chandan Chavadi, Presidency Business School, Presidency College, Bengaluru, India
    G. Manoj, Vel Tech Rangarajan Dr. Sagunthala R&D Institute of Science and Technology, India
    Sathis Kumar Ganesan, Populus Empowerment Network, India
    Sendhilkumar Manoharan, Presidency Business School, Presidency College, Bengaluru, India
    Dhanabalan Thangam, Presidency Business School, Presidency College, Bengaluru, India

In the present era of information, social media has risen as the primary channel for engagement. Platforms like Facebook, Twitter, YouTube, and others possess the capability to bring about significant changes. They have been instrumental in activities ranging from the downfall of governments to the amplification of political campaigns, the facilitation of public protests, the enablement of social demonstrations, and the initiation of social campaigns. Moreover, these platforms promote communication, dialogue, and awareness within public forums, serving as immediate sources of news and information. Within the dynamic landscape of communication evolution, the interconnected population now enjoys unprecedented access to information, expanded opportunities for public discourse, and enhanced potential for collective action.

Chapter 2
    Nadia Sha, Dhofar University, Oman
    Bitha S. Mani, Rajadhani Business School, India
    B. Ganesh, Am Maxwell International Institute for Education and Research, India
    Sankar Ganesh, Veltech Rangarajan Dr. Sagunthala R&D Institute of Science and Technology, India
    R. Velmurugan, Karpagam Academy of Higher Education, India
    J. Sudarvel, Karpagam Academy of Higher Education, India

Social media's influence extends to policymaking, as governments are now more attentive to public sentiment and demands voiced on these platforms. Additionally, social media enables international collaboration and diplomacy, enhancing global governance efforts. In conclusion, social media's influence on governments' operational aspects is undeniable. While it has fostered greater transparency, public engagement, and crisis communication, its impact also necessitates careful management to mitigate potential risks. Governments must harness the power of social media responsibly to ensure a positive and transformative influence on their operations and better serve their citizens.

Mirshad Rahman, Department of Social Work, Acharya Institute of Graduate Studies, India
Madhusudanan Sundaresan, Department of Social Work, Dwaraka Doss Goverdhan Doss Vaishnav College, India
Akhila, Department of Social Work, Sree Sankaracharya University of Sanskrit, India
Bagavathi C., Department of Social Work, Vellalar College for Women, India
Kumaraswamy Channabasaiah, Department of Social Work, Acharya Institute of Graduate Studies, India

Social workers must navigate issues related to client privacy, boundary management, and maintaining professional integrity online. The potential risks of misinformation, cyberbullying, and burnout demand careful attention and responsible usage. Despite these challenges, social media's positive impact on social workers cannot be ignored. It has empowered them to stay informed about the latest developments, trends, and best practices in their profession. As social media continues to evolve, it is crucial for social workers to embrace these technological tools thoughtfully and responsibly, harnessing their potential for enhancing collaboration and advancing social work practice.

David Winster Praveenraj D, CHRIST University (Deemed), India
E. Sudha, CHRIST University (Deemed), India
R. Hariharan, CHRIST University (Deemed), India
R. Vedapradha, Mount Carmel College (Autonomous), India
J. Ashok, CHRIST University (Deemed), India

A digital transformation endeavor is the use of technology and digital processes to enhance business operations and consumer experiences. These projects frequently include the use of new technology like social media platforms, artificial intelligence (AI), and analytics, as well as the execution of digital processes like cloud computing, omnichannel commerce, data analytics, and automation. An organization needs to integrate digital transformation initiatives into its current systems if it wants to stay current with the rapidly evolving technology landscape of today. Social media is now an essential part of contemporary life, and businesses are increasingly using it to connect with their clients and other stakeholders. To take advantage of social media's huge potential, businesses are incorporating it into their digital transformation initiatives.

Chapter 5

Thirupathi Manickam, CHRIST University (Deemed), India
S. Gopalakrishnan, East Point College of Higher Education, India
P. K. Hridhya, CHRIST University (Deemed), India
V. Ravi, CHRIST University (Deemed), India
Devarajanayaka Kalenahalli Muniyanayaka, University of Buraimi, Oman
Haritha Muniraju, Triveni Institute of Commerce and Management, India
B. Seenivasan, Sacred Heart College (Autonomous), India

Due to technological innovation, the economy is transitioning from a market-driven to a network-oriented status, and social media has seized the leading I.T. trends in the technology sector. A paradigm change in banking and finance operations has occurred due to the upswing in innovation, transformation, and digitalisation in Indian banking and financial organisations. The development of online banking, mobile apps, mobile banking, and tools like debit and credit cards has changed how customers utilise banking and financing services. Thanks to social media and digital marketing, banks may now be practical tools for supporting customers' enterprises and gaining target prospects. To provide customers with rapid and efficient service in the post-pandemic age, Indian banks and financial institutions are rushing to modernise their technology infrastructure and digital goods. Social media offers users attractive options for 24-hour access to information and the use of financial services across temporal and geographic boundaries.

Chapter 6

S. Baranidharan, CHRIST University (Deemed), India
Amirdha Vasani Sankarkumar, SRM Institute of Science and Technology, India
G. Chandrakala, Dayananda Sagar University, India
Raja Narayanan, Dayananda Sagar University, India
K. Sathyanarayana, Presidency University, India

This systematic review examined the role of social media in enhancing financial literacy among individuals by collecting and reviewing 60 articles published from 2021 to 2023. The findings revealed that social media has a positive impact on financial literacy through the dissemination of financial education, promotion of financial awareness, and sharing of financial experiences. The review also identified digital financial literacy, entrepreneurial learning, and financial knowledge as significant determinants of financial literacy, while demographic characteristics, social media usage behavior, risk attitude, and overconfidence played a role in determining financial literacy. The study recommends that financial institutions, policymakers, and educators leverage social media for promoting financial literacy, and social media usage skills to improve financial literacy among individuals. Overall, the study suggests that the use of social media can democratize financial literacy and enable individuals from diverse backgrounds to access financial education and information.

Satheesh Pandian Murugan, Arumugam Pillai Seethai Ammal College, India

Rani J. Devika, Department of Economics, Mannar Thirumalai Naicker College, India

Vimala Govindaraju, University Malaysia Sarawak, Malaysia

Ramakrishna Narasimhaiah, Department of Economics, Jain University (Deemed), Bengaluru, India

H. L. Babu, Srinidhi College of Education, Bengaluru, India

Ravindran Kandasamy, Presidency Business School, Presidency College, India

Shouvik Sanyal, Department of Marketing and Entrepreneurship, Dhofar University, Oman

Climate change remains a threatening issue to humanity, and lots of people still think of climate change as a growing issue that needs regular measures to curtail it. However, it is not such an easy task to influence a huge mass, but now it has become possible by social media. Because the role played by social media is enormously huge nowadays and many are relying on the internet to gain knowledge, gather data, and socialize. A 16 year old Swedish environmental activist Greta Thunberg has used social media to raise her voice against climate change and started her first school strike, Fridays For Future, against this in August 2018 at the Swedish parliament. In propagating this narrative, she uses various social media and digital platforms to attract people and institutions in developing a climate activist movement with a united voice and intention. This chapter reveals Greta's social media activity, how Greta uses the affordances of social media to frame the climate crisis and to build a worldwide action-based conversation.

Chapter 8

Vidhya Shanmugam, Amity Business School, Amity University, Haryana, India

V. Gowrishankkar, Sri Krishna College of Technology, India

S. Sibi, School of Management, Sri Krishna College of Technology, India

Sudha Maheswari T., PSGR Krishnammal College for Women, India

Vijay Bose S, Vaagdevi College of Engineering, India

Murali Mora, Vaagdevi College of Engineering, India

Senthilkumar Chandramohan, Arsi University, Ethiopia

M. Maruthamuthu, Department of Business Administration, Government Arts and Science College, Kadayanallur, India

Irshad Nazeer, Presidency Business School, Presidency College, India

In the digital age, social media has emerged as a powerful tool for communication, networking, and information sharing. Its widespread popularity and accessibility have led to its adoption by governments worldwide to reach the public effectively. This chapter explores the role of social media in bridging the gap between government initiatives for human resource development (HRD) and the public. It examines how social media platforms have transformed the way governments communicate HRD policies, initiatives, and opportunities to citizens, fostering greater engagement, transparency, and inclusivity. The chapter also highlights the potential challenges and ethical considerations associated with the use of social media in HRD initiatives. Social media's integration with government HRD initiatives has immense potential to enhance access to resources, promote skill development, and empower individuals in the modern workforce.

The pandemic is anticipated to have a significant economic impact, and it already has a terrible effect on schooling worldwide. Due to the coronavirus's quick spread, educational institutions worldwide are making the drastic leap from delivering course materials in person to doing so online. The rapid use of digital technology represents a significant paradigm change that may ultimately transform the Indian educational system. The COVID-19 scenario provides an opportunity to test new tools and technology to make education more relevant for students who cannot travel to campuses. With online learning and evaluation, there is a chance to increase knowledge and productivity while acquiring new skill sets and expedited professional talents. In this chapter, the authors have examined the educational difficulties and opportunities brought on by the sudden COVID-19 epidemic, followed by a discussion of how the Indian educational system has to be recalibrated.

The topic of media psychology is multidisciplinary, and people's interactions with media in many spheres of their lives from work to education to entertainment to social engagement are ever-evolving. By fusing a comprehension of human behaviour, cognition, and emotion with a comparable comprehension of media technology, media psychologists seek to provide answers to these problems. As the globe gets more linked, media is now present in practically every aspect of life and is becoming a more essential field of study. Media psychology, in contrast to some media studies, is not merely about the content. Media psychology takes the entire system into account. Understanding the effects of technology depends heavily on psychology. By merging their knowledge of human behaviour, cognition, and emotion, media psychologists seek out answers and solutions.

Chapter 11

Durairaj Duraisamy, School of Management, CMR University, India
Chethan Shivaram, Department of Management Studies, Acharya Institute of Graduate
Studies, India
N. Nethravathi, Department of Business Administration, Acharya Institute of Technology, India
K. Y. Anusha, Department of Management Studies, Acharya Institute of Graduate Studies, India
Kanchan Rajput, ISBR Research Centre, India
Mathiraj Subramanian, Department of Cooperate Secretaryship, Alagappa University, India
Shaila Kedla, Department of Commerce, Acharya Institute of Graduate Studies, India
Raghu Narayana Reddy, Presidency Business School, Presidency College, India
Kiran Hiremath, Presidency Business School, Presidency College, India

This chapter emphasizes the importance of compliance with data protection regulations and maintaining customer privacy. Finally, the framework offers strategic recommendations for Indian banks to optimize their social media presence, including the development of robust social media policies, integration with existing customer service channels, and investment in analytics to gain valuable insights from user interactions. Overall, this framework provides valuable insights for Indian banks seeking to harness the potential of social media to stay competitive, build customer trust, and enhance their overall operational efficiency in the dynamic digital landscape.

Chapter 12

Ravishankar Krishnan, Vel Tech Rangarajan Dr. Sagunthala R&D Institute of Science and
Technology, India
Rajalakshmi Vel, Sri Ramachandra Institute of Higher Education and Research, India
Priyanka Zala, GLS University, India
S. Thandayuthapani, Vel Tech Rangarajan Dr. Sagunthala R&D Institute of Science and
Technology, India
H. Moideen Batcha, B.S. Abdur Rahman Crescent Institute of Science and Technology, India
Kalyani Velusamy, DMI-St. Eugene University, Malawi
Theju Kumar Chandrappa, Department of Criminology and Forensic Science, Acharya
Institute of Graduate Studies, India

Social media offers great power and potential to all kinds of users, and it is not free from threats and risks that come along with the adoption of new tools and innovations. There is cyber stalking, sexting, bullying happening substantially. Anonymity of the virtual world has contributed to online harassment and lack of awareness. This research assesses the awareness and perception of female college students of Indian universities. The opinion of senior government officials in regulating social media to improve cyber resilience is sought. Using judgement sampling technique, 463 responses were collected through questionnaire method. The majority of respondents perceive social media as a useful place for infotainment. There is awareness however that respondents don't want to limit themselves and they are open to posting pictures, tweeting, commenting on unknown posts. Among many online platforms, incidence of cyber harassment is high on social media platforms. The main contribution of this study is to emphasize the need to treat cyber behaviour as a foundational course in today's parallel world.

Chapter 13

Munir Ahmad, Survey of Pakistan, Pakistan

This chapter explored the use of social media geographic information in governance and policy-making. Social media geographic information has great potential to impact decision-making, citizen engagement, service delivery, crisis management, innovation, policy formation and evaluation, and public opinion assessment. However, challenges such as data quality, privacy concerns, data overload, standardization, limited access, ethics, technical issues, language barriers, and limited geographic coverage also arose. To address these challenges, policymakers should establish clear guidelines, ensure data accuracy, address privacy concerns, manage data overload, and promote ethical practices. Real-world applications in disaster response, traffic management, urban planning, air quality monitoring, disease outbreak tracking, and flood monitoring are also described. By harnessing social media geographic information while addressing challenges, policymakers can make informed decisions that benefit society.

Chapter 14

Yosephina Ohoiwutun, Cenderawasih University, Indonesia
M. Zaenul Muttaqin, Cenderawasih University, Indonesia
Ilham Ilham, Cenderawasih University, Indonesia
Vince Tebay, Cenderawasih University, Indonesia

This chapter aims to explore further how forms of public service innovation are applied in Jayapura City during the pandemic. Several highlights are the chapter's main focus, so the authors divide them into several sections. The first section reviews the implementation of electronic governance (e-governance). Then the second part describes how electronic-based services at the Jayapura City Disdukcapil were before the pandemic. The last section reveals the electronic-based service system during the pandemic. This study is a qualitative study using a research approach based on a literature study. The Jayapura City Population and Civil Registration Service (Disdukcapil) utilizes advances in digital technology by giving birth to various innovations to improve the quality of public service delivery in the field of population administration. The innovations are accessed online without coming to the Dukcapil office.

Chapter 15

Rebant Juyal, Assam University, India

This chapter explores the importance of the right to privacy, its impact on society, and the threats to privacy rights from technology. The right to privacy is a fundamental human right that protects individuals from unwarranted intrusion into their personal lives. It has a significant impact on society by ensuring that individuals can exercise their rights and freedoms without interference from others. However, with the rise of technology, the right to privacy has come under threat. The use of digital technology has led to an unprecedented level of surveillance and data collection, raising concerns about the potential for abuse of power by governments and private entities. This chapter examines the various ways in which privacy rights are being eroded and the measures that can be taken to protect these rights. The conclusion highlights the importance of respecting individuals' privacy rights and the need to ensure that they are protected in today's digital age.

Chapter 16

> *S. P. W. S. K. Karunarathna, Sabaragamuwa University of Sri Lanka, Sri Lanka*
> *U. A. Piumi Ishanka, Sabaragamuwa University of Sri Lanka, Sri Lanka*
> *Banujan Kuhaneswaran, Sabaragamuwa University of Sri Lanka, Sri Lanka*

The emergence of COVID-19 emanating from Wuhan, China in December 2019 has deeply affected society at every level, impacting areas like public health, social well-being, and local economies globally. The study highlights mental health and its impact on social behavior during pandemics. The authors analyze Sri Lankan individuals' mental health issues through tweets presented using sentiment analysis techniques. A rigorous data preparation process was completed before filtering categorized data into three distinct groups: 'experience', 'information', and 'counseling'. Three different machine learning algorithms were utilized for sentiment analysis, including ANN, LSTM, and SVM. In addition, the Latent Dirichlet Allocation technique was employed to identify topics from tweets during four waves of the COVID-19 outbreak, analyzing people's mental status and identifying conditions present. The findings contribute significantly to the evolving field of psychology during these trying times caused by COVID-19, providing much-needed guidance on implementing relevant support mechanisms.

Chapter 17

> *Suvarna V. Nimbagal, KLE Technological University, India*
> *Ansumalini Panda, KLE Technological University, India*
> *Srushti Kulkarni, KLE Technological University, India*
> *Shrushti Bilebhavi, KLE Technological University, India*
> *G. S. Hiremath, KLE Technological University, India*

Governments recognized that an increasing number of citizens are present on social networks rather than government websites. Reviewing the effects that social media have had on government, as well as the role that these new technologies have played and the implications they have for the future, appears pertinent. This is true given that the Indian government predicts that information and communication technologies-enabled services will significantly affect economic growth, inclusion, and quality of life, and that the extensive use of social media for communication ensures awareness and transparency in the government's objectives and strategies for implementing various schemes. Social networking software and social media have evolved into tools for communication, entertainment, and change, and it is reasonable to believe that they will continue to have an impact on our world. This chapter uses applications like Facebook, Twitter, and Instagram to develop a case study-based framework for assessing communication effectiveness on social networks in India.

This study investigates the factors influencing youth intention to adopt digital currency and explores the impact of social media and government initiatives on their attitudes and behaviors. The variables perceived ease of use, dissemination of information, responsibility, liability, translucency, and perceived usefulness are used to study the impact of digital adoption. Employing a judgmental study approach, including questionnaire survey and qualitative inputs, this research covered 337 samples and aims to provide comprehensive insights. The findings of this research hold significant implications for policymakers, financial institutions, and social media platforms. By understanding the role of social media and government initiatives, effective strategies can be developed to encourage digital currency adoption among the youth. Addressing potential barriers and leveraging influencers and trusted sources can enhance youth engagement with digital currencies and stimulate economic growth.

Foreword

In an age defined by unprecedented connectivity and rapid technological advancement, the emergence of social media has ushered in a paradigm shift in the way governments interact with their citizens and the global community. The book you hold in your hands, *Global Perspectives on Social Media Usage Within Governments*, delves into the multifaceted tapestry of this digital transformation, offering a comprehensive exploration of the complex interplay between social media and governance on a global scale.

The 21ˢᵗ century has borne witness to an extraordinary confluence of events that have reshaped the contours of political discourse, public engagement, and diplomatic communication. From the Arab Spring movements that showcased the power of digital mobilization to the real-time diplomacy conducted on platforms like Twitter, Facebook, and Instagram, the landscape of governance is being redrawn. This book stands as a critical lens through which we can examine the intricate dynamics of this new era.

As our world becomes increasingly interconnected, the ways in which governments use social media have evolved beyond mere communication tools. These platforms have become vehicles for shaping public opinion, disseminating policy information, and fostering participatory democracy. The book's contributors, a distinguished array of scholars, practitioners, and analysts, come together to unpack this phenomenon through a series of thought-provoking essays that traverse continents, cultures, and contexts.

The volume opens with a panoramic view of the global landscape, setting the stage for deeper exploration. It emphasizes the diverse ways in which governments have embraced social media, from the integration of digital platforms into traditional governance structures to the creation of innovative digital governance models. The chapters that follow delve into specific case studies, each shedding light on a unique aspect of the complex relationship between social media and governmental functions.

Through richly detailed case studies, we witness the spectrum of possibilities that social media presents for governmental engagement. We delve into the digital town halls that bridge the gap between leaders and citizens, enabling direct participation and fostering a sense of ownership in governance. We explore how governments leverage social media to enhance transparency, providing citizens with a window into decision-making processes. From these examples, it becomes clear that social media has the potential to not only improve the efficiency of governance but also to bolster the legitimacy of government actions.

Yet, the book does not shy away from the challenges that this digital revolution poses. The perils of misinformation, the erosion of privacy, and the potential for manipulation are all examined with a critical eye. As the digital sphere blurs the lines between fact and fiction, the book underscores the importance of media literacy and ethical governance. It warns against the pitfalls of digital echo chambers, where information is curated to fit preconceived notions, and emphasizes the need for robust mechanisms to counter the spread of false information.

Central to this exploration is the concept of digital diplomacy, a new modality in international relations that reshapes the way nations interact on the global stage. The book elucidates how social media has transformed diplomacy into a real-time, interactive affair, allowing diplomats to communicate directly with citizens and foreign counterparts, transcending traditional diplomatic protocols. This transformation demands a nuanced understanding of cultural sensitivities, linguistic nuances, and the complexities of global communication.

As we navigate this brave new world, ethical considerations loom large. The book delves into the delicate balance governments must strike between security imperatives and the right to privacy and free expression. It highlights the ethical dilemmas surrounding data collection, surveillance, and the potential misuse of personal information. In a time when governments wield vast amounts of digital power, the responsible and ethical use of social media becomes an imperative.

Global Perspectives on Social Media Usage Within Governments is an invaluable compendium that captures the pulse of digital governance in the modern age. Its pages resonate with the voices of scholars who have meticulously dissected the dynamics of social media within the governmental sphere. Their insights, drawn from a rich mosaic of experiences and expertise, offer readers a panoramic view of the opportunities and challenges that lie ahead.

In closing, I commend the contributors for their scholarly rigor and commitment to unearthing the complexities of this ever-evolving landscape. Their collective efforts have yielded a volume that is both timely and timeless, providing a roadmap for navigating the uncharted terrain of digital governance. As we continue to grapple with the implications of social media on governance and society, may this book serve as an enduring source of knowledge, inspiration, and reflection.

Best Wishes,

Jin Yong Park
Konkuk School of Business, Konkuk University, Seoul, South Korea

Preface

In an era characterized by the rapid evolution of digital communication, the book *Global Perspectives on Social Media Usage Within Governments* offers a comprehensive exploration of the intricate interplay between social media platforms and the governing processes of nations worldwide. This volume brings together a diverse range of scholars, practitioners, and experts to illuminate the multifaceted dimensions of how governments across the globe leverage social media to engage with citizens, facilitate diplomatic communication, and shape public opinion.

The subject matter of this book delves into the complex relationship between social media and governance, examining the ways in which digital platforms have transformed the landscape of modern politics, diplomacy, and public administration. The chapters contained within provide an in-depth analysis of various facets of this relationship, offering a panoramic view of the opportunities, challenges, and ethical considerations that arise from the fusion of social media and governmental activities.

Hence, this book addresses the imperative to analyze and assess the concept of *Global Perspectives on Social Media Usage Within Governments* within the context of the digital world. With this objective in mind, the book delves into a variety of information from diverse contexts, aiming to connect the realms of social media, government, and socio-economic development.

This comprehensive book imparts valuable insights by encompassing crucial elements and facets of Social Media Usage within Governments. It sheds light on the current advancements amidst a social media-dominated world, capturing emerging trends and tendencies in both theory and practice. While exploring significant concerns, it evaluates the benefits, advancements, and contributions linked to the effective utilization of Social Media within the realm of government.

In this vein, the book seamlessly integrates theoretical and practical frameworks, merging conceptual viewpoints with real-world examples that include case studies from numerous countries, along with findings from conducted empirical studies. Encompassing a wide array of academic subjects, including Electronic-Based Service Innovation, Social Media's Impact on the Banking Sector, Media Psychology and Human Communication, Global Perspectives on Social Media Usage within Governments, the Dynamics of Social Media and Government Operations, Social Media's Influence on Social Workers, Smart Governance and Policy Formulation, Privacy Threats in the Digital Era, Government's Role in Combating Cyber Harassment and Cybercrime, Social Media's Role in Government Initiatives for Human Resource Development, Social Media's Contribution to Climate Action, Social Media's Role in Business Digital Transformation, Social Media and Digital Financial Literacy, and the Collaboration between Social Media and Government in the Realm of Digital Currency.

This book is structured into four principal sections, encompassing a total of seventeen chapters. These chapters have been meticulously chosen through a rigorous peer-review process. Furthermore, the book intentionally features diverse global regions, offering readers insights into country-specific instances, examples, and intricacies. A succinct overview of each chapter follows.

Chapter 1, "Global Perspectives on Social Media Usage Within Governments," points to the current information age being dominated by social media as the primary avenue for engagement. Platforms such as Facebook, Twitter, YouTube, and others have emerged as influential agents capable of catalyzing significant transformations. They have played pivotal roles, spanning from toppling governments to amplifying political movements, facilitating public protests, enabling social demonstrations, and kickstarting social campaigns. Furthermore, these platforms foster communication, dialogue, and awareness in public arenas, swiftly disseminating news and information. Amid the ever-evolving landscape of communication, the interconnected population now revels in unparalleled access to information, expanded prospects for public discourse, and heightened potential for unified action. Social media has become woven into the fabric of global civil society, involving a diverse spectrum of participants, ranging from ordinary citizens and activists to NGOs, telecommunications firms, software providers, and governments.

Chapter 2, "Impact of Social Media on Government Operational Dynamics," reveals that the sway of social media reaches into the realm of policy formulation, prompting governments to be increasingly attuned to the public's feelings and requests expressed through these channels. Moreover, social media facilitates cross-border teamwork and diplomacy, enriching endeavors in global governance. To sum up, the impact of social media on the functional aspects of governments is indisputable. While it has nurtured heightened openness, civic involvement, and crisis correspondence, its effects also call for cautious handling to minimize potential pitfalls. Governments must prudently wield the potential of social media to guarantee a constructive and revolutionary impact on their operations, thereby enhancing their service to citizens.

Chapter 3, "Impact of Social Media on Social Workers in the Digital Age," depicts within their role, social workers face the task of skillfully maneuvering through concerns associated with client confidentiality, establishing boundaries, and upholding their professional ethics in the online realm. The potential hazards tied to misinformation, cyberbullying, and burnout necessitates vigilant consideration and judicious engagement. Notwithstanding these hurdles, the favorable influence of social media on social workers remains undeniable. It has provided them with the means to stay attuned to the latest advancements, trends, and optimal strategies within their field. As social media progresses, it becomes imperative for social workers to prudently and conscientiously embrace these technological tools, leveraging their potential to foster collaboration and propel the advancement of social work practices.

Chapter 4, "Role of Social Media in the Digital Transformation of Business," presents digital transformation initiative involves leveraging technology and digital methodologies to elevate both business operations and consumer interactions. These undertakings commonly encompass the adoption of novel technologies such as social media platforms, artificial intelligence (AI), and analytics. Furthermore, they encompass the implementation of digital processes including cloud computing, omnichannel commerce, data analytics, and automation. For an organization to remain current in today's swiftly evolving technological landscape, it's imperative to seamlessly integrate digital transformation endeavors into its existing systems. Given the integral role that social media now plays in modern life, businesses are progressively utilizing it as a means to engage with their clients and other stakeholders. To tap into the vast potential offered by social media, businesses are incorporating it into their broader digital transformation initiatives.

Chapter 5, "Social Media Usage in Indian Banking and Financial Institutions," discloses that Owing to technological advancements, the economy is undergoing a shift from being market-driven to becoming more network-oriented. Social media has emerged as a frontrunner in the prevailing information technology trends within the technology sector. A significant shift in banking and financial operations has been brought about by the surge in innovation, transformation, and digitization within Indian banking and financial entities. The emergence of online banking, mobile apps, mobile banking, and tools like debit and credit cards has revolutionized the way customers engage with banking and financial services. Leveraging the potential of social media and digital marketing, banks are now positioned as practical resources to support customer businesses and attract potential clients. In response to the demands of the post-pandemic era, Indian banks and financial institutions are actively racing to modernize their technological infrastructure and digital offerings to provide customers with swift and efficient services. Through social media, users are presented with appealing avenues for round-the-clock access to information and the utilization of financial services, transcending both time and geographical constraints.

Chapter 6, "The Role of Social Media in Empowering Digital Financial Literacy," divulges that the impact of social media on enhancing individuals' financial literacy, comprising a comprehensive review of 60 articles published between 2021 and 2023. The outcomes illuminated that social media exerts a favorable influence on financial literacy by facilitating the distribution of financial education, fostering awareness about financial matters, and facilitating the exchange of personal financial experiences. Additionally, the assessment pinpointed digital financial literacy, entrepreneurial learning, and financial knowledge as key factors influencing financial literacy, while demographic characteristics, patterns of social media usage, risk propensity, and overconfidence emerged as pivotal determinants. Consequently, the research suggests that financial institutions, policymakers, and educators can capitalize on social media to bolster financial literacy and enhance social media proficiency, ultimately heightening financial knowledge among individuals. In summation, the study underscores the potential of social media to democratize financial literacy, rendering financial education and information accessible to individuals from varied backgrounds.

Chapter 7, "Role of Social Media in Greta Thunberg's Climate and Sustainability Action," portrays that the specter of climate change continues to cast a looming shadow over humanity, prompting the recognition that it's an escalating concern requiring consistent measures to combat. Yet, effecting change on a vast scale is no simple feat. Fortunately, the advent of social media has rendered this endeavor feasible. The role assumed by social media has grown exponentially, given the internet's pivotal role in information acquisition, data aggregation, and social interaction. An exemplary illustration of this is embodied by Greta Thunberg, a 16-year-old Swedish environmental advocate. Using the power of social media, she raised her voice against climate change and ignited the "Fridays for Future" school strike movement in August 2018 outside the Swedish parliament. Employing diverse social media platforms and digital channels, she has orchestrated a concerted global effort to shape a collective narrative and intent among individuals and institutions striving for environmental change.

Chapter 8, "Role of Social Media on Government Initiatives Towards Human Resource Development," exposes that Social media has ascended as a potent instrument for communication, networking, and the exchange of information. Its widespread popularity and easy accessibility have prompted governments worldwide to embrace it as a means of effectively connecting with the public. This piece of writing delves into the role social media plays in bridging the divide between governmental endeavors in Human Resource Development (HRD) and the general populace. It scrutinizes how social media platforms have revolutionized the manner in which governments disseminate HRD policies, initiatives, and opportunities to citizens, fostering heightened engagement, transparency, and inclusiveness. Moreover, this article sheds light on the potential obstacles and ethical considerations associated with employing social media in HRD initiatives. The integration of social media with government HRD endeavors holds substantial potential for enriching resource accessibility, stimulating skill cultivation, and empowering individuals within the contemporary workforce.

Chapter 9, "Usage of Social Media in Education: A Paradigm Shift in the Indian Education Sector," represents In light of the swift transmission of the coronavirus, educational institutions worldwide are undergoing a profound shift from traditional in-person teaching methods to virtual instruction. The rapid adoption of digital technology signifies a momentous paradigm shift that holds the potential to reshape the landscape of the Indian education system. The COVID-19 situation presents an occasion to explore novel tools and technologies that can render education more pertinent for students unable to physically attend campuses. Through online learning and assessment, an avenue emerges to augment knowledge and efficiency, concurrently fostering the acquisition of fresh skill sets and accelerating professional competencies. Within this chapter, we have examined the educational challenges and prospects stemming from the sudden outbreak of COVID-19. This is followed by a discourse on the imperative need to recalibrate the Indian educational system to effectively respond to these transformative circumstances.

Chapter 10, "Exploring the Significance of Media Psychology in Human Communication During the Era of Digitalization," demonstrates media psychology operates at the crossroads of multiple disciplines, encompassing individuals' interactions with media across diverse spheres of their lives, ranging from work and education to entertainment and social involvement. As these interactions continue to transform, media psychologists amalgamate insights into human behavior, cognition, and emotion with a parallel understanding of media technology to address these evolving challenges. In a world increasingly interconnected, media has permeated nearly every facet of existence, underscoring its growing significance as a field of study. Unlike certain branches of media studies, media psychology transcends a focus solely on content; it encompasses the entire intricate system. Comprehending the impacts of technology relies significantly on insights from psychology. By uniting our grasp of human behavior, cognition, and emotion, media psychologists diligently pursue resolutions and approaches to these inquiries.

Chapter 11, "Exploring the Impact of Social Media on the Indian Banking Sector: A Comprehensive Social Media Framework," explores the significance of adhering to data protection regulations and safeguarding customer privacy takes precedence. Conclusively, the framework furnishes strategic suggestions to Indian banks, aimed at refining their standing on social media. This encompasses the establishment of resilient social media guidelines, fusion with pre-existing customer service avenues, and channeling resources into analytics to extract meaningful insights from user engagements. At its core, this framework supplies invaluable perspectives for Indian banks aspiring to leverage social media's capabilities. This endeavor not only bolsters competitiveness but also cultivates customer confidence and amplifies overall operational efficacy within the ever-evolving digital sphere.

Chapter 12, "Promoting Online Safety: The Government's Role in Combating Cyber Harassment and Cybercrime Through Social Media Platforms," exposes that India is currently undergoing a swift expansion of its presence on social media, with users actively participating across various platforms. However, this surge in engagement does not provide immunity to social media users from encountering the negative aspects of online harassment. Frequently, the terms "online harassment" and "online abuse" are employed interchangeably. As outlined by PEN America, online harassment denotes the consistent or severe targeting of an individual or group through harmful behavior within the digital sphere. Let's delve into the core elements of this definition. It's worth noting that a single isolated incident might not meet the threshold for harassment. Yet, when such occurrences persist, they can escalate into abusive or harassing behavior. Conversely, even a solitary instance can cause profound distress and fall within the domains of abuse and harassment.

Chapter 13, "Leveraging Social Media Geographic Information for Smart Governance and Policy Making: Opportunities and Challenges," expresses that the utilization of geographic information from social media is becoming increasingly relevant within governance and policy-making realms. The potential impact of social media geographic information is vast and extends to influencing decision-making, enhancing citizen engagement, optimizing service delivery, facilitating crisis management, fostering innovation, shaping policy development and assessment, and gauging public sentiment. Nonetheless, there are several hurdles to overcome, including issues related to data quality, privacy considerations, information overload, standardization, restricted access, ethical concerns, technical limitations, language barriers, and limited geographical coverage. To effectively tackle these challenges, policymakers need to establish well-defined guidelines, ensure the accuracy of data, address privacy apprehensions, manage information overload, and promote ethical standards. The article also highlights practical applications in various domains such as disaster response, traffic management, urban planning, air quality monitoring, disease outbreak tracking, and flood monitoring. By capitalizing on the potential of social media geographic information while proactively addressing its associated challenges, policymakers can make informed decisions that yield benefits for society as a whole.

Chapter 14, "Electronic-Based Service Innovation: Evidence From the Jayapura City Population and Civil Registration Office, Indonesia," states that the initial section of this study centers on the adoption of electronic governance (E-Governance). Subsequently, the second segment outlines the state of electronic-based services at the Jayapura City Population and Civil Registration Service (Disdukcapil) prior to the pandemic. The concluding portion unveils the operational framework of electronic-based services during the pandemic. Employing a qualitative approach grounded in a literature review, this study delves into the transformative use of digital technology by the Jayapura City Disdukcapil. Various innovations have been introduced to enhance the quality of public service provision in the domain of population administration. These innovations, accessible online without necessitating a visit to the Dukcapil office, were initiated in 2016 and have continued to be operational during the pandemic.

Chapter 15, "Preserving Personal Autonomy: Exploring Importance of Privacy Right, Its Impact on Society, and Threats to Privacy in Digital Age," explains the significance of the right to privacy, its societal ramifications, and the challenges it faces due to technological advancements. The right to privacy stands as a foundational human right, safeguarding individuals against undue intrusion into their personal domains. Its impact on society is profound, preserving individuals' ability to exercise their rights and liberties devoid of external interference. Nevertheless, the proliferation of technology has posed a formidable threat to the right to privacy. The surge in digital technology adoption has given rise to an unprecedented level of surveillance and data gathering, triggering concerns regarding potential abuses of authority by both governmental bodies and private entities. This article scrutinizes the diverse avenues through which privacy rights are undergoing erosion and proposes strategies to shield these rights. The article's culmination underscores the imperative of upholding individuals' privacy rights and underscores the urgency of safeguarding them within the contemporary digital landscape.

Chapter 16, "Machine Learning-Based Sentiment Analysis of Mental Health-Related Tweets by Sri Lankan Twitter Users During the COVID-19 Pandemic," explicates that the advent of COVID-19, originating in Wuhan, China, in December 2019, has profoundly impacted society on a global scale. It has brought about extensive repercussions, affecting facets such as public health, societal well-being, and local economies. Our study specifically sheds light on the sphere of mental health and its correlation with social behavior during pandemics. We undertake an examination of the mental health concerns among individuals in Sri Lanka by analyzing their tweets through sentiment analysis methodologies. To ensure robustness, a meticulous process of data preparation was executed, followed by the categorization of data into three distinct groups: 'experience,' 'information,' and 'counseling.' We then employed three distinct machine learning algorithms – ANN, LSTM, and SVM – for the purpose of sentiment analysis. In addition to this, the Latent Dirichlet Allocation technique was harnessed to unveil prevailing topics from tweets during the four waves of the COVID-19 outbreak. This enabled us to scrutinize the mental state of people and identify prevalent conditions.

Chapter 17, "Revolutionizing Government Communication: A Framework for Harnessing the Power of Social Media," addresses that governments have recognized the prevailing trend wherein an increasing number of citizens are engaging on social networks as opposed to government websites. It becomes relevant, therefore, to delve into the impact of social media on government operations, the role these emerging technologies have played, and the implications they carry for the future. This significance is accentuated by the Indian government's projection that services empowered by Information and Communication Technologies will notably influence economic growth, inclusivity, and quality of life. Additionally, the extensive utilization of social media for communication serves to bolster awareness and transparency in the government's pursuits, strategies, and implementation of various initiatives.

Chapter 18, "Youth Intention Towards Implementing Digital Currency: Role of Social Media and Government," demonstrates the determinants that influence the inclination of young individuals to adopt digital currency. It also delves into the effects of social media and governmental endeavors on shaping their attitudes and behaviors towards this subject. The research examines variables such as Perceived Ease of Use, Dissemination of Information, Responsibility, Liability, Translucency, and Perceived Usefulness to gauge the impact of digital adoption. Employing a methodological approach based on judgmental sampling, which encompasses a questionnaire survey and qualitative inputs, this study encompasses a sample of 337 participants. The objective is to furnish comprehensive insights into the matter at hand. The research outcomes bear substantial relevance for policymakers, financial institutions, and social media platforms. By unraveling the roles played by social media and government initiatives, the groundwork can be laid for the formulation of effective strategies to foster the adoption of digital currency among young individuals. Addressing potential barriers and harnessing the influence of thought leaders and trusted sources can amplify youth engagement with digital currencies, thereby stimulating economic growth.

Relevance of the Book

Global Perspectives on Social Media Usage Within Governments is a comprehensive and insightful exploration of the intricate relationship between social media platforms and the machinery of governance across the globe. This meticulously curated collection of essays brings together leading scholars, practitioners, and experts to dissect the multifaceted ways in which governments utilize social media to communicate, engage with citizens, and navigate the complexities of modern politics and diplomacy.

The book is divided into distinct sections, each offering a deep dive into various aspects of the topic. It begins by providing a panoramic view of the digital governance landscape, showcasing the diversity of approaches governments adopt to harness the power of social media for effective governance. Moving forward, the book delves into how governments leverage social media to enhance citizen engagement, foster transparency, and bridge the gap between leaders and citizens. It further examines the transformation of diplomacy in the digital age, emphasizing how governments use social media for real-time international communication and public diplomacy. The book also takes a critical look at the challenges that arise, such as the spread of misinformation, ethical considerations, and the potential for abuse of power within the digital realm.

The Relevance in Today's World

In an era defined by technological interconnectivity, *Global Perspectives on Social Media Usage Within Governments* offers a timely and relevant exploration of a subject that has profound implications for the present and the future. As societies worldwide grapple with the implications of digitalization, the topic of social media's role within governments is more pertinent than ever.

Social media platforms have become central to public discourse, serving as conduits for information dissemination, citizen participation, and political mobilization. Governments are navigating uncharted territory as they harness these platforms to connect with citizens, solicit feedback, and communicate policy decisions. The book's analysis of various strategies employed by governments to engage their citizens offers invaluable insights for policymakers seeking to create transparent and inclusive governance structures.

The global political landscape is also undergoing a seismic shift due to the rise of digital diplomacy. Governments are increasingly turning to social media as a tool to shape international narratives, communicate directly with foreign populations, and engage in real-time diplomacy. This transformation in diplomatic communication underscores the urgency of understanding the nuances, cultural sensitivities, and ethical implications associated with digital engagement on the global stage.

Furthermore, the book's examination of challenges such as misinformation and data privacy is particularly pertinent in an era where the boundaries between truth and falsehood are increasingly blurred. As governments and societies grapple with the consequences of disinformation campaigns and data breaches, the ethical considerations outlined in the book become indispensable guidelines for responsible governance in the digital age.

Global Perspectives on Social Media Usage Within Governments is a thought-provoking compilation that offers a panoramic view of a rapidly evolving landscape. By shedding light on the opportunities, challenges, and ethical dilemmas posed by the intersection of social media and governance, the book equips readers with the knowledge needed to navigate the complexities of the digital era. As societies worldwide continue to grapple with the implications of digital transformation, this volume serves as a guiding compass for scholars, policymakers, practitioners, and engaged citizens seeking to understand and shape the future of governance in an interconnected world.

Target Audience

Global Perspectives on Social Media Usage Within Governments is a comprehensive and insightful book that appeals to a diverse range of individuals, professionals, and institutions. The book's rich exploration of the complex interplay between social media and governance offers valuable insights for various segments of the academic, policy, and practitioner communities. The following groups are among the primary target audience for this thought-provoking volume:

Academics and Researchers: Scholars and researchers in the fields of political science, international relations, communication studies, digital media, public administration, and technology studies will find this book to be an invaluable resource. The book's comprehensive coverage of the topic provides a wealth of case studies, analyses, and theoretical frameworks that contribute to a deeper understanding of the evolving landscape of governance in the digital age. Academics will benefit from the multidisciplinary perspectives presented, which can inform further research and scholarship.

Policymakers and Government Officials: Government officials, policymakers, and public administrators seeking to navigate the complexities of incorporating social media into governance strategies will find practical insights within this book. The case studies and real-world examples offer actionable ideas for enhancing citizen engagement, transparency, and diplomacy through digital platforms. The book's examination of challenges and ethical considerations also equips policymakers with the knowledge needed to make informed decisions about social media usage within government frameworks.

Practitioners in Communication and Diplomacy: Professionals working in the fields of communication, public relations, and diplomacy will benefit from the book's in-depth analysis of how social media has transformed communication strategies in the digital age. The insights into digital diplomacy, crisis management, and international relations offer practical guidance for practitioners seeking to effectively engage with diverse audiences and navigate the nuances of digital communication channels.

Students and Educators: Educators teaching courses related to political science, communication studies, international relations, and public administration can integrate this book into their curricula. The comprehensive exploration of the subject matter, coupled with case studies from around the world, provides students with a well-rounded understanding of the role of social media in governance. The book can serve as a foundational resource for classroom discussions, research projects, and assignments.

Media and Journalism Professionals: Journalists, media professionals, and media literacy advocates will find the book's analysis of misinformation, fake news, and ethical considerations within the digital sphere particularly relevant. The insights into the challenges and pitfalls of social media usage within governments provide valuable context for media practitioners reporting on political developments and diplomatic affairs in the digital age.

Civil Society Organizations and Activists: Individuals and organizations engaged in civil society, activism, and advocacy can gain insights into how governments leverage social media to communicate with citizens and respond to public concerns. The book's exploration of citizen engagement, transparency, and accountability offers perspectives that can inform their efforts to promote democratic participation and influence policy decisions.

In essence, *Global Perspectives on Social Media Usage Within Governments* addresses a diverse and global audience that seeks to understand, navigate, and harness the transformative power of social media within the realm of governance. With its balanced insights, multidisciplinary perspectives, and real-world case studies, the book serves as a bridge between theory and practice, offering actionable insights for individuals and institutions engaged in shaping the future of governance in an increasingly digital world.

Impact on the Field and Subject Matter

The book *Global Perspectives on Social Media Usage Within Governments* significantly impacts the field of political science, communication studies, and governance by offering a nuanced and comprehensive exploration of the intricate relationship between social media and governmental processes. Its contributions are far-reaching and extend to various dimensions of research, policy formulation, and practice within this rapidly evolving landscape:

Advancing Scholarly Understanding: The book enriches the scholarly discourse by presenting a diverse array of perspectives, case studies, and analyses that deepen our understanding of the evolving relationship between social media and governance. By examining real-world examples from around the globe, the book provides scholars with a wealth of material to study and analyze, contributing to the development of new theories and frameworks.

Bridging Theory and Practice: The book's practical insights bridge the gap between theoretical discussions and real-world application. It equips policymakers, practitioners, and government officials with actionable ideas to enhance citizen engagement, transparency, and diplomatic communication through social media platforms. This bridge between theory and practice enhances the relevance and applicability of academic research.

Informing Policy and Governance: By dissecting the strategies governments use to leverage social media, the book informs policy decisions related to digital communication, citizen engagement, and diplomacy. Policymakers can draw upon the insights provided to craft more effective and ethical strategies for using social media as a governance tool, thereby improving the quality of governance in the digital age.

Navigating Ethical Challenges: The book provides an in-depth exploration of the ethical considerations inherent to social media usage within governments. It raises awareness about the challenges of misinformation, privacy breaches, and the potential manipulation of public sentiment. This awareness empowers policymakers, researchers, and practitioners to develop ethical guidelines and frameworks that mitigate the negative consequences of digital governance.

Shaping the Future of Diplomacy: The book's insights into digital diplomacy illuminate how governments engage in international communication and relations through social media. It contributes to the field of diplomacy by exploring the opportunities and challenges posed by this new modality of statecraft, ultimately shaping the way nations communicate on the global stage.

Fostering Cross-Disciplinary Collaboration: The multidisciplinary nature of the book encourages collaboration among various academic disciplines and professional fields. Scholars from political science, communication, technology, public administration, and international relations can draw inspiration from the diverse perspectives presented, leading to cross-disciplinary research and innovation.

Enhancing Media Literacy and Awareness: The book's analysis of misinformation and fake news within the digital space raises awareness about the importance of media literacy. It equips readers with the tools to critically evaluate information, fostering a more informed and discerning citizenry capable of navigating the complexities of the digital information landscape.

In summary, *Global Perspectives on Social Media Usage Within Governments* has a transformative impact on the field and subject matter by advancing academic understanding, informing policy and practice, navigating ethical challenges, and shaping the future trajectory of governance, diplomacy, and communication. By offering a comprehensive and multidimensional exploration, the book becomes a guiding compass for scholars, policymakers, practitioners, and engaged citizens seeking to navigate the evolving landscape of governance in the digital age.

Chandan Chavadi
Presidency Business School, Presidency College, Bengaluru, India

Dhanabalan Thangam
Presidency Business School, Presidency College, Bengaluru, India

Acknowledgment

We writing to express my sincere gratitude for providing me with the opportunity to publish book project titled *Global Perspectives on Social Media Usage Within Governments* in IGI Global Publishing house, which is set to be released under your esteemed publishing house. It is an honor to collaborate with IGI Global and to contribute to the scholarly discourse within my field.

We would also like to extend our heartfelt appreciation to the chapter contributors, anonymous reviewers, and all those involved in the publication process for their dedication and expertise. Your guidance, feedback, and support have been invaluable in refining and enhancing the quality of my work.

We truly excited about the prospect of sharing this book with the academic community and contributing to the ongoing advancement of knowledge in digital age. The platform provided by IGI Global will undoubtedly allow for a broader reach and impact of my research findings.

Once again, we wish to express our deepest gratitude for the opportunity to publish with IGI Global. We look forward to our continued collaboration and to being a part of your reputable publishing network.

Thank you for your trust in our work and for your commitment to advancing scholarly research.

Sincerely,

The editors of this book.

Chapter 1
Global Perspectives on Social Media Usage Within Governments

Chandan Chavadi

 https://orcid.org/0000-0002-7214-5888

Presidency Business School, Presidency College, Bengaluru, India

G. Manoj

Vel Tech Rangarajan Dr. Sagunthala R&D Institute of Science and Technology, India

Sathis Kumar Ganesan

Populus Empowerment Network, India

Sendhilkumar Manoharan

 https://orcid.org/0000-0001-5116-8696

Presidency Business School, Presidency College, Bengaluru, India

Dhanabalan Thangam

 https://orcid.org/0000-0003-1253-3587

Presidency Business School, Presidency College, Bengaluru, India

ABSTRACT

In the present era of information, social media has risen as the primary channel for engagement. Platforms like Facebook, Twitter, YouTube, and others possess the capability to bring about significant changes. They have been instrumental in activities ranging from the downfall of governments to the amplification of political campaigns, the facilitation of public protests, the enablement of social demonstrations, and the initiation of social campaigns. Moreover, these platforms promote communication, dialogue, and awareness within public forums, serving as immediate sources of news and information. Within the dynamic landscape of communication evolution, the interconnected population now enjoys unprecedented access to information, expanded opportunities for public discourse, and enhanced potential for collective action.

DOI: 10.4018/978-1-6684-7450-1.ch001

INTRODUCTION

The technological revolution of the 1990s, known as the internet, has undergone a profound transformation of global connectivity. From a scattered few million connected individuals, we have evolved into a digital network of a billion people, transcending borders and boundaries. Modern individuals are increasingly immersed in digital devices such as laptops, smartphones, and computers. These devices serve as portals for activities such as reading newspapers, booking travel, enjoying music and videos, seeking information, making online purchases, and participating in public forums and discussions (Bennet, 2015). This digital age has also ushered in the era of social media, where interactions with friends, family, businesses, and governments occur on platforms like Facebook, Twitter, MySpace, YouTube, and LinkedIn (Balbi & Magaudda, 2018). The only requisites are an internet connection and a computer. The advent of Information and Communications Technology (ICT) and the widespread penetration of broadband in urban, semi-urban, and rural areas have interconnected people like never before, achieved through a simple "click" of a mouse (Olan et al, 2015).

Social media has emerged as the primary medium for engagement in this era of information. Platforms such as Facebook, Twitter, YouTube, and others wield the power to effect change – from toppling governments to boosting political campaigns, fostering public protests, facilitating social demonstrations, and catalyzing social campaigns. These platforms also foster communication, discussion, and awareness on public forums, serving as instant sources of news and information (Magro, 2012). Amidst the evolving communications landscape, the networked population is gaining unprecedented access to information, increased opportunities for public discourse, and enhanced capabilities for collective action (riado, Sandoval-Almazan, & Gil-Garcia, 2013). Social media has woven itself into the fabric of global civil society, engaging diverse stakeholders ranging from ordinary citizens and activists to NGOs, telecommunications companies, software providers, and governments (Mansoor, 2021). As the integration of social media into everyday life deepens, governmental agencies are establishing their online presence on platforms like Facebook, Twitter, and YouTube, recognizing their efficacy as channels of communication.

Initially met with skepticism, governments worldwide are gradually embracing social media to improve governance. In the 21st century, governments seek openness and transparency in their operations, and social networking sites offer avenues to foster a participatory, innovative, and inclusive governing model (Chen et al., 2020). These platforms not only disseminate information about policies and plans but also enable two-way communication, allowing for immediate citizen feedback and the incorporation of suggestions from the public. This evolving landscape underscores the transformative potential of social media in shaping the relationship between governments and their constituents.

SOCIAL MEDIA AND GOVERNMENT

The phenomenon known as social media has swept across the globe with unprecedented force, witnessing an exponential growth trajectory. This is evident from the fact that radio took 38 years to garner 50 million users, television achieved the same milestone in 14 years, and the internet accomplished it within just 4 years (Liao et al,. 2020). The iPod reached this mark in 3 years, while Facebook astonishingly added 100 million users in less than 9 months. Social networking has risen to become one of the predominant activities on the internet, with virtually every major global brand establishing a presence on social media platforms. This has become a new marketing tool at their disposal, even prompting governments, which were initially hesitant, to embrace social media as a communication channel (Croucher, Nguyen, & Rahmani, 2020).

Social media encompasses web-based and mobile technologies that transform communication into interactive dialogues among organizations, communities, and individuals. In the words of Andreas Kaplan and Michael Haenlein, it encompasses "a group of Internet-based applications that build on the ideological and technological foundations of Web 2.0 and that allow the creation and exchange of user-generated content." Its accessibility is nearly universal, powered by scalable communication methods (Kaplan & Haenlein, 2020).

At its core, social media represents a convenient means of generating, publishing, and engaging with content on the internet. This term encapsulates how both organizations and individuals share textual, visual, and audiovisual content while fostering discussions online. Its influence extends to revolutionizing business practices and interpersonal interactions, providing a platform for previously marginalized voices (Zhuravskaya, Petrova, & Enikolopov, 2020). Moreover, social media is reshaping the dynamics between elected officials, council members, and the public.

Central to understanding social media is its inherently social nature, emphasizing communication and empowering individuals much like the transformative impact of the printing press in the past. Just as political pamphlets and coffeehouse debates laid the groundwork for liberal democracy, social media is poised to exert a comparable influence on governance and commerce. Today, anyone can publish and disseminate their opinions, engaging in conversations with others through a few simple clicks (Shaher & Radwan, 2022). Social media platforms generally foster openness, facilitating widespread viewing, commenting, and collaboration on content. These tools are often cost-effective and user-friendly, requiring minimal technical expertise. Additionally, the design of social media emphasizes shareability, enabling easy forwarding, linking, and republishing of content. This translates to minimal barriers for expressing opinions and reaching a potentially extensive audience (Zhuravskaya, Petrova, & Enikolopov, 2020).

The term "Web 2.0" is often used to succinctly describe how social media has shifted the internet landscape. It has transitioned from predominantly one-way publishing and e-commerce to a greater emphasis on user-generated words, images, music, and videos, all open for sharing, commenting, and interaction (Kaplan & Haenlein, 2020). "Government 2.0" characterizes the transformation in the relationship between governmental bodies and citizens catalyzed by social media. Increasingly, citizens and service users demand open governance and greater involvement in local decision-making, often discussing community matters online. This concept encompasses open data initiatives to enhance transparency and accountability, as well as the utilization of social media tools to engage in conversations, shape policies, foster local democracy, and enhance services (Croucher, Nguyen, & Rahmani, 2020).

GROWING IMPORTANCE OF SOCIAL MEDIA IN GOVERNANCE

Social media has achieved widespread adoption among citizens across the world, but government utilization of social media remains largely untapped. This observation is particularly striking considering that social media represents an ideal avenue for government departments to connect with their primary audience the citizens (Gorwa, 2019). Businesses and prominent brands have adeptly harnessed this medium for over half a decade, offering valuable lessons for governmental engagement online. According to the Yellow Social Media Report 2020, nearly eight out of ten Australians are now active social media users. Furthermore, over 40% of large businesses utilize social media as a means to communicate and advertise to their target demographic (Yellow Social Media Report, 2020).

In Australia, Facebook continues to dominate as the preferred social media platform for businesses of all sizes, closely followed by LinkedIn and Twitter. Instagram and YouTube are also popular choices for medium-sized businesses (Zhuravskaya, Petrova & Enikolopov, 2020). While businesses reap the rewards of social media interaction, decision-makers within government entities are still grappling with the most effective ways to utilize these platforms for citizen engagement. As the number of social media users escalates daily, users consistently voice concerns about privacy policies and platform functionality (Virender Jeet, 2015). Notably, platforms like Facebook have responded to these concerns by making policy changes. In essence, social media empowers users to voice their opinions.

In the present digital landscape, a larger proportion of people are online than ever before. The SSMR reveals that the average Australian accesses social media more than five times a day. Over the past couple of years, Twitter and Instagram have gained significant traction across all age groups. This serves as a wakeup call for government entities that have yet to establish a robust presence on social media or utilize these platforms effectively to engage with citizens (Jaime de Guzman, 2023). Social media is where citizens reside digitally, presenting a direct path to reach them; government social media can bridge the gap between departments and citizens.

Therefore, it's imperative for government departments to adopt social media channels to foster meaningful and valuable communication with the public, a necessity to achieve policy objectives. However, to facilitate this transition, a fundamental shift in understanding is necessary. Accepting that social media channels have revolutionized public communication is pivotal (Al-Dmour et al,.2020). Communication is now instant, enabling relationship-building and addressing concerns at unparalleled speeds. Especially with the advent of COVID-19, the need for crisis communication platforms has been expedited, with social media serving as the preferred method to relay immediate messages (Jennings et al., 2021).

Social media has now emerged as the dominant avenue for two-way communication, empowering senders to gather feedback and gauge sentiment. According to the SSMR, 9% of Australians now prefer to engage with customer service via social media instead of traditional means like email or phone. This percentage is poised to grow annually. While some government departments may still debate the role of social media, others have wholeheartedly embraced it (Yellow Social Media Report, 2020). Noteworthy instances include the Australian Federal Government's Department of Human Services, which established the Facebook page "Family Update" to aid families relying on social security payments. Additionally, local Australian governments, like Brisbane City Council, employed social media during the 2010/11 floods to provide essential information and connect with evacuees (Zhuravskaya, Petrova & Enikolopov, 2020).

Government social media channels are invaluable, particularly for building trust. Without audience trust, messages go unheard. The rigidity of traditional media within government PR needs recalibration. A blend of traditional and digital communication is required, a shift that certain departments have successfully undertaken. As noted in the WPP Leaders Report, communication departments investing in digital communication are reallocating resources from traditional avenues (Oh, Lee, & Han, 2021). In the private sector, numerous large businesses and renowned brands effectively utilize social media to promptly address issues, monitor sentiment, manage brand reputation, and foster loyalty. The government must exhibit courage and embrace social media akin to global businesses. For instance, responding to customer complaints or seeking their opinions not only provides resolution opportunities but also mitigates brand damage (Yarchi, Baden, & Kligler-Vilenchik, 2021).

With this backdrop this present chapter has developed for exposing the Historical Context of Social Media Adoption in Governments, Benefits and Opportunities of Social Media Usage in Governments, Challenges and Risks of Government Social Media Usage with cases, Strategies for Effective Government Social Media Usage, and The Future of Government Social Media Usage. Where section one presents the introduction of concept and it includes social media and society, and growing importance of social media in governance. Section two reveals Historical Context of Social Media Adoption in Governments, Benefits and Opportunities of Social Media Usage in Governments explained in section three, section four depicts the Challenges and Risks of Government Social Media Usage with cases, section five presents the Future of Government Social Media Usage, and the last section concludes the work.

HISTORICAL CONTEXT OF SOCIAL MEDIA ADOPTION IN GLOBAL GOVERNMENTS

The historical trajectory of social media adoption within global governments has been marked by notable shifts, reflecting the evolving nature of communication and governance in the digital age. From early experimentation to widespread integration, governments around the world have traversed a dynamic path in their utilization of social media platforms. This essay delves into the historical context of social media adoption in global governments, highlighting key milestones, statistics, and the implications of this evolution.

Early Experimentation and Emergence (2000s)

The dawn of the 21st century witnessed the initial forays of governments into the realm of social media. As digital platforms gained traction, governments recognized the potential of these tools for enhancing public engagement and transparency. In 2009, Twitter emerged as a prominent platform for governmental communication. The U.S. State Department, for instance, launched its Twitter presence, recognizing the platform's ability to swiftly disseminate information to a global audience (Khan, & Khan, 2019).

Proliferation and Expansion (2010s)

The subsequent decade saw a proliferation of government engagement on social media platforms. The "Arab Spring" uprisings in 2010 and 2011 underscored the transformative power of social media, as citizens harnessed these platforms to mobilize mass protests and amplify their voices. Governments worldwide took note of the impact, leading to a surge in social media adoption for both communication and policy initiatives. This part reveals the historical context of social media adoption by governments across a diverse range of nations, including the USA, UK, European countries, Russia, India, China, Japan, and South Korea (Dwivedi et al, 2021). By examining statistics and trends, we gain insights into the transformative journey of government communication in the digital age.

United States: Forging New Communication Channels

The United States, known for its tech innovation, played a pivotal role in shaping the early landscape of government social media adoption. It was among the first to recognize the potential of platforms like Twitter and Facebook for official communication. As of 2021, approximately 84% of U.S. federal agencies use social media platforms, with 95% of them on Twitter and 85% on Facebook. The U.S. State Department's active Twitter diplomacy, White House's Facebook Town Halls, and NASA's space updates on social media showcase the government's engagement (Yellow Social Media Report, 2020).

United Kingdom: Bridging the Gap

The UK embraced social media as a bridge between government and citizens, offering a platform for direct interaction. Around 3,500 Twitter accounts representing various UK government departments were active as per 2020 statistics (Manacorda & Tesei, 2020). Social media enables real-time updates on policies, crises, and initiatives, fostering transparency and public trust.

European Countries: A Tapestry of Engagement

European countries present a varied picture of social media adoption, reflecting cultural diversity and regional priorities. European countries like Germany, France, and the Netherlands have actively engaged with citizens through platforms like Twitter, Facebook, and Instagram. Social media adoption varies, with countries like Estonia pioneering e-governance and others gradually embracing digital communication (Griffith & Leston-Bandeira, 2020).

Russia: Unique Digital Landscape

Russia's government has taken a distinctive approach to social media engagement. Russia's largest social media platform, VKontakte (VK), hosts official government accounts that engage with citizens on policies and information dissemination (Kompella, 2020).

India: Democratizing Government Communication

India's burgeoning social media landscape has allowed governments to directly communicate with citizens. The Indian government's Digital India initiative aims to enhance governance through technology, utilizing social media for transparency and citizen engagement (Shukla, & Mathur, 2020).

China: Controlled Engagement

China's government has harnessed social media platforms within its unique digital ecosystem. China's government utilizes platforms like WeChat, Weibo, and Douyin (TikTok), while tightly controlling content to align with its narratives (El-Ebiary et al., 2020).

Japan: Balancing Tradition and Innovation

Japan has struck a balance between embracing modern communication and preserving cultural norms. Governmental bodies in Japan leverage platforms like Twitter and Facebook to provide updates, without deviating from traditional communication channels (Hussain, H. (2019).

South Korea: Embracing Connectivity

South Korea's tech-savvy society has embraced social media as an extension of its interconnected culture: Government agencies in South Korea use platforms like Naver and KakaoTalk to engage citizens in real-time updates and crisis management (Hussain, H. (2019).

The historical context of social media adoption by governments unveils a global transformation in communication strategies. From early experimentation to active engagement, governments have recognized the potential of these platforms to enhance transparency, connect with citizens, and shape public narratives. As governments worldwide continue to evolve in the digital age, the statistics and trends demonstrate the power of social media as a tool for citizen engagement, policy dissemination, and fostering a more connected and informed society.

BENEFITS AND OPPORTUNITIES OF SOCIAL MEDIA USAGE IN GOVERNMENTS

The rapid evolution of digital technology has transformed the way governments interact with citizens, manage public affairs, and communicate policies. Social media, once primarily associated with personal communication, has emerged as a powerful tool for governments worldwide to engage with constituents, foster transparency, and unlock new opportunities for efficient governance. This article explores the manifold benefits and opportunities of social media usage in governments, substantiated by compelling statistics that underscore its transformative impact (Sobaci, 2016).

Enhancing Citizen Engagement and Participation

One of the most significant advantages of social media adoption by governments is the enhancement of citizen engagement and participation in the democratic process. By providing platforms for direct interaction and feedback, governments can tap into the pulse of public sentiment and gather valuable insights. According to a Pew Research Center report, 70% of Americans believe that government officials should use social media to engage with citizens. The European Commission's Digital Economy and Society Index (DESI) report highlights that 51% of EU citizens use social media to communicate with public authorities (Khan, Swar & Lee, 2014).

Fostering Transparent Governance

Social media acts as a bridge between governments and citizens, fostering transparency by providing real-time updates, announcements, and policy changes. The World Economic Forum's Global Risks Report 2021 reveals that social media enables governments to respond more rapidly to crises, facilitating transparent communication during emergencies. In the UK, as reported by Gov.uk, government departments and agencies published over 500,000 social media posts in 2020, enhancing transparency and accessibility to vital information (Khan & Khan, 2019).

Dissemination of Critical Information

Social media enables governments to rapidly disseminate crucial information to citizens, ensuring timely communication during emergencies, natural disasters, or public health crises. The International Telecommunication Union (ITU) highlights that during the COVID-19 pandemic, governments leveraged social media to share health advisories, guidelines, and updates, reaching a wider audience swiftly (Chen et al., 2020).

Catalyst for Public Services and Initiatives

Governments can utilize social media platforms to amplify public service initiatives, campaigns, and policy awareness. The Indian government's "Swachh Bharat Abhiyan" (Clean India Campaign) leveraged social media to encourage citizen participation, resulting in over 12 million citizens taking the "Swachh Bharat" pledge. The World Bank reports that social media played a pivotal role in promoting government-led initiatives, such as financial literacy campaigns and healthcare awareness programs (Al-Dmour,2020).

Direct Communication with Citizens

Social media provides an unprecedented avenue for governments to directly communicate with citizens, bypassing traditional intermediaries. The European Parliament's 2021 report highlights that over 71% of EU institutions engage directly with citizens through social media, fostering a sense of accessibility and approachability (Khan & Khan, 2019). The Government Social Media Conference & Expo (GSMCON) reveals that 63% of government social media professionals consider direct citizen engagement as the primary purpose of their social media presence.

Global Diplomacy and Diplomatic Outreach

Social media has extended the realm of diplomacy, enabling governments to engage in public diplomacy and cross-border interactions. The Pew Research Center states that 91% of U.S. embassies are active on Twitter, facilitating diplomatic discourse and promoting cross-cultural understanding. The use of social media by governments for diplomatic purposes has become commonplace, as evidenced by the active presence of leaders and diplomats on platforms like Twitter and Instagram. The benefits and opportunities of social media usage in governments are undeniable (Zhuravskaya, Petrova & Enikolopov, 2020). From fostering transparency and direct citizen engagement to disseminating critical information swiftly, social media has revolutionized governance. Governments worldwide are leveraging these platforms to enhance public service, bridge the communication gap, and build a more informed and participatory society. As social media continues to evolve, its potential to shape the future of governance remains limitless.

CHALLENGES AND RISKS OF GOVERNMENT SOCIAL MEDIA USAGE

The integration of social media into government operations has brought about transformative benefits in communication, citizen engagement, and transparency. However, along with these advantages come a range of challenges and risks that governments must navigate effectively to ensure the responsible and secure use of these platforms. This article explores the key challenges and risks associated with government social media usage, supported by relevant statistics that underscore the complexities of this digital landscape.

Misinformation and Disinformation

The rapid spread of misinformation and disinformation on social media poses a significant challenge for governments. A survey by the Pew Research Center found that 64% of Americans believe that fake news has caused "a great deal" of confusion about basic facts of current events. The European Commission's report on disinformation highlights that more than half of Europeans (56%) are concerned about the spread of fake news (Bertot, Jaeger & Hansen, 2012).

Data Privacy and Security

Governments must navigate the complexities of data privacy and security while leveraging social media platforms. A survey by the International Association of Privacy Professionals (IAPP) revealed that 84% of privacy professionals view data protection as a top priority. The Ponemon Institute's report states that the average cost of a data breach in 2020 was $3.86 million, underscoring the financial implications of inadequate data security (Chen & Wang, 2021).

Cybersecurity Threats

The increasing digitization of government operations exposes them to cyber threats and attacks. A report by the Center for Strategic and International Studies (CSIS) states that the average annual cost of cybercrime globally is $13 million per organization. The U.S. Federal Bureau of Investigation (FBI) reported a 400% increase in cybercrime complaints during the COVID-19 pandemic (Ismagilova et al., 2020)

Hate Speech and Online Abuse

Government social media accounts are susceptible to hate speech, online abuse, and harassment. Amnesty International's "Toxic Twitter" report revealed that female politicians and journalists are more likely to experience abuse on Twitter, with women of color being disproportionately targeted. A study by the European Parliamentary Research Service (EPRS) found that 67% of European female politicians had experienced psychological violence on social media (Matamoros-Fernández & Farkas, 2021).

Regulatory Compliance and Policy Enforcement

Governments must navigate regulatory challenges while enforcing policies on social media platforms. The European Commission's Digital Services Act package aims to enhance online safety by holding platforms accountable for content moderation and addressing illegal content. The U.S. Congress has grappled with issues related to misinformation, leading to discussions about Section 230 of the Communications Decency Act and its implications (Fagherazzi et al, 2020).

Accountability and Transparency

Maintaining accountability and transparency in government communication on social media platforms can be complex. A survey by the Pew Research Center indicated that 73% of Americans believe that elected officials should face "strong consequences" for posting false information on social media. The Centre for the Analysis of Social Media found that the majority of false information shared during the 2019 UK General Election originated from political party leaders and elected officials (Katzenbach & Ulbricht, 2019).

While government social media usage offers numerous benefits, the challenges and risks are significant and cannot be ignored. Misinformation, data privacy concerns, cybersecurity threats, and online abuse present formidable obstacles that governments must address. As technology evolves, governments must adopt proactive strategies, robust policies, and effective partnerships to navigate this dynamic digital landscape responsibly, ensuring that social media remains a tool for positive engagement, informed communication, and transparent governance.

EXAMINING CASES: WORLDWIDE ILLUSTRATIONS OF GOVERNMENT SOCIAL MEDIA APPLICATION

United Kingdom: In October 2008, the United Kingdom's Labour government introduced their vision of community empowerment, advocating for the incorporation of social media by local authorities to engage with communities. The Department for Communities and Local Government expressed their commitment to supporting technological innovation, whether through active deliberation with the government or inventive applications of community and social media.

Recent years have seen a proactive adoption of social media by UK Councils, including platforms such as blogs, Facebook, Twitter, and YouTube, to foster meaningful connections with local communities. Monmouthshire County Council, a noteworthy example, has transcended the realm of social technology, using platforms like Yammer for policy support and YouTube for creative recruitment initiatives (Abi-Jaoude, Naylor & Pignatiello, 2020). Notably, Monmouthshire County Council became the first to transform their town into a Wikipedia town using QR codes. Helen Reynolds, Communications Officer for the council, emphasized the significance of engaging in social spaces where citizens are active and delivering relevant, timely, and valuable information to bolster government influence.

In accordance with guidelines issued by the U.K. government's digital service on May 17, 2012, a strong emphasis has been placed on incorporating public engagement through social media into the daily operations of civil servants. Francis Maude, the minister for cabinet office, highlights that opening dialogues with the public provides a more profound understanding of citizens' genuine needs and concerns (Paul, & Das, 2023). The document underscores that social media should be employed responsibly, only when it aligns with the core responsibilities of civil servants.

Canada: In Canada, a significant number of politicians are actively engaged on social media platforms, and some government departments are going a step further by integrating these platforms into official government operations. Glen Murray, serving as the Minister of Research and Innovation for Ontario, exemplifies this approach. Following a social innovation summit, Murray aimed to foster public participation in the discourse. Collaborating with two other ministries, a crowdsourced wiki was established to develop an official policy paper outlining the government's stance on social innovation. This innovative approach allows users to contribute articles and edit submissions collectively, much like the collaborative nature of Wikipedia (Wike et al, .2020). Additionally, gov.politwitter.ca serves as a complementary tool to Politwitter, monitoring social media engagement by Canadian government institutions and organizations. This resource offers insights into Canadian Government Social Media activities and trends. Internationally, world leaders from various nations are leveraging social media platforms to wield their influence. Nations including Brazil, Mexico, Venezuela, Argentina, and the United Arab Emirates are actively exercising their presence on different social media platforms to engage with their constituents and communicate their policies (Barrett-Maitland & Lynch, 2020). Notably, the use of platforms like Twitter has enabled these leaders to reach wider audiences and disseminate information in real-time.

Russia: In alignment with its commitment to modernization and technology advancement, the Russian government has embarked on a proactive journey to establish a robust online presence. This concerted effort has seen government ministries and agencies not only develop official websites but also venture into social networks and blogging communities (Enikolopov, Makarin & Petrova, 2020). The overarching goal of this digital outreach extends beyond merely informing the Russian populace about governmental actions; it actively seeks to foster a two-way dialogue, encouraging citizens to provide feedback and engage in discussions. An exemplar of this strategy is the presidential commission's approach, where each item on its agenda is open for online deliberation through the dedicated platform i-Russia.ru. This interactive space allows individuals interested in government affairs to contribute their insights and opinions via widely used social networks like Facebook, Twitter, and VKontakte (Nekliudov et al, 2020).

India: India has witnessed a substantial surge in broadband penetration and mobile phone subscriptions. Standing as the world's second-largest mobile phone user base, India boasts a staggering 919 million users as of March 2012 (Gajendran, 2020). With over 121 million internet users by December 2011, the nation ranks third globally. Notably, India's telecom market has transformed into one of the most competitive and fastest-growing worldwide (Zhuravskaya, E., Petrova, M., & Enikolopov, 2020).

The realm of social media has also experienced a significant footprint within India. Social media platforms extend their reach to approximately 60 percent of the online Indian audience. Facebook and Orkut stand out, collectively catering to nearly 90 percent of the users within the social media sphere. Impressively, Facebook's user base in India has nearly doubled in the past six months, making it the predominant social network in the country (Sahoo, 2020). Currently, social networking garners the highest online engagement among Indians. According to data from marketing research firm ComScore, a staggering 84 percent of India's internet users access social networking sites. Consequently, India ranks as the world's seventh-largest social networking market, trailing only the U.S., China, Germany, the Russian Federation, Brazil, and the U.K (Dutta, 2020).

Global social network utilization has experienced a monumental surge, and India mirrors this trend. LinkedIn, for instance, derives approximately 33 percent of its revenue from international markets. With 51 million users in India and over 900 million users worldwide, Facebook exemplifies the widespread influence of social networks. The significance of social networking is further evidenced by its claim to more than 25 percent of global online user engagement, a remarkable shift from its negligible presence in 2005, as reported by Avendus Capital in November 2011 (Yadav, Bagga, & Johar, 2020).

At the 11th India Today Conclave in New Delhi, Kirthiga Reddy, the Head of Facebook India, emphasized the centrality of people, especially those in rural areas, in the web revolution. Highlighting the potential of community initiatives, Reddy exemplified how Facebook facilitated farmers in Sangli, Maharashtra to counteract the plummeting price of turmeric (Guess et al, .2020). She also underscored the transformative impact of collaborating with government initiatives, illustrating the potential for societal change through such partnerships.

STRATEGIES FOR EFFECTIVE GOVERNMENT SOCIAL MEDIA USAGE

In an era of rapid technological evolution, governments worldwide are harnessing the power of social media platforms to connect with citizens, share information, and engage in meaningful dialogue. Effective utilization of these digital platforms requires well-defined strategies that leverage their potential while addressing the unique challenges presented by the digital landscape. This part delves into the key strategies for successful government social media usage, supported by relevant statistics that underscore the significance of these approaches.

Purposeful Goal Setting

Establishing clear objectives is the foundation of successful government social media usage. A survey conducted by the International City/County Management Association (ICMA) revealed that 85% of local governments in the U.S. employ social media to increase community engagement. The U.S. Government Accountability Office (GAO) reported that 88% of federal agencies employ social media to achieve specific goals, such as increasing public awareness (Hyland-Wood et al,.2020).

Targeted Audience Engagement

Identifying and engaging the right audience is crucial for effective communication. The Pew Research Center found that 68% of American adults are Facebook users, making it a prominent platform for government engagement (Hudders, De Jans, & De Veirman, 2021). The European Commission's Eurobarometer survey highlighted that 67% of Europeans aged 16-74 use the internet daily, indicating the potential for online engagement.

Consistent Branding and Messaging

Maintaining a consistent brand image and messaging across platforms enhances credibility. The Australian Government's Digital Transformation Office revealed that consistent branding across social media channels resulted in a 700% increase in visits to their website. A study by the Inter-American Development Bank indicated that 60% of citizens in Latin America consider social media a trustworthy source for government information (Mason, Narcum, & Mason, 2021).

Timely and Relevant Content

Sharing timely and relevant information fosters citizen trust and engagement. The Pew Research Center reported that 78% of social media users in the U.S. engage with political content on these platforms. The Social Media Examiner's 2021 report found that 66% of marketers believe sharing timely content is crucial for successful social media engagement (Yadav, Bagga, & Johar, 2020).

Responsive Communication

Promptly addressing queries and concerns demonstrates government responsiveness. The UK government's 2019 report highlighted that 61% of citizens expected a response to their queries on social media within six hours. Research by Socialbakers revealed that the average response time for governments on social media platforms is around 7.3 hours (Dutta, 2020).

Data-Driven Decision Making

Utilizing data analytics guides informed decision-making and content optimization. The Government Social Media Conference & Expo (GSMCON) noted that 61% of government social media professionals use analytics tools to measure effectiveness. Abi-Jaoude, Naylor and Pignatiello (2020) a survey by the Institute for Public Relations and Muck Rack found that 85% of PR professionals believe data analytics is important for demonstrating ROI on social media efforts (Mason, Narcum, & Mason, 2021).

Secure and Ethical Practices

Prioritizing cybersecurity and ethical conduct safeguards government and citizen interests. The National Association of State Chief Information Officers (NASCIO) revealed that 92% of states in the U.S. have cybersecurity policies for social media. The International Journal of Information Management highlighted the importance of ethical considerations in government social media usage to maintain trust and transparency (Mason, Narcum, & Mason, 2021).

Effective government social media usage requires a comprehensive strategy that aligns with organizational goals, engages the target audience, and ensures consistent communication. By leveraging the power of social media, governments can foster citizen participation, enhance transparency, and build a more informed and engaged society. As statistics highlight the impact of these strategies, governments around the world must continue to evolve their approaches to remain at the forefront of digital engagement in the modern era.

THE FUTURE OF GOVERNMENT SOCIAL MEDIA USAGE

As governments navigate an increasingly digitized world, the role of social media in shaping governance and public engagement has become paramount. The trajectory of government social media usage is poised to undergo transformative shifts, catalyzed by technological advancements, evolving citizen expectations, and innovative strategies. This part examines the emerging trends and future outlook of government social media usage, bolstered by compelling statistics that offer insight into the impending digital governance landscape.

Embracing Emerging Technologies

By 2025, the global Artificial Intelligence (AI) market is projected to reach $190.61 billion, and governments are keenly adopting AI-powered chatbots and automated services for citizen inquiries and support. Virtual Reality (VR) and Augmented Reality (AR) market is anticipated to surpass $72.8 billion by 2024, propelling governments to explore immersive experiences for public engagement and education (Chen & Wang, 2021).

Shift towards Personalization

A survey by Accenture found that 58% of citizens expect governments to anticipate their needs and deliver personalized experiences, prompting governments to curate content based on individual preferences. The use of predictive analytics to understand citizen behaviors and needs is anticipated to grow significantly, enabling governments to proactively address concerns (Appel et al, 2020).

Enhanced Data Privacy and Security

With data breaches on the rise, governments are projected to invest more in robust cybersecurity measures to safeguard citizen data. The global cybersecurity market is expected to reach $248.26 billion by 2023. The integration of blockchain for secure and transparent data management is gaining traction, with the global blockchain market forecasted to reach $39.7 billion by 2025 (Appel et al, 2020).

Amplified Citizen Engagement

A study by Deloitte indicated that 85% of government organizations believe social media has a positive impact on citizen engagement, indicating a continued emphasis on participatory governance. The growth of online civic platforms, akin to Estonia's "e-Residency" program, is expected to provide citizens with enhanced digital participation in government processes (Chen & Wang, 2021).

Leveraging Open Data

The global open data market is projected to surpass $69.87 billion by 2027, reflecting governments' efforts to make public data more accessible, fostering transparency and innovation. Governments are increasingly leveraging open data to collaborate with citizens in co-creating innovative solutions for urban planning, infrastructure, and public services (Mason, Narcum, & Mason, 2021).

Evolving Regulation and Ethical Guidelines

Governments are likely to implement ethical guidelines for social media usage, addressing concerns related to misinformation, privacy, and algorithmic biases. The proliferation of data protection regulations, like the European Union's GDPR, signifies a future where governments prioritize citizens' data privacy rights (Oh, Lee, & Han, 2021).

The future of government social media usage is poised to redefine the interaction between citizens and their governing bodies. As technology evolves and citizen expectations transform, governments have a unique opportunity to harness social media as a powerful tool for transparency, engagement, and innovation. By embracing emerging technologies, personalizing citizen experiences, and safeguarding data privacy, governments can pave the way for a digital governance landscape that is dynamic, inclusive, and responsive to the needs of its citizens. As statistics illuminate these forthcoming trends, governments worldwide must seize the moment to pioneer a new era of digital democracy and effective public service delivery.

CONCLUSION AND FUTURE DIRECTIONS OF RESEARCH

In the ever-changing landscape of technology, the book "Global Perspectives on Social Media Usage within Governments" has illuminated the profound impact of social media on the way governments interact with their citizens. Through a comprehensive exploration of diverse case studies, statistical insights, and analytical discussions, this book has unraveled the intricate threads that weave the fabric of modern governance. As the book's journey through the intricacies of social media adoption within governments draws to a close, it becomes evident that the interactions between governments and citizens are no longer confined to traditional channels. The digital era has ushered in a new paradigm where transparency, engagement, and responsiveness thrive in the virtual realms of social networks, forums, and online platforms. From enabling participatory decision-making to amplifying the reach of public services, social media has transformed the dynamics of government-citizen relationships, paving the way for a more connected and informed society.

The conclusion of this work is not a culmination, but rather a call to action. As we embrace the evolving nature of government-citizen interactions, it becomes imperative to acknowledge that the digital landscape is a dynamic realm that continuously reshapes itself. This chapter serves as a stepping stone, inviting further research, exploration, and adaptation. The journey of understanding how governments across the globe leverage social media to enhance governance, foster engagement, and promote transparency is ongoing. In the pages of this chapter, we have journeyed through the past, present, and emerging future of government social media usage. Yet, the story remains unfinished. To ensure that governments effectively harness the potential of social media and adapt to the changing technological currents, a commitment to ongoing research, innovation, and the cultivation of best practices is essential. Just as governments are required to evolve to meet the needs of their citizens, so too must the exploration of this transformative field of study. In closing, "Global Perspectives on Social Media Usage within Governments" invites scholars, policymakers, practitioners, and citizens alike to join hands in charting the course for a future where government-citizen interactions thrive in the digital age. Let this book inspire an unyielding pursuit of knowledge and an unwavering commitment to harnessing the power of social media for the betterment of societies around the world. The story continues, and the narrative is in our collective hands.

REFERENCES

Abi-Jaoude, E., Naylor, K. T., & Pignatiello, A. (2020). Smartphones, social media use and youth mental health. *Canadian Medical Association Journal, 192*(6), E136–E141. doi:10.1503/cmaj.190434 PMID:32041697

Al-Dmour, H., Masa'deh, R. E., Salman, A., Abuhashesh, M., & Al-Dmour, R. (2020). Influence of social media platforms on public health protection against the COVID-19 pandemic via the mediating effects of public health awareness and behavioral changes: Integrated model. *Journal of Medical Internet Research, 22*(8), e19996. doi:10.2196/19996 PMID:32750004

Appel, G., Grewal, L., Hadi, R., & Stephen, A. T. (2020). The future of social media in marketing. *Journal of the Academy of Marketing Science, 48*(1), 79–95. doi:10.100711747-019-00695-1 PMID:32431463

Balbi, G., & Magaudda, P. (2018). *A history of digital media: An intermedia and global perspective.* Routledge. doi:10.4324/9781315209630

Barrett-Maitland, N., & Lynch, J. (2020). Social media, ethics and the privacy paradox. *Security and privacy from a legal, ethical, and technical perspective, 49.*

Bennet, A. (2015). *Social Media: Global Perspectives, Applications and Benefits and Dangers.* Novinka.

Chen, J., & Wang, Y. (2021). Social media use for health purposes: Systematic review. *Journal of Medical Internet Research, 23*(5), e17917. doi:10.2196/17917 PMID:33978589

Chen, Q., Min, C., Zhang, W., Wang, G., Ma, X., & Evans, R. (2020). Unpacking the black box: How to promote citizen engagement through government social media during the COVID-19 crisis. *Computers in Human Behavior, 110*, 106380. doi:10.1016/j.chb.2020.106380 PMID:32292239

Criado, J. I., Sandoval-Almazan, R., & Gil-Garcia, J. R. (2013). Government innovation through social media. *Government Information Quarterly, 30*(4), 319–326. doi:10.1016/j.giq.2013.10.003

Croucher, S. M., Nguyen, T., & Rahmani, D. (2020). Prejudice toward Asian Americans in the CO-VID-19 pandemic: The effects of social media use in the United States. *Frontiers in Communication, 5*, 39. doi:10.3389/fcomm.2020.00039

Dutta, A. (2020). Impact of digital social media on Indian higher education: alternative approaches of online learning during COVID-19 pandemic crisis. *International journal of scientific and research publications, 10*(5), 604-611.

El-Ebiary, Y. A. B., Bamansoor, S., Abu-Ulbeh, W., Amir, W. M., Saany, S. I. A., & Yusoff, M. H. (2020). A prognosis of Chinese E-governance. *IJETT, 68*, 86–89. doi:10.14445/22315381/CATI1P215

Enikolopov, R., Makarin, A., & Petrova, M. (2020). Social media and protest participation: Evidence from Russia. *Econometrica, 88*(4), 1479–1514. doi:10.3982/ECTA14281

Fagherazzi, G., Goetzinger, C., Rashid, M. A., Aguayo, G. A., & Huiart, L. (2020). Digital health strategies to fight COVID-19 worldwide: Challenges, recommendations, and a call for papers. *Journal of Medical Internet Research, 22*(6), e19284. doi:10.2196/19284 PMID:32501804

Gajendran, N. (2020). Web-sites and social media technologies as implements of E-Governance: A study of North East India. *Indian Journal of Science and Technology, 13*(31), 3188–3197. doi:10.17485/IJST/v13i31.1016

Gorwa, R. (2019). What is platform governance? *Information Communication and Society, 22*(6), 854–871. doi:10.1080/1369118X.2019.1573914

Griffith, J., & Leston-Bandeira, C. (2020). How are parliaments using new media to engage with citizens? In *The Impact of Legislatures* (pp. 380–397). Routledge. doi:10.4324/9781003033783-20

Guess, A. M., Lerner, M., Lyons, B., Montgomery, J. M., Nyhan, B., Reifler, J., & Sircar, N. (2020). A digital media literacy intervention increases discernment between mainstream and false news in the United States and India. *Proceedings of the National Academy of Sciences of the United States of America, 117*(27), 15536–15545. doi:10.1073/pnas.1920498117 PMID:32571950

Guzman, J. (2023). Social Media Statistics for Australia. *Melt Water.* https://www.meltwater.com/en/blog/social-media-statistics-australia

Hudders, L., De Jans, S., & De Veirman, M. (2021). The commercialization of social media stars: A literature review and conceptual framework on the strategic use of social media influencers. *International Journal of Advertising, 40*(3), 327–375. doi:10.1080/02650487.2020.1836925

Hussain, H. (2019). Barriers and Drivers of using social media in e-goverance: A global case study. In *2019 IEEE International Symposium on Signal Processing and Information Technology (ISSPIT)* (pp. 1-6). IEEE. 10.1109/ISSPIT47144.2019.9001764

Hyland-Wood, B., Gardner, J., Leask, J., & Ecker, U. K. (2021). Toward effective government communication strategies in the era of COVID-19. *Humanities & Social Sciences Communications, 8*(1), 30. doi:10.105741599-020-00701-w

Ismagilova, E., Hughes, L., Rana, N. P., & Dwivedi, Y. K. (2020). Security, privacy and risks within smart cities: Literature review and development of a smart city interaction framework. *Information Systems Frontiers,* 1–22. PMID:32837262

Jeet, V. (2015). *The Growing Relevance of Social Media in Governance.* New Gen Soft. https://newgen-soft.com/blog/the-growing-relevance-of-social-media-in-governance/

Jennings, W., Stoker, G., Bunting, H., Valgarðsson, V. O., Gaskell, J., Devine, D., McKay, L., & Mills, M. C. (2021). Lack of trust, conspiracy beliefs, and social media use predict COVID-19 vaccine hesitancy. *Vaccines, 9*(6), 593. doi:10.3390/vaccines9060593 PMID:34204971

Kaplan, A., & Haenlein, M. (2020). Rulers of the world, unite! The challenges and opportunities of artificial intelligence. *Business Horizons, 63*(1), 37–50. doi:10.1016/j.bushor.2019.09.003

Katzenbach, C., & Ulbricht, L. (2019). Algorithmic governance. *Internet Policy Review*, *8*(4), 1–18. doi:10.14763/2019.4.1424

Khan, G. F., Swar, B., & Lee, S. K. (2014). Social media risks and benefits: A public sector perspective. *Social Science Computer Review*, *32*(5), 606–627. doi:10.1177/0894439314524701

Khan, N. A., & Khan, A. N. (2019). What followers are saying about transformational leaders fostering employee innovation via organisational learning, knowledge sharing and social media use in public organisations? *Government Information Quarterly*, *36*(4), 101391. doi:10.1016/j.giq.2019.07.003

Kompella, L. (2020). Socio-technical transitions and organizational responses: Insights from e-governance case studies. *Journal of Global Information Technology Management*, *23*(2), 89–111. doi:10.1080/1097198X.2020.1752082

Liao, Q., Yuan, J., Dong, M., Yang, L., Fielding, R., & Lam, W. W. T. (2020). Public engagement and government responsiveness in the communications about COVID-19 during the early epidemic stage in China: Infodemiology study on social media data. *Journal of Medical Internet Research*, *22*(5), e18796. doi:10.2196/18796 PMID:32412414

Magro, M. J. (2012). A review of social media use in e-government. *Administrative Sciences*, *2*(2), 148–161. doi:10.3390/admsci2020148

Manacorda, M., & Tesei, A. (2020). Liberation technology: Mobile phones and political mobilization in Africa. *Econometrica*, *88*(2), 533–567. doi:10.3982/ECTA14392

Mansoor, M. (2021). Citizens' trust in government as a function of good governance and government agency's provision of quality information on social media during COVID-19. *Government Information Quarterly*, *38*(4), 101597. doi:10.1016/j.giq.2021.101597 PMID:34642542

Mason, A. N., Narcum, J., & Mason, K. (2021). Social media marketing gains importance after Covid-19. *Cogent Business & Management*, *8*(1), 1870797. doi:10.1080/23311975.2020.1870797

Matamoros-Fernández, A., & Farkas, J. (2021). Racism, hate speech, and social media: A systematic review and critique. *Television & New Media*, *22*(2), 205–224. doi:10.1177/1527476420982230

Nekliudov, N. A., Blyuss, O., Cheung, K. Y., Petrou, L., Genuneit, J., Sushentsev, N., Levadnaya, A., Comberiati, P., Warner, J. O., Tudor-Williams, G., Teufel, M., Greenhawt, M., DunnGalvin, A., & Munblit, D. (2020). Excessive media consumption about COVID-19 is associated with increased state anxiety: Outcomes of a large online survey in Russia. *Journal of Medical Internet Research*, *22*(9), e20955. doi:10.2196/20955 PMID:32788143

Oh, S. H., Lee, S. Y., & Han, C. (2021). The effects of social media use on preventive behaviors during infectious disease outbreaks: The mediating role of self-relevant emotions and public risk perception. *Health Communication*, *36*(8), 972–981. doi:10.1080/10410236.2020.1724639 PMID:32064932

Olan, F., Jayawickrama, U., Arakpogun, E. O., Suklan, J., & Liu, S. (2022). Fake news on social media: The Impact on Society. *Information Systems Frontiers*, 1–16. doi:10.100710796-022-10242-z PMID:35068999

Paul, S., & Das, S. (2023). Investigating information dissemination and citizen engagement through government social media during the COVID-19 crisis. *Online Information Review, 47*(2), 316–332. doi:10.1108/OIR-06-2021-0307

Sahoo, N. (2020). *Mounting majoritarianism and political polarization in India.* Political Polarization in South and Southeast Asia.

Shaher, M. A. A., & Radwan, A. F. (2022). The Role of Social Media in Government Communication during Covid-19 Pandemic: The Case of KSA. *Journal of Emergency Management and Disaster Communications, 3*(02), 131–150. doi:10.1142/S2689980922500099

Sobaci, M. Z. (2016). Social media and local governments: An overview. Social media and local governments. *Theory into Practice*, 3–21.

Wike, R., Silver, L., Fetterolf, J., Huang, C., Austin, S., Clancy, L., & Gubbala, S. (2022). *Social media seen as mostly good for democracy across many nations, but US is a major outlier.* Pew Research Center's Global Attitudes Project.

Yadav, R. K., Bagga, T., & Johar, S. (2020). E–governance impact on ease of doing business in India. *PalArch's Journal of Archaeology of Egypt/Egyptology, 17*(7), 6188-6203.

Yarchi, M., Baden, C., & Kligler-Vilenchik, N. (2021). Political polarization on the digital sphere: A cross-platform, over-time analysis of interactional, positional, and affective polarization on social media. *Political Communication, 38*(1-2), 98–139. doi:10.1080/10584609.2020.1785067

Yellow, S. M. R. (2020). *Social Media Report.* Yellow. https://www.yellow.com.au/social-media-report/ accessed on August 12, 2023.

Zhuravskaya, E., Petrova, M., & Enikolopov, R. (2020). Political effects of the internet and social media. *Annual Review of Economics, 12*(1), 415–438. doi:10.1146/annurev-economics-081919-050239

Chapter 2
Impact of Social Media on Government Operational Dynamics

Nadia Sha
Dhofar University, Oman

Bitha S. Mani
Rajadhani Business School, India

B. Ganesh
Am Maxwell International Institute for Education and Research, India

Sankar Ganesh
https://orcid.org/0000-0003-0708-8327
Veltech Rangarajan Dr. Sagunthala R&D Institute of Science and Technology, India

R. Velmurugan
https://orcid.org/0000-0002-7925-9757
Karpagam Academy of Higher Education, India

J. Sudarvel
https://orcid.org/0000-0001-6656-1992
Karpagam Academy of Higher Education, India

ABSTRACT

Social media's influence extends to policymaking, as governments are now more attentive to public sentiment and demands voiced on these platforms. Additionally, social media enables international collaboration and diplomacy, enhancing global governance efforts. In conclusion, social media's influence on governments' operational aspects is undeniable. While it has fostered greater transparency, public engagement, and crisis communication, its impact also necessitates careful management to mitigate potential risks. Governments must harness the power of social media responsibly to ensure a positive and transformative influence on their operations and better serve their citizens.

DOI: 10.4018/978-1-6684-7450-1.ch002

INTRODUCTION

Over the past few years, the emergence of new technologies and the widespread adoption of social media have significantly transformed the way people communicate. This shift has not only impacted personal interactions but has also brought about changes in the way public administration operates. Social media's growing popularity and capacity to cater to broad social demands have turned it into a potent tool for network communication. As a result, it has become a means of mutual communication between governments and society, fostering government transparency and the development of democratic societies. Advanced information plays a pivotal role in achieving transparency in public administration. Social networks offer easy and interactive ways for people to connect, allowing them to share various types of content, including text, audio, and video materials. These networks are widely utilized by private, public, and non-governmental organizations, as people seek information and form relationships. As the administration of government functions evolves, interactive multimedia communication becomes an integral part of these networks. The decision for the government to embrace and improve these networks or remain on the periphery lies with them. However, to achieve effective governance, collaboration with citizens in daily tasks and the pursuit of long-term goals is essential.

The role of social media in public administration has become a prominent area of research. Citizens now use information and communication technologies not only for professional purposes but also for social interactions, leading to the expectation of modern, open, and efficient government services. Simultaneously, government institutions facing financial constraints and budgetary pressures are compelled to seek innovative solutions. Responding to citizens' desire for seamless communication and unbiased information, government bodies are increasingly turning to new digital technology and Web 2.0 tools. This approach can help alleviate financial difficulties and enhance the quality of government services, making the exploration of social media's role in shaping and managing e-government a pressing matter. In recent years, the application of Web 2.0 technologies in e-government environments has given rise to various research directions. Studies focused on Web 2.0, social media, social networks, and their usage in the government sector underscore the intricate nature of social media's impact on public administration. As a result, the subject of social media and its role in shaping government practices has become a subject of considerable research interest. The literature review highlights the effectiveness of social media as a tool for the government to bolster citizens' trust by improving their perception of government transparency. A specific case study investigated how citizens' engagement with social media in the context of government activities can influence their trust in the government. This study provided empirical evidence of how perceived government transparency plays a crucial role in connecting the use of e-government with citizens' trust in the government.

In Linders' (2012) research, the focus is on examining the evolution of citizen coproduction in the context of social media, web 2.0 interactivity, and widespread connectivity. The study proposes a comprehensive typology consisting of three overarching categories: "Citizen Sourcing," "Government as a Platform," and "Do-It-Yourself Government." The aim is to facilitate systematic analysis and explore the potential implications for public administration. The research highlights the increasing role of the public in actively participating in government functions. Park, Kang, et al. (2016) investigate the policy role of social media in fostering public trust. Their study specifically observes the impact of tweets from prominent government figures, such as ministers, on citizens' perception of credibility in governmental Twitter feeds. The research demonstrates the mediating effect of such tweets in enhancing trust. In another study by Chen,et al. (2020), an initial assessment is made regarding the use of Facebook by Western

European municipalities, with a focus on two aspects: citizens' engagement and municipalities' activity. The research reveals that Facebook usage has become prevalent among Western European local governments. Additionally, the study proposes a methodology to measure citizen engagement on social media, which can be valuable for future research. Alcaide Muñoz, Rodríguez Bolívar and López Hernández, (2017) delves into governance models for delivering public services through Web 2.0 technologies in local initiatives. The research explores the debate surrounding Web 2.0 technologies and their implications for local governance. It identifies different governance models that local governments may adopt if they choose to implement Web 2.0 technologies for providing public services. The results indicate that majority governments tend to favor collaborative governance models, while minority governments lean towards non-collaborative solutions.

The research focuses on several key areas related to the role of social media in e-government and its impact on citizen-government feedback. These main research directions include the establishment of feedback channels between e-government and citizens through social media, the importance of having long-term agreed goals for fostering mutual links between government institutions and citizens, the use of social media in e-government, the influence of social culture on administrative forms, and the transformation of administrative processes. Considering the significance of these research areas, investigating the role of social media in the e-government environment and developing efficient feedback mechanisms remain highly relevant. Effective administrative mechanisms in e-government implementation are crucial, and the integration of social media tools and social networks can greatly enhance administrative efficiency and feedback mechanisms. Analyzing social networks and their application in transforming and improving public administration processes serves as a potent approach. The development of social media analysis tools plays a vital role in fostering mutual communication between citizens and the government, thereby improving the administration of e-government and the establishment of feedback mechanisms. This study delves into the utilization of social media tools in the e-government context and explores the prominent development trends in this area. It also reviews positive and negative impacts of social media in government. It sheds light on the futures of social media usage in government.

EMERGENCE OF SOCIAL MEDIA INTO THE BUSINESS WORLD

The rise of electronic commerce in 1995 sparked a series of new trends, leading governments to develop reliable electronic business practices that offer customer self-service. This shift enabled faster access to information and streamlined citizen-government processes, such as updating automobile registration and paying taxes. E-government initiatives have primarily focused on enhancing service delivery and efficiency through various investments. Today, e-government has transformed the state into an electronic environment, making information and services more accessible through online channels and optimizing business processes. Social media, encompassing platforms like Facebook, Google+, Twitter, blogs, wikis, and sharing websites such as YouTube and Flickr, is an integral part of Web 2.0 technologies, characterized by user-generated content and interconnected networks. Social media holds great potential for fostering electronic participation (Magro, 2012), and many saw promising opportunities for its application in government between 2007 and 2009. In some developed countries, digital disparities have been reduced (Couldry, 2007). However, a portion of the population still lacks access to these new opportunities, making them feel like "second-class citizens" (Couldry, 2007; Bertot, Jaeger, & Grimes, 2010; Magro, 2012). Some have expressed concerns that the mere adoption of technology does not automatically lead to increased civil participation (Breind & Francq, 2008). Governments, after facing challenges with earlier Web 2.0 experiments and failed transformative initiatives, have come to realize that their innovative actions might cause more harm than benefits (Magro, 2012).

Research conducted from the citizens' perspective has revealed a positive attitude and willingness to establish a mutual link with government bodies through e-government initiatives. Citizens tend to trust the government more than the private sector when it comes to handling private information. Starting from 2009, certain issues have been identified as potential threats in the realm of e-government. Experts emphasize the importance of achieving success in areas such as participation and accountability, accessible information, cooperation among government institutions, multi-channel delivery, and identification within the government sectors. While participation and accountability were primary objectives of e-government social media projects, their implementation has led to unexpected outcomes. Some propose that social media serves as a platform for mutual cooperation between citizens and the government through information sharing, potentially shaping a positive opinion about governments (Park & Cho, 2009). In 2009, experts were still deprived of the use of social media in government, but it was revealed that its adoption by the government could facilitate broader opportunities for citizen participation and increase the satisfaction of individuals who might otherwise be uninformed and disengaged (Magro, 2012). The year 2010 witnessed rapid growth in research on social media and e-government, with increased attention given to new challenges, leading to the development of detailed guidelines. Although social media and Web 2.0 have been utilized in Europe, their full potential has not been fully harnessed by the government, which has lagged behind in effectively utilizing these technologies. Many have come to recognize that adopting new technologies requires a shift in approach. Governments have been compelled to embrace everyday technologies used by people, leading to necessary changes in leadership and policies for comprehensive use of social media (Magro, 2012). Some institutions anticipated that incorporating social media technologies would increase their participation levels. However, experts caution that digital technologies cannot shield us from our own tendencies; in fact, they might amplify existing behaviors. For social media to be a solution, governments must adapt to the current agenda, moving away from a model of information collection and limitation towards a paradigm of information exchange that fosters e-participation and government innovation (Lindqvist, & Östling, 2010; Parvcek & Sachs, 2010). Over the last five years, Web 2.0 has empowered passive web users to become active content creators who are willing to share their knowledge and participate. Enterprises have been flexible in investing in social media to attract and satisfy customers, encourage their participation in discussions, get to know them better, and leverage their insights for industrial manufacturing.

Governments have observed the successful application of Web 2.0 technologies in election campaigns and have shifted their attention towards investing in social media as part of their IT strategies. However, further research is needed to explore how social media can be effectively utilized in government, drawing from experiences and limitations encountered by business sectors. To ensure successful investments in social media, it is crucial for the government not to merely follow corporate trends and use social media without a proper plan. Instead, the government's approach to social media should be well-planned, just, and focused on promoting mutual aid and transparency (Magro, 2012). An e-government approach can lead to the development of advanced ICT tools, changes in the existing environment, and organizational improvements (Magro, 2012). Experts have proposed eight key elements for a successful social media policy: employee availability, account management, satisfactory use, situation, content, security, legal considerations, and citizen engagement. Since 2011, the increasing power of social media in the hands of users has become evident. Early forms of e-government initiatives worldwide showed limited use, but expanding social media usage has been suggested as a solution to foster more extensive, deeper, and advanced electronic participation (Chun, & Reyes, 2012). Some government agencies have encountered challenges with their social media proposals. For example, contradictory announcements on a government's Facebook page can raise concerns about reliability. Additionally, Facebook privacy issues have been a point of contention. Citizens may have difficulty distinguishing between social media sources and government institutions. Accessing undesirable websites, format and design limitations, and the government's ability to reach specific citizen groups are other issues of concern. Analyzing the Arab Spring in the Near East, experts found that social media tools, including Facebook and Twitter, played a significant role in spreading information and contributing to the dramatic changes in the region (Magro, 2012). Instructions for using social media in government, particularly non-commercial tools like Facebook and Twitter, have continued to be developed. Governments are encouraged to devise specific strategies and use alternative platforms to improve access (Hellman, 2011). Studies have shown that 65% of all enterprises, including state enterprises, lack appropriate policies regarding employees' use of social media and 50% of those enterprises do not regularly monitor social media (Mcnamara, 2011; Magro, 2012). Various Web 2.0 technologies have been adopted to varying degrees by local, regional, and national governments in advanced countries, including the USA. Representative Web 2.0 technologies utilized in government include Social cooperation and Blogs, Wikis for collaborative authoring and editing, podcasting, photo and video sharing, Social Bookmarking, News Sharing, Tagging, Social networks, Mashups, Widgets, and more. This section provides a concise overview of these technologies, and their respective implementations have been identified through sources such as Firstbrook & Wollan (2001).

SOCIAL MEDIA IN E-GOVERNANCE

Social media has become widely utilized by commercial organizations, academic institutions, and individuals for various purposes, including online presence, promoting goods and services, gathering customer feedback, sharing experiences, engaging in consumer and customer interactions, collaborative content creation, e-learning, communication, and social interaction. In recent times, social media's impact has extended beyond the private sector to the political landscape. Politicians, citizens, and governments worldwide, including those from least developed countries, have harnessed the power of social media tools to transform governance arrangements, mobilize movements both for and against governments, conduct election campaigns, and maintain government-citizen communication during challenging times. Prominent examples include Barack Obama and Mitt Romney, who effectively used Twitter and other social networking sites as campaign tools during the 2012 presidential contest, allowing direct communication with supporters and shaping the political conversation on a broader scale. Additionally, various governments and officials, whether in their official capacity or personal capacity, employ social media platforms for foreign affairs, administration, and information dissemination (Banday & Mattoo, 2013). Countries like the USA, UK, Australia, and Sweden are highly active in using social media for digital diplomacy. A significant portion of USA Government agencies, around 66 percent, actively use social media websites in some form. According to the UN e-Governance survey 2012, approximately 48 percent, which amounts to 78 member states, include statements like "follow us on Facebook" or "follow us on Twitter" on their government websites. Moreover, about 7 percent of such websites provide chat rooms or instant messaging features to gather public opinion. India also has a strong presence on social media, with various ministers and officials actively using these platforms to communicate with citizens.

Overall, social media has become a crucial tool for shaping public discourse, facilitating government-citizen engagement, and advancing digital diplomacy on a global scale (Dadashzadeh, 2010).

The expansion of electronic awareness and the rapid development of e-government and e-administration indicate a significant trend towards the formation of an information society. Many international and national organizations closely monitor these trends. In advanced countries, the expenditure on e-government projects has been steadily increasing, making the efficient implementation of such initiatives a key topic of discussion. The primary objectives of e-government programs include enhancing the efficiency of economic and governmental administration and providing a material-technical foundation for the development of civil society through free access to information. In international practice, e-government projects are categorized into three main conceptual models: G2G (Government-to-Government), G2B (Government-to-Business), and G2C (Government-to-Citizen). These models aim to provide citizens with easy access to government services and streamline various functional aspects, such as e-services for registries in different sectors and e-document flow within government institutions. Social media has a wide audience due to its use of visual and audio content, making it an integral part of the network used for decision-making in public administration. It serves as a communication tool between the government and society, fostering government transparency and democratic society (Sinclair, Peirson-Smith, & Boerchers, 2017). Government transparency is achieved through the provision of advanced information, ensuring that citizens have accessible and transparent information (Landsbergen, 2010; Song & Lee, 2013; Banday & Mattoo, 2013). Social media continues to rapidly evolve to meet significant social demands. Governments, in order to effectively utilize social media, must understand how it meets these social demands. People seek easy access to information and desire to build relationships. Interactive multimedia communication is becoming increasingly integrated into networks to handle various government affairs. The government has the choice to improve or support these networks, integrate into them, or remain on the periphery. The government's role includes conducting daily transactions and developing long-term goals alongside its citizens. Multimedia proves powerful in conveying information through text, visuals, and audio (Landsbergen, 2010; Banday & Mattoo, 2013).

Trust in public administration is a delicate balance between decision-makers and citizens, or the trust citizens have in each government decision. Administrative bodies must have faith in the sovereignty of civil democracy. Unlike static web pages, social media tools enable direct appeals and proposals to citizens, creating social networks that support the government's reliability. Social media greatly facilitates network communication, including unofficial networks within the government, and can be more effective when utilized as a source of trust-building for the government. As a communication tool, social media offers advantages for both government and the people. It enables prompt, mutual, and individual interactions, making it desirable for citizens. However, the government must find new ways to engage with citizens and monitor their activities effectively. Social media's power lies in cooperation, participation, competence, and timeliness. It serves as a tool to bring together government institutions, citizens, and information, promoting government services and cooperation. Social media expands the possibilities of electronic administration by intensifying and monitoring services while reducing costs and raising efficiency (Alguliyev, Aliguliyev, & Yusifov, 2018).

Governments can use social media pages to post job announcements, promote services, seek public feedback, and collaborate with geographically diverse institutions. Increased use of social media enhances transparency, leading to greater trust in the government. Electronic transparency through social media involves sharing information about organizations' performance and outcomes and their openness to evaluation and criticism from external groups and individuals. Active information sharing fosters government transparency and helps reduce corruption. The internet plays a vital role in expanding government transparency due to its cost-effective way of disseminating large volumes of information to connected individuals. Governments strive to increase transparency through electronic administration, and social media is recognized as an alternative channel for achieving this goal, particularly in reaching groups that may lag in using online government services. The adoption of social technologies by government institutions, though slow, is gradually altering the traditional model of the state sector. These technologies offer new opportunities that can enhance government transparency and reliability, foster new forms of civil participation and engagement, and improve inter- and intra-organizational cooperation between the government and citizens. This evolving cooperation between the government and citizens is leading to a transformation in how public issues are addressed (Karakiza, 2014). In today's world, citizens use information and communication technologies (ICT) not only for professional purposes but also in their social lives. Consequently, they expect to establish similar connections with governments, seeking a modern, open, and effective government. However, government institutions often face economic challenges, including harsh measures and tight budget control, prompting them to explore new and innovative approaches. Simultaneously, citizens' increasing desire for more comfortable, seamless communication with the government, and their demand for unbiased information serve as drivers for government bodies to adopt new digital technology and leverage Web 2.0 tools. These measures aim to alleviate financial difficulties and enhance the overall quality of government services (Karakiza, 2014).

SOCIAL MEDIA IN E GOVERNANCE: BENEFITS

Various impediments hinder the adoption of e-governance, including the lack of awareness of e-services, limited access to these services, citizens' interest in utilizing them, government support, the digital divide, and the low usability of government websites. Building trust in the government is crucial for successful adoption of new technologies required for e-governance. Effective communication with citizens has been recognized as the most significant measure to establish this trust.

Social media sites offer four major potential strengths: collaboration, participation, empowerment, and time efficiency. Governments can leverage these strengths to better serve their citizens by promoting government information, services, and collaboration with stakeholders, bringing together government agencies, citizens, and relevant information (Carlo Bertot, Jaeger, & Grimes, 2012). Social media's utilization can expand the benefits of e-governance by intensifying and monitoring services while reducing costs and enhancing quality. Government agencies can use social media platforms to post job advertisements, promote services, announce events, seek public feedback and cooperation, and foster collaboration across geographically diverse agencies.

The extensive usage of social media by the public could lead to increased transparency, thereby enhancing trust in the government. Social media's potential impact on citizen usage of e-services and e-participation further supports its relevance for e-governance. A recent review of social media use in e-government has identified various other applications in e-governance. The Centre for Technology in Government at the University at Albany identified three distinct ways in which employees use social media at work: for official agency interests, professional interests, and personal interests (Lee-Geiller, & Lee, 2019). These uses are often intertwined, and clear lines may not always separate them.

SOCIAL MEDIA IN E-GOVERNANCE: NEGATIVE ASPECTS

Government information systems, including its infrastructure, individuals, agencies, employees, and information, are facing persistent, pervasive, and aggressive threats. These risks are further amplified by the ever-changing environment of social media, which utilizes Web 2.0 technologies and poses multiple challenges related to behavior, ergonomic configuration, regulation, and technology. Addressing one risk may inadvertently intensify others due to their interconnected nature.

In the Web 2.0 environment, users are empowered to collaborate, share, and interact, but this can lead to practices that infringe on the rights of others. Common risks associated with user behavior on the Web include threats to reputation, privacy, intellectual property, and the dissemination of personal or illegal content (Kadam, & Atre, 2020). Social media has the potential to fuel campaigns both in favor of and against governments or groups, and its misuse has been evident during events such as the 2011 riots in the UK and the separatist movement in Kashmir. Technological advancements in Web 2.0, including social media, have resulted in user-friendly interfaces and services that permit easy sharing of documents, videos, audio, and the creation of online communities.

Some configurations even allow users to perform these actions anonymously, which can inadvertently lead to privacy violations, intellectual property infringements, and other illegal activities. The legal frameworks governing online communication vary significantly from country to country, while social media operates on a global scale (Bennett et al, 2019). Enforcing appropriate punishments for violating these laws can be challenging in a social networking environment where multiple stakeholders have varying roles and responsibilities. Additionally, users may lack sufficient knowledge of the laws governing social media usage, making them susceptible to engaging in online offenses and crimes unknowingly. Cyber attacks, such as spear phishing, social engineering, and web application vulnerabilities, pose risks to individuals, agencies, employees, and information within the social media space (Al-Dmour et al, 2020). Even users with moderate computing skills can become targets for highly skilled cyber attackers, leading to unlawful activities and compromising information security and privacy.

IMPACT OF SOCIAL MEDIA IN E- GOVERNANCE

Information and communication tools have become increasingly crucial in people's lives, with the Internet significantly influencing communication and cooperation among individuals. The rise of blogs, websites, and social networks like Facebook, Twitter, and Google Plus has created a favorable environment for governments to engage with these new platforms. Social media serves as a platform that provides easy Internet access for everyone, enabling governments to communicate and enhance citizen participation and engagement (Abu-Shanab, 2012). As people, private enterprises, and government institutions embrace social media and information tools, governments must carefully consider how to leverage these platforms to increase citizen engagement and participation. While e-government websites serve citizens' needs, social networks facilitate communication among people, allowing governments to bridge the gap and connect more closely with their citizens (Sawalha, & Abu-Shanab, 2013). Social media has become a preferred communication tool for a broad audience with Internet access. Governments are recognizing the potential of social media to strategically manage their communication with citizens and improve overall efficiency (Sawalha & Abu-Shanab, 2013). Harris and Rea (2009) describe social media as a project that facilitates second-generation web development, fostering communication, contacts, cooperation, and information sharing. Social media's primary function revolves around communication and building mutual connections, contrasting with the historical evolution of e-government, which primarily focused on information exchange in two main stages. A key advantage of social media lies in its ability to enable information exchange through private user profiles, making content sharing and creation accessible to a broader audience (Khasawneh & Abu-Shanab, 2013). Social media empowers individuals to become content creators and publishers, offering a valuable feedback mechanism for two-way information flow. Users can share various types of content, including news, advertisements, documents, videos, and music, fostering an environment of sharing and disseminating information among networks.

E-government refers to the use of information and communication technologies by the government to engage in mutual communication with citizens and conduct state affairs through various electronic media, such as telephones, tablets, fax, smart cards, self-service kiosks, email, Internet, and EDI (Electronic Data Exchange) (Alma et al., 2021). The conceptual model of e-government is categorized based on proposed services and their efficiency, encompassing government institutions, social and political organizations, businesses, employees, and non-governmental organizations. Social media plays a significant role in the implementation of government affairs, offering strategic opportunities to engage citizens, businesses, and organizations. However, when governments decide to join social media platforms, they must exercise caution and consider important factors. Being active users on these platforms and providing timely, sustainable, and updated information while establishing mutual communication with citizens are essential for effective engagement. Experts believe that social media can contribute to a more transparent government by providing better services and information access, opening active communication channels with citizens, and empowering citizens with more influence and participation in society (Khasawneh & Abu-Shanab, 2013). Social media offers new communication tools for governments to deliver messages and news rapidly and effectively, encouraging online discussions on public matters and fostering open and transparent relations between citizens and governments. To effectively manage social media websites, governments can adopt various approaches, including the "Four R" approach used by corporations: React by monitoring what people say online, Respond by maintaining active communication channels, and Redirect to other resources to help others with similar issues. Governments should explore how to leverage these approaches creatively and efficiently on social media platforms (Khasawneh & Abu-Shanab, 2013). Having a presence on social media websites is crucial for governments to maintain high levels of trust among citizens and provide them with an active information channel. Social media also allows governments to effectively communicate with citizens and utilize valuable resources available on these platforms through innovative methods (Gohary, (2019).

DISCUSSIONS AND FUTURE RESEARCH DIRECTIONS

Governments are highly sensitive to the legal and ethical implications of technology usage, and privacy attacks on state institutions through social media have raised concerns about compiling and using online user-generated content. Despite these threats, social media remains an ideal solution for supporting awareness and future-oriented policy making. The benefits of social media tools for governments should not be overlooked. The various advantages of social media, such as collaboration, empowerment, and participation, have attracted governments to utilize it in governance to unite citizens, agencies, local municipalities, and organizations (Chun & Reyes, 2012). It helps expand government services, enhance governmental trust, strengthen democracy mechanisms, and increase transparency. However, its implementation in e-governance also poses risks of exclusion, addiction, reputation damage, isolation, privacy violation, fraud and scams, security threats, and lost productivity. Governments need to develop comprehensive frameworks, best practices, guidelines, feedback mechanisms, and policies to enable local government agencies to effectively implement social media in e-government. These policies should focus on different components and emphasize the adaptation of existing rules and regulations to ensure information and data security (Song & Lee, 2016). The application of social networks in e-government is a new direction in research and empirical applications, aiming to achieve effective administration based on the analysis of massive electronic documents and information space monitoring. Administrative decision-making proposals are developed based on data analysis, and outcomes are obtained through feedback evaluation. The final phase involves making decisions based on acquired information. Building e-government and developing effective administrative mechanisms are priorities for state development. E-government building aligns with the stages of transformation and development in public administration, contributing to economic growth, connecting remote regions with urban centers, and improving the standard of living (Dadashzadeh, 2010).

The advancement and application of new methods and mechanisms in e-government administration go beyond merely increasing electronic services and building internal networks and databases in public institutions. It also involves ensuring transparency in government activities, providing access to information, improving government efficiency, enhancing democracy, enabling citizen participation regardless of physical abilities, fostering direct democracy, offering state services online, and ensuring security (Picazo-Vela, Fernández-Haddad & Luna-Reyes, 2016). Social media plays a crucial role in the e-government environment, and analyzing social media and social networks is a significant and purposeful area of research. Given the widespread popularity of social media, implementing and analyzing social media tools is of utmost importance. Advanced analytical tools allow for the analysis of unstructured data in social media, identifying user interests and profiles on specific subjects. These tools can improve the accuracy of big data analysis and assess the effectiveness of various marketing and political campaigns. Future research should focus on developing feedback tools based on social media analytics to enhance the efficiency of e-government services. In-depth analysis of citizen information gathered from social media can create user groups with similar interests, characteristics, and preferences in various e-government domains (Lee & VanDyke, 2015). This information can be utilized for forecasting and recommending the most relevant services among the existing ones. As a result, customized services can be provided based on citizen interests and requests obtained from their profiles, ultimately increasing their satisfaction with e-government services.

CONCLUSION

Governments have been drawn to the advantages of social media, such as collaboration, participation, and empowerment, for fostering cohesion among agencies, citizens, and information in governance. It serves as a platform to promote e-services, enhance transparency, and build trust in government. However, this adoption of social media also exposes government information systems to persistent and aggressive threats, further intensified in the social media environment, encompassing risks related to behavior, ergonomic configuration, regulation, and technology. In the context of e-governance, social media may also present risks like isolation, exclusion, privacy violations, misuse of information, and security threats (Bertot, Jaeger, & Hansen, 2012). To address these challenges, governments have developed comprehensive frameworks, policies, guidelines, and best practices as essential enablers for effectively using social media in governance. While different policies emphasize various elements, most underscore adherence to existing laws and regulations to secure data and information. Some policies propose that incorporating social media in e-governance at an agency should be supported by strong business justifications, along with adequate security and privacy controls, while others consider it necessary for inclusion without providing sufficient guidelines for security and data privacy (Madyatmadja, Nindito, & Pristinella, 2019). The Indian government's framework aligns with such policies and also considers its multilingual cultural context. However, there is room for improvement, particularly in the guidelines concerning security controls, third-party service acquisition, risk assessment, employee training, account management, and legal considerations. The rapid development of ICT has significantly influenced people's lifestyles, interactions, and communication. These notable changes affect how people engage in various activities and impact the implementation of government functions. Meanwhile, existing media tools and websites, such as blogs and social media, are widely used by individuals and organizations, prompting e-government administrators to contemplate the potential benefits of joining such platforms. The growing importance and role of social media in societies, including political communication and civil activities, enable social media analysis, analysis of social networks, knowledge detection, creation of user profiles, and the use of feedback mechanisms (Yuan et al., 2023). These facilitate the expansion of government services and enhance administrative efficiency. Consequently, social media analytics tools are predominantly used in the political process and by private companies for commercial purposes. While various approaches to social media and social analytics tools exist in international practice, they undeniably exert a significant influence on improving public administration. Many governments express interest in promoting their presence on social media while also utilizing it to gather feedback on their activities.

REFERENCES

Abu-Shanab, E., & Alsmadi, N. (2019, March). Blogs as an Effective Social Media Tool in Education. In *Society for Information Technology & Teacher Education International Conference* (pp. 367-373). Association for the Advancement of Computing in Education (AACE).

Alcaide Muñoz, L., Rodríguez Bolívar, M. P., & López Hernández, A. M. (2017). Transparency in governments: A meta-analytic review of incentives for digital versus hard-copy public financial disclosures. *American Review of Public Administration*, *47*(5), 550–573. doi:10.1177/0275074016629008

Alguliyev, R., Aliguliyev, R., & Yusifov, F. (2018). Role of social networks in E-government: Risks and security threats. *Online Journal of Communication and Media Technologies*, *8*(4), 363–376.

Allam, A. A., AbuAli, A. N., Ghabban, F. M., Ameerbakhsh, O., Alfadli, I. M., & Alraddadi, A. S. (2021). Citizens satisfaction with E-Government mobile services and M-Health application during the COVID-19 pandemic in Al-Madinah Region. *Journal of Service Science and Management*, *14*(6), 636–650. doi:10.4236/jssm.2021.146040

Arumugam, T., Latha Lavanya, B., Karthik, V., Velusamy, K., Kommuri, U. K., & Panneerselvam, D. (2022). Portraying Women in Advertisements: An Analogy Between Past and Present. *American Journal of Economics and Sociology*, *81*(1), 207–223. doi:10.1111/ajes.12452

Arumugam, T., Sethu, S., Kalyani, V., Shahul Hameed, S., & Divakar, P. (2022). Representing Women Entrepreneurs in Tamil Movies. *American Journal of Economics and Sociology*, *81*(1), 115–125. doi:10.1111/ajes.12446

Banday, M. T., & Mattoo, M. M. (2013). *Social media in E-governance: A study with special reference to India.*

Bennett, N. J., Di Franco, A., Calò, A., Nethery, E., Niccolini, F., Milazzo, M., & Guidetti, P. (2019). Local support for conservation is associated with perceptions of good governance, social impacts, and ecological effectiveness. *Conservation Letters*, *12*(4), e12640. doi:10.1111/conl.12640

Bertot, J. C., Jaeger, P. T., & Grimes, J. M. (2010). Using ICTs to create a culture of transparency: E-government and social media as openness and anti-corruption tools for societies. *Government Information Quarterly*, *27*(3), 264–271. doi:10.1016/j.giq.2010.03.001

Bertot, J. C., Jaeger, P. T., & Hansen, D. (2012). The impact of polices on government social media usage: Issues, challenges, and recommendations. *Government Information Quarterly*, *29*(1), 30–40. doi:10.1016/j.giq.2011.04.004

Brandes, L., Franck, E., & Nüesch, S. (2008). Local heroes and superstars: An empirical analysis of star attraction in German soccer. *Journal of Sports Economics*, *9*(3), 266–286. doi:10.1177/1527002507302026

Carlo Bertot, J., Jaeger, P. T., & Grimes, J. M. (2012). Promoting transparency and accountability through ICTs, social media, and collaborative e-government. *Transforming government: people, process and policy, 6*(1), 78-91.

Chen, Q., Min, C., Zhang, W., Wang, G., Ma, X., & Evans, R. (2020). Unpacking the black box: How to promote citizen engagement through government social media during the COVID-19 crisis. *Computers in Human Behavior*, *110*, 106380. doi:10.1016/j.chb.2020.106380 PMID:32292239

Chun, S. A., & Reyes, L. F. L. (2012). Social media in government. *Government Information Quarterly*, *29*(4), 441–445. doi:10.1016/j.giq.2012.07.003

Couldry, N. (2009). Does 'the media' have a future? *European Journal of Communication*, *24*(4), 437–449. doi:10.1177/0267323109345604

Dadashzadeh, M. (2010). Social media in government: From eGovernment to eGovernance. [JBER]. *Journal of Business & Economics Research*, *8*(11). doi:10.19030/jber.v8i11.51

Gohary, E. E. (2019). The impact of financial technology on facilitating e-government services in Egypt. *Journal of Distribution Science*, *17*(5), 51–59. doi:10.15722/jds.17.5.201905.51

Hellman, R. (2011, October). The cloverleaves of social media challenges for e-governments. In *Proceedings of eChallenges e-2011 Conference* (pp. 1-8).

Kadam, A. B., & Atre, S. R. (2020). Negative impact of social media panic during the COVID-19 outbreak in India. *Journal of Travel Medicine*, *27*(3), taaa057. doi:10.1093/jtm/taaa057 PMID:32307545

Kalyani, V. (2017). Empowering Women Farmers Participation In Organic Agricultural Development. *International Journal of Multidisciplinary Educational Research*, *6*(2), 187.

Kalyani, V. (2018). Organic farming in Tamil Nadu: Status, Issues and Prospects. American International Journal of Research in Humanities. *Arts and Social Sciences*, *21*(1), 82–86.

Kalyani, V. (2020). *Perception of Certified Organic Farmers towards Organic Farming Practices in Pudukkottai District of TamilNadu (No. 4784)*. Easy Chair.

KalyaniV. (2021). A Study of Effect of Social Networking Sites on the Self-Esteem of Adolescent Girl Students Belonging to Urban Areas of Sivaganga District. Available at SSRN 3879915. doi:10.2139/ssrn.3879915

Kalyani, V. (2021). *Marketing Intelligence Practices on Fmcg Consumer Preferences and Buying Behaviour Pattern Using Social Network Analysis (No. 5857)*. EasyChair.

Kalyani, V. (2021). *Parental Involvement in Improving Children's Learning in Social Work Perspective (No. 5107)*. Easy Chair.

Kalyani, V. (2021). *The Employee Engagement on Human Resources Information System Practice Through E-Learning Training (No. 5856)*. EasyChair.

Kalyani, V. (2023). Regression Analysis in R: A Comprehensive View for the Social Sciences. *Journal of the Royal Statistical Society. Series A, (Statistics in Society)*, qnad081. doi:10.1093/jrsssa/qnad081

Kalyani, V., Arumugam, T., & Surya Kumar, M. (2022). Women in Oppressive Societies as Portrayed in Kollywood Movies. *American Journal of Economics and Sociology*, *81*(1), 173–185. doi:10.1111/ajes.12450

Karakiza, M. (2015). The impact of social media in the public sector. *Procedia: Social and Behavioral Sciences*, *175*, 384–392. doi:10.1016/j.sbspro.2015.01.1214

Landsbergen, D. (2010, June). Government as part of the revolution: Using social media to achieve public goals. In *Proceedings of the 10th European conference on e-government* (pp. 243-250).

Lee, N. M., & VanDyke, M. S. (2015). Set it and forget it: The one-way use of social media by government agencies communicating science. *Science Communication*, *37*(4), 533–541. doi:10.1177/1075547015588600

Lee-Geiller, S., & Lee, T. D. (2019). Using government websites to enhance democratic E-governance: A conceptual model for evaluation. *Government Information Quarterly*, *36*(2), 208–225. doi:10.1016/j.giq.2019.01.003

Linders, D. (2012). From e-government to we-government: Defining a typology for citizen coproduction in the age of social media. *Government Information Quarterly*, *29*(4), 446–454. doi:10.1016/j.giq.2012.06.003

Lindqvist, E., & Östling, R. (2010). Political polarization and the size of government. *The American Political Science Review*, *104*(3), 543–565. doi:10.1017/S0003055410000262

Madyatmadja, E. D., Nindito, H., & Pristinella, D. (2019, November). Citizen attitude: Potential impact of social media based government. In *Proceedings of the 2019 3rd International Conference on Education and E-Learning* (pp. 128-134). ACM. 10.1145/3371647.3371653

Magro, M. J. (2012). A review of social media use in e-government. *Administrative Sciences*, *2*(2), 148–161. doi:10.3390/admsci2020148

Manikandan, G., Murugaiah, S., Velusamy, K., Ramesh, A. B. K., Rathinavelu, S., Viswanathan, R., & Jageerkhan, M. N. (2022). Work Life Imbalance and Emotional Intelligence: A Major Role and Segment Among College Teachers. *International Journal of Professional Business Review*, *7*(6), e0832. doi:10.26668/businessreview/2022.v7i6.832

MCNAMARA, L. (2011). Social media: What role should it play in the courts? [Law Society of South Australia]. *Bulletin*, *33*(4), 22–23.

Park, J., & Cho, K. (2009, September). Declining relational trust between government and publics, and potential prospects of social media in the government public relations. In *Proceedings of EGPA Conference 2009 The Public Service: Service Delivery in the Information Age*. ACM.

Park, M. J., Kang, D., Rho, J. J., & Lee, D. H. (2016). Policy role of social media in developing public trust: Twitter communication with government leaders. *Public Management Review*, *18*(9), 1265–1288. doi:10.1080/14719037.2015.1066418

Picazo-Vela, S., Fernández-Haddad, M., & Luna-Reyes, L. F. (2016). Opening the black box: Developing strategies to use social media in government. *Government Information Quarterly*, *33*(4), 693–704. doi:10.1016/j.giq.2016.08.004

Sachs, M., & Parycek, P. (2010). Open government-information flow in Web 2.0. *Euro. J. ePractice*, *9*, 1-70.

Sawalha, S., Al-Jamal, M., & Abu-Shanab, E. (2019). The influence of utilising Facebook on e-government adoption. *Electronic Government, an International Journal*, *15*(1), 1-20.

Sinclair, A. J., Peirson-Smith, T. J., & Boerchers, M. (2017). Environmental assessments in the Internet age: The role of e-governance and social media in creating platforms for meaningful participation. *Impact Assessment and Project Appraisal*, *35*(2), 148–157. doi:10.1080/14615517.2016.1251697

Song, C., & Lee, J. (2013, June). Can social media restore citizen trust in government? In *Public Management Research Conference*, Madison, Wisconsin.

Song, C., & Lee, J. (2016). Citizens' use of social media in government, perceived transparency, and trust in government. *Public Performance & Management Review*, *39*(2), 430–453. doi:10.1080/15309576.2015.1108798

Yuan, Y. P., Dwivedi, Y. K., Tan, G. W. H., Cham, T. H., Ooi, K. B., Aw, E. C. X., & Currie, W. (2023). Government digital transformation: Understanding the role of government social media. *Government Information Quarterly*, *40*(1), 101775. doi:10.1016/j.giq.2022.101775

Chapter 3
Impact of Social Media on Social Workers in the Digital Age

Mirshad Rahman

https://orcid.org/0009-0005-2488-9216

Department of Social Work, Acharya Institute of Graduate Studies, India

Madhusudanan Sundaresan

https://orcid.org/0000-0002-1916-0317

Department of Social Work, Dwaraka Doss Goverdhan Doss Vaishnav College, India

Akhila

Department of Social Work, Sree Sankaracharya University of Sanskrit, India

Bagavathi C.

https://orcid.org/0009-0009-2052-2299

Department of Social Work, Vellalar College for Women, India

Kumaraswamy Channabasaiah

Department of Social Work, Acharya Institute of Graduate Studies, India

ABSTRACT

Social workers must navigate issues related to client privacy, boundary management, and maintaining professional integrity online. The potential risks of misinformation, cyberbullying, and burnout demand careful attention and responsible usage. Despite these challenges, social media's positive impact on social workers cannot be ignored. It has empowered them to stay informed about the latest developments, trends, and best practices in their profession. As social media continues to evolve, it is crucial for social workers to embrace these technological tools thoughtfully and responsibly, harnessing their potential for enhancing collaboration and advancing social work practice.

DOI: 10.4018/978-1-6684-7450-1.ch003

INTRODUCTION

The advent of social media and the Internet has had a profound impact on the field of social work, revolutionizing how communication and information exchange occur. On one hand, it facilitates global connectivity, allowing people from diverse corners of the world to interact and access information effortlessly. However, the darker side of social media has also surfaced, with issues like fake news and cyberbullying having potentially dire consequences. Nevertheless, examining the positive influence of this 21st-century innovation on social work is essential. Social media has notably enhanced communication channels between social workers and their clients. Platforms like Facebook and WhatsApp have simplified, cost-effective, and expedited the process of reaching out to clients, eliminating the need for unnecessary transportation expenses (Mishna et al., 2012). Moreover, many social workers maintain active social media pages, offering interested clients a convenient means to contact them and book appointments with ease. The accessibility and efficiency provided by social media have transformed how social workers deliver their services, enabling quicker response times and expanding their outreach to a broader audience. By leveraging the power of these digital tools, social workers can engage with clients in real-time and establish meaningful connections across geographical boundaries (Fang et al., 2014). However, it is crucial to remain mindful of the potential negative consequences of social media in the context of social work. The proliferation of fake news can lead to misinformation and misunderstanding among clients, while cyberbullying poses serious threats to the mental well-being of both clients and professionals alike. Social workers must stay vigilant and implement strategies to address and mitigate these challenges. Social media's impact on social work has been substantial, transforming the way professionals communicate with clients and enhancing service delivery (Lee, 2020). It offers new opportunities for connection and engagement, but it also demands a responsible approach to address the challenges it brings. By harnessing the potential of social media while remaining mindful of its drawbacks, social workers can navigate this dynamic digital landscape effectively and make a positive difference in the lives of their clients (Mugisha, 2018).

The emergence of social media has opened unprecedented opportunities for social service workers, yet it also presents unique challenges and potential risks to their profession. While the digital revolution has impacted various disciplines, few face such blurred boundaries and complexities concerning social media usage as the field of social services. For the social care workforce, it is crucial to grasp the social media landscape and recognize its potential benefits for their practice (Voshel & Wesala, 2015). However, research and guidance have lagged behind the growing demand for support from professionals in this sector. Although there are anecdotal accounts of individuals leveraging social media to improve and enhance their practice, comprehensive research exploring the broader implications for the workforce remains limited. The existing studies primarily consist of small-scale investigations with specific caveats on social media usage, lacking large-scale, generalizable, and scalable research projects (Mishna et al., 2012). This Insight aims to address a part of this gap by delving into the understanding of 'social media,' examining perceived risks associated with its use, identifying the opportunities it provides, exploring its relationship to workforce well-being, and considering the future implications for social care practice. By shedding light on these aspects, this exploration seeks to equip social service workers with valuable insights to navigate the evolving landscape of social media and make informed decisions for their professional development and practice (Chan, 2016).

SOCIAL MEDIA FOR SOCIAL WORKERS

Social media has revolutionized how we communicate and access information, and various industries have recognized the benefits of a well-executed social media presence. Social work, with its focus on providing support to those in need, has also embraced social media to connect and strengthen its community. The appeal of social media lies in its accessibility, making it easier for social workers to engage in conversations with like-minded individuals (Thornton-Rice & Moran, 2022). Platforms such as LinkedIn and Facebook provide opportunities for social workers to build personal networks that foster education and support, as mentioned in the National Association of Social Workers and Association of Social Work Boards' Standards for Technology and Social Media Practice. Real-time communication on social media enables social workers to stay updated on critical topics and share relevant content with their peers (Boddy & Dominelli, 2017). They can learn about the latest treatments, cultural experiences of clients, and other developments that enhance the quality of their services (Willoughby, 2019). However, social workers must exercise caution in their use of social media. Some may unknowingly breach confidentiality by sharing intimate client details while trying to protect identities. Such actions undermine professional ethics and can harm clients' trust. Responsible use of social media is crucial for social workers. They should avoid sharing client stories without permission and focus on empowering their community through knowledge-sharing and support. By using social media responsibly, social workers can create a positive impact, advancing their profession and serving their clients effectively (Chan, 2016).

UTILIZING SOCIAL MEDIA AND TECHNOLOGY FOR ENHANCED COLLABORATION AMONG SOCIAL WORKERS

Social workers can leverage the power of social media and technology as valuable tools for connecting, learning, and sharing with both their peers and clients. However, making the most of these resources while upholding ethical standards demands specific skills and thoughtful strategies (Chan, & Ngai, 2019). The following are some of the steps need to follow for the effective utilization of social media among the social workers;

Selecting the Appropriate Platforms

Selecting the appropriate platforms is the initial step in effectively utilizing social media and technology for collaboration. Numerous options, such as Facebook, Twitter, LinkedIn, Instagram, YouTube, blogs, podcasts, webinars, and online forums, are available, each catering to distinct goals, preferences, and audiences. For instance, Facebook allows for group and page creation to foster communication among social workers, though it may expose one to privacy and security concerns. Twitter offers access to the latest trends and news in the field but can be overwhelming and distracting (Hitchcock & Young, 2016). LinkedIn facilitates the establishment of a professional network and showcases skills, though it may also come across as competitive and formal. Conducting research and experimenting with various platforms is necessary to determine the most suitable ones for both you and your collaborators, enabling effective and tailored collaboration efforts (Beaumont, Chester & Rideout, 2017).

Adhere to the Guidelines

The second crucial step in leveraging social media and technology for collaboration is to strictly follow the guidelines and standards set by your profession, organization, and platform. As a responsible social worker, upholding the values and ethics of your practice, including confidentiality, respect, integrity, and competence, is of utmost importance. It is equally essential to comply with your employer's policies and procedures concerning data protection, consent, and supervision (Best, Manktelow & Taylor, 2014). Additionally, respect the rules and norms of the specific platform you are using, which may encompass copyright regulations, terms of service, and netiquette. Staying well-informed and conscious of the guidelines and standards that govern your use of social media and technology is vital. By adhering consistently and diligently to these principles, you can maintain professionalism, protect clients' privacy, and ensure a positive and ethical collaboration experience (Boyd, 2010).

Strike a Balance Between Professional and Personal

The third key step to effectively utilize social media and technology for collaboration is to maintain a harmonious blend of professionalism and personality in your communication and interactions. Being professional entails using appropriate language, tone, and content suited to your purpose and audience. Avoid sharing or commenting on anything that might compromise your reputation, credibility, or relationships with clients, colleagues, or employers. Simultaneously, embrace the personal aspect by showcasing your personality, passion, and perspective in your posts and responses (Papacharissi, 2010). Engage with other social workers in a friendly, respectful, and supportive manner. Striking this delicate balance between being professional and personal in your use of social media and technology is essential to create a positive and authentic online presence. By doing so, you can effectively collaborate, connect with others, and maintain a trustworthy and relatable online identity (Chan, 2016).

Engage in Learning and Sharing

The fourth crucial step in effectively utilizing social media and technology for collaboration is to actively engage in learning from and sharing with other social workers. These digital tools provide a vast array of information, resources, and opportunities for professional development and growth. By leveraging them, you can stay updated on the latest research, best practices, and innovations in your field (Bonini, Caliandro & Massarelli, 2016). Additionally, social media and technology enable you to seek valuable feedback, advice, and mentorship from peers and experts. You can contribute to the collective learning by sharing your knowledge, experience, and insights with other social workers who can benefit from them. To make the most of this process, maintain curiosity and an open-minded approach in your use of social media and technology. By actively participating in learning and sharing, you contribute to the collaborative growth and advancement of your profession (Ellison, Gibbs & Weber, 2015).

Engage in Collaboration and Networking

The fifth pivotal step in utilizing social media and technology for collaboration is to actively engage in collaboration and networking with fellow social workers. These digital platforms offer the opportunity to connect with professionals from diverse backgrounds, locations, and specialties. You can leverage social media and technology to create or join communities of practice, interest, or action that align with your goals, values, and passions (Chan, 2018). Additionally, you can initiate or participate in projects, campaigns, or events that address common issues, challenges, or opportunities within your field. Furthermore, these platforms enable you to expand and diversify your professional network, establishing valuable relationships that offer mutual support, referral opportunities, and potential partnerships. To maximize the benefits, adopt a proactive and strategic approach in your use of social media and technology (Abidin, 2021). By leveraging these tools effectively, you can enhance collaboration and network with other social workers, fostering a sense of unity and growth within the profession.

Assess and Enhance

The sixth essential step in leveraging social media and technology for collaboration is to continually assess and enhance your usage. Given the ever-evolving nature of these tools and your evolving needs, goals, and expectations, regular evaluation is crucial. Monitoring and evaluating the impact and effectiveness of your collaboration efforts through qualitative and quantitative means, such as analytics, surveys, feedback forms, or self-reflection, are essential. These assessments help gauge the results, outcomes, and experiences derived from your use of social media and technology (Ellison, Gibbs & Weber, 2015). Moreover, such evaluations aid in identifying and addressing any gaps, issues, or risks that may arise during your collaboration endeavors. Being adaptable and flexible in your approach to using social media and technology is vital, as it allows you to continuously improve your skills and strategies for collaboration. By proactively seeking growth and refinement in your collaborative efforts, you can make the most of social media and technology as powerful tools for achieving meaningful and impactful collaborations with others (Abidin, 2021).

IMPACT OF SOCIAL MEDIA ON SOCIAL WORK

Social media and the Internet have profoundly impacted the field of social work. Their ability to facilitate communication across the globe and provide fast and easy access to information has been instrumental in transforming social work practices. However, this technological revolution has also given rise to challenges like the dissemination of fake news and the prevalence of cyberbullying, which can have severe consequences. Considering the most significant invention of the 21st century, it becomes crucial to explore its specific effects on social work. This examination reveals both positive and negative impacts (Cheung & Lee 2010). On the positive side, social media has enabled social workers to connect with individuals from diverse backgrounds, allowing for enhanced communication and the exchange of ideas on a global scale. Information sharing has become more efficient, empowering professionals to stay updated on the latest developments and best practices in their field. However, the darker aspects of social media, such as the spread of misinformation and cyberbullying, must not be overlooked (Banks et al., 2020). These harmful phenomena can compromise the well-being of individuals and communities, demanding vigilance and responsible use of social media within the social work profession. In summary, social media and the Internet have revolutionized social work, providing unprecedented opportunities for connection and information sharing (Siddiqui & Singh, 2016). Nonetheless, careful consideration of the potential risks and a commitment to ethical practice are essential to ensure the responsible and constructive use of these powerful tools within the field.

Positive Impact of Social Media Among Social Workers

Improved Communication

Social media has revolutionized how social workers communicate with their clients. Platforms like Facebook and WhatsApp have made it easier, more cost-effective, and faster for social workers to connect with their clients without the need for expensive transportation. Additionally, many social workers maintain active social media pages, enabling interested clients to effortlessly contact them and book appointments (Chan, 2016).

Globalization of Social Work

In the past, social workers were limited to addressing issues within their local communities. However, with the advent of social media platforms like Skype and Facebook Messenger, counselors in one part of the world can now offer their services to clients located in distant regions like Europe or Africa without incurring exorbitant expenses (Turner, 2016).

Streamlined Client Solicitation

Social media has become a powerful tool for social workers to attract and engage with clients. By establishing and maintaining active social media pages and regularly updating content, social workers can effectively market their services to a broader audience (Chan, 2016). Clients, in turn, can easily find available social workers and access a range of services, including spiritual, psychiatric, and anxiety counseling, all while maintaining their anonymity. The use of video content further enhances engagement and fosters a sense of trust in the online counseling process (Siddiqui & Singh, 2016).

Negative Impact of Social Media Among Social Workers

Ethical Challenges in Social Work and Social Media

Social workers who engage with their clients on social media encounter a multitude of ethical dilemmas in their practice. One such concern is the potential for inappropriate relationships to develop when being friends on platforms like Facebook, leading to conflicts of interest and compromising the social worker's effectiveness (Boddy & Dominelli, 2017).

Privacy Issues

Privacy and confidentiality are also significant concerns. The ease of accessing clients' social media pages may tempt social workers, including counselors and psychiatrists, to gather information without consent, infringing upon their clients' privacy and violating ethical and legal standards. Furthermore, social workers may face uncomfortable situations when clients send friend requests or initiate personal conversations on social media (Voshel & Wesala, 2015). The risk of clients stalking social workers and using their information or pictures for unprofessional purposes adds to the complexity of maintaining appropriate boundaries.

Regulatory Issues

Regulatory challenges pose additional difficulties for online social work. The field remains largely unregulated, making it challenging for regulatory bodies to oversee online practitioners who lack a physical office or address. The absence of a comprehensive regulatory framework for online social work further complicates matters, leaving clients with little means to verify their social worker's credentials or regulatory status, especially if they are from different countries (Siddiqui & Singh, 2016). Dealing with unregulated social workers exposes clients to potential dangers, including sexual harassment and fraud, making it imperative for the social work community to address these ethical challenges posed by social media and establish robust ethical guidelines and regulatory standards (Boddy & Dominelli, 2017).

ETHICAL CONSIDERATIONS FOR SOCIAL MEDIA AND SOCIAL WORK PRACTICE

The National Association of Social Workers (2008) does not directly mention social media and modern modes of communication in its Code of Ethics. However, the Code provides guidance on various ethical challenges that social workers encounter in social networking sites. While it may not offer immediate answers to all ethical dilemmas, social workers are expected to ensure their decisions and behavior aligns with the provisions of the Code (Boddy & Dominelli, 2017). One strength of the NASW Code of Ethics is its emphasis on upholding the dignity and autonomy of individuals. This principle applies to social media interactions as well, where social workers must prioritize their clients' needs and avoid crossing personal boundaries. Integrity, fairness, trustworthiness, and transparency, which are central to the Code, govern all actions in social work practice, including communication on social networking sites (Kimball & Kim, 2013). Confidentiality is another essential aspect highlighted by the NASW Code, with social workers entrusted to safeguard their clients' personal information. Ethical decision-making guidelines are provided when navigating situations that may compromise client confidentiality. Cultural competence is emphasized, encouraging social workers to be aware of their clients' backgrounds and how they may influence their perspectives (Turner, 2016).

Professional boundaries are critical in social work practice, and social workers must assess if social media blurs these boundaries. Steps to manage risks and protect integrity should be taken if multiple relationships in social media interfere with professional conduct. The need for ongoing skill development is underscored, prompting social workers to familiarize themselves with the benefits and risks of social media and stay informed about emerging platforms and technologies (Ricciardelli et al., 2020). By aligning their practices with the NASW Code of Ethics and being mindful of ethical considerations, social workers can navigate the complexities of social media while providing high-quality and responsible services to their clients. Experienced practitioners understand the appropriate boundaries for sharing information with colleagues, friends, and family members in both formal and informal settings (Barsky, 2017). Nevertheless, when utilizing social media, social workers must resist the temptation to publicly post private information about current or former clients. It is crucial to prioritize confidentiality and maintain the highest standards of privacy, regardless of whether the clients' identities are revealed or concealed (Baier, 2019).

AREAS NOT COVERED BY THE NASW CODE OF ETHICS CONCERNING SOCIAL MEDIA AND SOCIAL WORK PRACTICE

The NASW Code of Ethics provides comprehensive guidance for numerous ethical challenges faced by practitioners. However, in the realm of social networking, certain gray areas remain unaddressed, giving rise to ethical dilemmas (Duncan-Daston, Hunter-Sloan & Fullmer, 2013). One such issue involves non-therapeutic connections formed online, which can undermine the integrity of the practitioner-client relationship. Establishing cyberspace contacts with clients may blur boundaries, leading to potential conflicts, yet the NASW Code is ambiguous about addressing such online relationships (Reamer, 2013). Social media users often employ pennames and share distorted information, blurring the line between private and public personas. This raises questions about the confidentiality of data accessed online, an ethical paradox that the NASW Code does not explicitly tackle. Blogging poses another ethical challenge as practitioners and bloggers alike share personal experiences with the world. Some social workers post work-related protests on social media, but without precise guidance from the NASW Code, reprimands are rare, given the informal context of social media (Barsky, 2017). Institutions creating blogs for sharing clinical experiences also raise concerns about the credibility of information posted. The lack of mechanisms to deter misinformation may jeopardize the reputation of practitioners, as the NASW Code does not address this specific threat. Overall, these unaddressed areas in the context of social media present ethical complexities that require further examination and clarity from the NASW Code of Ethics (Brill, 2001).

THREE STANDARDS BY ASSOCIATION OF SOCIAL WORK BOARDS

Policy 3.08 emphasizes the utmost protection of client data obtained or stored digitally or through electronic means. However, certain exceptions allow for breaches of confidentiality under specific circumstances (Marson, DeAngelis, & Mittal, 2010). Social workers engage with clients through diverse platforms like social media, email, videoconferencing, text messaging, or online chat, as outlined by the ASWB. Policy 4.03 mandates that such communications remain strictly professional and relevant to the client's received services (Boland-Prom, 2009). On the other hand, Policy 6.02 prohibits invading or compromising a colleague's privacy, including disclosing their personal information (Comer & Bell, 2020). Regarding Policy 3.08, exceptions include situations where withholding information may cause harm to a verifiable individual, either the client or another known person. The risk must be foreseeable and imminent, with evidence supporting the potential consequences of non-disclosure. Additionally, disclosure is permissible when it is a legal requirement, compelled by a statute, regulation, or court order, in alignment with ASWB policies (Wagner, & Gilbert, 2018).

THE IMPACT OF ASWB ON SOCIAL MEDIA AND SOCIAL WORK PRACTICE

As per the Association of Social Work Boards, Policy 3.08 prioritizes safeguarding client information, especially in cases where social work services are provided to individuals or groups necessitating privacy due to the sensitive nature of the information involved, such as counseling or specialized treatment. Policy 4.03 mandates obtaining client consent for any communication (Kimball & Kim, 2013). While social media facilitates efficient information exchange and deeper client understanding, it also presents challenges. The accessibility of shared information on social media networks may inadvertently reveal client details that were not intended for public consumption. Policy 6.02 strictly prohibits sharing personal or work-related information about colleagues on social media without their consent, as once exposed, such information becomes challenging to retrieve (Boddy & Dominelli, 2017). The ease of information transmission through social media can be both advantageous and problematic. Information can rapidly spread to a large audience, posing a risk of destructive consequences when sensitive client data is disseminated without proper safeguards. Additionally, social media allows easy tracking and communication with clients, but it can also enable harassment or mistreatment when communication occurs without the client's explicit consent (Byrne, Kirwan, & Mc Guckin, 2019).

THE THREE STANDARDS' IMPLICATIONS FOR SOCIAL WORKERS

The implications of the Three Standards for Social Workers are significant in enhancing the quality of services provided and maintaining a professional relationship with clients. Policy 3.08's emphasis on confidentiality fosters a sense of security for clients, as they feel confident sharing their information with service providers, knowing it will not be disclosed on social media. This policy ensures clients are spared unnecessary distress resulting from mishandling their confidential information (Parker, 2020). Strict adherence to Policy 4.03 in maintaining communications related to the service provided preserves a professional dynamic throughout the treatment process. The requirement for explicit client consent before engaging in any communication minimizes the risk of client harassment and ensures all interactions are consensual (Torous et al., 2020). Furthermore, Policy 6.02 safeguards social workers from having their personal or work information shared on social media without their consent (Alston, 2020). This protection shields workers from potential harm to their career and personal life. By enforcing such boundaries and confidentiality, these policies promote professionalism in client interactions. The existence of penalties for breaching these policies reinforces their importance and encourages adherence, safeguarding both clients and social workers (Kaushik & Walsh, 2019). Overall, the Three Standards contribute to improved service quality and strengthened professionalism in social work practice.

Implications for Personal Wellbeing

A growing body of literature highlights the impact of stress, burnout, depression, and other work-related mental health issues on individual practice and team morale (McFadden et al., 2020; Greer, 2016). Social media's role in supporting personal wellbeing is also gaining recognition. Ravalier and Boichat's (2018) research delves into social worker wellbeing, analyzing the influence of workload, support, and working conditions on stress and job satisfaction levels. While not solely focused on social media, they do identify the stress caused by public criticism of social workers on social media platforms, an experience reported by 6 in 10 participants in their survey. Despite the challenges, social media can also be beneficial. Communities of practice offer professionals the chance to communicate with other social service workers, providing a positive therapeutic experience. Forums create a safe space for colleagues to connect, act as a support network, and offer a sounding board (Gandy-Guedes et al, 2016; Westwood, 2014). Social workers can engage in personal reflective practice through blogging and note-taking apps, using them as learning logs or diaries. These tools not only help individuals but can also be valuable resources for leadership, offering examples of good practice and opportunities for improvement (Ventola, 2014). From a management perspective, social media presents opportunities for remote staff to work flexibly through document sharing apps and video conferencing software, accessible on tablets or smartphones. Initiatives like Nottinghamshire Council providing iPads to staff enabled virtual paperwork completion and easy communication with colleagues (Donovan, Rose & Connolly, 2017). However, it is essential to remind staff of their right to "switch off," even with 24/7 connectivity-promoting technologies, as emphasized by Greer (2016). Maintaining a healthy work-life balance remains crucial.

Implications for Practice

The impact of social media on social services practice is extensive, but it should not replace traditional models. Instead, it serves as a valuable tool to enhance development and foster more effective and efficient practice, equipping practitioners with better tools to support their work. For the workforce and the profession, recognizing potential risks and offering solutions is crucial. Turner (2017) emphasizes the importance of initiating a dialogue between organizations and their workforce about the benefits and appropriate use of social media to support staff's practice needs. Wider implications include driving innovation within the workforce, promoting greater engagement and partnership among professionals, and facilitating integration across disciplines like health. Social media usage can also facilitate a more comprehensive integration of practice within social services teams, fostering closer collaboration and improved service alignment (Greer, 2016). Furthermore, social media offers opportunities for positive risk-taking within organizations. Encouraging and supporting staff to manage risks can lead to significantly improved outcomes for both individuals and services. It paves the way for innovative approaches in service delivery and fosters a culture of proactive risk management for better results.

CONCLUSION

As of today, there remains limited research and understanding about the immediate and long-term effects of social media on adolescent development. However, it is evident that social media, particularly social networking sites, profoundly impact and shape the lives of adolescents in multiple ways (Zeng, 2010). Numerous studies highlight the connections between social media and depression symptoms, eating disorders, harassment, and bullying. Our firsthand experience with adolescents reinforces the idea that social networking sites perpetuate a culture of idealized images, affecting the self-worth and mood of today's youth (Turner et al., 2018). Furthermore, our encounters with adolescents underscore the risks posed by social media and online communities as platforms for engaging in harmful behaviors. As professionals, it is imperative to grasp the cultural implications of these platforms to better comprehend the youth who use them. Social workers should educate themselves about these platforms to effectively support and build rapport with adolescent clients (Horng & Wu, 2020). To navigate the ever-evolving landscape of social media, social workers can develop screening tools to better understand its impact on adolescents, create online communities among themselves for knowledge exchange, and design continued education courses focusing on various social media platforms (Turner, 2017). As technology continues to advance and shape our world, social media will play an increasingly central role in communication, networks, and relationships among adolescents. These platforms are here to stay, and it is essential not only to identify their risks but also to encourage positive and responsible usage to promote healthy development among youth. As the social media possesses the potential to revolutionize social service work, research works emphasize that when used effectively with awareness of risks and uncertainties, creative and well-informed staff can drive innovation and development within the profession (Boddy & Dominelli, 2017). Such a strategic utilization of social media will enable the workforce to receive unprecedented support and benefits, benefiting both practitioners and the organizations they serve. This innovative approach not only empowers social service workers but also enhances the overall experience for service users, ultimately fostering a positive impact on the entire sector.

REFERENCES

Abidin, C. (2021). From "networked publics" to "refracted publics": A companion framework for researching "below the radar" studies. *Social Media + Society*, 7(1), 2056305120984458. doi:10.1177/2056305120984458

Alston, M. (2020). *Research for social workers: An introduction to methods*. Routledge. doi:10.4324/9781003117094

Baier, A. L. (2019). The ethical implications of social media: Issues and recommendations for clinical practice. *Ethics & Behavior*, 29(5), 341–351. doi:10.1080/10508422.2018.1516148

Banks, S., Cai, T., De Jonge, E., Shears, J., Shum, M., Sobočan, A. M., Strom, K., Truell, R., Úriz, M. J., & Weinberg, M. (2020). Practising ethically during COVID-19: Social work challenges and responses. *International Social Work*, 63(5), 569–583. doi:10.1177/0020872820949614

Barsky, A. (2017). Ethics alive! The 2017 NASW code of ethics: What's new. *New Social Worker*.

Barsky, A. E. (2017). Social work practice and technology: Ethical issues and policy responses. *Journal of Technology in Human Services*, 35(1), 8–19. doi:10.1080/15228835.2017.1277906

Beaumont, E., Chester, P., & Rideout, H. (2017). Navigating ethical challenges in social media: Social work student and practitioner perspectives. *Australian Social Work*, 70(2), 221–228. doi:10.1080/0312 407X.2016.1274416

Best, P., Manktelow, R., & Taylor, B. (2014). Online communication, social media and adolescent well-being: A systematic narrative review. *Children and Youth Services Review*, 41, 27–36. doi:10.1016/j. childyouth.2014.03.001

Boddy, J., & Dominelli, L. (2017). Social media and social work: The challenges of a new ethical space. *Australian Social Work*, 70(2), 172–184. doi:10.1080/0312407X.2016.1224907

Boland-Prom, K. W. (2009). Results from a national study of social workers sanctioned by state licensing boards. *Social Work*, 54(4), 351–360. doi:10.1093w/54.4.351 PMID:19780465

Bonini, T., Caliandro, A., & Massarelli, A. (2016). Understanding the value of networked publics in radio: Employing digital methods and social network analysis to understand the Twitter publics of two Italian national radio stations. *Information Communication and Society*, 19(1), 40–58. doi:10.1080/13 69118X.2015.1093532

Boyd, D. (2010). Social network sites as networked publics: Affordances, dynamics, and implications. In *A networked self* (pp. 47–66). Routledge.

Brill, C. K. (2001). Looking at the social work profession through the eye of the NASW Code of Ethics. *Research on Social Work Practice*, *11*(2), 223–234. doi:10.1177/104973150101100209

Chan, C. (2016). A scoping review of social media use in social work practice. *Journal of Evidence-Informed Social Work*, *13*(3), 263–276. doi:10.1080/23761407.2015.1052908 PMID:26176999

Chan, C. (2018). Analysing social networks for social work practice: A case study of the Facebook fan page of an online youth outreach project. *Children and Youth Services Review*, *85*, 143–150. doi:10.1016/j.childyouth.2017.12.021

Chan, C., & Ngai, S. S. Y. (2019). Utilizing social media for social work: Insights from clients in online youth services. *Journal of Social Work Practice*, *33*(2), 157–172. doi:10.1080/02650533.2018.1504286

Cheung, C. M., & Lee, M. K. (2010). A theoretical model of intentional social action in online social networks. *Decision Support Systems*, *49*(1), 24–30. doi:10.1016/j.dss.2009.12.006

Comer, M. J., & Bell, J. A. (2020). The Association of Social Work Boards. In Encyclopedia of Social Work. doi:10.1093/acrefore/9780199975839.013.1341

Donovan, J., Rose, D., & Connolly, M. (2017). A crisis of identity: Social work theorising at a time of change. *British Journal of Social Work*, *47*(8), 2291–2307. doi:10.1093/bjsw/bcw180

Duncan-Daston, R., Hunter-Sloan, M., & Fullmer, E. (2013). Considering the ethical implications of social media in social work education. *Ethics and Information Technology*, *15*(1), 35–43. doi:10.100710676-013-9312-7

Ellison, N. B., Gibbs, J. L., & Weber, M. S. (2015). The use of enterprise social network sites for knowledge sharing in distributed organizations: The role of organizational affordances. *The American Behavioral Scientist*, *59*(1), 103–123. doi:10.1177/0002764214540510

Fang, L., Mishna, F., Zhang, V. F., Van Wert, M., & Bogo, M. (2014). Social media and social work education: Understanding and dealing with the new digital world. *Social Work in Health Care*, *53*(9), 800–814. doi:10.1080/00981389.2014.943455 PMID:25321930

Gandy-Guedes, M. E., Vance, M. M., Bridgewater, E. A., Montgomery, T., & Taylor, K. (2016). Using Facebook as a tool for informal peer support: A case example. *Social Work Education*, *35*(3), 323–332. doi:10.1080/02615479.2016.1154937

Greer, J. (2016). Resilience and personal effectiveness for social workers. *Resilience and Personal Effectiveness for Social Workers*, 1-184.

Hitchcock, L. I., & Young, J. A. (2016). Tweet, tweet!: Using live Twitter chats in social work education. *Social Work Education*, *35*(4), 457–468. doi:10.1080/02615479.2015.1136273

Kaushik, V., & Walsh, C. A. (2019). Pragmatism as a research paradigm and its implications for social work research. *Social Sciences (Basel, Switzerland)*, *8*(9), 255. doi:10.3390ocsci8090255

Kimball, E., & Kim, J. (2013). Virtual boundaries: Ethical considerations for use of social media in social work. *Social Work*, *58*(2), 185–188. doi:10.1093wwt005 PMID:23724583

Lee, S. C. (2020). Social work and social media: Organizing in the digital age. *Journal of Public Health Issues and Practices*, *4*(1), 1–6. doi:10.33790/jphip1100158

Marson, S. M., DeAngelis, D., & Mittal, N. (2010). The Association of Social Work Boards' licensure examinations: A review of reliability and validity processes. *Research on Social Work Practice*, *20*(1), 87–99. doi:10.1177/1049731509347858

McFadden, P., Campbell, A., & Taylor, B. (2019). Corrigendum: This is a correction to: Resilience and Burnout in Child Protection Social Work: Individual and Organisational Themes from a Systematic Literature Review, The British Journal of Social Work, Volume 45, Issue 5, July 2015, Pages 1546–1563. *British Journal of Social Work*, *49*(2), 552–553. doi:10.1093/bjsw/bcw051

Mishna, F., Bogo, M., Root, J., Sawyer, J. L., & Khoury-Kassabri, M. (2012). "It just crept in": The digital age and implications for social work practice. *Clinical Social Work Journal*, *40*(3), 277–286. doi:10.100710615-012-0383-4

Mugisha, C. (2018). Social Work in a Digital Age: The Need to Integrate Social Media in Social Work Education in the UK. *Journal of Social Work Education and Practice*, *3*(4), 1–10.

Papacharissi, Z. (Ed.). (2010). *A networked self: Identity, community, and culture on social network sites*. Routledge. doi:10.4324/9780203876527

Parker, J. (2020). Social work practice: Assessment, planning, intervention and review. *Social Work Practice,* 1-264.

Ravalier, J., & Boichat, C. (2018). *UK social workers: Working conditions and wellbeing*. Bath Spa University.

Reamer, F. G. (2013). Social work in a digital age: Ethical and risk management challenges. *Social Work*, *58*(2), 163–172. doi:10.1093wwt003 PMID:23724579

Ricciardelli, L. A., Nackerud, L., Quinn, A. E., Sewell, M., & Casiano, B. (2020). Social media use, attitudes, and knowledge among social work students: Ethical implications for the social work profession. *Social Sciences & Humanities Open*, *2*(1), 100008. doi:10.1016/j.ssaho.2019.100008

Siddiqui, S., & Singh, T. (2016). Social media its impact with positive and negative aspects. *International journal of computer applications technology and research, 5*(2), 71-75.

Thornton-Rice, A., & Moran, N. (2022). The invisible frontier: Practitioner perspectives on the privacy implications of utilising social media in mental health social work practice. *British Journal of Social Work*, *52*(4), 2271–2290. doi:10.1093/bjsw/bcab184

Torous, J., Bucci, S., Bell, I. H., Kessing, L. V., Faurholt-Jepsen, M., Whelan, P., Carvalho, A. F., Keshavan, M., Linardon, J., & Firth, J. (2021). The growing field of digital psychiatry: Current evidence and the future of apps, social media, chatbots, and virtual reality. *World Psychiatry; Official Journal of the World Psychiatric Association (WPA)*, *20*(3), 318–335. doi:10.1002/wps.20883 PMID:34505369

Turner, D. (2016). 'Only connect': Unifying the social in social work and social media. *Journal of Social Work Practice*, *30*(3), 313–327. doi:10.1080/02650533.2016.1215977

Turner, D., Bennison, G., Megele, C., & Fenge, L. A. (2016). Social work and social media: Best friends or natural enemies? *Social Work Education*, *35*(3), 241–244. doi:10.1080/02615479.2016.1164283

Turner, F. J. (Ed.). (2017). *Social work treatment: Interlocking theoretical approaches*. Oxford University Press.

Ventola, C. L. (2014). Social media and health care professionals: Benefits, risks, and best practices. *P&T*, *39*(7), 491. PMID:25083128

Voshel, E. H., & Wesala, A. (2015). Social media & social work ethics: Determining best practices in an ambiguous reality. *Journal of Social Work Values and Ethics*, *12*(1), 67–76.

Voshel, E. H., & Wesala, A. (2015). Social media & social work ethics: Determining best practices in an ambiguous reality. *Journal of Social Work Values and Ethics*, *12*(1), 67–76.

Wagner, S. H., & Gilbert, M. C. (2018). Social work educators' evaluations of regulatory boards. *The Right for the Elderly to Commit Suicide*, *15*(2), 81.

Westwood, J. (2014). *Social work and social media: An introduction to applying social work principles to social media*.

Willoughby, M. (2019). A review of the risks associated with children and young people's social media use and the implications for social work practice. *Journal of Social Work Practice*, *33*(2), 127–140. doi:10.1080/02650533.2018.1460587

Zeng, D., Chen, H., Lusch, R., & Li, S. H. (2010). Social media analytics and intelligence. *IEEE Intelligent Systems*, *25*(6), 13–16. doi:10.1109/MIS.2010.151

Chapter 4
Role of Social Media in the Digital Transformation of Business

David Winster Praveenraj D
CHRIST University (Deemed), India

E. Sudha
CHRIST University (Deemed), India

R. Hariharan
CHRIST University (Deemed), India

R. Vedapradha
Mount Carmel College (Autonomous), India

J. Ashok
CHRIST University (Deemed), India

ABSTRACT

A digital transformation endeavor is the use of technology and digital processes to enhance business operations and consumer experiences. These projects frequently include the use of new technology like social media platforms, artificial intelligence (AI), and analytics, as well as the execution of digital processes like cloud computing, omnichannel commerce, data analytics, and automation. An organization needs to integrate digital transformation initiatives into its current systems if it wants to stay current with the rapidly evolving technology landscape of today. Social media is now an essential part of contemporary life, and businesses are increasingly using it to connect with their clients and other stakeholders. To take advantage of social media's huge potential, businesses are incorporating it into their digital transformation initiatives.

DOI: 10.4018/978-1-6684-7450-1.ch004

INTRODUCTION

A comprehensive digital transformation can significantly boost an organization's performance. Due to growing competition, client demand, and technology improvements, organizations are being driven to operate with a great deal more innovation and agility than ever before. Industry leaders from a variety of sectors are now using digital innovation and creativity to develop, and social media is one of their most successful strategies for achieving digital success. In 2021, digital transformation continued as a prominent topic in marketing, and for good reason. According to IFS analysis indicates that throughout the epidemic, 70% of firms increased or maintained their investment in digital transformation. The plans of 58% of enterprises that haven't yet started their transformation projects will be expedited by Covid-19. Even yet, it's important to consider what digital transformation includes before marketers rush to tick the box (Verhoef, 2021). It is a synthesis of all aspects of a business and contemporary digital technologies. Any firm, no matter how big or little, needs to undergo a digital transformation if it wants to survive and thrive in the contemporary business environment. Research studies, conventional news outlets, and online pieces have all utilized the phrase "digital transformation" in diverse situations. However, several corporate executives are still unaware of what it means to digitally change a corporation (The enterpriser's Project, 2023). According to some CEOs, the phrase "digital transformation" has become so overused that it is no longer relevant. It is challenging to communicate because digital transformation covers a wide range of topics.

It will vary from one business to the next; there is no such thing as a universal digital transformation. Using social media to increase digital visibility could be part of firm A's digital transformation. The digital transformation of firm B, however, can involve improving operations processes through robotics technology. The extent of your company's change has gone through several stages as well. It is best to start converting your organization as soon as you can, regardless of stage, to avoid being eliminated from the competition by natural selection (Tripathi, 2021). Nevertheless, no matter where you are in the process, it is better to start changing your organization as soon as you can to avoid being eliminated by natural selection. Utilizing social media for digital exposure may be a part of firm A's digital transformation. However, firm B's digital transformation may involve improving its operational systems using robotics. How far a business has come in its transition has also gone through several stages. No of the stage, it is preferable to start transforming the organization as soon as it can avoid being eliminated by natural selection (Argüelles, Cortés, Ramirez, & Bustamante, 2021)

One of the most important forums for feedback in the modern world is social media. Globally, more than 3.6 billion people use social media every day, and by 2025, that figure is expected to reach 4.41 billion. And when 4.41 billion people can offer real-time feedback on your modifications and initiatives, it's simpler to evolve more quickly. What about the businesses that creates the technology then? They are aware of this as well. A corporation can maintain its business plan current by incorporating social media into its digital transformation and basing it on customer feedback (Hai, Van, & Thi Tuyet, 2021).

There is increasing demand for organizations with numerous delivery channels to make sure their experiences are seamless and integrated. Social media also makes it easier for businesses to communicate with their clients (Thangam & Chavadi, 2023). Thus, businesses can immediately learn about the positive or negative experiences of their clients through social media and use this information to enhance their business plans. Therefore, businesses may utilize social media to brand themselves in a lighthearted and interesting way, with high engagement resulting in higher credibility. It is crucial to give the audience pertinent content and to urge them to share it with their family and friends for free advertising and instant visibility. To humanize its brand, a firm must treat social media like a physical asset rather than a digital one and provide interesting, engaging content for its audience (Murugan et al., 2023). Even while it's not a good idea to only post about the company's goods and services, the business can still add value by running competitions, daily info-graphics, and factual material on this network.

Since the majority of businesses in the current digital age use social media, it is simple to access and contrast competitors' strategies. In the same manner, all businesses may use social media to understand current trends, enabling them to remain relevant in a cutthroat and always-shifting environment (Sriram, 2023). To be competitive, organizations need to be flexible, and the ability to react rapidly to market changes is a key quality. If the majority of your consumers are devoted to your business, effective social media management will foster strong customer loyalty and help you stay ahead of the competition (Karumban, 2023). Social media is increasingly being used by people to communicate with businesses, and it has quickly established itself as a fundamental part of any digital transformation.

Importance of Digital Transformation for Business

No matter the size or industry of the business, digital transformation should be a top priority because it is not only necessary for successful marketing and sales alignment but also for several other crucial outcomes that will be extremely advantageous for the organization in question. Using the professional direction and advice of the hired digital marketing agency is not only recommended but vital (Thangam, 2022). When the marketing and sales teams are aligned with digital marketing, detailed information, and insights about lead prospects and clients also become available. On the one side, sellers frequently have thorough and helpful insights that the marketing team may use to produce content expressly for nurturing. On the other hand, marketers usually have a broad perspective of a market or potential customer (Park Et al., 2022). Customers' comments, third-party data, content interaction, or even one-on-one customer conversations can all yield customer insights.

To convert leads into sales, brands must use personalization. According to McKinsey, the majority of consumers said that personalized communication influenced their choice to buy a particular brand, and 78% of those consumers said it led them to make additional purchases from the company in question. Since personalization increases customer engagement, which frequently results in the development of client loyalty, it follows that digital transformation is essential for marketing and sales alignment (Thangam, 2022). But when the sales and marketing teams collaborate to discuss the target demographic and develop pertinent and interesting campaigns, personalization is made feasible through the correct and efficient marketing.

Consumers today are not limited to a single channel. They use smartphone apps, make physical purchases online, and contact customer care for help and questions. Therefore, it is possible to digitally connect all of these platforms that customers use to try to contact businesses. The client services are tailored to the needs of the customers and are continuously upgraded (Jennifer Lund, 2023). Today's services are available around-the-clock and are quick, easy, and convenient. This is feasible with digital transformation and puts organizations in a stronger position in terms of consumer satisfaction (Holly Briedis, Anne Kronschnabl, Alex Rodriguez, and Kelly Ungerman, 2020).

If they haven't already, businesses in today's social media-connected, fast-paced technology environment have been seriously considering the execution of the digital transformation strategy (Einsatz, Wiegand, & Imschloss, 2019). Businesses now have essential knowledge about the significance of digital marketing thanks to the marketing firms' guidance on the best plan for digital transformation, which enables these brands to interact with consumers and meet their individual needs. The current business is all about how effective digital transformation tactics are applied, to the seamless customer experience (Saldanha, 2019).

Role of Social Media in the Digital Business Transformation

An endeavor for digital transformation uses technology and digital processes to enhance business operations and consumer experiences. The deployment of digital processes like cloud computing, omnichannel commerce, data analytics, and automation, as well as the adoption of new technologies like social media platforms, artificial intelligence (AI), and analytics, are typical elements of these projects (Urbach, Drews & Ross, 2017). For an organization to stay current with the rapidly evolving technology landscape of today, digital transformation initiatives must be integrated into the organization's current systems.

Social media is now an essential part of contemporary life, and businesses are increasingly using it to connect with their clients and other stakeholders. To take advantage of social media's huge potential, businesses are incorporating it into their digital transformation initiatives (Simangunsong & Handoko, 2020). For instance, businesses utilize it to increase customer engagement, produce leads, offer customer service, increase brand recognition, reach a wider audience, and gather crucial consumer data. Additionally, it enables firms to forge close bonds with their clientele. Social networking is now a crucial tool for companies looking to stay competitive in today's economy (Sedera, Tan, & Xu, 2022).

Businesses must first address several issues before they can start integrating social media into their digital transformation programs. For instance, many businesses lack the technical resources necessary for the effective administration and implementation of social media-based digital transformation initiatives (Aral, Dellarocas, & Godes, 2013). Businesses must also ensure that their content conforms to several laws covering privacy and intellectual property rights to avoid paying hefty fines or penalties. To maximize their return on investment (ROI), businesses demand a clear strategy defining how they intend to use social media (Gruner, Power & Bergey, 2013).

As technology has developed, social media has emerged as one of the most useful tools for organizations to connect with target audiences, engage customers, and gather data. Social media platforms like Facebook, Instagram, and Twitter give them unmatched access to a sizable audience of potential customers who are eager to buy their goods or services (Sivarajah, Irani, Gupta, & Mahroof, 2020). Social media platforms also enable businesses to interact more personally with both current and potential customers. Social media is being extensively utilized by businesses as a digital transformation tool as well as a platform for promotion. They can leverage the trends they find in customer behavior and preferences to plan their digital activities by analyzing user data collected through social media channels (Barmuta et al, 2020).

By regularly updating clients, businesses may quickly tell them of new product releases or planned modifications to existing digital products and services. Additionally, interacting with customers on social media can strengthen the bonds between brands and consumers and boost overall loyalty among both current and potential customers (Bican, & Brem, 2020). By utilizing the many analytical tools offered by major platforms, like Facebook Insights or Twitter Analytics service, businesses can also actively track user interaction with their content across a variety of channels while also gaining valuable insights into user interests and behaviors (Priyono, Moin & Putri, 2020).

By better understanding the kinds of content that resonate with consumers, they may adjust their plan to more effectively target their target audiences. Additionally, businesses may use this information to develop tailored online marketing efforts based on the tastes of the target market, which raises engagement rates even higher (Udovita, 2020). Businesses have also started to take advantage of influencer marketing by working with well-known individuals or bloggers who have a large following on well-known social media platforms like Instagram or YouTube to promote their goods or services more successfully.

This kind of marketing increases brand recognition across several channels, which encourages customers from the targeted influencer audiences to engage with those businesses more, improving total conversion rates for such campaigns (Ziyadin, Suieubayeva, & Utegenova, 2020). Overall, it is clear that social media has evolved into a crucial instrument for digital transformation initiatives because it grants businesses unparalleled access to vast volumes of customer data and allows them to interact directly and at scale with particular target groups. Organizations today must fully utilize everything that these potent platforms have to offer to remain competitive in the rapidly evolving digital business landscape. These platforms enable targeted marketing campaigns and provide invaluable insights into customer behaviors and interests.

Social Media and Digital Transformation: The Process

Social media acts as an important component in digital transformation, which is the process of moving an organization from its current state to one that is more effective and efficient. Changes to an organization's internal procedures as well as how it engages with clients and partners may be part of this process (Ulas, 2019). Even though other elements go into a successful digital transformation, social media may be a useful tool for businesses trying to enhance their operations and strengthen relationships with clients and partners. For the same, the following process has been used;

Discover the Prospects for Social Media Innovation

Innovation in social media connects users, promotes goods, gathers data, and involves stakeholders. Irrespective of the size all the businesses may function better and compete with competitors through social media. For the same companies or businesses need to find the greatest short- and long-term answers before using social media and need to examine the technical and social media landscape. Moreover, current and future demands should also be estimated. While many businesses market on Facebook and Twitter, Pinterest is also quickly emerging as a vital platform for digital or online marketing (Priyono, Moin, & Putri, 2020).

Researching Current Trends in the Market

When implementing social media innovation into your business, market research should come first. Businesses can learn more about consumer wants and rivals' tactics by conducting market research. This aids in the development of distinctive marketing initiatives that draw in and retain clients. When conducting market research, businesses could look at client reviews of previous social media marketing campaigns (Ulas, 2019). They can use this to identify the most persuasive messaging and underperforming procedures. They should also look at the social media pages of their competitors in the same field to determine what content techniques they are doing and how effective they are at building user engagement and brand awareness (Warner, & Wäger, 2019).

Businesses should research the digital marketing tactics of their rivals to identify opportunities. Businesses can gain knowledge about what works by seeing how their rivals approach their target market. A competitive strategy can also be developed with the aid of customer evaluations of competing goods and services. To uncover prominent industries or specialized terms for competitive analysis, companies could do keyword searches on Google and Bing (Vial, 2019). Using this data, content plans for social media postings and other digital advertisements on websites and other platforms, such as display ads and banner ads, can be developed. Businesses may also wish to look at pertinent blogs and websites that concentrate on current industry trends to better understand what themes to explore when promoting goods or services through digital channels like social media (Pucihar, 2020).

Select the Right Platforms to Use

The next step is to decide which platforms to use after selecting how to incorporate social media innovation into your business. It's critical to pick platforms that connect with your target market and boost engagement and value. Select the material that best serves your company's objectives first. The way that images, videos, texts, and infographics behave varies depending on the platform ((Pucihar, 2020). While LinkedIn and Facebook favor longer-form material, Instagram and Twitter favor visual content. As an illustration, Pinterest might be effective for a fashion business but not for a B2B firm that targets decision-makers (Vial, 2019).

After deciding on the content kind, the business can investigate the appropriate platforms for its objectives. To determine whether a platform will assist in achieving corporate objectives, examine its primary features and analytical tools. Businesses can utilize this information to inform future initiatives by better understanding how users engage with various sorts of content on various platforms (Benavides, et al, 2020). To make data collecting or performance tracking simpler, take into account technologies or applications that interface with platforms. Finally, keep your budget in mind when you research platforms. The organization may need to restrict the amount of social media accounts it uses or user accounts with shared logins for team members, depending on the budget (Mergel, Edelmann & Haug, 2019). Because adopting social media innovation in any business depends on choosing the appropriate social media platform or platforms.

Developing a Detailed Social Media Strategy

Companies must establish an objective before organizing social media initiatives. The rest will be simpler once businesses are aware of their social media objectives. Create a thorough plan to attain your business goals after selecting them. Social media strategy must include audience targeting, content generation, platform management, analytics, and reporting.

Targeting the Audience

Target is essential for effective social media efforts. Surveys and interviews offer useful information on the interests, needs, and behaviors of potential target audiences that can be used to create messages that appeal to them. Businesses can give demographics higher priority in upcoming advertisements by understanding what has interacted with their content.

Content Development

The effectiveness of social media marketing hinges on interesting and compelling content! Platform-specific content creation requires planning and time, but the correct tools can make it simpler. Users can schedule posts ahead of time and follow brand conversations across networks in real-time with the help of well-known content planning tools like Hootsuite and Sprout Social. An organized library of excellent photos and videos can help you post content more quickly to many channels.

Platform Administration

To increase engagement with followers and potential customers, a business must be present on the platforms it has chosen. Increasing your visibility on social media may also be accomplished by keeping up with trends and forming connections with other influencers. Success is increased by creating eye-catching Twitter hashtags or inventive Instagram Stories images!

Data Analytics and Reporting

Social media platforms include a variety of analytical tools that allow businesses to modify their strategy in response to the success of campaigns. Users may assess if ads are effective or need to be optimized by measuring follower interaction over time in addition to other key performance indicators (KPIs) such as link clicks and platform mentions. By routinely tracking these findings, brands may pinpoint audience patterns and enhance long-term strategy and product development.

Analyzing Social Media Campaign Results

A corporation should assess the success of its efforts after establishing a presence on various social media sites. It is vital to keep track of indicators that demonstrate how well campaigns and projects are doing across various platforms (Bonanomi,202). The business will receive quantitative data about the success or failure of social media marketing as a result.

It is critical to establish fundamental metrics that a company may use for benchmarking and tracking development over time. The general level of engagement is one of these metrics: How many shares, tweets, likes, and other interactions does company material get overall? It includes reach, conversation rates, and audience expansion.

These fundamental metrics should be regularly tracked so that the organization can assess progress and make appropriate strategic adjustments. In addition to the important indicators like engagement, reach, and audience growth, deeper KPIs can help to better understand how well the company campaigns are performing (Reinartz, Wiegand & Imschloss, 2019). A few KPIs that could be employed include the click-through rate (CTR), cost per click (CPC), cost per acquisition (CPA), lead generation rate (LGR), and brand sentiment (positive/negative customer feedback on social media networks).

Data can be gathered from a variety of sources, such as website analytics, hashtag monitoring tools, surveys, or polls, among others, and then analyzed and evaluated for potential future improvements in social media initiatives. Accurate data is necessary to comprehend customer preferences and shifts in industry trends (Chanias, Myers, & Hess, 2019). Companies will be able to identify key areas for improvement or development in terms of integrating cutting-edge social media practices by analyzing these findings.

For instance, if a certain campaign doesn't produce the desired results, a firm can look into possible reasons such as inefficient targeting or message, a dearth of original material, timing issues, and poor platform selection. Finding areas for improvement can help with both improving current campaigns and creating new ones with greater results (Li, Larimo & Leonidou, 2021). By understanding what works best for each platform from results analysis, businesses can maximize the success of any prospective campaigns on each one.

Business Value/Benefits of Social Media in Digital Transformation

Many current business trends are circulating on the internet right now. Social media is one of the most widely used online outlets. Millions of individuals use several social media platforms daily. Because of its popularity, many people check it out as soon as they wake up and as soon as they turn in for the night. Any computer with an internet connection can access these social media websites. Among them are smartphones, laptops, computers, and other technological devices. Some of the most well-known social media networks available today include Facebook, Instagram, Snapchat, Twitter, LinkedIn, and Pinterest (Pfister & Lehmann, 2023).

Knowing that a website has a significant number of users is a huge asset for many online businesses, both large and small. The use of social media marketing has skyrocketed due to all the advantages it provides. Social media marketing should be taken into consideration while attempting to grow a business. Some advantages of utilizing social media marketing include the following:

Audience Focus

This is one of the most important benefits social media networks have given to business. A corporation designates the person whose profile they want to see when they post an advertisement on a social media platform. As a result, businesses are better able to reach their target customers (Teng, Wu, & Yang, 2022). Before social media, businesses had difficulty determining how well their advertisements were targeted and whether they had reached their target demographic.

Brand Recognition

If a business has a social media presence, current and potential customers will be able to recognize and interact with your business more readily. Thus the business will have the ability to reach a significant number of fresh eyes and viewers due to the large number of people who utilize social media today (Teng, Wu, & Yang, 2022). Social media platforms can also be utilized to tell the brand's story and explain the company's mission to the public.

Connect Customers Directly

Through social media platforms, businesses can reach out to and stay in touch with their customers directly (Pfister & Lehmann, 2023). A corporation should communicate directly with its customers rather than via other channels if it has new products, promotions, or other news to provide.

Considerable Growth in Website Traffic

Thanks to social media, alternatives for driving inbound visitors to a company website are expanding. Every social media account the firm has is a potential route to the website, and every post is an opportunity to add value and persuade followers and visitors to the website why they should do so. In the end, these visits might generate more leads and conversions (Teng, Wu, & Yang, 2022).

Easy to Quantify the Impact of Campaigns

Using social media, a company may easily and swiftly evaluate the success or failure of its marketing strategy. Real-time counts of individuals participating in business interaction on social media platforms are possible (El Hilali, & El Manouar, 2019). The number of people that clicked through or liked the post allows businesses to determine how many people responded to the call and liked or clicked through the post.

Accurate Client Insights

Today, a tremendous amount of consumer data is generated by all social media users who are engaged. By utilizing social listening and interacting with company followers, a company can discover more about whom its true consumers are, where they want to spend their time, what interests them, and what they think about the brand, competitors, and industry. As a result, the business may better engage them with content, advertisements, and message ((Pfister & Lehmann, 2023).

Building Better Community

Building communities around their brands is another advantage social media offers businesses. Loyal customers may swiftly and easily communicate with the rest of the world and the business about their products (El Hilali, & El Manouar, 2019). In light of this, the organization is in a position to deliver the necessary data as quickly as practicable.

Increasing Brand Loyalty

Through social media, brands have unmatched potential to participate in conversations and interact with their audience. When delivered appropriately and repeatedly, these interactions foster brand loyalty. Social media can help businesses build trust more rapidly, even though it takes time to acquire client loyalty.

Omni Channel Campaigns

Nowadays, customers may simply transfer between platforms, such as from a website to social media and back again via email. Social media can be beneficial on its own, but when it is included in marketing and strategy activities, its effectiveness increases significantly. Social networking posts give you another chance to connect with your audience, no matter where they are, and they promote and reinforce your message on other platforms (El Hilali, & El Manouar, 2019).

Generation of Leads and Sales

Social media has the potential to be a potent tool for generating leads and advancing them through the purchase cycle. By combining organic and pay-per-click techniques, social media marketers may broaden their reach and generate more leads. B2B sales teams can then employ social listening and other social media monitoring to convert these leads into sales.

Confronts/Difficulties in Integrating Social Media in the Digital Transformation

The term "digital marketing transformation" refers to an altogether new, inventive manner of carrying out a task that is essential to your organization, rather than simply referring to the adoption of new software, technologies, and processes that are more effective and automated than conventional business practices and processes. Therefore, before embarking on a digital transformation program, businesses must take into account a variety of factors, including how employees will react to the change, how it will affect customer relations, how much it will cost, how it will connect with corporate objectives, and so on. Digital transformations enable businesses to move into the future and position them to compete effectively and expand into new markets (Schnader, 2019). All of that is easier said than done, though, as evidenced by the fact that only 16% of employees believe their company's digital transformation efforts have improved their performance or are sustainable, and that 70% of all digital transformation programs fail because of employee resistance and a lack of management support. While digital transformation offers organizations distinctive chances for innovation and growth, it also encourages critical thinking and may require reimagining certain areas of the business that are fundamental (Mogaji, Soetan, & Kieu, 2020). The top nine challenges to take into account when implementing digital transformation are explained as follows;

Unpreparedness for Change Management

A detailed change management strategy is more likely to help an organization achieve its goals for digital transformation. A solid change management culture is essential for the success of any organization. Any new project or implementation strategy that doesn't have a change strategy is doomed to failure. Building relationships with all stakeholders and employees is important for any organization while preparing a project by determining the underlying causes of problems are key components of an effective change management strategy(Mogaji, Soetan, & Kieu, 2020).

Multifaceted Technology and Software

The complexity of enterprise software is intrinsic. Innovative technologies can be frightening. This is a significant barrier for businesses going through a digital transformation, both in terms of implementation and data integration as well as end-user experience. When a transformation project is in its early phases, leaders should take this into account and look for the most user-friendly, integrated systems (Schnader, 2019).

Promoting the Use of New Methods and Tools

The adoption of new procedures and technology is frequently hampered by the reluctance of long-tenured staff members, who believe that the way things are done now is fine. To enable employees quickly become productive and proficient with a tool and comprehend the benefits of these new procedures, organizations must adopt new software while also providing thorough onboarding training and ongoing employee performance support (Schnader, 2019).

The Constant Change in Customer Needs

Organizations constantly change, and Covid-19 has hastened this process. Think about what a client would like. That alters as the world and many industries alter. An intense transformation effort might take years to complete, and digital transformation is not a simple project. What happens if the customer's needs change during that time? Customer issues will progress over time. When the time comes to implement new digital technologies, don't be shocked and prepare to be flexible (Mogaji, Soetan, & Kieu, 2020).

Digital Transformation Strategy Absence

Why are businesses switching to new digital systems instead of human processes and outdated systems? Is there a need for or plan for the organization to install sophisticated systems? Are the businesses prepared to appropriately transition from old systems to new ones? All of these queries need to be addressed before a digital transformation strategy is put into place. Without a set strategy, a transformation project cannot be successful. Don't buy into hyped-up ideas and assumptions (Mogaji, Soetan, & Kieu, 2020). Know the parts of your business that need to be upgraded and where improvements may be made, then start there.

Inadequate IT Skills

Businesses need a talented, effective IT workforce if they are to be successful in their business transformation initiatives. And putting that together is challenging, particularly given the present shortage of computer workers. An industry survey found that 54% of organizations claimed that a shortage of technically trained workers is the reason why they are unable to achieve their goals for digital transformation. Mogaji, Soetan, & Kieu, (2020) Organisations have difficulties due to a lack of expertise in data analytics, application architecture, software integrations, cybersecurity, and data transfer. By outsourcing this work to outside consultants and digital transformation specialists, businesses that lack IT personnel can overcome this difficulty and close the implementation and migration gap. However, for organizations that are serious about digital transformation, having an internal team or an IT team member who is responsible for managing digital transformation is essential.

Security Issues

Privacy and cybersecurity worries are a rebuttal that many enterprise organizations in data-sensitive industries have. That is true, too. The majority of digital transformation initiatives entail moving away from on-premise solutions and merging all of a company's data into a single, centralized system. Naturally, this raises the potential of hackers that steal client information and business secrets. Online attacks can target weak points in systems, shoddy setups, and unwary users. Make sure you have a strategy in place to prevent these threats from materializing. Hire a cyber security specialist to help you find areas of vulnerability in your defense and train your staff in cyber security (Woodcock & Johnson, 2019).

Budgetary Restrictions

Investment in digital transformation is not inexpensive. Scope creep can gradually start to delay deadlines and add new work for organizations with a less-than-stellar transformation plan, all of which raise the cost of a project. The price of digital transformation keeps rising when you factor in any consulting work, adjustments in your customers' expectations, or IT issues. Recognize the organization's long-term objectives and the ROI the business expects from the transformation effort (Mogaji, Soetan, & Kieu, 2020). This will make it easier for the company to determine what spending is excessive and where budget growth is needed.

The Mindset of a Culture

Organizations with manual procedures and older systems frequently have an antiquated mindset. Things evolve slowly, automation is despised, and it's challenging to adapt to new technologies. The cultural aspect of digital transformation is a major barrier. Everyone must agree, even senior management and new hires (Schnader, 2019). Everyone needs to be open to sweeping changes in their daily life and unafraid to pick up new skills.

Ways to Overcoming the Challenges in Digital Transformation

The following five techniques can prevent the social media digital transformation from happening, even though there are a lot of obstacles in its way. Businesses can use the same strategy to overcome the difficulties of digital transformation and realize their full potential by utilizing new digital systems and technology.

Invest in a Platform for Digital Adoption

A new digital tool or procedure won't necessarily be more efficient; as a result, businesses must properly onboard, teach, and assist their staff or end users to enable them to make better use of these tools. Invest in a digital adoption platform (DAP) to make sure that your organization's digital transformation initiative is successful. DAPs give businesses the no-code tools they need to develop in-app content for contextual onboarding and ongoing performance support (Almeida, Santos & Monteiro, 2020).

Develop a Leadership Team for Change

Identify the important, creative, and reliable members of the organization's present staff. These top performers should be brought together to form a cross-functional team that will serve as the change leadership team. This team will assist in developing a vision for your digital transformation process that is generated by those who are familiar with the internal operations of your organization and that is in line with business objectives (Li, Larimo & Leonidou, 2021). As a result, businesses may approach digital transformation programs with a proactive mindset that emphasizes the human side of change, which ultimately speeds up the process.

Employ a Consultant for Digital Transformation

Digital transformation is not just any change; it is a complete realignment of fundamental processes, resources, and user interfaces. It provides a frightening challenge to organizations that may feel frightened by this magnitude because the majority of organizations have never gone through a complete transformation process like this. By hiring a digital transformation consultant, the company will have the assurance that they are working with experts who have done this previously and are familiar with the process (Li, Larimo & Leonidou, 2021). They will offer the company a plan and a basis for success, along with a track record to support this.

Business Objectives and Digital Transformation Strategy Alignment

What is the organization's digital transformation being driven by? When you're putting new processes in place, this should be your top priority. Businesses should be aware of the needs of their customers as well as the sources of friction in their offerings, goods, and services. To identify old systems that require infrastructure upgrading, the business or corporation must analyze its current procedures (Mogaji, Soetan, & Kieu, 2020). The organizational transformation process should ultimately be in direct alignment with the primary business objectives. It should enable staff to perform their jobs more effectively, improve the customer experience with more user-friendly systems that address more customer issues, and increase income for our company.

Be Flexible

Awareness of organizational vulnerability lies at the heart of digital transformation initiatives. Leaders understand that innovation and change are necessary to adapt to and compete in a global, digital environment. But more people than ever are unaware of how quickly technology is evolving. Being nimble means having no fear of changing course. It entails seizing chances when they present themselves (Li, Larimo & Leonidou, 2021). Lean into this even though the firm is already agile because you are through digital transformation.

Future of Social Media and Digital Transformation

It is more crucial than ever to ensure that the company is set up to survive and grow in the digital age as social media and the internet become ingrained in society. When it comes to the potential of social media marketing, the majority of small businesses are practically in their infancy. And while it is OK for the time being, it is a problem that needs to be resolved as quickly as possible. Having a solid internet presence will only become more essential over time. Typically, a firm will be set up with at least these three components as Facebook page, a Yelp page, and Web site (Iivari, Sharma, & Ventä-Olkkonen, 2020).

If a company simply lists the first three, it is doing itself and the competitors a disservice because they will be easier to recognize. Currently, Twitter, Facebook, Instagram, Snapchat, Reddit, YouTube, and TikTok are some of the well-known social media platforms. Each of these offers countless opportunities to advertise the company and its goods. The business decides which platform is best for it based on how the material is tailored specifically to each platform's user base (Li, Larimo & Leonidou, 2021). The company must comprehend each platform to avoid wasting time and resources on advertising on a platform that is not appropriate for them.

When discussing the future of social media marketing, analytics is another important factor that must be taken into consideration. The company must comprehend the function that analytics will play to maximize the benefits of social media marketing. Analytics enables the company to keep track of how well specific campaigns are performing or to identify which kinds of advertisements are more effective on which platforms (Fletcher & Griffiths, 2020). The good news is that most of these platforms have the capabilities needed to monitor and track these kinds of activities on the profile of the business, which may enable it to save money by avoiding the need for additional software or services.

Having a solid online reputation will soon become crucial when it comes to the future of social media marketing. Since the invention of the internet, news has spread more quickly than before. There was a time when the adage "any advertising is good advertising" may have been true, but that is no longer the case (Li, Larimo & Leonidou, 2021). One tweet, Facebook post, Reddit thread, or YouTube video criticizing a good or service is all it takes to ruin a brand's reputation. A company must have primarily positive reviews, pay attention to complaints or comments on posts, produce fresh content, stay current on trends, and put a strong emphasis on customer relations if it wants to maintain a positive public image (Fletcher & Griffiths, 2020). Most firms should be well-positioned for success in the future of social media marketing if they abide by these guidelines.

CONCLUSION

As social media continues to expand, its significance for activities related to digital transformation will increase. It can assist businesses in attracting clients, hiring personnel, and edging out rivals. To take advantage of social media's enormous reach and expanding user base, businesses can employ it as a component of a digital transformation strategy. To fully reap the rewards of social media, it must be used responsibly and with awareness of its hazards and difficulties. Businesses need to have robust network security to prevent social media-related attacks and data breaches. Businesses should be careful about how they communicate with customers on social media, making sure to reply to questions right away, and only share legal information. Organizations should stay abreast of social media trends and digital transformation technology to maintain their competitive edge. While maximizing the potential for a truly integrated approach that employs conventional methods and cutting-edge technology, firms may do this by keeping their digital transformation initiatives current with industry standards.

REFERENCES

Almeida, F., Santos, J. D., & Monteiro, J. A. (2020). The challenges and opportunities in the digitalization of companies in a post-COVID-19 World. *IEEE Engineering Management Review*, *48*(3), 97–103. doi:10.1109/EMR.2020.3013206

Aral, S., Dellarocas, C., & Godes, D. (2013). Introduction to the special issue social media and business transformation: A framework for research. *Information Systems Research*, *24*(1), 3–13. doi:10.1287/isre.1120.0470

Argüelles, A. J., Cortés, H. D., Ramirez, O. E. P., & Bustamante, O. A. (2021). Technological Spotlights of Digital Transformation: Uses and Implications Under COVID-19 Conditions. In Information Technology Trends for a Global and Interdisciplinary Research Community (pp. 19-49). IGI Global.

Barmuta, K. A., Akhmetshin, E. M., Andryushchenko, I. Y., Tagibova, A. A., Meshkova, G. V., & Zekiy, A. O. (2020). Problems of business processes transformation in the context of building digital economy. *Entrepreneurship and Sustainability Issues*, *8*(1), 945–959. doi:10.9770/jesi.2020.8.1(63)

Benavides, L. M. C., Tamayo Arias, J. A., Arango Serna, M. D., Branch Bedoya, J. W., & Burgos, D. (2020). Digital transformation in higher education institutions: A systematic literature review. *Sensors (Basel)*, *20*(11), 3291. doi:10.339020113291 PMID:32526998

Bican, P. M., & Brem, A. (2020). Digital business model, digital transformation, digital entrepreneurship: Is there a sustainable "digital"? *Sustainability (Basel)*, *12*(13), 5239. doi:10.3390u12135239

Bonanomi, M. M., Hall, D. M., Staub-French, S., Tucker, A., & Talamo, C. M. L. (2020). The impact of digital transformation on formal and informal organizational structures of large architecture and engineering firms. *Engineering, Construction, and Architectural Management*, *27*(4), 872–892. doi:10.1108/ECAM-03-2019-0119

Chanias, S., Myers, M. D., & Hess, T. (2019). Digital transformation strategy making in pre-digital organizations: The case of a financial services provider. *The Journal of Strategic Information Systems*, *28*(1), 17–33. doi:10.1016/j.jsis.2018.11.003

Chavadi, C. (2021). Growth drivers, characteristics, preference and challenges faced by Fast Moving Consumer Goods-A study with reference to Bengaluru. *Turkish Online Journal of Qualitative Inquiry, 12*(7).

Chavadi, C. A., Arul, M. J., & Sirothiya, M. (2020). Modelling the effects of creative advertisements on consumers: An empirical study. *Vision (Basel)*, *24*(3), 269–283. doi:10.1177/0972262920926074

Chavadi, C. A., Hiremath, C. V., & Hyderabad, R. L. (2014). Customer loyalty appraisal based on store characteristics: An alternative approach. *Indian Journal of Marketing*, *44*(5), 18–29. doi:10.17010/ijom/2014/v44/i5/80375

Chavadi, C. A., & Kokatnur, S. S. (2008). Consumer Expectation and Perception of Fast Food Outlets: An Empirical Study in Davangere. *ICFAI Journal Of Services Marketing, 6*(2).

Chavadi, C. A., & Kokatnur, S. S. (2009). Impact of Short-Term Promotional Ads on Food Retailing. *ICFAI Journal of Consumer Behavior, 4*(1).

Chavadi, C. A., & Kokatnur, S. S. (2009). RFID Adoption by Indian Retailers: An Exploratory Study. *The Icfai University Journal of Supply Chain Management, 6*(1), 60–77.

Chavadi, C. A., Menon, S. R., & Sirothiya, M. (2019). Measuring Service Quality Perceptions of Indian E-retailers: An Evaluative Study. *Metamorphosis, 18*(2), 92–102. doi:10.1177/0972622519886232

Chavadi, C. A., Menon, S. R., & Sirothiya, M. (2019). Modelling the Effects of Brand Placements in Movies: An Investigative Study of Event Type and Placement Type. *Vision (Basel), 23*(1), 31–43. doi:10.1177/0972262918821227

Chavadi, C. A., Vishwanatha, M. R., & Mubeen, S. (2018). Ghee with Glee: A Study of How Consumers Evaluate Product Packaging. *Metamorphosis, 17*(2), 100–110. doi:10.1177/0972622518817407

El Hilali, W., & El Manouar, A. (2019, March). Towards a sustainable world through a SMART digital transformation. In *Proceedings of the 2nd International Conference on Networking, Information Systems & Security* (pp. 1-8). ACM. 10.1145/3320326.3320364

Fletcher, G., & Griffiths, M. (2020). Digital transformation during a lockdown. *International Journal of Information Management, 55*, 102185. doi:10.1016/j.ijinfomgt.2020.102185 PMID:32836642

Gruner, R. L., Power, D., & Bergey, P. K. (2013). Leveraging social media technology for business transformation: The case of corporate social communities. In *Social media in strategic management* (Vol. 11, pp. 27–42). Emerald Group Publishing Limited. doi:10.1108/S1877-6361(2013)0000011006

Hai, T. N., Van, Q. N., & Thi Tuyet, M. N. (2021). Digital transformation: Opportunities and challenges for leaders in the emerging countries in response to COVID-19 pandemic. *Emerging Science Journal, 5*(1), 21–36. doi:10.28991/esj-2021-SPER-03

Hiremath, C. V., Chavadi, C. A., & Yatgiri, P. Y. (2013). Cloud Technology as an Alternative for Marketing Information System: An Empirical Study. *International Journal of Management. Research and Business Strategy, 2*(4).

Iivari, N., Sharma, S., & Ventä-Olkkonen, L. (2020). Digital transformation of everyday life–How COVID-19 pandemic transformed the basic education of the young generation and why information management research should care? *International Journal of Information Management, 55*, 102183. doi:10.1016/j.ijinfomgt.2020.102183 PMID:32836640

Jennifer Lund. (2023). How Customer Experience Drives Digital Transformation. Available at: https://www.superoffice.com/blog/digital-transformation/

Karumban, S., Sanyal, S., Laddunuri, M. M., Sivalinga, V. D., Shanmugam, V., Bose, V., & Murugan, S. P. (2023). Industrial Automation and Its Impact on Manufacturing Industries. In Revolutionizing Industrial Automation Through the Convergence of Artificial Intelligence and the Internet of Things (pp. 24-40). IGI Global.

Li, F., Larimo, J., & Leonidou, L. C. (2021). Social media marketing strategy: Definition, conceptualization, taxonomy, validation, and future agenda. *Journal of the Academy of Marketing Science, 49*(1), 51–70. doi:10.100711747-020-00733-3

Li, F., Larimo, J., & Leonidou, L. C. (2021). Social media marketing strategy: Definition, conceptualization, taxonomy, validation, and future agenda. *Journal of the Academy of Marketing Science*, *49*(1), 51–70. doi:10.100711747-020-00733-3

Manickam, T., Vinayagamoorthi, G., Gopalakrishnan, S., Sudha, M., & Mathiraj, S. P. (2022). Customer Inclination on Mobile Wallets With Reference to Google-Pay and PayTM in Bengaluru City. [IJEBR]. *International Journal of E-Business Research*, *18*(1), 1–16. doi:10.4018/IJEBR.293295

Menon, S. R., & Chavadi, C. A. (2022). A Research-based Approach to Identify the Health-conscious Consumers in India. *Metamorphosis*, *21*(2), 118–128. doi:10.1177/09726225221098783

Mergel, I., Edelmann, N., & Haug, N. (2019). Defining digital transformation: Results from expert interviews. *Government Information Quarterly*, *36*(4), 101385. doi:10.1016/j.giq.2019.06.002

Mogaji, E., Soetan, T. O., & Kieu, T. A. (2020). The implications of artificial intelligence on the digital marketing of financial services to vulnerable customers. *Australasian Marketing Journal, j-ausmj.*

Murugan, S. P., Shivaprasad, G., Dhanalakshmi, A., Sriram, V. P., Rajput, K., Mahesh, B. N., & Kedla, S. (2023). The Impact of COVID-19 on the Indian Microfinance Industry and Its Sustainability. In *Transforming Economies Through Microfinance in Developing Nations* (pp. 160–188). IGI Global. doi:10.4018/978-1-6684-5647-7.ch009

Park, J. Y., Perumal, S. V., Sanyal, S., Ah Nguyen, B., Ray, S., Krishnan, R., Narasimhaiah, R., & Thangam, D. (2022). Sustainable Marketing Strategies as an Essential Tool of Business. *American Journal of Economics and Sociology*, *81*(2), 359–379. doi:10.1111/ajes.12459

Pfister, P., & Lehmann, C. (2023). Measuring the Success of Digital Transformation in German SMEs. *Journal of Small Business Strategy*, *33*(1), 1–19. doi:10.53703/001c.39679

Priyono, A., Moin, A., & Putri, V. N. A. O. (2020). Identifying digital transformation paths in the business model of SMEs during the COVID-19 pandemic. *Journal of Open Innovation*, *6*(4), 104. doi:10.3390/joitmc6040104

Pucihar, A. (2020). The digital transformation journey: Content analysis of Electronic Markets articles and Bled eConference proceedings from 2012 to 2019. *Electronic Markets*, *30*(1), 29–37. doi:10.100712525-020-00406-7

Reinartz, W., Wiegand, N., & Imschloss, M. (2019). The impact of digital transformation on the retailing value chain. *International Journal of Research in Marketing*, *36*(3), 350–366. doi:10.1016/j.ijresmar.2018.12.002

Reinartz, W., Wiegand, N., & Imschloss, M. (2019). The impact of digital transformation on the retailing value chain. *International Journal of Research in Marketing*, *36*(3), 350–366. doi:10.1016/j.ijresmar.2018.12.002

Saldanha, T. (2019). *Why digital transformations fail: The surprising disciplines of how to take off and stay ahead.* Berrett-Koehler Publishers.

Schnader, J. (2019). The Implementation of Artificial Intelligence in Hard and Soft Counterterrorism Efforts on Social Media. *Santa Clara High-Technology Law Journal*, *36*, 42.

Sedera, D., Tan, C. W., & Xu, D. (2022). Digital business transformation in innovation and entrepreneurship. *Information & Management*, *59*(3), 103620. doi:10.1016/j.im.2022.103620

Simangunsong, E., & Handoko, R. (2020). The role of social media in Indonesia for business transformation strategy. *International Research Journal of Business Studies*, *13*(1), 99–112. doi:10.21632/irjbs.13.1.99-112

Sirothiya, M., & Chavadi, C. (2020). Compressed biogas (cbg) as an alternative and sustainable energy source in India: Case study on implementation frameworks and challenges. *Invertis Journal of Renewable Energy*, *10*(2), 49–64. doi:10.5958/2454-7611.2020.00007.7

Sirothiya, M., & Chavadi, C. (2020). Evaluating marketing strategies ofcompressed biogas (CBG) companies in India using decision tree analysis. *IIMS Journal of Management Science*, *11*(3), 219–237. doi:10.5958/0976-173X.2020.00012.0

Sirothiya, M., & Chavadi, C. (2020). Role of compressed biogas to assess the effects of perceived value on customer satisfaction and customer loyalty. *BIMTECH Bus. Perspect*, *1*, 70–89.

Sivarajah, U., Irani, Z., Gupta, S., & Mahroof, K. (2020). Role of big data and social media analytics for business to business sustainability: A participatory web context. *Industrial Marketing Management*, *86*, 163–179. doi:10.1016/j.indmarman.2019.04.005

Sriram, V. P., Sanyal, S., Laddunuri, M. M., Subramanian, M., Bose, V., Booshan, B., & Thangam, D. (2023). Enhancing Cybersecurity Through Blockchain Technology. In Handbook of Research on Cybersecurity Issues and Challenges for Business and FinTech Applications (pp. 208-224). IGI Global.

Teng, X., Wu, Z., & Yang, F. (2022). Research on the Relationship between Digital Transformation and Performance of SMEs. *Sustainability (Basel)*, *14*(10), 6012. doi:10.3390u14106012

Thangam, D., Arumugam, T., Velusamy, K., Subramanian, M., Ganesan, S. K., & Suryakumar, M. (2022). COVID-19 Pandemic and Its Brunt on Digital Transformation and Cybersecurity. In Cybersecurity Crisis Management and Lessons Learned From the COVID-19 Pandemic (pp. 15-42). IGI Global.

Thangam, D., & Chavadi, C. (2023). Impact of Digital Marketing Practices on Energy Consumption, Climate Change, and Sustainability. *Climate and Energy*, *39*(7), 11–19. doi:10.1002/gas.22329

Thangam, D., Malali, A. B., Subramanian, G., Mohan, S., & Park, J. Y. (2022). Internet of things: a smart technology for healthcare industries. In *Healthcare Systems and Health Informatics* (pp. 3–15). CRC Press.

Thangam, D., Malali, A. B., Subramanian, G., & Park, J. Y. (2022). Transforming Healthcare through Internet of Things. In *Cloud and Fog Computing Platforms for Internet of Things* (pp. 15–24). Chapman and Hall/CRC. doi:10.1201/9781003213888-2

Thangam, D., Malali, A. B., Subramaniyan, G., Mariappan, S., Mohan, S., & Park, J. Y. (2022). Relevance of Artificial Intelligence in Modern Healthcare. In *Integrating AI in IoT Analytics on the Cloud for Healthcare Applications* (pp. 67–88). IGI Global. doi:10.4018/978-1-7998-9132-1.ch005

Thangam, D., Malali, A. B., Subramaniyan, S. G., Mariappan, S., Mohan, S., & Park, J. Y. (2021). Blockchain Technology and Its Brunt on Digital Marketing. In Blockchain Technology and Applications for Digital Marketing (pp. 1-15). IGI Global. doi:10.4018/978-1-7998-8081-3.ch001

Thangam, D., Vaidya, G. R., Subramanian, G., Velusamy, K., Selvi Govindarajan, K., & Park, J. Y. (2022). The Portrayal of Women's Empowerment in Select Indian Movies. *American Journal of Economics and Sociology*, *81*(1), 187–205. doi:10.1111/ajes.12451

The Enterprisers Project. (2023). *what is digital transformation?* The Enterprisers. https://enterprisersproject.com/what-is-digital-transformation

Thirupathi, M., & Gopalakrishnan, D. S. (2019). Impact of E-Media Among College Students. *Journal of Emerging Technologies and Innovative Research*, *6*(5), 185–192.

Thirupathi, M., Vinayagamoorthi, G., Gopalakrishnan, S., Sriram, V. P., & Kavitha, S. (2019). Accessibility and Adaptability of Emerging Technology among Mobile Wallet Customer using TAM model. *Journal of Contemporary Issues in Business and Government*, *27*(2), 2411–2435.

Thirupathi, M., Vinayagamoorthi, G., &Mathiraj, S. P. (2019). Effect Of cashless payment methods: A case study perspective analysis. *International Journal of scientific & technology research, 8*(8), 394-397.

Thirupathi, M, V. B., Kolur, V. P. ,Sriram, D. N. K. M, S., B. & P., S. K. (2022). *A Meta-Appraisal on UTAUT Model towards Accessibility and Adaptability of Digital Mobile Wallet Usage in India.* 2022 International Conference on Innovative Computing, Intelligent Communication and Smart Electrical Systems (ICSES), Chennai, India. . doi:10.1109/ICSES55317.2022.9914089

Tripathi, S. (2021). Determinants of Digital, Transformation in the Post-Covid-19 Business World. IJRDO-. *Journal of Business and Management*, *7*(6), 75–81.

Udovita, P. V. M. V. D. (2020). Conceptual review on dimensions of digital transformation in modern era. *International Journal of Scientific and Research Publications*, *10*(2), 520–529. doi:10.29322/IJSRP.10.02.2020.p9873

Ulas, D. (2019). Digital transformation process and SMEs. *Procedia Computer Science*, *158*, 662–671. doi:10.1016/j.procs.2019.09.101

Urbach, N., Drews, P., & Ross, J. (2017). Digital business transformation and the changing role of the IT function. *MIS Quarterly Executive*, *16*(2), 1–4.

Verhoef, P. C., Broekhuizen, T., Bart, Y., Bhattacharya, A., Dong, J. Q., Fabian, N., & Haenlein, M. (2021). Digital transformation: A multidisciplinary reflection and research agenda. *Journal of Business Research*, *122*, 889–901. doi:10.1016/j.jbusres.2019.09.022

Vial, G. (2019). Understanding digital transformation: A review and a research agenda. *The Journal of Strategic Information Systems*, *28*(2), 118–144. doi:10.1016/j.jsis.2019.01.003

Vinayamoorthi, G., & Thirupathi, M. (2020). Consumer's Adoption of Digital Wallets With Special Reference to Bangalore City. *Shanlax International Journal of Management*, *8*(2), 108–113. doi:10.34293/management.v8i2.3429

Warner, K. S., & Wäger, M. (2019). Building dynamic capabilities for digital transformation: An ongoing process of strategic renewal. *Long Range Planning*, *52*(3), 326–349. doi:10.1016/j.lrp.2018.12.001

Woodcock, J., & Johnson, M. R. (2019). Live streamers on Twitch. tv as social media influencers: Chances and challenges for strategic communication. *International Journal of Strategic Communication*, *13*(4), 321–335. doi:10.1080/1553118X.2019.1630412

Ziyadin, S., Suieubayeva, S., & Utegenova, A. (2020). Digital transformation in business. In Digital Age: Chances, Challenges and Future 7 (pp. 408-415). Springer International Publishing. doi:10.1007/978-3-030-27015-5_49

Chapter 5
Social Media Usage in Indian Banking and Financial Institutions

Thirupathi Manickam
https://orcid.org/0000-0001-7976-6073
CHRIST University (Deemed), India

S. Gopalakrishnan
https://orcid.org/0000-0002-2158-7483
East Point College of Higher Education, India

P. K. Hridhya
CHRIST University (Deemed), India

V. Ravi
CHRIST University (Deemed), India

Devarajanayaka Kalenahalli Muniyanayaka
https://orcid.org/0000-0003-0853-4085
University of Buraimi, Oman

Haritha Muniraju
Triveni Institute of Commerce and Management, India

B. Seenivasan
Sacred Heart College (Autonomous), India

ABSTRACT

Due to technological innovation, the economy is transitioning from a market-driven to a network-oriented status, and social media has seized the leading I.T. trends in the technology sector. A paradigm change in banking and finance operations has occurred due to the upswing in innovation, transformation, and digitalisation in Indian banking and financial organisations. The development of online banking, mobile apps, mobile banking, and tools like debit and credit cards has changed how customers utilise banking and financing services. Thanks to social media and digital marketing, banks may now be practical tools for supporting customers' enterprises and gaining target prospects. To provide customers with rapid and efficient service in the post-pandemic age, Indian banks and financial institutions are rushing to modernise their technology infrastructure and digital goods. Social media offers users attractive options for 24-hour access to information and the use of financial services across temporal and geographic boundaries.

DOI: 10.4018/978-1-6684-7450-1.ch005

INTRODUCTION

People now spend more time on their laptops, smartphones, and computers, whether it be to read newspapers online, book travel tickets, listen to music or watch videos for entertainment, find information, purchase any product through online shopping, participate in public forums and discussions, read e-books, e-journals, share pictures and videos, or interact with friends, family, coworkers, businesses, or government organisations via popular social networking sites like Facebook and Twitter. All they require is a computer and an internet connection. Mass internet connections have been made possible by developing information and communications technology and expanding broadband penetration in urban, semi-urban, and rural regions.

In this digital age, social media is the new medium for people, businesses, organisations, the government, and civil society to communicate and participate. Social networking sites like Facebook, Twitter, YouTube, etc., can bring about public protests, organise social demonstrations, mobilise social campaigns, and enable communications and discussions on public forums. They can also overthrow political regimes, support political campaigns, and help candidates win the presidency. Most of the time, social networking has taken up a significant amount of space in the lives of millions of individuals worldwide. These days, social media platforms serve as a means of communication, information access, commerce, networking with clients, and a wide range of comparable activities (Bawre & Kar, 2019; Miranda et al., 2013). Blogs, microblogs, Wikipedia, virtual worlds, and social networking sites are the main components of social media (Kaplan & Haenlein, 2010; Miranda et al., 2013). Although there isn't a clear definition of social media yet, (Bryer & Zavattaro, 2011) claim that "social media are technologies that encourage social contact, make it feasible for cooperation, and allow for stakeholder discourse." These technologies include wikis, blogs, networking sites like Facebook, and tools for sharing media (music, photos, videos, and text).

Organisations can connect with the public through social media (Aula, 2010). In recent years, banks worldwide have been utilising social media platforms to communicate with their clients and build their reputations. According to Banerjee (2017), social media facilitates the real-time connection between banks and their clients, allowing the latter to detect and address any issues swiftly. Social media aids banks in developing their digital offerings. Also, banks are running financial literacy campaigns on social media to pique users' interest in the advantages of savings accounts and investing in other financial products.

With the development of innovation and Technology in the finance sector, the ideology of the Indian financial sector has been transformed in a digital access way. With the development of the financial industry in India, financial products and services have become easily accessible to every familiar people in India. In India, the process of digitising banks began about 30 years ago. The Digital India initiative, which emphasises giving India digital empowerment through better online infrastructure and enhanced internet access, has also helped speed up this process. According to Gadekar (2016), certain Indian banks (State Bank of India, ICICI, HDFC, and Kotak Mahindra Bank) have added services for their clients on Facebook and Twitter, including balance inquiries, financial counselling, financial transactions, and more. It is essential to investigate how much the financial industry uses social media to its advantage in this age of digitalisation and social networking (Bawre & Kar, 2019).

Customers may develop closer ties with financial institutions and learn more about them through social media. Social media has emerged as the platform that will determine many winners in tomorrow's linked company. Initial financial service endeavours saw banks looking to learn what customers thought of bank services and products. Subsequently, it changed to play a more proactive role by promptly reacting to client input. Financial institutions worldwide are working extra hard to create the Connected Client Strategy (K.S. Venkateswara Kumar, Dr V. Rama Devi).

Given that India has a sizable population of young (under 35) social media users, this market symbolises the consumer of the future in many aspects. Financial institutions must create a channel and engagement strategy that can cater to the needs of various consumers, each with their tastes and wants. Financial institutions will be able to design their interaction strategy with their existing and potential consumers by comprehending the factors underlying social networking engagement (Dwivedi et al., 2021).

Social Media

"social media" refers to a series of online communication networks focused on a specific group-based input where individuals may engage, exchange material, and form relationships and alliances (Pan & Crotts, 2016). Social media comprise several web portals and online programmes that speed up the adequate and suitable distribution of material to the intended consumers (Wahi et al., 2014).

Employing extremely accessible and scalable communication tools via social media. Using web-based and mobile Technology, social media transforms communication into a participatory discussion (Wikipedia).

Gadekar (2016), certain Indian banks (State Bank of India, ICICI, HDFC, and Kotak Mahindra Bank) have added services for their clients on Facebook and Twitter, including balance inquiries, financial counselling, financial transactions, and more. It is essential to investigate how much the financial industry uses social media to its advantage in this age of digitalisation and social networking. (Bryer & Zavattaro, 2011) Social media enable collaboration, social interaction, and stakeholder-wide deliberation." These technologies include wikis, blogs, networking sites like Facebook, and tools for sharing media (music, photos, videos, and text). According to (Bawre & Kar, 2019), Facebook, Twitter, and LinkedIn are the most popular social networking sites for discovering new markets, developing novel ideas, marketing financial goods, interacting with clients, and managing customer relationships (CRM).

Additionally, it has been observed that banks and NBFCs use these media pages to post significant financial announcements, which spurs customers' interest in investment opportunities. The study offers a perspective on using social media regarding cost savings and consumer satisfaction. However, some risks are connected with social media, including operational risks, data and information risks, and reputational risks. (Chikandiwa et al., 2013) Most South African banks utilise Facebook and Twitter as their most popular social media platforms for advertising, sales promotion, brand management, and customer support. Facebook, Twitter and LinkedIn have emerged as the most popular social media sites among Turkish banks, and links to each can be found on the official websites of individual banks, making them professional areas as well (Mucan & Özeltürkay, 2014). Social media users may be effectively targeted for all types of financial transactions. There are three primary types of Internet banking: informative level, communicative level, and transactional level. Regarding Net Banking, all Indian banks have completed the first two stages and are currently at the transactional level. This study sought to understand the disconnect between knowledge and the use of social media banking services (Thamaraiselvi G, 2019).

To provide customers with rapid and efficient service in the post-pandemic period, Indian banks are rushing to modernise their technology infrastructure and digital goods. Social media offers users engaging chances to acquire information and take advantage of financial services around-the-clock, without regard to time or place. To meet the high expectations of the digitally empowered consumer and provide a personalised, immersive experience, marketers must create new customer-centric tactics. Customers must also be informed of how certain banking brands may help them and improve the returns on their financial investments (Sawhney et al., 2022) usage of Facebook, in particular by India's public and commercial banks on social networking platforms. The information for this study is based on a review of 47 banks' Facebook pages, which were looked at between February and March of 2015. The study is based on a tool called the Facebook Assessment Index (FAI), which measures a company's Facebook page's popularity, engagement, and content in three different areas. According to the findings, only 48.9% of the banks under observation had an official Facebook page. New private sector banks (ICICI Bank and Axis Bank) outperformed other banks in each FAI category (Malhotra & Singh, 2016). Consumers now have an exponentially greater capacity to affect company behaviour and business strategy in unexpected and, at times, disagreeable ways. In less than 24 hours, a sore client's viral, entertaining complaint can become a significant issue. Understanding what customers feel, think, and say about a firm in real time is increasingly important in this context. Financial services organisations need to use social media's immense potential to improve customer service, manage their reputation, and gain a competitive edge. Social media makes information more accessible, humanises customer service, and ties companies to their stakeholders (Kumar & Devi, 2014).

Social Media in India

Both the use of broadband and the number of mobile phone customers have surged in India. India, ranking second in user numbers, reached 755 million social media users in 2022 and is estimated to reach 1.17 billion by 2027. The United States has the third largest social network audience, followed by Indonesia and Brazil. In recent years, India has developed into one of the world's most competitive and rapidly expanding telecom markets. Social media reaches 60% of the country's internet population in India. About 90% of social media users are served by Facebook and Orkut combined (Srivastava, 2013).

The social media platforms in India that have had the highest growth—almost tripling in users over the past six months—are WhatsApp, Instagram, and Facebook. Indians now spend the majority of their internet time socialising. The most recent statistics from marketing research firm ComScore show that 84% of Internet users in India use social networking sites. India now ranks globally as the seventh-largest social networking market after the U.S., China, Germany, Russian Federation, Brazil, and the U.K. The CEO of Facebook India, Kirthiga Reddy, launched her remarks at the 11th India Today Conclave, held on March 16 in New Delhi, by emphasising how the success of the online revolution hinged on placing people at the core, particularly those living in rural regions. Reddy emphasised the value of community actions by describing how farmers in Sangli, Maharashtra, stopped the price decline of turmeric by using Facebook. She continued by explaining how collaborating with government programmes may alter society. The term "government 2.0" is occasionally used to describe how social media is changing the dynamic between the public and institutions of government. Citizens and service users are undoubtedly already discussing local issues online and are increasingly demanding more transparent government and a more significant role in how things happen where they live. Government 2.0 refers to using social media platforms to participate in these debates, influence policy, promote local democracy, enhance services, and open data to make government more accessible and accountable (Srivastava, 2013).

Figure 1. Penetration of leading social networks in India
Source: https://www.statista.com/statistics/284436/india-social-media-penetration/

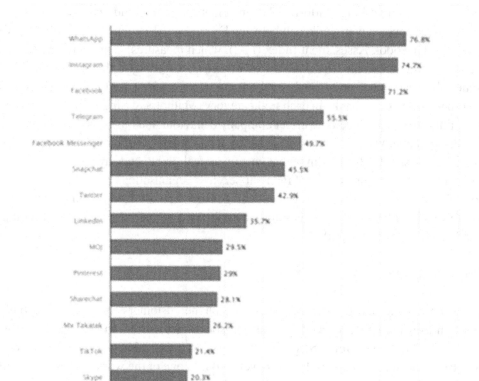

Indian Banking and Financial Institutions

Social media is occasionally seen to be less significant in the financial services industry. There are well-known arguments against increasing social media spending in the financial services industry. However, the examples in this section will demonstrate that creative options are still within the bounds of compliance. Financial institutions successfully interact with their digital clients and set themselves apart using real-time social media communication. With the industry perceiving social media posts as participatory communication rather than static advertising, there has been a clear transition from pre- and post-review.

India's financial institutions (F.I.s) are divided into three broad divisions based on their core activity. Institutions that specialise in term loans and investments, which are direct lending activities; Banks and non-banking financial institutions are the primary recipients of refinancing from organisations like the National Bank for Agriculture and Rural Development (NABARD), the Small Industries Development Bank of India (SIDBI), and the National Housing Bank (NHB). Marketable securities are where most investments are made by investment companies like Life Insurance Corporation (LIC). Institutions at the state or regional level are another distinct category.

A sizeable portion of SIDBI's overall exposure (SFCs) is to State Finance Corporations. SIDBI is the Small Industries Development Bank of India. The SFCs' poor financial standing negatively impacts SIDBI's financial health. The Government of India occasionally issues particular securities (such as oil bonds and bonds for fertilisers) that do not meet bank SLR requirements. These government securities have a more significant degree of liquidity spread and are subject to a unique set of terms and restrictions.

Social Media in Banking and Financial Institutions

In India, the process of digitising banks began about 30 years ago. But in the most recent decade, its pace has multiplied. It has also been made possible by the Digital India campaign, which emphasises giving India greater digital empowerment through better online infrastructure and improved internet connectivity (Bawre & Kar, 2019). According to Suvarna and Banerjee (2014), social media is a significant trend in the banking sector. These analyses explained how social media would inevitably play a function in the banking sector in retaining consumers who are particularly adept at using Technology. The banking industry must step up the integration of social media trends with banking services as social media is becoming a more popular media outlet among consumers, and over 89% of customers surveyed reported having a social media account. Bank institutions are aware of the power of social media and actively engage with their customers there Because they want to meet the growing customer demand for personalisation (Fasnacht, 2018).

Banks adapt their attitudes and behaviour to the opportunities social media provide for contact with their customers. We provide four models for how banks might use social media to interact with their clients: as a marketing tool, a communication channel, a channel for feedback and responses, and a model for social media transactional banking (Silvia Parusheva, 2017). Any emerging economy's foundation is its banking sector. Banks play a crucial role in putting the economic changes into action. Any banking industry transformation brought on by the use of Technology will significantly influence the expansion of an economy. Banks are looking for novel methods to offer and set themselves apart from the competition. Customers today want the ability to complete financial transactions at any time and location that suits them (Jayasuriya & Azam, 2018). Social media has altered every aspect of business and marketing, and the banking sector is no different, given that customer interaction is crucial in this sector. Banks may rely on social media since it is widespread and global today. Banks and their clients are increasingly using digital communication as a method of communication. This medium demonstrates how crucial it is for reaching out to potential customers. By enabling money transfers, credit applications, and even the simple establishment of bank accounts, it has enhanced customer services, strengthening client relationships. Understanding people's emotions is a huge and challenging task, especially in the case of the service sector. Social media has an exceptional capacity for establishing and maintaining client relationships and improving customer relations (Kim et al., 2016).

The company's success as a brand may be influenced by the bank's social media marketing strategy in a media environment where social media is becoming more and more dominant. Banks must maintain a high level of social media activity and create tailored strategies to strengthen their brand, attract customers, and yield a high return on investment. Social media is becoming vital for banks to communicate with people worldwide. Because traditional banking methods, such as interest rates and product differentiation, are challenging them to attract new clients and sustain existing clients, banks are adapting to social media (Shah, Khan & Sadiqa, 2015). To investigate how social media impacts the perception of service quality and client loyalty in the West Bengal banking sector. In the Indian banking sector, the quality of social media services can be used to increase customer loyalty (Potgieter & Naidoo, 2017).

Need & Role of Social Media in Banking and Financial Institutions

Since social media has recently become very political, it's critical to consider potential controversies as you develop your strategy. There is also a lot of debate on the psychological harm these websites do and how they use user information. Keep in mind that these discussions include your consumers as you post. Maintaining social media accounts takes a lot of effort and money. After all, banking is a business; thus, it is crucial to consider the value to your institution's bottom line. Social media is the most significant outlet that might offer banks the much needed conduit for establishing client relationships. Most of us are accustomed to using social media for connection development and communication as individual consumers. But using social media for banking or business is still a relatively new phenomenon. Some priceless benefits that social media strategy might provide banks include the enormous potential to deliver client solutions, raise brand recognition, grow their customer base, and establish continuous personal connections. Traditional banks realise the urgency of rethinking their customer relationship strategies in light of fintech companies' ability to provide innovative digital value propositions and their capacity to interact with customers through social media platforms to understand their purchasing processes better.

Social Media- Aid to financial institutions

Communication: Social media platforms like Facebook, Twitter, LinkedIn, and others link thousands of investors. Social media offers the chance to reach out to and educate customers. The financial institutions must speak to the public in a language they can comprehend. Social media transparency will aid institutions in developing trust. A social media plan (Kumar & Devi, 2014). Real-time information updates may be found on social media. Limited product offers and time-sensitive industry information might be posted on the social media platform. Since the products and offers will only be made available through social media and not traditional media streams, consumers who interact with the financial institution's social media page may have a sense of exclusivity.

Solving the Customer's Concerns

Social media may help engage consumers with their questions and complaints. A financial institution representative can promptly respond when queries or grievances are posted on the social media page. If any exchange of sensitive information is necessary for the activity, the financial institution may contact the client directly via a secure communication channel. Social media may therefore be effectively employed as the initial level of question. Since this non-core activity is removed from the branch and other delivery channels, the company saves money (Financial et al., 2010). Customers can submit complaints or problems on social media, and financial institutions can address them there. This will aid financial companies in keeping customers and building their brands (Kumar & Devi, 2014).

Content

Financial institutions must produce the appropriate material for their target investors. To provide financial services, the material must reflect how investors converse with one another. For different types of investors, the information must be specifically tailored.

Identify and Address the Public Sentiment

Due to the multidirectional nature of social media, clients may express opinions about the business. As a result, it would be wise for financial institutions to be active on social media to monitor client sentiment. When people express unpleasant opinions publicly, the financial institution can respond quickly to control the problem (Financial et al., 2010). Social media helps communicate with customers – knowing their needs and wants. Financial institutions must understand customers' perceptions (Kumar & Devi, 2014).

Crowdsourcing: Financial institutions engage in many non-banking activities such as CSR, social and environmental initiatives etc. Such non-core activities are usually identified and executed internally. Customers can be effectively involved in these activities as it entails minimal risk to the institutions while allowing customers to develop a strong sense of ownership and decision-making through such participation (Financial et al., 2010).

Create brand awareness: Brand awareness is the most important purpose that a social network may fulfil for a financial institution. Financial institutions can interact with social media users in a variety of ways, including by promoting deals and discounts, polling or posing questions, sharing information about the business, etc. Compared to traditional media, engaging social media users successfully may enhance brand exposure for a far lesser expenditure (Kumar & Devi, 2014).

Customer feedback: Customers who interact with their financial institutions on social media may receive frequent updates on their social media profiles from the financial institution. Financial institutions may use this element of social media, especially social networks, to poll customers about their opinions of the goods and services they offer. Financial companies may precisely determine their client's needs using social media. A blog or forum has to be set up by the financial institutions. Inviting customers to provide and post feedback online is one of the most excellent ways to use social media (Kumar & Devi, 2014).

Hire employees: The way financial organisations hire staff is changing due to social media. Talent is become simpler to locate on professional social media platforms like LinkedIn because of the expansion of social media. Senior management, which headhunters often hire, is increasingly introduced through specialised social media platforms. Financial companies can cut expenditures on hiring by using technological and social media platforms (Financial et al., 2010).

Employee engagement: Employees can publish on the financial institution's social media page using their social media accounts, giving the financial organisation a more personal feel. As a result of employee interaction, a sense of community and belonging develops (Financial et al., 2010).

CONCLUSION

Today Social media is global, omnipresent, and of rising importance because it makes it easier for businesses to build and maintain long-lasting relationships with their target audience. As a result, as part of their overall marketing strategy, banks must evaluate and implement numerous digital marketing and social media content marketing tactics (Sawhney & Ahuja, 2022). Social media will be increasingly embraced as a component of retail banking in the upcoming years. To use social media to its maximum potential, banks must strongly emphasise their comprehension of it. However, there is still a disconnect between banks' services and how clients wish to utilise social media for banking and finance institutions (Askar et al., 2022).

In the current environment, banks must carefully plan their strategies under the needs of their clients to retain them. The next generation's attitude towards the banking industry and their current youth varies significantly from the previous one. As a result, the banking industry and other financial institutions use social media marketing to keep in touch with their clients and simplify their jobs. Social media content marketing is a popular digital marketing approach that is necessary for the entire banking marketing strategy. The primary goal of a content strategy put out by banks is to raise awareness of, provide information to, and educate target audiences about financial goods and services as well as to further develop the customer relationship by encouraging the target audience to show loyalty and trust (Sawhney & Ahuja, 2022). Banking and financial institutions should do in-depth research to tailor their social media content marketing strategies to their target audience's requirements and expectations. As a result, social media content marketing techniques are essential for educating and enlightening their target audience and boosting brand loyalty by creating lasting connections.

REFERENCES

Askar, M., Aboutabl, A. E., & Galal, A. (2022). Utilising Social Media Data Analytics to Enhance Banking Services. *Intelligent Information Management*, *14*(1), 1–14. doi:10.4236/iim.2022.141001

Aula, P. (2010). Social media, reputation risk and ambient publicity management. *Strategy and Leadership*, *38*(6), 43–49. doi:10.1108/10878571011088069

Bawre, S., & Kar, S. (2019). Social media and financial institutions in the Indian context. *International Journal of Economics and Business Research*, *18*(3), 343–355. doi:10.1504/IJEBR.2019.102734

Bryer, T. A., & Zavattaro, S. M. (2011). Social media and public administration: Theoretical dimensions and introduction to the symposium. *Administrative Theory & Praxis, 33*(3), 325-340.

Chavadi, C. (2021). Growth drivers, characteristics, preference and challenges faced by Fast Moving Consumer Goods-A study with reference to Bengaluru. *Turkish Online Journal of Qualitative Inquiry, 12*(7).

Chavadi, C. A., Arul, M. J., & Sirothiya, M. (2020). Modelling the effects of creative advertisements on consumers: An empirical study. *Vision (Basel)*, *24*(3), 269–283. doi:10.1177/0972262920926074

Chavadi, C. A., Hiremath, C. V., & Hyderabad, R. L. (2014). Customer loyalty appraisal based on store characteristics: An alternative approach. *Indian Journal of Marketing*, *44*(5), 18–29. doi:10.17010/ijom/2014/v44/i5/80375

Chavadi, C. A., & Kokatnur, S. S. (2008). Consumer Expectation and Perception of Fast Food Outlets: An Empirical Study in Davangere. *ICFAI Journal Of Services Marketing, 6*(2).

Chavadi, C. A., & Kokatnur, S. S. (2009). Impact of Short-Term Promotional Ads on Food Retailing. *ICFAI Journal of Consumer Behavior, 4*(1).

Chavadi, C. A., & Kokatnur, S. S. (2009). RFID Adoption by Indian Retailers: An Exploratory Study. *The Icfai University Journal of Supply Chain Management, 6*(1), 60–77.

Chavadi, C. A., Menon, S. R., & Sirothiya, M. (2019). Measuring Service Quality Perceptions of Indian E-retailers: An Evaluative Study. *Metamorphosis, 18*(2), 92–102. doi:10.1177/0972622519886232

Chavadi, C. A., Menon, S. R., & Sirothiya, M. (2019). Modelling the Effects of Brand Placements in Movies: An Investigative Study of Event Type and Placement Type. *Vision (Basel), 23*(1), 31–43. doi:10.1177/0972262918821227

Chavadi, C. A., Vishwanatha, M. R., & Mubeen, S. (2018). Ghee with Glee: A Study of How Consumers Evaluate Product Packaging. *Metamorphosis, 17*(2), 100–110. doi:10.1177/0972622518817407

Chikandiwa, S. T., Contogiannis, E., & Jembere, E. (2013). The adoption of social media marketing in South African banks. *European Business Review, 25*(4), 365–381. doi:10.1108/EBR-02-2013-0013

Dwivedi, Y. K., Ismagilova, E., Hughes, D. L., Carlson, J., Filieri, R., Jacobson, J., Jain, V., Karjaluoto, H., Kefi, H., Krishen, A. S., Kumar, V., Rahman, M. M., Raman, R., Rauschnabel, P. A., Rowley, J., Salo, J., Tran, G. A., & Wang, Y. (2021). Setting the future of digital and social media marketing research: Perspectives and research propositions. *International Journal of Information Management, 59*, 2021. doi:10.1016/j.ijinfomgt.2020.102168

Fasnacht, D. (2018). Banking for the Next Generation, Management for Professionals. Open Innovation Ecosystems, 2(8), 231-243. doi:10.1007/978-3-319-76394-1_8

Financial, D., Consumer, S., & Series, I. (2010). Social Media in Financial Services. *Insight (American Society of Ophthalmic Registered Nurses).*

Jayasuriya, N., & Azam, F. (2018). The Impact of Social Media Marketing on Brand Equity: A Study of Fashion-Wear Retail in Sri Lanka. *International Review of Management and Marketing, 7*(5), 178–183.

Kaplan, A. M., & Haenlein, M. (2010). Users of the world, unite! The challenges and opportunities of Social Media. Business Horizons, 53(1), 59-68. doi:10.1016/j.bushor.2009.09.003

Kim, Y., Wang, Y., & Oh, J. (2016). Digital Media Use and Social Engagement: How Social Media and Smartphone Use Influence Social Activities of College Students. *Cyberpsychology, Behavior, and Social Networking, 19*(4), 264–269. doi:10.1089/cyber.2015.0408 PMID:26991638

Kumar, K. S. V., & Devi, V. R. (2014). Social Media in Financial Services – A Theoretical Perspective. *Procedia Economics and Finance, 11*, 306–313. doi:10.1016/S2212-5671(14)00198-1

Malhotra, P., & Singh, B. (2016). Presence of banking in social media: Indian evidence. *International Journal of Business Forecasting and Marketing Intelligence, 2*(2), 117 - 127. doi:10.1504/IJBFMI.2016.078149

Miranda, F. J., Chamorro, A., Rubio, S., & Morgado, V. (2013). Evaluation of social networks sites in the banking sector: An analysis of top 200 international banks. *Journal of Internet Banking and Commerce, 18*(2), 1–17.

Mucan, B., & Özeltürkay, E. Y. (2014). Social Media Creates Competitive Advantages: How Turkish Banks Use This Power? A Content Analysis of Turkish Banks through their Webpages. *Procedia: Social and Behavioral Sciences*, *148*, 137–145. doi:10.1016/j.sbspro.2014.07.027

Pan, B., & Crotts, J. C. (2016). Theoretical models of social media, marketing implications, and future research directions. In Social Media in Travel, Tourism and Hospitality: Theory, Practice and Cases, pp. 73-85

Potgieter, L. M., & Naidoo, R. (2017). Factors explaining user loyalty in a social media-based brand community. *S.A. Journal of Information Management, 19*. . doi:10.4102/sajim.v19i1.744

Sawhney, A., & Ahuja, V. (2022). Drivers of Social Media Content Marketing in the Banking Sector. In Research Anthology on Social Media Advertising and Building Consumer Relationships, 12(3), pages 54-72. doi:10.4018/978-1-6684-6287-4.ch023

Sawhney, A., Ahuja, V., & Sharma, P. (2022). *Role of Social Media in the Indian Banking Sector*. Multidisciplinary Perspectives Towards Building a Digitally Competent Society., doi:10.4018/978-1-6684-5274-5.ch002

Shah, Khan, I., & Sadiqa, M. (2015). Impact of Service Quality on Customer Satisfaction of Banking Sector Employees: a Study of Lahore, Punjab. *Vidyabharati International Interdisciplinary Research Journal*.

Sriram, V. P., Sanyal, S., Laddunuri, M. M., Subramanian, M., Bose, V., Booshan, B., & Thangam, D. (2023). Enhancing Cybersecurity Through Blockchain Technology. In Handbook of Research on Cybersecurity Issues and Challenges for Business and FinTech Applications (pp. 208-224). IGI Global.

Srivastava, M. (2013). Social Media and Its Use by the Government. *Journal of Public Administration and Governance*, *3*(2), 161–172. doi:10.5296/jpag.v3i2.3978

G. Thamaraiselvi (2019), A Gap Analysis on Awareness and Utilization of Social Media Banking – The New Line of Self Service Banking. (2019). *International Journal of Innovative Technology and Exploring Engineering, 9*, 456-459. doi:10.35940/ijitee.B1215.1292S219

Thangam, D., Arumugam, T., Velusamy, K., Subramanian, M., Ganesan, S. K., & Suryakumar, M. (2022). COVID-19 Pandemic and Its Brunt on Digital Transformation and Cybersecurity. In Cybersecurity Crisis Management and Lessons Learned From the COVID-19 Pandemic (pp. 15-42). IGI Global.

Thangam, D., & Chavadi, C. (2023). Impact of Digital Marketing Practices on Energy Consumption, Climate Change, and Sustainability. *Climate and Energy*, *39*(7), 11–19. doi:10.1002/gas.22329

Thangam, D., Malali, A. B., Subramanian, G., Mohan, S., & Park, J. Y. (2022). Internet of things: a smart technology for healthcare industries. In *Healthcare Systems and Health Informatics* (pp. 3–15). CRC Press.

Thangam, D., Malali, A. B., Subramanian, G., & Park, J. Y. (2022). Transforming Healthcare through Internet of Things. In *Cloud and Fog Computing Platforms for Internet of Things* (pp. 15–24). Chapman and Hall/CRC. doi:10.1201/9781003213888-2

Thangam, D., Malali, A. B., Subramaniyan, G., Mariappan, S., Mohan, S., & Park, J. Y. (2022). Relevance of Artificial Intelligence in Modern Healthcare. In *Integrating A.I. in IoT Analytics on the Cloud for Healthcare Applications* (pp. 67–88). IGI Global. doi:10.4018/978-1-7998-9132-1.ch005

Thangam, D., Malali, A. B., Subramaniyan, S. G., Mariappan, S., Mohan, S., & Park, J. Y. (2021). Blockchain Technology and Its Brunt on Digital Marketing. In Blockchain Technology and Applications for Digital Marketing (pp. 1-15). IGI Global. doi:10.4018/978-1-7998-8081-3.ch001

Thangam, D., Vaidya, G. R., Subramanian, G., Velusamy, K., Selvi Govindarajan, K., & Park, J. Y. (2022). The Portrayal of Women's Empowerment in Select Indian Movies. *American Journal of Economics and Sociology*, *81*(1), 187–205. doi:10.1111/ajes.12451

Wahi, A. K., Medury, Y., & Misra, R. K. (2014). Social Media: The Core of Enterprise 2.0. [July.]. *International Journal of Service Science, Management, Engineering, and Technology*, *5*(3), 1–15. doi:10.4018/ijssmet.2014070101

Chapter 6
The Role of Social Media in Empowering Digital Financial Literacy

S. Baranidharan
iD https://orcid.org/0000-0002-7780-4045
CHRIST University (Deemed), India

Amirdha Vasani Sankarkumar
SRM Institute of Science and Technology, India

G. Chandrakala
Dayananda Sagar University, India

Raja Narayanan
Dayananda Sagar University, India

K. Sathyanarayana
Presidency University, India

ABSTRACT

This systematic review examined the role of social media in enhancing financial literacy among individuals by collecting and reviewing 60 articles published from 2021 to 2023. The findings revealed that social media has a positive impact on financial literacy through the dissemination of financial education, promotion of financial awareness, and sharing of financial experiences. The review also identified digital financial literacy, entrepreneurial learning, and financial knowledge as significant determinants of financial literacy, while demographic characteristics, social media usage behavior, risk attitude, and overconfidence played a role in determining financial literacy. The study recommends that financial institutions, policymakers, and educators leverage social media for promoting financial literacy, and social media usage skills to improve financial literacy among individuals. Overall, the study suggests that the use of social media can democratize financial literacy and enable individuals from diverse backgrounds to access financial education and information.

DOI: 10.4018/978-1-6684-7450-1.ch006

INTRODUCTION

Social media platforms have gained immense popularity in recent years and are now an integral part of people's daily lives. With more than 3.8 billion active users worldwide, social media is a powerful tool for communication and information sharing. Social media platforms like Facebook, Twitter, Instagram, LinkedIn, and YouTube have revolutionized the way people interact with each other, and it has become a key source of information for individuals. In recent years, the use of social media in the financial sector has increased significantly. Financial institutions, as well as individuals, are utilizing social media to educate, promote, and sell financial products and services. This trend has led to the emergence of a new term called "social media financial literacy."

Financial literacy is the knowledge and skills required to make informed and effective decisions about money management. It includes understanding financial products and services, managing money, making investments, and planning for retirement. Financial literacy is essential for individuals to make informed decisions about their financial well-being. However, studies have shown that a significant proportion of the population lacks financial literacy, which can lead to poor financial decisions and outcomes. In recent years, social media has emerged as a powerful tool for promoting financial literacy.

Evaluation of social media and its impact on financial literacy:

Social media can be an effective tool for promoting financial literacy. Social media platforms provide an opportunity for financial institutions to engage with customers and provide financial education. Social media platforms allow financial institutions to disseminate information about financial products and services, and customers can ask questions and receive immediate responses. This interactive communication can help individuals better understand financial products and services and make informed decisions.

Additionally, social media can help individuals access financial education resources. Many financial institutions, government agencies, and nonprofit organizations offer financial education resources through social media platforms. Social media can help individuals access these resources and learn about financial topics such as budgeting, investing, and debt management. Furthermore, social media can also help individuals connect with peers and experts who can provide financial advice and guidance. Social media platforms allow individuals to join groups and communities focused on financial education and connect with financial experts. These connections can help individuals learn about financial topics and get advice from experts.

However, social media also poses some challenges for promoting financial literacy. The information provided on social media may not always be accurate, reliable, or unbiased. Financial institutions may use social media to promote their products and services, which can be misleading for individuals who lack financial literacy. Additionally, the overwhelming amount of information available on social media can make it challenging for individuals to distinguish between reliable and unreliable sources of financial information.

Social media has the potential to be an effective tool for promoting financial literacy. Social media platforms provide an opportunity for financial institutions to engage with customers and provide financial education. Social media can also help individuals access financial education resources and connect with peers and experts who can provide financial advice and guidance. However, social media also poses some challenges for promoting financial literacy, including the accuracy and reliability of information provided and the overwhelming amount of information available. Therefore, it is essential to ensure that the information provided on social media is accurate, reliable, and unbiased to promote financial literacy effectively.

Statement of the Problem

Based on the above reviewed articles, it is clear that there is a growing interest in the relationship between social media and financial literacy. Many studies have found that social media can have both positive and negative effects on financial literacy, depending on factors such as demographics, risk attitudes, and overconfidence. While digital financial literacy is becoming increasingly important, particularly in rural areas, there are still many challenges to ensuring that individuals have access to the education and resources they need. The multidimensional nature of financial literacy means that it is important to take a holistic approach, incorporating factors such as social capital, entrepreneurship, and digitalization. Overall, there is a need for further research to better understand the relationship between social media and financial literacy, and to develop effective strategies for improving financial literacy in the digital age.

Research Questions

1. To what extent does social media usage impact financial literacy levels among different demographic groups?
2. How do social media platforms shape individuals' financial attitudes, behaviors, and decision-making processes?
3. What are the most effective strategies for leveraging social media to promote financial literacy and improve financial outcomes for individuals and communities?

Objectives of the Study

Objective 1: To identify the relationship between social media usage and financial literacy levels among individuals.

Objective 2: To determine the impact of social media-based financial education programs on individuals' financial literacy levels.

Objective 3: To examine the effectiveness of social media as a tool for promoting financial literacy among different age groups and demographic segments.

METHODOLOGY

This study is a systematic review that aims to investigate the role of social media on financial literacy. The review articles were selected based on the criteria of social media and financial literacy, and only articles published between 2021 and 2023 were included. The articles were collected from various sources, including Scopus database, Web of Science, Proquest, Ebsco, and Google Scholar.

Research Design: The research design for this study is a systematic review. This approach involves identifying relevant research studies, appraising their quality and relevance, and synthesizing their findings to draw conclusions about the topic of interest. Systematic reviews are a useful research design for exploring complex research questions and synthesizing evidence from multiple studies.

Type of Research: This study is a qualitative research as it aims to synthesize and analyze the findings of previously conducted research studies on the role of social media on financial literacy.

Data Collection: The data for this study were collected through a systematic search of relevant articles in various databases. The search terms used were "social media" AND "financial literacy". Only articles published between 2021 and 2023 were included in the study. The 60 articles were collected from different sources, such as Scopus database, Web of Science, Proquest, Ebsco, and Google Scholar.

Data Analysis: The data collected for this study will be analyzed using a thematic analysis approach. This involves identifying and coding themes from the collected articles, and then synthesizing the findings to draw conclusions about the role of social media on financial literacy. The themes will be identified based on the research questions and objectives of the study.

Literature Review Discussion

Kumar, Pillai, Kumar, and Tabash (2023) conducted a study on the interplay of skills, digital financial literacy, capability, and autonomy in financial decision-making and well-being. The study found that digital financial literacy, along with autonomy and capability, significantly impact individuals' financial decision-making and well-being. Moreover, the study showed that financial literacy skills, particularly in digital contexts, play a vital role in financial decision-making and well-being. Koskelainen, Kalmi, Scornavacca, and others (2023) proposed a research agenda for exploring financial literacy in the digital age. The authors suggest that future studies should investigate the relationships between digital financial literacy and financial outcomes, the impact of new technologies on financial decision-making, and the role of financial education and regulation in enhancing financial literacy.

Almeida and Costa (2023) examined the perspectives of undergraduate students on financial literacy. The study found that students perceive financial literacy as a valuable skill, but they lack sufficient knowledge and experience in managing finances effectively. The authors suggest that incorporating financial literacy education into the undergraduate curriculum could help students develop financial management skills and enhance their financial well-being. Haudi (2023) investigated the role of financial literacy, financial attitudes, and family financial education on personal financial management and locus of control among university students. The study found that financial literacy and positive financial attitudes positively influence personal financial management, while family financial education does not have a significant impact. The study also showed that students with a strong internal locus of control exhibit better financial management practices.

Widyastuti and Hermanto (2022) studied the effect of financial literacy and social media on micro capital through financial technology in the creative industry sector in East Java. The study found that financial literacy and social media positively impact micro capital, and financial technology plays a crucial role in facilitating financial transactions in the creative industry sector. The study suggests that enhancing financial literacy and leveraging digital technologies could promote financial inclusion and economic development in the creative industry sector. Seldal and Nyhus (2022) investigated the relationship between financial vulnerability, financial literacy, and the use of digital payment technologies. The study found that individuals with low financial literacy and high financial vulnerability are less likely to adopt digital payment technologies. The study suggests that enhancing financial literacy and reducing financial vulnerability could promote the adoption of digital payment technologies and improve financial inclusion.

Ingale and Paluri (2022) conducted a bibliometric analysis of the relationship between financial literacy and financial behavior. The study found that financial literacy positively influences financial behavior, and financial education programs play a vital role in enhancing financial literacy. The study suggests that future research should explore the effectiveness of financial education programs and identify the most effective approaches to promoting financial literacy. Khan and Ahmad (2022) examined the effects of financial literacy and social media on financial behavior. The study found that financial literacy positively influences financial behavior, while social media has a negative impact on financial behavior. The study suggests that financial education programs could help individuals develop effective financial management skills, while social media platforms should provide more accurate financial information to their users. Klein (2022) explored the impact of the GameStop short squeeze on financial literacy and autodidactic herding behavior. The study suggests that the GameStop short squeeze and subsequent media attention may have increased individuals' interest in financial literacy and prompted them to educate themselves about financial markets.

Twumasi, Jiang, Ding, Wang, and others (2022) investigated the mediating role of access to financial services in the relationship between financial literacy and household income in rural Ghana. The study found that access to financial services mediates the positive relationship between financial literacy and household income. The study suggests that enhancing financial literacy and expanding access to financial services could promote economic development and poverty reduction in rural areas. In "Fintech, financial literacy, and financial education," Morgan (2022) explores the intersection of financial technology (fintech) and financial literacy. The chapter discusses how fintech can be used as a tool for financial education, as well as the potential risks and challenges associated with its use. The author highlights the importance of financial education in helping consumers make informed decisions in a rapidly changing financial landscape.

Yanto et al. (2022) investigate the roles of entrepreneurial skills, financial literacy, and digital literacy in maintaining micro, small, and medium enterprises (MSMEs) during the COVID-19 pandemic. The study found that all three factors were positively related to MSME resilience during the pandemic. The authors suggest that policymakers and business owners should prioritize the development of these skills and literacies to better prepare for future crises. Setiawan et al. (2022) examine the relationship between digital financial literacy, saving and spending behaviors, and future foresight. The study found that individuals with higher levels of digital financial literacy were more likely to engage in positive financial behaviors and have greater future foresight. The authors suggest that digital financial literacy education can help individuals improve their financial decision-making skills and prepare for the future. Dwijayanti et al. (2022) explore the role of Islamic fintech peer-to-peer lending (P2PL) in promoting financial inclusion and literacy among MSMEs. The study found that Islamic P2PL can help MSMEs access financing and improve their financial literacy, leading to greater business growth and sustainability. The authors suggest that Islamic P2PL can be a valuable tool for promoting financial inclusion and literacy in Muslim communities.

Rahim et al. (2022) provide an overview of the key drivers of financial literacy and behavior. The study found that individual characteristics, such as age, education, and income, as well as cultural and environmental factors, such as social norms and financial regulation, are important determinants of financial literacy and behavior. The authors suggest that policymakers and educators should consider these factors when designing financial literacy interventions. Ridho (2022) conducted a study to compare social media as a platform for financial literacy source. The author analyzed the content of financial literacy on social media and compared it with traditional financial literacy sources such as books and seminars. The study found that social media is a promising platform for financial literacy, as it provides easy access, up-to-date information, and interactive features. However, the quality and credibility of the information shared on social media should be carefully evaluated.

Garai-Fodor et al. (2022) explored the generation-specific perceptions of financial literacy and digital solutions. The study investigated the attitudes of different age groups towards financial literacy and digital financial services. The authors found that younger generations are more open to digital solutions and have higher levels of financial literacy. The study suggests that financial education should be adapted to different age groups and their specific needs and preferences. Nahar et al. (2022) examined the factors affecting the financial literacy rate of millennials in Malaysia. The study used a survey to gather data on the financial literacy levels of millennials and analyzed the factors that influence their financial literacy. The study found that financial literacy is positively influenced by education, income, and exposure to financial information. The study suggests that financial education programs should target millennials and provide relevant and engaging content. Zaitul and Ilona (2022) investigated the association between financial literacy and SME sustainability during COVID-19. The study analyzed the financial literacy levels of SME owners and their financial performance during the pandemic. The study found that SMEs with higher levels of financial literacy were more resilient and adaptable during the pandemic. The study highlights the importance of financial literacy for SME owners and suggests that financial education can improve SME sustainability.

Gunawan et al. (2022) studied the consumption behavior of Medan city students during the pandemic and the role of financial literacy in e-commerce. The study used a survey to gather data on the students' consumption behavior and financial literacy levels. The study found that financial literacy has a positive effect on e-commerce adoption and usage. The study suggests that financial education can promote e-commerce adoption and improve financial management skills among students. Putri et al. (2022) conducted a literature review on digital financial literacy in Indonesia. They found that digital financial literacy is crucial for financial inclusion and economic growth, but there are still gaps in understanding the impact of digital financial literacy programs. Majid and Nugraha (2022) studied the role of financial literacy in crowdfunding and Islamic securities. They found that financial literacy positively influences crowdfunding participation and that Islamic financial literacy has a positive impact on investors' trust and intention to invest in Islamic securities. Nguyen et al. (2022) conducted a study on financial literacy and associated factors among adults in a low-middle income country. They found that financial literacy was positively associated with income, education, and employment status. Additionally, financial literacy was found to be a significant predictor of financial behavior.

Nyakurukwa and Seetharam (2022) explored the role of financial literacy and social interactions in household stock market participation in South Africa. They found that financial literacy and social interactions have a positive effect on stock market participation, with financial literacy being a stronger predictor. Meitriana et al. (2022) conducted a narrative review on social capital-based financial literacy to improve business performance. They found that social capital can positively affect financial literacy and business performance, but there is a need for further research on the specific mechanisms and interventions that can improve social capital-based financial literacy. Meoli, Rossi, and Vismara (2022) investigated the effect of financial literacy on security-based crowdfunding. The study found that financial literacy has a significant positive impact on investment performance, with financially literate investors achieving higher returns. The authors conclude that promoting financial literacy among investors can improve investment performance and encourage the development of the crowdfunding market. Hermansson, Jonsson, and Liu (2022) examined the relationship between learning channels, financial literacy, and stock market participation. The study found that formal education and financial literacy positively affect stock market participation. The authors suggest that promoting financial education can increase the likelihood of stock market participation, especially for those with low levels of financial literacy.

Zhu and Xiao (2022) studied the impact of consumer financial education on risky financial asset holding in China. The study found that financial education reduces the likelihood of holding risky financial assets, especially for those with low levels of financial literacy. The authors suggest that financial education can improve financial decision-making and reduce financial risks for consumers. Leviastuti, Santika, and colleagues (2022) evaluated a social media-based financial literacy education program for women in Indonesia. The study found that the program improved participants' financial knowledge, attitudes, and behaviors. The authors suggest that social media can be an effective platform for financial literacy education, especially for women who face barriers to accessing traditional financial education programs.

Sari, Fatimah, Rika, Ilyana, and colleagues (2022) developed an augmented reality-based sharia financial literacy system for young learners. The study found that the system improved participants' financial literacy and attitudes toward sharia finance. The authors suggest that the system can be a useful tool for promoting financial literacy and sharia finance education among young learners. Wijayanti and Kartawinata (2022) investigated the effect of financial literacy, financial confidence, and external locus of control on personal finance management among students in East Java. The study found that financial literacy and financial confidence had a positive impact on personal finance management, while external locus of control had a negative impact. Mullappallykayamkulath (2022) conducted an empirical investigation into the impact of digital financial literacy on the financial behavior of millennials. The study found that digital financial literacy had a significant positive impact on financial behavior, including saving, investing, and using digital financial services. Padil et al. (2022) explored the relationship between financial literacy and awareness of investment scams among university students. The study found that higher financial literacy was associated with greater awareness of investment scams and a lower likelihood of falling victim to them.

Suchocka et al. (2022) investigated the role of modern media in shaping the financial literacy of young people. The study found that exposure to different forms of media, such as social media and online news sources, was positively associated with financial literacy among young people. Sugiarto et al. (2022) examined the role of a micro-business development program in improving the performance of micro, small, and medium enterprises (MSMEs) through financial literacy and digital marketing. The study found that the program had a positive impact on MSME performance, particularly for those who had high levels of financial literacy and digital marketing skills. Kakinuma (2022) conducted a study on the relationship between financial literacy, fintech adoption, leisure, and quality of life. The study found that fintech adoption has a mediating effect on the relationship between financial literacy and quality of life, and that leisure moderates this relationship. Dewi (2022) investigated how demographic and socioeconomic factors affect financial literacy and its variables. The study found that factors such as age, education level, income, and occupation have significant effects on financial literacy, financial attitude, and financial behavior. Ozdemir, Sari, and Irwandi (2021) studied the influence of motivation, financial literacy, and social media financial platforms on student investment interest. The study found that financial literacy and social media financial platforms have a significant positive effect on student investment interest, while motivation has a weak effect. Yanto, Ismail, Kiswanto, and Rahim (2021) explored the roles of peers and social media in building financial literacy among Indonesian economics and business students. The study found that both peers and social media have a positive influence on financial literacy, with social media being more effective in building financial knowledge. Kuchciak and Wiktorowicz (2021) examined the effectiveness of social media as a channel for empowering financial education by banks. The study found that social media can be an effective tool for providing financial education to customers, and that banks can use it to build customer relationships and increase their financial literacy. The study by Muñoz-Céspedes et al. (2021) investigates the relationship between financial literacy and sustainable consumer behavior. The findings suggest that financial literacy plays a significant role in promoting sustainable consumption practices. Specifically, individuals with higher financial literacy are more likely to engage in sustainable behaviors such as recycling, reducing energy consumption, and making environmentally conscious purchases. Lyons and Kass-Hanna (2021) provide a methodological overview of defining and measuring "digital" financial literacy. The study highlights the need to define digital financial literacy separately from traditional financial literacy, as it encompasses a distinct set of skills, including the ability to use digital tools for financial management and decision-making. The authors propose a framework for measuring digital financial literacy that considers both cognitive and behavioral aspects.

Estelami and Florendo (2021) investigate the role of financial literacy, need for cognition, and political orientation in consumers' use of social media for financial decision-making. The study finds that financial literacy is a significant predictor of social media use for financial purposes, and individuals with high financial literacy are more likely to use social media to seek financial information. Additionally, the study suggests that individuals with high need for cognition and liberal political orientation are more likely to engage in active information-seeking behavior. Shvaher et al. (2021) examine the effect of social media on financial literacy. The study finds that social media can have a positive impact on financial literacy by providing access to financial information and resources, as well as creating opportunities for financial education and training. However, the study also highlights the potential negative effects of social media, including misinformation and overload, which can lead to confusion and poor financial decision-making. Andreou and Anyfantaki (2021) explore the influence of financial literacy on internet banking behavior. The study finds that individuals with high financial literacy are more likely to use internet banking services, including online account management and electronic payments. The authors suggest that financial education and training can play a crucial role in promoting internet banking adoption, as it helps individuals understand the benefits and risks of using digital financial services.

Goyal and Kumar (2021) conducted a systematic review and bibliometric analysis of the literature on financial literacy. The study identified a rising trend in research on financial literacy and concluded that most studies focus on financial literacy as a predictor of financial behavior. The authors recommended that future research should explore the effectiveness of different interventions for improving financial literacy. Hidayati, Kartikowati, and colleagues (2021) investigated the influence of income level, financial literacy, and social media use on teachers' consumption behavior. The study found that financial literacy and social media use have a significant positive effect on teachers' consumption behavior, while income level has no significant effect. Jannah, Murwatiningsih, and colleagues (2021) examined the effect of financial literacy, social media, and social environment on the consumptive behavior of students at a high school in Indonesia. The study found that financial literacy has a significant negative effect on consumptive behavior, while social media and social environment have no significant effect. Voomets, Riitsalu, and Siibak (2021) explored the effectiveness of using social media to improve financial literacy, using the case of Kogumispäevik, a personal finance management app in Estonia. The study found that social media can be an effective tool for improving financial literacy, as it can increase engagement and provide personalized and interactive content.

Rizon, Anastasia, and Evelyn (2021) investigated the influence of demographic factors, social media use, risk attitude, and overconfidence on the financial literacy of social media users in Indonesia. The study found that social media use has a positive effect on financial literacy, while overconfidence has a negative effect. The authors recommended that financial education programs should consider these factors to be more effective. Zhao and Li's (2021) study in Frontiers in Psychology examines the relationship between social capital, financial literacy, and rural household entrepreneurship in China. They found that financial literacy has a mediating effect on the relationship between social capital and entrepreneurship, and that social capital has a positive effect on financial literacy and entrepreneurship. Mudasih and Subroto's (2021) study in Technium Soc. Sci. J. investigates the effect of financial literacy, digital literacy, and entrepreneurial learning outcome on the entrepreneurial behavior of students in Indonesia. Their findings suggest that all three factors have a positive and significant effect on entrepreneurial behavior. Selvia et al. (2021) explore the effect of financial knowledge, financial behavior, and financial inclusion on financial well-being in Indonesia. Using a sample of university students, they found that financial knowledge and behavior have a positive effect on financial well-being, while financial inclusion did not have a significant effect.

Lyons and Kass-Hanna (2021) propose a multidimensional approach to defining and measuring financial literacy in the digital age. They argue that financial literacy should be viewed as a set of inter-related skills, including financial knowledge, financial behavior, and financial confidence. Thomas and Gupta's (2021) study in Frontiers in Psychology examines the role of knowledge sharing in enhancing financial well-being. Drawing on social exchange theory and social cognitive theory, they found that financial literacy and knowledge sharing have a positive effect on financial well-being, and that knowledge sharing moderates the relationship between financial literacy and well-being. Azeez and Akhtar (2021) conducted an empirical study in rural India to identify the determinants of digital financial literacy. The study found that education, income, age, gender, and access to technology were significant factors influencing digital financial literacy.

Munna and Khanam (2021) analyzed the value and advantages of financial literacy and digitalization to individuals. The study found that financial literacy and digitalization can help individuals make informed financial decisions and access financial services more easily. JECONIAH and Anastasia (2021) investigated the influence of demography, social media, risk attitude, and overconfidence on the financial literacy of social media users. The study found that age, education, income, and social media use were significant factors affecting financial literacy. Akimova et al. (2021) discussed the challenges and opportunities of digital educational support for financial literacy education. The study highlighted the importance of incorporating digital technologies in financial literacy education to enhance the effectiveness of the learning process. Lyons and Kass-Hanna (2021) examined the relationship between financial inclusion, financial literacy, and economically vulnerable populations in the Middle East and North Africa. The study found that financial literacy was positively associated with financial inclusion and financial well-being among the economically vulnerable populations in the region. The core of all literature reviews discussed in this study is the role of social media on financial literacy. The reviews indicate that social media has a significant impact on financial literacy, with various factors affecting the relationship. Some of the factors include demographic characteristics, level of education, income level, risk attitude, and digital literacy. The reviews also suggest that financial literacy can be enhanced through various strategies, such as financial education programs, digital literacy training, and financial inclusion programs. Additionally, the reviews indicate that social media can be an effective tool for disseminating financial information, promoting financial literacy, and facilitating financial transactions. However, the reviews also highlight the potential risks and challenges associated with social media, such as misinformation, fraud, privacy concerns, and addiction. Overall, the literature reviews provide valuable insights into the role of social media on financial literacy and suggest practical implications for policymakers, educators, financial institutions, and individuals.

Findings

Based on the reviewed articles, the study on the role of social media in financial literacy reveals several major findings:

1. Financial literacy is recognized as a critical factor in promoting various aspects of individuals' financial well-being, including entrepreneurial behavior, financial inclusion, and overall financial health. The articles consistently emphasize the importance of enhancing financial literacy to empower individuals in making informed financial decisions.
2. Digital financial literacy and digitalization are identified as significant contributors to improving financial literacy, particularly in rural areas. The articles highlight the potential of digital platforms and technologies in reaching a wider audience, delivering financial education, and providing access to financial resources and services.
3. Social media platforms are identified as valuable tools for promoting financial literacy. They facilitate the dissemination of financial education materials, raise financial awareness, and provide a space for individuals to share their financial experiences and knowledge. However, it is also recognized that social media presents challenges, such as the risk of overconfidence and the spread of misinformation. These issues need to be addressed to maximize the benefits of social media in enhancing financial literacy.
4. The determinants of financial literacy are found to be multifaceted. The reviewed articles highlight the influence of demographic factors, such as age, gender, and socioeconomic status, on individuals' financial literacy levels. Moreover, individuals' social media usage patterns, risk attitudes, and financial behaviors are identified as significant factors shaping their financial literacy outcomes.
5. The concept of financial literacy is acknowledged to be multidimensional and evolving in the digital age. The articles emphasize the need for a comprehensive approach to defining and measuring financial literacy that considers various dimensions, including knowledge, skills, attitudes, and behaviors. This multidimensional perspective helps capture the complexity of financial literacy and ensures that interventions address the diverse needs of individuals.
6. The mediating effect of social capital is explored in the relationship between financial literacy and entrepreneurial behavior among rural households. The articles suggest that social capital, such as social networks and community connections, can play a significant role in bridging the gap between financial literacy and entrepreneurial activities, particularly in rural settings.
7. Entrepreneurial learning outcomes, such as digital literacy and financial knowledge, are found to have a positive impact on entrepreneurial behavior among students. The articles highlight the importance of incorporating entrepreneurial education that includes financial literacy and digital literacy components to foster entrepreneurial skills and behaviors.
8. The role of knowledge sharing is emphasized in enhancing the effects of financial literacy on financial well-being. Drawing from social exchange theory and social cognitive theory, the articles suggest that knowledge sharing can amplify the positive impact of financial literacy on individuals' financial outcomes by facilitating learning, influencing attitudes, and promoting behavior change.
9. The potential of digital educational support is recognized in promoting financial literacy education. The articles highlight the importance of adapting financial education programs to changing times by utilizing digital platforms and tools. Digital educational support can provide innovative and engaging ways to deliver financial literacy content and reach a broader audience.

10. The importance of financial inclusion and financial literacy for economically vulnerable populations in the Middle East and North Africa region is emphasized. The articles shed light on the unique challenges faced by these populations and highlight the role of financial inclusion initiatives and tailored financial literacy programs in improving their financial well-being.

The reviewed articles collectively provide valuable insights into the role of social media in enhancing financial literacy. The findings underscore the significance of digital financial literacy, the potential of social media platforms, and the need for comprehensive approaches to promoting financial literacy. The identified determinants, mediating factors, and outcomes contribute to a deeper understanding of the complex relationship between social media and financial literacy. These findings have implications for policymakers, financial institutions, educators, and researchers in designing effective interventions and strategies to improve financial literacy levels among individuals.

Suggestions

Based on the findings of the reviewed articles, some practical suggestions are:

1. Social media platforms can be utilized to promote financial literacy among individuals by providing them with accessible and easy-to-understand financial information.
2. Schools and universities can incorporate financial literacy courses that include digital financial literacy into their curriculum to prepare students for the digital age.
3. Governments and financial institutions can collaborate to provide financial literacy programs that cater to the needs of financially vulnerable populations, including those in rural areas.
4. Individuals can take the initiative to increase their digital financial literacy by taking advantage of the numerous online resources available, such as blogs, podcasts, and social media pages.
5. Financial institutions can make use of social media platforms to reach out to their customers and provide them with personalized financial advice and assistance.

Overall, the suggestions above aim to promote financial literacy through the use of social media and digital platforms, which can be effective in increasing financial knowledge and improving financial behaviors among individuals

Implications

Social implications: The study's findings have broad social implications, as they highlight the potential of social media platforms to address the financial literacy gap among individuals. By leveraging social media for financial education, policymakers and organizations can reach a wider audience and promote financial inclusion. This can help empower individuals from diverse backgrounds to make informed financial decisions, improve their financial well-being, and reduce economic disparities.

Practical implications: The study's practical implications are manifold. Financial institutions can harness the power of social media to engage with their customers, provide financial education resources, and enhance customer experiences. Educators can incorporate social media into their teaching methods to make financial literacy more interactive and accessible to students. By leveraging social media platforms, financial educators can reach a larger audience, facilitate discussions, and deliver personalized content.

Furthermore, the study suggests that individuals themselves can leverage social media as a self-learning tool by following reputable financial experts, participating in online financial communities, and accessing reliable financial resources.

Research implications: The study opens avenues for future research in the field of social media and financial literacy. Researchers can explore the effectiveness of different social media strategies in delivering financial education and fostering behavior change. They can investigate the role of social media influencers and peer networks in promoting financial literacy and examine the long-term impact of social media interventions on individuals' financial knowledge, attitudes, and behaviors. Additionally, researchers can delve deeper into understanding the relationship between demographic factors, social media usage patterns, and financial literacy outcomes to design targeted interventions. Exploring the potential of emerging social media platforms, such as TikTok and Instagram, in enhancing financial literacy can also be an interesting area for future research.

Overall, this study underscores the transformative role of social media in advancing financial literacy. By harnessing the power of social media platforms, policymakers, financial institutions, educators, and individuals themselves can contribute to building a financially literate society, fostering economic empowerment, and enabling individuals to make informed financial decisions.

CONCLUSION

In conclusion, this study conducted a systematic review of articles published between 2021 and 2023 to examine the role of social media on financial literacy. The review identified relevant articles and found that social media can have both positive and negative impacts on financial literacy. The key findings of the study revealed that social media platforms can be effective in promoting financial literacy among different groups of people, including rural households and students. However, social media can also pose risks to financial literacy, particularly among vulnerable populations, such as low-income individuals, who may be exposed to fraudulent financial schemes.

Based on these findings, practical suggestions were proposed, such as developing tailored financial education programs that incorporate social media platforms as a tool for enhancing financial literacy. It is also important to establish effective regulatory frameworks and consumer protection policies that can help mitigate the risks associated with social media use. This study has several social, practical, and research implications. Socially, the findings suggest that social media can play an important role in promoting financial literacy, which can contribute to the overall financial well-being of individuals and communities. Practically, this study offers insights into the design of effective financial education programs that leverage the potential of social media platforms.

Research implications include the need for more research to explore the effectiveness of social media-based financial education programs and to identify strategies to mitigate the risks associated with social media use. Additionally, future research should explore the impact of social media on financial decision-making and the potential of social media as a tool for promoting financial inclusion. Overall, this study highlights the complex relationship between social media and financial literacy and underscores the need for a holistic approach that takes into account the potential benefits and risks of social media use in promoting financial literacy.

REFERENCES

Akimova, E., Korshunova, N., Fedorov, A., Shatayeva, O., & Shipkova, O. (2021). New challenges in changing times: the digital educational support for financial literacy education. *SHS Web of Conferences, 98*, 05020. 10.1051hsconf/20219805020

Almeida, F., & Costa, O. (2023). Perspectives on financial literacy in undergraduate students. *Journal of Education for Business, 98*(1), 1–8. doi:10.1080/08832323.2021.2005513

Andreou, P. C., & Anyfantaki, S. (2021). Financial literacy and its influence on internet banking behavior. *European Management Journal, 39*(5), 658–674. doi:10.1016/j.emj.2020.12.001

Azeez, N. P. A., & Akhtar, S. M. J. (2021). Digital financial literacy and its determinants: An empirical evidences from rural India. *South Asian Journal of Social Studies and Economics, 11*(2), 8–22. doi:10.9734ajsse/2021/v11i230279

Candra Sari, R., Rika Fatimah, P. L., Ilyana, S., & Dwi Hermawan, H. (2022). Augmented reality (AR)-based sharia financial literacy system (AR-SFLS): A new approach to virtual sharia financial socialization for young learners. *International Journal of Islamic and Middle Eastern Finance and Management, 15*(1), 48–65. doi:10.1108/IMEFM-11-2019-0484

Dewi, V. I. (2022). How do demographic and socioeconomic factors affect financial literacy and its variables? *Cogent Business & Management, 9*(1), 2077640. Advance online publication. doi:10.1080/23311975.2022.2077640

Dwijayanti, N., Iqbal, M., & Zulfikar, M. (2022). The role of Islamic fintech P2PL in increasing inclusion and financial literacy of MSMEs. *Journal of Islamic Finance, 11*(1), 94–101. https://journals.iium.edu.my/iiibf-journal/index.php/jif/article/view/638

Estelami, H., & Florendo, J. (2021). The Role of Financial Literacy, Need for Cognition and Political Orientation on Consumers' Use of Social Media in Financial Decision Making. *Journal of Personal Finance, 20*(2).

Garai-Fodor, M., Varga, J., & Csiszarik-Kocsir, A. (2022). Generation-specific perceptions of financial literacy and digital solutions. *2022 IEEE 20th Jubilee World Symposium on Applied Machine Intelligence and Informatics (SAMI)*. IEEE. 10.1109/SAMI54271.2022.9780717

Goyal, K., & Kumar, S. (2021). Financial literacy: A systematic review and bibliometric analysis. *International Journal of Consumer Studies, 45*(1), 80–105. doi:10.1111/ijcs.12605

Gunawan, A., Sadri, M., Pulungan, D. R., & Koto, M. (2022). Study of phenomenon on consumption behavior of Medan City students during pandemic: Financial literacy on E-commerce. *Webology, 19*(1), 2853–2872. doi:10.14704/WEB/V19I1/WEB19190

Haudi, H. (2023). The role of financial literacy, financial attitudes, and Family Financial Education on personal financial management and Locus of Control of university students. *International Journal of Social and Management Studies, 4*(2), 107–116. doi:10.5555/ijosmas.v4i2.289

Hermansson, C., Jonsson, S., & Liu, L. (2022). The medium is the message: Learning channels, financial literacy, and stock market participation. *International Review of Financial Analysis*, *79*(101996), 101996. doi:10.1016/j.irfa.2021.101996

Hidayati, N., Kartikowati, S., & Gimin, G. (2021). The influence of income level, financial literature, and social media use on teachers consumption behavior. *Journal of Educational Sciences*, *5*(3), 479. doi:10.31258/jes.5.3.p.479-490

Ingale, K. K., & Paluri, R. A. (2022). Financial literacy and financial behaviour: A bibliometric analysis. *Review of Behavioral Finance*, *14*(1), 130–154. doi:10.1108/RBF-06-2020-0141

Jannah, A. M., Murwatiningsih, M., & Oktarina, N. (2021). The effect of financial literacy, social media, and social environment towards the consumptive behavior of students at SMA Negeri Kabupaten Jepara. *The Journal of Economic Education*, *10*(1), 85–93. doi:10.15294/jeec.v9i2.43986

Kakinuma, Y. (2022). Financial literacy and quality of life: A moderated mediation approach of fintech adoption and leisure. *International Journal of Social Economics*, *49*(12), 1713–1726. doi:10.1108/IJSE-10-2021-0633

Khan, M. S., & Ahmad, Z. (2022). The effects of financial literacy and social media on financial behaviour. In Mixed Methods Perspectives on Communication and Social Media Research (pp. 144–164). doi:10.4324/9781003265887-12

Klein, T. (2022). A note on GameStop, short squeezes, and autodidactic herding: An evolution in financial literacy? *Finance Research Letters*, *46*(102229), 102229. doi:10.1016/j.frl.2021.102229

Koskelainen, T., Kalmi, P., Scornavacca, E., & Vartiainen, T. (2023). Financial literacy in the digital age – A research agenda. *The Journal of Consumer Affairs*, *57*(1), 507–528. doi:10.1111/joca.12510

Kuchciak, I., & Wiktorowicz, J. (2021). Empowering financial education by banks—Social media as a modern channel. *Journal of Risk and Financial Management*, *14*(3), 118. doi:10.3390/jrfm14030118

Kumar, P., Pillai, R., Kumar, N., & Tabash, M. I. (2023). The interplay of skills, digital financial literacy, capability, and autonomy in financial decision making and well-being. *Borsa Istanbul Review*, *23*(1), 169–183. doi:10.1016/j.bir.2022.09.012

Leviastuti, A., Santika, T. D., & Prasetyo, I. (2022). Empowering women through social media-based financial-literacy education program. *RSF Conference Series: Business, Management and Social Sciences, 2*(1), 88–95. doi:10.31098/bmss.v2i1.520

Lyons, A., & Kass-Hanna, J. (2021). A multidimensional approach to defining and measuring financial literacy in the digital age. SSRN *Electronic Journal*. doi:10.4324/9781003025221-7

Lyons, A. C., & Kass-Hanna, J. (2021). A methodological overview to defining and measuring "digital" financial literacy. *Financial Planning Review*, *4*(2). doi:10.1002/cfp2.1113

Lyons, A. C., & Kass-Hanna, J. (2021). Financial inclusion, financial literacy and economically vulnerable populations in the middle east and north Africa. *Emerging Markets Finance & Trade*, *57*(9), 2699–2738. doi:10.1080/1540496X.2019.1598370

Majid, R., & Nugraha, R. A. (2022). The CROWDFUNDING AND ISLAMIC SECURITIES: THE ROLE OF FINANCIAL LITERACY. *Journal of Islamic Monetary Economics and Finance*, 8(1), 89–112. doi:10.21098/jimf.v8i1.1420

Meitriana, M. A., Yuliarmi, N. N., Utama, M. S., & Marhaeni, A. A. I. N. (2022). Social capital-based financial literacy to improve business performance: A narrative review. *International Journal on Social Science. Economics and Art*, 12(2), 83–90. doi:10.35335/ijosea.v12i2.97

Meoli, M., Rossi, A., & Vismara, S. (2022). Financial literacy and security-based crowdfunding. *Corporate Governance*, 30(1), 27–54. doi:10.1111/corg.12355

Mohd Padil, H., Kasim, E. S., Muda, S., Ismail, N., & Md Zin, N. (2022). Financial literacy and awareness of investment scams among university students. *Journal of Financial Crime*, 29(1), 355–367. doi:10.1108/JFC-01-2021-0012

Morgan, P. J. (2021). Fintech, financial literacy, and financial education. In The Routledge Handbook of Financial Literacy (pp. 239–258). doi:10.4324/9781003025221-21

Mudasih, I., & Subroto, W. T. (2021). The effect of financial literacy, digital literacy, and entrepreneurial learning outcome on entrepreneur behavior of students at SMK Negeri 1 Surabaya. *Technium Soc. Sci. J.*, 15, 303.

Mullappallykayamkulath, M. A. (2022). Digital Financial Literacy and its Impact on the Financial Behaviour of Millennials: An Empirical Investigation. *International Journal of Financial Management*, 12(3).

Munna, A. S., & Khanam, R. (2021). Analysis of the value and advantages of financial literacy and digitalization to the individual. *International Journal of Asian Education*, 2(2), 141–152. doi:10.46966/ijae.v2i2.80

Muñoz-Céspedes, E., Ibar-Alonso, R., & de Lorenzo Ros, S. (2021). Financial literacy and sustainable consumer behavior. *Sustainability (Basel)*, 13(16), 9145. doi:10.3390u13169145

Nahar, A. I. M., Shahrul, S. N. S., Rozzani, N., & Saleh, S. K. (2022). Factors affecting financial literacy rate of millennial in Malaysia. *International Journal of Publication and Social Studies*, 7(1), 1–11. doi:10.55493/5050.v7i1.4433

Nyakurukwa, K., & Seetharam, Y. (2022). Household stock market participation in South Africa: The role of financial literacy and social interactions. *Review of Behavioral Finance*. doi:10.1108/RBF-03-2022-0083

Ozdemir, M., Sari, A. L., & Irwandi, I. (2021). The influence of motivation, Financial Literacy, and social media Financial Platforms on student investment interest. *Komitmen: Jurnal Ilmiah Manajemen*, 2(2), 68–82. doi:10.15575/jim.v2i2.14381

Putri, A. M., Damayanti, S. M., & Rahadi, R. A. (2022). DIGITAL FINANCIAL LITERACY IN INDONESIA: A LITERATURE REVIEW. *Central Asia & the Caucasus (14046091)*, 23(1).

Rahim, N., Ismail, N., & Karmawan, K. (2022). Financial literacy and financial behaviour: An overview of key drivers. *Proceedings of the 1st International Conference on Social, Science, and Technology, ICSST 2021*, Tangerang, Indonesia. 10.4108/eai.25-11-2021.2319348

Ridho, W. F. (2022). Comparison of social media as a platform for financial literacy source. *Jurnal Aplikasi Manajemen Dan Bisnis, 3*, 1–14. doi:10.5281/ZENODO.7260311

Rizon, R., Anastasia, N., & Evelyn, E. (2021). The influence of demography, social media, risk attitude, and overconfidence on the financial literacy of users social media in Surabaya. [IJFIS]. *International Journal of Financial and Investment Studies, 2*(1), 10–19. doi:10.9744/ijfis.2.1.10-19

Rizon, R., Anastasia, N., & Evelyn, E. (2021). The influence of demography, social media, risk attitude, and overconfidence on the financial literacy of users social media in Surabaya [Masters] [IJFIS]. *International Journal of Financial and Investment Studies, 2*(1), 10–19. doi:10.9744/ijfis.2.1.10-19

Seldal, M. M. N., & Nyhus, E. K. (2022). Financial vulnerability, financial literacy, and the use of digital payment technologies. *Journal of Consumer Policy, 45*(2), 281–306. doi:10.100710603-022-09512-9 PMID:35283545

Selvia, G., Rahmayanti, D., Afandy, C., & Zoraya, I. (2021). *The effect of financial knowledge, financial behavior and financial inclusion on financial well-being*. Proceedings of the 3rd Beehive International Social Innovation Conference, BISIC 2020, Bengkulu, Indonesia. 10.4108/eai.3-10-2020.2306600

Setiawan, M., Effendi, N., Santoso, T., Dewi, V. I., & Sapulette, M. S. (2022). Digital financial literacy, current behavior of saving and spending and its future foresight. *Economics of Innovation and New Technology, 31*(4), 320–338. doi:10.1080/10438599.2020.1799142

Shvaher, O. A., Degtyarev, S. I., & Polyakova, L. G. (2021). The effect of social media on financial literacy. *International Journal of Media and Information Literacy, 6*(1), 211–218. doi:10.13187/ijmil.2021.1.211

Sriyono, H., Sugiarto, G. B., Dearelsa, D., Anisyah, F., & Nur, A. (n.d.). *Peran Mbkm Dalam Peningkatan Kinerja Umkm Melalui Literasi Keuangan Dan Digital Marketing Di Desa Ketanireng Kecamatan Prigen Kabupaten Pasuruan*. PSSH. https://pssh.umsida.ac.id/index.php/pssh/article/download/301/233

Suchocka, L., Yarasheva, A., Medvedeva, E., Aleksandrova, O., Alikperova, N., & Kroshilin, S. (2022). Modern media space and financial literacy of young people. *Humanities and Social Sciences Quarterly, 29*(1), 61–71. doi:10.7862/rz.2022.hss.05

Thomas, A., & Gupta, V. (2021). Social capital theory, social exchange theory, social cognitive theory, financial literacy, and the role of knowledge sharing as a moderator in enhancing financial well-being: From bibliometric analysis to a conceptual framework model. *Frontiers in Psychology, 12*, 664638. doi:10.3389/fpsyg.2021.664638 PMID:34093360

Twumasi, M. A., Jiang, Y., Ding, Z., Wang, P., & Abgenyo, W. (2022). The mediating role of access to financial services in the effect of financial literacy on household income: The case of rural Ghana. *SAGE Open, 12*(1), 215824402210799. doi:10.1177/21582440221079921

Van Nguyen, H., Ha, G. H., Nguyen, D. N., Doan, A. H., & Phan, H. T. (2022). Understanding financial literacy and associated factors among adult population in a low-middle income country. *Heliyon, 8*(6), e09638. doi:10.1016/j.heliyon.2022.e09638 PMID:35677404

Voomets, K., Riitsalu, L., & Siibak, A. (2021). Improving financial literacy via social media: The case of Kogumispäevik. *Eesti Haridusteaduste Ajakiri =. Estonian Journal of Education, 9*(2), 127–154. doi:10.12697/eha.2021.9.2.06

Widyastuti, M., & Hermanto, Y. B. (2022). The effect of financial literacy and social media on micro capital through financial technology in the creative industry sector in East Java. *Cogent Economics & Finance*, *10*(1), 2087647. doi:10.1080/23322039.2022.2087647

Wijayanti, N., & Kartawinata, B. R. (2022). Effect of financial literacy, financial confidence, external locus of control, on personal finance management (object of study on East Java students). *Budapest International Research and Critics Institute-Journal (BIRCI-Journal), 5*(4), 30106–30114. doi:10.33258/birci.v5i4.7171

Yanto, H., Ismail, N., Kiswanto, K., Rahim, N. M., & Baroroh, N. (2021). The roles of peers and social media in building financial literacy among the millennial generation: A case of indonesian economics and business students. *Cogent Social Sciences*, *7*(1), 1947579. doi:10.1080/23311886.2021.1947579

Yanto, H., Kiswanto, Baroroh, N., Hajawiyah, A., & Rahim, N. M. (2022). The roles of entrepreneurial skills, financial literacy, and digital literacy in maintaining MSMEs during the COVID-19 pandemic. *Asian Economic and Financial Review*, *12*(7), 504–517. doi:10.55493/5002.v12i7.4535

Zaitul, Z., & Ilona, D. (2022). Is financial literacy associated with SME sustainability during COVID-19? *KnE Social Sciences*, 100–115. doi:10.18502/kss.v7i6.10613

Zhao, J., & Li, T. (2021). Social capital, financial literacy, and rural household entrepreneurship: A mediating effect analysis. *Frontiers in Psychology*, *12*, 724605. doi:10.3389/fpsyg.2021.724605 PMID:34512479

Zhu, T., & Xiao, J. J. (2022). Consumer financial education and risky financial asset holding in China. *International Journal of Consumer Studies*, *46*(1), 56–74. doi:10.1111/ijcs.12643

KEY TERMS AND DEFINITIONS

Digital Financial Literacy: This refers to the ability of individuals to understand and use digital technologies to manage their financial affairs, such as online banking, mobile payments, and digital wallets.

Entrepreneurial Learning: This refers to the process of developing the knowledge, skills, and attitudes needed to create and manage a business venture.

Financial Literacy: This refers to the knowledge, skills, and attitudes that enable individuals to understand financial concepts and make informed decisions about money management, investment, and debt.

Overconfidence: This refers to an individual's belief that they are more skilled, knowledgeable, or successful than they actually are, leading to overestimation of their abilities and underestimation of risk.

Risk Attitude: This refers to an individual's inclination to take risks in decision making, including financial decision making.

Social Media: This refers to a web-based technology that allows people to create, share, and exchange information and ideas in virtual communities and networks.

Systematic Review: This refers to a research method that involves a comprehensive and structured review of published studies to synthesize and summarize the evidence on a particular research question or topic.

Chapter 7
Role of Social Media in Greta Thunberg's Climate and Sustainability Action

Satheesh Pandian Murugan
(iD) https://orcid.org/0009-0002-4301-9521
Arumugam Pillai Seethai Ammal College, India

Rani J. Devika
Department of Economics, Mannar Thirumalai Naicker College, India

Vimala Govindaraju
(iD) https://orcid.org/0000-0001-8799-4770
University Malaysia Sarawak, Malaysia

Ramakrishna Narasimhaiah
Department of Economics, Jain University (Deemed), Bengaluru, India

H. L. Babu
Srinidhi College of Education, Bengaluru, India

Ravindran Kandasamy
Presidency Business School, Presidency College, India

Shouvik Sanyal
Department of Marketing and Entrepreneurship, Dhofar University, Oman

ABSTRACT

Climate change remains a threatening issue to humanity, and lots of people still think of climate change as a growing issue that needs regular measures to curtail it. However, it is not such an easy task to influence a huge mass, but now it has become possible by social media. Because the role played by social media is enormously huge nowadays and many are relying on the internet to gain knowledge, gather data, and socialize. A 16 year old Swedish environmental activist Greta Thunberg has used social media to raise her voice against climate change and started her first school strike, Fridays For Future, against this in August 2018 at the Swedish parliament. In propagating this narrative, she uses various social media and digital platforms to attract people and institutions in developing a climate activist movement with a united voice and intention. This chapter reveals Greta's social media activity, how Greta uses the affordances of social media to frame the climate crisis and to build a worldwide action-based conversation.

DOI: 10.4018/978-1-6684-7450-1.ch007

INTRODUCTION

Social Media, is comparatively a powerful slogan in our recent society. The phenomenon of social media has begun its operations in the new millennium, when the first social media network called Myspace has attracted a large number of users and enables them to create a bespoke wall, thus facilitating their friends to visit the digital wall. It was also the platform to share the things that the users have in their minds. After the success of the Myspace network, many other similar social media networks such as Facebook, LinkedIn, Twitter, YouTube, and Google+ have come to the scene and are popular today. Social media has helped a lot of different users to communicate their idea and information across the globe within a short period and make the people up-to-date about the happenings. Though the usage of social media is wide-ranging, its common goal is the same. The ultimate objective of each social media is to reach the information to the users (Ortiz-Ospina, 2019). Thus the role of social media is a tremendous one and it supports all sorts of user segments such as individuals and businesses. Even there are political leaders and activists have been using this social media to propagate their intention and ideology toward the betterment of the society, environment, economy, and country (Bria, 2013). Greta Thunberg is one among those who use this social media to propagate her climate actions and to reach millions of people throughout the world, as it is more effective and powerful. Greta Thunberg is a 19-year Swedish girl who initiated the largest movement called "Fridays for Future". It is one of the most prevalent social movements in history, as it was initiated by a quite small girl in front of the Swedish Parliament in August 2018. Further a single child potholed in opposition to the adults, a child against the global political system (Jung, Petkanic, Nan, & Kim, 2020). The same has been tweeted immediately and reached hurriedly and this phenomenon received global attention. Thus one single girl in Sweden shortly became six million remonstrate children throughout the world. All these possibilities are because of social media. Thus, social media have played a major part in Greta Thunberg's climate movements and made her a Global icon single-handedly. However, Greta Thunberg's efforts cannot be removed from the social media atmosphere in which it placed (Prakoso, Timorria, & Murtyantoro, 2021). Regarding the same Thomas Olesen explained that it is difficult to envisage the iconization relating this way and to this degree with no social media. He also revealed that the smattering of social media features influences the course of the iconization progression. They also diminish the communication cost, highlight visual depiction, maintain intimacy between icon and spectators, consist of a fresh and younger audience, and disseminate communication throughout different media platforms. Through this, Greta Thunberg was capable to attain young minds and direct them towards her climate actions and therefore she could achieve the status that she is today, bearing in mind her feeble starting point and absence of resources, being a girl child and haulage a load of psychological challenges (Olesen, 2022). As a result, Greta Thunberg, the name has familiarised in all households as she initiated omitting school to begin actions against climate change in August 2018, as she was motivated by the Parkland school students in the USA, they started nationwide school strikes to remonstration against the inaction of government on gun violence (Beckett, 2019). She demands political leaders of all the country to follow the conditions of the Paris agreement and, if she has to contain any other demands, these would be to announce a global climate crisis (Vice, 2019). Hence, she initiated the Fridays for Future movement and thereby skipped school and sit in front of the Swedish parliament with a slogan board "skol strejk för klimatet" ("school strike for climate" in Swedish). Though this movement started by her alone, very soon she became familiar with her remarkable actions and stimulated the School Strike meant for the Climate movement (Alter, Haynes, & Worland, 2019).

In connection with this movement, Greta has been posting a photo on Twitter and Instagram each Friday, with a heading that explains which week of school wallop. It hence looks like a hybrid method of both online and offline platforms to create awareness about climate change with the help of a mixed media system. This phrase reveals that various forms of media not only co-exist but form a structure that progresses through common actions amongst newer and older media logic (Chadwick, Dennis, & Smith, 2016). It is a common ideology that a single medium cannot propagate all the information successfully, but all the information can be propagated successfully by the manifold media collaboration and concurrently being in stable power combat. Chadwick and colleagues (2016) mentioned in their research work that, campaign information considered online can be categorized as a hybrid, at first its life starts offline either through television or in the print media, which after that goes on to digital media through promotional campaigns. This same kind of hybrid also happened in Thunberg's case as her awareness campaign information took place with her offline strike; it then passed through online since the media exposure on it, as well as national conversation, and soon after as a sort of movement promotion to obtain others to join in her climate change movement. As a result, the phrase hybrid media structure is helpful in this background as it cannot converse simply like old or new media; all sorts of media have supported Greta Thunberg's reputation and as a result, her Fridays for Future movement has stretched throughout the world (Hakala, 2021). With this backdrop present paper has proposed to address three questions:

Question 1: What made Greta Thunberg present on social media?
Question 2: what type of media platform she has used to motivate and mobilize people to join the strike?
Question 3: How the social media support Greta Thunberg's strike and climate movement?

These questions have been answered in the following sections by reviewing the existing published articles and materials. Where section one explains Greta Thunberg's Social Media Presence and activism, section two speaks about Greta's media Transition from social media to a hybrid media platform, the Role of social media in Greta's Global Climate change movement presented in section three, section four depicts Greta's Digital media and climate striking Interconnection through Social Media and final part of the paper concludes in section five.

Greta Thunberg's Social Media Presence and Activism

Greta has very clear about her goal and taking numerous steps to reach it. She has chosen social media as the right platform to share her information and message. Greta has posted her first strike photo on Twitter and Instagram; however, the other social media accounts have taken up her quickly as a cause. Well-profile young social activists have augmented her climate strike photo on Instagram, as a result on the second day, the number has increased from one to many, due to social media. Thus social media supports her a lot to Greta, and now she is having more than 14.5 million followers. Further, Greta's social media account fascinated more local news reporters, as Greta's stories attracted more international coverage in the short span of a week. Further, a Swedish-based social media company called We Don't Have Time (WDHT) observed the activities of Greta, as this company also focuses more on climate change-related activities. The founder of this company Ingmar Rentzhog joined hands with Greta in her climate change movement. Regarding this, he told that Greta's school strike has started to attract the attention of the public, only after the company has posted Greta's photo on his Twitter, Facebook, and Instagram accounts. There was a video also prepared in English and the same has posted on the

WDHT's YouTube channel, thereby they have attracted millions of followers and popularised her climate action-related messages. As a result, Greta's climate action has become popular all over Europe, to her demonstrations including several rich-profile public speeches, and thereby she has been mobilizing a huge number of supporters on social media platforms (Bergmann, & Ossewaarde, 2020). Later 2018 October she formed her so-called movement "Fridays for Future," thereby every Friday has been used for a school strike. Through this movement, she has inspired millions of school students throughout the world and made them take part in school strikes. Thus more than 25,000 students have conducted strikes in more than 275 cities (Boulianne, Lalancette, & Ilkiw, 2020).

Greta also has used social media to raise her voice not only for the climate but also for various issues happening around the world. She has also talked a lot about the National Eligibility cum Entrance Test for Undergraduate coerces and Joint Entrance Examinations arranged in the year 2020, September in India. She revealed that these entrance exams are unfair for students to materialize for exams amid the global pandemic. In an interview, Greta said to the reporters that all these protests have been possible because of social media. Further, she knows the power of the messages and their importance for all sorts of communication. Because, when a message is utilized successfully, someone comes to occupy their message in the act of propagating. It is like, how a politician's message is an essential part of politics (Thunberg, 2020). Moreover, a piece of information or a message is a result of promotion and it can be perceived as somewhat related to the brand. In the same manner, all the politicians will be using online messages and offline messages. While a big shot is on the message, they will disseminate some notion, with certain genuineness that will help to appeal to the audience targeted. Thus a message supplies a reliable, increasing, and substantial image among the audience when it propagates by someone famous in the area. Further, messages utilize some styles strategically to generate an image in a significant way. This image not essentially is visual, as it is a conceptual representation of distinctiveness. Good speaker creates an image about themselves through their communication and the suitability of the times (Olesen, 2022). Even though Greta Thunberg's climate change message and her image turned around in the society, still Greta requires the politicians' support at this juncture to achieve some more. As she is in her young age, it is being an obstacle to her efforts and she has to overcome it. Since she is eighteen; it does not influence the people seriously to listen to her message and support her movement. 60 years old tope gear presenter Jeremy Clarkson mentioned in his interview that Greta Thunberg is a "moron" and wants to say herself a "good girl, shut up and allow them to acquire on with it. You won't stay out past 10. And you won't go out in a sarong that small" (Radford, 2019). Moreover, the actuality that he calls Thunberg a moron and reprimands her to stay away from this movement, as he is focusing on her age of hers, by performing like he is fining Thunberg like a father would his daughter. In the same way, Donald Trump, former president of the USA has also criticized Thunberg's "Fridays for Future" movement, and he also has mentioned in his Tweeted that "Greta is so ludicrous. She has to learn how to manage anger, as she is having an anger management problem, further she should also need to watch the good fashioned film with her friend! Cool Greta, cool!" Greta has then responded to Trump's tweet by altering her Twitter bio that' A teenage girl is good in anger management, and watching an old fashioned with her friend with cool mindset." Thus Greta has changed her Twitter bio in response to Trump's messages about her, and this is not the first time she is changing her Twitter bio. Thunberg has given a talk at United Nations in the year 2019, about the climate change reasons and steps that need to take by the nations. Followed by her talk, Trump has written ironically that "Thunberg looks like a cheerful young girl gazing ahead a magnificent and vivid future. It is good to see her on this platform!", as Greta had conveyed annoyance and bitterness towards the world leaders who have congregated to listen to her address. However, Greta had altered her Twitter bio this time stating that "a cheerful young girl gazing ahead to a magnificent and vivid future (Juliette Berndsen, 2020). While Greta tweets, she also had been using a green image as part of her message. Regarding the same, there was a question asked by Democracy Now, towards Thunberg, "of course, your image spins around climate change; you will become a charlatan if you are not following your suggestion. Thunberg has answered this question stated that "not only my image but I am also green because I am eating vegetarian foods, I have avoided flights to travel and I am a shop stop. A shop stop means not buying anything unnecessarily unless there is a necessity (Democracy Now, 2019). This shop stop concept reveals that it is a no-buy defied by influencers, they may have diverse rules for each one but the ideology remains the same. Thus no one should buy anything unless there is a need. However in many cases, people have some exceptions for reinstating existing goods they need when they run out or not working anymore, but in addition, one is not permitted to purchase something. Further, Greta and her entire family follow a vegetarian food style. Thereby they are ensuring ecological benefits by not consuming animal protein and milk, and the same has been proved by several research works (Carrington, 2018; Harrabin, 2019).

Further Greta has determined not to use the flights for the travel, and it would be the benefit for saving the environment from various pollution, and she also has been using the electric vehicles, cars, trains, and sometimes boats. Though Greta has been using the boats for various travel purposes, her first choice to travel to various areas is by train. Thus Greta is walking as per her talk, and people from different parts of the world eulogize her climate actions or efforts, however, she is not free from the criticism, as still many censures her for her actions. Greta has posted her train travel photo a day, where she was sitting on the floor of the train. It happened when Greta traveled to her hometown after attending the Climate conference held at the UN in 2019 (Bergmann & Ossewaarde, 2020). For the same, a Germanian train company called "Deutsche Bahn" offered a first-class seating facility; however, she has been traveled on the floor of the train. The company tweeted the same that, though we had given a first class travel facility to Greta, she simply traveled on the floor for making herself as fame (Connolly, 2019). Once she sees this tweet, responds immediately that she was sitting on the floor of the train for four hours after spending two hours on the seat. Further, she said that I didn't consider this issue as a problem of course and I never said it was. Overfull train travels are revealed that the demand for train travel is increasing day by day and it also seems like a good sign. On the other side, Greta has been traveling to various parts of the world to disseminate the impact of climate change and the actions that need to take. However, she has been using her mother tongue Swedish to communicate the information, but it won't be much effective. Further, all her tweets were in Swedish in the initial stage. She had received some suggestions to change her communication language to make her efforts to be more effective. After such suggestions, she started to use English to tweet and respond to other tweets, thus she has made her efforts more effective and easy to understand. Meantime she has also been using the Swedish language, whenever she is responding to Swedish tweets. As Greta has gotten more media attention from all parts of the world, she has changed her communication language from Swedish to English, to expand public coverage, and to make it more sense (Boulianne, Lalancette, & Ilkiw, 2020).

Greta's Media Transition From Social Media to Hybrid Media Platform

Greta Thunberg could inspire the entire world and make them involved in the Fridays for Future movement. As per the statistics available on of Fridays for Future website, more than 14,000,000 people have participated in this movement from 7500 cities across 140 countries. All this was not possible by a single person or a single group; however, the entire world has participated collectively in this Friday for Future movement (fridaysforfuture.org, 2022). So many teams are working for this movement to make sure those activists gather in their country in various cities, or any one particular city; however these teams are working jointly and communicating with each other team to share the ideas, tips, and data. In a manner, this movement has become a hybrid mobilization, and such kinds of movements will not be functioning without the Internet and communication technology, as these technologies set up multifaceted communications between the offline and online atmosphere (Chadwick, 2007). Further, this type of movement will also not work properly without a multifaceted spatial and sequential relationship of political life and it has been established by digital communication (Chadwick & Dennis, 2017). Thus, the Fridays for Future movement become a strong one as it has moved from online to offline in a flourishing manner. As a result, this movement becomes a successful one as it is being a slacktivism type; it means good activism will not have a political or societal brunt however as a substitute it will generate a delusion of having a significant brunt on the globe not demanding something more than unification in a Facebook cluster (Gerbaudo, 2012).

However, this movement cannot be considered slacktivism, as it is letting it expand worldwide. Because this movement made climate change an important issue in global politics and it also influence the school-going teens to enter this movement throughout the world. As social media played a major role in this movement to communicate movement-related information, its effectiveness seems to be an extraordinary one. A German climate activist Luisa Neubauer mentioned that Greta and her friends initially shared the strike information through a Whatsapp group, where they have been texting each other to share their ideas, and information, thereby they have prepared the ways and means of the first strike (Ted.com, 2019). After some time the climate activists have started to use some other social media platforms in addition to WhatsApp, of which Facebook played a major role in organizing more participants through different Facebook groups throughout the world, very specifically some towns have formed their groups for the same. There is one Facebook group called "#ClimateStrike" is having more than 30,000 followers, and it has been administered by Greta Thunberg. Where they have shared the posts related to climate change, share the ideas about climate change control, strike plans from members, and the clips of the strikes. The countries which are having Fridays for Future facebook group also used one more social media platform called Instagram to share strike-related information. Where the strike photos and participants' details have been shared, and the forthcoming strike information such as place, time, and other pertinent details have been shared. Furthermore, this Friday for Future movement's Instagram account has more than 5, 00,000 followers all over the world. Thus various social media played a major role to organize and expand this movement, and this phenomenon can be considered an assembly of choreography. Because this movement is a process of developing common space through various symbolic actions and it has been revolving around a psychological setting and make the participants be assembled physically (Boulianne, Lalancette, & Ilkiw, 2020). Further, this physical assembly can be divided into two segments. The first segment is developed through common characteristics into a widespread prejudice with the competence to function as a combined subject with control over their accomplishments. All these accomplishments are possible by disseminating the information along with psychological investment on the group members' side (Gerbaudo, 2012). The same situation has also been explained by Luisa Neubauer in Greta's case, Greta used to arrange weekly meetings to discuss how the Fridays for Future should be in Germany. In the meeting Greta mentioned that "we need people those who are ready to mingle, get to know each other and willing to work together, hence the like meeting has been arranging in every week". Further, she used a mobile phone to communicate with the group organizers and members, however, the members have understood quickly that people need to have a personal bond towards the strikes, if not the self-commitment won't happen (Videovice.com, 2019). Gerbaudo (2012) explained substance precipitation in the second segment, through a radio example. When there was a problem between Algerians and French colonizers, this Radio has been used as a community symbol for the Algerians; thereby it has attracted more people in public places to raise voices against the French colonizers. In the same way, Greta's Fridays for Future movement has been using internet technology as a tool for attracting people to raise their voices against climate change. However, Greta realized that using internet technology and mobile phones will not be enough to organize people for this movement, hence planned to organize the weekly meetings under this movement. Thus, Greta has used social media as a complementary to various forms of face-to-face meetings and not as an alternative for them (Gerbaudo (2012). As a result, people who have engaged themselves in this movement were inspired by Greta for her worldwide movement. Further people have expressed their emotions, as they have been seeing Greta as the first personality who unfastened this discussion and encouraged other youth activists. A Belgium climate activist Anuna de Wever told that "No one talked about before Greta started this" (Maeve Campbell, 2020). Anuna de Wever also told a lot about Greta and her meeting "this movement is amazing and Greta is my motivation to initiate this, and with the Global support, we jointly have made this insurrection, as Greta is being a vehicle of this movement". Even though such positive things have been made by Greta, it not essentially perceived as a leader. Gerta by herself called a "messenger" not a leader. Further, Greta has never expected that her Fridays for Future movement will go viral. All such things reveal the fact that Greta is not willing to be a leader in the first situation, however, her efforts and the message that she is using in the movement will make the people participate spontaneously with innovative participation the movements. Even though social media have not been the reason for the leaderlessness, to certain extent assists in the rise of multifaceted leadership which makes use of the collective and cooperative character of the novel communication technologies. Greta has initiated strikes through conversation, it has expanded to various countries through social media platforms and it is also supported by climate activists of various countries in the world (Gerbaudo, 2012).

ROLE OF SOCIAL MEDIA IN GRETA'S GLOBAL CLIMATE CHANGE MOVEMENT

Social media have contributed a lot to Greta's Fridays for Future movement. The contribution of Twitter in this movement is extraordinary, as it has extended much coverage support to Greta's Swedish parliament strike. Around 18,00,00 tweets have been generated by 6,00,000 members of this movement within 14 months from August 2018 to October 2019, about Greta and her Movement around 14.5 million followers have been following Greta on Twitter as of 27th, May 2022, and 849 uploads have been done. On Facebook 20million followers have been following this movement, as far as Instagram is concerned, the Fridays for Future movement is having 4, 81, 733 followers, and posted 528 photos as of 30th, May 2022 (fridaysforfuture.org, 2022). In the same manner on the Fridays for Future YouTube channel, 21,500 subscribers are engaged, and around 280 videos have been uploaded about climate change, and movement-related (thesocialflame.com, 2022). Thus, if a single message or video has been uploaded by Greta; it will be reached throughout the world in a matter of a few minutes. As a result, Greta's strike-related information once posted will go viral and become a trend worldwide, ultimately it can be seen and understood by so many people in the world, about Greta's actions. The same has been mentioned and tweeted by Barrack Obama in 2019, "Just 16, @GretaThunberg is already one of our planet's greatest advocates. Recognizing that her generation will bear the brunt of climate change, she's unafraid to push for real action. She embodies our vision at the @ObamaFoundation: A future shaped by young leaders like her. - Barack Obama (@BarackObama) September 17, 2019" against this tweet, Barrack Obama received 54,763 re-tweets and 452,726 likes (The Indian Express, 2022). Thus, the propaganda of this movement has been utilized by Greta as a tool of communal activism. Further, Greta has started to use various social media to attract people and organize a mega strike throughout the world. Thus, people around the world could understand and recognize the seriousness of climate change, and the action needs to take to curtail this issue gravely. The same also has been discussed earlier by Postmes and Brunsting that social media activism has the power to attract the public and promotes collective action among them (Jung, Petkanic, Nan, and Kim, 2020).) As a result, more people have been joining every day in her movement; thereby it is increasing the possibility of taking the climate change-related concerns to the knowledge of the politicians, governments, and the global leaders. Further, the people's mass participation in this movement could attract the attention of the politicians and have a look at it. The number of strikes conducted this Friday for the Future and the stability of the strikes can be considered as one of the yardsticks to measure the success of the movement. It can also understand that, if the people are conducting the climate strike continuously and discussing the seriousness of climate change, it means the real purpose of the movement has been served. All these things can be possible only through social media. Thus social media are having the power to transform the society's existing social and political structure and ensure a new system that can be removing the problem associated with the society. However, such kind of social change through social media is comparatively new.

GRETA'S DIGITAL MEDIA AND CLIMATE STRIKING INTERCONNECTION THROUGH SOCIAL MEDIA

Greta has organized the climate change movement on various social media, particularly Twitter. Though Greta has posted many posts on various social media platforms, however the first Twitter post was anticipated to inform and attract the common public to join her movement on December 14, 2018. As it was expected, the first post has received a huge response, all this success is because of the post shared among the public, and as a result, many people have the same opinion of Greta and have a similar idea to save the Globe from climate change. There was a conference conducted at the United Nations to discuss the seriousness of the Climate Change in 2018, where several school students also participated by skipping their school, and thereby they supported Greta. However, the conference committee members have mentioned that "it is very difficult to understand the climate change at the age of 12, even it is impossible to know about the entire overhaul of the worldwide energy system. But in the conference, the students have sung a song that reflects their hope that they could prevent climate change and its impacts on their better future. Al this thing has happened because, Greta has asked the students worldwide, to raise their voices against climate change and global warming (Prakoso, Timorria, and Murtyantoro, 2021). The rationale behind this is very obvious and simple youngsters will reinstate adults eventually in the future. If the youngsters do not participate in such movements, the place where they are living now will be smashed and too perilous for their lives and health. Hence, Greta has targeted global youths and appealed to them to discuss the jeopardy of global warming and climate change to the global. Thus it seems that Greta has followed the theory of Jonathan Steven's Collaborative Internet Utilities, with the help of internet technology and social media, posted apprehensions, ideas, and views, by anticipating reaching the same to everyone, and thus making them join in the Fridays for Future Movement. As Greta expected the posts have gone viral and gained the interest of the public, especially the youngsters who have joined more than the elders. As a result, Greta has realized the biggest outreach of posts among the youngsters, as the majority of the youngsters have been involved in various social media and dominating the same. As Greta's intention, global youths are started to concentrate on the climate issues and started the Fridays for Future movement, to spot their steps to skip the class and arrange a strike every Friday. This movement also leads to establishing global connectivity towards the Fridays for Future movement and acting against global warming and climate change. Stevens (2010) stated in his work that when more people join the movement, it will have a higher possibility to influence particular stakeholders to pay attention and give a response to the budding movement. However, if the government is reacting to the movement, it would be expected to collapse the social and political condition and situation of a country. Hence, the leaders and politicians should consider their requests to continue stability in the political realm. In the same way, Greta's Fridays for Future movement has been stretched to more than 124 countries, and it is also expected that the number to increase (theguardian.com, 2019). Throughout the world, the political leaders, and experts are wondering about Greta's sudden raise against Global warming and climate change, and all this because of the support of digital media. A young girl and her initiatives have got popularized throughout through social media, as they have written articles about Greta and her strikes; they also have published her speeches, and activities through famous social media platforms such as Twitter, Facebook, and Instagram. Greta also demands the global political leaders follow the crux of the Paris agreement, and also reverberated with global youths, who consider Greta as an instance and started to participate in the climate striking activities. As a result, the Fridays for Future movement have been organized throughout the world, and around 4.5 million people have participated in the climate strike to fight for our environment. This has happened as possible because of the support of digital media. They have helped a lot to disseminate the idea to the entire world and as a result, people felt an individual bond and accountability to the case. Though Greta is still involved in the climate strike, and it inspires people, it does not denote that Greta is their leader. However, Greta has been treated as a catalyst for other activists to raise voices against climate change, throughout the world (mavenroad.com, 2019).

DISCUSSION AND CONCLUSION

This work has attempted to provide insights into how social media have been supporting Greta Thunberg to organize and achieve her climate action movement called Fridays for Future, how Greta connects with people, and how she interacts with the public online. Supporters who have participated in the Fridays for Future movement become more vibrant politically as well as socially, they have also become active to take care of their futures by saving their environment. It could be taken into consideration of various published works and their findings, it could understand that climate change is a serious issue as it is determining the quality of the environment and future life. Despite this issue, global nations have come up with various climate change agreements to manage this issue; many also see that the actions are more like argot. Meantime many individual social activists have also organized various movements to raise voices against climate change and its impacts. As a result, a trigger of activities needs to organize essentially to tune the things towards creating awareness about climate change. In line with this, a young Swedish girl Greta Thunberg has taken initiatives to create awareness about climate change, for the same she has also announced a strike called Fridays for Future. For promoting the strike Greta has been using different social media platforms for disseminating the strike information such as date, time, and place. She has been using social media platforms, called Facebook, Twitter, Instagram, and some others to broaden her concerns and thoughts about climate change. Greta has received lots of feedback in return for her strike, and the majority of the supporters have seen her as a youngster, especially school-going students, as they are concerned about their future and the generation to come (Brooks, 2021). Greta has been calling and approaching the youths who are worried about climate change and global warming to support strikes. Millions of youths from various cities and countries join hands with Greta and speed up the school strikes every Friday to display their concern and anxiousness. Social activism theory and collaborative internet utilities (Dumitrascu, 2015) reveals that when more join for a reason, the better the opportunity that exertion or the issue will be brought to the knowledge of a particular stakeholder, thereby the presumed goal can be achieved easily and effectively. Thus, Greta has good goals and tried to reach them through her activities, however, it is not free from opposition. Greta has received so many negative thoughts about the strike from all sides. Many political leaders too disparaged Greta's school strike, such as Trump, the former American president tweeted that "Greta must work on her anger management problem, and then go to a good old fashioned movie with a friend! Chill Greta, Chill!" (Theindianexpress.com, 2020). Australian Prime Minister Scott Morrison told that school students should not skip school and try to learn new things instead of protesting. He also mentioned in some places that students must stop climate strikes and do fewer activities (AAP, 2018). In some cases, some told that politicians purposively use the students to accomplish their political agenda. Its hidden meaning is that the students should not involve in any such protest in the future. However, some governments announce through social media that action will be taken against the participants who have joined the movement. Meantime, Greta replied with this statement that no actions control the participants; instead, the threats may be put into a museum, as these actions look old-fashion. It can be understood from this paper that social media plays a major role in interconnecting the people with the events, as per the requirement, and the same has also happened in Greta's case.

The authors have identified that even though many people and the world leaders were criticizing, and commenting on Greta's climate actions, to put her efforts down and endorse their perspective. But, Greta herself turns into a well-renowned figure globally with a huge number of followers on social media, especially on Twitter. The use of Social Media data has become a modern approach among researchers, though any field; in the same way the present paper assesses the role of social media communications in connection with a social figure, and it is a subject that has not been explored much so far. Hence the authors recommend that more new studies should conduct on the user profiles, as it is a comparatively new research area in social media research. Accordingly, some of the implications have been found and summarized in the study.

IMPLICATIONS OF THE STUDY

The first implication is the usage of social media can be a platform for attracting and connecting to leaders, and thereby required information and actions can be circulated swiftly through influential connections. Greta has utilized social media effectively to communicate climate movement activities among the interested people, organizations, and social entrepreneurs, and it has helped to enlarge her exposure in a short time, as her followers have responded to her message actively. The global political leaders have wondered how effectively a teenage girl has been using social media as a communication channel.

The second implication reveals that, those who are using social media platforms to attract and encourage supportive people in a common opinion place. Social media made available a common sharing platform for the minority faction to exchange ideas and thoughts with other similar parties easily and directly, rather than depending on conventional media, to disseminate their events and thoughts. The same has been proved in Greta's case, as she has used Twitter and Facebook for sharing information among her followers. Thus social media has transformed the communication process more speedily, easy, and more convenient than the conventional media have done so far.

It is observed from the Third implication that, Greta's social media interactions replicate the different forms of contemporary societal conflict happening globally. Social media has been used as a political combat zone for fighting each other. Further, the Climate changes problems have become a notable issue globally; as a result, it is progressively related to government policies and political perspective. The same has happened in Donald Trump's election case, as it was unpredictably related to Greta's climate actions endorsed in a political perspective in the United States. But, the discussion also developed to take in similar other social and political problems such as gender discrimination, and culture and social divisions.

LIMITATIONS AND DIRECTIONS FOR FUTURE STUDY

As the present paper has been formatted based on the review of available literature related to Greta Thunberg's climate action, future studies should apply some methodologies such as sentiment analysis to assess social media effectiveness. Though climate change seems one of the most important discussions on social media, almost many of the messages look as not taking sides. However, many of the posts look pertinent to climate change. Hence there may be a possibility for conducting feedback analysis, by assessing social media messages generated by the followers or users. Further, there are possibilities for researching social media content and it can be assessed besides user profiles to establish whether the attitudes of the users are different among various user groups. The present study analyzed the role of social media in organizing the campaigns, and how it has supported Greta. This facet of the study can be used in various promising directions by consequent research. Future researchers may also include messages or posts shared by Asians so that the attitude of the Asians towards climate actions can be studied. Thus, it would help to improve the accuracy of the research, particularly when comparing with the Global level data.

REFERENCES

AAP. (2018). Scott Morrison tells students striking over climate change to be 'less activist'. *The Guardian*.

Alter, C., Haynes, S., & Worland, J. 2019. Greta Thunberg: TIME's Person of the Year 2019. *Time Magazine*.

Bergmann, Z., & Ossewaarde, R. (2020). Youth climate activists meet environmental governance: Ageist depictions of the FFF movement and Greta Thunberg in German newspaper coverage. *Journal of Multicultural Discourses*, *15*(3), 267–290. doi:10.1080/17447143.2020.1745211

Boulianne, S., Lalancette, M., & Ilkiw, D. (2020). "School strike 4 climate": Social media and the international youth protest on climate change. *Media and Communication, 8*(2), 208–218. doi:10.17645/mac.v8i2.2768

Bria, F. (2013). *Social media and their impact on organisations: building Firm Celebrity and organisational legitimacy through social media* [Doctoral dissertation, Imperial College London].

Brooks, L. 2021. COP26 protesters' anger and frustration tinged with optimism. *The Guardian.* https://www.theguardian.com/environment/2021/nov/03/cop26-protesters-anger-and-frustration-tinged-with-optimism

Carrington, D. (2018). Avoiding meat and diary is 'single biggest way' to reduce your impact on Earth. *The Guardian.* https://www.theguardian.com/environment/2018/may/31/avoiding-meat-and-dairy-is-single-biggest-way-to-reduce-your-impact-on-earth

Chadwick, A., & Dennis, J. (2017). Social Media, Professional Media and Mobilisation in Contemporary Britain: Explaining the Strengths and Weaknesses of the Citizens' Movement 38 Degrees. *Political Studies, 65*(1), 42–60. doi:10.1177/0032321716631350

Chadwick, A., Dennis, J. W., & Smith, A. P. (2016). Politics in the age of hybrid media: power, systems, and media logics. In A. Bruns, G. Enli, E. Skogerbø, A. Olof Larsson, & C. Christensen (Eds.), *The Routledge Companion to Social Media and Politics* (pp. 7–22). Routledge.

Chavadi, C. (2021). Growth drivers, characteristics, preference and challenges faced by Fast Moving Consumer Goods-A study with reference to Bengaluru. *Turkish Online Journal of Qualitative Inquiry, 12*(7).

Chavadi, C. A., Arul, M. J., & Sirothiya, M. (2020). Modelling the effects of creative advertisements on consumers: An empirical study. *Vision (Basel), 24*(3), 269–283. doi:10.1177/0972262920926074

Chavadi, C. A., Hiremath, C. V., & Hyderabad, R. L. (2014). Customer loyalty appraisal based on store characteristics: An alternative approach. *Indian Journal of Marketing, 44*(5), 18–29. doi:10.17010/ijom/2014/v44/i5/80375

Chavadi, C. A., & Kokatnur, S. S. (2008). Consumer Expectation and Perception of Fast Food Outlets: An Empirical Study in Davangere. *ICFAI Journal Of Services Marketing, 6*(2).

Chavadi, C. A., & Kokatnur, S. S. (2009). Impact of Short-Term Promotional Ads on Food Retailing. *ICFAI Journal of Consumer Behavior, 4*(1).

Chavadi, C. A., & Kokatnur, S. S. (2009). RFID Adoption by Indian Retailers: An Exploratory Study. *The Icfai University Journal of Supply Chain Management, 6*(1), 60–77.

Chavadi, C. A., Menon, S. R., & Sirothiya, M. (2019). Measuring Service Quality Perceptions of Indian E-retailers: An Evaluative Study. *Metamorphosis, 18*(2), 92–102. doi:10.1177/0972622519886232

Chavadi, C. A., Menon, S. R., & Sirothiya, M. (2019). Modelling the Effects of Brand Placements in Movies: An Investigative Study of Event Type and Placement Type. *Vision (Basel), 23*(1), 31–43. doi:10.1177/0972262918821227

Chavadi, C. A., Vishwanatha, M. R., & Mubeen, S. (2018). Ghee with Glee: A Study of How Consumers Evaluate Product Packaging. *Metamorphosis*, *17*(2), 100–110. doi:10.1177/0972622518817407

Connolly, K. (2019). Greta Thunberg in Twitter spat with German rail firm. *The Guardian*. https://www.theguardian.com/environment/2019/dec/15/greta-thunberg-in-twitter-spat-with-german-rail-firm

Democracy Now. (2019). School Strike for Climate: Meet 15-Year-Old Activist Greta Thunberg, Who Inspired a Global Movement. *Democracy Now*. https://www.democracynow.org/2018/12/11/meet_the_15_year_old_swedish

Dumitraşcu, V. (2015). Social activism: theories and methods. *Revista Universitară de Sociologie, 11*(1), 84-94. https://www.ceeol.com/search/article-detail?id=716528

Gerbaudo, P. (2012). *Tweets and the streets: Social media and contemporary activism*. Pluto Press. https://www.jstor.org/stable/j.ctt183pdzs

Hakala, F. P. (2021). *The Greta Effect on Global Environmental Governance: Testing the Applicability of Frame Theory*.

Harrabin, R. (2019). Plant-based diet can fight climate change. *BBC News*. https://www.bbc.com/news/science-environment-49238749

Hiremath, C. V., Chavadi, C. A., & Yatgiri, P. Y. (2013). Cloud Technology as an Alternative for Marketing Information System: An Empirical Study. *International Journal of Management. Research and Business Strategy, 2*(4).

Berndsen, J. (2020). Greta Thunberg: the climate striking catalyst. *Diggit Magazine*. https://www.diggitmagazine.com/articles/greta-thunberg-climate-striking-catalyst

Jung, J., Petkanic, P., Nan, D., & Kim, J. H. (2020). When a girl awakened the world: A user and social message analysis of Greta Thunberg. *Sustainability (Basel), 12*(7), 2707. doi:10.3390u12072707

Karumban, S., Sanyal, S., Laddunuri, M. M., Sivalinga, V. D., Shanmugam, V., Bose, V., & Murugan, S. P. (2023). Industrial Automation and Its Impact on Manufacturing Industries. In Revolutionizing Industrial Automation Through the Convergence of Artificial Intelligence and the Internet of Things (pp. 24-40). IGI Global.

Campbell, M. (2020). Ecological disaster' develops in Slovakia as river contaminated by orange iron. *Euronews*. https://www.euronews.com/green/2022/05/23/ecological-disaster-develops-in-slovakia-as-river-is-contaminated-by-iron

Mavenroad.com. (2019). Fridays for Future: The Social Media Impact of Greta Thunberg: How the young climate change activist is raising awareness within social media. *Maven Road*. https://mavenroad.com/fridaysforfuture-the-social-media-impact-of-greta-thunberg/

Menon, S. R., & Chavadi, C. A. (2022). A Research-based Approach to Identify the Health-conscious Consumers in India. *Metamorphosis*, *21*(2), 118–128. doi:10.1177/09726225221098783

Murugan, S. P., Shivaprasad, G., Dhanalakshmi, A., Sriram, V. P., Rajput, K., Mahesh, B. N., & Kedla, S. (2023). The Impact of COVID-19 on the Indian Microfinance Industry and Its Sustainability. In *Transforming Economies Through Microfinance in Developing Nations* (pp. 160–188). IGI Global. doi:10.4018/978-1-6684-5647-7.ch009

Olesen, T. (2022). Greta Thunberg's iconicity: Performance and co-performance in the social media ecology. *New Media & Society*, 24(6), 1325–1342. doi:10.1177/1461444820975416

Ortiz-Ospina, E. (2019). The rise of social media. *Our world in data, 18.*

Park, J. Y., Perumal, S. V., Sanyal, S., Ah Nguyen, B., Ray, S., Krishnan, R., Narasimhaiah, R., & Thangam, D. (2022). Sustainable Marketing Strategies as an Essential Tool of Business. *American Journal of Economics and Sociology*, 81(2), 359–379. doi:10.1111/ajes.12459

Prakoso, S. G., Timorria, I. F., & Murtyantoro, A. P. (2021, November). Social media interconnection between people: Greta Thunberg's influence on the climate movement. [). IOP Publishing.]. *IOP Conference Series. Earth and Environmental Science*, 905(1), 012136. doi:10.1088/1755-1315/905/1/012136

Radford, A. (2019). Jeremy Clarkson says Greta Thunberg is an 'idiot' who has killed the car show. *SBS.* https://www.sbs.com.au/news/article/jeremy-clarkson-says-greta-thunberg-is-an-idiot-who-has-killed-the-car-show/1857ddhh5

Sirothiya, M., & Chavadi, C. (2020). Compressed biogas (cbg) as an alternative and sustainable energy source in India: Case study on implementation frameworks and challenges. *Invertis Journal of Renewable Energy*, 10(2), 49–64. doi:10.5958/2454-7611.2020.00007.7

Sirothiya, M., & Chavadi, C. (2020). Evaluating marketing strategies ofcompressed biogas (CBG) companies in India using decision tree analysis. *IIMS Journal of Management Science*, 11(3), 219–237. doi:10.5958/0976-173X.2020.00012.0

Sirothiya, M., & Chavadi, C. (2020). Role of compressed biogas to assess the effects of perceived value on customer satisfaction and customer loyalty. *BIMTECH Bus. Perspect*, 1, 70–89.

Sriram, V. P., Sanyal, S., Laddunuri, M. M., Subramanian, M., Bose, V., Booshan, B., & Thangam, D. (2023). Enhancing Cybersecurity Through Blockchain Technology. In Handbook of Research on Cybersecurity Issues and Challenges for Business and FinTech Applications (pp. 208-224). IGI Global.

Stevens, J.C. (2010). *Homeland Security.* Webeucracy: The Collaborative Revolution)

Ted.com. (2019). *Why you should be a climate activist.* TED. https://www.ted.com/talks/luisa_neubauer_why_you_should_be_a_climate_activist

Thangam, D., Arumugam, T., Velusamy, K., Subramanian, M., Ganesan, S. K., & Suryakumar, M. (2022). COVID-19 Pandemic and Its Brunt on Digital Transformation and Cybersecurity. In Cybersecurity Crisis Management and Lessons Learned From the COVID-19 Pandemic (pp. 15-42). IGI Global.

Thangam, D., & Chavadi, C. (2023). Impact of Digital Marketing Practices on Energy Consumption, Climate Change, and Sustainability. *Climate and Energy*, 39(7), 11–19. doi:10.1002/gas.22329

Thangam, D., Malali, A. B., Subramanian, G., Mohan, S., & Park, J. Y. (2022). Internet of things: a smart technology for healthcare industries. In *Healthcare Systems and Health Informatics* (pp. 3–15). CRC Press.

Thangam, D., Malali, A. B., Subramanian, G., & Park, J. Y. (2022). Transforming Healthcare through Internet of Things. In *Cloud and Fog Computing Platforms for Internet of Things* (pp. 15–24). Chapman and Hall/CRC. doi:10.1201/9781003213888-2

Thangam, D., Malali, A. B., Subramaniyan, G., Mariappan, S., Mohan, S., & Park, J. Y. (2022). Relevance of Artificial Intelligence in Modern Healthcare. In *Integrating AI in IoT Analytics on the Cloud for Healthcare Applications* (pp. 67–88). IGI Global. doi:10.4018/978-1-7998-9132-1.ch005

Thangam, D., Malali, A. B., Subramaniyan, S. G., Mariappan, S., Mohan, S., & Park, J. Y. (2021). Blockchain Technology and Its Brunt on Digital Marketing. In Blockchain Technology and Applications for Digital Marketing (pp. 1-15). IGI Global. doi:10.4018/978-1-7998-8081-3.ch001

Thangam, D., Vaidya, G. R., Subramanian, G., Velusamy, K., Selvi Govindarajan, K., & Park, J. Y. (2022). The Portrayal of Women's Empowerment in Select Indian Movies. *American Journal of Economics and Sociology*, *81*(1), 187–205. doi:10.1111/ajes.12451

The Indian Express. (2022). 'You and me are a team': When Barack Obama met a 16-year-old climate change activist. *The Indian Express*. https://indianexpress.com/article/trending/trending-globally/barack-obama-met-environmentalist-greta-thunberg-6005450/

Theguardian.com. (2019). The Swedish 15-year-old who's cutting class to fight the climate crisis. *The Guardian*. https://www.theguardian.com/science/2018/sep/01/swedish-15-year-old-cutting-class-to-fight-the-climate-crisis

Theindianexpress.com. (2020). Greta Thunberg recycles Donald Trump's tweet to her in 2019, tells him to 'chill'. *The Indian Express*. https://indianexpress.com/article/trending/trending-globally/greta-thunberg-recycles-trump-old-mockery-tweet-as-he-tries-to-stop-vote-count-6976467/

Thesocialflame.com. (2022). Greta Thunberg on Instagram. *The Social Flame*. https://thesocialflame.com/en/influencer/gretathunberg

Thunberg, G. (2020). *Greta Thunberg. Climate Change 'as Urgent' as Coronavirus*. Justin Rowalt BBC Interview.

Videovice.com. (2019). Make the World Greta Again. *Vice*. https://video.vice.com/en_us/video/vice-make-the-world-greta-again/5ca5f6cbbe40770ec567d7b7

Chapter 8
Role of Social Media on Government Initiatives Towards Human Resource Development

Vidhya Shanmugam
https://orcid.org/0000-0002-6181-5268
Amity Business School, Amity University, Haryana, India

V. Gowrishankkar
Sri Krishna College of Technology, India

S. Sibi
School of Management, Sri Krishna College of Technology, India

Sudha Maheswari T.
PSGR Krishnammal College for Women, India

Vijay Bose S
Vaagdevi College of Engineering, India

Murali Mora
Vaagdevi College of Engineering, India

Senthilkumar Chandramohan
Arsi University, Ethiopia

M. Maruthamuthu
https://orcid.org/0009-0008-2848-1922
Department of Business Administration, Government Arts and Science College, Kadayanallur, India

Irshad Nazeer
Presidency Business School, Presidency College, India

ABSTRACT

In the digital age, social media has emerged as a powerful tool for communication, networking, and information sharing. Its widespread popularity and accessibility have led to its adoption by governments worldwide to reach the public effectively. This chapter explores the role of social media in bridging the gap between government initiatives for human resource development (HRD) and the public. It examines how social media platforms have transformed the way governments communicate HRD policies, initiatives, and opportunities to citizens, fostering greater engagement, transparency, and inclusivity. The chapter also highlights the potential challenges and ethical considerations associated with the use of social media in HRD initiatives. Social media's integration with government HRD initiatives has immense potential to enhance access to resources, promote skill development, and empower individuals in the modern workforce.

DOI: 10.4018/978-1-6684-7450-1.ch008

INTRODUCTION

In recent years, social media has emerged as a powerful tool that is revolutionizing the way governments approach human resource development (HRD) initiatives. With its wide reach, instantaneous communication, and interactive features, social media platforms have transformed the landscape of HRD, enabling governments to engage with a broader audience, deliver targeted training programs, and bridge the gap between education and industry requirements. Social media platforms, such as Facebook, Twitter, LinkedIn, and YouTube, have become virtual hubs where governments can disseminate information, provide learning resources, and foster collaboration among individuals, trainers, industry professionals, and policymakers (Kiran Jason Samuel, 2014). These platforms offer a unique opportunity to tap into the digital behaviors and preferences of a diverse population, allowing governments to tailor HRD initiatives to meet specific needs and maximize their impact.The integration of social media in government initiatives for HRD has opened up new possibilities for effective communication, engagement, and collaboration. By leveraging the power of social media, governments can reach a wider audience, break down geographical barriers, and provide access to learning opportunities to individuals who may have limited resources or face physical constraints. This transformative shift has the potential to empower individuals, enhance employability, and contribute to sustainable socio-economic development. In this era of digital connectivity, social media has emerged as a catalyst for change in HRD (Hecklau, Galeitzke, Flachs& Kohl, 2016). It enables governments to adapt their strategies, leverage emerging technologies, and stay at the forefront of skills development. By harnessing the capabilities of social media, governments can create innovative approaches to training, foster lifelong learning, and bridge the skills gap between educational institutions and industry demands (Bennett, 2012).However, with this revolution come challenges and ethical considerations that needs to be carefully addressed. Governments must navigate issues of privacy, data security, misinformation, and digital literacy to ensure that the benefits of social media in HRD are harnessed responsibly and inclusively. This article explores the transformative power of social media in government initiatives for HRD. It delves into the various ways social media is reshaping the HRD landscape, highlights successful case studies, discusses best practices, and provides insights into future directions and emerging trends. By understanding the potential and harnessing the capabilities of social media, governments can unlock new opportunities to nurture human capital, foster economic growth, and create a more inclusive and skilled workforce.

IMPORTANCE OF HUMAN RESOURCE DEVELOPMENT (HRD) INITIATIVES BY GOVERNMENTS

Human Resource Development (HRD) initiatives are vital for the overall growth and progress of a nation. They refer to the planned and systematic activities undertaken by governments to enhance the skills, knowledge, and capabilities of individuals within their workforce (Metcalfe & Rees, 2005).Here are some key reasons why HRD initiatives are important:

Economic development: HRD initiatives help develop a skilled and knowledgeable workforce, which is essential for economic growth. By investing in education, training, and skill development, governments can create a highly competent workforce capable of driving innovation, productivity, and competitiveness.

Job creation and employability: HRD initiatives focus on improving employability and job prospects for individuals. By equipping people with relevant skills and knowledge, governments can enhance their chances of finding suitable employment. This, in turn, reduces unemployment rates and contributes to overall socio-economic development.

Social inclusion and poverty reduction: HRD initiatives promote social inclusion by providing equal opportunities for individuals from diverse backgrounds to access education and skill development programs. By narrowing the skills gap, governments can uplift marginalized communities, reduce poverty, and promote social equity (Hecklau, Galeitzke, Flachs& Kohl, 2016).

Adaptation to technological advancements: Rapid technological advancements require a workforce that can adapt and thrive in the digital era. HRD initiatives help individuals acquire digital literacy skills, upskill or reskill to meet changing industry demands, and navigate the digital landscape effectively.

Improved productivity and competitiveness: A well-trained and competent workforce leads to increased productivity and competitiveness at both individual and national levels. HRD initiatives foster a culture of continuous learning, enabling employees to enhance their productivity, contribute to innovation, and drive economic progress.

THE ROLE OF SOCIAL MEDIA IN BRIDGING THE GAP BETWEEN HRD INITIATIVES AND THE PUBLIC

Social media plays a crucial role in bridging the gap between HRD initiatives by governments and the public. Here's how it facilitates this connection:

Accessible communication channel: Social media provides a direct and accessible communication channel for governments to disseminate information about HRD initiatives. It allows them to reach a wide audience instantly, bypassing traditional barriers of time and location (Bruns&Highfield, 2015). Governments can share updates, announcements, and resources related to HRD initiatives, ensuring that the public remains informed.

Engagement and feedback: Social media platforms enable governments to engage with the public and gather feedback on HRD initiatives. They can conduct surveys, host online discussions, and receive direct inputs from citizens, fostering a sense of participation and ownership. This feedback can inform policy decisions and help governments tailor HRD initiatives to better meet public needs.

Awareness and promotion: Social media platforms serve as effective tools for raising awareness about HRD initiatives. Governments can leverage social media's viral nature to promote their programs, campaigns, and educational resources. By utilizing targeted advertising and influencer partnerships, they can reach specific demographics and communities, ensuring a wider reach and engagement (Kusumasari&Alam, 2012).

Collaboration and partnerships: Social media facilitates collaboration between governments, educational institutions, and other stakeholders involved in HRD initiatives. It allows for the exchange of ideas, best practices, and resources, creating synergies and improving the effectiveness of HRD programs. Social media also enables governments to connect with experts, organizations, and professionals who can contribute to HRD initiatives through mentorship, training, or knowledge sharing.

Skill development and learning opportunities: Social media platforms offer diverse learning opportunities for individuals seeking to enhance their skills and knowledge. Governments can leverage these platforms to provide educational content, online courses, webinars, and interactive resources related to HRD initiatives. Social media also enables peer-to-peer learning, networking, and access to professional communities, enriching the learning experience (Shirmohammadi, HedayatiMehdiabadi, Beigi& McLean, 2021).

Social media acts as a powerful bridge between governments' HRD initiatives and the public by facilitating communication, engagement, awareness, collaboration, and learning. It enhances the effectiveness of HRD initiatives by creating a more inclusive, informed, and participatory environment.

THE TRANSFORMATIVE POWER OF SOCIAL MEDIA IN HRD

Social media has emerged as a transformative force in the field of Human Resource Development (HRD), revolutionizing the way organizations approach learning, training, and employee development (Bruns&Highfield, 2015). Here are some key ways in which social media has transformed HRD practices:

Accessible and flexible learning: Social media platforms provide convenient and flexible avenues for learning and skill development. Organizations can create dedicated online learning communities, where employees can access training materials, interactive modules, and collaborative learning opportunities. This accessibility allows employees to engage in learning at their own pace and convenience, irrespective of geographical boundaries or time constraints (Shirmohammadi, HedayatiMehdiabadi, Beigi& McLean, 2021).

Collaborative and peer-to-peer learning: Social media fosters collaborative learning environments, enabling employees to engage in discussions, share knowledge, and learn from one another. Platforms like enterprise social networks or internal communication tools facilitate the exchange of ideas, best practices, and expertise among employees. Peer-to-peer learning through social media encourages a culture of continuous learning and knowledge sharing within organizations.

Personalized and targeted learning experiences: Social media platforms enable HRD professionals to customize learning experiences based on individual needs and preferences. By analyzing user data and engagement patterns, organizations can deliver personalized learning content, recommendations, and targeted training interventions. This personalized approach enhances the effectiveness and engagement of HRD initiatives (Booth, Strudwick& Fraser, 2017).

Amplifying employee voices and recognition: Social media provides a platform for employees to share their achievements, ideas, and experiences, allowing for recognition and appreciation from peers and leaders. Through employee-generated content, organizations can showcase success stories, highlight employee contributions, and create a positive work culture. This recognition and visibility on social media platforms can boost employee morale, motivation, and engagement (Gideon, Lang &Benbunan-Fich, 2010).

Expanding professional networks and connections: Social media allows employees to expand their professional networks and connect with industry experts, thought leaders, and peers beyond their immediate organizational boundaries. Platforms like LinkedIn enable employees to build meaningful connections, participate in industry discussions, and access valuable career resources (Gideon, Lang &Benbunan-Fich, 2010). These expanded networks facilitate knowledge exchange, career development, and opportunities for collaboration.

Fostering innovation and creativity: Social media platforms provide spaces for employees to share innovative ideas, seek feedback, and collaborate on projects. By leveraging social media tools, organizations can tap into the collective intelligence of their workforce, encouraging innovation and creativity.

Employees can contribute to problem-solving, ideation, and co-creation, leading to organizational growth and improvement (Fuchs, 2014).

Enhancing employer branding and recruitment: Social media plays a significant role in shaping an organization's employer brand and attracting top talent. HRD initiatives can leverage social media platforms to showcase a company's culture, values, and employee development programs. Engaging and interactive content, such as employee testimonials, behind-the-scenes videos, or virtual tours, can attract potential candidates and enhance the recruitment process.

Social media has transformed HRD practices by providing accessible learning, fostering collaboration, personalization, and recognition, expanding professional networks, fostering innovation, and enhancing employer branding. Its transformative power lies in its ability to facilitate continuous learning, connect employees, and create a dynamic and engaging learning ecosystem within organizations (Fuchs, 2014).

BENEFITS OF GOVERNMENT ADOPTION OF SOCIAL MEDIA FOR HRD INITIATIVES

In an era of rapid technological advancements, governments around the world are recognizing the transformative power of social media in various aspects of governance. One area where social media has gained significant traction is in the field of Human Resource Development (HRD). Governments are increasingly adopting social media platforms as a means to enhance the effectiveness of their HRD initiatives, fostering a culture of continuous learning, and improving workforce capabilities (Parise, 2007). This part of the chapter explores the reasons behind government adoption of social media for HRD initiatives and highlights the benefits and challenges associated with this approach.

Increased Accessibility and Reach: Social media platforms offer a vast user base and widespread accessibility. By adopting social media for HRD initiatives, governments can reach a larger audience, including employees, job seekers, and the general public. The wide reach of social media enables governments to disseminate information about HRD programs, training opportunities, and job vacancies, ensuring that the public remains informed and engaged (Poba-Nzaou, Lemieux, Beaupré&Uwizeyemungu, 2016).).

Improved Communication and Engagement: Social media platforms provide a direct and interactive communication channel between governments and individuals. Governments can leverage these platforms to engage with citizens, answer queries, and address concerns related to HRD initiatives. The real-time nature of social media allows for immediate feedback and fosters a sense of participation, promoting transparency and accountability in government HRD efforts (Parise, 2007).

Cost-effective Dissemination of Information: Compared to traditional media channels, social media offers a cost-effective way for governments to disseminate information about HRD initiatives. It eliminates the need for extensive advertising campaigns and enables governments to target specific demographics and communities. Through creative and engaging content, governments can effectively promote HRD programs and opportunities, maximizing their impact within limited budgets (Fuchs, 2014).

Collaboration and Partnerships: Social media facilitates collaboration between government agencies, educational institutions, and other stakeholders involved in HRD. Governments can establish online communities or groups where experts, trainers, and HRD professionals can share best practices, resources, and experiences. This collaboration helps governments stay updated with the latest HRD trends and fosters innovation in the design and delivery of HRD programs (Parise, 2007).

Data-driven Decision Making: Social media platforms provide governments with valuable data and insights on user engagement, preferences, and feedback. By analyzing this data, governments can make informed decisions regarding the design, implementation, and evaluation of HRD initiatives. This data-driven approach helps governments tailor their programs to better meet the needs and expectations of the target audience, improving the overall effectiveness of HRD efforts.

SOCIAL MEDIA STRATEGIES FOR EFFECTIVE HRD COMMUNICATION

In the realm of Human Resource Development (HRD), effective communication plays a crucial role in engaging employees, promoting learning initiatives, and fostering a culture of continuous development. Social media platforms provide a unique and powerful avenue to enhance HRD communication (Girard, Fallery&Rodhain, 2014). Here are some key strategies for leveraging social media effectively in HRD communication:

Establish Clear Objectives: Before implementing social media strategies for HRD communication, it is essential to establish clear objectives. Determine what you aim to achieve through social media, whether it's to disseminate information about training programs, encourage employee engagement, or create a knowledge-sharing culture. Having defined objectives will guide your content creation, platform selection, and measurement of success (Delello, McWhorter& Camp, 2015).

Identify the Right Platforms: Different social media platforms cater to different audiences and purposes. Identify the platforms that align with your HRD communication objectives and target audience. LinkedIn, for example, is ideal for professional networking and sharing industry insights, while internal communication tools like Yammer or Slack can foster collaboration within the organization. Consider the demographics and preferences of your employees to choose the most effective platforms.

Tailor Content to Suit the Medium: Each social media platform has its unique characteristics and limitations. Tailor your content to suit the medium and maximize engagement. Use visually appealing graphics, videos, and infographics to capture attention. Keep your messages concise, compelling, and easy to consume. Incorporate storytelling techniques to make your content relatable and memorable. Remember to include a call-to-action to encourage employee participation and interaction(Delello, McWhorter & Camp, 2015).

Encourage Employee-generated Content: Encouraging employees to generate content can significantly enhance HRD communication on social media. Create opportunities for employees to share their success stories, lessons learned, and best practices. Employee testimonials, case studies, and knowledge-sharing posts not only inspire others but also create a sense of ownership and pride within the organization. Highlight and recognize employee contributions to foster a positive and collaborative work culture.

Foster Two-Way Communication: Social media platforms offer a unique opportunity for two-way communication. Encourage employees to provide feedback, ask questions, and share their opinions on HRD initiatives. Respond promptly and engage in meaningful conversations to build trust and demonstrate that their voices are valued. Actively listen to employee concerns, suggestions, and ideas, and incorporate them into your HRD strategies. Two-way communication fosters a sense of inclusion and strengthens the impact of HRD initiatives.

Utilize Multimedia and Interactive Features: Social media platforms provide various multimedia and interactive features that can enhance HRD communication. Consider utilizing live video streaming for webinars or training sessions, conducting Q&A sessions through live chats, or creating polls and surveys to gather feedback. Gamification elements, such as quizzes or challenges, can also make learning more interactive and engaging. These features create a dynamic and participatory learning environment (Parise, 2007).

Analyze and Optimize: Monitor the performance of your social media HRD communication efforts and analyze the data to measure success and identify areas for improvement. Track metrics such as engagement rates, reach, and conversion to assess the effectiveness of your strategies. Use insights from data analysis to optimize your content, posting schedules, and communication tactics. Continuously adapt and refine your social media strategies based on the feedback and results you receive (Parise, 2007).

By implementing these social media strategies for HRD communication, organizations can create an inclusive, engaging, and effective communication ecosystem. Social media platforms offer the opportunity to foster collaboration, facilitate knowledge-sharing, and empower employees to take ownership of their development, ultimately contributing to the growth and success of the organization.

CHALLENGES AND ETHICAL CONSIDERATIONS OF GOVERNMENT SOCIAL MEDIA INITIATIVES FOR HUMAN RESOURCE DEVELOPMENT

While government social media initiatives for Human Resource Development (HRD) bring numerous benefits, they also come with unique challenges and ethical considerations that need to be carefully addressed. Understanding and addressing these challenges is crucial for ensuring the responsible and ethical use of social media in HRD (Berman, Bowman, West & Van Wart, 2021). Here are some key challenges and ethical considerations to consider:

Privacy and Data Security: One of the primary concerns in government social media initiatives is the privacy and security of personal data. Governments must establish robust data protection policies and frameworks to safeguard sensitive information shared on social media platforms. It is essential to comply with data protection regulations and ensure that user data is securely stored and used only for the intended purposes (Berman, Bowman, West & Van Wart, 2021).

Digital Divide and Accessibility: While social media has the potential to reach a wide audience, there is a risk of excluding certain populations due to the digital divide. Governments need to ensure that HRD initiatives on social media are accessible to all individuals, irrespective of their socio-economic background, location, or level of digital literacy (Rotich, 2015). Measures should be taken to bridge the digital divide, provide internet access, and offer training programs to promote digital inclusion.

Misinformation and Fake News: The prevalence of misinformation and fake news on social media platforms is a significant challenge for government HRD initiatives. Governments should be cautious about disseminating accurate information and actively combat misinformation related to HRD programs. It is important to promote media literacy among citizens and encourage critical thinking skills to help individuals discern reliable information from misinformation.

Bias and Discrimination: Social media platforms can inadvertently perpetuate bias and discrimination if not managed carefully. Governments must be mindful of the content they share and ensure that it is inclusive, unbiased, and does not reinforce stereotypes or discriminatory practices (Rotich, 2015). HRD initiatives should promote equal opportunities and fairness in training, recruitment, and career development.

Maintaining Transparency and Accountability: Government social media initiatives should maintain transparency and accountability in their HRD communication. Clear guidelines should be established regarding the type of information that can be shared, ensuring that it aligns with the government's objectives and values. It is crucial to engage in open and honest communication, addressing queries, concerns, and feedback from citizens in a timely and transparent manner.

Balancing Personal and Professional Boundaries: Social media blurs the lines between personal and professional lives, and this can create challenges for government HRD initiatives. Employees participating in social media initiatives may inadvertently disclose personal information or engage in inappropriate behavior that reflects poorly on the organization. Governments must provide clear guidelines and training to employees on responsible social media usage, ensuring that personal and professional boundaries are respected (Berman, Bowman, West & Van Wart, 2021).

Ensuring Equality and Fairness: Governments should ensure that their social media HRD initiatives promote equality and fairness in access to learning opportunities. Measures should be taken to prevent any bias or favoritism in the selection process for training programs, mentorship opportunities, or career advancement. Transparent and merit-based systems should be established to ensure that HRD initiatives benefit all individuals based on their skills and capabilities.

Ethical Handling of User Data: Governments must handle user data collected through social media platforms ethically and responsibly. It is essential to obtain proper consent from users when collecting their data and use it only for the intended purposes. Governments should have clear policies on data retention, sharing, and deletion to protect user privacy and prevent any misuse of personal information.

By addressing these challenges and ethical considerations, governments can ensure that their social media initiatives for HRD are conducted responsibly, respecting privacy, promoting equality, and fostering a positive and inclusive learning environment. Open dialogue, stakeholder engagement, and continuous evaluation of social media practices can help navigate these challenges and uphold ethical standards in government HRD initiatives (Berman, Bowman, West & Van Wart, 2021).

CASE STUDY: SUCCESSFUL IMPLEMENTATION OF SOCIAL MEDIA IN HRD INITIATIVES—NATIONAL SKILL DEVELOPMENT CORPORATION (NSDC)

The National Skill Development Corporation (NSDC) is a government-owned organization in India focused on skill development and training initiatives to enhance employability and bridge the gap between industry requirements and workforce capabilities. NSDC recognized the potential of social media in HRD and successfully implemented social media strategies to enhance their communication, engagement, and impact in skill development initiatives (NSDC, 2023). This case study examines the successful implementation of social media in HRD initiatives by NSDC.

Objectives

Improve Communication: NSDC aimed to enhance communication channels and reach a larger audience, including potential trainees, trainers, and industry partners. They wanted to disseminate information about skill development programs, training opportunities, and industry trends effectively.

Increase Engagement: NSDC sought to foster engagement among stakeholders by encouraging active participation, knowledge-sharing, and collaboration. They aimed to create a vibrant community where trainees, trainers, and industry professionals could interact, learn from each other, and contribute to the skill development ecosystem.

Enhance Brand Visibility: NSDC aimed to increase brand visibility and establish them as a reliable authority in skill development. They wanted to leverage social media platforms to showcase success stories, highlight industry partnerships, and promote the impact of their initiatives, thereby attracting more participants and industry support.

Social Media Strategies Implemented by NSDC

Multi-Platform Approach: NSDC adopted a multi-platform approach to maximize their reach and engagement. They utilized popular social media platforms such as Facebook, Twitter, LinkedIn, and YouTube, tailoring their content to suit the specific platform and target audience. This approach allowed them to reach diverse demographics and engage with stakeholders across different platforms.

Engaging Content Creation: NSDC focused on creating engaging and informative content to attract and retain the attention of their target audience. They shared success stories of individuals who benefited from skill development programs, industry insights, training resources, and expert interviews. The content was designed to be visually appealing, concise, and shareable, with a call-to-action to encourage audience participation (NSDC, 2023).

Two-Way Communication: NSDC actively engaged with their audience through social media, responding to queries, addressing concerns, and encouraging discussions. They employed community management strategies to ensure timely and meaningful interactions, fostering a sense of belonging and participation. Regular engagement helped build trust and credibility among their followers.

Collaboration with Partners: NSDC collaborated with industry partners, training providers, and other stakeholders to leverage their expertise and expand the reach of their social media initiatives. They co-created content, conducted webinars, and promoted joint initiatives, enhancing the value and relevance of their social media presence. Collaboration strengthened their network and amplified their impact.

Results and Impact

Increased reach and engagement: NSDC's social media initiatives significantly expanded their reach, with a substantial increase in followers and engagement across platforms. The use of visually appealing content, industry insights, and success stories resonated with their audience, resulting in higher engagement rates, shares, and comments.

Enhanced Communication and Feedback Loop: Social media enabled NSDC to establish a direct and transparent communication channel with their stakeholders. They received feedback, suggestions, and queries from potential trainees, trainers, and industry professionals, allowing them to address concerns promptly and improve their programs based on real-time insights.

Strengthened Industry Partnerships: NSDC's social media initiatives facilitated collaborations with industry partners and training providers. These partnerships resulted in joint initiatives, increased industry participation, and improved alignment between skill development programs and industry needs. The engagement on social media platforms fostered stronger connections and knowledge-sharing opportunities.

Improved Brand Visibility and Trust: NSDC's social media presence helped them establish a strong brand identity and build trust among their stakeholders. By sharing success stories and industry partnerships, they showcased the impact of their initiatives, increasing credibility and attracting more participants, trainers, and industry support.

The successful implementation of social media in HRD initiatives by NSDC demonstrates the transformative power of social media in skill development and training. By leveraging multiple platforms, creating engaging content, fostering two-way communication, and collaborating with industry partners, NSDC significantly enhanced their reach, engagement, and impact. The use of social media facilitated better communication, feedback loop, and trust-building, ultimately contributing to the success of their skill development programs and their mission of creating a skilled workforce in India. This case study serves as a valuable example for organizations looking to harness the potential of social media in their HRD initiatives.

BEST PRACTICES AND RECOMMENDATIONS ON GOVERNMENT SOCIAL MEDIA USAGE FOR HUMAN RESOURCE DEVELOPMENT

The effective utilization of social media platforms by governments for Human Resource Development (HRD) requires careful planning, strategic implementation, and adherence to best practices (Hosain, 2023). Here are some recommendations for government agencies to maximize the benefits and minimize the risks associated with social media usage in HRD initiatives:

Establish Clear Objectives: Clearly define the objectives and goals of using social media for HRD initiatives. Determine the desired outcomes, such as increased engagement, improved communication, or better access to learning resources. Align these objectives with the overall HRD strategy of the government to ensure consistency and effectiveness.

Understand the Target Audience: Gain a deep understanding of the target audience for HRD initiatives. Identify their demographics, preferences, and needs. This understanding will help tailor content, platform selection, and communication strategies to effectively engage the target audience and deliver relevant information.

Select Appropriate Platforms: Choose the social media platforms that align with the target audience and the objectives of HRD initiatives. Each platform has its own strengths and characteristics, so consider factors such as user base, engagement levels, and content formats. Use a mix of platforms to maximize reach and engagement while considering the resources available for content creation and management (Hosain, 2023).

Create Engaging and Informative Content: Develop compelling and informative content that resonates with the target audience. Use a variety of formats such as videos, info graphics, and articles to cater to different learning preferences. Focus on delivering value through educational resources, success stories, industry insights, and practical tips. Maintain a consistent posting schedule to keep the audience engaged.

Encourage Two-Way Communication: Foster a culture of open communication and engagement by actively encouraging and responding to comments, questions, and feedback from the audience. Promptly address queries and concerns, and use feedback to improve HRD initiatives. Actively listen to the audience and incorporate their suggestions and ideas into future initiatives, creating a sense of ownership and participation (Waring& Buchanan, 2010).

Collaborate with Stakeholders: Collaborate with relevant stakeholders, such as industry associations, educational institutions, and training providers, to amplify the impact of HRD initiatives. Seek partnerships for content co-creation, webinars, workshops, or mentorship programs. Collaboration helps diversify perspectives, expand reach, and ensure the relevance of HRD initiatives to the needs of various stakeholders.

Ensure Accessibility and Inclusivity: Make HRD initiatives on social media accessible and inclusive to all individuals, regardless of their backgrounds or abilities. Provide captions, transcripts, and alternative formats for multimedia content to accommodate individuals with disabilities. Ensure that content is available in multiple languages, considering the linguistic diversity of the target audience (Waring& Buchanan, 2010).

Monitor and Measure Performance: Regularly monitor the performance of social media initiatives for HRD. Track key metrics such as engagement rates, reach, website traffic, and audience demographics. Use analytics tools to gain insights into the effectiveness of different content types, platforms, and communication strategies. Continuously evaluate and optimize social media strategies based on data-driven insights (Tripathy, M.R. and Kaur, 2012).

By following these best practices and recommendations, governments can harness the full potential of social media for human resource development. Effective use of social media platforms will enhance communication, engagement, and accessibility of HRD initiatives, ultimately leading to a skilled and empowered workforce for socio-economic development.

FUTURE DIRECTIONS AND EMERGING TRENDS OF GOVERNMENT SOCIAL MEDIA USAGE FOR HUMAN RESOURCE DEVELOPMENT

As technology continues to evolve and shape the way we communicate and access information, government social media usage for Human Resource Development (HRD) is expected to undergo significant advancements. Here are some future directions and emerging trends that can be anticipated. Government social media initiatives for HRD will increasingly focus on providing personalized learning experiences. Utilizing data analytics and artificial intelligence, governments can analyze user preferences, learning styles, and skill gaps to deliver tailored content and recommendations. This approach will enhance engagement and cater to the specific needs of individuals, leading to more effective skill development outcomes (Kapoor, Tamilmani, Rana, et al. 2018). Augmented reality (AR) and virtual reality (VR) technologies offer immersive and interactive experiences that can revolutionize HRD initiatives. Governments can leverage AR/VR to provide realistic simulations, virtual training environments, and hands-on experiences for skill development. These technologies enable learners to practice tasks, explore complex scenarios, and receive immediate feedback, enhancing the effectiveness of training programs (Fenech, Baguant, &Ivanov, 2019).Gamification techniques will play a significant role in government social media usage for HRD. By incorporating game elements such as challenges, rewards, and leaderboards, governments can make skill development engaging and enjoyable. Gamification enhances motivation, encourages active participation, and fosters healthy competition, resulting in increased knowledge retention and skill acquisition.With shrinking attention spans and the need for on-the-go learning, microlearning and bite-sized content will gain prominence in government social media initiatives. Governments will deliver concise and focused learning modules that can be accessed anytime, anywhere (Vrontis, Christofi, Pereira, Tarba, Makrides& Trichina, 2022). Short videos, infographics, and interactive quizzes will facilitate quick and digestible learning, catering to the preferences of modern learners.Future government social media usage for HRD will emphasize social collaboration and peer learning. Online communities and collaborative platforms will be created where learners, trainers, and industry professionals can connect, share knowledge, and engage in discussions. Governments can facilitate mentorship programs, group projects, and knowledge-sharing networks, fostering a culture of continuous learning and collaboration (Ivanov, 2019).

AI-powered chatbots and virtual assistants will become integral components of government social media initiatives for HRD. These automated systems can provide instant responses to queries; offer personalized recommendations, and guide individuals through various HRD programs. Chatbots can also assist in career guidance, suggesting suitable training opportunities and career paths based on user preferences and skill sets.As mobile devices become the primary means of accessing the internet, government social media initiatives for HRD will prioritize a mobile-first approach. Responsive design and mobile-friendly interfaces will ensure that content and learning resources are easily accessible on smartphones and tablets (Fernandez, & Gallardo-Gallardo, 2021). Mobile applications specifically designed for HRD purposes will provide seamless learning experiences on the go.Governments will increasingly rely on data-driven insights to make informed decisions regarding HRD initiatives. Advanced analytics tools will help analyze user behavior, engagement patterns, and learning outcomes, enabling governments to optimize content, delivery methods, and program effectiveness. Data-driven decision making will lead to targeted interventions, improved resource allocation, and continuous improvement of HRD initiatives.As new social media platforms and technologies emerge, governments will explore their potential for HRD initiatives (Vrontis, Christofi, Pereira, Tarba, Makrides& Trichina, 2022). Platforms like TikTok, Instagram, and LinkedIn will be leveraged to reach diverse audiences, engage with specific professional communities, and promote skill development opportunities. Governments will adapt to the evolving social media landscape, staying abreast of emerging platforms and trends.As government social media usage for HRD expands, ethical considerations and privacy concerns will become increasingly important. Governments will need to ensure transparent data practices, secure handling of personal information, and compliance with privacy regulations. Ethical guidelines will be developed to govern the collection, storage, and usage of user data, prioritizing the protection of individual privacy rights.By embracing these future directions and emerging trends, governments can leverage the power of social media to enhance HRD initiatives, promote lifelong learning, and develop a skilled workforce ready for the challenges of the future (Fernandez, & Gallardo-Gallardo, 2021). The dynamic nature of technology and social media will continue to shape the landscape of HRD, presenting exciting opportunities for governments to engage, educate, and empower their citizens.

CONCLUSION

The revolution of social media in government initiatives for human resource development (HRD) has brought about a paradigm shift in the way governments engage, educate, and empower individuals. Through its expansive reach, real-time communication, and interactive features, social media has become a catalyst for transforming HRD practices and bridging the gap between education and industry requirements. The integration of social media platforms into government initiatives has enabled a broader dissemination of information, the creation of targeted training programs, and the fostering of collaboration among diverse stakeholders. Governments now have the ability to tap into the digital behaviors and preferences of their population, tailoring HRD initiatives to meet specific needs and maximizing their impact.By leveraging social media, governments can reach individuals who may have limited resources or face geographical constraints, providing them with access to learning opportunities and empowering them to enhance their employability. This inclusivity is a significant step towards creating a skilled workforce that can contribute to sustainable socio-economic development.The use of social media in HRD also encourages lifelong learning and the acquisition of skills that are in line with emerging technologies and industry demands. Governments can adapt their strategies, harness emerging technologies, and stay at the forefront of skills development, ensuring that their workforce remains competitive in a rapidly evolving digital landscape.However, as governments embrace the transformative power of social media, it is crucial to address the challenges and ethical considerations that arise. Privacy, data security, misinformation, and digital literacy must be carefully managed to ensure responsible and inclusive use of social media in HRD initiatives.In conclusion, social media is revolutionizing government initiatives for HRD, enabling governments to redefine their approach to skill development and education. Through strategic utilization of social media platforms, governments can engage a wider audience, break down barriers to access, and create innovative approaches to training. By embracing the potential of social media, governments can cultivate a skilled workforce, foster economic growth, and build a future where individuals have the tools and opportunities to thrive in a rapidly changing world.

REFERENCES

Anuradha, A., Shilpa, R., Thirupathi, M., Padmapriya, S., Supramaniam, G., Booshan, B., & Thangam, D. (2023). Importance of Sustainable Marketing Initiatives for Supporting the Sustainable Development Goals. In *Handbook of Research on Achieving Sustainable Development Goals With Sustainable Marketing* (pp. 149–169). IGI Global. doi:10.4018/978-1-6684-8681-8.ch008

Bennett, W. L. (2012). The personalization of politics: Political identity, social media, and changing patterns of participation. *The Annals of the American Academy of Political and Social Science, 644*(1), 20–39. doi:10.1177/0002716212451428

Berman, E. M., Bowman, J. S., West, J. P., & Van Wart, M. R. (2021). *Human resource management in public service: Paradoxes, processes, and problems.* CQ Press.

Booth, R. G., Strudwick, G., & Fraser, R. (2017, May). The transformative power of social media: Considerations for practice and emerging leaders. [). Sage CA: Los Angeles, CA: SAGE Publications.]. *Healthcare Management Forum, 30*(3), 138–141. doi:10.1177/0840470417693017 PMID:28929851

Bruns, A., & Highfield, T. (2015). Is Habermas on Twitter?: Social media and the public sphere. In The Routledge companion to social media and politics (pp. 56-73). Routledge.

Delello, J. A., McWhorter, R. R., & Camp, K. M. (2015). Using social media as a tool for learning: A multi-disciplinary study. In EdMedia+ Innovate Learning Online 2022 (Vol. 14, pp. 163-180). Association for the Advancement of Computing in Education (AACE).

Fenech, R., Baguant, P., & Ivanov, D. (2019). The changing role of human resource management in an era of digital transformation. *Journal of Management Information & Decision Sciences, 22*(2).

Fernandez, V., & Gallardo-Gallardo, E. (2021). Tackling the HR digitalization challenge: Key factors and barriers to HR analytics adoption. *Competitiveness Review*, *31*(1), 162–187. doi:10.1108/CR-12-2019-0163

Gideon, F., Lang, G., & Benbunan-Fich, R. (2010). the transformative Power of social Media on emergency and Crisis Management. *International Journal of Information Systems for Crisis Response and Management*, *2*(1), 1–10. doi:10.4018/jiscrm.2010120401

Girard, A., Fallery, B., & Rodhain, F. (2014). Integration of social media in recruitment: a delphi study. In *Social Media in Human Resources Management* (Vol. 12, pp. 97–120). Emerald Group Publishing Limited. doi:10.1108/S1877-6361(2013)0000012009

Hecklau, F., Galeitzke, M., Flachs, S., & Kohl, H. (2016). Holistic approach for human resource management in Industry 4.0. *Procedia CIRP*, *54*, 1–6. doi:10.1016/j.procir.2016.05.102

Hosain, M. S. (2023). Integration of social media into HRM practices: A bibliometric overview. *PSU Research Review*, *7*(1), 51–72. doi:10.1108/PRR-12-2020-0039

Ivanov, S. (2019). Ultimate transformation: How will automation technologies disrupt the travel, tourism and hospitality industries? *Zeitschrift für Tourismuswissenschaft*, *11*(1), 25–43. doi:10.1515/tw-2019-0003

Kapoor, K. K., Tamilmani, K., Rana, N. P., Patil, P., Dwivedi, Y. K., & Nerur, S. (2018). Advances in Social Media Research: Past, Present and Future. *Information Systems Frontiers*, *20*(3), 531–558. doi:10.100710796-017-9810-y

Karumban, S., Sanyal, S., Laddunuri, M. M., Sivalinga, V. D., Shanmugam, V., Bose, V., & Murugan, S. P. (2023). Industrial Automation and Its Impact on Manufacturing Industries. In Revolutionizing Industrial Automation Through the Convergence of Artificial Intelligence and the Internet of Things (pp. 24-40). IGI Global.

Kiran Jason Samuel. (2014). The Human Resources & Social Media Revolution. *Torry Harris*. https://www.torryharris.com/blog/the-human-resources-and-social-media-revolution

Kusumasari, B., & Alam, Q. (2012). Bridging the gaps: The role of local government capability and the management of a natural disaster in Bantul, Indonesia. *Natural Hazards*, *60*(2), 761–779. doi:10.100711069-011-0016-1

Metcalfe, B. D., & Rees, C. J. (2005). Theorizing advances in international human resource development. *Human Resource Development International*, *8*(4), 449–465. doi:10.1080/13678860500354601

Murugan, S. P., Shivaprasad, G., Dhanalakshmi, A., Sriram, V. P., Rajput, K., Mahesh, B. N., & Kedla, S. (2023). The Impact of COVID-19 on the Indian Microfinance Industry and Its Sustainability. In *Transforming Economies Through Microfinance in Developing Nations* (pp. 160–188). IGI Global. doi:10.4018/978-1-6684-5647-7.ch009

NSDC. (2023). *Skilling India's Youth, Shaping India's Future*. NSDC. https://nsdcindia.org/sites/default/files/files/NSDC-Annual-Report-2019-20.pdf

Parise, S. (2007). Knowledge management and human resource development: An application in social network analysis methods. *Advances in Developing Human Resources*, *9*(3), 359–383. doi:10.1177/1523422307304106

Park, J. Y., Perumal, S. V., Sanyal, S., Ah Nguyen, B., Ray, S., Krishnan, R., Narasimhaiah, R., & Thangam, D. (2022). Sustainable Marketing Strategies as an Essential Tool of Business. *American Journal of Economics and Sociology*, *81*(2), 359–379. doi:10.1111/ajes.12459

Rotich, K. J. (2015). History, evolution and development of human resource management: A contemporary perspective. *Global Journal of Human Resource Management*, *3*(3), 58–73.

Shanmugam, V., Asha, N., Samanvitha, C., Murthy, L. N., & Thangam, D. (2021). An analysis of bilateral trade between india and korea. *Journal of Contemporary Issues in Business and Government*, *27*(2).

Sriram, V. P., Sanyal, S., Laddunuri, M. M., Subramanian, M., Bose, V., Booshan, B., & Thangam, D. (2023). Enhancing Cybersecurity Through Blockchain Technology. In Handbook of Research on Cybersecurity Issues and Challenges for Business and FinTech Applications (pp. 208-224). IGI Global.

Thangam, D., Arumugam, T., Velusamy, K., Subramanian, M., Ganesan, S. K., & Suryakumar, M. (2022). COVID-19 Pandemic and Its Brunt on Digital Transformation and Cybersecurity. In Cybersecurity Crisis Management and Lessons Learned From the COVID-19 Pandemic (pp. 15-42). IGI Global.

Thangam, D., & Chavadi, C. (2023). Impact of Digital Marketing Practices on Energy Consumption, Climate Change, and Sustainability. *Climate and Energy*, *39*(7), 11–19. doi:10.1002/gas.22329

Thangam, D., Malali, A. B., Subramanian, G., Mohan, S., & Park, J. Y. (2022). Internet of things: a smart technology for healthcare industries. In *Healthcare Systems and Health Informatics* (pp. 3–15). CRC Press.

Thangam, D., Malali, A. B., Subramanian, G., & Park, J. Y. (2022). Transforming Healthcare through Internet of Things. In *Cloud and Fog Computing Platforms for Internet of Things* (pp. 15–24). Chapman and Hall/CRC. doi:10.1201/9781003213888-2

Thangam, D., Malali, A. B., Subramaniyan, G., Mariappan, S., Mohan, S., & Park, J. Y. (2022). Relevance of Artificial Intelligence in Modern Healthcare. In *Integrating AI in IoT Analytics on the Cloud for Healthcare Applications* (pp. 67–88). IGI Global. doi:10.4018/978-1-7998-9132-1.ch005

Thangam, D., Vaidya, G. R., Subramanian, G., Velusamy, K., Selvi Govindarajan, K., & Park, J. Y. (2022). The Portrayal of Women's Empowerment in Select Indian Movies. *American Journal of Economics and Sociology*, *81*(1), 187–205. doi:10.1111/ajes.12451

Tripathy, M. R., & Kaur, T. (2012). Perceptions of employees on information checks by employers using social networking sites in IT sector. *Management and Labour Studies*, *37*(4), 345–358. doi:10.1177/0258042X13484866

Vrontis, D., Christofi, M., Pereira, V., Tarba, S., Makrides, A., & Trichina, E. (2022). Artificial intelligence, robotics, advanced technologies and human resource management: A systematic review. *International Journal of Human Resource Management*, *33*(6), 1237–1266. doi:10.1080/09585192.2020.1871398

Waring, R. L., & Buchanan, F. R. (2010). Social networking web sites: The legal and ethical aspects of pre-employment screening and employee surveillance. *Journal of Human Resources Education*, *4*(2), 14–23.

Chapter 9
Usage of Social Media in Education:
A Paradigm Shift in the Indian Education Sector

Thirupathi Manickam
https://orcid.org/0000-0001-7976-6073
CHRIST University (Deemed), India

Macherla Bhagyalakshmi
CHRIST University (Deemed), India

Kavitha Desai
CHRIST University (Deemed), India

G. Vinayagamoorthi
Alagappa University, India

M. Sudha
Acharya Institute of Graduate Studies, India

Joel Jebadurai Devapictahi
https://orcid.org/0000-0002-6947-8497
St. Joseph's College of Engineering, India

ABSTRACT

The pandemic is anticipated to have a significant economic impact, and it already has a terrible effect on schooling worldwide. Due to the coronavirus's quick spread, educational institutions worldwide are making the drastic leap from delivering course materials in person to doing so online. The rapid use of digital technology represents a significant paradigm change that may ultimately transform the Indian educational system. The COVID-19 scenario provides an opportunity to test new tools and technology to make education more relevant for students who cannot travel to campuses. With online learning and evaluation, there is a chance to increase knowledge and productivity while acquiring new skill sets and expedited professional talents. In this chapter, the authors have examined the educational difficulties and opportunities brought on by the sudden COVID-19 epidemic, followed by a discussion of how the Indian educational system has to be recalibrated.

DOI: 10.4018/978-1-6684-7450-1.ch009

INTRODUCTION

In recent times, especially after Covid-19, educational institutions are now incorporating social media innovations into their curriculum and relying on group resources and procedures to enhance the student experience. Social media use in the classroom enables students, teachers, and parents to connect with learning communities and other convenient educational systems and get more helpful information. Thanks to social networking applications, students and institutions have much potential to improve learning methods. Institutions can implement social media plugins that allow sharing and interaction through these networks. Online lessons on YouTube, distance learning courses from other universities through Skype, and a wealth of information shared on social media are all helpful to students.

Social media can provide helpful information for research purposes, such as analytics and insights on numerous topics or concerns. Being involved on as many social media platforms as possible as a school is essential because it helps you develop better student training programmes and shapes student culture. The benefit of social media in education is that students quickly discover who the authorities are in various sectors and subjects. Students are given the tools they need to accomplish outstanding results when they begin following these professionals and learning more from them.

Social media can broaden students' perspectives on various topics and instantly provides enlightening, new knowledge. As a result, students can consult professionals to get solutions to their questions. Educational institutions can communicate with students through social media platforms like Facebook, Google Plus groups, and YouTube. These platforms can be utilised to notify students about important information, disseminate school news, and make announcements. This increases interaction between the college and the students, which aids in resolving many student difficulties through group discussions.

Institutions can distribute encouraging and uplifting posts to all students on the networks and pages. So that students can participate in helpful online debates, academic institutions might start hashtag campaigns on social media. A video is a popular and beneficial tool in social media trends that can disseminate content that motivates students and aids them in their academic subjects. The exchanges between students and the school can be maintained using social media platforms like YouTube, Facebook, or Instagram live video. Social media's educational advantages need not end with the teacher-student interaction. Social networking usage at higher levels can also yield various additional benefits. Administrators or principals, for instance, can devise fresh ways to incorporate social media. Like disseminating school information via social media, they hosted an online parent meeting or even started fundraising efforts for various projects. Our fast-paced lives mean that social media can swiftly replace other forms of communication as parents are frequently preoccupied with work and unable to attend school events. However, this does not imply that they should not be aware of current affairs or be able to check in on their children periodically.

Social media is one of the best venues for data extraction because it provides valuable audience and subject-monitoring tools. Using tools like Instagram/Facebook polls, surveys with Google Forms or Survey Monkey, or online discussion boards like Quora, you may learn how most people feel about a given problem. This can assist students in gathering and producing pertinent study information. Some of the best data and outcomes may be gleaned from social media, whether students are working on an assignment, working on a project, or seeking more insight on a subject. Presentations of such data may be made with the aid of Slideshare. A learning management system (LMS) networking programme allows institutions to carry out additional administrative tasks and deliver educational programmes. In Learning Management Systems, social media learning can be accessed through video chat, forums for information sharing, and other lesson resources for students.

The LMS system improves student engagement and facilitates team project collaboration. This method was implemented to address concerns with students and learning to enhance educational programmes. Institutions should adopt well-known learning management systems with social media integration for the highest reach and impact through the system. Live conferencing tools, webinar functionality, the opportunity to share group reviews, blogs, and a lot more are further advantages of social learning. Additionally, teachers use social media as a networking tool and stay up to date on what is going on in classrooms around the world and find new resources to support their lessons, activities to teach specific concepts, ideas for bulletin boards, and information on new apps.

The bottom line is that social media plays a significant role in our daily lives. Thus there is no need to exclude it from the educational process. Staff at schools, colleges, and universities should be encouraged to use technology to communicate with parents and students. The advantages are clear, beginning with improved parent-teacher interactions and extending all the way to a long-term transformation of our children's learning.

Thus, everyone has been forced by 2020 to rely on social media platforms to the point where we are now social media-dependent creatures rather than just social animals. Every industry, including education, has become so reliant on social media platforms for staff productivity, efficiency, and output that they cannot envision operating without them. The COVID-19 spread has wholly shattered the world economy(Ahuja & Bala, 2021; Chahrour et al., 2020). Educational institutions have shifted from traditional classroom instruction to online instruction. The pandemic has caused the higher education system in most countries to move online, reflecting a need for additional digital technology training for teachers, particularly in nations and institutions adopting e-learning for the first time. There aren't many formal online learning management systems in public institutions, especially in developing countries like India. India's government has made it mandatory for higher education students to get their instruction online or in virtual classrooms rather than in person, following the lead of governments in many other nations. Asynchronous learning will require wisdom from instructors in real-time classrooms (Thangam & Chavadi, 2023). Al-Azawei, (2019) revealed that closing institutions/universities has disrupted students' studies globally, impeded crucial assessment times, and forced the postponement or cancellation of several university exams. Numerous schools or educational governing/regulatory authorities have directly promoted pupils to high levels.

In contrast, many institutions and colleges in higher education now choose online exams over traditional ones (Murugan et al., 2023). Covid-19 has ushered in a new age of education for instructors and students by causing a huge paradigm change in the educational field (Dill et al., 2020; Spina et al., 2020). So, to reach students in various geographic regions, today's educational system must urgently transition from traditional teaching to distant learning programmes and platforms. Governments and schools are looking at ways to let pupils get an education from home.

Continuing education is more crucial than ever in the current situation since doing so might negatively affect students' mental growth and well-being. Education is one of the few industries on the way to a good transformation after this devastating epidemic. With the help of e-learning, young students may become immersed in their studies without losing interest in their topics throughout the lockdown (Sriram et al., 2023). Adaptive learning gives teachers more flexibility when creating lesson plans and allows students to revisit these lessons as often as they choose. Social media is a tremendous asset to the nation's educational system regarding internet access. Social media play a huge role in education.

Given that the pandemic is still present, I don't believe we could continue living without social media. This chapter has covered the initial difficulties the educational community will experience in abruptly switching to digital learning platforms (Karumban et al., 2023). After providing a summary of some of the easily accessible online options used to provide students with online education, we recommended the procedures that educational institutions must follow to restart operations following Covid-19.

Existing Studies in This Field

Abu Elnasr E. Sobaih et al. (2022), In light of the COVID-19 pandemic, this study investigates the views of higher education students in India on using social media for online learning. An online survey was sent to a sample of Indian students enrolled in higher education for this purpose via a personal network. The findings demonstrated that students' evaluations of social media's usability and usability made them more satisfied with their use of it. Most students spend 1-2 hours daily on social media (p 0.01). The preferred platform among all respondents (n = 154; 36%) was YouTube. The findings supported students' perceptions that social media sites significantly improve academic performance (p 0.01). Maha Abdullah Al Shaher (2022) this research study uses a case study of KSA to perform an in-depth analysis of social media's role in government communication during the COVID-19 pandemic. The study aims to gain a thorough understanding of how the KSA government uses social media for official communications (Thangam et al., 2022). The study uses both primary and secondary sources of information, and the deductive method of analysis and the descriptive research methodology are used. According to the research report, the government of KSA has used social media extensively for official communications. Guru Charan Sharma (2021) examined how using social media in the teaching and learning process improved the results compared to not using it. As a result, it was determined that the Bihar government permits students and teachers to use smartphones for educational purposes and changes the "Mukhyamantri Cycle Yojana Scheme" to the "Mukhyamantri Mobile Yojana Scheme," which will result in a revolution in the digitisation of education.

Muhammad Naeem Khan et al. (2021), This study examines how college students use social media to address the crucial idea of CL during the COVID-19 pandemic. Understanding the connection between student performance and social media use is essential to comprehending social media's function during a pandemic. The technological acceptance model and constructivism theory are the foundations of this investigation. Using Smart PLS, structural equation modelling was utilised to examine the conceptual model (Park et al., 2022). According to the research's conclusions, social media is crucial during the pandemic because it allows students to improve their CL in the circumstances mentioned earlier. Jamal Abdul Nasir Ansari and Nawab Ali Khan (2020), This study found that students' academic performance was significantly impacted by the usage of online social media for collaborative learning, which also had a substantial impact on students' interaction with peers, teachers, and online knowledge sharing. Rodrigo Sandoval-Almazan (2021), this paper examines a case study that the ISSEMyM local Mexican government agency used.

The information from October 2017 to June 2020 is examined. According to the findings, the ISSEMyM government agency consistently uses Twitter and Facebook for communication. Also, it shows an improvement in communication flow and engagement over the past three years. We discovered that official local government correspondence remained unaltered over the whole time. However, the COVID-19 epidemic significantly changes interactions, followers, and user engagement. We found no interaction, follower count, or message structure change throughout this time. Priyanka Khurana (2019),

According to perceived convenience, efficacy, and perceived reliability, social networking sites are currently the most popular information sources, according to this survey. They have a beneficial impact on students and are regarded as cutting-edge digital tools for information transfer. Shahbaz Ahmed and Deepak Kumar (2019), According to this survey, high school students use social media more frequently for instructional and entertainment objectives than for social contact. Considering student inclinations and effectively utilising social media in teaching and learning can benefit teachers. Jehangir Pheroze Bharucha (2017), social media will undoubtedly continue to play a significant part in Indian education, but there are challenges in effectively integrating its use into curricula. Although social media will never completely replace traditional education in India, it does aid with evaluative procedures and enhance student learning, which may help students in future competitive job markets. Anindita Bose (2016) and Thangam et al. (2022), as per this study, use social media as a platform to communicate information, brand a product, stimulate word-of-mouth advertising, and drive customer involvement and connection. Still, according to this study, it cannot completely replace conventional promotional techniques.

Problem Statement

Due to the world's technological changes moving forward to socialisation, social media platforms have played a crucial role among the present generations. The connectivity of the current generations is more vibrant with users and spending more time in that. The marketers have understood this, and the government also understands the importance of social media and its inevitable among the youth. So the government had an idea to promote education through social media platforms, and later Covid-19 has boosted the entire world of education through social media platforms. This chapter discusses the benefits of social media education in India and how it's boomed in the Indian education sector.

Growth and Development of Social Media in the Education Sector

India's education sector is growing as a result of ongoing media backing. Media and education have a crucial role in the learning process. Media has the power to alter our perceptions of the world and our perceptions of ourselves. Older forms of media, including radio, television, newspapers, periodicals, and journals, helped spread knowledge and awareness. But in the 21st century, social media has revolutionised communication. People and organisations may stay in touch and informed by using numerous social media networks like Facebook, Twitter, YouTube, blogs, and webpages.

After the 1980s, during the surge in computer innovation that characterised the 1990s and 2000s, CD-ROMS were first introduced, making the Internet easier to use. 95% of adolescent students have access to a smartphone as of 2018, and 45% report being online nearly continuously. As technology and social media use increased, some parents and teachers contended that they were too distracting for the classroom setting. As a result, many schools blocked access to the Internet, including social media websites, and even outlawed cell phone use in class. These rules have been ineffectual as long as kids can bring their phones to style and can access social media sites despite the precautions made by school officials.

Because of these difficulties, several schools now have a "Bring Your Own Device" (BYOD) policy. In accordance with this policy, students are permitted to bring their own internet-enabled devices, such as a phone or iPad, to class so they can use the Internet for in-class projects and research. Although some administrators and teachers have seen other advantages, such as improved student enthusiasm and engagement and broader access to information, the BYOD concept was primarily adopted to cut departmental IT costs. Video calls, stories, feeds, and game playing on social media can all positively impact learning, both inside and outside of the classroom. Yet, social media-based language learning raises concerns about the possible difficulty of speaking with academics and lecturers in an informal setting.

Social media enables the classroom to continue after school hours and allows students to work together in a different format. Social media can divert children, but with self-control and self-direction, it can also be a tremendous tool. Because of social media, there are many new learning opportunities. One study advises appropriately separating social media learning into informal and formal academic education to address these opportunities (Thangam, 2022).

Educators are more and more recognising the relative benefits of social media in the teaching and learning process. Social media has established itself as a reliable tool for classroom learning and communication, from setting up school Facebook pages to connecting students with professionals via Twitter. Social media's highly linguistic nature enables us to produce and consume ideas and information in ways that have never been possible.

The use of social media in the classroom and among the school community is crucial since it is a potent communication facilitator. Parents, particularly moms, use social media platforms like Facebook to maintain relationships with their friends and the local community. Schools may easily transmit announcements, updates, and crucial information to parents via social media platforms like Facebook and Twitter. It may also open contact channels between teachers and students that aren't always present. By speaking privately to a teacher online, students who are reserved in person may become more open. It would also probably help to foster a stronger sense of community for the teacher and students to have an online communication channel. The Indian government is developing digital pedagogy for e-learning as part of a long-term plan for the education sector. It has aided in the development of a new, non-school learning era. To develop an improved learning environment for the students, the Ministry of Education is currently working on the idea of learning by all, with all, and for all. Major government initiatives for digital education are PM E-Vidya, Diksha, SWAYAM Prabha TV, and VidyaDaan.

Importance of Social Media in the Education Sector

Social media in education is utilising social media websites to improve student learning. "A range of Internet-based applications that build on the theoretical and technological foundations of the Web and that enable the creation and exchange of user-generated content" is the definition of social media. Because so many students waste their time and money on social media, the site has come under fire from many educators. Nonetheless, it provides numerous opportunities and options for interaction and information gathering, which can enhance their learning. Thus social media has played various vital roles in the education section, and they are explained as follows;

Aids Students to Succeed in Their Education.

People are constantly logged into social media sites and their phones today. Online learning has increased as a result of this. Students are using online content to learn in more significant numbers. Students can utilise social media as a powerful tool to interact with the outside world. It enables people to interact with individuals who can provide resources, discuss their work, and provide comments. Social media has advantages for academics, but it may also be a tool for students with emotional or mental health problems to take care of themselves.

Quick Online Conversations

Communication through social media is widespread. Connecting with like-minded individuals is possible for students, faculty, staff, prospective students, alumni, stakeholders, and the general public. They can establish networks, meet new people, and get their questions answered.

Effective Communication Channel

Effective communication between students and teachers is essential. Social media lets students connect online with friends, family, coworkers, peers, and teachers. Students become engaged participants who actively participate in learning.

Improves Learning and Networking

Students can attend lessons from e-learning websites and participate in discussions and information sharing using various social media platforms like YouTube, Udemy, Facebook, Instagram, etc. Apart from these, universities can use social media to connect with current and prospective students, researchers, other organisations, and staff members. But at its core, social media is about forming connections. Further, Students can connect with classmates, other university students, students studying in the same field at other institutions, and professionals in their area.

Enhanced Research Tool

Any student or instructor may quickly get top-notch research materials via social media in the classroom. They can find pertinent information by searching on Twitter, Facebook, Instagram, and YouTube about any subject about your institution.

Knowledge Transfer

Social media is a platform where students may share their knowledge and gain the respect of others in their chosen field(s) and specialisation (s). In an online community, students can also learn from people who are in comparable situations to suit their own or who have completed previous research of a similar nature.

Parental Satisfaction

Parents may choose the best Institute for their kids by quickly accessing and viewing the curriculum of the Institute better understand classes and professors. This aids in their understanding of the educational institution.

Reach Out Anytime

Social media is always in use. A person at three in the morning might be unable to respond immediately. However, since most social networks are not geographically restricted, there is a good chance that people will always be able to connect with people from around the world. People can also ask questions and wait for responses because social media communication is asynchronous.

Using YouTube to Help Students Learn New Skills

Although many people know that YouTube is an excellent resource for learning new skills, they might not be aware that it can also be used to impart knowledge. There are channels dedicated to particular topics, like knitting or cooking. These films can assist students in learning new skills without the need for additional teacher effort.

Student's Perceptive On the Usage of Social Media in Education

People may have unsettling ideas when they consider how students use social media. The inevitable conjunction is typically associated with something terrible. Adults worry that kids cannot conduct themselves maturely and appropriately out of fear or a lack of trust. These concerns can be legitimate, but if students are constantly taught how to use social media properly, they are more likely to share responsibly and constructively. Adults should get more involved with pupils' social media use to ease worries. For instance, parents should always friend or follow their children on all social media platforms they use. Social media access should be revoked for students who refuse to let their parents' friends follow them. Students are less likely to post, favourite, like, share, or retweet inappropriate content when parents actively monitor their online behaviour.

Clear boundaries and a positive approach are crucial when talking to pupils about inappropriate behaviour on social media. By maintaining this balance, kids will recognise that social media should be used responsibly and feel as though they have a committed support structure at home and school. Adults might adopt a more motivating strategy rather than reprimanding students and concentrating only on their shortcomings. If students feel supported and are reminded that they have a variety of adults to turn to for guidance, they are more likely to respond appropriately. Additionally, if adults and students understand social media equally, student use may increase positively. Adults could point pupils in the proper direction and recommend educational resources if they had a solid understanding of social media. This means that both adults and students should explore new social media platforms.

It can be challenging to address the subject of social media usage with pupils unless you've built up their trust. Students should be made aware of social media as soon as possible to make the topic easy to address. Early discussion of the subject and direction-finding by parents and teachers are essential. A teacher may use an intriguing item they found on Twitter as bell work at the start of the class. Students are demonstrated how social media can be used for education in this way. Students are more likely to understand the message that they are not invincible if they receive counsel on social media at home and at school. One of the most pervasive myths about social media that students have is undoubtedly this one. Boundaries appear to elude many kids since they have grown up in a time when having social media at their fingertips is entirely normal.

Although adults want to shield students from the harmful content on social media, it's essential to let them know it's there. Students learn that they are not free to post, like, or share whatever they want by watching a video or reading an article about someone who was punished for inappropriately using social media. Additionally, because they typically aren't exposed to the idea, most students don't use social media for educational purposes. While tweeting famous people or posting pictures of one's lunch online isn't harmful, it doesn't seem to have the same impact as being made aware of resources that could aid one's educational development.

Teachers and parents should share any trustworthy social media sources that may be used to advance education immediately. Students may be motivated to go above and above and conduct independent research by being given the easy task of reading an article for homework or writing down a few social media resources on the classroom whiteboard. Students become more conscious of their social media use with the assistance of committed parents and teachers. If the idea of responsibly using the resource is repeatedly brought up during the school day, it will become a universally accepted expectation that kids follow.

Social Media in Education: Teachers' Perspective

Social media has ingrained itself into every student's life with the development of internet technology. Social networks make communicating, sharing information, and staying connected more uncomplicated and comfortable. Social media platforms allow teachers and students to keep in touch while serving instructional purposes. Thanks to social networks, students and educational institutions now have more opportunities to enhance teaching-learning. Students benefit from online tutorials offered by sites like SlideShare, Quora, and ResearchGate. These platforms provide helpful informational resources for improving knowledge bases.

Students can make contacts on social media that can help them in their future jobs. Educational institutions must be active on as many social media platforms as possible since this promotes better student engagement techniques and more participatory, inclusive learning. Professors can organise live sessions, provide extra support to students, and broaden the scope of learning outside the classroom by using their Twitter, Facebook, or even messaging platforms like WhatsApp. They can coordinate discussions about their subjects or homework assignments on social media platforms. Thus, social media facilitates communication between educators and students away from the classroom.

The ability to undertake personal branding on social media is one of the primary factors driving academics to adapt to social media in and outside the classroom. This helps them establish a reputation in the academic community. Professors can promote their expertise on social media platforms, including Facebook, Twitter, numerous blogging platforms, and YouTube. These websites are very well-liked by students and can therefore aid in building a solid reputation.

By doing so, the teaching fraternity realises how social media impacts personal and professional lives. Social media is increasingly being used to establish connections outside of the classroom. It promotes enrollment and enhances the Institute's reputation in the community. College student welfare offices use social media to interact with students and solve their concerns. Additionally, it is being used to promote campus life and create robust alumni networks. Social media platforms are utilised in the classroom to facilitate contact with classmates and, possibly, those beyond the school. Through Facebook live sessions, you can communicate with subject-matter experts.

Institutional Perceptive on Social Media in the Education

Everyone has been forced by 2020 to rely on social media platforms to the point where we are now social media-dependent creatures rather than just social animals. Every industry, including education, has become so reliant on social media platforms for staff productivity, efficiency, and output that they cannot envision operating without them. As an educator, the response is now required from the beginning to the end. In this case, social media tools like WhatsApp and emailing are used for direct communication. In the same vein, social media has shown to be helpful for educators and students during this pandemic.

These days, social media is moving in a more positive direction, keeping people occupied working on projects for their respective industries. People share important notifications, electronic certificates of achievement, and newsletters on social media instead of sharing meaningless content. Instead of playing online games, kids are more engaged in an online exploration of 3-D modelling and animation and sharing these creations and activities with their peers and teachers.

A study on worldwide social media conducted in August 2020 indicates that the growth rate is as follows:Globally, 3.81 billion individuals were actively using social media in 2020, up 9.2% from 3.48 billion in 2019, according to data from Statista. There were just 2.07 billion users in 2015. Digital India estimates 400 million social media users in India as of January 2020, an increase of 130 million from April 2019. It will be essential to remember that social media had an unlimited and immeasurable scope while discussing its potential future characteristics.

The Global Web Index predicts that social media will significantly impact product research and markets among mobile customers by 2030. According to Facebook, 80% of smartphone users are expected to use a mobile messaging app by 2030. According to Mark Zuckerberg, the video will be the more critical business driver and determining factor over the coming years. The latest statistics on social video adoption from Global Web Index show that audience demand is still rising. 56% of internet users view videos on Facebook, Twitter, Snapchat, or Instagram each month, while 81% of people aged 55 to 64 do the same.

On the other hand, social networking should enhance your life rather than take over your entire existence. It's essential to cease doom-scrolling because it might generate anxiety and sadness. According to Esther, the founder of the law of attraction, your life only reflects how dominantly you think. Most platforms use artificial intelligence to provide you control over the posts and the channels you wish to engage with the most on social media. These clever tools assist you in curating your feeds and removing the posts you want to see less of.

Social media use should be limited to prevent it from dominating private lives. Everyone has a right to their personal space. Every problematic situation teaches a lesson, and this year we faced a challenging position where our only alternative was to increase our screen usage. The new strategy will take a hybrid approach that balances our connections and social media since time is rapidly ending. I pray Corona leaves us soon, going through just the beneficial lessons it has imparted.

Social Media in the Education Sector: During and After Covid-19

Platforms for social media are among the simplest and most efficient ways to spread information. Social media has emerged as the main channel for mass digital communication across various groups over the last ten years. The power of the Internet to promote networking is making it more and more frequent to interact with people with similar beliefs, interests, or objectives. Self-regulation of learning is crucial for coping with e-learning since students are in charge of their own education in online contexts. Worldwide school closures are a result of Covid-19 (Thangam, 2022). Almost 1.2 billion youngsters are not in school worldwide. As a result, education has undergone a significant transformation because of the particular growth of e-learning, in which lessons are delivered online and through digital platforms. Online learning has been demonstrated to improve retention of information and require less time, according to research, suggesting that the alterations brought on by the coronavirus may be long-lasting; teachers can improve connections with students, students and instructors, and with individuals and resources beyond the classroom by using social media. These are crucial for a student to feel a part of the educational community. By using social media themselves, teachers can get professional advantages through just-in-time teaching resources and social or emotional support from institutions outside of their own.

Social media and technology are an essential part of daily life. Because so many individuals are accustomed to them, incorporating their use into the classroom is more natural than ever. Every social media site has a variety of educational applications, including sharing announcements, hosting live lectures, and much more. First, social media gives students, instructors, and parents a smoother, more direct way to communicate; they can check in and ask or answer questions. Social networking may assist in teaching students how to work remotely, which is a vital lesson as remote employment and online education grow in popularity. Before adopting social media in education, it's critical to understand its effects, but we firmly believe that it will increase students' technological proficiency. Online learning has always been seen as a viable alternative, especially for students looking for higher education alternatives. Nonetheless, the COVID-19 pandemic's rise has forced educators and students at all educational levels to acclimate to online courses quickly. Numerous new developments in education will have made widespread acceptance of online learning a reality. Access is a significant issue. Many issues still exist in this area, such as the fact that some areas, particularly rural ones, lack Internet connectivity, and those different family members have varying demands for home technology usage. Innovative solutions have evolved to give students and families the facilities and resources they require to participate in and effectively complete the curriculum (Thangam, 2022). For example, school buses have been used to provide mobile hotspots, class packets have been sent by mail, and instructional presentations aired on local public broadcasting stations. 2020 has also seen increased availability and adoption of electronic resources and activities that can now be integrated into online learning experiences. Synchronous online conferencing systems, such as Zoom and Google Meet, have allowed experts from anywhere in the world to join online classrooms and have allowed presentations to be recorded for individual learners to watch at the most convenient time.

Suggestion

Social media is very beneficial for students and gives them a lot of exposure while they are learning. During COVID-19, social media technologies also became more practical, demonstrating a new learning method in the educational sector and assisting in times of crisis. Students, however, became more reliant, self-isolated and addicted without any awareness of the consequences. As a result, students can set up a social media schedule, which is a terrific approach to encourage discipline and allow kids to use social media or replace the time on social media with other activities. Due to security concerns, social media is a contributing factor in cyberbullying. This may impact the institutions, teachers, and students. Hence establishing rigorous privacy rules that limit access to your profile is necessary to maintain the highest level of safety.

Social media occasionally contains a lot of unsuitable stuff that is destructive and goes beyond moral bounds. The government must implement a new age verification system for adults to access social media. This will help adults avoid harsh repercussions and safeguard children from inappropriate content.

It is of utmost importance for students to be physically and mentally well. Students who use social media too much may endanger their health by skipping sleep and developing a sedentary lifestyle. It is common knowledge that students spend their days and nights glued to their phones or computer displays. To maximise the benefits of social media, students should use it sparingly and to further their academic goals. Government initiatives to bring several programs to improve education in rural areas receive little technical backing. Hence, free mobile phones that provide all notes without network connectivity must be available to students in remote areas.

CONCLUSION

Digitalization has helped the education sector as a result of global technical improvements. Digital education is the newest cutting-edge method for rapidly and widely disseminating knowledge. Also, other states worldwide are concerned about the standard of education. Everyone now has more convenient access to information and means of timely communication because of the rapid development of social media and social networking sites, particularly in developing nations like India. It is becoming a significant daily life component for teachers and students. Students who desire the ease and flexibility of learning remotely have a valued and feasible choice in online education. While it has its obstacles and limitations, it can give several benefits, including decreased costs and the ability to access educational resources anywhere in the world.

REFERENCES

Abu Elnasr, E. (2022). Social Media Use in E-Learning amid COVID 19 Pandemic: Indian Students' Perspective. *International Journal of Environmental Research and Public Health, 19*(9), 5380. doi:10.3390/ijerph19095380 PMID:35564771

Ahmed, S., & Kumar, D. (2019, March). The influence of Social media in Education system: The Case of Digital India. *International Journal of Research in Advent Technology*, (Special Issue), 175–179.

Al-Azawei, A. (2019). What Drives Successful Social Media in Education and E-Learning? A Comparative Study on Facebook and Moodle. *Journal of Information Technology Education, 18*, 18. doi:10.28945/4360

Anindita, B. (2016). Social Media and Education Sector: Enriching Relationship. *Commentary-4 Global Media Journal–Indian Edition Sponsored by the University of Calcutta, 7*(1). https://www.caluniv.ac.in/global-mdia-journal/COMMENT-2016-NOV/C4.pdf

Ansari, J. A. N., & Khan, N. A. (2020). Exploring the role of social media in collaborative learning the new domain of learning. *Smart Learn. Environ., 7*(1), 9. doi:10.118640561-020-00118-7

Bharucha, J. (2018). Exploring education-related use of social media: Business students perspectives in a changing India. *Education + Training, 60*(2), 198–212. doi:10.1108/ET-07-2017-0105

Bose, A. (2016),"Social Media And Education Sector: Enriching Relationship"Global Media Journal – Indian Edition Sponsored by the University of Calcutta, 7.

Chavadi, C. (2021). Growth drivers, characteristics, preference and challenges faced by Fast Moving Consumer Goods-A study with reference to Bengaluru. *Turkish Online Journal of Qualitative Inquiry, 12*(7).

Chavadi, C. A., Arul, M. J., & Sirothiya, M. (2020). Modelling the effects of creative advertisements on consumers: An empirical study. *Vision (Basel), 24*(3), 269–283. doi:10.1177/0972262920926074

Chavadi, C. A., Hiremath, C. V., & Hyderabad, R. L. (2014). Customer loyalty appraisal based on store characteristics: An alternative approach. *Indian Journal of Marketing, 44*(5), 18–29. doi:10.17010/ijom/2014/v44/i5/80375

Chavadi, C. A., & Kokatnur, S. S. (2008). Consumer Expectation and Perception of Fast Food Outlets: An Empirical Study in Davangere. *ICFAI Journal Of Services Marketing, 6*(2).

Chavadi, C. A., & Kokatnur, S. S. (2009). Impact of Short-Term Promotional Ads on Food Retailing. *ICFAI Journal of Consumer Behavior, 4*(1).

Chavadi, C. A., & Kokatnur, S. S. (2009). RFID Adoption by Indian Retailers: An Exploratory Study. *The Icfai University Journal of Supply Chain Management, 6*(1), 60–77.

Chavadi, C. A., Menon, S. R., & Sirothiya, M. (2019). Measuring Service Quality Perceptions of Indian E-retailers: An Evaluative Study. *Metamorphosis, 18*(2), 92–102. doi:10.1177/0972622519886232

Chavadi, C. A., Menon, S. R., & Sirothiya, M. (2019). Modelling the Effects of Brand Placements in Movies: An Investigative Study of Event Type and Placement Type. *Vision (Basel), 23*(1), 31–43. doi:10.1177/0972262918821227

Chavadi, C. A., Vishwanatha, M. R., & Mubeen, S. (2018). Ghee with Glee: A Study of How Consumers Evaluate Product Packaging. *Metamorphosis, 17*(2), 100–110. doi:10.1177/0972622518817407

Guru Charan Sharma. (2021). The Digitalization of Education Through Social Media. *International Journal of Creative Research Thoughts, 9*(5). https://ijcrt.org/papers/IJCRT2105473.pdf

Hiremath, C. V., Chavadi, C. A., & Yatgiri, P. Y. (2013). Cloud Technology as an Alternative for Marketing Information System: An Empirical Study. *International Journal of Management. Research and Business Strategy, 2*(4).

Karumban, S., Sanyal, S., Laddunuri, M. M., Sivalinga, V. D., Shanmugam, V., Bose, V., & Murugan, S. P. (2023). Industrial Automation and Its Impact on Manufacturing Industries. In Revolutionizing Industrial Automation Through the Convergence of Artificial Intelligence and the Internet of Things (pp. 24-40). IGI Global.

Khan, M. N., Ashraf, M. A., Seinen, D., Khan, K. U., & Laar, R. A. (2021). Social Media for Knowledge Acquisition and Dissemination: The Impact of the COVID-19 Pandemic on Collaborative Learning Driven Social Media Adoption. *Frontiers in Psychology, 12*, 648253. doi:10.3389/fpsyg.2021.648253 PMID:34135814

Radwan, M. (2022). The Role of Social Media in Government Communication during Covid-19 Pandemic: The Case of KSA. *Journal of Social Sciences, 10*, 368–383.

Menon, S. R., & Chavadi, C. A. (2022). A Research-based Approach to Identify the Health-conscious Consumers in India. *Metamorphosis, 21*(2), 118–128. doi:10.1177/09726225221098783

Murugan, S. P., Shivaprasad, G., Dhanalakshmi, A., Sriram, V. P., Rajput, K., Mahesh, B. N., & Kedla, S. (2023). The Impact of COVID-19 on the Indian Microfinance Industry and Its Sustainability. In *Transforming Economies Through Microfinance in Developing Nations* (pp. 160–188). IGI Global. doi:10.4018/978-1-6684-5647-7.ch009

Park, J. Y., Perumal, S. V., Sanyal, S., Ah Nguyen, B., Ray, S., Krishnan, R., Narasimhaiah, R., & Thangam, D. (2022). Sustainable Marketing Strategies as an Essential Tool of Business. *American Journal of Economics and Sociology, 81*(2), 359–379. doi:10.1111/ajes.12459

Khurana, P. (2019). Digital Education: Impact of Social Media in Quality Higher Education, *An international peer-Reviewed open Access. Journal of Interdisciplinary Studies, 2*(1). https://www.gapinterdisciplinarities.org/res/articles/(372-375).pdf

Sandoval-Almazan, R., & Valle-Cruz, D. (2021). Social Media Use in Government Health Agencies: The COVID-19 Impact. *Information Polity, 26*(4), 459–475. doi:10.3233/IP-210326

Sirothiya, M., & Chavadi, C. (2020). Compressed biogas (cbg) as an alternative and sustainable energy source in India: Case study on implementation frameworks and challenges. *Invertis Journal of Renewable Energy, 10*(2), 49–64. doi:10.5958/2454-7611.2020.00007.7

Sirothiya, M., & Chavadi, C. (2020). Evaluating marketing strategies ofcompressed biogas (CBG) companies in India using decision tree analysis. *IIMS Journal of Management Science, 11*(3), 219–237. doi:10.5958/0976-173X.2020.00012.0

Sirothiya, M., & Chavadi, C. (2020). Role of compressed biogas to assess the effects of perceived value on customer satisfaction and customer loyalty. *BIMTECH Bus. Perspect, 1*, 70–89.

Sriram, V. P., Sanyal, S., Laddunuri, M. M., Subramanian, M., Bose, V., Booshan, B., & Thangam, D. (2023). Enhancing Cybersecurity Through Blockchain Technology. In Handbook of Research on Cybersecurity Issues and Challenges for Business and FinTech Applications (pp. 208-224). IGI Global.

Thangam, D., Arumugam, T., Velusamy, K., Subramanian, M., Ganesan, S. K., & Suryakumar, M. (2022). COVID-19 Pandemic and Its Brunt on Digital Transformation and Cybersecurity. In Cybersecurity Crisis Management and Lessons Learned From the COVID-19 Pandemic (pp. 15-42). IGI Global.

Thangam, D., & Chavadi, C. (2023). Impact of Digital Marketing Practices on Energy Consumption, Climate Change, and Sustainability. *Climate and Energy, 39*(7), 11–19. doi:10.1002/gas.22329

Thangam, D., Malali, A. B., Subramanian, G., Mohan, S., & Park, J. Y. (2022). Internet of things: a smart technology for healthcare industries. In *Healthcare Systems and Health Informatics* (pp. 3–15). CRC Press.

Thangam, D., Malali, A. B., Subramanian, G., & Park, J. Y. (2022). Transforming Healthcare through Internet of Things. In *Cloud and Fog Computing Platforms for Internet of Things* (pp. 15–24). Chapman and Hall/CRC. doi:10.1201/9781003213888-2

Thangam, D., Malali, A. B., Subramaniyan, G., Mariappan, S., Mohan, S., & Park, J. Y. (2022). Relevance of Artificial Intelligence in Modern Healthcare. In *Integrating AI in IoT Analytics on the Cloud for Healthcare Applications* (pp. 67–88). IGI Global. doi:10.4018/978-1-7998-9132-1.ch005

Thangam, D., Malali, A. B., Subramaniyan, S. G., Mariappan, S., Mohan, S., & Park, J. Y. (2021). Blockchain Technology and Its Brunt on Digital Marketing. In Blockchain Technology and Applications for Digital Marketing (pp. 1-15). IGI Global. doi:10.4018/978-1-7998-8081-3.ch001

Thangam, D., Vaidya, G. R., Subramanian, G., Velusamy, K., Selvi Govindarajan, K., & Park, J. Y. (2022). The Portrayal of Women's Empowerment in Select Indian Movies. *American Journal of Economics and Sociology*, *81*(1), 187–205. doi:10.1111/ajes.12451

Chapter 10
Exploring the Significance of Media Psychology in Human Communication During the Era of Digitalization

R. Sankar Ganesh

https://orcid.org/0000-0003-0708-8327

Veltech Rangarajan Dr. Sagunthala R&D Institute of Science and Technology, India

B. Ganesh

Am Maxwell International Institute for Education and Research, India

Nadia Sha

College of Commerce and Business Administration, Oman

M. S. R. Mariyappan

Veltech Rangarajan Dr. Sagunthala R&D Institute of Science and Technology, India

T. Srividhya

Periyar University, India

R. Lakshmi Priya

Am Maxwell International Institute for Education and Research, India

ABSTRACT

The topic of media psychology is multidisciplinary, and people's interactions with media in many spheres of their lives from work to education to entertainment to social engagement are ever-evolving. By fusing a comprehension of human behaviour, cognition, and emotion with a comparable comprehension of media technology, media psychologists seek to provide answers to these problems. As the globe gets more linked, media is now present in practically every aspect of life and is becoming a more essential field of study. Media psychology, in contrast to some media studies, is not merely about the content. Media psychology takes the entire system into account. Understanding the effects of technology depends heavily on psychology. By merging their knowledge of human behaviour, cognition, and emotion, media psychologists seek out answers and solutions.

DOI: 10.4018/978-1-6684-7450-1.ch010

INTRODUCTION

In the past decade, media has undergone significant transformations, driven by the explosion of new communication technologies. These advancements have brought waves of change to the lives of individuals worldwide who have access to these technologies. Media psychology, as a field of study, explores how individuals perceive, interpret, apply, and respond to a world dominated by media. It is important to recognize that media psychology is a relatively new academic and practical discipline that has emerged in response to the prevalence of communication technology over the past 50 years. The field has evolved into a professional domain due to its social and practical relevance, incorporating psychological frameworks within media contexts (Rutledge, 2012). The multidisciplinary nature of media psychology, along with the evolving ways in which people interact with media across various aspects of their lives, including work, education, entertainment, and social engagement, is constantly changing. The goal of media psychologists is to address these evolving dynamics by combining an understanding of human behavior, cognition, and emotion with an equivalent understanding of media technology. In today's interconnected world, where media is present in almost every area of life, the study of media has become increasingly important as the world becomes more connected. Unlike some media studies that solely focus on content, media psychology takes a holistic view of the system as a whole. Psychology plays a crucial role in understanding the impact of technology. Media psychologists strive to find answers and solutions by combining our understanding of human behavior, cognition, and emotion with insights into media technology.

Media psychology is a newly emerged field within psychology that focuses on examining how individuals are influenced by mediated communication. While it draws heavily from psychology and communication, media psychology also integrates insights from various other scientific disciplines such as sociology, media studies, anthropology, and fan studies. However, the field remains scattered across multiple disciplines, with many researchers investigating the effects of media on individuals who do not primarily identify as psychologists. It is worth noting that media psychology represents an ongoing, interconnected cycle involving technology developers, content producers, content awareness, and user reactions. Its approach differs from previous research by providing a fresh perspective for comprehending and clarifying the theoretical structure of communication. On another front, digitalization and globalization have significantly altered human interactions. Human communication revolves around fulfilling the fundamental needs of association and interaction, encompassing collective activities involving the exchange of ideas, facts, and data between individuals. Prior to the development of spoken language, human communication relied on cues and gestures for centuries (Meyer, Allen & Smith, 1993). Since the advent of mobile phones and social media in the late 2000s, extensive research has explored the impact of technology on social interaction and personal communication (Przybylski and Weinstein, 2013). In one study, researchers examined the correlation between the presence of mobile devices and the quality of face-to-face social interactions in real-world settings. From a near-natural perspective, conversations conducted without mobile communication technology received significantly higher ratings compared to those involving mobile devices (Misra, Cheng, Genevie, and Yuan, 2014). It was observed that individuals who engaged in conversations without using a mobile device reported higher levels of empathic concern, whereas those who conversed in the presence of a mobile device reported lower levels of empathy (Reeve, 2016).

Another study yielded similar results, indicating that the presence of mobile communication devices in social settings has an impact on relationships (Przybylski& Weinstein, 2013). From an educational science perspective, the choice of technical terminology in the digital realm and the presentation approach that emphasizes analog elements are of great importance. Incorrect selection of digital elements can lead to significant disruptions for both individuals and the social environment. This holds true for new media technologies in academic as well as non-intellectual environments. Psychology plays a vital role in comprehending the implications of integrating media technology into society. The field encompasses a wide range of human experiences with media, including effectiveness, cognition, and behavior. Moreover, it greatly influences events, activities, theoretical models, and their practical applications. Media encompasses various forms of intermediary communication, such as images, sounds, and other mediums. Additionally, new technologies are an integral part of the media landscape. Media psychology presents a significant opportunity to creatively and innovatively employ media by understanding the interaction between psychology and media (Piocuda, et al,. 2015). Psychological theories can be applied to pioneering approaches in emerging fields like social media, e-learning, and digital technology. Exploring the relationship between media psychology and diverse fields such as sociology, communication, international relations, and anthropology is also crucial (Rutledge, 2012). As media-driven technology rapidly spreads in society, there is a growing need for media psychology. With new gadgets entering the market every day, it is important to acknowledge that these technologies are reshaping the way we work, play, and communicate on a daily basis. Media psychologists can assist individuals in adapting to higher levels of technological advancement. Discipline is also essential to ensure that journalists and other media professionals adhere to professional requirements and ethical standards (Weiner, 2012). Furthermore, this field serves as a reminder that individuals have diverse experiences with media technology based on their culture, personality, and other attitudinal factors.

IMPORTANCE OF MEDIA PSYCHOLOGY IN THE DIGITAL AGE

Media psychology is crucial in today's society due to the omnipresence of media technologies. These technologies are constantly evolving at an unprecedented pace, presenting us with both exciting opportunities and complex challenges. They have a profound impact on various aspects of our lives, transforming our work patterns, recreational activities, modes of communication, and even our cognitive processes (Chen & Li, 2017). Consequently, media psychology plays a vital role in understanding and navigating this dynamic landscape. As a result Media psychology is important, for the following reasons;

Hurried Change Is Difficult

Navigating rapid technological change can be challenging for individuals as it elicits a range of reactions, from excitement to skepticism. Adapting our perspectives to embrace these changes is not strength inherent in human nature. To address this dilemma, media psychology emerges as a valuable field. It delves into the interactions between individuals, groups, society, and technology, offering insights to consumers, developers, communicators, and society as a whole, aiding them in making informed decisions. Media and technology possess immense power, capable of promoting tremendous good or unleashing unchecked harm. Like psychology in general, media psychology aims to alleviate problems and foster positive and productive outcomes (Hanna, 2014).

Although media psychology officially became an academic discipline in the early 1980s, it has gained prominence with the advent of the Internet and social media. Drawing upon years of valuable theory and research from diverse fields and disciplines, this field has been fueled by our collective concern over the impact of traditional media on individuals and society. Topics such as the influence of media on children, portrayals of violence, manipulation of consumers, and information overload have driven extensive research (Roberts & David, 2020). The introduction of social media has further complicated and interconnected the media landscape.

Transitioning From Traditional Broadcast Media to Networked Media

Information flows back and forth, shaping the narratives that shape our worldview. The abundance of media sources exceeds any individual's capacity to consume and process, leading to the creation of self-curated filter bubbles and eroding trust. It is understandable that this complexity breeds anxiety and prompts researchers to address societal issues (Klinger &Svensson, 2015). However, finding easy answers is challenging, particularly because media and technology behaviors occur within real-life contexts, rather than isolated laboratory settings.

Even well-intentioned researchers are susceptible to biases and tunnel vision when responding to social and moral panics. It is natural to idealize the "good old days" and use previous eras as a benchmark for how things should operate and how the world should be. This tendency skews research by framing the past as a gold standard and measuring the present as a deviation. As our understanding of media becomes more nuanced, a growing body of research focuses on the positive applications of media technologies and envisions the potential benefits of what could be, rather than solely identifying what is lacking (Roberts & David, 2020).

Even Socrates Worried About Media

The fear of change is a common human response that dates back to ancient times. In Ancient Greece, Socrates expressed concerns about the advent of writing, fearing that it relied too heavily on external objects, neglected the power of the mind, and lacked flexibility due to the permanence of written words. This distrust towards new technology can be seen throughout history, as evidenced by early references to writing in the Western tradition. Today, our fears have shifted towards the fluidity of electronic media and the blurred boundaries between authors and readers. We worry about the impact of social media and data science, which have made us feel exposed and vulnerable. These concerns extend beyond the loss of privacy; they encompass the spread of misinformation and the erosion of trust in institutions, official processes, and even science itself. Nugent (2005), the President of Kenyon College, aptly compares this fear to a narrative pattern of "killing the bearer of the message." When faced with unfamiliar technology, those who do not understand it often seek to control the easy exchange between the internal and external worlds facilitated by the technology. Similar anxieties were voiced by Homer and Plato, who worried about the potential secrecy arising from individual writings. Today, our worries center on the risks posed by social media, the manipulation of data, and the consequences of information being readily available.

Hardwired to Perceive Change, Not to Like It

Given that a change in the environment increases the likelihood of danger, it is known that human brains are programmed to detect change. It was crucial to pay attention to anything moving on the Savannah. Tigers with sabre teeth could manoeuvre and posed a threat. Trees had no harmful effects. Nothing was more crucial to staying alive. Despite the fact that our brains are hardwired for an older world and that we live in a new one, change is not the threat that it may seem to be (Misra, Cheng, Genevie, & Yuan, 2014).The idea of equilibrium is alluring because it makes the universe predictable and comprehensible. But even physics falls short for us. The rules of thermodynamics explain how energy in a system fluctuates, leading to abrupt rather than gradual changes when matter transitions between states. These phase changes, such as when water turns into ice, happen all at once rather than gradually (Rutledge, 2015). Systems adhere to unique mathematical rules that, like our incapacity to deal logically with probability, are frequently in opposition to our ingrained cognitive biases.

Conflict Is Caused by Change

We want to believe there are obvious solutions and explanations because it helps us feel secure and at ease. We wouldn't have to be concerned about the effects of things we don't fully comprehend if everything remained in place. However, they don't. Sometimes they undergo significant modification. The printing press, the telegraph, and the internet all heralded a sudden transformation with broad social repercussions (Rutledge, 2015). Technology that makes it more difficult to control information is not particularly well liked by gatekeepers, if knowledge is power. Conflict results, and there is an unsettling degree of change in both the political climate and how we go about our daily lives.

ROLE OF MEDIA PSYCHOLOGY IN UNDERSTANDING AND ANTICIPATING CHANGE

In order to better understand and prepare for change, media psychology fills this gap. In order to help consumers and producers make better decisions, researchers hypothesise, operationalize, and measure the influence of media. Each of us performs the functions of a consumer, a producer, and a distributor, and our decisions have an impact on our perceptions as well as those of others.When we want to assign causation to events in order to make them understandable because we are order-seeking beings (Akhmetzyanova, 2016). It gets harder and harder to accomplish that. Even in the field of psychological science, as in any other, the standard of the research varies, as do the inferences that can be made from it. The way a question is posed, what is measured, how it is measured, and how the results are interpreted all have a significant impact on the research. This is complicated by a number of cognitive biases: we assume that numbers are facts, some of which are representative of "truth;" we frequently look for information that supports our worldview; we prioritise items that we have recently seen; and we are vulnerable to framing (Akhmetzyanova, Artemyeva, Nigmatullina, &Tvardovskaya, 2017). It's easy to see how research isn't always as straightforward as you'd like when you consider the widespread misunderstanding of the distinction between correlation (related to) and causation (caused by). The fact that many "findings" that ultimately affect public opinion and public policy are based on press releases from the sponsoring organisations or on a journalist's interpretation only serves to muddle matters further.

Mass media is the primary focus of the majority of studies that we would classify as media psychology, and with good reason. Mass media changed the game by making information, pictures, and culture accessible to a larger portion of society and the global community. The public was thought to be subject to a one-way flow of influence from media conglomerates, advertisers, and governmental entities (Mossbridge, Tressoldi, & Utts, 2012). This tradition of media effects has given rise to a number of theories, such as the silver bullet, media framing and uses and gratifications (people use media to gratify needs), and they have changed the way we think about media consumers from seeing them as a passive and homogenous audience to one that is driven by individual differences and motivations. Bandura's model of social cognitive theory is one of few psychological or media theories that is system-based, integrating the effects of a system of actions and influences among individual consumers, providers, and the social environment despite the unique dynamics of social networks. This is in contrast to arguments for reciprocity between individuals and our cultural environment (Mossbridge, Tressoldi, & Utts, 2012).

UNDERSTANDING MEDIA PSYCHOLOGY AND HUMAN COMMUNICATION

Media psychology, one of the most recent developing subfields of dynamic psychology, focuses on understanding how media technology and human behaviour interact in our increasingly digital world. Psychology is extending its reach to better understand the psychological impact of human connection with technology around the globe at various societal levels because research indicates that 90% of our everyday communications are now screen-based through mobile technologies. Social media's success is greatly influenced by psychology, which also has an impact on how company owners use various social media platforms to advertise their goods and services. In order to appeal to customers, you must appeal to their emotions (Ivanovna, 2016). It is crucial for creating lasting customer ties.By fusing knowledge of human behaviour, cognition, and emotions with a similar knowledge of media technology, media psychologists hope to provide some answers to these problems. Media psychology, in contrast to some media studies, is not just focused on the content. The psychological examination of the origins and effects of human media consumption is known as media psychology. The goal of media psychology research is to comprehend and provide explanations for the functions, applications, methods, and outcomes of mediated communication (Patwardhan & Ramaprasad, 2005). It is interdisciplinary in nature and draws from a variety of fields, including social, developmental, and personality psychology, public opinion, marketing, sociology, communication, and political science. Media psychology serves as a bridge between the media and how people react to it. There are occasionally difficult and unusual legal and ethical issues with implications. Psychology is typically learned one theory at a time, and as one gains more knowledge, one starts to combine and apply theories. Media psychology is both an art and a science and is the result of applying psychology to media, technology, and communication (Ivanovna, 2016).

The study of media psychology is concerned with the way that media and technology affect human behaviour. It emphasises technological development and uses critical analysis in conjunction with the investigation to create a model of how people perceive the media. It is used to society as a whole or even to an individual (Saifullina & Akhmetzyanova, 2018). In order to liberate positive capabilities, empower technology users, producers, and distributors in ways that satisfy the fundamental motivations behind human behaviour, and advance society as a whole across all domains, media psychology plays a key role. According to a survey, middle school students use social media to keep up with classmates' activities, share photos, and communicate with them. According to a survey, middle school students use social media to interact with peers, upload images, and find out what their pals are up to. Depression, anxiety, attachment, self-identity, and the drive to fit in are other psychological aspects of social media (Palermo, Benedetti, Costa & Amanzio, 2015). Media psychology encompasses all forms of mediated communication and media technology-related behaviours, including the usage, design, impact, and sharing behaviours. It is not just concerned with mass media or media content. Because of technological improvement, this branch is a relatively recent subject of study. Research indicates that long-term media exposure leads to insensitivity in a person and makes them less sensitive to events that might have in the past had a significant impact on them. For example, long-term media exposure to violence changes how a person views violence.

Media Psychology in Information Processing

From a biological standpoint, we are aware that because environmental change increases the likelihood of danger, human brains are designed to detect change. There are various hypotheses on how we comprehend what we see and hear. According to the culturalist perspective, media meaning or interpretation is arbitrary or personal. Different people can interpret the same material in different ways since perception requires using all of the senses and providing meaning to all of the information that is taken in (Mustaffa, 2013). The memory is organised in recurring patterns known as scripts or schemata, which contain associations that are triggered by fresh events. Every time we encounter something new, more informational tidbits are added to the scripts that already exist. Our belief systems, attitudes, and wants have an impact on perception as well. For instance, if you are a passivist, or someone who never condones violence, you might see a movie about war and go away with the impression that the story was illustrating the sorrow that can result from violence (Eveland Jr & Dunwoody, 2000). Someone who is patriotic or interested by weapons may view the same film and believe it to be celebrating war and showcasing some of the best firearms ever manufactured. It is argued that this is an example of selective perception or "the principle of least effort." It is simpler to understand messages that support your expectations or beliefs (McCombs & Stroud, 2014). Every information consumer has a unique frame of reference, or starting point, when they consume new material.

Due to the psychological theory of mind and emotional connection, communication via technology devices is simpler than face-to-face contact. The divider, together with a second party, is in control of resource distribution in an ultimatum game. The resource that the divider typically controls and has the most freedom to chose is money. If the recipient is happy with the share, he must accept the resultant offer. Alternatively, if the money does not meet the intended needs, he can refuse it in protest (Wicks, 2013). Both players have no financial shares if the share cannot be agreed upon.

Due to its rich history and rising multidisciplinary scope, media psychology is in a unique position to involve both researchers and practitioners. The mental processes that were looked into included reflexive reactions, thoughtful decision-making, and many other processes in between (Wicks, 2013). Every area of communication and communication professions, from advertising to entertainment, computer games to computer collaboration systems, require a grasp of brain processes. Children's reactions to health messages, emotional contagion in instant messaging, entertainment narratives in health communication, and decision-making in computer-mediated work teams are some of the specific media psychology studies that our department has been working on (McCombs & Stroud, 2014).

The connection with the public forged through the media permits the dissemination of knowledge gleaned from psychological research, but going beyond that, offering general advice through the media also necessitates knowledge of the best ways to produce media so as to enable comprehension of such research. The ability to accurately communicate new social science discoveries with the general public is a crucial application of psychological media research, which is developing at an accelerated rate. Students studying psychology from any discipline can benefit from the research and educational opportunities provided by the rapidly growing field of media psychology.

Benefits of Social Media

Advantages Mental Health

When a friend or family member posts on our Facebook wall, we feel accepted because everyone aspires to fit in to some extent.

Makes it simple to discover role models: Social media makes it possible to interact with individuals who have similar interests or concerns. Connecting with your running hero on social media can inspire you when you're struggling to go the extra mile during your Boston marathon training.

Increases trust: According to a study by Valenzuela, Park, and Kee, Facebook users are more likely to have faith in their contacts since the detailed information offered by contacts makes it less uncertain what their intents and behaviours are.

Strengthens relationships while reducing loneliness: A Carnegie Mellon University study found that when people engage in one-on-one communication on social media (such as receiving a "like," "instant message," or "comment"), they feel more linked.

It makes People happy: In spite of all the chatter about "Facebook depression," social media actually improves our moods but only when we are actively using it. Researchers from the University of Missouri found that the test subjects who were actively engaged had a physiological reaction that suggested an improvement in happiness. But soon participants returned to passive browsing, the elevated enjoyment subsided.

Spreads pleasure to others: According to research, there are at least three degrees of separation between two people who are happy.

Physical Health

Has a positive impact on how individuals manage their health: More than 40% of users say that as a result of what they read on social media, their health practises have improved. Having a phone app on hand helps users stay focused on exercise, nutrition, and weight, and some apps include social elements so that other users can offer further assistance.

Improves healthcare quality: According to 60% of doctors, social media has helped them deliver better treatment.

THEORIES IN MEDIA PSYCHOLOGY

Various theories encompass the perception, cognition, and human factors in relation to the environment and experiences. These theories draw upon developmental psychology, narrative psychology, and even neuroscience. They serve as the foundation for the field of psychology and guide its exploration. These theories encompass dimensions such as semiotics, semantics, social cognition, and neuroscience.

Currently, several prominent theories have emerged in the field:

1. *Affective Disposition Theory (ADT):* This theory focuses on differentiating individuals' perspectives on various forms of media, with an emphasis on attentional focus. ADT explores the emotions, opinions, enjoyment, and appreciation that individuals have towards media characters. It also examines how people form positive or negative feelings towards characters, conflicts depicted in the media, and how individuals react to them.
2. *Simulation Theory (ST):* ST proposes that mental simulations involve incorporating external information from the user's surroundings. These simulations are then transformed into memories to generate internal experiences. This theory explains how individuals can create experiences without relying solely on technology, as internal processing plays a significant role in shaping their perception and interaction with the world.
3. *Theory of Play:* This psychological theory emphasizes the importance of play in media enjoyment, highlighting its conceptual connection to presence. According to this theory, play is characterized by intrinsic motivation, an implied shift in perceived reality, and frequent repetition. The Theory of Play draws on explanations from various psychologists and explores how individuals utilize media to satisfy their needs and how media influences their lives. While play is self-contained, individuals are both positively and negatively affected by the stimuli in their environment. By examining different forms of play, this theory sheds light on how individuals respond to their desires within their environment.

These theories play a crucial role in understanding how humans interact with different aspects of media and the resulting positive and negative impacts on individuals.

CONCLUSION, IMPLICATIONS, AND DIRECTIONS FOR FUTURE RESEARCH

Focused on are the numerous roles psychologists play in the media, such as but not limited to radio, television, film, video, newsprint, periodicals, and more recent technology. Instead of an integration where media development and analysis are informed by psychology, the emphasis on media as a distribution channel suggests separate realms for media and psychology. According to research, playing action video games has a beneficial effect that enhances visual attention. As a result, research is pointing out both drawbacks and advantages of the connection between media stimulation and attention. There is promise for understanding how media influences and impacts are perceived. Although a common response, the data left many concerns regarding the respondents' concept of agency in relation to media unanswered, i.e. whether people and society are perceived as interactive participants or victims of media impact. As they have consequences for the efficacy of media applications in domains including education, healthcare, and public policy, both areas will be crucial for further research. New information is developing. Right now, we know a lot more than we comprehend. But the instruments of media psychology can only be of use if each of us is prepared to accept personal accountability for our part in the system.

This article provided a better perspective and explanation of the theoretical developments of human communication theory and practice in media psychology, which has practical ramifications. The subject of media psychology, a fast developing area of journalism theory and practice, is the description of how exposure to the media affects people's behavior. Study of the psychological patterns of human attitudes and behaviors in a multicultural media environment as well as the fundamental elements of media culture. Investigating media psychology phenomena and perceptual mechanisms, maximizing understanding of a person's mental capacities, and media manipulation.

This corpus of literature still needs to be clarified and expanded upon by adding works from high impact journals. It should be stressed, nonetheless, that theoretical underpinnings and rigour must be further established for future research endeavours. In order to better understand the problems with human communication theory in the nation, more basic and theoretically driven study is required. Insights, direction, and development of theoretical application and development in media psychology study can be improved using theory-based research.

REFERENCES

Aishwarya, S., & Millath, M.A. (2019) Effectiveness of online marketing and hedonism among university students in Singapore. *International Journal of Recent Technology and Engineering*, 8(2), 727–734.

Akhmetzyanova, A. I. (2016). The Theoretical Analysis of the Phenomenon of Anticipation in Psychology. *International Journal of Environmental and Science Education*, 11(7), 1559–1570.

Akhmetzyanova, A. I., Artemyeva, T. V., Nigmatullina, I. A., & Tvardovskaya, A. A. (2017). Anticipation in the Structure of Psychological Mechanisms of Deviance: Analytical Research. *Man in India*, 97(14), 251–265.

Berthet, V. (2022). The Impact of Cognitive Biases on Professionals' Decision-Making: A Review of Four Occupational Areas [Review]. *Frontiers in Psychology*, 12, 802439. Advance online publication. doi:10.3389/fpsyg.2021.802439 PMID:35058862

Chavadi, C. (2021). Growth drivers, characteristics, preference and challenges faced by Fast Moving Consumer Goods-A study with reference to Bengaluru. *Turkish Online Journal of Qualitative Inquiry*, 12(7).

Chavadi, C. A., Arul, M. J., & Sirothiya, M. (2020). Modelling the effects of creative advertisements on consumers: An empirical study. *Vision (Basel)*, 24(3), 269–283. doi:10.1177/0972262920926074

Chavadi, C. A., Hiremath, C. V., & Hyderabad, R. L. (2014). Customer loyalty appraisal based on store characteristics: An alternative approach. *Indian Journal of Marketing*, 44(5), 18–29. doi:10.17010/ijom/2014/v44/i5/80375

Chavadi, C. A., & Kokatnur, S. S. (2008). Consumer Expectation and Perception of Fast Food Outlets: An Empirical Study in Davangere. *ICFAI Journal of Services Marketing*, 6(2).

Chavadi, C. A., & Kokatnur, S. S. (2009). Impact of Short-Term Promotional Ads on Food Retailing. *ICFAI Journal of Consumer Behavior*, 4(1).

Chavadi, C. A., & Kokatnur, S. S. (2009). RFID Adoption by Indian Retailers: An Exploratory Study. *The Icfai University Journal of Supply Chain Management, 6*(1), 60–77.

Chavadi, C. A., Menon, S. R., & Sirothiya, M. (2019). Measuring Service Quality Perceptions of Indian E-retailers: An Evaluative Study. *Metamorphosis, 18*(2), 92–102. doi:10.1177/0972622519886232

Chavadi, C. A., Menon, S. R., & Sirothiya, M. (2019). Modelling the Effects of Brand Placements in Movies: An Investigative Study of Event Type and Placement Type. *Vision (Basel), 23*(1), 31–43. doi:10.1177/0972262918821227

Chavadi, C. A., Vishwanatha, M. R., & Mubeen, S. (2018). Ghee with Glee: A Study of How Consumers Evaluate Product Packaging. *Metamorphosis, 17*(2), 100–110. doi:10.1177/0972622518817407

Chen, H. T., & Li, X. (2017). The contribution of mobile social media to social capital and psychological well-being: Examining the role of communicative use, friending and self-disclosure. *Computers in Human Behavior, 75,* 958–965. doi:10.1016/j.chb.2017.06.011

Eveland, W. P. Jr, & Dunwoody, S. (2000). Examining information processing on the World Wide Web using think aloud protocols. *Media Psychology, 2*(3), 219–244. doi:10.1207/S1532785XMEP0203_2

Faisal, M., Chandramohan, S., Millath, M. A., &Karthick, A. V. (2019). Influence of Fashion Behavior on Store Choice among the Arts College Students in Sivganga District. *International Journal of Recent Technology and Engineering, 8*(2), 672-676.

Hanna, E., Ward, L. M., Seabrook, R. C., Jerald, M., Reed, L., Giaccardi, S., & Lippman, J. R. (2017). Contributions of social comparison and self-objectification in mediating associations between Facebook use and emergent adults' psychological well-being. *Cyberpsychology, Behavior, and Social Networking, 20*(3), 172–179. doi:10.1089/cyber.2016.0247 PMID:28263683

Hiremath, C. V., Chavadi, C. A., &Yatgiri, P. Y. (2013). Cloud Technology as an Alternative for Marketing Information System: An Empirical Study. *International Journal of Management. Research and Business Strategy, 2*(4).

Karthick, A. V., & Millath, D. M. A. (2019). *Management of digital libraries for active learning environment: Trends and challenges.* Library Philosophy and Practice.

Karthick, A. V., Millath, D. M. A., & Thowseaf, S. (2018). Elucidating Water Supply, Demand and Contamination in Tamil Nadu. *Shanlax. International Journal of Management, 5*(3), 209–219.

Karthick, A. V., Millath, M. A., Karthik, R. R., & Faisal, M. (2019). Influence of social marketing on rain water harvesting practices for water recycling system. *International Journal of Recent Technology and Engineering, 8*(2), 654–661.

Karthik, R. R., Thowseaf, S., & Millath, M. A. (2018). Impact of demonetization and GST on stock price of automobile sector. *ZENITH International Journal of Multidisciplinary Research, 8*(11), 35–44.

Karumban, S., Sanyal, S., Laddunuri, M. M., Sivalinga, V. D., Shanmugam, V., Bose, V., . . . Murugan, S. P. (2023). Industrial Automation and Its Impact on Manufacturing Industries. In Revolutionizing Industrial Automation Through the Convergence of Artificial Intelligence and the Internet of Things (pp. 24-40). IGI Global.

Klinger, U., & Svensson, J. (2015). The emergence of network media logic in political communication: A theoretical approach. *New Media & Society, 17*(8), 1241–1257. doi:10.1177/1461444814522952

McCombs, M., & Stroud, N. J. (2014). Psychology of agenda-setting effects: Mapping the paths of information processing. *Review of Communication Research, 2,* 68–93. doi:10.12840/issn.2255-4165.2014.02.01.003

Menon, S. R., & Chavadi, C. A. (2022). A Research-based Approach to Identify the Health-conscious Consumers in India. *Metamorphosis, 21*(2), 118–128. doi:10.1177/09726225221098783

Meyer, J. P., Allen, N. J., & Smith, C. A. (1993). Commitment to organizations and occupations: Extension and test of a three-component conceptualization. *The Journal of Applied Psychology, 78*(4), 538–551. doi:10.1037/0021-9010.78.4.538

Millath. (2019a). Indian Tea production Overview and Price Analysis. *International Journal of Advanced Science and Technology, 28*(19), 1253 - 1259.

Millath. (2019b). Identifying Work-Family Conflict Among IT Employees of Infopark, Kochi, Kerala. *International Journal of Advanced Science and Technology, 28*(19), 1164 - 1176.

Millath. (2019c). A Study and Analysis on Sustainable Business Models for Indian Automotive Industry. *International Journal of Advanced Science and Technology, 28*(19), 953 - 959.

Millath, M. A., & Thowseaf, S. (2016). Export performance of Special Economic Zones in India and its economic contribution. *International Journal of Innovative Research in Management Studies, 1*(10), 24–28.

Millath, M. A., & Thowseaf, S. (2017). An investigative study on stock performance of selected companies in food and beverage sector listed under BSE. *ZENITH International Journal of Business Economics & Management Research, 7*(4), 59–70.

Misra, S., Cheng, L., Genevie, J., & Yuan, M. (2014). The iphone effect: The quality of in-person social interactions in the presence of mobile device. *Environment and Behavior,* 1–24.

Mossbridge, J., Tressoldi, P., & Utts, J. (2012). Predictive physiological anticipation preceding seemingly unpredictable stimuli: A meta-analysis. *Frontiers in Psychology, 3,* 390. doi:10.3389/fpsyg.2012.00390 PMID:23109927

Murugan, S. P., Shivaprasad, G., Dhanalakshmi, A., Sriram, V. P., Rajput, K., Mahesh, B. N., & Kedla, S. (2023). The Impact of COVID-19 on the Indian Microfinance Industry and Its Sustainability. In *Transforming Economies Through Microfinance in Developing Nations* (pp. 160–188). IGI Global. doi:10.4018/978-1-6684-5647-7.ch009

Mustaffa, N., Mahmud, W. A. W., Ahmad, F., & Mahbob, M. H., & AbdRahim, M. H. (2013). Kebergantungan Internet danaktiviti online remajadiLembahKelang. JurnalKomunikasi. *Malaysian Journal of Communication, 29*(1), 199–212.

Nair, D. S., & Millath, M. A. (2018). An analytical study on the influence of gender on the reasons for opting flexible working hours among faculties of engineering colleges in Trivandrum District of Kerala. *ZENITH International Journal of Multidisciplinary Research, 8*(12), 195–200.

Nair, D.S., & Millath, M.A. (2019) Identifying family-work conflict among employees of the travancore cements limited, Kottayam, Kerala. *International Journal of Recent Technology and Engineering*, *8*(2), 718–726.

Nugent, S. G. (2005). *If Socrates Had Email* [Commencement Speech]. https://www.kenyon.edu/x29475.xml

Palermo, S., Benedetti, F., Costa, T., & Amanzio, M. (2015). Pain anticipation: An activation likelihood estimation meta-analysis of brain imaging studies. *Human Brain Mapping*, *36*(5), 1648–1661. doi:10.1002/hbm.22727 PMID:25529840

Park, J. Y., Perumal, S. V., Sanyal, S., Ah Nguyen, B., Ray, S., Krishnan, R., Narasimhaiah, R., & Thangam, D. (2022). Sustainable Marketing Strategies as an Essential Tool of Business. *American Journal of Economics and Sociology*, *81*(2), 359–379. doi:10.1111/ajes.12459

Patwardhan, P., & Ramaprasad, J. (2005, May). Internet dependency relations and online activity exposure, involvement and satisfaction: A study of American and Indian internet users. In *Annual convention of the International Communication Association* (Vol. 13). Academic Press.

Piocuda, J. E., Smyers, J. O., Knyshev, E., Harris, R. J., & Rai, M. (2015). Trends of internationalization and collaboration in US psychology journals 1950–2010. *Archives of Scientific Psychology*, *3*(1), 82–92. doi:10.1037/arc0000020

Prensky, M. (2001). Digital Natives, Digital Immigrants: Do They Really Think Differently? *On the Horizon*, *9*(6), 1–8. doi:10.1108/10748120110424843

Przybylski, A. K., & Weinstein, N. (2013). Can you connect with me now? How the presence of mobile communication technology influences face-to- face conversation quality. *Journal of Social and Personal Relationships*, *30*(3), 237–246. doi:10.1177/0265407512453827

Przybylski, A. K., & Weinstein, N. (2019). Investigating the motivational and psychosocial dynamics of dysregulated gaming: Evidence from a preregistered cohort study. *Clinical Psychological Science*, *7*(6), 1257–1265. doi:10.1177/2167702619859341

Rajeswari, V., & Millath, A. (2003). Brand Preference towards Water Purifier-A Study. *Indian Journal of Marketing*, *13*, 9–15.

Reeve, J. (2016). A grand theory of motivation: Why not? *Motivation and Emotion*, *40*(1), 31–35. doi:10.100711031-015-9538-2

Roberts, J. A., & David, M. E. (2020). The social media party: Fear of missing out (FoMO), social media intensity, connection, and well-being. *International Journal of Human-Computer Interaction*, *36*(4), 386–392. doi:10.1080/10447318.2019.1646517

Rutledge, J. (2015). Economics as Energy Framework: Complexity, Turbulence, Financial Crises, and Protectionism. *Review of Financial Economics*, *25*(1), 10–18. doi:10.1016/j.rfe.2015.02.003

S, M., & Millath, A. (2019). Talent Management an Emerging Trend for Employee Effectiveness in Corporate Hospitals. *International Journal of Recent Technology and Engineering, 8*(4S5), 69–71

Saifullina, N. A., & Akhmetzyanova, A. I. (2018). Anticipation of Individuals with Communication Disabilities: Problem Current State Review. *HELIX, 8*(1), 2506–2511. doi:10.29042/2018-2506-2511

Saraladevi, E., Chandramohan, S., & Millath, M.A. (2019). Online shopping behavior pattern among school children. *International Journal of Recent Technology and Engineering, 8*(2), 695–699.

Sirothiya, M., & Chavadi, C. (2020). Compressed biogas (cbg) as an alternative and sustainable energy source in India: Case study on implementation frameworks and challenges. *Invertis Journal of Renewable Energy, 10*(2), 49–64. doi:10.5958/2454-7611.2020.00007.7

Sirothiya, M., & Chavadi, C. (2020). Evaluating marketing strategies ofcompressed biogas (CBG) companies in India using decision tree analysis. *IIMS Journal of Management Science, 11*(3), 219–237. doi:10.5958/0976-173X.2020.00012.0

Sirothiya, M., & Chavadi, C. (2020). Role of compressed biogas to assess the effects of perceived value on customer satisfaction and customer loyalty. *BIMTECH Bus. Perspect, 1*, 70–89.

Sriram, V. P., Sanyal, S., Laddunuri, M. M., Subramanian, M., Bose, V., Booshan, B., & Thangam, D. (2023). Enhancing Cybersecurity Through Blockchain Technology. In *Handbook of Research on Cybersecurity Issues and Challenges for Business and FinTech Applications* (pp. 208–224). IGI Global.

Thangam, D., Arumugam, T., Velusamy, K., Subramanian, M., Ganesan, S. K., & Suryakumar, M. (2022). COVID-19 Pandemic and Its Brunt on Digital Transformation and Cybersecurity. In Cybersecurity Crisis Management and Lessons Learned From the COVID-19 Pandemic (pp. 15-42). IGI Global.

Thangam, D., & Chavadi, C. (2023). Impact of Digital Marketing Practices on Energy Consumption, Climate Change, and Sustainability. *Climate and Energy, 39*(7), 11–19. doi:10.1002/gas.22329

Thangam, D., Malali, A. B., Subramanian, G., Mohan, S., & Park, J. Y. (2022). Internet of things: a smart technology for healthcare industries. In *Healthcare Systems and Health Informatics* (pp. 3–15). CRC Press.

Thangam, D., Malali, A. B., Subramanian, G., & Park, J. Y. (2022). Transforming Healthcare through Internet of Things. In *Cloud and Fog Computing Platforms for Internet of Things* (pp. 15–24). Chapman and Hall/CRC. doi:10.1201/9781003213888-2

Thangam, D., Malali, A. B., Subramaniyan, G., Mariappan, S., Mohan, S., & Park, J. Y. (2022). Relevance of Artificial Intelligence in Modern Healthcare. In *Integrating AI in IoT Analytics on the Cloud for Healthcare Applications* (pp. 67–88). IGI Global. doi:10.4018/978-1-7998-9132-1.ch005

Thangam, D., Malali, A. B., Subramaniyan, S. G., Mariappan, S., Mohan, S., & Park, J. Y. (2021). Blockchain Technology and Its Brunt on Digital Marketing. In Blockchain Technology and Applications for Digital Marketing (pp. 1-15). IGI Global. doi:10.4018/978-1-7998-8081-3.ch001

Thangam, D., Vaidya, G. R., Subramanian, G., Velusamy, K., Selvi Govindarajan, K., & Park, J. Y. (2022). The Portrayal of Women's Empowerment in Select Indian Movies. *American Journal of Economics and Sociology, 81*(1), 187–205. doi:10.1111/ajes.12451

Thawab, M. A., Thowseaf, S., Millath, M. A., & Ali, K. M. (2019) Reconnoitering the Impact of Economic Variables on Fruit Pulp Export from Tamil Nadu. *International Journal of Recent Technology and Engineering, 8*(4), 58-65.

Thowseaf, M. A. S., & Millath, M. A. (2016). A study on GST implementation and its impact on Indian industrial sectors and export. *International Journal of Management Research and Social Science, 3*(2), 27–30.

Thowseaf, S., & Millath, M. A. (2016). Factors Influencing Export - A Conceptual Analysis. *International Journal of Management, 7*(2), 150–158.

Thowseaf, S., & Millath, M. A. (2016). An analysis on Indian Forex for examining investment and trade option. *International Journal of Advanced Research in Management and Social Sciences, 5*(9), 47–54.

Thowseaf, S., & Millath, M. A. (2017). Delineation on Demonetization Impact on Indian Economy. *International Journal of Innovative Knowledge Concepts, 5*, 7.

Thowseaf, S., Millath, M. A., & Ali, K. M. Aftermath Effect Of GST On Consumer Purchasing Power. *Resturamt Business, 118*(5), 122-131.

Weiner, B. (2012). *An attributional theory of motivation and emotion.* Springer Science & Business Media.

Wicks, R. H. (2013). Media information processing. In *Psychology of entertainment* (pp. 103–120). Routledge.

Chapter 11
Exploring the Impact of Social Media on the Indian Banking Sector:
A Comprehensive Social Media Framework

Durairaj Duraisamy
School of Management, CMR University, India

Kanchan Rajput
ISBR Research Centre, India

Chethan Shivaram
Department of Management Studies, Acharya Institute of Graduate Studies, India

Mathiraj Subramanian
Department of Cooperate Secretaryship, Alagappa University, India

N. Nethravathi
Department of Business Administration, Acharya Institute of Technology, India

Shaila Kedla
Department of Commerce, Acharya Institute of Graduate Studies, India

K. Y. Anusha
Department of Management Studies, Acharya Institute of Graduate Studies, India

Raghu Narayana Reddy
Presidency Business School, Presidency College, India

Kiran Hiremath
Presidency Business School, Presidency College, India

ABSTRACT

This chapter emphasizes the importance of compliance with data protection regulations and maintaining customer privacy. Finally, the framework offers strategic recommendations for Indian banks to optimize their social media presence, including the development of robust social media policies, integration with existing customer service channels, and investment in analytics to gain valuable insights from user interactions. Overall, this framework provides valuable insights for Indian banks seeking to harness the potential of social media to stay competitive, build customer trust, and enhance their overall operational efficiency in the dynamic digital landscape.

DOI: 10.4018/978-1-6684-7450-1.ch011

INTRODUCTION

In the digital age, social media has become an integral part of people's lives, revolutionizing the way they connect, communicate, and access information. Beyond personal interactions, social media platforms have found their way into the business world, transforming industries in unprecedented ways. One such sector profoundly impacted by the advent of social media is the banking industry. Social Media has emerged as a powerful internet-based platform, building upon the foundations of Web 2.0, enabling users to create and exchange user-generated content (Heet al., 2015). The widespread availability of the internet at affordable tariffs has led to a significant rise in internet adoption, paving the way for the emergence of Social Media as a new medium of communication. Social media provides banks with an efficient and interactive means of engaging with their customers. Through platforms such as Facebook, Twitter, and Instagram, banks can establish direct communication channels with clients, responding to queries, providing real-time updates, and addressing concerns promptly (Vrontis, Makrides, Christofi & Thrassou, 2021). This direct engagement fosters stronger customer relationships and enhances brand loyalty, as customers feel more valued and appreciated.

Incorporating social media into their customer service strategies allows banks to offer more convenient and accessible support. Customers can reach out to the bank through social media channels, eliminating the need for long waiting times on customer service helplines. Banks can provide personalized assistance and address issues more efficiently, leading to greater customer satisfaction. Social media platforms offer banks an unparalleled opportunity to market their products and services to a vast audience. By creating engaging content, sharing informative posts, and leveraging targeted advertising, banks can effectively reach potential customers and showcase their offerings (Razmerita, Kirchner & Nielsen, 2016). Social media marketing campaigns can be tailored to specific demographics, allowing banks to attract new customers and expand their reach.

Social media provides a treasure trove of customer data and insights that banks can use to inform their strategies. By analyzing user behavior, preferences, and feedback on social media, banks can gain valuable insights into customer needs and expectations (Sawhney, & Ahuja, 2022). This information can be leveraged to tailor products, services, and marketing efforts to better suit customer preferences (Parusheva, 2017). Social media also serves as a platform for banks to promote financial literacy and awareness. Through informative content and educational campaigns, banks can help customers make informed financial decisions and understand various banking products. This fosters a more financially responsible customer base and strengthens the overall financial ecosystem. Social media enables banks to provide real-time updates and alerts to customers (Chatterjee & Kar, 2020). From notifying customers about transaction alerts to offering updates on new product launches and market developments, social media serves as an efficient channel for disseminating time-sensitive information.

The role of social media in the banking sector is undeniably significant, revolutionizing how banks interact with customers, market their products, and gather insights for informed decision-making. The integration of social media into banking operations has resulted in improved customer engagement, enhanced customer service, and targeted marketing efforts (Agnihotri, Kulshreshtha, & Tripathi, 2022). As technology continues to advance, banks must adapt to the changing landscape, embracing social media as a powerful tool to better serve their customers and stay ahead in a competitive market. While challenges exist, the potential benefits outweigh the risks, making social media a crucial component of modern banking operations.

SOCIAL MEDIA AND INDIAN BANKING SECTOR

In India, the increasing usage of smartphones and the availability of social media apps have further encouraged active participation in various social media networks. Around 40 million people in India access the internet through mobile handsets, and a substantial 82% of these users engage with social media applications on their phones. The vast user base on social media platforms provides a treasure trove of customer information, encompassing opinions, values, behaviors, likes, and dislikes. Users share a wide range of information, from their current state of mind to their thoughts on various subjects, making this data highly valuable for businesses (Agnihotri, Kulshreshtha, & Tripathi, 2022). Indian banks have recognized the potential of social media in their regular operations and are at different stages of integrating it into their strategies. Some private banks have already begun providing regular updates on the latest offers and enabling basic customer operations through popular social media sites (Uma Ganesh, 2022). For instance, a large private bank in India has developed a Facebook application hosted on secure servers, allowing customers to check their account balances, request a cheque book, and initiate stop payments. Moreover, some private banks utilize their Facebook pages to offer customers exclusive deals, share product details, and provide customer care services (Kumari & Jindal, 2021). As a few banks take the lead in adopting social media for online financial services, others are expected to follow suit in the near future.

The incorporation of social media into banking operations presents significant opportunities for banks to engage with their customers more effectively, gather valuable insights, and provide personalized services. As the trend gains momentum, banks in India are poised to leverage social media platforms as an integral part of their overall strategy to enhance customer experiences and offer online financial services. Indian banks have recognized the importance of social media in engaging with customers, promoting their services, and building brand loyalty (Sawhney, Ahuja & Sharma, 2022). They actively use various social media platforms to reach a wider audience and interact with their customers on a more personal level. Some common platforms that banks use for their social media presence include Facebook, Twitter, Instagram, LinkedIn, and YouTube.

The social media presence of Indian banks is usually measured based on several key indicators, such as the number of followers, engagement rate, response time to customer queries, and the quality of content posted (Malhotra, 2017). Here's a general overview of the social media presence of some top Indian banks:

- *State Bank of India (SBI):* SBI is the largest bank in India and has a significant presence on social media platforms. They have a massive following on Facebook and Twitter, where they regularly share updates, financial advice, and promotional content.
- *HDFC Bank:* HDFC Bank is one of the leading private sector banks in India and has a strong social media presence. They actively engage with customers on various platforms and provide informative content on personal finance and banking services.
- *ICICI Bank:* ICICI Bank is another major private sector bank with a substantial social media presence. They are known for their interactive campaigns and engaging content on platforms like Twitter and Instagram.
- *Axis Bank:* Axis Bank is among the top private banks in India and maintains an active presence on social media. They focus on promoting their digital banking solutions and offering personalized customer support.

- *Kotak Mahindra Bank:* Kotak Mahindra Bank has a considerable presence on social media, particularly on Twitter and LinkedIn. They share insights on financial matters and engage with their audience through quizzes and contests.
- *Yes Bank:* Yes Bank is known for its innovative social media campaigns and has a growing presence on platforms like Twitter and YouTube.
- *Punjab National Bank (PNB):* PNB is one of the leading public sector banks in India and has been actively expanding its social media presence in recent years.
- *Bank of Baroda (BoB):* BoB has also been increasing its social media presence and uses platforms like Facebook and Twitter to engage with customers.
- *IndusInd Bank:* IndusInd Bank actively interacts with its customers on social media platforms and shares informative content on various financial topics.
- *IDFC FIRST Bank:* IDFC FIRST Bank is known for its vibrant social media presence and creative campaigns on platforms like Instagram.

SOCIAL MEDIA AND ITS VARIOUS APPLICATIONS IN BANKING SECTOR

Social media has become an integral part of modern society, and the banking sector has not been left behind in embracing its potential. Banks have recognized the importance of social media as a powerful tool for customer engagement, marketing, brand building, and providing personalized customer service (Miranda, Chamorro, Rubio, & Morgado, 2013). Here are some of the various applications of social media in the banking sector:

Social CRM and the Expectations of Customer 3.0

Customer 3.0, also known as the new age Customer or Gen Y customers, have unique expectations from banks, particularly in how they want to engage. They exhibit a strong inclination to trust advice from friends and acquaintances when it comes to products and services, relying on them as guides for decision-making. As a result, customers are increasingly turning to social networking, social bookmarking, and social shopping as powerful mediums for gathering information, sharing experiences, and making informed choices (Miranda, Chamorro, Rubio, & Morgado, 2013). This growing reliance on social media as an essential source of information necessitates organizations to evolve beyond the boundaries of traditional marketing, sales, and customer service. To meet the demands of Customer 3.0, businesses must leverage social media as a means to build lasting relationships, actively listen to customer feedback, and engage with individuals and communities in a more personalized, collaborative, and transparent manner. Incorporating social media into their strategies allows banks to stay relevant and connected with their customers (Manzira, & Bankole, 2018). By actively participating in social conversations, addressing concerns promptly, and providing valuable insights, banks can cultivate trust and loyalty among their clientele. Furthermore, embracing social media empowers banks to be more accessible and responsive to customer needs, creating a sense of community and fostering a positive brand image. Additionally, social media offers an opportunity for banks to identify and leverage brand advocates within their customer base (Singh, Chakraborty & Majumdar, 2020). These loyal customers can become influential advocates, spreading positive word-of-mouth and attracting new clients through referrals.

Educating Customers

Social Media offers a rapid, cost-effective, and engaging platform for spreading information. It can be utilized for various purposes in the banking industry, (Sarigianni, Thalmann & Manhart, 2016).such as:

Raising Awareness: Social Media can be used to educate customers about the basics of Banking and Finance, as well as government regulations that impact them, such as KYC (Know Your Customer) and AML (Anti-Money Laundering) requirements. Awareness campaigns can take the form of visual content, informative text, or interactive games like crosswords and puzzles.

Financial Literacy: Social Media can play a vital role in educating customers about the do's and don'ts of Credit/Debit card usage, how to identify fake notes, the importance of data confidentiality and privacy, and other essential financial topics.

By leveraging the power of Social Media, banks can effectively reach out to a wider audience, empower customers with knowledge, and foster a more informed and financially responsible community.

Consumer Insights 2.0

Social Media serves as a valuable data mine for banks, providing a wealth of information about both current and potential customers (Mohamed, Yehia, & Marie, 2022). The generation of insights is facilitated through the following means:

Voice of Analysis: Banks can leverage text analytics tools to scrutinize social conversations related to their products and services. By doing so, they can identify customer pain points, areas of satisfaction, prevailing topics, sentiments, and customer demographics. These insights are highly useful in understanding customer preferences and behaviors.

Content Aggregation: It is essential to aggregate data from various sources in a unified manner to gain deeper insights and analytics. By adopting an aggregated 'all-source' approach, banks can develop a comprehensive 360-degree view of their customers, enabling more informed decision-making.

Early Detection: Social Media offers valuable insights into emerging trends and themes among customer conversations. By promptly identifying these insights, banks can take corresponding actions to mitigate risks to their brand reputation and address potential issues before they escalate.

By tapping into the potential of Social Media analytics, banks can enhance their understanding of customers, refine their strategies, and foster better customer relationships.

Customer Acquisition 2.0

Social Media serves as a powerful tool for banks to expand their customer base, achieving the following benefits:

Brand Building: Social Media enables banks to differentiate their brands and make them more relevant to consumers. By involving consumers in brand conversations and giving them a sense of ownership, Social Media significantly impacts reputation and trust.

Marketing: Social Media redefines the way banks build and manage customer relationships with the 5Rs - Relationship, Response, Relevance, Recognition, and Reach. This shift in mindset leads to more effective marketing strategies.

Viral Marketing: Social Media amplifies Word-of-Mouth, directly influencing customer growth and the spread of positive or negative feedback about products or services among the target audience.

Influence on Purchase Decision: Customers use Social Media for market research and rely on reviews, ratings, and testimonials from other customers to make informed purchase decisions.

Targeted Advertising: Social Media allows banks to tailor advertisements according to specific customer preferences and behaviors, reducing marketing costs compared to traditional channels. Pixel tracking enables precise tracking of customer conversions.

Better Leads: Social Media technology enhances insight into potential leads and facilitates lead generation through consumer referrals and influencers. This enriched lead generation process improves customer acquisition and engagement (Kazemi, et al., 2013).

By leveraging Social Media effectively, banks can strengthen their market presence, engage with customers more meaningfully, and drive business growth.

Customer Experience 2.0

Banks can harness the power of Social Media to create a seamless and comprehensive customer experience. By adopting a customer-centric approach, banks can foster deeper engagement, drive recommendations, increase sales, and mitigate customer frustrations (Rootman & Cupp, 2016). Several strategies contribute to an improved customer experience:

Customer Empowerment: Leveraging Social Media allows banks to tap into the collective wisdom of their customer base. Customers can become service representatives, assisting others with queries and enriching the overall customer experience.

Monitoring and Engagement: Banks can effectively monitor social media platforms frequented by their customers. This proactive approach enables service representatives to promptly identify and resolve any customer issues, preventing negative sentiments from spreading and safeguarding the brand's reputation.

Swift Issue Resolution: Social media's real-time nature demands quick responses to customer concerns. Addressing issues promptly not only prevents potential reputation damage but also showcases the bank's commitment to excellent customer service (Ying et al., 2021).

Building a Community: By engaging customers through Social Media, banks can create a strong sense of community and brand loyalty. A branded online community encourages supporters to become advocates, sharing positive experiences and recommendations with a wider audience.

Incorporating Social Media into the customer experience strategy empowers banks to proactively engage with customers, build a positive brand image, and create a dynamic and responsive community of advocates.

Customer Innovation 2.0

Social media acts as a powerful tool, connecting various spheres of influence within the banking industry, including internal, trusted, and global networks. In the fast-paced world of ever-changing market and customer demands, social media enables banks to keep pace with shortened product lifecycles. By utilizing social media, banks can better understand and target customer niches with new and innovative offerings (Broby, 2021). To enhance their understanding of customer segments, banks can employ various strategies:

Buzz Monitoring and Sentiment Analysis: By closely monitoring and analyzing customer conversations on social media, banks can gauge the sentiments and opinions of their target customer base regarding their products and services. This data provides valuable insights into explicit and implicit customer needs, behaviors, and values, helping banks define new customer segments and tailor customer experiences accordingly.

Crowd sourcing: Banks can tap into the collective intelligence of the masses through crowdsourcing. By engaging customers as a think tank, banks can co-create products and services that meet customers' desires and requirements while adhering to regulatory guidelines. For example, a public sector bank in India designed an internal collaborative platform to understand field officers' sentiments and used this information to innovate and redesign products using technology (Bekmamedova, & Shanks, 2014).

Building Customer Attachment: Active engagement through social media fosters emotional attachment between banks and their customers. Customers who feel connected and appreciated are more likely to become brand champions, advocating for the bank and promoting its products and services.

By harnessing the potential of social media, banks can gain valuable customer insights, foster innovation, and strengthen their bond with customers, ultimately driving growth and success in the competitive banking landscape.

INTERNAL COLLABORATION, TRAINING, AND RECRUITMENT IN THE DIGITAL AGE

The younger generation workforce, like Customer 3.0 (Gen Y customers), prefers communication through social networking sites. For banks, Social Media offers an excellent opportunity to engage and empower their staff, fostering a collaborative culture within the organization. Utilizing social networking and collaboration applications, banks can bring employees together to streamline processes, share experiences, celebrate successes, and learn from temporary setbacks (Bekmamedova, & Shanks, 2014). Employees with common interests or related roles can form communities, providing support and learning opportunities.

Training Support: Social Media can enhance the effectiveness of training programs in several ways:

- Delivering content just-in-time and at the point of need for specific employee groups.
- Providing video reviews of new processes with direct links to additional procedure steps.
- Offering immediate support for process-related questions and effective knowledge management.
- Listening to employee feedback and identifying key skill gaps to inform training design and delivery.

Before implementing social media in the public domain, banks must train employees on handling difficult questions, conflict management, and familiarize them with social media language used in conversations.

Recruitment

Private Banks are leveraging social media for various recruitment purposes, including:

- Personal branding and job searches.
- Employment branding to showcase the company's culture and values.
- Streamlining the hiring process and employee development.
- Expanding networks, attracting talent, and building the bank's business brand.

By following pioneers and implementing best practices in social media recruitment, banks can effectively connect with potential candidates, communicate with employees, and strengthen their brand presence.

APPROACH FOR BANKS NEEDS TO BE FOLLOWED BY BANKS FOR EMPOWERING THE SOCIAL MEDIA JOURNEY

Social media has become an indispensable channel for banks to enhance their customer relationships and provide personalized experiences. It offers a multitude of benefits, including improved customer touchpoints, lead generation, data sharing, emotional targeting, and ensuring an omnichannel experience. Enhancing Customer Touch points: Embracing social media allows banks to interact with customers more frequently, building stronger connections (Dery, Sebastian, & van der Meulen, 2017). Personalized content and engagement on platforms like Facebook and Instagram help foster real relationships, branding, and customer satisfaction. While social media should focus on value-driven content, a proportion can be dedicated to self-promotion, including offers, special rates, and personalized solutions. It's a chance to connect with potential customers actively seeking financial solutions. Social media provides new insights and data sources, enabling banks to offer industry insights, valuable financial tips, and market overviews (Vandana Ahuja, 2020). Building trust through helpful content strengthens customer loyalty and drives product awareness. Connecting with customers on an emotional level gives banks a competitive edge. Tailoring content to specific audiences and highlighting emotional aspects of financial decisions boosts trust and brand loyalty. Consistency across all channels, including social media, is crucial for a seamless customer experience. Banks should ensure that messaging and customer service remains consistent, reinforcing brand reliability. Social media marketing for banks is ever-evolving, but when utilized effectively, it creates a more personalized and engaging banking experience. By understanding customer needs, targeting emotions, and maintaining a consistent brand image, banks can capitalize on the power of social media to build lasting customer relationships and offer tailored financial solutions (Kuchciak & Wiktorowicz, 2021). Here's how banks can empower their social media journey:

Fixing the Strategy for Social Media: Social Media permeates throughout the fabric of the bank, impacting various aspects of its operations. It necessitates a comprehensive strategy and approach to ensure a seamless experience, reliable content creation, data governance, and adherence to regulatory compliance. To kickstart the implementation, it is vital to identify the pilot business division(s) that will spearhead the Social Media Strategy, aligning it with the bank's vision and mission. Understanding the existing business goals of these divisions is key to crafting a tailored Social Media approach that harmonizes with the bank's overall strategic objectives.

Once the existing business goals are identified, potential Social Media options can be explored and analyzed to create a robust strategy. The viability and attractiveness of each option should be carefully discussed, considering factors like audience engagement, reach, and potential impact. Moreover, defining Key Performance Indicators (KPIs) is crucial to gauge the success of the Social Media initiatives (Kaplan, & Haenlein, 2010).

While measuring Return on Investment (ROI) is essential in most business aspects, in the context of Social Media, it can be more complex. Many of the benefits derived from Social Media efforts are intangible and may take time to manifest, such as enhanced brand awareness, positive sentiments, and increased fan base. Therefore, focusing solely on tangible ROI may not accurately capture the full value of Social Media efforts in the long run (Dery, Sebastian, & van der Meulen, 2017). By thoughtfully implementing these steps and crafting a well-tailored Social Media strategy, the bank can effectively harness the power of digital platforms to achieve its goals, strengthen brand presence, and build enduring relationships with its customers and stakeholders.

Social Media Administration Framework: A comprehensive Social Media Management Framework must encompass critical factors to establish and scale social media capabilities effectively. This framework comprises six key elements and the same presented in Figure 1.

Context: This element takes into account external factors, such as regulations and competitive dynamics, as well as insights gathered through social media listening activities. It also considers internal priorities and initiatives. Social media can also aid in promoting Corporate Social Responsibility and community outreach activities.

Figure 1. Social media management framework

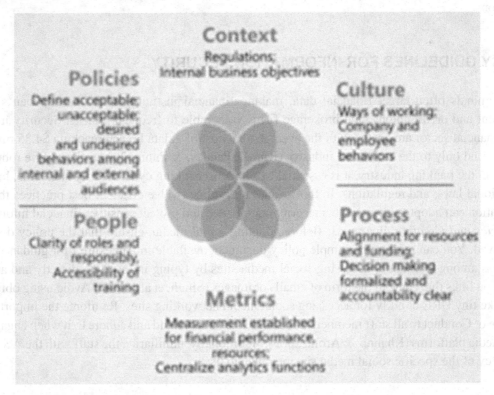

Culture: Culture encompasses the habits, behaviors, and ways of working within the bank. Successful adoption of social media involves fostering a collaborative culture both within and outside the bank, leveraging technology for seamless communication and engagement (Kumari, Jindal, & Mittal, 2023).

Process: Beyond the processes that social media supports or influences, it is vital to establish a structured approach to managing social media within the bank. Implementing cross-divisional processes for social media management ensures consistency and coherence in the bank's social media activities.

Metrics: Banks should define key performance metrics for each line of business engaged in social media. These metrics may include the number of fans, likes, shares, and tweets to gauge the effectiveness of their social media efforts.

People: Identifying the necessary skills to execute the Social Media Strategy is crucial for achieving desired business outcomes. Various roles emerge or are impacted in banks utilizing social media, including Executive Director (Champion), Marketing and Community Managers, Monitoring Analysts, Chief Information Security Officer, Legal and Inspection teams, Content Makers, Advertisers, Web Crawler Architects, Recruiters, Social Learning Architects, and Employee Community Managers.

Policies: Establishing clear policies is essential to govern acceptable, unacceptable, desired, and undesired behavior for both internal and external audiences, including employees, contractors, vendors, customers, and prospects. These policies help ensure proper use and representation of the bank's brand across social media platforms.

As the number of social media platforms continues to grow, each catering to distinct audience groups and purposes, banks must conduct thorough research to understand the available options and where their customer base resides before deciding on their social media presence. By integrating these key elements into the Social Media Management Framework, banks can build a strong and successful social media strategy, connecting with their audience effectively while adhering to industry best practices and regulations.

POLICY GUIDELINES FOR INFORMATION SECURITY

Cybercriminals often target financial data, making financial institutions like banks, loan services, investment and credit unions, and brokerage firms vulnerable to frequent attacks. Security incidents in the financial sector are costly, with the average total cost of a data breach reaching $4.35 million in 2022, second only to the healthcare industry (Kumar, Pandey, & Punia, 2014). To achieve robust data security in the banking industry, it is essential to adhere to banking cybersecurity standards, local and international laws, and regulations. In this article, we outline twelve efficient best practices that your organization can adopt to ensure cybersecurity compliance and protect sensitive financial information.

Policies and Creating Awareness: Before adopting social media, ensure that the policy document is approved. You can refer to the sample policy document available in Annexure I for guidance. Raise awareness among staff about accessing social media sites by typing in the URL directly and avoiding clicking on links that come in the form of emails or images (Singh, et al., 2013). Avoid using obfuscated URLs like tiny URL or bit.ly for accessing social media networking sites. Reinforce the importance of the Code of Conduct to all staff members. Make sure they understand and adhere to it when engaging on social media platforms (Khanna, & Arora, 2009). Additionally, familiarize the staff with the Acceptable Use policy of the specific social media site they plan to use.

Effective Management of Access: Use a different email ID for each social media site and adopt the bank's password policy to ensure strong and secure passwords. Implement mailbox spam and content filtering to prevent malicious emails and content from reaching the staff's inbox. Identify the content/campaign designer, approver, and publisher for social media posts, and restrict access to these roles only (Ghelani, Hua, & Koduru, 2022). Create a security group and implement IP-based restrictions to control access to social media sites. Avoid allowing remote desktop connections to machines used for social media interactions. Allow bank's authorized personnel to post on social media sites only from bank-provided smart phones to ensure secure access (Chaturvedi, Gupta, & Bhattacharya, 2008). If the bank outsources the social media platform to a third party, ensure adequate controls are in place to prevent confidential data exposure through social media. Regularly review the third party's security controls.

Monitoring and Logging: Keep a record of previous and current login details and validate postings for every logon. Implement re-authentication on session timeout and use CAPTCHA/Virtual Keyboard-based authentication for added security. Keep computers and browsers up-to-date and virus-free to reduce the risk of cyberattacks (Singh, et al., 2013). Clear all browser history, cookies, and other temporary files before and after accessing social media sites to minimize the risk of unauthorized access. Implement Intrusion Detection Systems (IDS), Intrusion Prevention Systems (IPS), Firewalls, web content filters, and layered proxies to monitor and secure data being posted on social media platforms from the bank.

REGULATIONS, LEGAL, AND COMPLIANCE

Information and Communication Technology (ICT) laws are taking a proactive approach in regulating organizations by defining new entities, types of cybercrimes, and contraventions. These laws create regulatory infrastructure, outline requirements and obligations, and mandate the provision of access to information for law enforcement purposes (Alawode, & Kaka, 2011). Additionally, they impose information retention requirements, set expectations for security and privacy implementation, and enforce fines for non-compliance. When deploying a social media policy, considerable efforts should be dedicated to determining the applicability of these legal provisions (Agboola, 2006). Organizations must ensure that their social media policies align with the relevant ICT laws to avoid any legal repercussions and to ensure the protection of sensitive information and data.

The Indian Penal Code, 1860: The Indian Penal Code, 1860, specifically sections 499 and 500, addresses the act of harming a person's reputation. Banks and their staff must exercise caution to avoid expressing personal emotions, frustrations, or anger on social media platforms; as such posts can quickly go viral and cause reputational damage. Language used on social media should be professional and validated by the Communications/PR department before posting (Ahmad, 2019).

Know Your Customer (KYC) Norms: Banks can utilize social media as an additional means of validating customer identity, in compliance with Know Your Customer (KYC) norms, Anti-Money Laundering (AML) standards, Combating of Financing of Terrorism (CFT) regulations, and the obligations under the Prevention of Money Laundering Act, 2002 (Kapsoulis, et al., 2020). However, customer profile data cannot be used for cross-selling purposes, as per the guidelines.

The Reserve Bank of India's Master Circular on Wilful Defaulters, dated July 01, 2011, mandates banks to identify and report data related to willful defaulters. Social media can be a useful tool in identifying defaulters. Additionally, the Reserve Bank of India regulates payment/fund transfer processes initiated through social media channels as per the Payment and Settlement System Act, 2007. Banks must comply with settlement and reporting requirements detailed in the Act (Chandani, Divekar, Neeraja, Mehta, & Atiq, 2022).

National Cyber Security Policy 2013: Banks with social media apps for financial/non-financial transactions must also adhere to the National Cyber Security Policy 2013, ensuring a secure computing environment and instilling trust and confidence in transactions and services. Staff participating in social media campaigns and interactions should avoid making damaging statements, including those that are dangerous, obstructing, insulting, injurious, promote criminal activities, intimidate, spread hatred/enmity, or incite ill will (Bagga, 2018).

Information Technology Act, 2008: In cases where customers make derogatory or inflammatory comments, the Communications/Public Relations department should consult the bank's legal department to understand the applicability of Section 66A to 66F of the Information Technology Act, 2008. Banks that create social media properties fall under the category of 'intermediary' as they allow end-users to share comments on their platforms (Gupta & Yadav, 2017). The obligations for intermediaries have been defined separately under Section 79. Banks deploying social media analytics tools may collect customer interaction/behavior data, which should be handled with care and in compliance with privacy regulations. As per the Right to Information Act, 2005, Section 8(1) (e), information available to a person in his fiduciary relationship cannot be shared unless the competent authority determines that the larger public interest justifies its disclosure. Therefore, banks should refrain from sharing such details with outside parties unless directed by the regulator, the Reserve Bank of India (Uppal, 2008).

Information Technology (Amendment) Act, 2008: Sections 43A and 72A of the Information Technology (Amendment) Act, 2008, necessitate banks to adopt reasonable security practices to safeguard sensitive personal data or information from compromise. Rules notified under Section 43A define privacy and security requirements, and banks must adhere to these norms when collecting and using sensitive personal information in social media transactions. Rules 3, 4, 5, 6, 7, and 8 outline privacy requirements and lay down expectations for reasonable security practices (Gupta & Yadav, 2017). Under Section 8(1) (j) of the Right to Information Act, 2005, disclosure of personal information unrelated to any public activity or interest or that could lead to an unwarranted invasion of an individual's privacy is exempted. Consequently, sharing customer details, such as loans and deposits, on social media for more referrals should be avoided.

The Trade Marks Act 1999: The Trade Marks Act 1999 can be utilized by banks to take action against unofficial social media sites. However, banks must be cautious not to infringe on any Intellectual Property Rights while posting images and content on social media platforms. The Telecom Commercial Communication Customer Preference Regulations, 2010, issued by TRAI, outlines methods to curb the menace of unsolicited commercial calls and messages. Banks possessing customer contact details through social media sites should adhere to these regulations and avoid violations. The collection, accessing, processing, storing, and sharing of data have raised concerns among end customers, partners, and governments (Castaldi, 2020). Information collected and used for specific purposes may inadvertently lead to privacy concerns. While gathering and using information, banks must ensure it does not harm the end-user or customer. Business proposals, product ideas, and partnership deals intending to collect and use personal information should follow ethical practices. Collection of information should be fair, the purpose of non-core operations should be disclosed, informed choice should be provided for information usage, and the organization's policies regarding personal information should be transparent (Gupta & Yadav, 2017).

DISCUSSION AND CONCLUSIONS

The significance of Social Media in BANK's communications can no longer be ignored. Research shows that around two-thirds of the global internet population regularly visits social networking sites, and the time spent on these platforms is increasing at a faster rate than the overall internet usage. As a non-traditional method of interaction, Social Media is gaining importance across all sectors, including the banking industry, presenting a valuable opportunity for banks. In the international banking world, there is an ongoing discussion about the role of Social Media in business. Banks are gradually realizing that social media can play a pivotal role in their overall business strategy (Pejić Bach, Krstić, Seljan, & Turulja, 2019). However, true evolution doesn't occur simply by adopting new tools; it necessitates a shift in behavior and a cultural change, not just a technological shift. Embracing this change will enable banks to fully harness the potential of Social Media and enhance their business prospects.

The widespread adoption of social media by consumers is undeniable. It's not just merchants who are leveraging social networks to engage with customers; businesses across various industries, including banks, have embraced this new way of interaction with clients, employees, and stakeholders. The rise of social media signifies a new era for banks, presenting both significant opportunities and challenges. Banks are actively utilizing social network sites to share information about their community service and philanthropic activities, market their products and services, provide customer support, foster engagement, and to some extent, offer access to banking services. However, the growth of commerce and payments on social networks also brings forth potential risks related to money laundering, fraudulent activities, and privacy violations (Mhlanga, 2020). In addition to fraud risks, social network users may unknowingly expose themselves to identity theft through social engineering, hacking, or unintentional data exposure. Even users' data can be inadvertently revealed. To unlock the full potential of the social channel, providers, users, and policymakers must stay vigilant and proactively guard against these risks to ensure a safe and secure environment for all stakeholders involved.

The provided policy and guideline framework offer valuable assistance to banks as they strategize their use of social media. By leveraging social media, banks can enhance their communication and engage with customers more effectively. Adopting the Social Media Governance Model will enable banks to maintain consistent customer experiences, ensure reliable content creation, uphold data governance, and comply with regulatory requirements. Additionally, the Information Security Guidelines will aid banks in mitigating risks associated with social network usage, thus promoting a secure and trustworthy social media presence (Gupta & Yadav, 2017).

Social media's immense popularity is undeniable, particularly among the youth who are not just enamored by it but also deeply involved in its use. While banks have expressed valid concerns about privacy and security, there are vast opportunities for them to enhance customer engagement, service, acquisition, and advocacy through social media. Some traditional players often argue that their customer profiles do not align with alternative delivery channels. However, even if only 10 percent of a bank's customer base is on social media and growing at a significant rate, it can still make a substantial impact. A technology fit study conducted on a Danish bank's social media initiative revealed that social media and banking tasks exhibit a high to medium fit across various parameters. Utilizing social media is a cost-effective way for banks to build their brand in sync with Gen Y and future generations.

The platform presents opportunities for co-creating products with customers through crowdsourcing. Dedicated Twitter accounts and blogs are effective in facilitating real-time conversations with small groups or individuals, thereby enhancing the customer experience. Online customer surveys in real-time can also be conducted, enabling open communication and interaction with customers. Even if some banks choose to avoid social media due to fears and doubts, the impact of customers on social media can still affect them, often negatively. Instances of poor customer service can quickly go viral, and delays in response can significantly harm a bank's image and reputation, potentially resulting in the loss of new business. Being present on social media allows banks to address issues before they escalate out of control and enables them to tap into emerging customer trends and preferences. To remain relevant and appeal to Gen Y, incumbent players must recognize the significant value proposition that these young customers offer.

The choice to have a social media presence is no longer optional; it has become a business imperative. While brick-and-mortar establishments are not disappearing, they can complement and reinforce each other effectively. Banks possess vast amounts of detailed information on their customers, and social media can be a valuable resource for mining and harvesting rich data. By leveraging social media insights, banks can conduct economic and customer research and identify important trends to optimize their strategies for growth and improved customer relationships. The future lies in finding a balance between physical and digital channels, harnessing the power of social media to augment traditional banking methods. This approach allows banks to capitalize on their vast information repositories and truly understand and cater to their customers' needs and preferences.

REFERENCES

Agboola, A. (2006). *Information and communication technology (ICT) in banking operations in Nigeria: An evaluation of recent experiences*. Academic Press.

Agnihotri, D., Kulshreshtha, K., & Tripathi, V. (2022). Emergence of social media as new normal during COVID-19 pandemic: A study on innovative complaint handling procedures in the context of banking industry. *International Journal of Innovation Science*, *14*(3/4), 405–427. doi:10.1108/IJIS-10-2020-0199

Ahmad, T. (2019). Law and Policy Relating to Bank Fraud and its Prevention and Control. *Int'l JL Mgmt. & Human.*, *2*, 7.

Alawode, A. J., & Kaka, E. U. (2011). Information and communication technology (ICT) and banking industry. *Mediterranean Journal of Social Sciences*, *2*(4), 71–74.

Arumugam, T., Latha Lavanya, B., Karthik, V., Velusamy, K., Kommuri, U. K., & Panneerselvam, D. (2022). Portraying Women in Advertisements: An Analogy Between Past and Present. *American Journal of Economics and Sociology*, *81*(1), 207–223. doi:10.1111/ajes.12452

Arumugam, T., Sethu, S., Kalyani, V., Shahul Hameed, S., & Divakar, P. (2022). Representing Women Entrepreneurs in Tamil Movies. *American Journal of Economics and Sociology*, *81*(1), 115–125. doi:10.1111/ajes.12446

Bagga, R. (2018). The National Cyber Security Policy of India 2013: An Analytical Study. *Indian JL & Just.*, *9*, 164.

Bekmamedova, N., & Shanks, G. (2014, January). Social media analytics and business value: a theoretical framework and case study. In *2014 47th Hawaii international conference on system sciences* (pp. 3728-3737). IEEE. 10.1109/HICSS.2014.464

Broby, D. (2021). Financial technology and the future of banking. *Financial Innovation*, *7*(1), 1–19. doi:10.118640854-021-00264-y

Castaldi, C. (2020). All the great things you can do with trademark data: Taking stock and looking ahead. *Strategic Organization*, *18*(3), 472–484. doi:10.1177/1476127019847835

Chandani, A., Divekar, R., Neeraja, B., Mehta, M., & Atiq, R. (2022, February). A Study to Analyze Use of Social Media by Private and Public Sector Banks in India. In *Achieving $5 Trillion Economy of India: Proceedings of 11th Annual International Research Conference of Symbiosis Institute of Management Studies* (pp. 135-152). Singapore: Springer Nature Singapore. 10.1007/978-981-16-7818-9_8

Chatterjee, S., & Kar, A. K. (2020). Why do small and medium enterprises use social media marketing and what is the impact: Empirical insights from India. *International Journal of Information Management*, *53*, 102103. doi:10.1016/j.ijinfomgt.2020.102103

Chaturvedi, M. M., Gupta, M. P., & Bhattacharya, J. (2008). *Cyber security infrastructure in India: a study. Emerging Technologies in E-Government.* CSI Publication.

Dery, K., Sebastian, I. M., & van der Meulen, N. (2017). The digital workplace is key to digital innovation. *MIS Quarterly Executive*, *16*(2).

GhelaniD.HuaT. K.KoduruS. K. R. (2022). Cyber Security Threats, Vulnerabilities, and Security Solutions Models in Banking. Authorea Preprints. doi:10.22541/au.166385206.63311335/v1

Gupta, S., & Yadav, A. (2017). The impact of electronic banking and information technology on the employees of banking sector. *Management and Labour Studies*, *42*(4), 379–387. doi:10.1177/2393957517736457

He, W., Wu, H., Yan, G., Akula, V., & Shen, J. (2015). A novel social media competitive analytics framework with sentiment benchmarks. *Information & Management*, *52*(7), 801–812. doi:10.1016/j.im.2015.04.006

Kalyani, V. (2017). Empowering Women Farmers Participation In Organic Agricultural Development. *International Journal of Multidisciplinary Educational Research*, *6*(2), 187.

Kalyani, V. (2018). Organic farming in Tamil Nadu: Status, Issues and Prospects. American International Journal of Research in Humanities. *Arts and Social Sciences*, *21*(1), 82–86.

Kalyani, V. (2020). *Perception of Certified Organic Farmers towards Organic Farming Practices in Pudukkottai District of TamilNadu (No. 4784).* Easy Chair.

KalyaniV. (2021a). *A Study of Effect of Social Networking Sites on the Self-Esteem of Adolescent Girl Students Belonging to Urban Areas of Sivaganga District.* Available at SSRN 3879915. doi:10.2139/ssrn.3879915

Kalyani, V. (2021b). *Marketing Intelligence Practices on Fmcg Consumer Preferences and Buying Behaviour Pattern Using Social Network Analysis (No. 5857).* Easy Chair.

Kalyani, V. (2021c). *Parental Involvement in Improving Children's Learning in Social Work Perspective (No. 5107).* Easy Chair.

Kalyani, V. (2021d). *The Employee Engagement on Human Resources Information System Practice Through E-Learning Training (No. 5856).* EasyChair.

Kalyani, V. (2023). Regression Analysis in R: A Comprehensive View for the Social Sciences. *Journal of the Royal Statistical Society. Series A, (Statistics in Society)*, qnad081. Advance online publication. doi:10.1093/jrsssa/qnad081

Kalyani, V., Arumugam, T., & Surya Kumar, M. (2022). Women in Oppressive Societies as Portrayed in Kollywood Movies. *American Journal of Economics and Sociology*, *81*(1), 173–185. doi:10.1111/ajes.12450

Kaplan, A. M., & Haenlein, M. (2010). Users of the world, unite! The challenges and opportunities of Social Media. *Business Horizons*, *53*(1), 59–68. doi:10.1016/j.bushor.2009.09.003

Kapsoulis, N., Psychas, A., Palaiokrassas, G., Marinakis, A., Litke, A., & Varvarigou, T. (2020). Know your customer (KYC) implementation with smart contracts on a privacy-oriented decentralized architecture. *Future Internet*, *12*(2), 41. doi:10.3390/fi12020041

Kazemi, A., PaEmami, V. M., Abbaszadeh, A., & Pourzamani, J. (2013). Impact of brand identity on customer loyalty and word of mouth communications, considering mediating role of customer satisfaction and brand commitment (Case study: Customers of Mellat Bank in Kermanshah). *International Journal of Academic Research in Economics and Management Sciences*, *2*(4), 1–14. doi:10.6007/IJAREMS/v2-i4/1

Khanna, A., & Arora, B. (2009). A study to investigate the reasons for bank frauds and the implementation of preventive security controls in Indian banking industry. *International Journal of Business Science and Applied Management*, *4*(3), 1–21.

Kuchciak, I., & Wiktorowicz, J. (2021). Empowering financial education by banks—Social media as a modern channel. *Journal of Risk and Financial Management*, *14*(3), 118. doi:10.3390/jrfm14030118

Kumar, V. A., Pandey, K. K., & Punia, D. K. (2014). Cyber security threats in the power sector: Need for a domain specific regulatory framework in India. *Energy Policy*, *65*, 126–133. doi:10.1016/j.enpol.2013.10.025

Kumari, S., & Jindal, P. (2021). The Impact of Social Media on Customer Satisfaction in the Indian Banking Industry. *Journal of Management Information and Decision Sciences*, *24*, 1–15.

Kumari, S., Jindal, P., & Mittal, A. (2023). Employee Productivity: Exploring the Multidimensional Nature with Acculturation, Open Innovation, Social Media Networking and Employee Vitality in the Indian Banking Sector: An Analytical Approach. *International Journal of Professional Business Review*, *8*(7), e02535–e02535. doi:10.26668/businessreview/2023.v8i7.2535

MalhotraD. P. (2017). Impact of social networking sites on financial performance: A case study of Indian banks. Available at SSRN 2965888. doi:10.2139/ssrn.2965888

Manikandan, G., Murugaiah, S., Velusamy, K., Ramesh, A. B. K., Rathinavelu, S., Viswanathan, R., & Jageerkhan, M. N. (2022). Work Life Imbalance and Emotional Intelligence: A Major Role and Segment Among College Teachers. *International Journal of Professional Business Review*, *7*(6), e0832. doi:10.26668/businessreview/2022.v7i6.832

Manzira, F. M., & Bankole, F. (2018, October). Application of Social Media Analytics in the banking sector to drive growth and sustainability: A proposed integrated framework. In *2018 Open Innovations Conference (OI)* (pp. 223-233). IEEE. 10.1109/OI.2018.8535833

Mhlanga, D. (2020). Industry 4.0 in finance: The impact of artificial intelligence (ai) on digital financial inclusion. *International Journal of Financial Studies, 8*(3), 45. doi:10.3390/ijfs8030045

Miranda, F. J., Chamorro, A., Rubio, S., & Morgado, V. (2013). Evaluation of social networks sites in the banking sector: An analysis of top 200 international banks. *Journal of Internet Banking and Commerce, 18*(2), 1–18.

Mohamed, S. M., Yehia, E., & Marie, M. (2022). Relationship between E-CRM, Service Quality, Customer Satisfaction, Trust, and Loyalty in banking Industry. *Future Computing and Informatics Journal, 7*(2), 51–74. doi:10.54623/fue.fcij.7.2.5

Parusheva, S. (2017). Social Media Banking Models: A case study of a practical implementation in banking sector. *Икономически изследвания,* (3), 125-141.

Pejić Bach, M., Krstić, Ž., Seljan, S., & Turulja, L. (2019). Text mining for big data analysis in financial sector: A literature review. *Sustainability (Basel), 11*(5), 1277. doi:10.3390u11051277

Razmerita, L., Kirchner, K., & Nielsen, P. (2016). What factors influence knowledge sharing in organizations? A social dilemma perspective of social media communication. *Journal of Knowledge Management, 20*(6), 1225–1246. doi:10.1108/JKM-03-2016-0112

Rootman, C., & Cupp, N. (2016). The impact of social media on customer satisfaction and retention in the banking industry: Views of clients and managers. *Journal of Chemical Information and Modeling,* 281–298.

Sarigianni, C., Thalmann, S., & Manhart, M. (2016, January). Protecting knowledge in the financial sector: An analysis of knowledge risks arising from social media. In *2016 49th Hawaii International Conference on System Sciences (HICSS)* (pp. 4031-4040). IEEE.

Sawhney, A., & Ahuja, V. (2022). Drivers of social media content marketing in the banking sector: A literature review. *Research Anthology on Social Media Advertising and Building Consumer Relationships,* 396-418.

Sawhney, A., Ahuja, V., & Sharma, P. (2022). Role of Social Media in the Indian Banking Sector. In Multidisciplinary Perspectives Towards Building a Digitally Competent Society (pp. 31-50). IGI Global. doi:10.4018/978-1-6684-5274-5.ch002

Singh, A. N., Picot, A., Kranz, J., Gupta, M. P., & Ojha, A. (2013). Information security management (ism) practices: Lessons from select cases from India and Germany. *Global Journal of Flexible Systems Managment, 14*(4), 225–239. doi:10.100740171-013-0047-4

Singh, N., Chakraborty, A., Biswas, S. B., & Majumdar, M. (2020). Impact of social media in banking sector under triangular neutrosophic arena using MCGDM technique. *Neutrosophic Sets and Systems, 35,* 153-176.

Uma Ganesh. (2022). *Need of the hour: Social media an absolute must for banks*. Available at: https://www.financialexpress.com/industry/banking-finance/need-of-the-hour-social-media-an-absolute-must-for-banks/2416559/

Uppal, R. K. (2008). Information Technology Changing Performance of Banking Industry-Emerging Challenges and New Potentials. *Gyan Management Journal*, 2(1), 76–99.

Vandana Ahuja. (2020). *The 7 Functional Benefits of social media for the banking industry*. Available at: https://customerthink.com/the-7-functional-benefits-of-social-media-for-the-banking-industry/

Vrontis, D., Makrides, A., Christofi, M., & Thrassou, A. (2021). Social media influencer marketing: A systematic review, integrative framework and future research agenda. *International Journal of Consumer Studies*, *45*(4), 617–644. doi:10.1111/ijcs.12647

Ying, F., Dartey, S., Ahakwa, I., Odai, L. A., Bright, D., & Amoabeng, S. M. (2021). Ascertaining the perceived risks and benefits of social media usage on the behavioural intent of employees: study of the banking sectors in Ga-West municipality: mediating role of user satisfaction. *International Research Journal of Advanced Engineering and Science*, *6*(1), 109–116.

Chapter 12
Promoting Online Safety:
The Government's Role in Combating Cyber Harassment and Cybercrime Through Social Media Platforms

Ravishankar Krishnan

Vel Tech Rangarajan Dr. Sagunthala R&D Institute of Science and Technology, India

Rajalakshmi Vel

Sri Ramachandra Institute of Higher Education and Research, India

Priyanka Zala

GLS University, India

S. Thandayuthapani

Vel Tech Rangarajan Dr. Sagunthala R&D Institute of Science and Technology, India

H. Moideen Batcha

https://orcid.org/0000-0003-0708-8327

B.S. Abdur Rahman Crescent Institute of Science and Technology, India

Kalyani Velusamy

https://orcid.org/0000-0003-1795-9632

DMI-St. Eugene University, Malawi

Theju Kumar Chandrappa

Department of Criminology and Forensic Science, Acharya Institute of Graduate Studies, India

ABSTRACT

Social media offers great power and potential to all kinds of users, and it is not free from threats and risks that come along with the adoption of new tools and innovations. There is cyber stalking, sexting, bullying happening substantially. Anonymity of the virtual world has contributed to online harassment and lack of awareness. This research assesses the awareness and perception of female college students of Indian universities. The opinion of senior government officials in regulating social media to improve cyber resilience is sought. Using judgement sampling technique, 463 responses were collected through questionnaire method. The majority of respondents perceive social media as a useful place for infotainment. There is awareness however that respondents don't want to limit themselves and they are open to posting pictures, tweeting, commenting on unknown posts. Among many online platforms, incidence of cyber harassment is high on social media platforms. The main contribution of this study is to emphasize the need to treat cyber behaviour as a foundational course in today's parallel world.

DOI: 10.4018/978-1-6684-7450-1.ch012

INTRODUCTION

The internet has become a significant communication channel in the modern era, and social media holds a significant portion of internet usage. It is predicted that a large number of users would have used social media in 2021. The increased usage of the internet and social media has led to cybersecurity being recognized as a critical issue in most countries. This may be attributed to the growing trend of high social media usage, which allows for reaching a wide audience in a short period. The presence of numerous social media platforms, their unreliable design and construction, the abundance of unstructured content, and the increased opportunities for malicious activities have made social media vulnerable to high-level cyber threats. The history of cybercrimes in the IT industry can be traced back to the late 1970s. Over time, these crimes have evolved from simple spam to more sophisticated forms like viruses and malware (Soomro, & Hussain, 2019). The term "cybercrimes" encompasses a wide range of illegal activities carried out by cybercriminals through internet-connected electronic devices. Cybercriminals often target easy and vulnerable individuals, leveraging their knowledge of technology and its vulnerabilities. These criminals exploit gullible users using various methods to collect personal data (Soomro, & Hussain, 2019). The internet has become an integral part of society, serving as a platform for connecting and sharing information. Consequently, it has become a prime target for a range of cyber threats, including hacking, identity theft, fraud, cyber espionage, terrorism, and warfare. Cybercrimes cover a broad spectrum of threats, including child pornography, email abuse, stalking, copyright violations, and more. The impact of these threats varies based on factors such as globalization, security environment, awareness, and education levels of administrators and users (Alguliyev, Aliguliyev & Yusifov, 2018). The consequences can range from data loss and financial damage to harm to individuals' health and well-being.

CYBER HARASSMENT: A MOUNTING WORRY IN THE AGE OF COVID WORLDWIDE

The COVID-19 pandemic has brought about significant transformations in various aspects of our daily lives. With widespread lockdown measures in place worldwide, our new "normal" heavily relies on digital platforms. Since March 2020, there has been a remarkable increase in global internet usage, soaring by 50-70%. The advancements in digital technologies have enabled the world to adapt by moving jobs and services online, facilitating remote work, online grocery shopping, virtual communication with distant family members, and telehealth appointments. However, along with increased connectivity, the digital space has also witnessed a surge in cyber harassment. This form of violence manifests in different ways, including online bullying, cyber stalking, hate speech, and public shaming (Lallie, et al, 2021). Similar to offline violence, cyber harassment inflicts negative psychological, social, and reproductive health impacts on its victims and can even escalate to physical and sexual violence offline. Moreover, it has significant economic consequences. For instance, recent research from the Australian Institute estimates that online harassment and cyberhate have cost Australia approximately \$3.7 billion in health expenses and lost income (Amarullah, A. H., Runturambi, & Widiawan, 2021).

During the 16 Days of Activism against Gender-Based Violence, it is crucial to address all forms of violence against women, particularly prioritizing actions to combat cyber harassment intensified by the pandemic. Despite the digital divide hindering many women from accessing and utilizing internet services, they remain disproportionately affected by digital abuse. Even before the pandemic, women, especially young women, were more likely to be targeted by cyber violence. In the United States, for example, 21% of women aged 18 to 29 reported experiencing online sexual harassment, a significantly higher percentage compared to their male counterparts at 9%. Since the onset of the COVID-19 pandemic, there has been a global rise in online harassment targeting women and girls, with reports from countries like the Philippines, Australia, India, and regions such as the Middle East and North Africa (Lessard, & Puhl, 2021). Addressing online sexual harassment is essential for creating a safe digital environment. However, legislation to protect women from such harassment lags behind, deterring women from seeking justice due to concerns of not being taken seriously. According to recent data from Women, Business and the Law, only 29% of economies (56 out of 190) have legislation specifically addressing cyber harassment. Regionally, South Asia leads with 50% of economies providing legal protection, followed by Latin America and the Caribbean at 38% and the Middle East and North Africa at 35%. Other regions, including OECD high-income countries, have relatively higher percentages than the global average. However, there is room for improvement in Europe and Central Asia, East Asia and the Pacific, and Sub-Saharan Africa to promote legal reforms and policy recommendations on cyber harassment (Dye et al., 2021) same has explained in Figure 1.

Figure 1. Legal reforms and policy recommendations on cyber harassment
Source: Women Business and the Law database

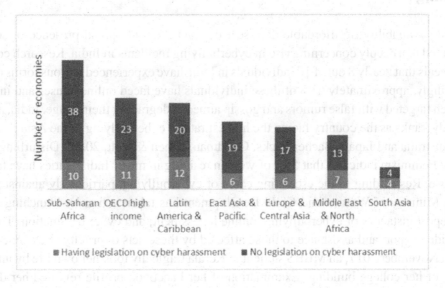

In the absence of legal protections, the harmful consequences of the hostile online environment can limit women's access to various e-services, undermining their freedom of expression and information. Additionally, the existing digital gender gap hinders women from acquiring the necessary skills to enter the digital sector and secure tech jobs. However, creating a safe, affordable, and inclusive digital space has the potential to increase women's online participation, bridging the digital gender gap and generating positive economic outcomes (ain, Gupta, Satam, & Panda, 2020). Fortunately, in some economies, governments and civil society organizations (CSOs) have implemented effective practices to combat cyber harassment. For instance, the Philippines has enacted the Safe Spaces Act, which defines and penalizes gender-based online sexual harassment. Australia has established the world's first government agency, the eSafety Commissioner, to address cyber violence complaints and promote online safety. The Association of Media Women in Kenya (AMWIK) has provided digital security training to empower Kenyan women journalists in countering online harassment. Bangladesh has introduced an all-woman police unit to encourage women to report digital abuse and harassment (Kee et al,.2022).

The Covid-19 pandemic has heightened our reliance on digital tools, leading to an increase in cyber harassment incidents. Therefore, it is crucial to promptly adopt urgent measures, including legislative protections, to address this new reality and safeguard women and girls from digital abuse. Civil society organizations can also play a vital role in raising public awareness, building capacity to identify and report cyber harassment, and facilitating access to tools and services that mitigate its impact (Rodriguez-Rivas et al., 2022). Collaborative efforts involving international society, governments, and policymakers are necessary to gradually bring about legal changes that promote equal access to a safe online environment for both men and women.

THE CURRENT STATE OF CYBER BULLING AND CYBERCRIME IN INDIA: ALARMING GROUND REALITY

Cyber Bulling

The increasing availability of affordable data services and the widespread presence of social media have contributed to a deeply concerning rise in cyberbullying incidents in India. Research conducted by Symantec reveals that nearly 8 out of 10 individuals in India have experienced various forms of cyberbullying. Shockingly, approximately 63% of these individuals have faced online abuses and insults, while 59% have been targeted with false rumors and gossip aimed at degrading their image. India, according to the same study, ranks as the country facing the highest rate of cyberbullying in the Asia Pacific region, surpassing Australia and Japan (Bacher-Hicks, Goodman, Green & Holt, 2022). Disturbingly, a survey conducted by Feminism indicates that 50% of women residing in major Indian cities have fallen victim to online abuse. Responding to the escalating cases of cyberbullying, particularly against women and children, the Ministry of Women and Child Development has taken action by launching a dedicated helpline to report instances of cyberbullying, online harassment, and cyber defamation. This initiative aims to provide support and assistance to those affected by these acts of cruelty (Kaur & Saini, 2023). Tragically, in November 2017, an MBBS student in Kerala tragically took her own life by jumping from the top floor of her college building. Examination of her Facebook profile revealed her distress over the cruel comments made by one of her peers, leading the police to suspect that cyberbullying played a significant role in her decision to take such a tragic step. In another incident, back in February 2017, students participating in a literary event at Delhi's Ramjas College were attacked by members of the Akhil Bharatiya Vidyarthi Parishad (ABVP). At that time, little did a 20-year-old student from Lady Shri Ram College, Delhi, imagine that her online campaign against the violence would forever change her life (Kethineni, 2020). Since then, the student, Gurmehar Kaur, has been subjected to relentless trolling and extensive abuse on various social media platforms. To make matters worse, she has even received death and rape threats. These incidents shed light on the distressing state of cyberbullying in

India. Each day, another innocent life becomes subjected to online torment and cyberbullying. It is an unfortunate reality that requires urgent attention and concerted efforts to protect individuals from such acts of cruelty (Srivastava, 2012).

Cybercrime

The prevalence of affordable data services and widespread social media presence has led to a distressing increase in cyberbullying incidents in India. Research conducted by Symantec reveals that nearly 8 out of 10 individuals in India have experienced various forms of cyberbullying. Shockingly, around 63% of these individuals have faced online abuses and insults, while 59% have been targeted with false rumors and gossip aimed at degrading their image. In the Asia Pacific region, India ranks highest in cyberbullying cases, surpassing countries like Australia and Japan. Disturbingly, a survey conducted by Feminism indicates that 50% of women in major Indian cities have become victims of online abuse. Responding to the rising cases of cyberbullying, particularly against women and children, the Ministry of Women and Child Development has launched a dedicated helpline to report instances of cyberbullying, online harassment, and cyber defamation. This initiative aims to provide support and assistance to those affected (Deep & Sharma, 2018). Tragically, in November 2017, an MBBS student in Kerala took her own life by jumping from the top floor of her college building. Examination of her Facebook profile revealed her distress over the malicious comments made by one of her peers, leading the police to suspect that cyberbullying played a significant role in her decision to take such a drastic step. In another incident, in February 2017, students participating in a literary event at Delhi's Ramjas College were attacked by members of the Akhil Bharatiya Vidyarthi Parishad (ABVP). Unbeknownst to a 20-year-old student from Lady Shri Ram College, Gurmehar Kaur, her online campaign against the violence would forever change her life. Since then, she has been subjected to relentless trolling and extensive abuse on various social media platforms. To make matters worse, she has even received death and rape threats. These instances highlight the distressing reality of cyberbullying in India (Tanwar et al, 2020). Each day, innocent lives are subjected to torment and bullying online, reflecting the urgent need for concerted efforts to address and combat this pervasive issue.

The prevailing cybercrime scenario in our country fails to accurately depict the true state of affairs on the ground. According to data from the National Crime Records Bureau (NCRB), the number of registered cybercrime cases in India witnessed an increase from 11,331 cases in 2015 to 12,187 cases in 2016. This reflects a 20.50 percent rise in cybercrime cases in 2015 compared to 2014, followed by a 6.3 percent increase in cases in 2016 compared to 2015. In terms of the distribution of cybercrime cases, Uttar Pradesh recorded the highest number with 2,639 cases, followed by Maharashtra (2,380) and Karnataka (1,101). Tamil Nadu witnessed a decline from 172 cases in 2014 to 142 cases in 2015, with a marginal increase to 144 cases in 2016. Among the metropolitan cities, Mumbai topped the list with 980 cases, followed by Bengaluru with 762 cases, and Jaipur with 532 cases. Chennai, with 26 cases, ranked 16th among the metro cities (Pradheep, Sheeba, Yogeshwaran, & Pradeep Devaneyan, 2017). During my tenure as Additional Director General of Crime Branch CID, I encountered various types of cybercrime cases. I vividly recall an incident where a distraught woman approached my office, tearfully recounting how her husband had been defrauded of Rs 45 lakh through WhatsApp under the false promise of employment in Auckland, New Zealand. Fortunately, we were able to detect the case and recover a portion of the money (Verma, Verma, Pal, & Verma, 2022).

The Cyber Cell also handled several diverse cases, including instances of child pornography, resulting in the detention of the accused under the Goondas Act. The key point I want to emphasize here is that Tamil Nadu, like the rest of the world, is not immune to cybercrime. Social media users in Tamil Nadu are equally vulnerable to cybercriminals, and they face the same risks of cyber-stalking, harassment, hacking, spoofing, cheating, fraud, spamming, squatting, trespassing, white-collar crimes, embezzlement, spying, child pornography, cyber trafficking, identity theft, cyber-bullying, and more, as individuals in other regions do. The widespread adoption of social media in Tamil Nadu has proven to be a double-edged sword when it comes to maintaining law and order. On one hand, social media platforms have facilitated tremendous contributions by volunteers during events like the Chennai floods in December 2015 and the aftermath of Cyclone Vardah (Sudhahar, & Fernandez, 2016). However, on the other hand, social media has played a sinister role in the rapid dissemination of fake messages, leading to incidents of lynching and assaults fueled by unfounded fears of child trafficking in the northern districts of Tamil Nadu. Unfortunately, social media has taken an antisocial turn in the hands of rumor-mongers, with over 20 reported cases of lynching in our country in the past two months. Tamil Nadu, known for its high number of protests, witnessed 20,450 agitations in 2015. The advent of social media appears to have added fuel to the fire, enabling organizers and opposition parties to quickly, easily, and cheaply mobilize large crowds whether for causes like Jallikattu or to spread dissent against government policies (Sharma, & Kataria, 2022).

Undeniably, social media has played a crucial role in organizing and mobilizing major protests in Tamil Nadu, such as those against the nuclear power plant in Kudankulam, the hydrocarbon project in Neduvasal, Pudukottai, the Neutrino Observatory in Theni district, the Jallikattu ban, the Cauvery river dispute, and the Sterlite project in Thoothukudi. To combat cybercrime and defend against growing cyber attacks, the Tamil Nadu government is implementing several measures. It plans to establish Cyber Crime Police Stations in all districts and cities, as well as a state-of-the-art technology center called "Cyber Arangam" in Chennai, with an allocated budget of Rs 3.24 crore (Abaido, 2020). These initiatives aim to develop a cyber-resilient ecosystem through collaboration with top IT professionals. Furthermore, the government has recently sanctioned a dedicated Cyber cell for the Department of Vigilance and Anti-Corruption, in addition to the existing cyber cells at the CBCID and Chennai City Police headquarters. Despite these efforts, it is essential to acknowledge the challenges in combating cybercrime in our country. The foremost challenge lies in the reluctance of cybercrime victims to report cases. In 2016, only 142 cases were reported in the entire state of Tamil Nadu, with a mere 26 cases in the metropolitan city of Chennai. The National Crime Agency in the UK has reported that cybercrime has surpassed traditional crimes like burglary and car theft. If reporting of cyber cases improves in India, we may witness a similar trend (Alamri, Almaiah, & Al-Rahmi, 2020). Another concerning factor is the alarmingly low conviction rate in the few reported cases due to a lack of adequate technical expertise among police officers in investigating cybercrime and gathering cyber evidence. Many officers lack knowledge about the functioning of domains and servers. Addressing these challenges requires a concerted effort to encourage reporting, enhance technical expertise, and equip law enforcement agencies with the necessary resources to combat cybercrime effectively. Only then can we strive towards a safer digital environment for Tamil Nadu and the country as a whole. Another critical challenge in investigating cyber cases is the fact that 80 percent of cybercrimes occur on international servers. When a crime takes place on platforms like Facebook, we face limitations if Facebook refuses to release the data. Before the emergence of Facebook, the social media site Orkut was popular in Brazil (Cassidy, Faucher, & Jackson, 2017). Unfortunately, Google's Orkut platform became a convenient tool for cybercriminals in Brazil, enabling crimes ranging from child pornography to kidnappings and murders.

When the Brazilian Court ordered Google to share the data, Google refused to cooperate, citing jurisdictional issues. In our own country, Orkut faced similar challenges due to the propagation of hatred. It is evident that there is a need for globally accepted standards of sovereignty, governance, and net neutrality. From a legal standpoint, although India has an effective IT Act, amendments are necessary to provide effective support to the IT Act. Neglecting cybercriminals would be a grave mistake that puts us in great danger. We must not forget the havoc wreaked by the ill-gotten gains of cybercrime during the 2008 terrorist siege in Mumbai by Lashkar-e-Taiba (LeT) (Rana, & Singhal, 2015). The entire operation was funded by a Filipino hacking cell working on behalf of Jamaah Islamiyah, an associate of Al-Qaeda. The cybercriminals recruited by this cell siphoned off millions of dollars, which were then channeled to manipulators in Saudi Arabia. These manipulators laundered the funds to the Lashkar-e-Taiba team in Pakistan, who carried out the brutal attack on Mumbai. Ten individuals, armed not only with weapons but also with technology such as Blackberry phones, Skype, Google Earth, and GSM handsets, were able to bring a city of 12 million people, the fourth-largest metropolis in the world, to a complete standstill. The world watched the live telecast of this event. While guns and bombs have been used in terrorist operations before, these operatives utilized the power and brilliance of technology and social media, making them a new breed of attackers. Social media and technology became their arsenal (Sharma, & Kataria, 2022). They demonstrated their capability to gather open-source intelligence in real-time during the attack, not only from broadcast media but also by mining the internet and social media. The intelligence they obtained was used to target more people and outwit the authorities. This occurred in 2008, and now, we can only imagine what cybercriminals and terrorists are capable of in the present era of exponential technologies like artificial intelligence, 3D printing, robotics, nanotechnology, and more. It is essential that we take action to rein them in, or else the consequences could be dire (Rana, & Singhal, 2015).

AVAILABLE LEGAL RECOURSE FOR COMBATING CYBER BULLYING AND CYBERSECURITY

Cyberbullying refers to the act of bullying carried out through digital technologies, as defined by UNICEF. It takes place on various platforms such as social media, messaging apps, gaming platforms, and mobile phones. Cyberbullying involves repetitive behavior aimed at frightening, angering, or shaming the targeted individuals. It encompasses a wide range of actions, including posting hurtful words, derogatory comments, spreading false information on public platforms, as well as making threats of rape or violence (Kintonova, Vasyaev, & Shestak, 2021). The increased usage of the internet in a digitally empowered society has heightened the risk of youth falling victim to cyberbullying on social networking platforms. According to a survey conducted by Child Rights and You (CRY), a non-governmental organization, 22.4% of respondents aged 13-18 years, who spent more than three hours per day on the internet, were vulnerable to online bullying. Cyberbullying can have severe consequences on victims, leading to anxiety, depression, and other stress-related conditions. To combat this menace, there are legal provisions that can be utilized to penalize cyberbullies and address the issue of cyberbullying effectively (Nandhini, & Sheeba, 2015).

Indian Penal Code (IPC)

The Indian Penal Code encompasses various sections that address different forms of cyberbullying and prescribe penalties for offenders. Here are some relevant sections:

Section 354C: This section deals with the illegal act of clicking or photographing women without their consent, as well as following them without permission when they desire solitude. Offenders charged under this section may face a fine and imprisonment ranging from one to three years. If a cyberbully falls within this category and proceeds to upload such images, they may face legal consequences (Shah, 2019).

Section 499: This section targets individuals who send defamatory messages to others, regardless of the platform used, including email or any other internet-based platform. If such actions occur on social media or online, it may be considered cyberbullying, as it can have a detrimental impact on the victim's psychological well-being.

Section 507: According to this section, individuals who engage in criminal intimidation through anonymous communication can face up to two years of imprisonment. This provision aims to discourage threats made to others using anonymous means.

These sections of the Indian Penal Code serve as legal measures to address and penalize cyberbullying offenses, helping to protect individuals from the harmful effects of online harassment and intimidation (Shah, 2019).

Information Technology Act

The Information Technology (IT) Act encompasses several sections that address different forms of cyberbullying and prescribe penalties for offenders. Here are the relevant sections:

Section 66A: This section outlines the penalty for sending objectionable, derogatory, abusive, or hurtful messages or material via the internet on any social media or web chat room platform. Violators of this provision may face legal consequences.

Section 66D: Under this section, if a person deceives or cheats someone through the internet on a social media or any other online platform, they can be sentenced to up to three years in prison and fined up to Rs. 1 lakh.

Section 66E: Section 66E of the IT Act provides penalties for privacy violations. Knowingly violating the privacy of others by transmitting, capturing, or publishing personal photographs can lead to imprisonment for up to three years or a fine of up to three lakh rupees (Halder & Jaishankar, 2021).

Section 67: Section 67 of the Information Technology Act of 2000 deals with the transmission of obscene or lascivious material. Offenders may face imprisonment for up to five years and a fine of up to one lakh rupees.

These sections within the Information Technology Act serve as legal measures to address cyberbullying and related offenses, aiming to ensure the safety and protection of individuals in the digital realm (Halder & Jaishankar, 2021).

National Cyber Crime Reporting Portal

The National Cyber Crime Reporting (NCCR) portal is an initiative by the Government of India that provides a platform for victims, especially women and children, to lodge online complaints related to cyber crimes. This portal enables individuals to report incidents of cyber bullying, harassment, fraud, and other digital offenses. Once a complaint is filed through the NCCR portal, prompt action is taken by collaborating with local law enforcement agencies to ensure timely resolution and appropriate investigation of the reported cases. This initiative aims to provide a user-friendly and efficient system for reporting cyber crimes, contributing to a safer digital environment for all individuals in India (Srivastava, 2012).

TIPS TO AVOID CYBER BULLYING AND CYBER SECURITY

The online world offers numerous opportunities for connection, learning, and sharing what matters to you. However, it also poses challenges. If you've ever felt stressed, envious, lonely, or experienced a decline in self-esteem or social anxiety due to social media or the internet, please know that you're not alone (Cilliers, L., & Chinyamurindi, 2020). Here are five tips to prioritize your mental well-being and foster kindness online:

Refrain From Doomscrolling

Pay careful attention to how social media and online content influence your emotions, thoughts, and actions. How do they make you feel? Does reading the news leave you informed or stressed? Do photos of your friends at parties bring joy or envy? Do you habitually check your phone first thing in the morning for news updates? Identifying your online motivations and emotional responses can help you establish personal boundaries for the amount of time spent on social media or other apps. While it may not always be feasible to unfollow or report every person who affects your emotions negatively, you can try muting or limiting content from accounts that don't make you feel good. Remember, not everything you see online is real, even when it comes from your friends, but it's crucial to consider how it impacts you (Cilliers, L., & Chinyamurindi, 2020).

Practice Mindfulness

The internet offers a plethora of valuable resources and content that can aid in supporting various aspects of mental health and well-being. You can find meditation apps that assist in relaxation and focus, as well as platforms that facilitate personal growth, identity development, and fostering connections while offering mutual support. Explore the abundance of online learning tools that enable you to try new activities like drawing or yoga, fostering cognitive and creative skills. Additionally, you can access online exercise classes to promote physical health and unwind. Strive to discover positive and inspiring content and creators to follow, such as athletes, singers, home cooks, authors, or young individuals who advocate for causes close to their hearts. Remember, the internet and social media can also serve as avenues to seek professional assistance and access mental health information should the need arise (Cilliers, L., & Chinyamurindi, 2020).

Ensure Online Safety for Yourself and Others

Take the necessary steps to safeguard your online presence. Review the privacy settings of all your social media profiles. When your webcams are not in use, cover them to protect your privacy. Exercise caution when signing up for apps and online services, especially when providing personal information like your full name, address, or photos. If you come across something online that worries or disturbs you, it's important to reach out to a trusted adult, such as a parent or teacher. Report the incident on the relevant platform (remember to take a screenshot as evidence) and seek additional support by accessing safety helplines and mental health services available in your country. You can also contribute to the well-being of others by being attentive to their online experiences. Learn to recognize signs of distress or unwellness in classmates, friends, or even strangers. Extend a helping hand and assist them in seeking the support they may require (Elbedour, 2020).

Embrace Kindness

Utilize social media as a force for good by sharing uplifting and supportive content and messages with your friends, family, and classmates. Take the opportunity to reach out and let someone know that they are in your thoughts or leave a positive comment on a post they've shared. If you feel inclined to respond with negativity to a message or post, take a moment to pause and consider if there's another way to frame your thoughts or if an in-person conversation might be more appropriate. Should you encounter or receive bullying or abusive messages or content, promptly block and report it. Remember, our words hold weight, so it's crucial to thoughtfully consider what we share. Each of us possesses the power to spread kindness and brighten someone's day, so let's choose to spread love instead of hate.

Embrace the Present Moment and Real-Life Connections

The boundaries between our online and offline lives can often become blurred, making it challenging to truly live in the present and fulfill our natural desire for human interaction. Have you ever caught yourself interrupting a meaningful experience just to share it on social media or prioritizing scrolling through your friends' stories over actually reaching out and connecting with them? It's essential to consciously disconnect from social media and take regular breaks, allowing yourself the opportunity to spend quality time with friends and family in the real world, as long as it's safe to do so. Consider setting realistic and personal goals for yourself, such as refraining from using your phone or going online for the first hour of the day (as it drains your energy and conditions you to absorb unfiltered information), or avoiding screen time just before bed (Thakur, Hayajneh & Tseng, 2019). Engaging in activities like meditation, going for a walk, or having a phone call with a friend can provide similar stimulation while leaving you feeling more focused and relaxed. Prioritizing these experiences will enable you to stay present, nurture meaningful connections, and find balance in both the online and offline aspects of your life.

CONCLUSION AND RECOMMENDATIONS

As technology continues to advance and blended learning becomes a prominent paradigm in higher education, the number of social media users is increasing, particularly among youngsters. Unfortunately, the lack of awareness about social media ethics and the easy accessibility of the internet have led to a rise in cyberbullying. While social networking sites offer valuable collaborative learning environments, especially during events like the COVID-19 pandemic, they also expose students to hate speech and aggressive behavior online, making them vulnerable to cyberbullying victimization (Karmakar & Das,

2021). Some students misuse social media platforms to humiliate or harass their peers. Therefore, despite the convenience offered by social media, constant exposure and communication through online technologies put users' safety, emotional well-being, and psychological health at risk.

Over time, the Indian Government has launched various schemes (such as the Nirbhaya Scheme, CCPW Scheme, and I4C Scheme), established online reporting portals (such as the National Cybercrime Reporting Portal), introduced helpline numbers for women and children, and made amendments to the IT Act and Indian Penal Code 1860 to address cyberbullying. State governments have also initiated numerous awareness campaigns. Educational institutions, in compliance with UGC regulations, have implemented anti-bullying policies. However, the effectiveness of these initiatives depends on the responses received from the survey participants. It has been observed that students are generally unaware of these laws against cyberbullying. More than half of the participants have experienced cyberbullying, and a significant number admitted to bullying others as well. Cyberbullying victimization is influenced by various factors, including parental guidance and the duration of social media usage. Adequate parental advice and limited social media usage may help prevent students from being bullied. Peer bullying is most prevalent among male students in colleges and universities. Cyberbullying has detrimental psychological and physical effects on students, and it impairs their academic or professional performance (Rodzalan, Arif, & Noor, 2021). Victims commonly experience anger and depression. Two-thirds of the students surveyed are unaware of cyberbullying policies and laws.

Based on the study's findings, it is recommended that institutions and authorities organize seminars and counseling sessions to raise awareness about cyberbullying. Strict measures should be implemented to address cyberbullying, appropriate actions should be taken, and complaint portals should be established at the college and university level. This study sheds light on existing initiatives and provides insights into the current cyberbullying landscape in Indian higher education institutions. It concludes that more campaigns and seminars should be conducted to familiarize students with relevant legal provisions. However, the study also acknowledges a few limitations. Firstly, it only lists a few government initiatives and legal provisions based on popularity, without discussing state-specific programs and campaigns (Jean-Baptiste, 2021). Secondly, the sample size may be constrained due to survey length, resulting in limited responses from respondents who may belong to similar environments and face similar problems. In the future, efforts will be made to overcome these limitations.

REFERENCES

Abaido, G. M. (2020). Cyberbullying on social media platforms among university students in the United Arab Emirates. *International Journal of Adolescence and Youth*, *25*(1), 407–420. doi:10.1080/02673843.2019.1669059

Aishwarya, S., & Millath, M.A. (2019) Effectiveness of online marketing and hedonism among university students in Singapore. *International Journal of Recent Technology and Engineering*, *8*(2), 727–734.

Alamri, M. M., Almaiah, M. A., & Al-Rahmi, W. M. (2020). Social media applications afecting students' academic performance: A model developed for sustainability in higher education. *Sustainability (Basel)*, *12*(16), 6471. doi:10.3390u12166471

Alguliyev, R., Aliguliyev, R., & Yusifov, F. (2018). Role of social networks in E-government: Risks and security threats. *Online Journal of Communication and Media Technologies*, 8(4), 363–376.

Amarullah, A. H., Runturambi, A. J. S., & Widiawan, B. (2021, June). Analyzing cyber crimes during Covid-19 time in Indonesia. In *2021 3rd International Conference on Computer Communication and the Internet (ICCCI)* (pp. 78-83). IEEE. 10.1109/ICCCI51764.2021.9486775

Bacher-Hicks, A., Goodman, J., Green, J. G., & Holt, M. K. (2022). The COVID-19 pandemic disrupted both school bullying and cyberbullying. *American Economic Review: Insights*, 4(3), 353–370. doi:10.1257/aeri.20210456

Cassidy, W., Faucher, C., & Jackson, M. (2017). Adversity in University: Cyberbullying and Its Impacts on Students, Faculty and Administrators. *International Journal of Environmental Research and Public Health*, 14(8), 14. doi:10.3390/ijerph14080888 PMID:28786941

Chavadi, C. (2021). Growth drivers, characteristics, preference and challenges faced by Fast Moving Consumer Goods-A study with reference to Bengaluru. *Turkish Online Journal of Qualitative Inquiry, 12*(7).

Chavadi, C. A., Arul, M. J., & Sirothiya, M. (2020). Modelling the effects of creative advertisements on consumers: An empirical study. *Vision (Basel), 24*(3), 269–283. doi:10.1177/0972262920926074

Chavadi, C. A., Hiremath, C. V., & Hyderabad, R. L. (2014). Customer loyalty appraisal based on store characteristics: An alternative approach. *Indian Journal of Marketing, 44*(5), 18–29. doi:10.17010/ijom/2014/v44/i5/80375

Chavadi, C. A., & Kokatnur, S. S. (2008). Consumer Expectation and Perception of Fast Food Outlets: An Empirical Study in Davangere. *ICFAI Journal Of Services Marketing, 6*(2).

Chavadi, C. A., & Kokatnur, S. S. (2009). Impact of Short-Term Promotional Ads on Food Retailing. *ICFAI Journal of Consumer Behavior, 4*(1).

Chavadi, C. A., & Kokatnur, S. S. (2009). RFID Adoption by Indian Retailers: An Exploratory Study. *The Icfai University Journal of Supply Chain Management, 6*(1), 60–77.

Chavadi, C. A., Menon, S. R., & Sirothiya, M. (2019). Measuring Service Quality Perceptions of Indian E-retailers: An Evaluative Study. *Metamorphosis, 18*(2), 92–102. doi:10.1177/0972622519886232

Chavadi, C. A., Menon, S. R., & Sirothiya, M. (2019). Modelling the Effects of Brand Placements in Movies: An Investigative Study of Event Type and Placement Type. *Vision (Basel), 23*(1), 31–43. doi:10.1177/0972262918821227

Chavadi, C. A., Vishwanatha, M. R., & Mubeen, S. (2018). Ghee with Glee: A Study of How Consumers Evaluate Product Packaging. *Metamorphosis, 17*(2), 100–110. doi:10.1177/0972622518817407

Cilliers, L., & Chinyamurindi, W. (2020). Perceptions of cyber bullying in primary and secondary schools among student teachers in the Eastern Cape Province of South Africa. *The Electronic Journal on Information Systems in Developing Countries, 86*(4), e12131. doi:10.1002/isd2.12131

Deep, V., & Sharma, P. (2018, December). Analysis and Impact of Cyber Security Threats in India using Mazarbot Case Study. In *2018 International Conference on Computational Techniques, Electronics and Mechanical Systems (CTEMS)* (pp. 499-503). IEEE.

Dr, M., & Ayisha Millath, A. C. (2019). Indian Tea production Overview and Price Analysis. *International Journal of Advanced Science and Technology*, *28*(19), 1253–1259.

Dr, M., & Ayisha Millath, D. S. N. (2019). Identifying Work-Family Conflict Among IT Employees of Infopark, Kochi, Kerala. *International Journal of Advanced Science and Technology*, *28*(19), 1164–1176.

Dr, M., & Ayisha Millath, R. K. R. (2019). A Study and Analysis on Sustainable Business Models for Indian Automotive Industry. *International Journal of Advanced Science and Technology*, *28*(19), 953–959.

Dye, T. D., Alcantara, L., Siddiqi, S., Barbosu, M., Sharma, S., Panko, T., & Pressman, E. (2020). Risk of COVID-19-related bullying, harassment and stigma among healthcare workers: An analytical cross-sectional global study. *BMJ Open*, *10*(12), e046620. doi:10.1136/bmjopen-2020-046620 PMID:33380488

Elbedour, S., Alqahtani, S., Rihan, I. E. S., Bawalsah, J. A., Booker-Ammah, B., & Turner, J. F. Jr. (2020). Cyberbullying: Roles of school psychologists and school counselors in addressing a pervasive social justice issue. *Children and Youth Services Review*, *109*, 104720. doi:10.1016/j.childyouth.2019.104720

Faisal, M., Chandramohan, S., Millath, M. A., & Karthick, A. V. (2019) Influence of Fashion Behavior on Store Choice among the Arts College Students in Sivganga District. *International Journal of Recent Technology and Engineering, 8*(2), 672-676.

Halder, D., & Jaishankar, K. (2021). Cyber governance and data protection in India: A critical legal analysis. In *Routledge Companion to Global Cyber-Security Strategy* (pp. 337–348). Routledge. doi:10.4324/9780429399718-28

Hiremath, C. V., Chavadi, C. A., & Yatgiri, P. Y. (2013). Cloud Technology as an Alternative for Marketing Information System: An Empirical Study. *International Journal of Management. Research and Business Strategy, 2*(4).

Jain, O., Gupta, M., Satam, S., & Panda, S. (2020). Has the COVID-19 pandemic affected the susceptibility to cyberbullying in India? *Computers in Human Behavior Reports, 2*, 100029. doi:10.1016/j.chbr.2020.100029 PMID:34235292

Jean-Baptiste, C. B. (2021). *Cyberbullying: The Digital World of Awareness and Emerging Concerns* [Doctoral dissertation]. Long Island University, CW Post Center.

Karmakar, S., & Das, S. (2021). Understanding the rise of Twitter-based cyberbullying due to COVID-19 through comprehensive statistical evaluation. *Proceedings of the 54th Hawaii international conference on system sciences*. 10.24251/HICSS.2021.309

Karthick, A. V., & Millath, D. M. A. (2019). *Management of digital libraries for active learning environment: Trends and challenges*. Library Philosophy and Practice.

Karthick, A. V., Millath, D. M. A., & Thowseaf, S. (2018). Elucidating Water Supply, Demand and Contamination in Tamil Nadu. *Shanlax. International Journal of Management, 5*(3), 209–219.

Karthick, A. V., Millath, M. A., Karthik, R. R., & Faisal, M. (2019). Influence of social marketing on rain water harvesting practices for water recycling system. *International Journal of Recent Technology and Engineering*, 8(2), 654–661.

Karthik, R. R., Thowseaf, S., & Millath, M. A. (2018). Impact of demonetization and GST on stock price of automobile sector. *ZENITH International Journal of Multidisciplinary Research*, 8(11), 35–44.

Karumban, S., Sanyal, S., Laddunuri, M. M., Sivalinga, V. D., Shanmugam, V., Bose, V., . . . Murugan, S. P. (2023). Industrial Automation and Its Impact on Manufacturing Industries. In Revolutionizing Industrial Automation Through the Convergence of Artificial Intelligence and the Internet of Things (pp. 24-40). IGI Global.

Kaur, M., & Saini, M. (2023). Indian government initiatives on cyberbullying: A case study on cyberbullying in Indian higher education institutions. *Education and Information Technologies*, 28(1), 581–615. doi:10.100710639-022-11168-4 PMID:35814802

Kee, D. M. H., Al-Anesi, M. A. L., & Al-Anesi, S. A. L. (2022). Cyberbullying on Social Media under the Influence of COVID-19. *Global Business and Organizational Excellence*, 41(6), 11–22. doi:10.1002/joe.22175

Kethineni, S. (2020). Cybercrime in India: Laws, regulations, and enforcement mechanisms. The Palgrave Handbook of International Cybercrime and Cyberdeviance, 305-326.

Kintonova, A., Vasyaev, A., & Shestak, V. (2021). Cyberbullying and cyber-mobbing in developing countries. *Information and Computer Security*, 29(3), 435–456. doi:10.1108/ICS-02-2020-0031

Lallie, H. S., Shepherd, L. A., Nurse, J. R., Erola, A., Epiphaniou, G., Maple, C., & Bellekens, X. (2021). Cyber security in the age of COVID-19: A timeline and analysis of cyber-crime and cyber-attacks during the pandemic. *Computers & Security*, 105, 102248. doi:10.1016/j.cose.2021.102248 PMID:36540648

Lessard, L. M., & Puhl, R. M. (2021). Adolescent academic worries amid COVID-19 and perspectives on pandemic-related changes in teacher and peer relations. *The School Psychologist*, 36(5), 285–292. doi:10.1037pq0000443 PMID:34292037

Menon, S. R., & Chavadi, C. A. (2022). A Research-based Approach to Identify the Health-conscious Consumers in India. *Metamorphosis*, 21(2), 118–128. doi:10.1177/09726225221098783

Millath, M. A., & Thowseaf, S. (2016). Export performance of Special Economic Zones in India and its economic contribution. *International Journal of Innovative Research in Management Studies*, 1(10), 24–28.

Millath, M. A., & Thowseaf, S. (2017). An investigative study on stock performance of selected companies in food and beverage sector listed under BSE. *ZENITH International Journal of Business Economics & Management Research*, 7(4), 59–70.

Murugan, S. P., Shivaprasad, G., Dhanalakshmi, A., Sriram, V. P., Rajput, K., Mahesh, B. N., & Kedla, S. (2023). The Impact of COVID-19 on the Indian Microfinance Industry and Its Sustainability. In *Transforming Economies Through Microfinance in Developing Nations* (pp. 160–188). IGI Global. doi:10.4018/978-1-6684-5647-7.ch009

Nair, D. S., & Millath, M. A. (2018). An analytical study on the influence of gender on the reasons for opting flexible working hours among faculties of engineering colleges in Trivandrum District of Kerala. *ZENITH International Journal of Multidisciplinary Research, 8*(12), 195–200.

Nair, D.S., & Millath, M.A. (2019) Identifying family-work conflict among employees of the travancore cements limited, Kottayam, Kerala. *International Journal of Recent Technology and Engineering, 8*(2), 718–726.

Nandhini, B. S., & Sheeba, J. I. (2015, March). Cyberbullying detection and classification using information retrieval algorithm. In *Proceedings of the 2015 international conference on advanced research in computer science engineering & technology (ICARCSET 2015)* (pp. 1-5). 10.1145/2743065.2743085

Park, J. Y., Perumal, S. V., Sanyal, S., Ah Nguyen, B., Ray, S., Krishnan, R., Narasimhaiah, R., & Thangam, D. (2022). Sustainable Marketing Strategies as an Essential Tool of Business. *American Journal of Economics and Sociology, 81*(2), 359–379. doi:10.1111/ajes.12459

Pradheep, T., Sheeba, J. I., Yogeshwaran, T., & Pradeep Devaneyan, S. (2017, December). Automatic Multi Model Cyber Bullying Detection from Social Networks. *Proceedings of the International Conference on Intelligent Computing Systems.* 10.2139srn.3123710

Rajeswari, V., & Ayisha Millath, M. (2003). Brand Preference towards Water Purifier-A Study. *Indian Journal of Marketing, 13*, 9–15.

Rana, R., & Singhal, R. (2015). Chi-square test and its application in hypothesis testing. *Journal of the Practice of Cardiovascular Sciences*, 69–71.

Rodriguez-Rivas, M. E., Varela, J. J., González, C., & Chuecas, M. J. (2022). The role of family support and conflict in cyberbullying and subjective well-being among Chilean adolescents during the Covid-19 period. *Heliyon, 8*(4), e09243. doi:10.1016/j.heliyon.2022.e09243 PMID:35445156

Rodzalan, S. A., Arif, H., & Noor, N. N. M. (2021). Formal Generalization of Cyber Bullying: A Review Study. *Annals of the Romanian Society for Cell Biology*, 3105–3117.

S, M., & Millath M, A. (2019). Talent Management an Emerging Trend for Employee Effectiveness in Corporate Hospitals. *International Journal of Recent Technology and Engineering, 8*(4S5), 69–71

Saraladevi, E., Chandramohan, S., & Millath, M.A. (2019). Online shopping behavior pattern among school children. *International Journal of Recent Technology and Engineering, 8*(2), 695–699.

Shah, R. (2019). Cyber Crimes In India: Trends And Prevention. *International Journal of Research and Analytical Reviews, 6*(1).

Sharma, B., & Kataria, G. (2022). Surge in Cybercrime against Children in India amid the Pandemic. *Int'l JL Mgmt. & Human., 5*, 1279.

Sirothiya, M., & Chavadi, C. (2020). Compressed biogas (cbg) as an alternative and sustainable energy source in India: Case study on implementation frameworks and challenges. *Invertis Journal of Renewable Energy, 10*(2), 49–64. doi:10.5958/2454-7611.2020.00007.7

Sirothiya, M., & Chavadi, C. (2020). Evaluating marketing strategies ofcompressed biogas (CBG) companies in India using decision tree analysis. *IIMS Journal of Management Science*, *11*(3), 219–237. doi:10.5958/0976-173X.2020.00012.0

Sirothiya, M., & Chavadi, C. (2020). Role of compressed biogas to assess the effects of perceived value on customer satisfaction and customer loyalty. *BIMTECH Bus. Perspect*, *1*, 70–89.

Soomro, T. R., & Hussain, M. (2019). Social Media-Related Cybercrimes and Techniques for Their Prevention. *Appl. Comput. Syst.*, *24*(1), 9–17. doi:10.2478/acss-2019-0002

Sriram, V. P., Sanyal, S., Laddunuri, M. M., Subramanian, M., Bose, V., Booshan, B., . . . Thangam, D. (2023). Enhancing Cybersecurity Through Blockchain Technology. In Handbook of Research on Cybersecurity Issues and Challenges for Business and FinTech Applications (pp. 208-224). IGI Global.

Srivastava, S. (2012). Pessimistic side of information & communication technology: Cyber bullying and legislature laws. *International Journal of Advances in Computer Science and Technology*, *1*(1).

Sudhahar, M., & Fernandez, N. N. (2016). A Study on Effectiveness of Social Networking Sites in Advertising with Special Reference to Erode District-Tamilnadu (India). *International Journal of Management and Social Sciences*, *4*(9), 509–518.

Tagaymuratovna, P. D. (2022). Cyberbullying as a socio-psychological problem and legal ways to solve it abroad. *EPRA International Journal of Research and Development*, *7*(2), 28–31.

Tanwar, S., Paul, T., Singh, K., Joshi, M., & Rana, A. (2020, June). Classification and imapct of cyber threats in India: a review. In *2020 8th International Conference on Reliability, Infocom Technologies and Optimization (Trends and Future Directions) (ICRITO)* (pp. 129-135). IEEE. 10.1109/ICRITO48877.2020.9198024

Thakur, K., Hayajneh, T., & Tseng, J. (2019). Cyber security in social media: Challenges and the way forward. *IT Professional*, *21*(2), 41–49. doi:10.1109/MITP.2018.2881373

Thangam, D., Arumugam, T., Velusamy, K., Subramanian, M., Ganesan, S. K., & Suryakumar, M. (2022). COVID-19 Pandemic and Its Brunt on Digital Transformation and Cybersecurity. In Cybersecurity Crisis Management and Lessons Learned From the COVID-19 Pandemic (pp. 15-42). IGI Global.

Thangam, D., & Chavadi, C. (2023). Impact of Digital Marketing Practices on Energy Consumption, Climate Change, and Sustainability. *Climate and Energy*, *39*(7), 11–19. doi:10.1002/gas.22329

Thangam, D., Malali, A. B., Subramanian, G., Mohan, S., & Park, J. Y. (2022). Internet of things: a smart technology for healthcare industries. In *Healthcare Systems and Health Informatics* (pp. 3–15). CRC Press.

Thangam, D., Malali, A. B., Subramanian, G., & Park, J. Y. (2022). Transforming Healthcare through Internet of Things. In *Cloud and Fog Computing Platforms for Internet of Things* (pp. 15–24). Chapman and Hall/CRC. doi:10.1201/9781003213888-2

Thangam, D., Malali, A. B., Subramaniyan, G., Mariappan, S., Mohan, S., & Park, J. Y. (2022). Relevance of Artificial Intelligence in Modern Healthcare. In *Integrating AI in IoT Analytics on the Cloud for Healthcare Applications* (pp. 67–88). IGI Global. doi:10.4018/978-1-7998-9132-1.ch005

Thangam, D., Malali, A. B., Subramaniyan, S. G., Mariappan, S., Mohan, S., & Park, J. Y. (2021). Blockchain Technology and Its Brunt on Digital Marketing. In Blockchain Technology and Applications for Digital Marketing (pp. 1-15). IGI Global. doi:10.4018/978-1-7998-8081-3.ch001

Thangam, D., Vaidya, G. R., Subramanian, G., Velusamy, K., Selvi Govindarajan, K., & Park, J. Y. (2022). The Portrayal of Women's Empowerment in Select Indian Movies. *American Journal of Economics and Sociology*, *81*(1), 187–205. doi:10.1111/ajes.12451

Thawab, M. A., Thowseaf, S., Millath, M. A., & Ali, K. M. (2019) Reconnoitering the Impact of Economic Variables on Fruit Pulp Export from Tamil Nadu. *International Journal of Recent Technology and Engineering, 8*(4), 58-65.

Thowseaf, M. A. S., & Millath, M. A. (2016). A study on GST implementation and its impact on Indian industrial sectors and export. *International Journal of Management Research and Social Science*, *3*(2), 27–30.

Thowseaf, S., & Millath, M. A. (2016). Factors Influencing Export - A Conceptual Analysis. *International Journal of Management*, *7*(2), 150–158.

Thowseaf, S., & Millath, M. A. (2016). An analysis on Indian Forex for examining investment and trade option. *International Journal of Advanced Research in Management and Social Sciences*, *5*(9), 47–54.

Thowseaf, S., & Millath, M. A. (2017). Delineation on Demonetization Impact on Indian Economy. *International Journal of Innovative Knowledge Concepts*, *5*, 7.

Thowseaf, S., Millath, M. A., & Ali, K. M. Aftermath Effect Of GST On Consumer Purchasing Power. *Resturamt Business, 118*(5), 122-131.

Chapter 13
Leveraging Social Media Geographic Information for Smart Governance and Policy Making:
Opportunities and Challenges

Munir Ahmad
🆔 https://orcid.org/0000-0003-4836-6151
Survey of Pakistan, Pakistan

ABSTRACT

This chapter explored the use of social media geographic information in governance and policy-making. Social media geographic information has great potential to impact decision-making, citizen engagement, service delivery, crisis management, innovation, policy formation and evaluation, and public opinion assessment. However, challenges such as data quality, privacy concerns, data overload, standardization, limited access, ethics, technical issues, language barriers, and limited geographic coverage also arose. To address these challenges, policymakers should establish clear guidelines, ensure data accuracy, address privacy concerns, manage data overload, and promote ethical practices. Real-world applications in disaster response, traffic management, urban planning, air quality monitoring, disease outbreak tracking, and flood monitoring are also described. By harnessing social media geographic information while addressing challenges, policymakers can make informed decisions that benefit society.

INTRODUCTION

Social media has transformed the way people communicate, offering a multitude of options such as Twitter, Facebook, Instagram, and YouTube. These digital platforms present numerous opportunities to impact governance and policy-making processes. It enables direct communication between the government and the people, facilitating their participation in decision-making and allowing them to express

DOI: 10.4018/978-1-6684-7450-1.ch013

their opinions on governmental regulations and businesses. Social media has revolutionized the methods of data collection, analysis, and sharing. Social media networks gather their data from a wide range of sources, including geo-tagged postings, check-ins, hashtags, and many others. It serves as a valuable source of data, including geographic information, which is crucial for informed governance and policy-making. Social media data provides governments with valuable insights into public demands, concerns, and behaviors regarding governmental policies. Therefore, governments can analyze social media data for data-driven policy-making and thereby improve governance.Marketing, public health, urban planning, and emergency management are just a few of the areas that have seen a rise in the utilization of geographic information from social media. For instance, researchers have tracked the spread of diseases, kept an eye on public emotion and attitudes, and discovered patterns of human mobility in cities using spatial data from social media(Carroll et al., 2014; Signorini et al., 2011).

The real-time and dynamic nature of social media geographic information, which enables researchers and practitioners to easily access and analyze data, is one of its main advantages. According to Stamati et al., (2015),this real-time characteristic of social media geographic information can help in decision-making, resource allocation, and policy-making in contemporary situations. However, there are several issues with data quality, privacy, and bias associated with the use of social media geolocation information. For instance, the type of device, software, and network that social media users use can affect the accuracy of geo-tagging data (H. Gao et al., 2011). Additionally, the use of social media geographic information raises concerns about ethical issues, as it involves the collection and use of personal data without explicit consent (Kitchin, 2014a).

To this effect, the objective of this chapter is to present an overview of social media geographic information and its potential for smart governance and policy making. The concept of smart governance, social media geographic information, its characteristics, and its sources are endorsed in this chapter. It also discussed the opportunities and challenges associated with leveraging this data for smart governance and policymaking, including improved decision-making, increased citizen engagement, enhanced service delivery, improved crisis management, and increased innovation. Another goal of this chapter is to provide policymakers, public administrators, and researchers insights into how social media geographic information might improve public services and decision-making processes by making them more responsive, effective, and efficient.

To achieve these objectives, the chapter is organized as follows. Section 2 highlighted the concept of smart governance. Section 3 described the characteristics, benefits, and sources of social media geographic information. Section 4 designated the opportunities offered by social media geographic information. Section 5 offeredassociated challenges and Section 6 presentedthe applications whereas the last section concluded the chapter.

SMART GOVERNANCE

Governance refers to the collaborative approach to achieving collective goals through coordinated efforts(Willke, 2007). According to Stoker, (1998), governance is creating a conducive environment for "ordered rule and collective actions". The goal of governance is to administer the citizens through effective management of citizens' affairs. Governance encompasses decision-making, policy formulation, and implementation, as well as developing strategies and mechanisms for accountability and transparency. Governance is a multifaceted process that is steered by authorities and mechanisms(Paquet, 1999). Governance has been in use through various terminologies such as good governance, open governance, digital governance, e-governance, g-governance,urban governance, smart governance, and many more.

Smart governance is an approach that combines technology and collaboration between local government and citizens to address urban issues with a focus on sustainability (Meijer &Thaens, 2018). It underscoresthe leveraging of digital tools, data analytics methods, and emerging technologies to maximize efficiency, effectiveness, and responsiveness in governance. Smart governance is the smart use of ICT in decision-making through the collaboration of different stakeholders including government and citizens(Pereira et al., 2018).Smart governance utilizes smart technologies like big data, the Internet of Things (IoT), and Artificial Intelligence (AI) to boost old-fashioned administrative systems for informed decision-making(Webster & Leleux, 2018).

Smart Governance and Policy Making

Data governance and collaborative governance are the main drivers of smart governance and policymaking. A strong legal framework, normative factors, guiding principles, effective techniques, valuable data assets, human resources, advanced IT infrastructure, and many other aspects also support these drivers in achieving smart governance and policymaking (Parycek& Viale, 2017). Smart governance is a wide-ranging approach increasingly embraced by policymakers that combines smart decision-making, smart management, and smart collaboration to facilitate effective urban development (Ruhlandt, 2018). Urban participatory policymaking must be evaluated using a comprehensive strategy as more cities adopt the idea of smart governance to advance urban development (Castelnovo et al., 2016).

Smart Governance and Citizen Engagement

Smart governance is centered on citizen participation (Scholl & Scholl, 2014).There is broad recognition of the significant role citizens play in the transition toward a more sustainable socioeconomic system(Osella et al., 2016). Citizens possess valuable local knowledge and expertise, which, when combined with the strategic knowledge of organizations, is crucial for setting priorities and allocating limited resources (Voorberg et al., 2015). Governance in smart cities is based on active public participation. examining the success of participatory policymaking requires examining the extent of citizen engagement, the methods for obtaining public input, and the inclusivity of the decision-making processes(Castelnovo et al., 2016; Z. Gao et al., 2020).

SOCIAL MEDIA GEOGRAPHIC INFORMATION

Social Media Platforms

The popularity of social networks and microblogging sites like Facebook, Twitter, Pinterest, Instagram, and Foursquare has significantly increased in recent years, creating enormous amounts of data. According to Statista, there are over 4.8 billion social media users worldwide, generating vast amounts of data daily(Ani, 2023). Followings are the few prominent social media platforms that are a potential source of geographic information.

1. Facebook: As of 2023, there were more than 2.96 billion active monthly users of this social networking platform(Dixon, 2023). It allows users to create profiles, connect with friends and family, and share text, photos, and videos.
2. Twitter: As of 2023, there were more than 556 million active monthly users on this microblogging service(Dixon, 2023). Twitter is frequently used for public discourse, social activism, and real-time news updates.
3. Instagram: As of 2023, Instagram had more than 2 billion active monthly users(Dixon, 2023). It is a platform for sharing photos and videos. Influencers, famous people, and companies all use Instagram to advertise and promote their brands.
4. YouTube: As of 2023, there were more than 2.5 billion active monthly users of this video-sharing website(Dixon, 2023). YouTube is well-known for its user-generated content, education, and entertainment.

These are just a few examples of popular social media platforms. Many others serve different purposes and cater to different audiences.

Geographic Information

Geographic information pertains to data that possesses spatial attributes and is meticulously organized and showcased through the utilization of a Geographic Information System (GIS) (Hua & Feng, 2021). The role of GIS is of paramount importance as it seamlessly amalgamates diverse datasets originating from both public and private domains, furnishing a contextual framework for scrutinizing and making informed choices (Barr & Masser, 2019). Geographic information constitutes a fundamental element within all information retrieval procedures geared towards facilitating effective decision-making(Ali et al., 2021).Numerous entities situated across different locations contribute to the generation of geographic data, forming a distinctly distributed environment. Within this context, a multitude of technical and institutional challenges must be addressed to facilitate seamless data sharing in such a setting and to ultimately foster progress. To tackle this, numerous nations have adopted Spatial Data Infrastructures (SDIs) over the past four decades(Ahmad et al., 2022; Ali & Imran, 2020).Rapid availability and easy accessibility of spatial data stand as primary goals within the realm of SDIs. The effectiveness of SDIs hinges upon the foundational spatial datasets that underlie their functioning(Ahmad et al., 2022).

Social Media and Geographic Information

Social media data includes enormous amounts of unstructured and semi-structured data that people have created on various social media sites using posts, comments, likes, and shares on these sites (Kietzmann et al., 2011). Businesses, researchers, and individuals looking to learn more about user behaviour, preferences, and sentiment can benefit greatly from this vast resource. The potential for users of social media platforms to include geographic information in the content they publish is noteworthy, and this has led to the development of Social Media Geographic Information (SMGI). SMDI pertains to data related to locations that are acquired from social media platforms The widespread adoption of mobile devices that come equipped with GPS sensors has made it even easier for users to share their location, thereby providing greater context to the content they share.

SMGI can be a valuable resource in spatial planning for the integration of both experiential and professional knowledge on places, events, and the environment, and has the potential to convey the community's collective preferences. This can enrich knowledge for decision-making and promote diversity in spatial planning (Campagna et al., 2018). It can be used to investigate the distribution of tourist attractions and hence assist tourist management and decision-making (Costa et al., 2019). Twitter data can be employed to explore critical algorithm studies, space conception, disciplinary areas, and ecological units through content analysis(C. C. De Falco et al., 2021). Similarly, the territorial distribution of geo-located tweets can be used to study the influence of geo-located data on social knowledge and the representativeness of big data(A. De Falco et al., 2022). SMGI can be employed to investigate human mobility patterns throughcorrelation analysis conducted at different periods, geographic scales, and flow directions(Liu et al., 2022). The study (Zhu et al., 2020) explored the application of social media data, particularly Sina Weibo check-in data, in urban research and planning. The data is analyzed using statistical techniques, such as kernel density analysis and price trend surface modeling, to identify hotspots and rental housing prices in Wuhan. The findings can assist the government in monitoring the real estate rental market.

In the study (X. Zhang et al., 2020),the influence of air pollution on tourists' experiences in Beijing is examined by utilizing geotagged social media data. The findings indicate that tourists tend to broaden their travel scope in response to higher concentrations and report fewer positive emotions. Similarly, the study (Muhammad et al., 2019), examined human check-in behavior in Guangzhou, China by analyzing location-based social network (LBSN) data from the microblog Sina Weibo. The results indicate that LBSN data is a dependable source for observing human check-in behavior and show that female users use social media more frequently than male users. The study (Ullah et al., 2019), explored the spatiotemporal patterns of park visits in Chinaby utilizing location-based social network data. The study revealed that location-based social network data is a more scalable and cost-effective method to analyze the spatiotemporal behavior of park visitors, which can be used to assist urban city planners in designing green spaces that reflect the preferences of visitors.The use of social media posts for understanding the spatial density and diversity of visitors in urban parks is experimented with in the study by Chuang et al., (2022). The findings revealed that different park characteristics influenced visitors' spatial density and diversity. Family-oriented facilities increased spatial density, while commercial areas and a wider range of amenities attracted more diverse visitors.

Potential use of social media data, specifically Flickr photos is explored in (Lotfian&Ingensand, 2021)for environmental monitoring, particularly in location-based contexts. By analyzing bird photos from Flickr and using a chi-square test, the study identified the correlation between bird species and land cover types in Switzerland. The study(S. Zhang et al., 2022) incorporated social media to better understand tourist preferences and plan infrastructure and services. Similarly, the study(Rizwan et al., 2020) employed location-based social media data to understand urban behavior at the city and district levels. Another study (Martí et al., 2021)utilized user-generated data from location-based social networks like Twitter, Instagram, Foursquare, Strava, and MapMyRunto explore urban planning. Geospatial social media (GSM) data is analyzed for infectious disease research in the study byJing et al., (2023). The potential of social media apps for geospatial research is evaluated inOwuor &Hochmair, (2020).

Terminologies Related to Social Media Geographic Information

Various terms interchangeably refer to social media geographic information, including geospatial social media data, social media location data, and geotagged social media data. Despite the differences in terminologies, all lead to a similar concept of location-based information shared through social media platforms. Table 1 described such terms.

Sources of Social Media Geographic Information

Social media platforms accumulate and present geographic information in different ways depending on the features and functionalities of a particular social media platform. It includes geotagged posts, check-ins, hashtags, user profile data, and other types of geotagged content are available which can be utilized to gain insights into the location, activities, and interests of social media users (Stefanidis et al., 2013).

Table 1. Terminologies related to social media geographic information

Terms	Reference
Spatial Social Networks	(Ye & Andris, 2021)
Ambient Geospatial Information	(Stefanidis et al., 2013)
Location-Based Social Media Data	(Cao et al., 2015; Gröbe& Burghardt, 2020; McKitrick et al., 2023; Ullah et al., 2019)
Geospatial Social Media Data	(Jing et al., 2023)
Location-Based Social Networks	(Martí et al., 2021)
Geotagged Social Media Data	(Liu et al., 2022; C. Yang et al., 2019)
Geolocated Social Media Data	(Chuang et al., 2022; Roy et al., 2019)
Social Media Big Data	(Muhammad et al., 2019)
Social Media Location Data	(Garcia-Rubio et al., 2018; Qian et al., 2020)
Geospatial Big Data	(Zhao & Sui, 2017)
Location Information in Social Media Data	(Hoffmann & Heft, 2020)
Geo-Social Media Data	(Bao et al., 2016)
Location-Centric Social Media data	(D. Yang et al., 2021)
Online Geo-Location Data	(Hasan &Ukkusuri, 2014)
Location-Based Big Data	(Huang et al., 2021)
Geolocation Data from social media	(Hasan et al., 2016)
Volunteered Geographic Information	(Ahmad &Khiyal, 2023; Goodchild, 2007)
Crowdsourced Geographic Information	(See et al., 2016)
Crowd-Sourcing Geospatial Information	(Kostanski, 2012)
Social Sensing Data	(Young et al., 2021)
Spatial Crowdsourcing Data	(Ogbe &Lujala, 2021)
Geofencing Data	(Dabh, 2016)
Crowdsourced Mapping Data	(Hunt & Specht, 2019)
Participatory Mapping Data	(Saija & Pappalardo, 2022)

Table 2. Sources of social media geographic information

Source	Definition	Examples	Social Media Platform
Social network data	• Social networking platforms that allow users to connect with others based on their location • Social media platforms also provide information about the social networks of their users, which can be used to understand social connections and interactions within and across communities.	User demographic information	Facebook, Instagram, Foursquare
Geotagged photos	• Photos that include location information • Location metadata embedded in social media content such as photos, videos, and posts	A photo was taken at a restaurant that includes the GPS coordinates of the restaurant's location	Instagram, Flickr, Twitter
Check-ins	• User-generated posts that indicate a user's location • The location indicated by a user's profile or check-in • User-generated location check-ins	A user's profile indicating that they live in New York City	Facebook, Foursquare
Hashtags	• User-generated tags that allow content to be grouped by topic or location • User-generated tags that indicate a specific location or point of interest	A tweet using the hashtag #centralpark to indicate a location #NYC, #Paris, #Beach	Twitter, Instagram
Location-based search	• Search functionality that allows users to find content based on location • Search queries based on geographical location	"Restaurants near me"	Google Maps, Yelp, TripAdvisor
Sensor networks	• Networks of physical sensors that collect and transmit location-based data • Data collected from physical sensors	Environmental data collected by IoT sensors	Weather stations, traffic cameras Weather monitoring devices
Crowdsourcing	• The practice of collecting data from a large group of people, often through mobile apps or social media platforms • Obtaining data by soliciting contributions from a crowd	Volunteered geographic information (VGI)	OpenStreetMap, iNaturalist
Public APIs	• Application programming interfaces that allow developers to access and use social media data • Application Programming Interfaces provide access to data	Twitter API, Google Maps API	Twitter, Google Maps
Web scraping	• The process of extracting data from websites, often through automated scripts or tools • Extracting data from websites through automated methods	Scraping location data from online directories	Yelp, Yellow Pages
Location-based advertising	• Advertising that is targeted to users based on their geographic location • Targeted ads based on the user's geographical location	Ads are shown based on the user's current location	Facebook Ads, Google Ads
Geotagged Posts	• Social media posts with embedded location tags	A tweet with location coordinates	Twitter, Instagram, Facebook

OPPORTUNITIES

Social media geographic information has great potential to impact various aspects of governance. This section will describe the key areas where social media geographical information can be smartly exploited. The applicability of social media governance spans several aspects that are summarized in Figure 1. This section describes the details of the opportunities offered by social media geographic information.

Improved Decision-Making

Social media geographic information can provide real-time and location-specific data that can inform policy decisions to act quickly on new challenges based on recent trends and patterns. For example, it can help governments identify areas that require more attention in terms of infrastructure, public services, or emergency response. In a study by Kim and Lee (2021), they demonstrated that social media geographic information can be used to identify areas with inadequate access to public transportation, enabling policymakers to develop more effective transportation policies.

Increased Citizen Engagement

Social media networks have billions of users, therefore the geographic information gathered can give information about huge, diverse populations, including hard-to-reach demographics. Social media can be used to engage citizens in policy-making processes, gather feedback, and foster collaboration. It can help to increase transparency, accountability, and trust between citizens and governments.In a study by Simonofski et al. (2021), they found that social media can improve citizen participation in public policy-making, leading to more effective policy outcomes.Social media geographic information empowers citizen engagement and participatory governance. Platforms like geotagged posts, check-ins, and user-generated content enable citizens to provide feedback, share ideas, and actively participate in decision-making processes. This fosters transparency, inclusivity, and collaboration between the government and its constituents.

Enhanced Service Delivery

Social media geographic information can give policymakers information about the demands and requirements of the general public, enabling them to better customize their policies to satisfy those demands. Social media can be used to monitor and evaluate the performance of public services, such as transportation, health care, and education. It can help to identify gaps and areas for improvement and ensure that services are delivered efficiently and effectively. In a study by Hamstead et al. (2018), they used social media geographic information to evaluate the accessibility of urban parks, finding that this approach can provide a cost-effective and efficient way to evaluate urban services.

Improved Crisis Management

Social media geographic information can be used to monitor and respond to crises, such as natural disasters, disease outbreaks, or social unrest. It can help to identify affected areas, communicate with citizens, and coordinate emergency response efforts. In a study by Ashktorab et al. (2014), they demonstrated the effectiveness of social media geographic information in disaster response, showing that it can provide real-time situational awareness and facilitate communication between disaster responders and affected communities.Another study (Kankanamge et al., 2020) demonstrated the potential of social media analysis for estimating the severity of disasters through the study of tweets related to the South East Queensland Flood. The results showed how crucial it is to incorporate social media analysis into disaster management plans to improve emergency response and resource allocation during crises.

Increased Innovation

Social media can be used to foster innovation and creativity in policy-making processes. It can help to identify emerging trends and best practices and enable collaboration and co-creation among different stakeholders. In a study (Granier & Kudo, 2016), they showed that social media geographic information can enable collaborative planning, facilitating engagement and co-creation among citizens, planners, and policy-makers in the context of Japanese Smart Communities. Another study (Cortés-Cediel et al., 2021) investigated the idea of collaborative decision-making and co-creation in European smart cities. The concept of empowering citizens in the context of sustainable urban development, focusing on their role in co-creating solutions for urban challenges is investigated in (Gutiérrez et al., 2018).

Policy Formation and Evaluation

Social media geographic information aids in policy formation and evaluation. It can be utilized to interact with citizens and gather feedback on proposed policies. As a result, the general people may participate more actively and develop a sense of responsibility and accountability for the decision-making process. By analyzing geospatial data, policymakers can gain insights into public opinions, concerns, and preferences related to specific geographic areas. This information can inform evidence-based policy decisions and enable ongoing monitoring and evaluation of policy effectiveness. The study (Oginni&Moitui, 2015) investigated how social media might improve policymaking in the digital age and its role in public policymaking in Africa.

Identifying Public Opinion and Needs

Social media geographic information can provide policymakers with a unique insight into public opinions and needs, which can help them make informed decisions. The study (Nguyen et al., 2016) highlighted the potential of social media data to provide insights into the well-being and health-related behaviours of people in certain localities. It provided useful information for urban planners and decision-makers working to build happier and healthier communities.

Assessing Public Perception

Social media geographic information can also help policymakers understand how the public perceives different policies and their implementation. Policymakers can get information about public attitudes and behaviours through social media at a fraction of the expense of doing so compared to more traditional survey approaches. For example, sentiment analysis of tweets can help policymakers gauge public perception of government actions or policies(Tsai & Wang, 2021).

Evaluating Policy Outcome

Social media geographic information can be used to evaluate the effectiveness of policies by analyzing the data before and after the policy implementation. Since social media data is frequently made available to the public, this can make the policy-making process more transparent and accountable by giving citizens access to and control over the information that is used to make choices. For example, analyzing geotagged tweets can help policymakers understand the impact of a policy on a specific region or population. The study (Lan et al., 2019) examined the impact of geotagged tweets as a gauge of the general population for the investigation of theft crimes in specific areas. In this way social media geographic information can help policymakers in developing proactive strategies to combat theft crimes.

Figure 1. Opportunities offered by social media geographic information

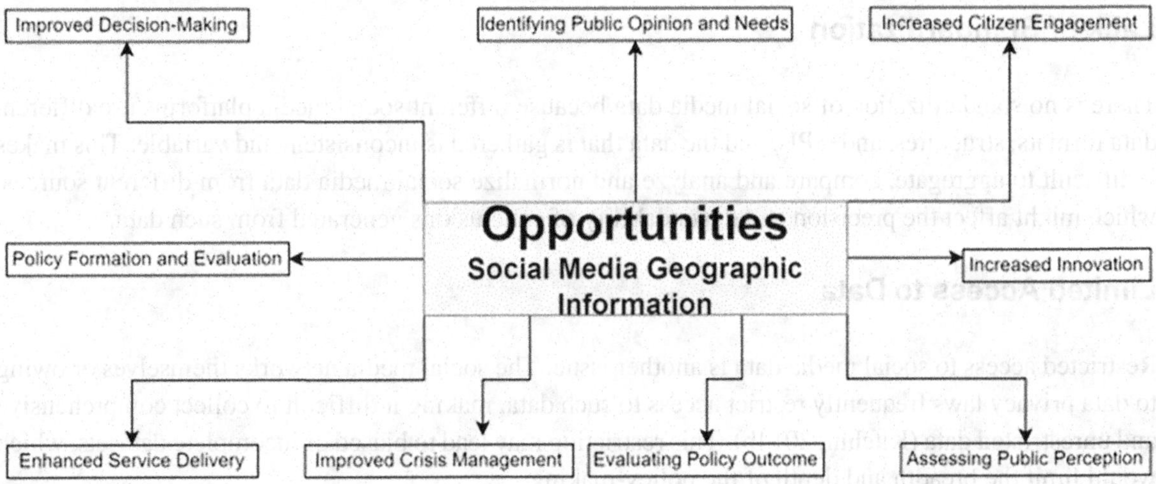

CHALLENGES

Although social media geographic information is helpful in policy-making and smart governance, it faced several challenges that are summarized in Figure 2. The section describes the details of the challenges.

Data Quality and Reliability

Social media data can be noisy, unstructured, and biased, making it difficult to extract meaningful insights. The accuracy and reliability of social media data can also be affected by factors such as fake accounts, bots, and deliberate misinformation campaigns (Himelein-Wachowiak et al., 2021; Moore, 2023).

Privacy Concerns

Social media platforms collect and store large amounts of personal data. However, the use of social media data raises privacy concerns, as personal information can be shared without consent (Kitchin, 2014b). There is a need for clear guidelines and regulations on the use of social media data to ensure that it is collected, stored, and analyzed ethically and securely.

Data Overload

The sheer volume of data generated by social media can be overwhelming, making it difficult to extract relevant information. For example, a flood of user-generated content resulted from the increased usage of social media platforms during emergencies, making it difficult for disaster management organizations to process and use this data efficiently (Schulz et al., 2012).

Lack of Standardization

There is no standardization of social media data because different social media platforms use different data formats, structures, and APIs, and the data that is gathered is inconsistent and variable. This makes it difficult to aggregate, compare and analyze and normalize social media data from different sources, which might affect the precision and dependability of conclusions generated from such data.

Limited Access to Data

Restricted access to social media data is another issue. The social media networks themselves or owing to data privacy laws frequently restrict access to such data, making it difficult to collect comprehensive and unrestricted data (Kitchin, 2014b). This restriction may lead to biased or incomplete datasets, which would limit the breadth and depth of the policy-making.

Ethical Issues

The use of social media data for policy-making raises ethical considerations around issues such as data ownership, consent, and privacy (Kitchin, 2014b). There is a need for clear guidelines and regulations on the use of social media data to ensure that it is collected, stored, and analyzed ethically and transparently.

Technical Challenges

Analyzing and interpreting social media data can be complex and requires specialized expertise and tools. There is a need for specialized expertise in data analytics and social media analysis to extract meaningful insights from social media data. This can create barriers to entry for policymakers who may not have the necessary resources or expertise to make use of social media data.

Language Barriers

People all around the world utilize social media platforms, which leads to the production of enormous amounts of social media data in numerous languages. The multilingual nature of social media data makes it difficult to extract pertinent data and conduct comprehensive analysis (Coşkun &Ozturan, 2018).

Digital Divide

Not all members of the public have equal access to social media platforms, which can create a digital divide in terms of who is represented in the data. This can lead to biased or incomplete insights, particularly for marginalized or underrepresented groups.

Limited Geographic Coverage

While social media data can provide insights into a wide geographic area, it may not be representative of the entire population. This can lead to biases and inaccuracies in social media data that can be misleading for policymakers. For example, it may not capture the opinions and behaviors of people who are not active on social media or who live in areas with poor internet connectivity.

Figure 2. Challenges of social media geographic information

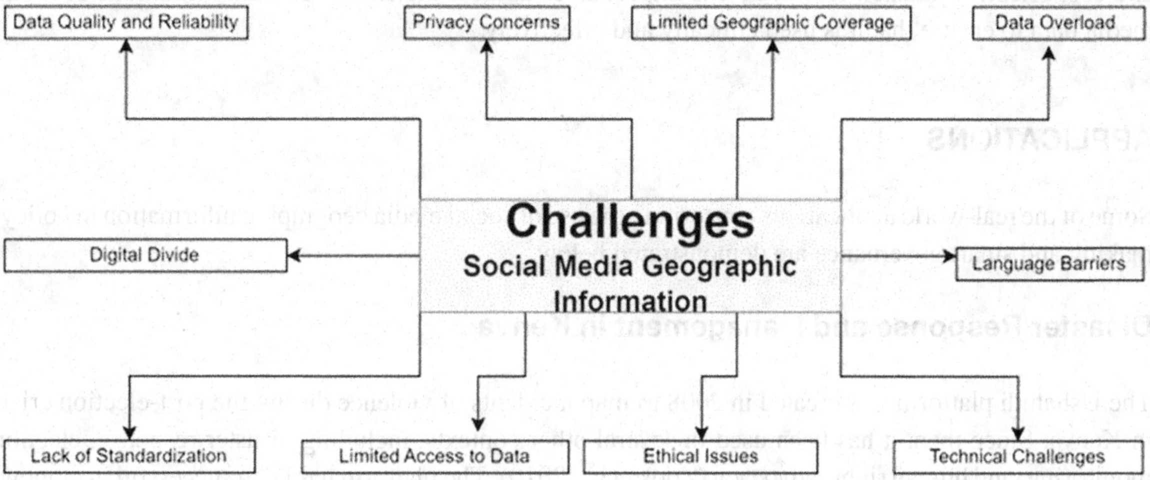

REMEDIES

Policymakers and stakeholders should work together to develop clear guidelines and regulations on the use of social media data. This includes guidelines on data privacy, security, and ethics, as well as guidelines on data ownership and consent.

When working with social media data, it is crucial to ensure data accuracy and dependability. Data quality assurance can be improved by using validation techniques, cross-referencing with existing datasets, and working with regional communities (Toivonen et al., 2019).

There isa need for policy interventions to address the problems brought on by bots and the dissemination of false information on social media. To encourage accountability, transparency, and responsible behaviour among social media sites and users, rules, and regulations can be created (Himelein-Wachowiak et al., 2021).

To stop the spread of false accounts, lessen epistemic uncertainty, and promote a more reliable online environment, independent auditing systems must be set up. Creating efficient auditing procedures requires collaboration and rigorous adherence to ethical principles (Moore, 2023).

The effective management and processing of structured user-generated material require integrated information management systems. These technologies make it possible for emergency management stakeholders to collaborate easily by enabling real-time data integration, analysis, and visualization. It helps to have reliable information management systems and technology fixes to deal with information overload in emergency management (Schulz et al., 2012).

Policymakers should be aware of the digital divide and take steps to ensure that social media data is representative of the entire population. This can include efforts to increase internet access and digital literacy, as well as the use of alternative data sources.

By implementing these recommendations, policymakers can maximize the potential of social media geographic information for governance and policy-making. Social media data can provide valuable insights into public opinion, behavior, and trends, and can help to inform policy decisions in a timely and cost-effective manner. However, it is important to address the challenges and limitations of social media data to ensure that it is used ethically and effectively.

APPLICATIONS

Some of the real-world applications concerning the use of social media geographic information in policy-making and smart governance are demonstrated below.

Disaster Response and Management in Kenya

The Ushahidi platform was created in 2008 to map incidents of violence during the post-election crisis in Kenya. Since then, it has been used in several other contexts, including disaster response, election monitoring, and human rights advocacy (Zook et al., 2010). The platform has been successful in empowering citizens to collect and share information and has been credited with saving lives during disasters and promoting transparency and accountability in governance.

Traffic Management in New York

In 2012, the New York City government launched the Twitter account @NYC311 to monitor and respond to citizen complaints about traffic congestion. The "311" service is a centralized system that allows citizens to report non-emergency issues such as graffiti, potholes, and noise complaints via phone, email, or social media. By leveraging social media platforms such as Twitter and Facebook, the city has been able to respond more quickly to complaints and resolve issues in a more timely and efficient manner (Duan et al., 2023). The service has been credited with improving the quality of life in the city and increasing citizen engagement in local governance.

Urban Planning in Buenos Aires

In 2018, the city of Buenos Aires in Argentina launched the Participatory Urbanism platform, which allows citizens to use social media to suggest improvements to their neighborhoods. The city government then uses the suggestions and votes to prioritize infrastructure improvements such as street lighting, sidewalk repairs, and park renovations (Felt, 2016). The platform has been successful in increasing citizen participation in local governance and improving the quality of life in neighborhoods across the city.

Air Quality Monitoring in London

The city government of London partnered with researchers at King's College London to analyze tweets with geolocation data that mentioned air pollution. The team used machine learning algorithms to analyze the content of the tweets and identify patterns related to air quality. The analysis of Twitter data provided the city government with real-time information on air quality levels and citizen perceptions of air pollution. The insights from the data helped the government make policy decisions to improve air quality in the city (Hswen et al., 2019).

Monitoring Infectious Diseases Outbreaks in Kenya

The Kenya Ministry of Health partnered with the University of Warwick and IBM Research to develop an early warning system for infectious disease outbreaks using social media data. They analyzed Twitter and Facebook posts for keywords related to symptoms and disease outbreaks and used machine-learning algorithms to identify potential outbreaks. Their system successfully detected outbreaks of cholera, malaria, and dengue fever in real-time, enabling healthcare workers to respond quickly and prevent the further spread of the diseases (Dion et al., 2015).

Tracking Floods in Jakarta, Indonesia

The Jakarta Smart City program partnered with Twitter to develop a real-time flood monitoring system using social media data. They analyzed Twitter posts for keywords related to floods and used geolocation data to map flood-prone areas. Their system enabled officials to quickly respond to floods and provide timely assistance to affected communities (Sitinjak et al., 2018).

Monitoring and Managing Urban Traffic

The government of Jakarta used social media data to monitor traffic patterns and optimize traffic flow. Specifically, they analyzed data from the Waze app, which provides real-time traffic information from drivers. By using this data, the government was able to identify congestion hotspots, adjust traffic signal timing, and reroute traffic as needed, resulting in a significant reduction in traffic congestion and air pollution (Luqman et al., 2019).

Tracking the Spread of Dengue Fever in Brazil

Researchers at the Federal University of Minas Gerais in Brazil developed a system that uses social media data to track the spread of dengue fever in real-time. The system uses natural language processing and machine learning algorithms to analyze posts on Twitter, looking for keywords and phrases that indicate the presence of the disease(Corbyn, 2011).

CONCLUSION AND FUTURE DIRECTIONS

The implications of social media geographic information for smart governance and policy-making are significant. The advantages, drawbacks, and solutions related to the use of social media spatial information in governance and policy-making are examined in this chapter. Decision-making, citizen involvement, service delivery, crisis management, innovation, policy creation and evaluation, and public opinion assessment could all be profoundly impacted by social media geographic information. Data quality and dependability, privacy issues, data overload, lack of standardization, restricted access to data, ethical concerns, technical difficulties, language obstacles, the digital divide, and limited geographic coverage are some of the issues that come up. Policymakers should create clear rules and regulations, guarantee data dependability and correctness, address privacy issues, control data overload with integrated information management systems, close the digital divide, and encourage moral behaviour to meet these difficulties.

The practical use of social media geographic information in policy-making and smart governance is further demonstrated by real-world applications in disaster response, traffic management, urban planning, air quality monitoring, disease outbreak tracking, flood monitoring, traffic optimization, and disease spread tracking. Policymakers can make more informed and timely decisions that are beneficial to society by utilizing the possibilities of social media spatial information while tackling its issues. New technologies such as machine learning and AI algorithms have the potential to enhance the use of social media geographic information, these areas need to be explored in future work. Further research is also needed to explore the potential of social media geographic information in other areas of governance and policy-making, such as public health, transportation, and environmental planning.

REFERENCES

Ahmad, M., Khayal, M. S. H., & Tahir, A. (2022). Analysis of Factors Affecting Adoption of Volunteered Geographic Information in the Context of National Spatial Data Infrastructure. *ISPRS International Journal of Geo-Information, 11*(2), 120. Advance online publication. doi:10.3390/ijgi11020120

Ahmad, M., & Khiyal, M. S. H. (2023). Assessment of land administration in Pakistan and the potential role of volunteered geographic information. In Handbook of Research on Driving Socioeconomic Development With Big Data. doi:10.4018/978-1-6684-5959-1.ch014

Ali, A., & Imran, M. (2020). The Evolution of National Spatial Data Infrastructure in Pakistan-Implementation Challenges and the Way Forward. *International Journal of Spatial Data Infrastructures Research, 15*(0).

Ali, A., Imran, M., Jabeen, M., Ali, Z., & Mahmood, S. A. (2021). Factors influencing integrated information management: Spatial data infrastructure in Pakistan. *Information Development*. Advance online publication. doi:10.1177/02666669211048483

Ani, P. (2023). *Worldwide Digital Population 2023*. Statista. https://www.statista.com/statistics/617136/digital-population-worldwide/

Ashktorab, Z., Brown, C., Nandi, M., & Culotta, A. (2014). Tweedr: Mining twitter to inform disaster response. *ISCRAM 2014 Conference Proceedings - 11th International Conference on Information Systems for Crisis Response and Management*.

Bao, J., Lian, D., Zhang, F., & Yuan, N. J. (2016). Geo-social media data analytic for user modeling and location-based services. *SIGSPATIAL Special*, *7*(3), 11–18. Advance online publication. doi:10.1145/2876480.2876484

Barr, R., & Masser, I. (2019). Geographic Information: a resource, a commodity, an asset or an infrastructure? In Geographic Information Systems to Spatial Data Infrastructures (pp. 87–108). CRC Press.

Campagna, M., Floris, R., Massa, P., & Mura, S. (2018). Social media geographic information: The community perspective in planning knowledge. In *Environmental Information Systems* (Vol. 1). Concepts, Methodologies, Tools, and Applications. doi:10.4018/978-1-5225-7033-2.ch003

Cao, G., Wang, S., Hwang, M., Padmanabhan, A., Zhang, Z., & Soltani, K. (2015). A scalable framework for spatiotemporal analysis of location-based social media data. *Computers, Environment and Urban Systems*, *51*, 70–82. Advance online publication. doi:10.1016/j.compenvurbsys.2015.01.002

Carroll, L. N., Au, A. P., Detwiler, L. T., Fu, T., Painter, I. S., & Abernethy, N. F. (2014). Visualization and analytics tools for infectious disease epidemiology: A systematic review. *Journal of Biomedical Informatics*, *51*, 287–298. doi:10.1016/j.jbi.2014.04.006 PMID:24747356

Castelnovo, W., Misuraca, G., & Savoldelli, A. (2016). Smart Cities Governance: The Need for a Holistic Approach to Assessing Urban Participatory Policy Making. *Social Science Computer Review*, *34*(6), 724–739. Advance online publication. doi:10.1177/0894439315611103

Chuang, I. T., Benita, F., & Tunçer, B. (2022). Effects of urban park spatial characteristics on visitor density and diversity: A geolocated social media approach. *Landscape and Urban Planning*, *226*, 104514. Advance online publication. doi:10.1016/j.landurbplan.2022.104514

Corbyn, Z. (2011). Twitter to track dengue fever outbreaks in Brazil. *New Scientist*, *211*(2821), 18. Advance online publication. doi:10.1016/S0262-4079(11)61685-0

Cortés-Cediel, M. E., Cantador, I., & Bolívar, M. P. R. (2021). Analyzing Citizen Participation and Engagement in European Smart Cities. *Social Science Computer Review*, *39*(4), 592–626. Advance online publication. doi:10.1177/0894439319877478

Coşkun, M., & Ozturan, M. (2018). #europehappinessmap: A framework for multi-lingual sentiment analysis via social media big data (a Twitter case study). *Information (Basel)*, *9*(5), 102. Advance online publication. doi:10.3390/info9050102

Costa, P. F., Badolato, I. da S., Borba, R. L. R., & Strauch, J. C. M. (2019). Strategy for extraction of foursquare's social media geographic information through data mining. *Boletim de Ciências Geodésicas*, *25*(1), e2019005. Advance online publication. doi:10.15901982-21702019000100005

Dabh, M. D. (2016). Geofencing: A Generic Approach to Real Time Location based Tracking System. *IRACST – International Journal of Computer Networks and Wireless Communications, 6*(6).

De FalcoA.De FalcoC. C.FerracciM. (2022). Geo-Social Media and Socio-Territorial Distribution: A Study on the Italian Case. *Italian Sociological Review, 12*(Special Issue 7). doi:10.13136/isr.v12i7S.577

De Falco, C. C., Crescentini, N., & Ferracci, M. (2021). *The Spatial Dimension in Social Media Analysis*. doi:10.4018/978-1-7998-8473-6.ch029

Dion, M., AbdelMalik, P., & Mawudeku, A. (2015). Big Data and the Global Public Health Intelligence Network (GPHIN). *Canada Communicable Disease Report*, *41*(9), 209–214. Advance online publication. doi:10.14745/ccdr.v41i09a02 PMID:29769954

Dixon, S. (2023). *Global Social Networks Ranked by Number of Users 2023*. Statista. https://www.statista.com/statistics/272014/global-social-networks-ranked-by-number-of-users/

Duan, H. K., Vasarhelyi, M. A., Codesso, M., & Alzamil, Z. (2023). Enhancing the government accounting information systems using social media information: An application of text mining and machine learning. *International Journal of Accounting Information Systems*, *48*, 100600. Advance online publication. doi:10.1016/j.accinf.2022.100600

Felt, M. (2016). Social media and the social sciences: How researchers employ Big Data analytics. *Big Data & Society*, *3*(1), 2053951716645828. doi:10.1177/2053951716645828

Gao, H., Barbier, G., & Goolsby, R. (2011). Harnessing the crowdsourcing power of social media for disaster relief. *IEEE Intelligent Systems*, *26*(3), 10–14. Advance online publication. doi:10.1109/MIS.2011.52

Gao, Z., Wang, S., & Gu, J. (2020). Public participation in smart-city governance: A qualitative content analysis of public comments in urban China. *Sustainability (Basel)*, *12*(20), 8605. Advance online publication. doi:10.3390u12208605

Garcia-Rubio, C., Redondo, R. P. D., Campo, C., & Vilas, A. F. (2018). Using entropy of social media location data for the detection of crowd dynamics anomalies. *Electronics (Basel)*, *7*(12), 380. Advance online publication. doi:10.3390/electronics7120380

Goodchild, M. F. (2007). Citizens as sensors: The world of volunteered geography. GeoJournal. doi:10.100710708-007-9111-y

Granier, B., & Kudo, H. (2016). How are citizens involved in smart cities? Analysing citizen participation in Japanese "smart Communities." *Information Polity*, *21*(1), 61–76. Advance online publication. doi:10.3233/IP-150367

Gröbe, M., & Burghardt, D. (2020). Micro diagrams: Visualization of categorical point data from location-based social media. *Cartography and Geographic Information Science*, *47*(4), 305–320. Advance online publication. doi:10.1080/15230406.2020.1733438

Gutiérrez, V., Amaxilatis, D., Mylonas, G., & Muñoz, L. (2018). Empowering Citizens Toward the Co-Creation of Sustainable Cities. *IEEE Internet of Things Journal*, *5*(2), 668–676. Advance online publication. doi:10.1109/JIOT.2017.2743783

Hamstead, Z. A., Fisher, D., Ilieva, R. T., Wood, S. A., McPhearson, T., & Kremer, P. (2018). Geolocated social media as a rapid indicator of park visitation and equitable park access. *Computers, Environment and Urban Systems*, *72*, 38–50. Advance online publication. doi:10.1016/j.compenvurbsys.2018.01.007

Hasan, S., & Ukkusuri, S. V. (2014). Urban activity pattern classification using topic models from online geo-location data. *Transportation Research Part C, Emerging Technologies*, *44*, 363–381. Advance online publication. doi:10.1016/j.trc.2014.04.003

Hasan, S., Ukkusuri, S. V., & Zhan, X. (2016). Understanding social influence in activity location choice and lifestyle patterns using geolocation data from social media. *Frontiers in ICT (Lausanne, Switzerland)*, *3*. Advance online publication. doi:10.3389/fict.2016.00010

Himelein-Wachowiak, M., Giorgi, S., Devoto, A., Rahman, M., Ungar, L., Schwartz, H. A., Epstein, D. H., Leggio, L., & Curtis, B. (2021). Bots and misinformation spread on social media: Implications for COVID-19. In Journal of Medical Internet Research (Vol. 23, Issue 5). doi:10.2196/26933

Hoffmann, M., & Heft, A. (2020). "Here, There and Everywhere": Classifying Location Information in Social Media Data - Possibilities and Limitations. *Communication Methods and Measures*, *14*(3), 184–203. Advance online publication. doi:10.1080/19312458.2019.1708282

Hswen, Y., Qin, Q., Brownstein, J. S., & Hawkins, J. B. (2019). Feasibility of using social media to monitor outdoor air pollution in London, England. *Preventive Medicine*, *121*, 86–93. Advance online publication. doi:10.1016/j.ypmed.2019.02.005 PMID:30742873

Hua, Y., & Feng, T. (2021). Geographic Information Systems. In J. Wang & F. Wu (Eds.), *Advances in Cartography and Geographic Information Engineering* (pp. 387–441). Springer Singapore. doi:10.1007/978-981-16-0614-4_11

Huang, H., Yao, X. A., Krisp, J. M., & Jiang, B. (2021). Analytics of location-based big data for smart cities: Opportunities, challenges, and future directions. *Computers, Environment and Urban Systems*, *90*, 101712. Advance online publication. doi:10.1016/j.compenvurbsys.2021.101712

Hunt, A., & Specht, D. (2019). Crowdsourced mapping in crisis zones: Collaboration, organisation and impact. *Journal of International Humanitarian Action*, *4*(1), 1. Advance online publication. doi:10.118641018-018-0048-1

Jing, F., Li, Z., Qiao, S., Zhang, J., Olatosi, B., & Li, X. (2023). Using geospatial social media data for infectious disease studies: a systematic review. In International Journal of Digital Earth (Vol. 16, Issue 1). doi:10.1080/17538947.2022.2161652

Kankanamge, N., Yigitcanlar, T., Goonetilleke, A., & Kamruzzaman, M. (2020). Determining disaster severity through social media analysis: Testing the methodology with South East Queensland Flood tweets. *International Journal of Disaster Risk Reduction*, *42*, 101360. Advance online publication. doi:10.1016/j.ijdrr.2019.101360

Kietzmann, J. H., Hermkens, K., McCarthy, I. P., & Silvestre, B. S. (2011). Social media? Get serious! Understanding the functional building blocks of social media. *Business Horizons*, *54*(3), 241–251. doi:10.1016/j.bushor.2011.01.005

Kim, J., & Lee, J. (2021). An analysis of spatial accessibility changes according to the attractiveness index of public libraries using social media data. *Sustainability (Basel)*, *13*(16), 9087. Advance online publication. doi:10.3390u13169087

Kitchin, R. (2014a). Big Data, new epistemologies and paradigm shifts. *Big Data & Society*, *1*(1). doi:10.1177/2053951714528481

Kitchin, R. (2014b). The Data Revolution: Big Data, Open Data, Data Infrastructures & Their Consequences. In The Data Revolution: Big Data, Open Data, Data Infrastructures & Their Consequences. doi:10.4135/9781473909472

Kostanski, L. (2012). Crowd-Sourcing Geospatial Information for Government Gazetteers. *Tenth United Nations Conference on the Standardization of Geographical Names*.

Lan, M., Liu, L., Hernandez, A., Liu, W., Zhou, H., & Wang, Z. (2019). The spillover effect of geotagged tweets as a measure of ambient population for theft crime. *Sustainability (Basel)*, *11*(23), 6748. Advance online publication. doi:10.3390u11236748

Liu, L., Wang, R., Guan, W. W., Bao, S., Yu, H., Fu, X., & Liu, H. (2022). Assessing Reliability of Chinese Geotagged Social Media Data for Spatiotemporal Representation of Human Mobility. *ISPRS International Journal of Geo-Information*, *11*(2), 145. Advance online publication. doi:10.3390/ijgi11020145

LotfianM.IngensandJ. (2021). Using geo geo-tagged flickr images to explore the correlation between land cover classes and the location of bird observations. *International Archives of the Photogrammetry, Remote Sensing and Spatial Information Sciences - ISPRS Archives, 43*(B4-2021). doi:10.5194/isprs-archives-XLIII-B4-2021-189-2021

Luqman, D., Marpaung, F. H., Marpaung, M. C., Girsang, A. S., & Muhamad Isa, S. (2019). City Traffic Analysis Based on Facebook Data. *Proceeding - 2019 International Conference on ICT for Smart Society: Innovation and Transformation Toward Smart Region, ICISS 2019*. 10.1109/ICISS48059.2019.8969835

Martí, P., Pérez del Hoyo, R., Nolasco-Cirugeda, A., Serrano-Estrada, L., & García-Mayor, C. (2021). The potential of location-based social networks for participatory urban planning. In Smart Cities and the un SDGs. doi:10.1016/B978-0-323-85151-0.00008-7

McKitrick, M. K., Schuurman, N., & Crooks, V. A. (2023). Collecting, analyzing, and visualizing location-based social media data: review of methods in GIS-social media analysis. In GeoJournal (Vol. 88, Issue 1). doi:10.100710708-022-10584-w

Meijer, A., & Thaens, M. (2018). Urban Technological Innovation: Developing and Testing a Socio-technical Framework for Studying Smart City Projects. *Urban Affairs Review*, *54*(2), 363–387. Advance online publication. doi:10.1177/1078087416670274

Moore, M. (2023). Fake accounts on social media, epistemic uncertainty and the need for an independent auditing of accounts. *Internet Policy Review, 12*(1).

Muhammad, R., Zhao, Y., & Liu, F. (2019). Spatiotemporal analysis to observe gender based check-in behavior by using social media big data: A case study of Guangzhou, China. *Sustainability (Basel)*, *11*(10), 2822. Advance online publication. doi:10.3390u11102822

Nguyen, Q. C., Kath, S., Meng, H. W., Li, D., Smith, K. R., VanDerslice, J. A., Wen, M., & Li, F. (2016). Leveraging geotagged Twitter data to examine neighborhood happiness, diet, and physical activity. *Applied Geography (Sevenoaks, England)*, *73*, 77–88. Advance online publication. doi:10.1016/j.apgeog.2016.06.003 PMID:28533568

Ogbe, M., & Lujala, P. (2021). Spatial crowdsourcing in natural resource revenue management. *Resources Policy*, *72*, 102082. Advance online publication. doi:10.1016/j.resourpol.2021.102082

Oginni, S. O., & Moitui, J. N. (2015). Social Media and Public Policy Process in Africa: Enhanced Policy Process in Digital Age. In *Consilience. Journal of Sustainable Development*, *14*(2).

Osella, M., Ferro, E., & Pautasso, E. (2016). Toward a Methodological Approach to Assess Public Value in Smart Cities. In Public Administration and Information Technology (Vol. 11). doi:10.1007/978-3-319-17620-8_7

Owuor, I., & Hochmair, H. H. (2020). An overview of social media apps and their potential role in geospatial research. In ISPRS International Journal of Geo-Information (Vol. 9, Issue 9). doi:10.3390/ijgi9090526

Paquet, G. (1999). Governance Through Social Learning. Governance Through Social Learning. doi:10.26530/OAPEN_578818

Parycek, P., & Viale, G. (2017). Drivers of smart governance: Towards to evidence-based policy-making. *ACM International Conference Proceeding Series, Part F128275*. 10.1145/3085228.3085255

Pereira, G. V., Parycek, P., Falco, E., & Kleinhans, R. (2018). Smart governance in the context of smart cities: A literature review. In Information Polity (Vol. 23, Issue 2). doi:10.3233/IP-170067

Qian, T., Chen, J., Li, A., Wang, J., & Shen, D. (2020). Evaluating spatial accessibility to general hospitals with navigation and social media location data: A case study in Nanjing. *International Journal of Environmental Research and Public Health*, *17*(8), 2752. Advance online publication. doi:10.3390/ijerph17082752 PMID:32316229

Rizwan, M., Wan, W., & Gwiazdzinski, L. (2020). Visualization, spatiotemporal patterns, and directional analysis of urban activities using geolocation data extracted from LBSN. *ISPRS International Journal of Geo-Information*, *9*(2), 137. Advance online publication. doi:10.3390/ijgi9020137

Roy, K. C., Cebrian, M., & Hasan, S. (2019). Quantifying human mobility resilience to extreme events using geo-located social media data. *EPJ Data Science*, *8*(1), 18. Advance online publication. doi:10.1140/epjds13688-019-0196-6

Ruhlandt, R. W. S. (2018). The governance of smart cities: A systematic literature review. *Cities (London, England)*, *81*, 1–23. Advance online publication. doi:10.1016/j.cities.2018.02.014

Saija, L., & Pappalardo, G. (2022). An Argument for Action Research-Inspired Participatory Mapping. *Journal of Planning Education and Research*, *42*(3), 375–385. Advance online publication. doi:10.1177/0739456X18817090

Scholl, H. J., & Scholl, M. C. (2014). Smart Governance: A Roadmap for Research and Practice. *IConference 2014 Proceedings*.

Schulz, A., Ortmann, J., & Probst, F. (2012). Getting user-generated content structured: Overcoming information overload in emergency management. *2012 IEEE Global Humanitarian Technology Conference*, 143–148. 10.1109/GHTC.2012.31

See, L., Mooney, P., Foody, G., Bastin, L., Comber, A., Estima, J., Fritz, S., Kerle, N., Jiang, B., Laakso, M., Liu, H. Y., Milèinski, G., Nikšieč, M., Painho, M., Podör, A., Olteanu-Raimond, A. M. R., & Rutzinger, M. (2016). Crowdsourcing, citizen science or volunteered geographic information? The current state of crowdsourced geographic information. *ISPRS International Journal of Geo-Information*, *5*(5), 55. Advance online publication. doi:10.3390/ijgi5050055

Signorini, A., Segre, A. M., & Polgreen, P. M. (2011). The use of Twitter to track levels of disease activity and public concern in the US during the influenza A H1N1 pandemic. *PLoS One*, *6*(5), e19467. doi:10.1371/journal.pone.0019467 PMID:21573238

Simonofski, A., Fink, J., & Burnay, C. (2021). Supporting policy-making with social media and e-participation platforms data: A policy analytics framework. *Government Information Quarterly*, *38*(3), 101590. Advance online publication. doi:10.1016/j.giq.2021.101590

Sitinjak, E., Meidityawati, B., Ichwan, R., Onggosandojo, N., & Aryani, P. (2018). Enhancing Urban Resilience through Technology and Social Media: Case Study of Urban Jakarta. *Procedia Engineering*, *212*, 222–229. Advance online publication. doi:10.1016/j.proeng.2018.01.029

Stamati, T., Papadopoulos, T., & Anagnostopoulos, D. (2015). Social media for openness and accountability in the public sector: Cases in the greek context. *Government Information Quarterly*, *32*(1), 12–29. Advance online publication. doi:10.1016/j.giq.2014.11.004

Stefanidis, A., Crooks, A., & Radzikowski, J. (2013). Harvesting ambient geospatial information from social media feeds. *GeoJournal*, *78*(2), 319–338. Advance online publication. doi:10.100710708-011-9438-2

Stoker, G. (1998). Governance as theory: Five propositions. *International Social Science Journal*, *50*(155), 17–28. Advance online publication. doi:10.1111/1468-2451.00106

Toivonen, T., Heikinheimo, V., Fink, C., Hausmann, A., Hiippala, T., Järv, O., Tenkanen, H., & Di Minin, E. (2019). Social media data for conservation science: A methodological overview. In *Biological Conservation* (Vol. 233). doi:10.1016/j.biocon.2019.01.023

Tsai, M. H., & Wang, Y. (2021). Analyzing twitter data to evaluate people's attitudes towards public health policies and events in the era of covid-19. *International Journal of Environmental Research and Public Health*, *18*(12), 6272. Advance online publication. doi:10.3390/ijerph18126272 PMID:34200576

Ullah, W., & Haidery, K. (2019). Analyzing the Spatiotemporal Patterns in Green Spaces for Urban Studies Using Location-Based Social Media Data. *ISPRS International Journal of Geo-Information*, *8*(11), 506. Advance online publication. doi:10.3390/ijgi8110506

Voorberg, W. H., Bekkers, V. J. J. M., & Tummers, L. G. (2015). A Systematic Review of Co-Creation and Co-Production: Embarking on the social innovation journey. *Public Management Review*, *17*(9), 1333–1357. Advance online publication. doi:10.1080/14719037.2014.930505

Webster, C. W. R., & Leleux, C. (2018). Smart governance: Opportunities for technologically-mediated citizen co-production. *Information Polity*, *23*(1), 95–110. Advance online publication. doi:10.3233/IP-170065

Willke, H. (2007). *Smart governance: governing the global knowledge society*. Campus Verlag.

Yang, C., Xiao, M., Ding, X., Tian, W., Zhai, Y., Chen, J., Liu, L., & Ye, X. (2019). Exploring human mobility patterns using geo-tagged social media data at the group level. In Journal of Spatial Science (Vol. 64, Issue 2). doi:10.1080/14498596.2017.1421487

Yang, D., Qu, B., & Cudre-Mauroux, P. (2021). Location-Centric Social Media Analytics: Challenges and Opportunities for Smart Cities. *IEEE Intelligent Systems*, *36*(5), 3–10. Advance online publication. doi:10.1109/MIS.2020.3009438

Ye, X., & Andris, C. (2021). Spatial social networks in geographic information science. In International Journal of Geographical Information Science (Vol. 35, Issue 12). doi:10.1080/13658816.2021.2001722

Young, J. C., Arthur, R., Spruce, M., & Williams, H. T. P. (2021). Social sensing of heatwaves. *Sensors (Basel)*, *21*(11), 3717. Advance online publication. doi:10.339021113717 PMID:34073608

Zhang, S., Zhen, F., Wang, B., Li, Z., & Qin, X. (2022). Coupling Social Media and Agent-Based Modelling: A Novel Approach for Supporting Smart Tourism Planning. *Journal of Urban Technology*, *29*(2), 79–97. Advance online publication. doi:10.1080/10630732.2020.1847987

Zhang, X., Yang, Y., Zhang, Y., & Zhang, Z. (2020). Designing tourist experiences amidst air pollution: A spatial analytical approach using social media. *Annals of Tourism Research*, *84*, 102999. Advance online publication. doi:10.1016/j.annals.2020.102999

Zhao, B., & Sui, D. Z. (2017). True lies in geospatial big data: Detecting location spoofing in social media. *Annals of GIS*, *23*(1), 1–14. Advance online publication. doi:10.1080/19475683.2017.1280536

Zhu, L., Yu, T., Liu, Y., & Zhou, L. (2020). Analyses on the Spatial Distribution Characteristics of Urban Rental Housing Supply and Demand Hotspots Based on Social Media Data. *2020 5th IEEE International Conference on Big Data Analytics, ICBDA 2020*. 10.1109/ICBDA49040.2020.9101317

Zook, M., Graham, M., Shelton, T., & Gorman, S. (2010). Volunteered Geographic Information and Crowdsourcing Disaster Relief: A Case Study of the Haitian Earthquake. *World Medical & Health Policy*, *2*(2), 6–32. doi:10.2202/1948-4682.1069

Chapter 14
Electronic–Based Service Innovation:
Evidence From the Jayapura City Population and Civil Registration Office, Indonesia

Yosephina Ohoiwutun
Cenderawasih University, Indonesia

M. Zaenul Muttaqin
ⓘ https://orcid.org/0000-0003-0627-7652
Cenderawasih University, Indonesia

Ilham Ilham
Cenderawasih University, Indonesia

Vince Tebay
Cenderawasih University, Indonesia

ABSTRACT

This chapter aims to explore further how forms of public service innovation are applied in Jayapura City during the pandemic. Several highlights are the chapter's main focus, so the authors divide them into several sections. The first section reviews the implementation of electronic governance (e-governance). Then the second part describes how electronic-based services at the Jayapura City Disdukcapil were before the pandemic. The last section reveals the electronic-based service system during the pandemic. This study is a qualitative study using a research approach based on a literature study. The Jayapura City Population and Civil Registration Service (Disdukcapil) utilizes advances in digital technology by giving birth to various innovations to improve the quality of public service delivery in the field of population administration. The innovations are accessed online without coming to the Dukcapil office.

DOI: 10.4018/978-1-6684-7450-1.ch014

INTRODUCTION

The demand for bureaucratic reform as the government's priority agenda begins with many complaints about the performance of government services that are not in line with community expectations (Solihah, 2021). In essence, bureaucratic reform3 is an effort to make a fundamental change concerning government administration, especially regarding the institutional aspects, management, and apparatus resources which stem from providing better services to the community (Wulan & Mustam, 2017). The achievement of bureaucratic reform and good governance, the quality of public services provided optimally, is one factor that also influences it (Anisa, 2019). In carrying out public services, it is not only aimed at fulfilling citizens' civil rights and basic needs. Service delivery is carried out optimally to realize good governance and effective, efficient, and accountable service delivery, which is undoubtedly part of the paradigm of new public administration (lapaslhoknga, 2021).

Along with the rapid development of technology, innovation has become an option, even a necessity, in public service. Through the dogma of a culture of innovation, the characteristics of a static and rigid public service system are believed to be able to be disbursed (Yanuar, 2019). It considers that implementing public services still causes many complaints, even though it is used as the main topic of news from various media in Indonesia.

The Population and Civil Registration Institution (Dukcapil) also develop innovations to accelerate the improvement of service quality in population administration. Through this innovation, a series of achievements were then successfully inscribed by the government concerning administrative services in Indonesia. For 3 (three) consecutive years, the Dukcapil agency has won the Top Innovation Award for the Public Service Innovation Competition (KIPP) from the Ministry of Administrative Reform and Bureaucratic Reform (PANRB) (dukcapil.kemendagri.go.id, 2021). The track was inscribed by the Dukcapil of the Ministry of Home Affairs in 2019 by winning the Top 45 (forty-five) KIPP. Through the innovation of the Statement of Absolute Responsibility (Super Sharp) in 2020, it was again obtaining the Top 45 award through the innovation of Indonesia's Population and Civil Registration Map (i -POP). Furthermore, in 2021 through the innovation "D'SIGN: Digital Signature Dukcapil," the Top 45 Public Service Innovations for 2021 were again achieved after previously being declared to have passed the TOP 99 KIPP or Synovik from the Ministry of PANRB (Dukcapil.kemendagri.go.id, 2021).

Network-based services (online) or trending with the term online services are an option and must be carried out by Disdukcapil agencies during the Covid-19 pandemic. It was then marked by the Minister of Home Affairs Regulation (Permendagri) issuance concerning Online Population Administration Services. Furthermore, the Ministry of Home Affairs (Kemendagri) has also issued a letter No. 443.1/2978/ Dukcapil dated March 16, 2020, regarding Corona Virus (Covid-19) Adminduk and Prevention Services to the Population and Civil Registry Office (Dukcapil) in the Province and Regency/City. This policy, as a form of government effort through the Ministry of Home Affairs to break the chain of Covid-19 disease, aims to ensure that the administration of public services in the administrative sector continues to run efficiently and effectively during the onslaught of the Covid-19 pandemic.

Innovation in public services is a meeting point for gaps that have so far been attached to public organizations. The community considers that the service model for public organizations tends to be rigid and convoluted and still uses manual methods. The rapidly developing dynamics of the environment amplifies the need for change in public organizations for the better and towards public welfare-oriented. However, research shows that public service innovation in Indonesia is not aligned with the internalization of the innovation values within it (Putri & Mutiarin, 2018). This problem occurs due to building the capacity of the bureaucratic apparatus and the minimal infrastructure supporting innovation. Other researchers confirm that innovation must present proper management, which allows the community to access services practically (Nasikhah, 2019). Another highlight submitted by Efendi et al. (2022) in their research shows that innovation during a pandemic is hampered due to changes in the budget's focus. Local governments must adapt their financial capabilities to the development of public service innovations during the pandemic. So program targets, as well as service innovations, are not per the stipulated time planned previously. These studies show that the pandemic has significantly influenced the implementation of innovation in public services.

Based on the challenges faced by public services during the pandemic, exploratory studies on service innovation before and during the pandemic are important. Thus, this study focuses on reviewing any innovations made by the Jayapura City Government through the Population and Civil Registration Service (Disdukcapil), with the intended innovations that were initiated before and during the outbreak of the Coronavirus Disease 2019 (Covid-19) in Indonesia.

THEORETICAL FRAMEWORK

E-Government

The development can be carried out through four levels: preparation, maturation, consolidation, and utilization (Ilham, 2021). First, the preparation stage includes creating a website as a medium of information and communication for government institutions, education and training of human resources, preparation of public access facilities such as internet cafes, and socialization of the existence of information services. Second, the maturation stage is creating interactive public service information sites and interfaces with other institutions. Third, the stabilization stage; providing electronic transaction facilities and making application and data interoperability with other institutions. Finally, the utilization stage includes creating applications for integrated G2G, G2B, and G2C services, developing effective and efficient e-government service processes, and improving the best service quality (Anggraeni, 2015).

a. G2C (Government to Citizen): Community Service Innovation

G2C services include the dissemination of information to the public as well as essential public services. Electronic or ICT-based G2C services are characterized by a government information exchange system and Internet-based applications that allow the public to access information and other services using a single window online portal. G2C Focus Dissemination of information to the community, essential community services such as renewal of licenses, ordering birth/death/marriage certificates, and payment of income tax, which helps the community with essential services such as education, health, hospital information, and library.

b. G2B (Government to Business Enterprises): Business Service Innovation

It is various services between the government and the business community, including the exchange of services between the government and the business community, including the dissemination of policies, warnings, rules, and laws. Business services obtain business information, application form, license renewal, company registration, license acquisition, and tax payment. Effective electronic G2B requires the application of ICT in an integrated e-procurement system, such as registration, tenders, contracts, and payments, carried out via the Internet. Furthermore, E-Commerce supports the sale and purchase of goods and services online.

c. G2G (Inter-Agency Relationship): Innovation of Government Work

The inter-agency relationship aims to reform the government's internal work processes to increase efficiency. This innovation is divided into two levels: the local or domestic level and the international level. G2G services are transactions between the central government and local governments and between departments and related representatives and bureaus. In addition, G2G services are intergovernmental transactions and can be used for international relations and diplomacy.

More specifically, reforming government work processes using ICT is expected to be able to make reporting system results between local and central governments connected, thereby increasing accuracy. In this system, information is exchanged between institutions in the form of a shared database. It increases efficiency, the exchange of ideas and resources between government agencies, and collaborative decision-making via video conferencing. The digitization of document processing in government institutions and the movement towards paperless government operations are the main movements of G2G. The e-Document exchange is expected to guarantee efficiency, security, and administrative reliability. The G2G system requires things such as the establishment of work processes electronically, electronic document processing, and a knowledge management system.

In the context of population administration services, Jayapura City Government is a manifestation of innovation in how the government works. The central and local governments coordinate regarding using certain information technologies in public service processes. However, each region must use a different approach to its implementation. The social context of society determines it.

Public Service Innovation

Kristiawan et al. (2018) explain that, in general, innovation can be interpreted as an idea, practical thing, method, and manufactured goods. It can be observed and felt as something new for a person or group, where the new thing can be in the form of discovery results or inventions that can be utilized in achieving specific goals and solving problems. Muluk (2008: 44) states that the success of an innovation is the creation and implementation of new processes, products, services, and service methods as a result of fundamental developments regarding efficiency, effectiveness, or quality of results. From this opinion, it can be seen that innovation is not only limited to service (product) and process innovation. Furthermore, Muluk (2008:44) explains that service/product innovation is a change in product/service form and design. In contrast, process innovation is a continuous quality change movement and refers to a combination of organizational changes, procedures, and policies needed to innovate.

Innovation has developed in terms of service methods into policy or strategic innovations (Baker in Muluk, 2008:44). Innovation regarding service methods is a renewal of interaction with customers or new methods of service delivery. In contrast, policy or strategy innovation refers to the vision and mission, including new goals and strategies used, along with the reasons that start from the existing reality. Furthermore, Muluk (2008:44) reveals that innovation in system interaction is also currently developing, which includes new methods of interacting with other actors or changes in governance. Public services are business services to improve services for the community's needs per the needs of their respective agencies (Sukarmin, 2020). Purwanti & Suharyadi (2018) Concluded that public services are service delivery activities carried out by the government as service providers in an agency. Alternatively, organizations in the context of meeting the community's needs, which in its implementation refers to the applicable regulations.

In simple terms, innovation can be carried out in all aspects with the meaning of everything that realizes new ideas as an alternative (Salam, 2021). It includes public service innovations. Regarding service quality, innovation in the public sector is a necessity today by providing cheap, easy, affordable, and equitable services (Suwarno in Anggraeny, 2013). After the implementation of regional autonomy, Indonesia's changes in the government system are also accompanied by demands for changes to the quality of services expected by the community (Anggraeny, 2013), with the creation of an innovation that will be an accurate measure of the success of regional autonomy. Service innovation in the public sector is oriented to improvement in service delivery (starting from input, process and output, and outcomes)—effective, efficient, and quality services in line with applicable laws and regulations (Rusmiyati, 2020).

Based on this description, innovation goes hand in hand with the needs and success of the objectives of the regional autonomy policy, namely, to increase the regions' independence in managing their households. However, from the available innovation literature, the application of public service innovation before and during the pandemic has not received much attention. So this paper fills this void by analyzing how the innovation model was before and during the pandemic, with a locus in the city of Jayapura. The description of the results of this study, which includes challenges and solutions for developing service innovation during a pandemic, contributes to the development of empirical studies for similar research elsewhere.

Research Methods

In conducting research, it is essential to use the method used. This method is necessary; therefore, this study was carried out using a qualitative approach. Many experts provide definitions of qualitative research; from a number of these definitions, Moleong (2017: 6) synthesizes qualitative research, which intends to understand the phenomena about those experienced by research subjects (such as behavior, perceptions, motivations, and actions) holistically, and descriptions in the form of words and language in a particular natural context by utilizing various natural methods. The data was obtained from observation, interviews, and documentation. In order to obtain data relevant to the topic or problem to be studied, this study also conducted a literature study or library research. Furthermore, cross-checking of data from the primary source and comparison with other sources is carried out to test the validity of the data (Muttaqin et al., 2021). The data analysis is carried out starting from the initial stage of data collection based on 3 (three) main stages, namely, data reduction, data presentation, and data verification/drawing conclusions.

Results and Discussion

a. The Implementation of E-Government

Wiryanto (2019) explains that the Disdukcapil agencies are spread across 34 (thirty-four) provinces, 416 (four hundred and sixteen) regencies, and 98 (ninety-eight) cities. The provision of services to each of these agencies has varying qualities due to geographical conditions; other causes are local problems, including different management capabilities in implementing each of the existing policies.

As a service provider agency, the Department of Population and Civil Registration (Disdukcapil) of Jayapura City has also responded to the progress of the times (advancement of digital technology) by giving birth to various innovations. It is done to improve the quality of public service delivery in population administration. These innovations are hoped to stem from implementing services that "make people happy," as Dukcapil agencies in Indonesia continually echo this slogan. As a public service provider agency in the field of population administration, under the captain of Merlan S. Uloli as the Head of Service (Kadis), the Jayapura City Disdukcapil succeeded in sparking various innovations. Thanks to his innovation, the Disdukcapil of Jayapura City was considered one of Indonesia's best administrative service providers representing the Papua Province. It was also conveyed by Merlan S. Uloli, who said that the Disdukcapil of Jayapura City was included in the top 10 best in Indonesia regarding the commitment to providing population document services representing the Papua Province. This achievement received direct appreciation from the Mayor of Jayapura, Dr. Drs. Benhur Tomi Mano, MM. He said that the achievements made by Disdukcapil could not be separated from the commitment of the leadership of the Regional Apparatus Organization (OPD) together with all their staff in order to improve the quality of public service delivery to the community (Friendly, 2017).

b. Jayapura City Dukcapil Innovation Before the Pandemic

In 2014, the Jayapura City Disdukcapil Innovation gave birth to innovations to bring the government into the midst of society. This innovation was later called the "Dukcapil Orderly Village." The ball pick-up activity is carried out directly to the village by the Disdukcapil officer of Jayapura City; the aim is to guarantee the ownership of population documents and civil registration for the entire community in one village. Then, in 2015 an innovation was born by the Disdukcapil of Jayapura City. The innovation is named "Daku Papua," Special Data for Indigenous Papuans (OAP). The program's benefit is the availability of OAP data (Port Numbay Tribe), which can later be used in policy-making, including preparing government programs that favor indigenous Papuans (jayapurakota.go.id, 2015). Furthermore, the innovation "Operation KaTePel," launched in 2016, is a program that aims to regulate population documents through the implementation of e-ID card legalization operations. This program takes place in the port area, highways, bars, and massage parlors, targeting boarding houses in Jayapura City (teraspapua, 2020).

Then the innovation "Anjungan Dukcapil Mandiri" (ADM), also presented in 2016, aims to regulate birth certificates, death certificates, marriage certificates, and divorces. This innovation can be accessed online without coming to the dukcapil office (teraspapua, 2020). At first glance, the ADM machine belonging to the Jayapura City Disdukcapil resembles an Automated Teller Machine (ATM) used by banks. To provide excellent service that is fast, precise, and accurate, including increasing the scope of ownership of marriage certificates, the Jayapura City Disdukcapil has again innovated through its program entitled "Nikah Fast Kilat" (Nik Capil Kilat), which was initiated in 2016. In the presence of this program, Married Couples (Couples) will receive a marriage certificate without having to go back and forth to the Disdukcapil Office shortly after they have registered their marriage (jayapurakota. go.id, 2016).

The "Electronic ID Card-Based Leadership Guest Book" program in 2017 was launched to create a sense of security, comfort, and order for leadership guests within the Jayapura City Government. This innovation is based on an application connected to a chip reader (card reader) in the e-KTP. It will provide convenience in registering guests who want to meet the leadership, such as; Mayor and Deputy Mayor, including the Regional Secretary (Sekda).

The "Tok Tok Pos" program is an innovation that was also initiated in 2017. By utilizing postal services to provide delivery services for population documents and civil registration to the public. This program is implemented without burdening the community as service users (Teraspapua, 2020). Referring to Gan (2017) said that although Jayapura City is in the easternmost region of Indonesia, the people have been spoiled with various conveniences in providing population administration services. One is the birth of the "Birth Plus" innovation initiated in 2017. The baby birth will immediately get a Family Card (KK), Birth Certificate, and Child Identity Card (KIA), including the innovation "Press Hp Akta So," which was also launched by Disdukcapil Jayapura City in 2017. This service will provide convenience to the public in managing population administration through smartphone devices/media owned by the community (nusakini.com, 2017). The welcome program in Jayapura City, "E-Waniambey," is a website-based application initiated in 2018. It is to register non-permanent (non-permanent) residents, including; residents outside the City of Jayapura, such as residents currently studying, working, or who have lived for approximately 6 (six) months. The E-Waniambey application is one step in the success of the Jayapura City Government in providing accessible services to the community (papuatoday, 2018). Furthermore, the "Population Service Package" innovation launched in 2018 is a program aimed at providing convenience and speeding up the process of managing and ownership of population documents and civil registration for the people of Jayapura City (teraspapua, 2020).

c. Jayapura City Dukcapil Innovation During the COVID-19 Pandemic

The Covid-19 pandemic was responded to in the public service sector by running digital technology-based services (online services). Public service providers are then expected to be able to adapt to advances in digital technology by giving birth to innovation during efforts to suppress the spread of the Covid-19 disease that has hit Indonesia. The Covid-19 pandemic period is a challenge for Dukcapil agencies in providing services. Seeing the needs of the community who continuously need government services, including services in the field of population administration (Adminduk), but the space for human movement must be temporarily limited as a result of the implementation of social distancing policies following physical distancing (satubanten.com in ombudsman.go.id, 2020). The policy of limiting human movement is carried out to break the chain of the spread of the coronavirus, therefore making the birth of an innovation a necessity to do so that it can ensure that people continue to receive government services.

To prevent the spread of Covid-19, the Jayapura City government temporarily closed schools and the State Civil Apparatus (ASN) for some time. The policy to close schools and ASN was carried out from March 17 to March 31, 2020, then extended to April 17, 2020 (Jayapura City Disukcapil, 2020). As a result, implementing public services, including the provision of services in the Adminduk, also impacts it. Panggabean & Saragih (2020) stated that to encourage the provision of digital-based public services during the Covid-19 outbreak. The Jayapura City Civil Registration and Civil Service Office continues to introduce an online service system to the public, one of the efforts made to socialize the implementation of e-government to the public intensely. The community through the provision of website-based services.

In addition to registration, management of population documents during the Covid-19 pandemic can be done through the official website of the Jayapura City Disdukcapil; the community can also register online by using the WhatsApp application and Short Message Service (SMS) (Jayapurakota.go.id, 2020). Furthermore, the delivery of residence documents is carried out by cooperating with the instant courier service owned by GrabExpress. Launching the pacificpos.com website, the collaboration between the Jayapura City Disdukcapil and GrabExpress is the first document delivery service in Papua. This innovation, packaged in the form of collaboration, aims to provide convenience for the community in managing population documents without requiring them to come directly to the Disdukcapil Office.

Kandipi (2021) explains that through the collaboration of the Jayapura City Disdukcapil with Grab-Express, the Disdukcapil will contact the public as service users when their residence documents have been issued by displaying a detailed description of the document. At the same time, the public will be given information about the GrabExpress service to assist with the delivery and pick-up of the document. In addition to collaborating with GrabExpress, during the Covid-19 pandemic, the Jayapura City Disdukcapil also collaborated with PT Pos Indonesia regarding document delivery through the postal shop innovation. The Disdukcapil of Jayapura City initiated this innovation before the Covid-19 pandemic broke out in Indonesia.

At the end of March 2020, the Jayapura City Government also launched the Mandiri Dukcapil Pavilion Machine, abbreviated as the ADM machine. In terms of shape, this machine is an Independent Dukcapil Pavilion Machine owned by the Jayapura City Government. The Mayor of Jayapura launched Benhur Tomi Mano resembles an ATM (Automated Teller Machine), or in Indonesia, it is called an Automated Teller Machine. Launching the news from ceposonline.com, the ADM machine was a phenomenal innovation from the Directorate General of Dukcapil, Ministry of Home Affairs, in 2019. This innovation was born from the realization of the Minister of Home Affairs Regulation (Permendagri) Number 7 of 2019 concerning Online Administrative Services (Wen, 2021).

Since April 2020, Disdukcapil Jayapura City has implemented four population administration applications: a Family Card application, an electronic ID card application, a Child Identity Card application (KIA), and Resident Transfer Letter Application (Panggabean & Saragih, 2020). In addition, this includes synchronization of (Non-permanent NIK/BPJS, Bank), e-Waniambey (Temporary/Non-Permanent Residence Certificate), and Civil Registration (Birth, Death, Marriage, and Divorce Certificates).

This go-digital public service transformation plays a role in preventing extortion, including preventing the spread of the Covid-19 disease, because this ADM public service innovation can be carried out with online access, without direct contact between service officers and the community who are taking care of Adminduk (Wen., 2021). The ADM machine has a function to print residence documents (e-KTP, Family Card, Child Identity Card, and Civil Registration Certificate). This breakthrough will provide convenience in providing services to the community during the Covid-19 pandemic. Convenience is given to the community because the machine is specifically designed to print population documents efficiently, quickly, free of charge, and at the same standard without discrimination. It does not complicate distance and time and makes the community happy as service users, which is also in line with the adaptation of new habits during the Covid-19 pandemic (Wen, 2021). The same thing was conveyed by Zul (2021) that using the ADM machine will provide convenience for the service user community. It has been specifically designed to print documents efficiently and quickly, without discrimination, and does not complicate distance and time; the services provided are free of charge and course in line with the adaptation of new habits during the Covid-19 pandemic. The ADM machine is very suitable to be applied during the Covid-19 outbreak. It is because the provision of services does not need to be done face-to-face or in direct contact with the community but with the help of IT (Information And Technology), which will make it easier to manage population documents and civil registration (Wen, 2021). In addition to launching the ADM machine, at that momentum, the Jayapura City Disdukcapil also entered into a Cooperation Agreement (PKS) with PT Jasa Raharja Papua branch by launching the NIK-Based Accident Victim Data Identification System Application (SIDAKK-NIK).

Entering a period of Adaptation to New Habits, the community is again given space to move as before but while still prioritizing the application of health protocols8, which previously had to stay at home, which was the government's recommendation to prevent the transmission of the Covid-19 disease in the community. During the adaptation period for this new habit, the ADM machine belonging to the Disdukcapil Jayapura City was placed in a shopping center to bring services closer to the community. One of them is at Saga Mall Abepura, Jayapura City, Papua. Therefore, people who want to take care of their population administration no longer need to come directly to the Disdukcapil office but can apply through the population service by utilizing the Pace Dukcapil application (Teraspapua, 2022). Regarding the ADM machine, Tribunnews Host Firda Ananda (2022), in his report, said that the collaboration was an agreement between the two parties (Jayapura City Government & Saga Mall Parties) to provide maximum service to the people of Jayapura City in the New Normal era. Government and private cooperation are very much needed because it determines more modern public sector management changes (Yusriadi, 2018). The adoption and development of information technology in the public sector have supported a service model that not only relies on government offices but can be carried out outside the office, indicating the route to the goal of innovation. From the perspective of public organizations, information technology facilitates the realization of efficient and effective services, and on the other hand, service innovation encourages public enthusiasm to participate in services.

CONCLUSION

Based on the results of this study, the Jayapura City Population and Civil Registration Service (Disdukcapil) utilizes advances in digital technology by giving birth to various innovations to improve the quality of public service delivery in the field of population administration. So that the Jayapura City Disdukcapil is included in the top 10 best in Indonesia regarding the commitment to providing population document services representing the Papua Province. The innovation of the Jayapura City Disdukcapil before the pandemic was the "Dukcapil Orderly Village" in 2014. In this activity, the Jayapura City Disdukcapil party picked up the ball by going directly to the village to ensure ownership of population documents and civil registration for all people living in one village. Furthermore, the innovation "Independent Dukcapil Anjungan" (ADM), also presented in 2016, is accessed online without coming to the Dukcapil office. The ADM machine belonging to the Jayapura City Disdukcapil resembles an Automated Teller Machine (ATM) used by banks. Furthermore, "Tok Tok Pos" is an innovation initiated in 2017. By utilizing postal services to provide delivery services for population documents and civil registration to the public. This program is implemented without having to burden the community as service users. Then the innovations "Birth Plus" and "Press Hp Akta Jadi" in 2017. This program is intended for services for Family Cards (KK), Birth Certificates, and Child Identity Cards (KIA) for mothers who have just given birth.

While the Adminduk innovation during the COVID-19 pandemic, Disdukcapil provides opportunities for managing population documents during the Covid-19 pandemic offline by complying with health protocols or through the official website to register online by utilizing the WhatsApp application and Short Message Service. There is the development of ADM innovation and "Tok Tok Pos" during the pandemic. Disdukcapil Jayapura City collaborated with GrabExpress. The mechanism for this service is that the Disdukcapil will contact the community as service users when their residence documents have been issued by displaying a detailed description of the document. At the same time, the public will be provided with information about GrabExpress and PT Pos Indonesia services to help deliver and pick up documents.

The population administration is fulfilled among the people, it helps the people in getting access to other public services such as fair social assistance. Meanwhile, the service innovation implemented by the Jayapura City Disdukcapil, especially ADM services that resemble ATM services, can be accessed by the public in shopping centers. This innovation can be used as a preference for other regional Dukcapil. In other words, it will provide useful information for local governments to develop their population service innovations. In addition, this study is limited to one locus that does not represent innovation in population and civil registration services elsewhere. Future studies could map dimensions of public service innovation beyond population services and broaden the scope of research loci to address comparative studies.

REFERENCES

Ananda, F. (2022). Facilitate the Community, Disdukcapil Launches the Automated Dukcapil Pavilion Machine (ADM) in Jayapura City. *Tribunnews.* https://bit.ly/3NOAASM

Anggraeni. (2015). Implementation of E-Government at the District Level: A Case Study of Pelalawan District, Riau. *Jurnal Sistem Informasi, 7*(2). https://doi.org/ doi:10.36706/jsi.v7i2.2269

Anggraeny, C. (2013). Health Service Innovation in Improving Service Quality at the Jagir Health Center, Surabaya City. *Kebijakan dan Manajemen Publik, 1*(1), 85–93. http://journal.unair.ac.id/filerPDF/11%20 Cindy_KMP%20V1%20N1%20Jan-April%202013.pdf. Accessed 05 April 2022.

Anisa, H. N. (2019). *Implementation of Three In One (3 In 1) Services in Population Administration Services of Karanganyar Regency.* Skripsi, Universitas Negeri Semarang. http://lib.unnes. ac.id/38869/1/3301415043.pdf

Disdukcapil Kota Jayapura. (2020). *Dukcapil Prevent Corona.* https://bit.ly/3tM6uY6

Dukcapil.kemendagri.go.id. (2021). *Dukcapil Wins KIPP's Top Commendable Innovations, Reverses Problems with Innovation.* https://bit.ly/3mJbtF6

Efendi, K., Tumija, T., Handayani, N., & Rifai, M. (2022). *Public Service Innovation Model in Sragen Regency.* Jurnal Media Birokrasi. doi:10.33701/jmb.v4i1.2327

Gan. (2017). *Jayapura City Government Uses Innovation to Make it Easier for Residents to Obtain Resident Documents.* https://bit.ly/3zHmnTc

Ilham, S. S. M. S. (2021). *E-Governance.* Deepublish.

Jayapurakota.go.id. (2015). *Daku Papua, Special Data for Indigenous Papuans (OAP).* https://bit. ly/3xMKlvg

Jayapurakota.go.id. (2016). *Nikcapil Kilat, Fast Execution and Obtaining of Marriage Certificate.* https://bit.ly/3twmjls

Jayapurakota.go.id. (2020). *Dukcapil Prevents Corona.* https://bit.ly/39uM1Qq

Kandipi, H. D. (2021). *Jayapura City Government Collaborates with GrabExpress to send residence documents.* https://bit.ly/3NNSwwR

Kristiawan, M., Suryani, I., Muntazir, M., Areli, A.J., Agustina, M., Kafarisa, R.F., Saputra, A.G., Diana, N., Agustina, E., Oktarina, R., & Hisri, T.B. (2018). *Educational Innovation*. Jawa Timur: WADE Publish.

Lapaslhoknga. (2021). *Bureaucracy Reform*. https://bit.ly/3zAH6Z8

Ministry of Home Affairs. (2019). *Pelayanan GISA Hadir di Kota Jayapura*. https://dukcapil.kemendagri. go.id/berita/baca/229/pelayanan-gisa-hadir-

Moleong, L. J. (2017). *Qualitative Research Methodology* (Revised Edition). Remaja Rosda Karya.

Muluk, K. (2008). *Knowledge Management: The Key to Success in Local Government Innovation*. Bayumedia Publishing.

Muttaqin, M. Z., Idris, U., & Ilham, I. (2021). The Challenge of Implementing the Neutrality of Civil Servants (Study of Symbolic Violence in Pilkada). *JWP*, *6*(1), 1–14. doi:10.24198/jwp.v6i1.32065

Nasikhah, M. A. (2019). *Information Technology-Based Public Transportation Service Innovations*. Jurnal Inovasi Ilmu Sosial Dan Politik. doi:10.33474/jisop.v1i1.2670

Nusakini.com. (2017). *Press HP Deed to Become Jayapura City*. https://bit.ly/39nZ6uY

Ombudsman.go.id. (2020). *Ombudsman Banten Holds Interactive Dialogue, Checks the Effectiveness and Innovation of Disdukcapil Administration Services*. https://bit.ly/3QfloQa

Panggabean, T. T. N., & Saragih, A. (2020). Implementation Of State Civil Service (ASN) Management Through E-Government In The New Normal Era. *Civil Service*, *14*(1), 93–103. https://jurnal.bkn.go.id/ index.php/asn/article/view/265/200

Papuatoday. (2018). *E-Waniambey App Promotes*. https://bit.ly/3zDD81I

Purwanti, T., & Suharyadi, R. (2018). Implementation of Government Policy on Population Administration (Study of the Study on the Population Service System in Sindang Beliti Ilir District, Rejang Lebong Regency). *MIMBAR : Jurnal Penelitian Sosial Dan Politik*, *7*(1), 59–67. doi:10.32663/jpsp.v7i1.425

Putri, L. D. M., & Mutiarin, D. (2018). *The effectiveness of public policy innovations; Its influence on the quality of public services in Indonesia*. Jurnal Ilmu Pemerintahan.

Ramah. (2017). *Jayapura City Dispendukcapil will take part in South Korea's education and training*. https://bit.ly/3O98QrI

Rusmiyati. (2020). Public Service Innovation at the One Stop Integrated Service Office 19 in the Autonomous Region of Depok City, West Java Province. *Jurnal Ilmiah Adminstrasi Pemerintah Daerah*, *12*(1), 19–25. https://doi.org/ doi:10.33701/jiapd.v12i1.1341

Salam, R. (2021). Changes and Innovations in Public Services in the New Normal Era of the Covid-19 Pandemic. *Journal of Public Administration and Government*, *3*(1), 28–36. https://doi.org/ doi:10.22487/ jpag.v3i1.138

Sukarmin. (2020). *Public Service Innovation Through Population Administration for Persons with Disabilities (Inclusive Administration) at the Population and Civil Registry Office of Bulukumba Regency*. Skripsi, Universitas Muhammadiyah Makassar. https://digilibadmin.unismuh.ac.id/upload/12604-Full_Text.pdf

Teraspapua. (2020). *Merlan Uloli, Create Innovations That Will Bear Rewards.* https://bit.ly/3mILoG0

Teraspapua. (2022). *Make Services Easy for the Community, Jayapura City Government Places ADM Machines at Saga Mall Abepura.* https://bit.ly/3Ql8Cjh

Wen. (2021). *Innovative, ADM Machine in Jayapura City Government Simplifies Administrative Affairs.* https://bit.ly/3MMtH2T

Wiryanto, W. (2019). Replication of the Population Administration Service Innovation Model in Indonesia. *INOBIS: Jurnal Inovasi Bisnis Dan Manajemen Indonesia, 3*(1), 27–40. doi:10.31842/jurnal-inobis. v3i1.118

Wulan, R. R., & Mustam, M. (2017). Improving Service Quality in the Context of Bureaucratic Reform in the Land Office of Semarang City. *Journal of Public Policy and Management Review, 6*(3), 1–20. doi:10.14710/jppmr.v6i3.16740

Yanuar, R. M. (2019). Public Service Innovation (Case Study: Public Safety Center (PSC) 119 Bantul Regency as Health and Emergency Services). *Jurnal Ilmu Pemerintahan, 04*(0274), 20. doi:10.31629/ kemudi.v4i1.1335

Yusriadi, Y. (2018). *Change Management in Bureaucratic Reform Towards Information Technology (IT).* Jurnal Mitra Manajemen. doi:10.52160/ejmm.v2i2.39

Zul. (2021). *Jayapura City Government Makes It Easy for People to Print Population Documents.* https:// bit.ly/3OaBvwr

Chapter 15

Preserving Personal Autonomy:
Exploring the Importance of Privacy Rights, Their Impact on Society, and Threats to Privacy in the Digital Age

Rebant Juyal
Assam University, India

ABSTRACT

This chapter explores the importance of the right to privacy, its impact on society, and the threats to privacy rights from technology. The right to privacy is a fundamental human right that protects individuals from unwarranted intrusion into their personal lives. It has a significant impact on society by ensuring that individuals can exercise their rights and freedoms without interference from others. However, with the rise of technology, the right to privacy has come under threat. The use of digital technology has led to an unprecedented level of surveillance and data collection, raising concerns about the potential for abuse of power by governments and private entities. This chapter examines the various ways in which privacy rights are being eroded and the measures that can be taken to protect these rights. The conclusion highlights the importance of respecting individuals' privacy rights and the need to ensure that they are protected in today's digital age.

I. INTRODUCTION

The right to privacy is a fundamental human right that has been recognized by many countries and international organizations (Privacy International, 2017). It is an essential aspect of personal autonomy, which enables individuals to make choices about their lives without fear of persecution or intrusion from others. The right to privacy has a significant impact on society, as it protects individuals from potential harm and promotes trust between individuals and the government (Hinailiyas, 2021). However, with the advancement of technology, the right to privacy has come under threat. The use of digital technology has led to an unprecedented level of surveillance and data collection, raising concerns about the potential

DOI: 10.4018/978-1-6684-7450-1.ch015

for abuse of power by governments and private entities. In this research article, we will discuss the importance of the right to privacy, its impact on society, and the threats to privacy rights from technology. We will examine the various ways in which privacy rights are being eroded and the measures that can be taken to protect these rights. By the end of this research article, we hope to provide a comprehensive understanding of the importance of privacy rights and the need to safeguard them in today's digital age

Technology has an impact on each and every facet of our civilization. The method of work and even the work itself has changed drastically. The facet of technology that is concerned with the accumulation of data to facilitates us with obtaining the targeted benefits require us to provide unique identification to the system established to hold such data. When the beneficiary forms the targeted group avails such benefit the unique identity that was submitted to identify her were then compared with the recorded data so as to ensure that the benefits are reached to targeted person. The unique identity of a person can be in the form of fingerprints, face, iris, such data do not change over time, easy to obtain and unique to everyone. Biometric is derived from Greek noun bio (life) and metric (measure) and means measurement of life. The integral part of biometric system is to verify the claim by comparing the biological identity already submitted in a database. The system of identifying a person with biological traits was done before manually, with the advent of technology the system automatically matches the identities of the person seeking access with the already stored data.

II. LITERATURE REVIEW

While, analysing and studying the broad bases available literature in the given subject, the author in this section attempts to provide a brief description of the literature used in preparation of this Chapter. DD Basu commentary on Article 21 stands as an essential literature to understand how the rights under Article 21 operates and can also be state's defenses for its inability to completely make these rights fully functional. Additionally, the constitutional law of India by Dr. J N Pandey guides for the correct interpretation of constitutional provisions and not to be muddle in the dark among principle of equity.

Furthermore, to understand the current development in the sphere of the Right to privacy in digital space several news articles are referred by the author some of them are namely, 'Fight for Data Privacy will not end with personal data protection bill' by the Mint, 'The data protection bill only weakens user rights' by The Hindu. News article and research papers throws light on current changes in technology and the trend followed elsewhere, which fundamentally stands crucial for understanding privacy laws in technology. Further the articles referred by the author poses a perception from which the point of issues must be seen. It brings out that how private corporations holding personal data have the capacity to negotiate with the government and such negotiation depends upon the policy of the state.

The primary source of the study of this research article is based on the judgments of the Supreme Court of India, as the documents of the cases bring out the philosophy behind the recognition of this essential right at first hand. The analysis of judgment brings forward the reasons for making preference on the question of competing rights against privacy.

III. BALANCING OF RIGHT TO PRIVACY AND OTHER RIGHTS UNDER ARTICLE 21

The Indian Supreme Court in the Justice K.S. Puttaswamy case recognised the Right to Privacy as a fundamental right under Article 21 of the Indian Constitution (Hinailiyas, 2021). While, expounding upon the constitutionality of Aadhar Act in the relevant case of Justice K.S. Puttaswamy Vs. Union of India,[1] the court went on to balance exercise of right to privacy and right to public benefits. The court observed that the purpose behind enacting Aadhar act was to provide subsidies or direct benefits to the beneficiary and therefore the biometrics were obtained to provide the essentials and enforce the proportional distribution of resources under the schemes of food security further it will be helpful to grant direct money transfers in the times of financial or health crisis.

In balancing the recently recognised right of privacy it is important to keep in mind that constitution is not to only to protect the rights of few but it aims to serve people at every stratum of our economy. The state has the obligation to equally distribute the resources and to have a just and egalitarian social order, in pursuance of the duty cast upon the state under directive principle of state policy the government has enacted the said law to distribute the targeted benefits in the form of subsidy and direct monetary benefits.

The state holds the public money as a trustee of public resources which it is obliged to use it for public good, this obligation of the state also stems from the fundamental rights of public under article 21 of life and liberty and right to life does not mean a mere animal like existence but the life of dignity therefore the governments must ensure that no one dies out of hunger or lack of medical care. The section 7 of the act empowers the government to use the collected date to use for transfer of benefits which are charged upon consolidated fund of India. In Minerva mills v. Union of India,[2] the court observed that directive principles of state policy cannot override fundamental rights, however the courts seem to construct the interplay of rights and directive principles by going through the balancing exercise.

The Act aims to provide food security for masses and other benefits on the contrary it was argued that right of privacy is infringed in the exercise obtaining biometrics of an individual. The court expounded upon the objective embraced in constitution and stated that the act passes the 3 tests to be sufficient to bypass the accusation of being violative of fundamental rights. The biometric information is obtained though act of the parliament which passes the test of legality, secondly the act is enacted for the legitimate aim of the state, which is to distribute public resources in the form of several benefits including food security, lastly the proportionality test, here the act of the parliament has direct nexus with the object sought to be achieved.

The proportionality test needs a further elaboration because as stated above the, it needs to be shown that whether the actions of the state does not exceed what is required which further possess a question that whether there is other substitute for the delivery of state benefits without hampering the privacy rights of an individual. It needs to be understood that whether the data stored in the form of biometric are sufficiently stored so that it cannot be breached easily. The court while upholding the constitutional validity of Aadhar act carved out certain provisions and declare them to be unconstitutional and incapable to pass the 3-fold test created in K.S. Puttaswamy v. Union of India[3]. In the context of competing balance, the right of autonomy and standard of living, the majority in its conclusion observed thus[4]:

There needs to be balancing of two competing fundamental rights, right to privacy on the one hand and right to food, shelter and employment on the other hand. Axiomatically both the rights are founded on human dignity. At the same time, in the given context, two facets are in conflict with each other.

The question here would be, when a person seeks to get the benefits of welfare schemes to which she is entitled to as a part of right to live life with dignity, whether her sacrifice to the right to privacy, is so invasive that it creates imbalance?[5]

Before considering the informational data apart from biometric that are used by social networking platforms, it is pertinent to further expounding upon the balance of rights under biometric data collection through Aadhar act, the majority opined that the balancing interest involve here is a right of dignified life and access to state benefits and on the other hand the digital privacy of an individual. While committing the balancing exercise the court stated that it is not the vision of the constitution to provide the dignified standard of living by robbing the right of liberty, however the act only accumulates the required data for the purpose it wants to achieve that is targeted delivery of benefits. The court further observed that the benefits and services refer to welfare benefits to the specific deprives class. On the issue of loopholes in technology the court said that the technology is proved to 99.27% secure and even if there are some loopholes which may exclude population on account solely on technological glitch then these loopholes can be remedied and the whole system of injecting benefits cannot be set aside merely on minimal glitches as the objective of the act is in greater good. Sikri J. took into the consideration the exclusion of population who due to some unfortunate accidents lost the biometric sought to be collected for example loss of finger prints or inefficient iris scan due to blindness, and it was observed that this class is taken into consideration and they are by no way can be excluded from any beneficial schemes and the government is bound to take separate measures for such population.

The technology must not create a divide and should not be operationalize in a manner which works on exclusion of population which does not fulfill the required criteria rather it must be used as a tool of inclusion, to assist the human efforts or labor and not be substitute it. The economic entitlements are the guarantee of the constitution and the government is bound to make efforts to actualize those guarantees through proportional means.

In so far section 33(2) is concerned which provides for disclosure of information in the interest of national security the court observed that such disclosure can only be made on the application of an officer not below the rank of joint secretary that too with the involvement of high court judge for the application of judicial mind in ascertaining whether there involves a security threat that requires the disclosure of such information. On section 57 which provide that the biometric authentication can be obtained on the basis of the agreement between two parties, the court observed that the information can only be obtained by the statutory backing and contractual provision are not backed by law therefore the private corporation cannot obtain or hold biometric authentication as it may lead to exposing the individual liberty for commercial exploitation, hence the court read down section 57 in its present form until a legal framework is developed around it.

On the front of financial privacy, the court regards the mandatory linking of Aadhar to existing and new accounts and their rendering as un-operative on being non-complied with the said seeding as un-constitutional as it would lead to invasion to financial privacy and further bereft the account holder of their property on non-compliance, the court found rule 9 of Money laundering act which is concerned with such seeding as unconstitutional. On the issue of linking of Aadhar with PAN the court found that such linking passes the triple test of constitutionality and relied on Binoy Viswam's case[6] to uphold the constitutionality.

IV. COLLECTION AND STORAGE OF PERSONAL INFORMATION BY PRIVATE CORPORATIONS

India is yet to implement its data protection law, which is going to be enacted as Personal Data Protection Bill, 2019 on the recommendation of the committee headed by B. N. Srikrishna J. India is not a party to any international convention on personal data protection like GDPR (Talwar Thakore & Associates, 2022). However, India is a long-standing member of Universal Declaration of Human Rights (article 12) and International Covenants on Civil and political rights (article 17) which recognize the right to privacy.

The ICCPR recognised the right to privacy in 1988 despite such recognition the challenges to privacy are ever increasing with advancement of communication technology the threat of global surveillance needs to be avoided with a well framed legal structure. In the wake of this the United Nations General Assembly Resolution on right to privacy in digital age was passed on December 18, 2013 (SFLC.IN, 2017). Until the specific legislation for data protection is enacted the parliament has amended Information technology Act (2000) to include section 43A and section 72A. Section 43A provides that if a body corporate who is possessing or handeling any sensitive data and due to its negligence in maintain reasonable security results in a wrongful loss or gain to any person then such body corporate is liable to pay compensation to person so effected. Section 73A provides that if there is a dissemination of personal information by any entity possessing such data without the consent of that person than such an entity is liable to pay compensation which can exceed to Rs. 5,00,000/-.

The government has notified the Information Technology (Reasonable Security Practices and Procedures and sensitive Personal Data or Information) Rules, 2011, these rules protects the sensitive data or information of a person, the rules prescribes for reasonable security practices to be followed by body corporate or any such person who is holding such information on behalf of body corporate, and in case of breach of duty in handling sensitive data or information then such body corporate is liable to compensate the concerned party. The sensitive information in the context of rules relates to (Dalmia, 2017) -

1. Password.
2. Physical, psychological and mental health condition.
3. Sexual orientation.
4. Biometric information.
5. Medical records and history.
6. Financial information like bank details, credit card or debit card or other instrument details.

V. DATA PROTECTION BILL 2019

The Data Protection Bill, 2019 was introduced in the Lok Sabha of Union Parliament with the fundamental objective of preserving and protecting the personal data of the people of India (PRS India, 2019). The Bill provisions that for obtaining the biometric information the Aadhar sought to attach the benefits it aims to transfer to the beneficiary. On the other hand, the big data companies who provide variety of other services while obtaining access to user's personal information. In K.S. Puttaswamy case, the court struck down section 57 which allowed the private corporation to obtain biometrics for authentication however while serving us with more advanced or feasible communication, these platforms often ask for several access of user so as to provide better services or oriented results. The introduction of technology to serve the population and collection of personal information to provide targeted or oriented services forms the premise for balancing exercise between right of privacy of beneficiary or user and standard of living which holds dignity as its core value or equal access to technology services which holds the emerging right of net neutrality.

To further enunciate the mechanism which the judicial exercise needs to take into account, it is useful to separate the collection of data for the purpose of benefits provided by the state for which the biometric data is allowed for authentication and information communication services by private corporation for which other data than biometric is collected. This separation is feasible for understanding the conceptual framework and consideration taken into account during judicial enquiry for weighing the claims.

In case of essential benefits as in Aadhar the balancing considerations are right to privacy and right to dignity whereas in access to information communication it is right of privacy and equal access to internet or right of net neutrality. The access to social networking applications and other utility applications asks for 'user consent' to provide the access to location, call logs, media, and on allowing the access the user is able to avail the services. In case the consent is not assigned by the user the platform denies the access further the terms are incomprehensible by every section of users therefore the consent obtained for access to personal information is not informed. The argument of consent is raised as it is argued that application platform work on consent-based model and if a user doesn't want to share her information with the platform operator, she is free to leave (Singh, 2021). The committee headed by Former Judge of the Supreme Court justice (retd) B N Srikrishna emphasized on informed consent of the user in the report submitted upon which the data protection bill was framed.

VI. CONSENT

According to Merriam Webster dictionary consent means to give assent or approval or to agree. Consent has been viewed as expression of an autonomy or control which has the consequence of allowing another partly to disclaim the liability of infringement to one's privacy. The committee recommended that platforms hold such information of their users in confidence and can only be used for the benefit of user or for the purpose for which consent is given therefore there must be a fiduciary relationship between platform and user (Sinha, 2018). The terms of the consent are communicated to the user as an obligation of formal communication.

It is further observed by the committee the consent obtained by fiduciaries are uninformed because users are unable to comprehend terms of consent further many of the users do not care about reading the terms altogether and even if they read, they don't have capacity to negotiate[7]. This is because the platform forms standard terms and conditions for all who want access to service and once the community relevant or necessary chose to be on the platform the individual even not willful of assigning the consent forced to do so. It is difficult to be in mainstream urban social life and remain secluded from social medial platforms or other utility applications therefore to raise the argument of user has the choice of not opting or leaving the platform serves very little or no use in resolution of the issue of privacy.

The committee observed that the general mode of obtaining consent leads to attaching of normative value to an individual's autonomy. The user consented to what she is not factually or in practice acquainted with. The general mode of obtaining consent therefore has lowered the value of autonomy an individual holds in digital space[8]. Due to collection of huge amount of uninformed data the consequences put forward a grim picture where users are helpless against the might of large data corporations which uses the weapon of standard non- negotiable contracts to enslave user's autonomy in exchange for making her a member of digital community.

The committee suggested an altogether different status to such contracts in order to have the practical implications of what they are required for in law. To have an effective consent and not just in its normative meaning the committee relying on Arther Leff's seminal article 'Contract as Thing' suggested that the contract between consumer and fiduciaries are to be treated as things or product, this would remove the 'contract of adhesion' and treat the notice of consent as a product thereby arising the product liability of a fiduciary, it empower the user to raise a dispute if the terms seems to subjugate the autonomy of a user or if the term goes against the law or if the term is such which gains the access to a user's profile which she reasonably did not presume or if it is more than what is required to serve her interest. When the consent notice is not treated as binding contract rather a product which can be contended and relief can be sought if the competent authority founds that there is a violation of law or unwarranted invasion to privacy than required, it can interfere to reinstate the position direct the fiduciaries to remove such data from there database.

VII. WHATSAPP PRIVACY POLICY

Recently new WhatsApp privacy policy is in news, and few are claiming that it would make user privacy vulnerable. WhatsApp collects meta data registration data like phone number, IP address, transaction details, usage data, purchase, user content (Singh, 2011). From 2016 WhatsApp has been sharing so much data with facebook, the 'affiliated companies' section of the privacy policy explains that facebook can use the data it gathers about the users and can use that to serve ads for example a person visits to particular store to often then it can recommend various other products or like products to the particular user (Sathe, 2021). In a podcast with NDTV' Gadget 360, Mishi Chaudhary an expert in cyber law said that in 2016 facebook gave choice to its users that if they don't want their information to be shared with other subsidiaries they can 'opt out' of this function but this right is taken away in recent policy.

WhatsApp in several FAQs have clarified that it is updating its policy to serve business better and the communication of business with its customers more efficient and therefore they are going to collect data about businesses to serve them better and individual's chat will remain end to end encrypted. One of the concerns that Ms. Chaudhary raised was that the data WhatsApp will collect with the inclusion of more and more functions like payment and shopping, this will generate large number of data points and that can be used for concluding several other derivative information. Further the WhatsApp in Europe has in its terms clearly mentioned the prohibition of using of data for its use however no such clause is present in Indian privacy policy, this amounts to discriminating the users in two countries treating the valuable right of privacy differently in different geographies (Alawadhi, 2021; Alawadhi, 2021).

The right to privacy under article 21 cannot be enforced against private tech companies and therefore their actions are not amenable to writ jurisdiction under article 32 or 226 of the constitution. The protection of personal data is regulated by Information and technology act 2000 and rules framed thereunder and the penalty for offending any provision will be penalized according to the rules.

The protection of data privacy is strengthened by new Data Protection Bill, 2019 which provides for informed consent to be obtained by users, the law gave the statutory right to a person over her personal data, if the consent is withdrawn the corporation will be require to eliminate the processing of data

(Lakshmikumaran, 2023). Fundamental rights cannot be enforced against private corporation therefore the balancing exercise that has been observed above will not come into force and the whole breach will be entertained in civil suit for obtaining the remedy, the nature of liability of a corporation is civil and therefore remedy in the form of compensation and specific relief is involved. However, as it is mentioned above that fundamental rights can be enforced against state and writ petition is amenable, in entertaining the writ the court will go through the exercise of enforcing the right of privacy while considering reasonable restrictions, the reasonableness of restriction is scrutinized on triple test of legality, legitimate state aim, proportionality.

The actions of state where it collects personal data are scrutinized on the anvil of 'triple test', if the act passed the triple test during judicial enquiry its constitutionality will be said to upheld. The argument above about net neutrality refers to elimination of discrimination in content provided to users on same platform, rather here the use of the term is in the sense that tech companies because of the huge size that they have already established in a country and therefore the population is largely reliant upon the platform cannot ask its users to either accept the terms or leave and therefore the removal of option to opt out of data sharing discriminates between section who willfully accepted the terms and those who didn't.

Further the differentiation created by the company on the basis of differential privacy terms creates a biased social networking environment for example in a global trade economy the transaction between two nations will have differential impacts in terms of collection of data in say Europe and India. The adoption of differential policy is *'user biased'*, and therefore to have a free global trade the platform cannot have differential terms of agreement further there need to have a basic standard below which the tech companies who are or will provide international trade services have to comply.

VIII. CONCLUSION

The right to privacy is an essential human right that protects individuals from unwarranted intrusion into their personal lives (European Data Protection Supervisor, 2023). It is recognized as a fundamental right in many countries, including the United States, and is enshrined in international law through the Universal Declaration of Human Rights (Diggelmann & Cleis, 2014; United Nations, 1948). The importance of the right to privacy cannot be overstated, as it has a significant impact on society and protects individuals from potential harm. However, with the advent of technology, the threat to privacy rights has become more pronounced (Banisar & Davies, 1991). The right to privacy is crucial for individuals to live their lives without fear of intrusion from others, including the government or private entities. It allows individuals to make choices about their personal lives, such as who they associate with and what they do in their free time, without fear of persecution. Additionally, the right to privacy protects sensitive information, such as medical records and financial information, from being disclosed to others without the individual's consent. Without the right to privacy, individuals could be subjected to surveillance, discrimination, or even harassment, which could have severe consequences for their physical and mental well-being.

The impact of the right to privacy on society is immense (Banisar & Davies, 1991). It ensures that individuals can exercise their rights and freedoms without interference from others. For example, journalists can report on issues of public interest without fear of retribution, and individuals can practice their religion or express their opinions freely. Furthermore, the right to privacy promotes trust between individuals and the government, as it prevents the government from abusing its power of surveillance or monitor its citizens. In this way, the right to privacy is crucial to maintaining a democratic society where individuals are free to express their opinions and participate in the democratic process.

However, with the proliferation of technology, the right to privacy is under threat. The use of digital technology, such as social media and mobile phones, has led to an unprecedented level of surveillance and data collection. Governments and private entities have access to vast amounts of personal data, which can be used to track individuals' movements, monitor their behaviour, and infer their preferences. This has led to concerns about the potential for abuse of power by these entities and the erosion of privacy rights.

In conclusion, the right to privacy persists as an essential human right that has a significant impact on society. It protects individuals from unwarranted intrusion into their personal lives and ensures that they can exercise their rights and freedoms without interference from others. However, with the rise of technology, the threat to privacy rights has become more pronounced. Governments and private entities must ensure that they respect individuals' privacy rights and do not abuse their power to collect and use personal data. In this way, individuals can continue to live their lives with the confidence that their privacy is being protected and that they can exercise their rights and freedoms without fear of persecution or harassment.

REFERENCES

Alawadhi, N. (n.d.). *Govt again asks WhatsApp to take back its contentious privacy policy update.* Business Standard. https://www.business-standard.com/article/technology/india-directs-WhatsApp-for-withdrawal-of-its-revised-privacy-policy-121051900594_1.html

Alawadhi, N. (2021). *India asks WhatsApp to withdraw new privacy policy, answer 14 questions.* Business Standard. https://www.business-standard.com/article/current-affairs/india-asks-WhatsApp-to-withdraw-new-privacy-policy-answer-14-questions-121011900741_1.html

Banisar, D., & Davies, S. (1991). Global Trends in Privacy Protection: An International Survey of Privacy, Data Protection, And Surveillance Laws and Developments. *The John Marshall Journal of Computer & Information Law*, 18.

Dalmia, V. P. (2017). *Data protection laws in india—Everything you must know—Data protection—India.* Mondaq Ltd. https://www.mondaq.com/india/data-protection/655034/data-protection-laws-in-india---everything-you-must-know

Diggelmann, O., & Cleis, M. N. (2014). How the right to privacy became a human right. *Human Rights Law Review*, *14*(3), 441–458. doi:10.1093/hrlr/ngu014

European Data Protection Supervisor. (2023, July 14). *Data protection.* European Union. https://edps.europa.eu/data-protection/data-protection_en

Hinailiyas. (2021). *Right to privacy under article 21 and the related conflicts.* Legal Services India; Legal Services India. https://www.legalservicesindia.com/article/1630/Right-To-Privacy-Under-Article-21-and-the-Related-Conflicts.html

India, P. R. S. (2021). *The personal data protection bill, 2019*. PRS Legislative Research. https://prsindia. org/billtrack/the-personal-data-protection-bill-2019

Lakshmikumaran, C. (2023, January 13). Digital Personal Data Protection Bill: What rights does it give individuals? *The Economic Times*. https://economictimes.indiatimes.com/wealth/legal/will/digital-personal-data-protection-bill-what-rights-does-it-give-individuals/articleshow/96535688.cms?from=mdr

Privacy International. (2017, October 23). *What is privacy?* Privacy International. https://privacyinter-national.org/explainer/56/what-privacy

Sathe, G. (2021). *WhatsApp Is Still Sharing a Lot of Your Data*. Gadgets 360. https://www.gadgets360. com/apps/opinion/WhatsApp-new-privacy-policy-sharing-data-with-facebook-2353796

SFLC.IN. (2017, October 24). *Right to privacy under udhr and iccpr*. Privacy Bytes; Privacy Bytes. https://privacy.sflc.in/universal/

Singh, J. (2021). *WhatsApp Privacy Policy Update: What Happens When You Don't Accept?* Gadgets 360. https://www.gadgets360.com/apps/news/WhatsApp-privacy-policy-update-changes-what-happens-if-you-dont-agree-details-facebook-data-2376020

Singh, S. R. (2021, January 18). Don't use WhatsApp if you don't like it: Delhi HC. *The Hindu*. https:// www.thehindu.com/news/national/dont-use-whatsapp-if-you-dont-like-it-delhi-hc/article33599671.ece

Sinha, R. (2018). *Committee Reports: Report Summary on A Free and Fair Digital Economy*, PRS Legislative Research. https://prsindia.org/policy/report-summaries/free-and-fair-digital-economy

Talwar Thakore & Associates. (2022). *Data Protected India*. Linklaters. https://www.linklaters.com/en/insights/data-protected/data-protected---india

United Nations. (1948). *Universal declaration of human rights*. United Nations. https://www.un.org/en/about-us/universal-declaration-of-human-rights

ENDNOTES

[1] (2017) 10 SCC 1

[2] AIR 1980 SC 1789

[3] (2017) 10 SCC 1.

[4] (2019) 1 SCC 1.

[5] Ibid.

[6] 2017 7 SCC 59.

[7] A Free and Fair Digital Economy: Protecting Privacy, Empowering Indians, Committee of Experts under the Chairmanship of Justice B.N. Srikrishna, 2018

[8] Ibid.

Chapter 16
Machine Learning–Based Sentiment Analysis of Mental Health–Related Tweets by Sri Lankan Twitter Users During the COVID–19 Pandemic

S. P. W. S. K. Karunarathna
Sabaragamuwa University of Sri Lanka, Sri Lanka

U. A. Piumi Ishanka
(iD) https://orcid.org/0000-0002-3664-5957
Sabaragamuwa University of Sri Lanka, Sri Lanka

Banujan Kuhaneswaran
(iD) https://orcid.org/0000-0002-0265-2198
Sabaragamuwa University of Sri Lanka, Sri Lanka

ABSTRACT

The emergence of COVID-19 emanating from Wuhan, China in December 2019 has deeply affected society at every level, impacting areas like public health, social well-being, and local economies globally. The study highlights mental health and its impact on social behavior during pandemics. The authors analyze Sri Lankan individuals' mental health issues through tweets presented using sentiment analysis techniques. A rigorous data preparation process was completed before filtering categorized data into three distinct groups: 'experience', 'information', and 'counseling'. Three different machine learning algorithms were utilized for sentiment analysis, including ANN, LSTM, and SVM. In addition, the Latent Dirichlet Allocation technique was employed to identify topics from tweets during four waves of the COVID-19 outbreak, analyzing people's mental status and identifying conditions present. The findings contribute significantly to the evolving field of psychology during these trying times caused by COVID-19, providing much-needed guidance on implementing relevant support mechanisms.

DOI: 10.4018/978-1-6684-7450-1.ch016

INTRODUCTION

The Coronavirus Disease of 2019 (COVID-19) has impacted billions of people worldwide, regardless of gender, nation, country, or area. During the pandemic, each country's health and economic and social difficulties had a significant detrimental influence. People who had jobs have lost their jobs and cannot go to work. School closures harmed nearly half of the world's children, which was a terrible outcome for their education. To limit the spread of the disease, each country's government decided to isolate certain sections, provinces, or the entire country. Although the lockdown helped to alleviate some of the difficulties, others arose. They had to stay at their houses with the loss of jobs. The situation affected people who earn daily wages and self-employed people. There were more obstacles to people's mental health worldwide than health, economic, and social issues. The typical day-to-day lifestyle had been altered, and they had to adjust to a new way of life; as a result, new difficulties arose in the place of old ones. These new difficulties included obtaining needed things such as money, food, and medicine, returning to work or, if fired, finding new employment, and caring for children and adults. However, their mentality deteriorated at the same time. The emotions and feelings have changed due to the epidemic. Among those feelings, negative ones such as fear, anxiety, depression, and distress are increased than positive ones. Therefore, the world should consider how people manage their emotions and cope with their mentality during an epidemic. We primarily focus on preventing the pandemic from spreading and minimising the number of illnesses, fatalities, and other physical conditions. However, we do not pay enough attention to the causes of poor mental health. People started using social media to express their ideas, feelings, and opinions with the rest of the globe. If social media data can be used to evaluate and analyse the facts mentioned above, many scenarios connected to mental health can be recognised. The purpose of the study is to identify the mental health status of Sri Lankans during the COVID-19 pandemic situation by analysing Twitter data as social media users' sentiments. This sentiment analysis identifies which mental health issues and conditions are affected during this pandemic. It focuses on Sri Lankans because people's mental health may change and vary according to their culture and geographical area. Sri Lanka is an island in the Indian Ocean with people with various cultures, religions. And their problems facing the pandemic may be different from other countries in the world.

SIGNIFICANCE OF THE STUDY

In the early days of the coronavirus outbreak, Sri Lanka became a low-infected country, but at the moment, there are a significant number of infections and deaths. With that fact, Sri Lankans are also staying with bad feelings, and their mental health gets down due to different reasons such as loss of jobs, falling economic level, inability to achieve their plans, barriers to usual lifestyle, and so on. This bad mental health has caused significant issues like suicide, child abuse, robbery, and murders. Failure to recognise their mentality and take appropriate actions may be the reason for their inability to prevent these harmful incidents. This study helps identify mental health conditions related to this crisis. In addition, the results of this study will be helpful to different parties in the country, such as; Healthcare professionals do a huge task during the pandemic. They can identify their patients' mentality and how normal people think and feel about this crisis. The awareness of that information will be important when treating patients. Government is the country's most important unit for making strategic decisions. Government officers are responsible in every aspect of the country, especially in an event like COVID-19. Before making plans for preventing or reducing the harmful effects of the event, the perception of the mental condition of people would be better. Citizens, who are the subjects of the study. They should know enough about their feelings and mentality because, during such a crisis, they can help each other and overcome the challenges together. They should know how to face a pandemic and how people react to those challenges.

STATEMENT OF THE HYPOTHESIS OR RESEARCH QUESTION

There are research questions that need to be answered through this study. They are;

RQ1: What is the mental health status among Sri Lankans? The proposed study covers which types of ideas, information, and thoughts are shared by Sri Lankans. It identifies the status of mentality by classifying tweets into three classes.

RQ2: What mental conditions/states people faced/endure during COVID-19? People face many mental conditions thatoccasionally change due to pandemics like COVID-19. This research question covers those conditions by analysing tweets.

RQ3: What are the issues that impacted mental health during covid pandemic? Some factors have impacted the public mentality in normal situations. In a pandemic like this coronavirus, these factors may be varied based on some circumstances. Those kinds of factors are discussed in this question.

RQ4: How does mental health vary according to the different waves of the pandemic? Mainly Sri Lanka faced four distinct COVID-19 waves in different periods in 2020 and 2021. Based on these waves, people's thoughts and feelings may be changed. Addressing those variations is the purpose of this research question.

LITERATURE REVIEW AND RELATED WORKS

Related work describes existing work related to the scope of the current study. It supports finding the gap between existing work and the proposed study. With the epidemic spreading around the world, researchers started to study it.The existing research publications can be divided into several parts as follows;

*Mental Health Detection*Studies are published based on the mentality of people, but they do not focus on any pandemic situation. M. Aragón et al. described a new approach for detecting depression and anorexia based on the modelling of fine-grained emotions stated by users using deep learning architectures with attention mechanisms (Aragón, López-Monroy, González, & Montes-y-Gómez, 2020). The potential for developing digital technologies to assist efforts to combat mental health stigma in low- and middle-income countries is examined in the analysis of J. Naslund et al., As a result, there are challenges with digital stigma reduction strategies, such as the need for cultural adaptation of these programs to various contexts and settings (Naslund & Deng, 2021).

Mental Health During COVID-19

Katongole et al. conducted in-depth interviews with health staff in two Ugandan and Ghanaian institutions that have treated COVID-19 patients (Katongole, Yaro, & Bukuluki, 2021). Based on many Machine learning forecast models, the goal of the study of R. Naiem et al. is to investigate the effects of COVID-19 on people's mental health, as the emergency has produced several difficulties such as stress, anxiety, and sadness (Naiem, kaur, Mishra, & Saxena, 2022).

Social Media Usage During COVID-19

A. Mugilan et al. examine Twitter data to see how the general public feels about the outbreak. According to this investigation, the public is adequately informed about the outbreak. In comparison to Severe Acute Respiratory Syndrome (SARS), Middle East Respiratory Syndrome (MERS), and other viruses, there is less circulation of misleading information about coronavirus (Mugilan, Kanmani, Deva Priya, Christy Jeba Malar, & Suganya, 2021).

Mental Health Issues During COVID-19 Using Social Media Context

Some researchers developed frameworks and systems by analysing COVID-19-related data on mental health. J. Kwan et al. discovered a system using public tweets. This system can understand public reactionsto the COVID-19 epidemic regarding attitudes, emotions, themes of interest, and contentious debates throughout various periods and locales (Kwan & Lim, 2021). H. Yin et al. provided a different framework for analysing COVID-19-related topics and sentiment trends from massive social media posts. They discovered that good sentiment outnumbers negative sentiment during the study period (Yin, Yang, & Li, 2020). J. Koh et al. discovered that given the widespread policy of isolation, loneliness is a public health issue projected to worsen throughout the COVID-19 pandemic. The study examined how loneliness was expressed on Twitter during the COVID-19 epidemic and identified critical areas of loneliness in various populations (Koh & Liew, 2022). According to R. Sabaruddin et al., Using unique keywords, a Malay Tweet dataset was created for analysing mental health tweets during the first Movement Control Order period. The sentiment of tweets was predicted using machine learning algorithms such as the Naive Bayes classifier and the Support Vector Machine (SVM). They assume the displayed data could give authorities insights into mental health issues related to local news and conditions at different times. There is a scarcity of information about frontline health workers' experiences during the COVID-19 pandemic and the consequences on their psychosocial well-being (Sabaruddin & Saee, 2021).

Sentiment Analysis on Mental Health During COVID-19 Using Social Media Context

According to A. Venigalla., Analysing real-time tweets in India during COVID-19 could aid in determining the country's sentiment. They presented a web platform that uses real-time Twitter data to depict India's sentiment during COVID-19. These tweets arecategorised into seven categories, including six basic emotions (Venigalla, Chimalakonda, & Vagavolu, 2020). K. Govindasamy et al. also mentioned that the researcher could determine whether or not the users are depressed using the data available on social media. The data may be classified into appropriate groups using a machine learning algorithm, and depressive and non-depressive data can be distinguished (Govindasamy & Palanichamy, 2021).

Mental Health Issues in Sri Lanka During COVID-19 Using Social Media Context

According to M. Chandradasa et al., COVID-19 affects healthcare workers and pregnant mothers suffering from anxiety for small and medium-scale enterprises and people in various sectors in Sri Lanka. They emphasise that health practitioners must be mindful of their own and the public's increased risk of psychological discomfort (Chandradasa & Kuruppuarachchi, 2020). The summary of selected studies is shown in Table 1, which helps to identify the gap between the proposed studies.

Table 1. Summary of selected literature reviews

Paper	Purpose	Findings
(Praveen, Ittamalla, & Deepak, 2021)	Examining how COVID-19 affects people's perceptions of what triggers stress, anxiety, and trauma. This research aims to comprehend Indian citizens in particular.	They identified the top ten topics that Indians generally talked about when expressing the stress, worry, and trauma brought on by the ongoing pandemic.
(Alles, Rohanachandra, Amarakoon, & Prathapan, 2021)	To evaluate the psychological discomfort, difficulties, and demands experienced by healthcare professionals in a tertiary care hospital in Sri Lanka during the COVID-19 epidemic.	The most prevalent psychological side effect was anxiety. Higher levels of stress, anxiety, and depression were seen among women, nurses, and people in their 25th to 34th years.
(Viviani et al., 2021)	Assessing the potential impact of several critical pandemic-related elements on people's mental health.	In topic modelling, topics were found as Social distancing and protection, Tests &hospitalisation, Politics, and in sentiment analysis, values obtained by Vader on the three considered target scenarios.
(Lenadora, Gamage, Haputhanthri, Meedeniya, & Perera, 2020)	To determine the causes of incidents and to pinpoint how the Sri Lankan people acted during this type of crisis.	There were both positive and negative behaviours. Examples of undesirable behaviours are political polarisation, unwarranted fury, and overreacting to specific situations.
(Rachman, 2020)	To use sentiment analysis to learn about mental health from Twitter users' opinions.	Most people express a neutral attitude, and the least express negative sentiments to conclude that everyone's mental health is still neutral and favourable.

METHODOLOGY

The research methodology section discusses and explains the methods utilised in this research's design, data collection, and analysis. It clearly describes how the study's objectives are fulfilled in a structured manner. This study discusses the research design, data collection, implementation, and data analysis under the research methodology section.

Research Design

The intuitive approach of extracting and analysing subjective assessments of various features of a thing or entity is called sentiment analysis. Using the sentimental analysis procedure, the writer's tone normally appears in their text as positive, negative, or neutral (Praveen et al., 2021). The sentiment analysis follows quantitative and qualitative methods since the data analysis with machine learning algorithms focuses on percentages like accuracy. In contrast, topic modelling focuses on the topic and its meanings. The proposed study follows the techniques to achieve the research results, as shown in Figure 1.

Figure 1. Research design of the proposed study

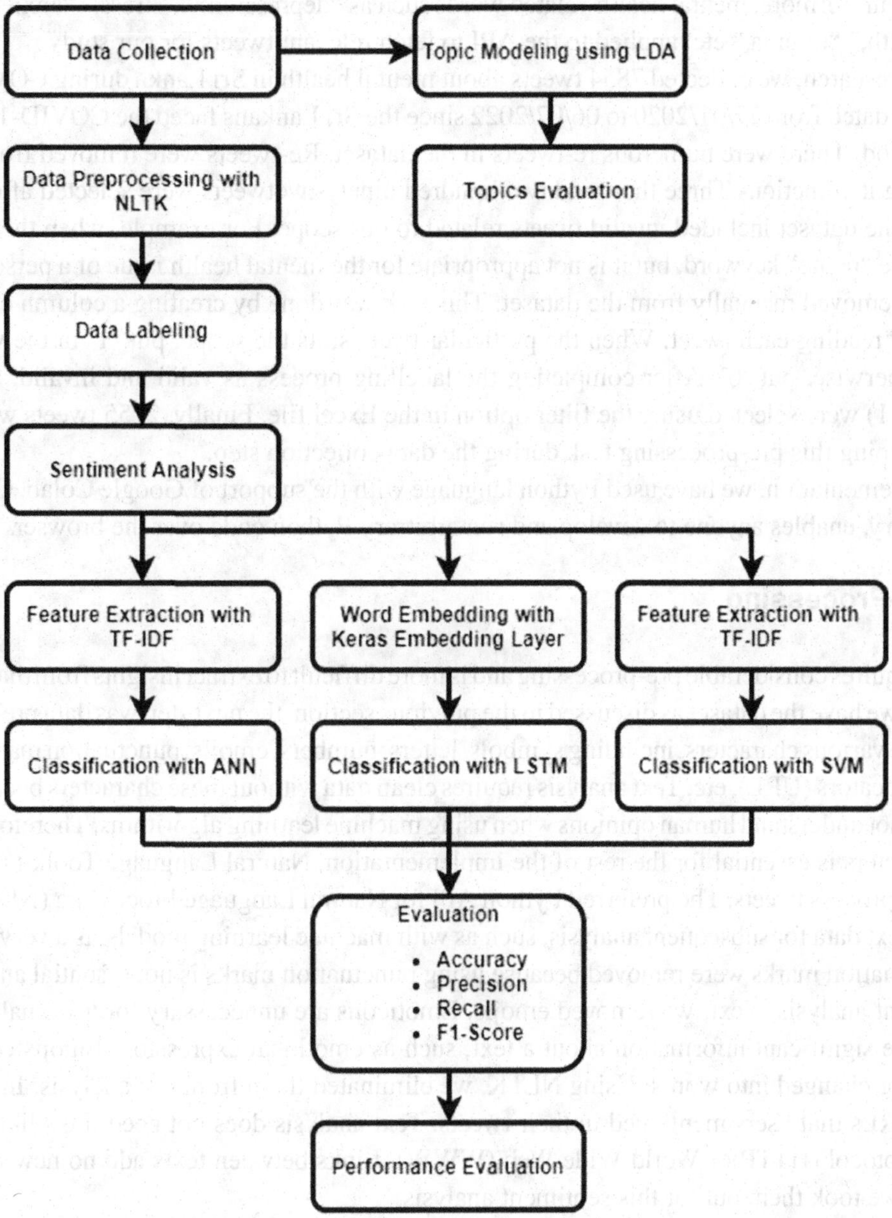

Data Collection

The dataset for analysis can be collected in different ways. These include social media, news, client testimonials, and public information. This study used social media data to gather user opinions, ideas, and sentiments. Twitter is used as social media and was collected using Twitter Application Programming Interface (API) Version 2 and Postman software. For access to retrieving Tweets, we created a developer account for Twitter. Postman software was used to add APIs and retrieve the tweets. The tweets from the Excel file are in a column in the dataset called "Full Text." The appropriate words as keywords were used to get the most relevant data for our research domain. When executing the Twitter API, the keywords should be mentioned properly. Since our scope relates to COVID-19, we used "covid19" and "covid" as the keywords and focused on Sri Lankan users. Therefore keywords "srilanka," "lka,"and "srilanka" were used. Furthermore, mental health-related words such as "depression"', "stress," "anxiety," "panic," "mentalhealth," "trauma," etc. applied to the API to fetch relevant tweets for our study.

For this research, we collected 7854 tweets about mental health in Sri Lanka during COVID-19. The tweets were dated from 27/01/2020 to 06/07/2022 since the Sri Lankans faced the COVID-19 crisis during this period. There were numerous re-tweets in the dataset. Re-tweets were removed from the Excel file by using its functions.Three thousand two hundred ninety-twotweets were selected after removing re-tweets. The dataset included invalid tweets related to our scope. For example, when there is a tweet including the "panic" keyword, but it is not appropriate for the mental health issue of a person, that kind of tweet is removed manually from the dataset. This task was done by creating a column called 'valid/invalid' and reading each tweet. When the particular tweet suits the scope, put '1' in the valid/invalid column; otherwise, put '0'. After completing the labelling process as valid and invalid, valid tweets (containing 1) were selected using the filter option in the Excel file. Finally, 2755 tweets were selected after performing this pre-processing task during the data collection step.

For implementation, we have used Python language with the support of Google Colab. Colab, called Collaboratory, enables anyone to develop and run arbitrary Python code over the browser.

Data Pre-Processing

Text data requires considerable pre-processing and is more difficult to extract insights from than structured data. Since we have the dataset as discussed in the previous section, the next step was data pre-processing. Tweets have various characters, including symbols, letters, numbers, emojis, punctuation marks, Uniform Resource Locators (URL), etc. Text analysis requires clean data without these characters because the machine does not understand human opinions when using machine learning algorithms. Therefore removing those characters is essential for the rest of the implementation. Natural Language Toolkit (NLTK) was used to pre-process tweets. The preferred Python API for Natural Language Processing (NLP) is NLTK. Preparing text data for subsequent analysis, such as with machine learning models, is a very potent tool. First, punctuation marks were removed because using punctuation marks is not essential and redundant for sentiment analysis. Next, we removed emojis. Emoticons are unnecessary for text analysis, even if they provide significant information about a text, such as emotional expression. Emojis can therefore be deleted or changed into words. Using NLTK, we eliminated them from our analysis. In the dataset, there are URLs that users mentioned in their tweets. Text analysis does not need links like HyperText Transfer Protocol (HTTP)or World Wide Web (WWW). Links between texts add no new information. Therefore, we took them out for this sentiment analysis.

Lowercasing the text is the next step we used in the pre-processing task. It aids in keeping the text mining and NLP operations moving along smoothly. For instance, there is a word in two formats, 'Stress' and 'stress,' which are considered two words despite having the same meaning. Such words are converted into a lowercase format for easy analysis. Removing stop words is an essential part of this phase. It is simply eliminating the words in every document in the corpus. Pronouns and articles are typically categorised as stop words. They consist of words that are often used in a language. Stop words in English include "a," "the," "is," "are," and others. We can customise the stop words by adding words we want to eliminate into the stop words list in the Python code. Lemmatising is converting words into their base or root form. For example, the word "affecting" is converted into "affect," which is useful when analysing texts. Stemming is the same as lemmatisation, which is cutting off the word's end while utilising a list of prevalent prefixes and suffixes. This slicing can be successful most of the time, but not always. This may result in words that have no context. Lemmatisation is favoured over stemming precisely because it uses a variety of linguistic insights specific to that word. In our study, we used lemmatisation to get a clear dataset. In addition to those techniques, we removed mentions since there are numerous mentions by Twitter users represented with @ symbol, which are not helpful for further analysis.

Data Labelling

Labelling the tweets is annotating the label of a document or text. Labelling can be conducted differently, such as manualand automatic labelling. For our study, manual tagging was used for each tweet. Commonly positive and negative sentiment classes are the focus of specific studies, whereas positive, negative, and neutral sentiment classes are used in others. According to our study, we focused on what type of information the users share opinions. Some people like sharing their personal experiences and information, which are more useful to other people for their awareness. At the same time, others share advice, and some people seek instructions for their situation during this challenging crisis period. Based on those facts, we decided to select three labels, 'experience (0)', 'information (1)', and 'counselling (2)', for tagging the data. Since our research aims to find the mental health status of people, reading each tweet and tagging 0,1, or 2 is better than going through an automatic labelling process. It supports increasing the accuracy of the data. The reason for choosing multi-labelling is that it gives better performance and accuracy for the developing analysis model instead of using two labels.

SENTIMENT ANALYSIS

Despite the comprehensive study being about sentiment analysis on mental health issues, the actual sentiment analysis is discussed in this section. The analysis of sentiments can be performed in many different ways based on the problem statement of the research. For the proposed study, three sub-steps were completed during this step: word embedding, classification, and model evaluation. Word embedding approaches assist in extracting data from the pattern and occurrence of words and also serve as a feature extraction technique by assisting in transforming unstructured input into meaningful word vector alignments in the embedding space, which the model can use more efficiently. After extracting features of the particular document, the classification process can be started by building a model. First, the dataset should be divided into two parts as a training and testing data set. The classification model is developed using a training set, and then the test data set is used to test the performance of the developed model. The dataset can be split as the developer's preference. Performing measurements of the model is done after the classification. The model can be evaluated using measurements like accuracy, precision, etc. High accuracy leads to decisions that the developed model performs better and is best for future analysis tasks.

This study applied the steps mentioned above to three machine learning algorithms. When using the first algorithm, data features were extracted using the Term Frequency-Inverse Document Frequency (TF-IDF) technique. The word weighting approach assigns weights (values) to individual terms inside a text. Inverse Document Frequency (IDF), normalisation, and Term Frequency (TF) are three factors that affect the term weighting scheme (Rachman, 2020). The features of documents were used to model buildings. For the classification, Artificial Neural Networks (ANN) algorithm was applied. Machine learning includes ANNs, which are a subset of it. ANNs comprise node layers, including an input layer, one or more hidden layers, and an output layer. In order to learn and increase their accuracy over time, neural networks rely on training data. This study split the dataset into 33% of test data; the rest was training data. Then the evaluation was performed by running the model on test data. It discovered model accuracy, precision, recall, and F1-score. Accuracy indicates how frequently the Machine Learning model was overall correct. The model's precision measures how well it can forecast a particular class. Recall indicates how frequently the model was able to identify a particular class. The F1 score gauges a model's precision. It combines a model's precision and recall ratings.

The second algorithm used for the classification was Long Short-Term Memory (LSTM). Before developing the model, Keras Embedding Layer was used as a word embedding technique. Textual data must be converted into numbers before feeding any machine learning model, including neural networks. We can turn each word into a fixed-length vector with a predetermined size owing to the embedding layer. Networks with LSTM are employed in deep learning. Using LSTM, data was split into 30% of test data and 70% of training data, and performed the model on test data was to evaluate them. Measurements like accuracy were found with the help of related codes.

SVM was used as the third algorithm for the analysis. A deep learning system known as the SVM uses supervised learning to classify or predict the behaviour of groupings of data. The algorithm produces a line or a hyperplane that divides the data into classes. Features of Tweets were extracted with the help of the TF-IDF vectorising technique and then used SVM to split data into 33% of test data, and the rest was training data same as the ANN model. Accuracy and other measurements were finally discovered using the results of running SVM models.

Performance Evaluation

As mentioned above, the mental health-related dataset is fed into three algorithms separately. After that,comparing those algorithms was performed by assessing each classification algorithm's performance measurements like accuracy, precision, and recall. This assessment is supported to address which is the best algorithm for analysing tweets in the future.

Data Analysis

In addition to sentiment analysis, topic modelling, an unsupervised method, was performed for this study. Using a forecasting model, topic modelling finds abstract subjects that appear in a corpus of documents (Praveen et al., 2021). It mentioned that Sentiment analysis does not reveal the elements that influence how individuals react to crises. The proposed study uses topic modelling to discover the primary mental health issues people faced during the pandemic. We performed Latent Dirichlet Allocation (LDA) to find out those issues mentioned in tweets. Latent represents the hidden issues in the data in LDA, while Dirichlet is a distribution type. The normal distribution and the Dirichlet distribution are distinct. Data analysis aims to determine solutions for the research questions discussed in this study. Topic modelling solves the research question (RQ2) by extracting words in tweets as keywords. The research question (RQ3) discusses reasons to affect Sri Lankans' mental health. The answer can also be found in the top frequent words discovered in topic modelling methods.

Sentiment analysis results can be applied as the answer tothe research question(RQ1), which means that the categorisation of the tweets gives more details about the status of the mentality of users. For the research question(RQ4), we found answers on how mental health varies according to different waves by running Python with matplotlib. For building dynamic and static graphics in Python, we can consider Matplotlib. Plots of publishing quality should be made, as should interactive charts that may be updated, zoomed, and panned. Since our Excel dataset contained the column "Date," mental health data were analysed with the particular date. In Sri Lanka, four distinct COVID-19 waves date from 2020 to 2021. We figured out relevant information based on the covid waves.

Using pre-processed data, a word cloud was performed by importing necessary Python libraries. A word cloud is a visualisation technique that shows the frequency of terms in a text by varying the size of each word. The words frequently appearing in the text are shown using it (Rachman, 2020). In case, we can get an idea of which Twitter users most frequently use words. After the completion of sentiment analysis, a confusion matrix was generated. A performance indicator for machine learning categorisation is the confusion matrix. The table has four possible anticipated and actual value combinations since we have used three classification classes.

RESULTS AND FINDINGS

The results and findings drive to fulfil the target of the proposed study by providing appropriate answers to the proposed research questions. In addition to that, we addressed results based on the performance of each machine learning algorithm. These results will be helpful in future analysis. Research question 1 focuses on the status of the mentality of people in Sri Lanka. During the pandemic, they were used to sharing their feelings with others through social media. The type of tweets they shared indicates at which level their mentality is. Therefore, we categorised all tweets into three classes: 'experience,' 'information,' or 'counselling.'the experience category includes tweets which are the personal experiences of users. If users are sharing some information about COVID-19 and mental health, that kind of tweet comes under the information category. Some people share their thoughts and opinions with advice, while others seek advice. Such people instruct others to behave or follow some activities, such as consulting. Those tweets were categorised under the counselling class. Examples of each type are shown in Table 2.

After completing data pre-processing, we found the number of tweets for each label (category). The visualisation of those facts is shown in Figure 2. It shows that the total tweets of label experience are 1037, 914 tweets for label information, and 804 tweets for counselling classification. Therefore, we discovered that Sri Lankans mainly shared their opinions, ideas, and personal experiences. In contrast, they shared information rather than advice, which means giving and seeking instructions is less than the other two types of tweets. It concludes that the mental status of people focused on their own experiences during the pandemic.

Table 2. Sample of tweets with labels

Sample of Tweet	Category (Label)
COVID messed with the bit of mental health I had. I'm so depressed all the time. I'm exhausted.	Experience (0)
The National Institute of Mental Health (NIMH) hotline is 1926#Mentalhealth #SriLanka https://t.co/W4AdISITjG	Information (1)
Join us on June 27 for a live discussion with Clinical Psychologist MsUvasaraArambewala on how young people can take care of their mental health during Covid-19.#COVID19 #MentalHealth #Youth #Wellbeing #SriLanka	Counselling (2)

Figure 2. Details of three labels

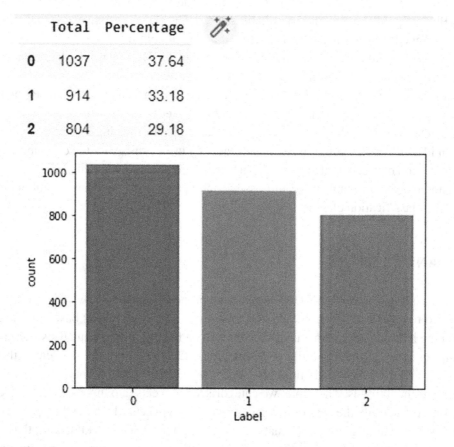

This research question covers the mental condition of people during the pandemic. When facing a crisis, people's mental health is also changed for good or bad. They can be discovered with topic modelling. We have performed the LDA model to find out three topics. Thirty top-frequency keywords were extracted for each topic scenario by the model. Table 3 shows these keywords and the relevant topics we suggested. The topics were identified through pyLDAvis, a highly interactive representation of the clusters produced by LDA that can be built and analysed using open-source Python software. It visualises the most frequent keywords for each topic. When we click on one circle(topic), the keywords appear on the left. Figure 3, Figure 4, and Figure 5 represent those visualisations.

Table 3. Suggested topics and their keywords

Topic	Keywords	Suggested Topic
Topic 1	Self, esteem, low, panic, people, srilanka, covid, covid19, health, coronavirus, covid19sl, stress, mentalhealth, time, motivated, fear, think, mental, need, lockdown, public, covid19lk, anxiety, depression, depressed, really, like, news, thing	Low self-esteem and panic of people in Sri Lanka during COVID-19
Topic 2	covid19, srilanka, covid, depressed, child, motivated, mentalhealth, home, time, stress, pandemic, people, year, work, disappointed, country, got, mental, lanka, good, life, frustrated, education, _srilanka, due, today, like, feel, health	Life and mental health of people in Sri Lanka during the pandemic
Topic 3	Covid, motivated, depressed, srilanka, covid19, year, people, mentalhealth, like, work, everyone, motivation, politically, stress, help, stay, feel, u, situation, keep, pandemic, since, need, exam, student, right, still, job, much	The situation of jobs and exams in Sri Lanka duringthe pandemic

Figure 3. Visualisation for Topic 1

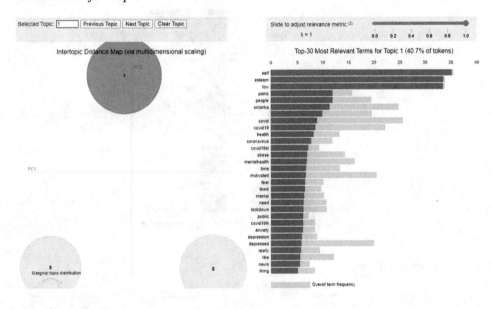

According to topic 1, the most relevant term is "low self-esteem." And the keywords of topic 1 show the numerous mental health conditions such as panic, fear, stress, anxiety, and depression, which are mental health issues. In contrast, it shows motivation, which would be a positive mental health condition for Sri Lankans. The topmost discussion of topic 2 is "people's lives and mental health." The reason to suggest that topic is that indicates some keywords 'frustrated,' 'disappointed,' and 'motivated' with 'work,' life, and 'education,' which are showing about public life and mental health together. Topic 3 discusses "exams, jobs in the pandemic." This topic also includes mental health issues like 'stress,' 'depressed,' and 'motivation.' This information gives us insight into people's mental conditions during the outbreak.

During the pandemic situation In Sri Lanka, which reasons that impacted the mentality are covered in this research question. Since sentiment analysis does not give these factors, we can find answers for RQ3 as well from topic modelling results. In topic 1, 'lockdown' and 'news' keywords indicate the topmost terms, whereas topic 2 includes 'work,' 'education,' and 'health,' and topic 3 consists of 'exam' and 'job.' These words appear as reasons to impact mental health because public health was the main reason in that period. Jobs and workloads affect workers, exams, and education for children, while lockdowns cause stress and anxiety. The news was also impacted since some wrong information about covid cases and other stuff was spread.

Like other countries, Sri Lanka also had COVID-19 waves in 2020 and 2021. The authors aimed to identify the way of varying mental health data based on these waves. The graphical visualisation for the data distribution among these four covid waves can be shown in Figure 6 and Figure 7. And Table 4 includes information about the four waves and how data is divided into relevant categories during these waves.

Figure 4. Visualization for Topic 2

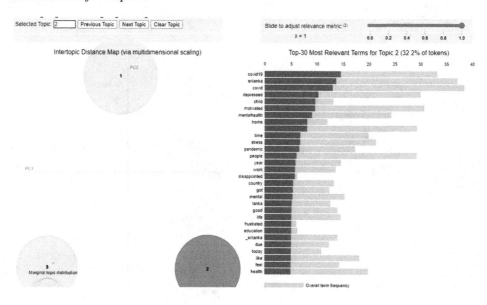

Figure 5. Visualization for Topic 3

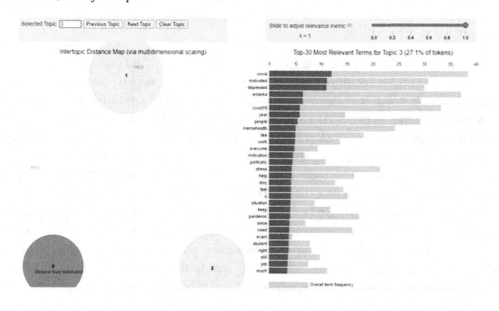

Table 4. Details of four covid waves

Wave	Date Range	Experience Class	Information Class	Counselling Class
Wave 1	27/01/2020 – 03/10/2020	266	266	292
Wave 2	04/10/2020 – 14/04/2021	143	209	158
Wave 3	15/04/2021 – 22/07/2021	211	168	130
Wave 4	23/07/2021 – 05/11/2021	308	211	155

Figure 6. Number of tweets in different covid waves

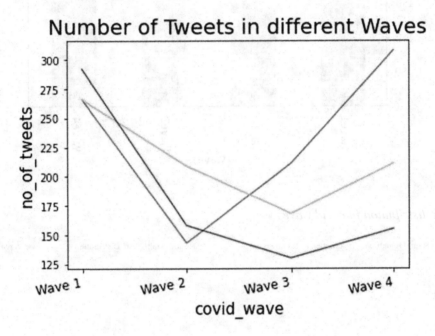

Figure 7 shows how three classes vary throughout four waves. Experience (shown in blue line) class becomes low in 2nd wave and high in 4th wave. It means most people share their experiences in the 4th wave. Information class (shown in yellow line) is high in 1st wave and low in 3rd wave. Counselling class (shown in green line) is high in 1st wave and low in 3rd wave.

The study has discovered how tweets are distributed in each wave. Figure 8 shows the data variation in the time duration of covid waves. It visualises most tweets being shared in March 2020 in 1st covid wave. Most data were shared in February of 2021 in the 2nd wave. The 3rd wave indicates that most tweets will be distributed in May 2021. 4th wave data is high in August of 2021.

Figure 7. Data distribution for three labels in four waves

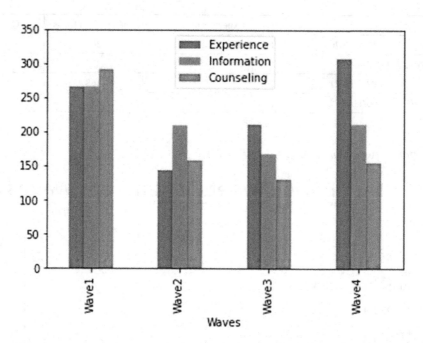

Figure 8. Data distribution in covid waves

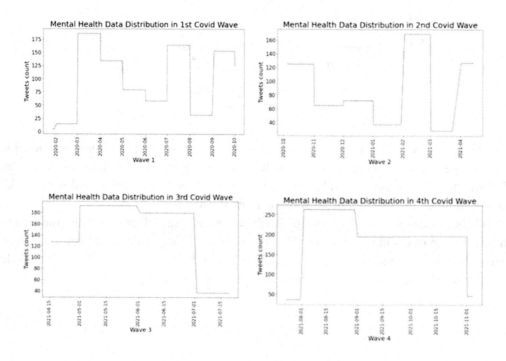

Performance Evaluation

The study has utilised three algorithms separately for sentiment analysis. The algorithmsare ANN, LSTM, and SVM. The comparison among these algorithms is shown in Table 5.

Table 5. Comparison of performance measurements of three algorithms

Algorithm	Accuracy	Precision	Recall	F1-Score
ANN	0.94	0.91	0.90	0.91
LSTM	0.89	0.86	0.81	0.83
SVM	0.63	0.63	0.62	0.63

According toTable 5, thestudy has addressed that the ANN model has high accuracy (94%). Other measurements of ANN also are better than the two other models. Therefore, the ANN algorithm is the best for analysing mental health data in future analysis.We have developed a confusion matrix using LSTM. It is shown in Figure 9.

Figure 9. Confusion matrix-LSTM

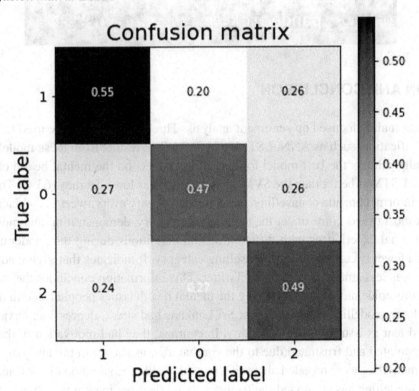

Word Cloud

Word cloud visualises the most frequent words in tweets. According to the word cloud shown in Figure 10, the words 'motivate,' 'mental health,' and 'self-esteem' appeared huge, while the words 'depress,' 'stress,' 'lockdown,' 'panic,' 'fear' are displayed in reasonably large size.

Figure 10. Word cloud for the mental health related tweets in Sri Lanka

DISCUSSION AND CONCLUSION

The research was mainly focused on sentiment analysis. Three algorithms were used to build separate models for classification, such as ANN, LSTM, and SVM. The results from these models demonstrate that the ANN algorithm is the best model for classifying tweets on the mental health of Sri Lankans. The accuracy of LSTM is better than the SVM model, which has low accuracy (63%). Three categories as, experience, information, and counselling, were used to classify every tweet in the dataset. The study discovered that most tweets come under the experience category, demonstrating that most Sri Lankans shared their personal experiences with different mental conditions during the pandemic. Among the tweets, there are fewer tweets under the counselling category. It indicates that giving advice or asking for counselling was less among people using Twitter. This information concludes the mental status of Sri Lankans in this epidemic. When discussing the mental health issues people faced in that period, the analysis using topic modelling discovered that Sri Lankans had stress, depression, anxiety, panic, low self-esteem, and fear as issues in their mentality. In contrast, they had motivation in that period. And they were disappointed and frustrated due to the coronavirus, as shown in the analysis. Further, three topics of topic modelling were revealed about life, mental health, the situation of jobs, and exams in the country. Topic modelling has addressed the factors which affect the mental well-being of Sri Lankans during the outbreak. These factors are workload, jobs, exams, education, lockdown, curfew, and news. Because of these factors, public mental health has been changed either negatively or positively.

The study aimed to find how data is distributed among four covid waves in Sri Lanka. It has been identified that in the 1st wave, counselling-related tweets are the highest, which means at the start of the virus outbreak, advice-related opinions were mainly shared. By the 2nd wave, it has changed that information-related tweets have been shared mostly among people. At the end of the coronavirus (in the 4th wave), experiences have been shared mainly in Sri Lanka. Currently, social media is the platform that allows users to freely broadcast content that is related to numerous elements of their private lives, including their mental health and psychological vulnerability. With facing the coronavirus epidemic, they were used to spending more time with social media.

These facts lead this study to analyse the mental status of the public during such a kind of health crisis since data can be gathered from social media easily. Twitter was selected for data collection because retrieving tweets via Twitter API is easy. The dataset is limited to 2755 tweets since Sri Lankans share fewer tweets about mental health during COVID-19. The public in Sri Lanka doesn't use Twitter, mostly. Due to the small size of the data set, analysis using the SVM model has been affected by the accuracy, and other measurements are less than the other two algorithms. However, this study demonstrates that the ANN algorithm is helpful in sentiment analysis of mental health data with higher accuracy. The second part of the study is topic modelling which reveals mental conditions and factors that impact the mental health of Sri Lankans in detail. The research findings are more valuable when getting knowledge about the mentality of Sri Lankans. The results of this study will assist mental health specialists and the government in better understanding the concerns of the general population during COVID-19 and in developing strategies to mitigate the harm COVID-19 has done to mental health. Public mental health awareness during a crisis is essential for preventing disasters like suicides. People can gain more knowledge from this study and realise each other's mentality will support them in overcoming such kinds of pandemics in the future.

The Social Implications of the study can be addressed through the findings. The study results are helpful to the public society and communities of social services. Because the society of people can know others' experiences on how to combat mental health issues in a pandemic, communities can improve counselling methods to develop public mental health. Since social media reflects society today, these results can be applied positively. Research findings can be translated into practical solutions, interventions, or strategies. Because policymakers like the government can apply the results when planning curfews and lockdown periods. Education institutions can decide on examination scheduling and education methods based on students' mental health since the study revealed that exams are the reason for their mentality. Healthcare sectors also can address mental disorders and take necessary actions in such a crisis. Some findings, such as addressing mentality among COVID-19 waves, are valuable to the academic community. Because researchers can gain insights about data distribution among different periods, and they can continue their studies by finding additional results. And researchers and workers dealing with data sets can analyse the mental health data of this study.

Data in the data set used for the study was retrieved using mental health problems like 'stress' and 'depression' as keywords. It has caused the limitation of tweets. In the future, the data set size should be increased for analysis, and then accuracy also can be increased in some models like SVM. The research can be extended by building classification models using more algorithms, especially the latest algorithms like BERT. Twitter is much less in Sri Lanka, while most users tend to share their thoughts and ideas on Facebook. So, it is better to extract data from Facebook for future studies. Moreover, topic modelling methods can be used widely to extract keywords related to people's mental health. Future research can focus more on that.

REFERENCES

Alles, P., Rohanachandra, Y., Amarakoon, L., & Prathapan, S. (2021). Psychological distress, challenges and perceived needs among doctors and nurses during the COVID-19 pandemic, in a tertiary care hospital in Sri Lanka. *Sri Lanka Journal of Psychiatry*, *12*(1), 4–10. doi:10.4038ljpsyc.v12i1.8279

Aragón, M. E., López-Monroy, A. P., González, L. C., & Montes-y-Gómez, M. (2020). *Attention to emotions: detecting mental disorders in social media*. Paper presented at the Text, Speech, and Dialogue: 23rd International Conference, TSD 2020, Brno, Czech Republic. 10.1007/978-3-030-58323-1_25

Arumugam, T., Latha Lavanya, B., Karthik, V., Velusamy, K., Kommuri, U. K., & Panneerselvam, D. (2022). Portraying Women in Advertisements: An Analogy Between Past and Present. *American Journal of Economics and Sociology*, *81*(1), 207–223. doi:10.1111/ajes.12452

Arumugam, T., Sethu, S., Kalyani, V., Shahul Hameed, S., & Divakar, P. (2022). Representing Women Entrepreneurs in Tamil Movies. *American Journal of Economics and Sociology*, *81*(1), 115–125. doi:10.1111/ajes.12446

Chandradasa, M., & Kuruppuarachchi, K. A. L. A. (2020). Mental health impact of the COVID-19 pandemic. *Sri Lanka Journal of Medicine*, *29*(2), 1. doi:10.4038ljm.v29i2.218

Dave, P., Master, K., Makwana, P., Goel, P., & Ganatra, A. (2021). *Mental Health Analysis of Indians during Pandemic*. Paper presented at the Data Science and Computational Intelligence: Sixteenth International Conference on Information Processing, ICInPro 2021, Bengaluru, India. 10.1007/978-3-030-91244-4_23

Dhesinghraja, J., & Sendhilkumar, M. (2015). An Overview of Supply Chain Management on Apparel Order Process in Garment Industries, Bangalore. *Journal of Exclusive Management Science, 4*.

Elaraby, N., Bolock, A. E., Herbert, C., & Abdennadher, S. (2021). *Anxiety Detection During COVID-19 Using the character computing ontology*. Paper presented at the Highlights in Practical Applications of Agents, Multi-Agent Systems, and Social Good. The PAAMS Collection: International Workshops of PAAMS 2021, Salamanca, Spain. 10.1007/978-3-030-85710-3_1

Govindasamy, K. A., & Palanichamy, N. (2021). *Depression detection using machine learning techniques on twitter data*. Paper presented at the 2021 5th international conference on intelligent computing and control systems (ICICCS). 10.1109/ICICCS51141.2021.9432203

Kalyani, V. (2017). Empowering Women Farmers Participation in Organic Agricultural Development. *International Journal of Multidisciplinary Educational Research*, *6*(2), 187.

Kalyani, V. (2018). Organic farming in Tamil Nadu: Status, Issues and Prospects. *American International Journal of Research in Humanities, Arts and Social Sciences*, *21*(1), 82–86.

Kalyani, V. (2020). *Perception of Certified Organic Farmers towards Organic Farming Practices in Pudukkottai District of TamilNadu (No. 4784)*. Easy Chair.

KalyaniV. (2021a). *A Study of Effect of Social Networking Sites on the Self-Esteem of Adolescent Girl Students Belonging to Urban Areas of Sivaganga District*. doi:10.2139/ssrn.3879915

Kalyani, V. (2021b). *Marketing Intelligence Practices on Fmcg Consumer Preferences and Buying Behaviour Pattern Using Social Network Analysis (No. 5857)*. Easy Chair.

Kalyani, V. (2021c). *Parental Involvement in Improving Children's learning in Social Work Perspective (No. 5107)*. Easy Chair.

Kalyani, V. (2021d). *The Employee Engagement on Human Resources Information System Practice through E-Learning Training (No. 5856)*. Easy Chair.

Kalyani, V. (2023). Regression Analysis in R: A Comprehensive View for the Social Sciences. *Journal of the Royal Statistical Society. Series A, (Statistics in Society)*. Advance online publication. doi:10.1093/jrsssa/qnad081

Kalyani, V., Arumugam, T., & Surya Kumar, M. (2022). Women in Oppressive Societies as Portrayed in Kollywood Movies. *American Journal of Economics and Sociology, 81*(1), 173–185. doi:10.1111/ajes.12450

Katongole, S. P., Yaro, P., & Bukuluki, P. (2021). *The impact of COVID-19 on mental health of frontline health workers in Ghana and Uganda Mental Health Effects of COVID-19*. Elsevier.

Koh, J. X., & Liew, T. M. (2022). How loneliness is talked about in social media during COVID-19 pandemic: Text mining of 4,492 Twitter feeds. *Journal of Psychiatric Research, 145*, 317–324. doi:10.1016/j.jpsychires.2020.11.015 PMID:33190839

Kulai, A., Sankhe, M., Anglekar, S., & Halbe, A. (2021). *Emotion analysis of Covid tweets using FastText supervised classifier model*. Paper presented at the 2021 International Conference on Communication information and Computing Technology (ICCICT). 10.1109/ICCICT50803.2021.9510156

Kumar, M. S., & Krishnan, D. S. G. (2020). *Perceived Usefulness (PU), Perceived Ease of Use (PEOU), and Behavioural Intension to Use (BIU): Mediating effect of Attitude toward Use (AU) with reference to Mobile wallet Acceptance and Adoption in Rural India*. Academic Press.

Kwan, J. S.-L., & Lim, K. H. (2021). *Tweetcovid: A system for analysing public sentiments and discussions about covid-19 via twitter activities*. Paper presented at the 26th International Conference on Intelligent User Interfaces-Companion. 10.1145/3397482.3450733

Lee, J. H. (2021). *Understanding Public Attitudes toward COVID-19 with Twitter*. Paper presented at the 2021 Systems and Information Engineering Design Symposium (SIEDS). 10.1109/SIEDS52267.2021.9483708

Lenadora, D., Gamage, G., Haputhanthri, D., Meedeniya, D., & Perera, I. (2020). *Exploratory analysis of a social media network in Sri Lanka during the COVID-19 virus outbreak*. arXiv preprint arXiv:2006.07855.

Lu, G., Kubli, M., Moist, R., Zhang, X., Li, N., Gächter, I., & Fleck, M. (2022). Tough times, extraordinary care: A critical assessment of chatbot-based digital mental healthcare solutions for older persons to fight against pandemics like covid-19. *Proceedings of Sixth International Congress on Information and Communication Technology: ICICT 2021, 1*. 10.1007/978-981-16-2377-6_68

Manikandan, G., Murugaiah, S., Velusamy, K., Ramesh, A. B. K., Rathinavelu, S., Viswanathan, R., & Jageerkhan, M. N. (2022). Work Life Imbalance and Emotional Intelligence: A Major Role and Segment among College Teachers. *International Journal of Professional Business Review*, 7(6), e0832. doi:10.26668/businessreview/2022.v7i6.832

Mugilan, A., Kanmani, R., Deva Priya, M., Christy Jeba Malar, A., & Suganya, R. (2021). Smart Sentimental Analysis of the Impact of Social Media on COVID-19. *Micro-Electronics and Telecommunication Engineering: Proceedings of 4th ICMETE 2020*. 10.1007/978-981-33-4687-1_42

Naiem, R., Kaur, J., Mishra, S., & Saxena, A. (2022). Impact of COVID-19 Pandemic on Mental Health Using Machine Learning and Artificial Intelligence. *International Conference on Innovative Computing and Communications: Proceedings of ICICC 2021*, 1. 10.1007/978-981-16-2594-7_21

Naslund, J. A., & Deng, D. (2021). Addressing mental health stigma in low-income and middle-income countries: A new frontier for digital mental health. *Ethics, Medicine, and Public Health*, 19, 100719. doi:10.1016/j.jemep.2021.100719 PMID:35083375

Praveen, S., Ittamalla, R., & Deepak, G. (2021). Analysing Indian general public's perspective on anxiety, stress and trauma during Covid-19-a machine learning study of 840,000 tweets. *Diabetes & Metabolic Syndrome*, 15(3), 667–671. doi:10.1016/j.dsx.2021.03.016 PMID:33813239

Rachman, F. H. (2020). *Twitter sentiment analysis of Covid-19 using term weighting TF-IDF and logistic regression*. Paper presented at the 2020 6th Information Technology International Seminar (ITIS).

Sabaruddin, R. A., & Saee, S. (2021). *Malay Tweets: Discovering Mental Health Situation during COVID-19 Pandemic in Malaysia*. Paper presented at the 2021 IEEE 19th Student Conference on Research and Development (SCOReD). 10.1109/SCOReD53546.2021.9652759

Samuel, J., Rahman, M. M., Ali, G. M. N., Samuel, Y., Pelaez, A., Chong, P. H. J., & Yakubov, M. (2020). Feeling positive about reopening? New normal scenarios from COVID-19 US reopen sentiment analytics. *IEEE Access : Practical Innovations, Open Solutions*, 8, 142173–142190. doi:10.1109/ACCESS.2020.3013933 PMID:34786280

Sanyal, S., Kalimuthu, M., Arumugam, T., Aruna, R., Balaji, J., Savarimuthu, A., & Patil, S. (2023). Internet of Things and Its Relevance to Digital Marketing. In *Opportunities and Challenges of Industrial IoT in 5G and 6G Networks* (pp. 138–154). IGI Global. doi:10.4018/978-1-7998-9266-3.ch007

Venigalla, A. S. M., Chimalakonda, S., & Vagavolu, D. (2020). *Mood of India during Covid-19-an interactive web portal based on emotion analysis of Twitter data*. Paper presented at the Conference companion publication of the 2020 on computer supported cooperative work and social computing. 10.1145/3406865.3418567

Viviani, M., Crocamo, C., Mazzola, M., Bartoli, F., Carrà, G., & Pasi, G. (2021). Assessing vulnerability to psychological distress during the COVID-19 pandemic through the analysis of microblogging content. *Future Generation Computer Systems*, 125, 446–459. doi:10.1016/j.future.2021.06.044 PMID:34934256

Yin, H., Yang, S., & Li, J. (2020). *Detecting topic and sentiment dynamics due to COVID-19 pandemic using social media*. Paper presented at the Advanced Data Mining and Applications: 16th International Conference, ADMA 2020, Foshan, China. 10.1007/978-3-030-65390-3_46

Chapter 17
Revolutionizing Government Communication:
A Framework for Harnessing the Power of Social Media

Suvarna V. Nimbagal
KLE Technological University, India

Ansumalini Panda
KLE Technological University, India

Srushti Kulkarni
KLE Technological University, India

Shrushti Bilebhavi
KLE Technological University, India

G. S. Hiremath
KLE Technological University, India

ABSTRACT

Governments recognized that an increasing number of citizens are present on social networks rather than government websites. Reviewing the effects that social media have had on government, as well as the role that these new technologies have played and the implications they have for the future, appears pertinent. This is true given that the Indian government predicts that information and communication technologies-enabled services will significantly affect economic growth, inclusion, and quality of life, and that the extensive use of social media for communication ensures awareness and transparency in the government's objectives and strategies for implementing various schemes. Social networking software and social media have evolved into tools for communication, entertainment, and change, and it is reasonable to believe that they will continue to have an impact on our world. This chapter uses applications like Facebook, Twitter, and Instagram to develop a case study-based framework for assessing communication effectiveness on social networks in India.

DOI: 10.4018/978-1-6684-7450-1.ch017

INTRODUCTION

The introduction of social media is changing the way individuals engage with one another as well as the way information is shared and transmitted. It differs from traditional media such as print, radio, and television in two ways: first, the amount of content that can be generated by users far outnumbers that generated by news/opinion makers; and second, its "viral" ability for potential exponential spread of information by word of mouth and interlinking of the various social media platforms, thereby significantly reducing control over the spread of any such information. These qualities represent a paradigm change from Web 1.0 technology, which allowed for simple information sharing and basic two-way interactions, to Web 2.0 - where absolutely anything is possible. The ubiquity of the Internet is flattering an imperative phenomenon in the changing world. Internet prejudiced every aspect of private and public lives, and changed the nature of service towards a click and mortar instead of brick and mortar nature. Governments recognized the importance of Internet, and started to provide their services electronically over e government websites. Social media has become an increasingly important tool for governments around the world to communicate with citizens, engage in public discourse, and gather feedback. Some of the ways in which social media is used by the government include information sharing, public engagement, crisis communication, transparency and accountability, campaigns, and elections. Governments use social media platforms like Twitter, Facebook, and Instagram to share important information such as news, announcements, and updates about policies and programs.

Social media has become an important tool for governments to quickly disseminate information during a crisis or emergency (Abbas et al., 2022; Fast et al., 2014). For example, during a natural disaster, social media can be used to provide real-time updates about the situation and inform citizens about emergency procedures. Social media platforms like Twitter and Facebook provide an opportunity for governments to engage with citizens and gather feedback on policies and programs. This engagement can help governments make more informed decisions and build trust with citizens. Governments can use social media to provide transparency into their decision-making processes and communicate their progress toward achieving their goals. Social media can also be used to hold governments accountable by providing a platform for citizens to voice their concerns and criticisms. Social media has become an important tool for political campaigns and elections (A.Mishaal & Abu-Shana, 2015). Governments can use social media platforms to The Indian government's use of social media has allowed citizens to participate in the policymaking process. Social media platforms provide a space for citizens to express their views and provide feedback on government initiatives. Social media has increased the transparency of the Indian government by providing citizens with access to information and updates on government activities (Lelisho et al., 2023). The government's use of social media also allows for greater accountability and scrutiny. The Indian government has used social media to mobilize citizens for various initiatives and campaigns. Social media platforms provide a space for citizens to connect with like-minded individuals and take collective action promote their campaigns, engage with voters, and provide information about the voting process.

Hofmann et al., (2013) argued that many governments have problems in their communications with their stakeholders due to the low budget and because they consider communication with stakeholders as a minor priority. Governments used traditional ways of communication such as newspapers, radio, and television to promote their policies and services. Such channels are one-way and miss the feedback of stakeholders, which leads to low participation from the stakeholder's side.

As of 2021, global social media penetration had surpassed 50%, meaning that more than half of the world's population was using social media. This indicates the widespread adoption of these platforms across various regions and demographics. Figure 1 shows the top ten countries in the world with the highest number of social media users in the millions. The number of social network users (social media and messaging apps) in India was expected to increase by more than 400 million in 2021, surpassing 1 billion by 2025.

Figure 1. Top 10 countries with highest number of social media users
Source: The Hindu Business Line.

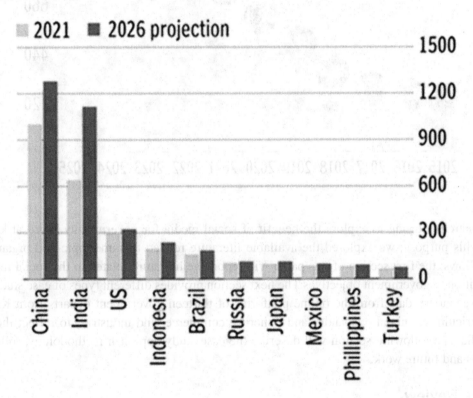

Overall, social media has become an integral part of modern governance, enabling governments to communicate more effectively with citizens, build trust and transparency, and foster greater engagement and participation in public affairs. where absolutely everyone is/can be a user as well as a provider of content. Social media is changing the way individuals interact with one another. To promote and enable government agencies to embrace this dynamic medium of engagement, the Government in Karnataka embraces the use of Social Media in different departments like agriculture, animal husbandry, primary and higher education, finance, industry and commerce, energy, governance, health and environment, ecology and forest, family welfare, and food and safety.

Figure 2 shows the penetration of social media users in India, 67% of the Indians are expected to use social media by 2025. Facebook remained one of the most widely used social media platforms globally. However, platform preferences varied by region.

Figure 2. Social media network user penetration
Source: The Hindu Business Line

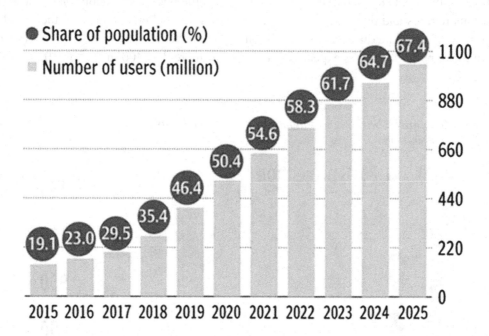

The research is trying to explore the benefit of social media for governments based at karnataks state. For this purpose, we explored the available literature related to same topic and organized the work as follows: the first section of this paper will report the literature related to the social media and its contribution to government objectives The next section provides different types of case study design including secondary data from the online platforms of thirteen government departs from Karnataka namely, agriculture, animal husbandry and fisheries, commerce, and industries to reflect the role of social media The following section will describe the case study approach methodology, followed by conclusions and future work.

Literature Review

According to Eric Qualman, author of Socialnomics, "The biggest change since the industrial revolution has been social media,". The phrase "web 2.0." is a succinct way to explain how social media has shifted the internet's content from being dominated by one-way publication or e-commerce to one that places more of a focus on words, pictures, music, and videos than regular people create, share, and comment on (Arora et al., 2023). Government 2.0 is a term sometimes used to describe how social media has altered citizen-government relations. Citizens and service users are undoubtedly already talking about local issues online and are expecting a more transparent government and a bigger influence on how things are done where they live. Government 2.0 is the use of open data to increase government accountability and transparency as well as the use of social media platforms to participate in these discussions, influence policy, and strengthen local democracy (Garg et al., 2020).

The utilization of social media in the Indian agriculture sector has the potential to revolutionize traditional practices, enhance communication, and improve farmers' livelihoods (Patel & Mallappa, 2022). By leveraging the power of these platforms, stakeholders can collaborate to build a more sustainable and prosperous agricultural future in India (Mamgain et al., 2020). Social media acts as a powerful tool for Animal Husbandry and Fisheries departments to communicate policies, regulations, and conservation initiatives. Twitter campaigns, Facebook posts, and Instagram stories to raise awareness about sustainable practices, endangered species, and the importance of responsible fishing. This engagement fosters a sense of responsibility among stakeholders (Kumar Mishra, 2022).

Social media is used by governmental entities, in 2011, the Ministry of External Affairs became the first government organization to use social media as part of the Department of Telecommunications (DoT) pilot initiative (Fast et al., 2014). It started to connect with people and project a positive image of India. While its Facebook page is now neglected, this is not true of Twitter. On Twitter, it has more than 42,000 followers, and the account is updated frequently. In fact, the effort received praise in particular for its contribution to the Libya conflict. They not only posted pertinent information about the situation, but they also assisted Indians who were stranded in Libya in returning safely home. Based on the information shared on Twitter by their relatives, they could contact those who were stranded in Libya (Lin, 2022).

The Traffic Police in different cities is another excellent example of a governmental organization that has used social media efficiently. Traffic Police Chandigarh, Traffic Police Bangalore, Traffic Police Delhi, and Traffic Police Mumbai are a few of these. Along with providing regular traffic updates, they also address complaints from the public and instruct people on how to drive safely (Bertot et al., 2012). A Delhi Traffic Police programme that asked its residents to upload photos of traffic rule violators and successfully apprehended over 20,000 of them has recently grabbed headlines. Similar efforts to catch rule breakers are also being made by the Bangalore Traffic Police. Both the traffic police in Bangalore and Delhi are making extensive use of Facebook, and both of these efforts are incredibly well-liked by the general public (https://www.firstpost.com/tech/news-analysis/indian-government-and-social-media-3609373.html).

Social media, which Indian Prime Minister Narendra Modi launched on July 1, 2015, is a crucial tool for other important government-run programs in India, including BharatNet, Make in India, Startup India, Standup India, industrial corridors, and Bharatmala and Sagarmala. India had 1.3 billion people as of December 31, 2018, 123 billion Aadhaar digital biometric identity cards, 121 billion mobile phones, 44.6 billion smartphones, and 56 billion internet users—an increase from 481 million users (35% of the population) in December 2017, and a growth of 51% in e-commerce (Wang et al., 2023).

The National e-Governance Plan aims to make all front-end government services accessible online. MyGov.in is a forum for discussing suggestions and ideas related to government and policy. It serves as a platform for citizen participation in government using the "Discuss," "Do," and "Disseminate" methods (Mastley, 2017). UMANG (Unified Mobile Application for New-age Governance) is a Government of India all-in-one secure multi-channel, multi-platform, multi-lingual, and multi-service freeware mobile app for accessing over 1,200 central and state government services in multiple Indian languages over Android, iOS (iPhone Operating system), Windows, and USSD (Unstructured Supplementary Service Data) devices. These services include AADHAAR, DigiLocker, Bharat Bill Payment System, PAN (Permanent Account Number) EPFO (Employees' Provident Fund Organization) services, Pradhan Mantri Kaushal Vikas Yojana (PMKVY) services, and AICTE. Aadhaar authentication combined with the e-Sign framework enables citizens to digitally sign documents online (Bertot et al., 2010).

The Indian government's use of social media can be analyzed through various dimensions, including communication, participation, transparency, and mobilization. Social media has become an essential tool for the Indian government to communicate with citizens. It allows the government to disseminate information quickly and efficiently, as well as to respond to citizen queries and concerns. The Indian government's use of social media has allowed citizens to participate in the policymaking process. Social media platforms provide a space for citizens to express their views and provide feedback on government initiatives. Social media has increased the transparency of the Indian government by providing citizens with access to information and updates on government activities (Lelisho et al., 2023). The government's use of social media also allows for greater accountability and scrutiny. The Indian government and Karnataka government has used social media to mobilize citizens for various initiatives and campaigns. Social media platforms provide a space for citizens to connect with like-minded individuals and take collective action.

Given its potential to give "voice to all," instant outreach, and 24*7 involvement, social media provides government departments with a unique chance to connect with their stakeholders, particularly citizens, in real time in order to make policy decisions that are citizen-centric. Numerous governments throughout the world, as well as numerous government departments in India, are using various social media platforms to reach out to residents, businesses, and experts in order to solicit input into policymaking, receive feedback on service delivery, and develop community-based activities, among other things.

However, many concerns remain, including, but not limited to, issues concerning authorization to speak on behalf of the department/agency, communication technologies and platforms to be used, scope of engagement, creating synergies between different channels of communication, compliance with existing legislation, and so on which the government of Karnataka has take n care by framing guidelines for usage of social media so that the departments can us the platforms effectively.

The Objectives of the Study

The use of social media by Indian government can be analyzed through communication, participation, transparency, and mobilization by citizen of India. Now a day, Social media has become an essential tool for the Indian government to connect with citizens. It allows the government to disseminate information quickly and efficiently, as well as to respond to citizen queries and concerns and allowed them to participate in the policymaking process. This study aims to conduct a literature review of knowledge sharing through social media with another aim to summarize previous research as well as to describe the novelty to advance research in this field. Further objectives are described in the following way.

a.   To identify the role of social media on Indian Government websites based at Karnataka state
b.   To find out the role of citizens in the policy-making process on different government websites in Karnataka state
c.   To determine the usages of social media on specific websites in the Karnataka state

Research Methodology

This research is carried out by secondary information including a case study approach, which is a comprehensive, multi-faceted investigation of any complex issues in real-life settings. The value of the case study approach is well-recognized in the fields of business, law, and policy (Crowe et al., 2011).

Based on our experiences of conducting several case studies, we reflect on the different types of case study design including secondary data from the online platforms of thirteen government departs from Karnataka namely, agriculture, animal husbandry and fisheries, commerce, and industries as shown in Table 1. Table 1 summarizes the usage of various online platforms based at Karnataka state.

The case study approach is primarily very useful to use when there is a need to obtain an in-depth appreciation of an issue, event, or phenomenon of interest, in its natural real-life context (Yin,2009). The sole objective in writing this piece is to provide insights into when to consider employing this approach and an overview of key methodological considerations in relation to the design, planning, analysis, interpretation, and reporting of case studies. According to Yin, case studies can be used to explain, describe or explore events or phenomena in the everyday contexts in which they occur (Yin, 2009). Here, we focus on the main stages of research activity when planning and undertaking a case study; the crucial stages are: defining the case; selecting the case(s); collecting and analyzing the data; interpreting data; (Yin,2005), and reporting the findings (George and Bennett,2005). Followed by this approach, we collected information from the online platforms of thirteen government departments namely, agriculture, animal husbandry and fisheries, commerce, and industries from Karnataka state.

The study used a case study approach based on secondary data from the literature and websites of the various departments. The study used secondary data from the online platforms of thirteen government departs from Karnataka namely, Agriculture, Animal Husbandry and Fisheries, Commerce, and Industries as shown in Table 1, and summarizes the usage of various online platforms.

Case Study: Agriculture Department

With the rapid growth of social media platforms worldwide, various sectors have begun exploring their potential for effective communication, outreach, and knowledge sharing. The agriculture sector plays a crucial role in India's economy, providing livelihoods to a significant portion of the population. To improve productivity, sustainability, and farmer welfare, the agriculture department has embraced the use of social media platforms. The data is gathered from official reports, social media analytics, and existing literature on social media usage in the agriculture sector. The study reveals that the agriculture department in India has adopted various social media platforms, including Facebook, Twitter, Instagram, and YouTube. These platforms provide opportunities for engaging with stakeholders, sharing agricultural information, and addressing farmer queries.

The integration of social media has facilitated direct communication channels between the agriculture department and farmers. Real-time updates, advisories, weather forecasts, market prices, and government schemes are disseminated to a wide audience through social media, enhancing outreach and information access. Social media platforms have become effective tools for knowledge sharing among farmers, experts, and agricultural organizations. Online forums, webinars, and live sessions are conducted to disseminate best practices, crop-specific information, and new technologies. Farmers can interact, share experiences, and seek guidance from experts, promoting capacity building and innovation(Vakeel & Panigrahi, 2018).

The study identifies challenges such as limited internet connectivity in rural areas, language barriers, and the digital divide. To overcome these challenges, the agriculture department has employed strategies such as mobile-based applications, multilingual content, and collaborations with local organizations. Training programs have also been conducted to enhance digital literacy among farmers (Silva et al., 2019).

Table 1. *Usage of various online platforms*

Sl.No.	Government Department	Facebook	Twitter	Instagram	Others	Purpose/Remarks Facebook	Purpose/Remarks Twitter	Purpose/Remarks Instagram	Purpose Remarks Other
1	Agriculture	YES	YES	Yes	NO	to share information, updates, and tips on farming, food safety,	Update News,	Marketing, Brand building	--
2	Animal Husbandry and Fisheries	YES	YES	YES	LINKEDIN	to give information, updates	updates and News	Share pictures and videos	Connecting with professionals (LinkedIn)
3	Commerce and Industries	YES	YES	YES	NO	Awareness (circulars, schemes)	notifications, connect with other government bodies	Share pictures and videos	--
4	Co-Operative Department	YES	YES	NO	YES(YOUTUBE)	Awareness (circulars, schemes)	notifications, connect with other government bodies	--	--
5	Personnel and Administrative Department.	YES	YES	NO		To publish policies	Guidance (service)	--	Administration work quality
6	Department of E-Governance	YES	YES	YES	YES(YOUTUBE)	Updates (initiatives and services)	Updates (services and events)	Share pictures,	Videos-related initiatives, services
7	Higher Education	YES	YES	NO	NO	Scholarships, schemes	policies, schemes, awareness, government orders	--	--
8	Primary and Higher Education	YES	YES	NO	YES	awareness about the services	to connect with all the stakeholders	--	To promote education and a new initiative
9	Energy	YES	YES	NO	YES(YOUTUBE)	awareness of new initiatives/ current updates	connecting with all stakeholders	--	Service
10	Finance	YES	YES	NO	NO	Notification (taxes, revenue, annual budget)	connecting with all stakeholders	--	--
11	Food and Civil Supplies	YES	YES	NO	YES	FSSAI certificate, quality certificate, tax	new initiatives, circulars	--	Food (hygienic, safety)
12	Forest, Ecology and Environment	YES	YES	NO	NO	awareness about environmental safety, recruiting posts,	notification, policy, scheme	--	--
13	Health and Family Welfare	YES	YES	NO	NO	circulars/schemes/policies	notifications, rights and duties	--	--

The social media usage in the agriculture department has significantly contributed to improving agricultural communication, outreach, and knowledge sharing in India. Farmers' access to timely information, government schemes, and expert guidance has enhanced productivity, sustainability, and their overall well-being. While challenges remain, continued efforts to bridge the digital divide and tailor social media initiatives to local needs can further strengthen the impact of social media in the agriculture sector (Baron & Kenny, 1986).

Case Study: Animal Husbandry and Fisheries

Animal Husbandry and Fisheries play pivotal roles in global food security and economic development. The integration of social media platforms within these sectors has introduced new dynamics in terms of communication, research, knowledge dissemination, and community engagement. Social media platforms offer an effective means for Animal Husbandry and Fisheries departments to communicate with stakeholders, including farmers, fishermen, researchers, and consumers. Facebook, Twitter, and Instagram have enabled real-time updates on livestock health, disease outbreaks, aquaculture techniques, fishing regulations, and market trends. This real-time communication enhances awareness and responsiveness in the face of challenges. Social media has revolutionized the way research findings, best practices, and technical information are shared with stakeholders. YouTube, TikTok, and WhatsApp groups provide platforms for video tutorials, webinars, and step-by-step guides. This facilitates the dissemination of practical knowledge to remote areas and less-privileged communities, improving production efficiency and resource management.

Social media bridges the gap between producers and consumers, enabling direct engagement and transparency in the supply chain. Farmers and fishermen can utilize platforms like LinkedIn, WhatsApp, and dedicated e-commerce websites to showcase their products, negotiate prices, and access wider markets. This empowerment can result in higher profits and reduced dependence on intermediaries. Online communities fostered by social media facilitate collaboration, knowledge sharing, and emotional support among practitioners. Forums, groups, and blogs on platforms like Facebook offer spaces for farmers and fishermen to exchange experiences, seek advice and collectively address challenges. This networking enhances resilience and adaptive capacity.

Social media acts as a powerful tool for Animal Husbandry and Fisheries departments to communicate policies, regulations, and conservation initiatives. Twitter campaigns, Facebook posts, and Instagram stories can raise awareness about sustainable practices, endangered species, and the importance of responsible fishing. This engagement fosters a sense of responsibility among stakeholders. While social media has transformative potential, challenges include digital divide, language barriers, misinformation, and data privacy concerns. Tailored strategies are required to ensure that information reaches all stakeholders, irrespective of their digital literacy or location. Efforts must be made to verify and authenticate information shared through these platforms.

The integration of social media platforms within Animal Husbandry and Fisheries departments presents a transformative opportunity to enhance communication, knowledge sharing, and community engagement. By leveraging the power of these platforms, these sectors can address challenges, improve resource management, and contribute to sustainable development. It is imperative for stakeholders to collaborate in designing strategies that maximize the benefits of social media while mitigating associated challenges, ensuring that the potential of these platforms is harnessed effectively.

Case Study: Commerce and Industries Department

In today's digital age, social media platforms have emerged as powerful tools for communication, outreach, and promotion. The Commerce and Industries Department has incorporated social media platforms into its operations with the purpose of fostering economic growth, attracting investments, and enhancing business competitiveness (Vakeel & Panigrahi, 2018). The Commerce and Industries Department in India plays a pivotal role in driving economic growth, attracting investments, and promoting business development. In recent years, the department has recognized the importance of social media in effectively reaching out to stakeholders and leveraging digital platforms for commerce and industries. Based on secondary data collected from official reports, and existing literature on social media usage in commerce and industries the study reveals that the Commerce and Industries Department in India has embraced various social media platforms, including Twitter, LinkedIn, Facebook, and YouTube. These platforms are utilized to engage with stakeholders, share industry updates, promote investment opportunities, and showcase success stories. Social media integration has facilitated direct communication channels between the department and businesses, investors, and the public. Real-time updates, policy announcements, business-related news, and industry-specific information are disseminated through social media, enhancing outreach and information access (Chauhan et al., 2019).

Social media platforms have become effective tools for promoting investment opportunities and attracting both domestic and foreign investors. The department utilizes social media to showcase investment-friendly policies, infrastructure developments, success stories, and business incentives. This approach has facilitated business growth, job creation, and economic development (Borkar et al., 2022).

The study identifies challenges such as managing online reputation, handling negative feedback, and maintaining the authenticity of the information shared. The Commerce and Industries Department has implemented strategies such as social media guidelines, content moderation, and proactive engagement to address these challenges. Regular monitoring and analysis of social media conversations also help in understanding public sentiment and addressing concerns promptly (Kumar, 2018).

The integration of social media platforms has proven instrumental in enhancing communication, outreach, investment promotion, and business development. The department's proactive approach to leveraging social media has contributed to economic growth, increased competitiveness, and improved stakeholder engagement (Singh, 2020).

Case Study: Cooperative Department

Social media enables cooperatives to share knowledge, best practices, and training resources more effectively. YouTube, webinars, and podcasts provide platforms for delivering educational content, skill development, and technical training. This empowerment enhances the capacity of cooperative members, contributing to improved productivity and sustainable growth. Cooperative department can utilize social media to build networks and collaborations with other cooperatives, NGOs, governmental agencies, and relevant stakeholders. LinkedIn and professional forums facilitate discussions, partnerships, and knowledge exchange, driving collective efforts toward common goals and shared interests.

Social media platforms act as tools for cooperative organizations to promote their products and services. Platforms like Instagram and e-commerce websites enable cooperatives to showcase their offerings, connect with potential buyers, and establish direct marketing channels. This aids in reaching wider markets and improving economic viability. Social media facilitates the creation of online communities centered around cooperatives. Facebook groups, forums, and online discussions foster a sense of belonging, enabling members to share experiences, seek advice, and support one another. This virtual community-building contributes to a stronger sense of trust and unity among members.

The integration of social media platforms within cooperative departments holds great promise for fostering communication, collaboration, and engagement among members. By leveraging these platforms, cooperatives can enhance their capacity to deliver services, promote sustainable practices, and achieve their social and economic objectives. To maximize the benefits while addressing challenges, cooperative organizations should adopt tailored strategies that ensure inclusivity, privacy, and effective utilization of social media tools.

Case Study: Personnel and Administrative Reforms

Administrative reforms are being implemented in accordance with the State Government's decision for maintaining vigilance on officials' performance, keep service records and accounting up to date, resolution of public grievance petitions, and promoting collaboration across government departments in order to achieve excellence in IT and related fields. Personnel and Administrative Reforms are critical components of modern governance and organizational efficiency. With the advent of social media, new avenues for communication, transparency, and engagement have emerged. This literature review aims to delve into the multifaceted applications of social media platforms in these sectors, shedding light on the implications for government bodies and organizations.

Social media facilitates cross-departmental and inter-agency collaboration and enhance communication and project management, breaking down traditional silos. This collaboration streamlines administrative processes, leading to faster implementation of reforms and better service delivery. Social media enables the rapid dissemination of training resources, manuals, and guidelines to employees. YouTube tutorials, webinars, and podcast series offer flexible learning opportunities, improving staff skills and ensuring uniform implementation of administrative reforms. Social media platforms offer channels for employees to voice their opinions, suggestions, and concerns. Dedicated forums, internal social networks, and anonymous feedback mechanisms provide platforms for open dialogue. This engagement leads to a sense of ownership in reforms and contributes to continuous improvement.

Social media enables government bodies to engage with citizens and stakeholders in shaping policies and reforms. Platforms like Facebook Live, Twitter polls, and online surveys has facilitated public participation, enabling more inclusive and informed decision-making. The utilization of social media in Personnel and Administrative Reforms presents challenges, including data privacy, information security, and the potential for misuse. Striking a balance between transparency and safeguarding sensitive information is crucial. Furthermore, digital literacy and inclusivity need to be addressed to ensure equitable engagement.

Case Study: Department of E-Governance

The integration of social media platforms within the realm of e-governance has revolutionized citizen engagement, service delivery, and policy formulation. By harnessing the power of these platforms, governments can create more transparent, efficient, and participatory governance systems. However, successful integration requires well-defined strategies that prioritize data security, inclusivity, and effective communication. The future of e-governance lies in a harmonious collaboration between traditional methodologies and innovative social media approaches. Social media acts as a bridge between citizens and government services. Chatbots, Facebook Messenger, and WhatsApp enable real-time communication for addressing queries, providing information, and resolving issues. This accessibility streamlines service delivery, reduces bureaucratic hurdles, and improves the overall citizen experience.

Social media is a crucial tool for disseminating real-time information during emergencies and crisis situations. Platforms such as Twitter and Facebook help governments deliver urgent updates, safety instructions, and disaster relief information to citizens promptly, ensuring their safety and well-being. Social media platforms play a pivotal role in promoting transparency and accountability. Governments can use platforms like Instagram, YouTube, and Snapchat to share multimedia updates on projects, policies, and initiatives. This visual storytelling fosters trust, increases understanding, and ensures that citizens are well-informed about government actions.

Social media platforms provide governments with direct channels to engage citizens in policy discussions, public consultations, and decision-making processes. Platforms like Twitter, Facebook, and online forums allow citizens to express their opinions, offer suggestions, and provide feedback on various government initiatives. This enhances the inclusivity of governance and strengthens the sense of democratic participation.

Case Study: Higher Education Department

With the widespread adoption of social media platforms globally, educational institutions have recognized their potential for communication, engagement, and knowledge dissemination. Higher education plays a crucial role in shaping the future of individuals and societies. With the increasing prevalence of social media platforms, educational institutions are leveraging these digital channels to improve communication, enhance learning experiences, and engage with stakeholders (Khairul & Aulia Putri, 2022). Based on secondary data gathered from official reports, social media analytics, and existing literature on social media usage in higher education the study reveals that the Higher Education Department in India has embraced various social media platforms, including Facebook, Twitter, LinkedIn, Instagram, and YouTube. These platforms are utilized to engage with students, faculty, alumni, and the wider community (Asghar et al., 2021).

Social media integration has facilitated direct communication channels between the department and students. Educational institutions use social media platforms to share important announcements, academic updates, event information, and opportunities for student involvement. Interactive features such as live chats, discussion forums, and polls foster student engagement and participation. Social media platforms provide avenues for faculty members to collaborate, share resources, and participate in professional development activities (Jyoti & Bhau, 2016). Online communities, webinars, and virtual conferences enable faculty members to connect with peers, exchange ideas, and stay updated on the latest research and teaching practices.

Social media platforms serve as effective tools for disseminating educational content, research findings, and institutional achievements. Educational institutions utilize social media to showcase their programs, facilities, and success stories, attracting prospective students and fostering institutional reputation. Open online courses, educational videos, and webinars are shared to promote lifelong learning and reach a wider audience (Islam et al., 2017).

Basu et al. (2020) identifies challenges such as maintaining privacy and security, managing online interactions, and ensuring responsible use of social media platforms. Strategies employed by the Higher Education Department include social media policies, training programs for faculty and staff, and regular monitoring of online activities. Collaboration with cybersecurity experts and social media platforms is also crucial in addressing these challenges.

This study demonstrates that social media integration within the Higher Education Department has significantly contributed to student engagement, faculty collaboration, and knowledge dissemination in India (Marongwe & Garidzirai, 2021). Social media platforms have transformed traditional educational practices, enabling seamless communication, fostering collaboration, and expanding the reach of higher education institutions.

Case Study: Primary and Higher Education

The integration of social media platforms into primary and higher education in India has been transformative. By embracing these platforms strategically, educators have enhanced communication, foster interactive learning experiences, and create a more inclusive educational environment. To mitigate challenges and maximize benefits, education stakeholders have designed approaches that prioritize student privacy, digital literacy, and effective use of social media tools. The future of education in India lies in harnessing the power of social media to create a more engaging, collaborative, and globally connected learning ecosystem.

Social media facilitates collaboration beyond borders. Platforms such as Skype, Zoom, and collaborative online spaces enable students to interact with peers from different cultures, enhancing their global awareness and cross-cultural communication skills. Social media platforms provide students with spaces for self-expression, creativity, and showcasing their work. Blogs, podcasts, and social networks enable students to showcase their projects, build personal brands, and receive feedback from a global audience, enhancing their sense of agency and empowerment.

Social media platforms offer opportunities for interactive and collaborative learning experiences. Teachers can utilize platforms such as YouTube, Facebook Groups, and virtual classrooms to share multimedia content, conduct discussions, and encourage peer-to-peer learning. This learner-centered approach promotes active participation and deeper understanding. Social media platforms have emerged as powerful tools for educators to communicate with students, parents, and peers. Platforms like WhatsApp, Instagram, and Twitter enable real-time updates, assignment notifications, and educational content sharing. This streamlined communication enhances engagement and collaboration within the educational community.

Case Study: Energy

By leveraging the power of social media platforms, the energy department can enhance public awareness, drive policy innovation, and accelerate the transition towards sustainable energy practices. In times of energy crises or disruptions, social media platforms offered a swift means of communication to provide real-time updates and instructions to the public. Platforms such as WhatsApp, Facebook Live, and Twitter updates helped disseminate accurate information, minimize panic, and ensure public safety.

Social media offers a direct channel for the energy department to engage with citizens, stakeholders, and industry players. Platforms like LinkedIn, online forums, and webinars facilitated discussions on energy policies, regulations, and incentives. This engagement fostered dialogues, enabling the department to gather feedback and shape more effective policies. Social media platforms provided a platform for showcasing technological advancements, research findings, and innovation in the energy sector. Platforms such as Instagram, TikTok, and LinkedIn allowed the energy department to share success stories, pilot projects, and collaborative efforts, inspiring further innovation and fostering a culture of sustainable development.

Case Study: Finance Department

The Finance Department is one of the Karnataka Government Secretariat's major departments. It is in charge of managing the State Government's finances, beginning with mobilization of resources (raising Tax and Non-Tax Revenue, borrowing from various sources such as internal debt, Small Savings and Provident Fund, etc.) and ending with efficient use of resources (formulation of Annual Budget and execution of Budget, Public Expenditure Management, keeping account of Receipt into and Expenditure from the State's Public Account, ensuring Accountability of Publ It also provides financial counselling, serves as a reference department for service and pension conditions, and facilitates credit from banks and other institutions.

The integration of social media platforms within the Finance Department of Karnataka has significantly enhanced transparency, citizen engagement, and financial accountability. By strategically harnessing these platforms, the department has created a more informed, engaged, and fiscally responsible society. Social media platforms have become powerful communication tools for the Finance Department to share budget updates, fiscal policies, and economic indicators. Platforms like Twitter, Facebook, and LinkedIn enable real-time dissemination of financial information, enhancing transparency and improving public awareness.

Social media platforms serve as platforms for sharing financial reports, audits, and budget documents. By utilizing platforms such as YouTube and SlideShare, the Finance Department can communicate complex financial information in accessible formats, fostering fiscal transparency and accountability. The Finance Department leveraged social media platforms for engaging citizens in budget consultations, public expenditure discussions, and policy formulation. Facebook Live sessions, online surveys, and interactive webinars enabled the public to participate in financial decision-making processes. Finance Department has used social media for effectively disseminate information about tax policies, subsidies, and financial literacy programs.

Case Study: Food and Civil Supplies

Karnataka Food and Civil Supplies Corporation Limited is a Government of Karnataka undertaking founded on September 7th, 1973 under the Companies Act with the primary goal of procuring, lifting, and distributing food grains through the Public Distribution System (PDS) and implementing various government schemes. The integration of social media platforms within the Food and Civil Supplies sector has the potential to enhance transparency, communication, and citizen engagement. By strategically leveraging these platforms, this department has improved distribution efficiency, reduced wastages, and empower citizens to actively participate in food security initiatives. Social media platforms provided a direct channel for Food and Civil Supplies departments to communicate with citizens. This transparent communication builds trust and helps citizens stay informed.

Social media offered avenues for citizens to provide feedback, report grievances, and suggest improvements in food distribution systems. Dedicated forums, online surveys, and helpline platforms created an interactive space where citizens can voice their concerns and contribute to policy discussions. Social media platforms played a significant role in optimizing distribution mechanisms. Social media allowed the Food and Civil Supplies departments to disseminate information about policy changes, subsidy schemes, and awareness campaigns. Social platforms provided a means for citizens and stakeholders to monitor food distribution processes and hold authorities accountable for any discrepancies.

Case Study: Forest Ecology and Environment

Karnataka's Department of Forest, Ecology, and Environment works to preserve and improve the quality of the natural environment, including water, air, and soil quality, as well as to conserve and safeguard the state's flora, fauna, and other natural resources. The integration of social media platforms within the Forest, Ecology, and Environment departments has immense potential for raising awareness, promoting sustainable practices, and driving positive environmental change. By harnessing the power of these platforms, departments can engage diverse audiences, mobilize collective action, and foster a deeper connection between people and the natural world.

Social media offered a platform for Forest, Ecology, and Environment departments to share information on conservation initiatives, endangered species, climate change, and sustainable practices. Social media allows organizations and departments to engage citizens in environmental conservation efforts.

Case Study: Health and Environment

The Indian Constitution lays out explicit provisions for people's rights as well as the Directive Principles of State Policy, which provide a purpose to which the state's activities are to be steered. On the basis of these Directive Principles and international instruments, the government is committed to regulating all economic activities for the management of workplace safety and health risks and to providing measures to ensure safe and healthy working conditions for all working men and women in the country. The government recognizes that worker safety and health have a positive impact on productivity as well as economic and social growth. As high safety and health standards at work are required, prevention is an essential component of economic activity.

The Health and Environment at Workplace departments play a crucial role in ensuring employee well-being and fostering sustainable practices. In the digital age, social media offered unique avenues to promote health, safety, and environmental awareness within the workplace. Social media enables the dissemination of environmental awareness campaigns and sustainability initiatives within the workplace. While social media presents numerous advantages, challenges include ensuring the privacy of sensitive health information, addressing misinformation, and managing potential distractions. Departments must establish clear guidelines and secure communication channels to address these concerns. The integration of social media platforms within Health and Environment at Workplace departments has the potential to create healthier, safer, and more environmentally responsible workplaces. By strategically leveraging these platforms, departments can promote employee well-being, drive sustainable practices, and enhance overall workplace culture.

Limitation

The study engages in the case method analysis of the usage of social media by government departments in Karnataka only. The paper might not adequately cover the challenges government departments face in adopting and implementing social media strategies. Effective utilization of social media by government departments involves a blend of communication, technology, governance, and public administration. The paper might not fully integrate insights from these various disciplines, leading to a less holistic understanding of the topic.

CONCLUSION

The usage of social media in Karnataka government departments has become increasingly prevalent, with a significant portion of departments actively utilizing various platforms. Facebook and Twitter are the most widely used platforms, followed by YouTube, Instagram, and LinkedIn. This indicates a recognition of the importance of social media as a communication and engagement channel (Jyoti & Bhau, 2016). Social media platforms have facilitated the creation of virtual agricultural communities where farmers can connect, share experiences, and seek advice. Farmers' groups on WhatsApp, Telegram, and other platforms allow them to discuss challenges, seek solutions, and celebrate successes. This networking not only enhances knowledge sharing but also provides emotional support and camaraderie among farmers.

In terms of posting frequency, a substantial number of departments post on social media daily or multiple times a week, ensuring a consistent flow of content and updates to their audience. This frequent posting demonstrates an effort to engage with citizens regularly and keep them informed about government initiatives and services (Sharma & Pandher, 2018).

The types of content posted by Karnataka government departments on social media primarily consist of news updates, event announcements, public service information, success stories, infographics, and videos. This diverse range of content allows departments to provide a comprehensive and engaging experience for their followers, catering to different information preferences and communication styles.

Engagement metrics, such as likes/followers, comments, shares/retweets, and click-through rates, reflect the level of interaction and interest generated by the departments' social media accounts. These metrics provide valuable feedback on the effectiveness of their social media strategies and content. The average engagement rates indicate a moderate level of user engagement, suggesting a reasonable level of interest and interaction from the audience.

Overall, the usage of social media in Karnataka government departments demonstrates a proactive approach to digital communication and citizen engagement. By leveraging various social media platforms, maintaining a consistent posting frequency, and delivering diverse content, these departments can effectively disseminate information, build awareness, and engage with citizens. Continued efforts to enhance social media strategies and monitor engagement metrics will further optimize their digital presence and communication with the public.

REFERENCES

Abbas, A. F., Jusoh, A., Mas'od, A., Alsharif, A. H., & Ali, J. (2022). Bibliometrix analysis of information sharing in social media. In Cogent Business and Management (Vol. 9, Issue 1). doi:10.1080/2331 1975.2021.2016556

Arora, N., Rana, M., & Prashar, S. (2023). How Does Social Media Impact Consumers' Sustainable Purchase Intention? *Review of Marketing Science*. doi:10.1515/roms-2022-0072

Asghar, M. Z., Iqbal, A., Seitamaa-Hakkarainen, P., & Barbera, E. (2021). Breaching learners' social distancing through social media during the covid-19 pandemic. *International Journal of Environmental Research and Public Health, 18*(21), 11012. Advance online publication. doi:10.3390/ijerph182111012 PMID:34769534

Baron, R. M., & Kenny, D. A. (1986). The Moderator-Mediator Variable Distinction in Social Psychological Research. Conceptual, Strategic, and Statistical Considerations. *Journal of Personality and Social Psychology, 51*(6), 1173–1182. doi:10.1037/0022-3514.51.6.1173 PMID:3806354

Basu, S., Marimuthu, Y., Sharma, N., Sharma, P., Gangadharan, N., & Santra, S. (2020). Attitude towards mobile learning among resident doctors involved in undergraduate medical education at a government medical college in Delhi, India. *Journal of Education and Health Promotion, 9*(1), 321. Advance online publication. doi:10.4103/jehp.jehp_443_20 PMID:33426125

Bertot, J. C., Jaeger, P. T., & Hansen, D. (2012). The impact of polices on government social media usage: Issues, challenges, and recommendations. *Government Information Quarterly, 29*(1), 30–40. Advance online publication. doi:10.1016/j.giq.2011.04.004

Bertot, J. C., Jaeger, P. T., Munson, S., & Glaisyer, T. (2010). Social media technology and government transparency. *Computer, 43*(11), 53–59. Advance online publication. doi:10.1109/MC.2010.325

Borkar, K. D. M., Rodrigues, P. A., & Mascarenhas, A. A. S. (2022). A Study on Trend and Pattern of Beneficiaries of Prime Minister Employment Generation Scheme. *Webology, 19*(1), 2019–2027. Advance online publication. doi:10.14704/WEB/V19I1/WEB19136

Chauhan, P., Sharma, P., Chauhan, R., & Jain, A. (2019). National eCommerce Policy: What India's new (Draft) eCommerce Policy outlines for Online Retailers and its Regulatory aspects. *International Journal of Drug Regulatory Affairs, 7*(3), 30–33. Advance online publication. doi:10.22270/ijdra.v7i3.335

Crowe, S., Cresswell, K., Robertson, A., Huby, G., Avery, A., & Sheikh, A. (2011). The case study approach. *BMC Medical Research Methodology, 11*(1), 100. doi:10.1186/1471-2288-11-100 PMID:21707982

Fast, I., Sørensen, K., Brand, H., & Suggs, L. S. (2014). Social Media for Public Health: An Exploratory Policy Analysis. *European Journal of Public Health, 25*(1), 162–166. doi:10.1093/eurpub/cku080 PMID:24942532

Garg, P., Gupta, B., Dzever, S., Sivarajah, U., & Kumar, V. (2020). Examining the Relationship between Social Media Analytics Practices and Business Performance in the Indian Retail and IT Industries: The Mediation Role of Customer Engagement. *International Journal of Information Management, 52*, 102069. Advance online publication. doi:10.1016/j.ijinfomgt.2020.102069

George, A. L., & Bennett, A. (2005). *Case studies and theory development in the social sciences. 2005.* MIT Press.

Hofmann, S., Beverungen, D., Räckers, M., & Becker, J. (2013). What makes local governments' online communications successful? Insights from a multi-method analysis of Facebook. *Government Information Quarterly, 30*(4), 387–396. doi:10.1016/j.giq.2013.05.013

Islam, T., Mukhopadhyay, S. C., & Suryadevara, N. K. (2017). Smart Sensors and Internet of Things: A Postgraduate Paper. *IEEE Sensors Journal, 17*(3), 577–584. Advance online publication. doi:10.1109/JSEN.2016.2630124

Jyoti, J., & Bhau, S. (2016). Empirical investigation of moderating and mediating variables in between transformational leadership and related outcomes: A study of higher education sector in North India. *International Journal of Educational Management, 30*(6), 1123–1149. Advance online publication. doi:10.1108/IJEM-01-2015-0011

Khairul, K., & Aulia Putri, R. (2022). *The correlation between the students' habit to watch English YouTube channel and their speaking skill.* ELECT. doi:10.37301/elect.v1i2.56

Kumar, S. (2018). An Assessment of Impact of GST on India's Online Retail Sector. *Economic Affairs, 63*(4). Advance online publication. doi:10.30954/0424-2513.4.2018.16

Lelisho, M. E., Pandey, D., Alemu, B. D., Pandey, B. K., & Tareke, S. A. (2023). The Negative Impact of Social Media during COVID-19 Pandemic. *Trends in Psychology, 31*(1), 123–142. Advance online publication. doi:10.100743076-022-00192-5

Lin, Y. (2022). Social media for collaborative planning: A typology of support functions and challenges. *Cities (London, England), 125*, 103641. Advance online publication. doi:10.1016/j.cities.2022.103641

Mamgain, A., Joshi, U., & Chauhan, J. (2020). Impact of Social Media in Enhancing Agriculture Extension. *Agriculture and Food: E-Newsletter, 2*(9).

Marongwe, N., & Garidzirai, R. (2021). Together but Not Together: Challenges of Remote Learning for Students Amid the COVID-19 Pandemic in Rural South African Universities. *Research in Social Sciences and Technology, 6*(3), 213–226. Advance online publication. doi:10.46303/ressat.2021.39

Mastley, C. P. (2017). Social Media and Information Behavior: A Citation Analysis of Current Research from 2008–2015. *The Serials Librarian, 73*(3–4), 339–351. doi:10.1080/0361526X.2017.1356420

Mishaal, D., & Abu-Shana, E. B. (2015). *The Effect of Using Social Media in Governments: Framework of Communication Success.* doi:10.15849/icit.2015.0069

Mishaal, D. A., & Abu-Shanab, E. A. (2017). Utilizing Facebook by the Arab World Governments. *International Journal of Public Administration in the Digital Age, 4*(3), 53–78. doi:10.4018/IJPADA.2017070105

Patel, P. K., & Mallappa, V. K. H. (2022). *Predictive Factors for Farmers' Knowledge of Social Media for Sustainable Agricultural Development.* Indian Journal of Extension Education. doi:10.48165/IJEE.2022.58412

Sharma, P., & Pandher, J. S. (2018). Quality of teachers in technical higher education institutions in India. Higher Education. *Skills and Work-Based Learning*, 8(4), 511–526. Advance online publication. doi:10.1108/HESWBL-10-2017-0080

Silva, P., Tavares, A. F., Silva, T., & Lameiras, M. (2019). The good, the bad and the ugly: Three faces of social media usage by local governments. *Government Information Quarterly*, 36(3), 469–479. Advance online publication. doi:10.1016/j.giq.2019.05.006

Singh, S. (2020). *Department for Promotion of Industry and Internal Trade Ministry of Commerce and Industry Government of India Consolidated FDI Policy (Effective from October 15, 2020).* Department for Promotion of Industry and Internal Trade Ministry of Commerce and Industry Government of India.

Vakeel, K. A., & Panigrahi, P. K. (2018). Social media usage in E-government: Mediating role of government participation. *Journal of Global Information Management*, 26(1), 1–19. Advance online publication. doi:10.4018/JGIM.2018010101

Wang, H., Xiong, L., Guo, J., Lu, M., & Meng, Q. (2023). Predicting the antecedents of discontinuous usage intention of mobile government social media during public health emergencies. *International Journal of Disaster Risk Reduction*, 87, 103582. Advance online publication. doi:10.1016/j.ijdrr.2023.103582

Yin, R. K. (2005). *Case study research, design and method.* London: Sage Publications Ltd. https://www.firstpost.com/tech/news-analysis

Yin, R. K. (2009). Case study research, design and method. London: Sage Publications Ltd.

Chapter 18
Youth Intention Towards Implementing Digital Currency:
Role of Social Media and Government

Ravishankar Krishnan

Vel Tech Rangarajan Dr. Sagunthala R&D Institute of Science and Technology, India

Logasakthi Kandasamy

Universal Business School, Universal AI University, India

Elantheraiyan Perumal

Vel Tech Rangarajan Dr. Sagunthala R&D Institute of Science and Technology, India

M. S. R. Mariyappan

VelTech Rangarajan Dr. Sagunthala R&D Institute of Science and Technology, India

K. Sankar Ganesh

Sharda University, Uzbekistan

Manoj Govindaraj

VelTech Rangarajan Dr. Sagunthala R&D Institute of Science and Technology, India

Anil B. Malali

Department of Commerce and Management, Acharya Institutes, India

ABSTRACT

This study investigates the factors influencing youth intention to adopt digital currency and explores the impact of social media and government initiatives on their attitudes and behaviors. The variables perceived ease of use, dissemination of information, responsibility, liability, translucency, and perceived usefulness are used to study the impact of digital adoption. Employing a judgmental study approach, including questionnaire survey and qualitative inputs, this research covered 337 samples and aims to provide comprehensive insights. The findings of this research hold significant implications for policy-makers, financial institutions, and social media platforms. By understanding the role of social media and government initiatives, effective strategies can be developed to encourage digital currency adoption among the youth. Addressing potential barriers and leveraging influencers and trusted sources can enhance youth engagement with digital currencies and stimulate economic growth.

DOI: 10.4018/978-1-6684-7450-1.ch018

INTRODUCTION

Development of Information communication and Technology (ICT) has redefined the financial economics in the global context. The revolution in the internet and software technology paved a way to improve the usage of digital currency (Aditya Kulkarni, 2022) Additionally, Reserve Bank of India initiated with Central Bank Digital Currently (CBDC) with intention of promoting the digital economy in India. However, numerous steps taken by the government to make the public to accept the digital currency and ensure the financial inclusion with safe transaction. The digital landscape is evolving gradually in India, as a result wide incremental growth on internet usage. (S. Adgaonkar, 2022) Digital currency referred as a kind of electronic form of fiat money used for contactless transactions where as a value of money protected by encryption is called as crypto currency. Digital currency is likely to appear in India during the 2023-24 FY, these currencies are already used by private companies in their wallet in different forms. Generally, social media become an instrumental on people's decision making in recent days. According to the global statistics the social media users are increasing to 467 million in 2023 (Global statistics report, 2023). Especially, Indians are spending 2.36 hours on an average in social media. It is an evident that how far the social media is occupying the people for different usages. The primary objective of the study is to portray the significance of digital economy and to trace out in what way government has been using social media as an instrument to penetrate the digital currency among the youth populationfor achieving the digital financial inclusion. Secondly, the study explores various factors which familiarize the digital currency among the youth, they are: perceived ease of use, perceived usefulness, responsibility, Quality information, Accountability, Trust and Intention. One of the ways to strengthen the monetary system and motivating element of financial inclusion is Central Bank Digital Currency (CBDC) and also it ensures execution of planned fiscal and financial policy with structured manner (Aditya Kulkarni, 2022). The unstoppable fintech revolution penetrated almost in all the sectors and the digital currency is an important part of the revolution which includes various areas of payment services and settlement system. Need to have enough study to understand the feasibility of the digital currency in India (Manpreet Kaur, 2019). The concept of digital payment is not a new one, digital payment services are already in practice in the name of Immediate Payment Services (IMPS), Real Time Gross Settlement (RTGS). Moreover, the scheme of Digital India enforced during the period of 2014-15 and it showed a way for cashless transaction through Unified Payment Services (UPS). It was a pioneering payment system which strengthened the cashless payment in nook and corner of the country through various applications such as Bharat Interface for Money (BHIM), Paytm, G-pay, phone pay etc. The major goal line of the digital payment service is to provide alternative for physical cash. And, also all these digital transactions can streamline the deposits and payments under the purview of bank account, it helps to include every citizen in the financial system (M.A. Haque & M. Shoaib, 2023). Union Budget of India 2022-23 insisted the significance of digital currency and it emerge to lift up the digital economy. India's dynamic potential is youth population, the biggest strength for the developing country is tremendous growth of young and energetic population. The positive force to develop the nation is depending on the skill driven opportunities given to the youth population (Youth in India, 2022). The present study will explore the youth intention towards implementing the digital currency and also the study highlights the digital currency's acceptance level among the youth population. Moreover, the study identifies how far the government has been using the social media as an instrument to influence the youth population on the acceptance of digital currency. The paper has been segregated in to nine section which includes introduction, theoretical framework, formulation of hypothesis, measurement, research model, discussion and conclusions, theoretical & managerial implications and Limitations & Scope for future study.

Operational Variable Definitions

Perceived Ease of Use (PEU)

Digital currency stronghold is that it helps the reserve bank in the execution of monetary procedures, framework tax policies and its expenditures, and empowers the economic ecosystem by the inclusion of citizens seldom with bank accounts in fiscal framework. The main kickbacks of this currency are the holders' issues with regards to their Privacy (Seth, 2021). Riquelme and Rios (2010) perceived that, the customers use unique equipment's and methods to carry out payments using electronic gizmos, client's assumption & promptness towards technology were significantly influenced by its user friendliness.

Perceived Usefulness (PUS)

According to Treiblmaier and Sillaber (2002), the propensity of individuals to utilize digital currency is significantly influenced by their exposure and comprehension towards it. It is important to focus that, according to San Martn and Camarero (2009), awareness is based on the available information about the advantages and disadvantages of technology adoption as well as the viable strategies in front of them. Customers' perspectives on cryptocurrency and willingness to accept it will shift if they believe they know and understand the pivotal components (Ayedh et al., 2020).

Dissemination of Information (DI)

Madnick et al. (2009) researches information quality as a data-intensive, knowledge-oriented economy stimulates the importance of data and information quality. In any circumstances, there is propensity to access reliable data to resolve significant and latent backlogs. Brunnermeier et al. (2019) opined that the Digital currencies may create ripples in the world's monetary system: Digitalization of money may be adopted by the group of similar nations, and the dominance of electronic framework paves way for the surge of e-money universally. The treatment of private money, the regulation of data ownership, and the independence of the central bank will all be affected by the rise of digital currencies. E-Currency utilization supports financial regulations to have an impact on risk sharing and credit provision. A system in where total deposits is exchangeable to electronic cash helps in the acceptance towards a digital economy in which the majority of activity is carried out through networks with their own monetary instruments.

Responsibility (RES)

Researcher Marmora (2022) states that, monetary policy proclaims that the sporadic rise in volume of transaction with regards to e-cash and its investor focus, but only if investors are wary about inflation. (Goodell, 2021) highlights the CBDCs, are completely different from cryptocurrencies because they are issued, managed, and backed by central banks, all CBDC-related transactions would be recorded for government monitoring. On the other hand, sovereign digital currencies offer opportunities for the people without bank account to financially mingle due to the ease of use of existing digital payment systems and e-wallets. As CBDCs will be amiable to savvy contracts, they will be serious with standard stage digital currencies in supporting developing scattered finance environments.

Liability (LIB)

Keister and Monnet (2022) expressed due to the emergence financial technology and electronic currency the bankers may do a smaller number of transactions and the depositors may take a lead by initiating transactions without the mediation of bankers. This will help the government to identify the underperforming banks and take suitable alternative actions to streamline the banking operations which prevents the customers from withdrawing their deposits from banks. Michel (2022) viewed that while Americans have long held cash in digital format, a CBDC would vary from the conventional digital currency viable to public. This digital money risks Central bank, instead of its subordinates. This is focal point preventing the Central bank from issuing digital money. The government rightly to gives surety to the people deposits unlike other banks which takes care of it in the conventional form, hence the government tightly grips the public money which is a much more safety for depositors.

Translucency (TRN)

Wust et al. (2021) implemented a completely intact digital currency transaction system by voiding block chain technology and aligning with conventional e-money and accounting models. To execute this framework, the depositor and beneficiary exhibit their then coded numbers of their current account, which are endorsed by the central bank, utilizing the cryptographic technology. The money is then transferred right away to the account of the recipient. Transparency and data integrity cannot be guaranteed by such a centralized digital transaction system. The only difference between a CBDC and conventional e-cash is privacy.

Trust (TST)

In a trade-off between digital currency, and bank deposits with regards to their privacy and security, Agur et al. (2022) viewed the potential framework of electronic money and exhibited that CBDC can be equally matched with the benefits rendered by a traditional cash deposit in bank. Additionally, this cashless digital platform may remove the banking middle men in future and eases the depositor's hassle of holding multiple gadgets for transaction purpose.

Intention to use (INT)

Xie et al. (2021) concentrated on factors that impacted people expectation to utilize digital currency is based the facilities like seamless internet availability of online wealth management systems strongly influences them towards these types of currencies rather than the usual one. According to Yi et al. (2021), positive attitudes toward technology adoption outputs are based on the technology awareness of the people who use it. Numerous researchers have discovered a correlation between behavioral measurements and technological advancement awareness (Granic & Maranguni, 2019). Innovation mindfulness of a society makes them to embrace new technology and its updated applications. They align themselves with new innovation when it enhances their abilities, capacities and task simplification guides them towards the adoption new technology towards financial system.

Research Hypotheses

The degree to which the youth population feel the ease to use the digital currency is termed as a 'perceived ease of use'. The study conducted by Davis (1989) revealed that citizens of the country haven't faced difficulty in accessing the e-government information through social media. The reach of information is quite ease when the government availing the information in social media. External factors are influencing directly on the acceptance of SAP and ERP solutions and it is correlated with perceived ease of ERP users (Sternad & Bobek, 2014). Availability of the information on the sustainability labels helps customers to understand the basics about the sustainability of labels on apparel products (Ma et al., 2017). Adequate environment and availability of the information helps the lecturers to learn the innovative technology in the learning management system, the perceived ease of use is associated with dissemination of technological information or sources (Samuel et al., 2018). Government of India is in a position to disseminate the information regarding the digital currency to the general public and youth population which will ensure the perceived ease of use. Thus, the study formulated a hypothesis to test the relationship between Perceived ease of use and Dissemination of Information.

H1: There is a positive relationship between PEU and DI.

Perceived ease of use is a key element to claim the environmental social responsibility on product and services by the consumers. It not only gives the sustainability labels on the apparel goods but also defines the consumer's intention to use products (Ma et al., 2017). Adnan Abd. Hamid et al. (2015) found that the PEU is a belief of individuals to use the e-government information with free of effort, it penetrates among the citizens easily when it is accessible by social media. Either directly or indirectly PEU creates a kind of responsibility among the individuals (Chahal & Rani, 2022). The extent to which people believe to accept the new technology referred as PEU and kind of self-responsibility generated when there is an accessibility and readily available information for user. Currently, fintech revolution is forcing the developing countries to shift from traditional economics in to digital economy where in which secured payment and settlement services happen with high reliability. Social Media plays an instrumental role to influence the youth population positively and creates the responsibility in understanding the digital currency. To check the relationship between reasonability of the youth and PEU, the study formulated the hypothesis as follows:

H2: There is a positive relationship between PEU and RES.

Accounting information system and its quality ensured with substantial impact of perceived ease of use. A definite system not only creates responsibility but also define the liability of the individuals who work under the particular system (Wiryanti & Fardinal, 2020; Nichols et al., 2012). Technological acceptance in the organization is based on the existence of organizational process liability and also study insisted that the liability of the individuals is interlinked in system itself. The present study emphasise that the Citizens of the country is to be aligned with emerging financial system which supports the new model, ease of use creates the liability among the individuals and also prepare their mindset to align with the new system which support the country to compete with global economic revolution. The following hypothesis was formulated to test further:

H3: There is a positive relationship between PEU and LIB.

The dictionary meaning of Transparency is 'being open and honest', information about the digital currency, regulatory framework and risk associated with digital transactions are needed to be transparent which facilitates the ease of use. However, money laundering and other fraudulent activities can be traced out easily when digital currency is in use, it has high transparency and possible to increase the financial transactions (Haque & Shoaib, 2023). Additionally, people can take the adequate decision based on the performance details shown by the government. There is a need of hardcore transparency while rearranging the structural design of the scheme or plans of the government; because it helps the users to connect with the system and leads to successful implementation (Sabani, 2021). Therefore, perceived ease of use and translucency are significantly associated and it reflects on the supporting system of any new implementation. The hypothesis is formulated as follows to test further:

H4: There is a positive relationship between PEU and TRN.

Chahal and Rani (2022) was conducted to explore e-learning acceptance among the students. It revealed the moderate relationship between perceived ease of use and perceived usefulness. Farahat (2012) perceived ease of use was directly influencing perceived usefulness. Ratna and Mehra (2015) reported that the PEU has indirect effect and plays a mediating role on PUS. In Chen and Aklikokou (2020) the community get benefit out of the continuous performance measures and availing the e-government information to the citizens of the country and also witnessed that perceived ease of use associated with usefulness. Therefore, there is a need to test the youth population's PEU and its association with PUS with regard to digital currency, the study coined a hypothesis as follows:

H9: There is a positive relationship between PEU and PUS.

Dissemination of Information (DI) With Trust (TST)

Presence of digital currency is fundamental requirement to compete with global digital economy. Equivalently, government needs to take appropriate measures for disseminating the relevant information about the digital currency with general public. Likewise, RBI is in a position to ensure the safe and reliable transaction through digital landscape and need to build the trust among the general public through demonstration on the use of the digital currency (S. Adgaonkar, 2022). The primary responsibility of the Government is to make the public to understand the risk associated with the digital currency in order to build the trust (Haque & Shoaib, 2023). Disseminating the quality of information has significant relationship with trust and it increases the level of e-government acceptance (Hutahaean et al, 2023). Thus, the study needs to test the relationship between disseminating the information and trust, the hypothesis was formulated as follows:

H5: There is a positive relationship between DI and TST.

Responsibility (RES) and Translucency (TRN) With Trust (TST)

The accountability of the government is to provide adequate information transparently and building long-standing trust with the public. Moreover, self-responsibility of the people to follow the guideless given by the RBI confirms the successful implementation of new plans or schemes (Kaur, 2019). The relationship of customer and corporate is to be strengthened by transparency (Waddock, 2004). Medina and Rufín (2015) highlighted that building the trust with customers is possible only through consistent transparency and it makes the customer to be loyal and responsible to the product. Behavioural intention of the customers is positively associated with transparency which paves a way for trust (Zhou et al., 2018). The study conducted by Kim and Kim (2016) found significantly positive relationship between overall trust of the customers and transparency. Therefore, hypothesis was developed to analyse the role of social media in sharing the transparent information, trust and responsibility of the youth population.

H6: There is a positive relationship between RES and TST.

Liability (LIB) With Trust (TST)

Liability is a kind of state in which people are responsible towards the plan or scheme or technology implemented by the government (Kaur, 2019). Previous studies emphasized that when customers are satisfied, they themselves build the bonding with the product & services and it ensure the loyalty of the customers towards the particular branded product (Hyun, 2010). Similarly, digital currency and its usages have to be explained clearly to the general public and youth population which creates the responsibility among the youngsters with complete trust. Hence, hypothesis was formulated to check the relationship between liability and trust.

H7: There is a positive relationship between LIB and TST.

Translucency (TRN) With Trust (TST)

The primary work of the government is to make the citizens to know the available information about the e-government. Naturally, the transparency has the power to influence the people and to build the trust among them (Hutahaean et al., 2023). Transparency is a conservative issue, it has to be implemented to build the trust among the people on e-government (Hung et al., 2020). And, also Gainey and Klaas (2003) have witnessed the positive relationship among the customer satisfaction, trust and transparency. Satisfaction had mediating role in connecting the trust and translucency. Thus, to check with present research context the hypothesis was formulated as follows:

H8: There is a positive relationship between TRN and TST.

Perceived Ease of Use (PEU) With Perceived Usefulness (PUS)

Perceived ease of use is a primary factor which shows that the degree to which users of the technology feels ease and consistency on the same reflects as a usefulness to the users (Davis, 1989). Perceived ease of use has significant positive relationship and it makes the possibility on achieving the perceived usefulness (Hutahaean et al., 2023). Youth population connected with social media predominantly and RBI can obtain its goal if the government use social media as a mediating factor to disseminate information with regard to digital currency and its benefits. Existing studies were witnessed on the positive association between perceived ease of use and perceived usefulness (Samuel, 2018). Therefore, the presented study has coined a hypothesis to test the relationship between these two variables.

H9: There is a positive relationship between PEU and PUS.

Trust (TST) With Intention (INT)

The major intention of the public and youth population with regard to digital currency is perceived usefulness. Trust can be built upon either directly or indirectly when PUS increases gradually (Kaur, 2019). Trust plays a primary role in converting the other variables such as intention, reliability towards the acceptance of e-government (Hutahaean et al., 2023). The intention of the government is quite clear in bringing the digital currency in to the market which strengthen the digital economy and improve the reputation of the country in the global economic context. Similarly, understanding the intention of the youth population on the digital currency facilitates on restructuring the promotional practices of the digital currency by the government. Trust and intentions are interconnected, each variable has significantly associated with one another (Samuel, 2018). Hence, the study formulated a hypothesis to test further and also to understand how far trust and intentions are associated each other to increase the acceptance level of digital currency.

H10: There is a positive relationship between TST and INT.

Figure 1. Proposed research model

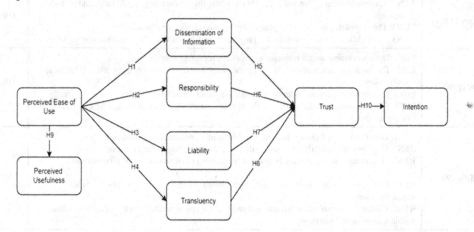

Research Model

Researchers developed the following conceptual framework for the current study by considering the results from the earlier-mentioned literature reviews and hypotheses. Perceived Ease of Use is shown in Figure 1 to be an independent variable that indirectly influences the intention to use digital currency. This model also builds relationship between Perceived Ease of Use (PEU), Perceived Usefulness (PUS), Dissemination of Information (DI), Responsibility (RES), Liability (LIB), Translucency (TRN), Trust (TST) and Intention to use (INT)

Table 1. Origin of construct: Intention to use digital currency

Factors	Items	Source
Dissemination of Information (DI)	DI1: Government will use social media to disseminate accurate information regarding 'digital currency'. DI2: Government will ensure that the information about 'digital rupees' shared through social media is kept up-to-date. DI3: I have confidence in the government's ability to provide information about 'digital currency' on social media that aligns with my specific needs. DI4: Government will share pertinent information about 'digital currency'. DI5: Government will provide easily comprehensible information about 'digital currency'.	(Khan et al., 2021)
Perceived Ease of Use (PEU)	PEU1: The chance of usability of digital currency is high. PEU2: Digital currency is easily grasped and understood. PEU3: User-friendly platforms are available for digital currency transactions.	(Venkatesh et al., 2012)
Perceived Usefulness (PUS)	PUS1: The utilization of social media for digital currency services can enhance the quality of the service. PUS2: Utilizing social media is enhancing my effectiveness in regards to e-rupee. PUS3: Leveraging social media can enhance my performance in exchanging information about digital currency. PUS4: Overall, I find it beneficial to access information about digital currency through social media.	(Khan et al., 2021)
Translucency (TRN)	TRN1: The government's plan and program regarding digital currency would be executed with transparency. TRN2: The complete process of the plan and program is transparently revealed. TRN3: The public can easily observe the progress and status of the administration of e-rupee.	(Hartanto et al., 2021)
Liability (LIB)	LIB1: The government would maintain a consistent reporting system. LIB2: The implementation of e-currency by the government would reflects its acknowledgment of responsibility. LIB3: The government would adhere to regulations at all times when implementing e-currency. LIB4: The government would guarantee the appropriate allocation of its budget for e-currency implementation.	(Hartanto et al., 2021)
Responsibility (RES)	RES1: Government pays close attention to public sentiments regarding e-currency. RES2: Government promptly addresses public requirements concerning e-rupee. RES3: Government would genuinely commit to assisting citizens in need of e-rupee-related support. RES4: Government would efficiently offer high-quality solutions to meet public demands regarding e-rupee. RES5: Citizens' requests to the government regarding e-rupee would be appropriately handled within a reasonable timeframe.	(Hartanto et al., 2021)
Trust (TST)	TST1: I have confidence in the reliability of this e-rupee. TST2: This e-rupee would be a dependable means for conducting public services. TST3: When it comes to performing public services, this e-rupee instils trust.	(Gefen et al., 2003)
Intention to use	INT1: Every time I have e-rupee access, I have the intention to utilize it. INT2: I anticipate utilizing e-rupee in the future. INT3: I have the intention to recommend e-rupee to others.	(Shankar & Datta, 2018)

Measurement

In this study, we conducted a review of existing literature to explore the adoption of digital currency in India. Based on our findings, we created a questionnaire. To evaluate the perceived ease of use (PEU), we included five items derived from Venkatesh et al. (2012b), which assess the convenience of public digital currency services. The construct of perceived usefulness (PUS) comprised four items sourced from (Khan et al., 2021). Similarly, the construct of Dissemination of Information (DI) included three items taken from (Khan et al., 2021). The constructs of Responsibility (RES), Liability (LIB), and Translucency (TRN) consisted of five, four, and three items, respectively, adopted from (Hartanto et al., 2021). For the Trust construct, three items were included from Gefen et al. (2003), while the items for the intention to use digital currency were adopted from Shankar & Datta (2018). Therefore, this research utilized established items from previous studies. The questionnaire development utilized five-point Likert scales, and each factor consisted of three to five items, as per the relevant literature. The construct measurement items are presented in Table 1.

Data Collection and Analysis

The data collection method employed in this study was judgmental sampling, which was chosen due to its simplicity, practicality, and affordability. Internet surveys, which offer various question types and require minimal human interaction, were used as they are typically cost-effective. Prior to conducting the research, pilot studies were conducted to enhance the reliability of the survey. Participants in the study consisted of young individuals aged 15 to 29 from different Indian states (*Youth_in_India_2022*, n.d.). The research was meticulously planned and executed over a period of four months using judgmental sampling, resulting in the collection of 361 responses, of which 337 were considered relevant for the study.

To validate the framework and examine the relationships between different factors, SmartPLS 3.0 software was utilized. This software facilitated data analysis and contributed to the overall improvement of the research outcomes. Structural equation modeling (SEM), which incorporates factor analysis and path estimation, was employed to understand and explore the various factors. The PLS-SEM method was specifically chosen for this investigation because it can handle small sample sizes and uncommon data, without assuming a specific data distribution. Previous studies by Hair et al. (2017) have supported the use of PLS-SEM in such cases. Since the PLS-SEM technique enables the inclusion of formative measures, which are helpful for understanding the link between a concept and its observable effects, it was used to produce important estimates.

Research Model Assessment and Results

Model Assessment

The model was evaluated using the PLS-SEM approach. In line with Truong and McColl's (2011) recommendation, all identified items exhibited factor loadings exceeding 0.50, validating the retention of the entire model for further analysis. To assess reliability, Cronbach's alpha value, denoting the consistency of study outcomes, was utilized. The relevant data is presented in Table 2, indicating good and sufficient reliability of survey responses. This is supported by Cronbach's alpha values for all variables surpassing 0.7, with the majority exceeding 0.8 (Narula et al., 2020).

Table 2. Results of the measurement model

Construct and Items	Indicator Loading	Cronbach's Alpha	rho_A	Composite Reliability	Average Variance Extracted (AVE)
Liability (LIB)					
LIB1	0.812				
LIB2	0.789	0.862	0.864	0.907	0.709
LIB3	0.875				
LIB4	0.889				
Intention to Use (INT)					
INT1	0.861				
INT2	0.871	0.881	0.892	0.918	0.736
INT3	0.841				
INT4	0.858				
Dissemination of Information (DI)					
DI1	0.864				
DI2	0.865				
DI3	0.842	0.765	0.765	0.865	0.680
DI4	0.859				
DI5	0.814				
Perceived Ease of Use (PEUS)					
PEUS1	0.815				
PEUS2	0.831	0.849	0.861	0.898	0.688
PEUS3	0.828				
Perceived Usefulness (PUS)					
PUS1	0.826				
PUS2	0.851	0.903	0.908	0.928	0.721
PUS3	0.864				
PUS4	0.774				
Responsibility (RES)					
RES1	0.787				
RES2	0.832				
RES3	0.833	0.889	0.893	0.919	0.693
RES4	0.845				
RES5	0.864				
Trust (TST)					
TST1	0.862				
TST2	0.773	0.818	0.819	0.892	0.733
TST3	0.820				
TST4	0.790				
Translucency (TRN)					
TR1	0.850				
TR2	0.854	0.828	0.834	0.885	0.659
TR3	0.865				

Source: Authors Calculation

Convergent validity was evaluated using the Average Variance Explained (AVE) and Composite Reliability measures. Each construct's metrics were required to meet certain standards, including a minimum AVE threshold score of 0.50 (Sarstedt et al., . 2021).Discriminant validity was assessed using the Fornell-Larcker criterion (FLC) and the Heterotrait-Monotrait ratio (HTMT). According to the Fornell-Larcker condition, the AVE values and their square roots should exceed the correlation values with other factors. Kline, (2010) recommend that the HTMT ratio figures be below 0.85 and can be considered up to 0.90. In Table 4, the connection scores of each dimension were found to be less than 0.90. The results of the FLC and HTMT validations were presented in Table 3 and 4 accordingly.

Table 3. Discriminant validity: Fornell-Larcker criterion

	1	2	3	4	5	6	7	8
Accountability (1)	0.842							
Intention (2)	0.611	0.858						
Perceived Ease of Use (3)	0.592	0.531	0.825					
Perceived Usefulness (4)	0.471	0.429	0.696	0.829				
Quality info (5)	0.52	0.453	0.771	0.663	0.849			
Responsibility (6)	0.871	0.691	0.616	0.466	0.575	0.833		
Transparency (7)	0.658	0.683	0.601	0.587	0.554	0.681	0.856	
Trust (8)	0.754	0.475	0.604	0.555	0.536	0.658	0.526	0.812

Table 4. Discriminant validity: Heterotrait monotrait ratio (HTMT)

	1	2	3	4	5	6	7	8
Accountability (1)								
Intention (2)	0.698							
Perceived Ease of Use (3)	0.727	0.644						
Perceived Usefulness (4)	0.544	0.494	0.854					
Quality info (5)	0.589	0.501	0.920	0.758				
Responsibility (6)	0.990	0.776	0.745	0.527	0.631			
Transparency (7)	0.780	0.804	0.759	0.701	0.643	0.792		
Trust (8)	0.889	0.540	0.750	0.656	0.613	0.758	0.631	

Source: Authors Calculation

Structural Model Assessment

Once the validity and reliability of the model were evaluated, the correlation between the factors comprising Perceived Ease of Use (PEU), Perceived Usefulness (PUS), Dissemination of Information (DI), Responsibility (RES), Liability (LIB), Translucency (TRN), Trust (TST), and Intention to Use (INT) was determined by calculating the coefficient of the multiple regression equation. The variance inflation factor (VIF) was used to assess the correlation strength among the exogenous variables in the regression analysis. To ensure the reliability of the regression results, the VIF values were examined, with a value below 3 indicating no multicollinearity issues (Kock & Lynn, 2012). In the current study, the VIF values ranged from 1.782 to 2.879, satisfying the threshold limit of 3.33 (Diamantopoulos & Siguaw, 2006). Hence, it can be affirmed that there are no issues of collinearity. Following the evaluation of VIF, an analysis of path coefficients was conducted. Within the PLS-SEM approach, the bootstrapping technique was employed to test the hypotheses within a structural model. This method allowed for the determination of the significance of path coefficients and the estimation of confidence intervals. Moreover, the regression value (R^2) was calculated for each regression equation in the structural equation model. The R^2 value measures the degree to which the independent variables explain the variability in each endogenous construct, serving as an indicator of the model's predictive capability. The utilization of the bootstrapping method was extensive in PLS-SEM to investigate the hypotheses, assess the significance of path coefficients, and establish confidence intervals. Consequently, the regression values (R^2) were computed to evaluate the variances in each exogenous variable and assess the predictive capacity of the model.

Figure 2. Path coefficient

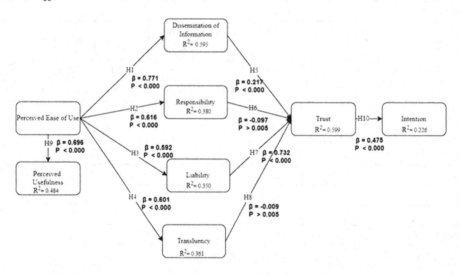

The proposed research model was assessed through the hypotheses, and the results were presented in Table 5 and Figure 2. The table results indicate that the model possesses high predictive power, as evidenced by R^2 values exceeding 0.20 (Table 4). In the field of behavioral sciences, an R^2 value of 0.20 or above is considered high. The R^2 values for Perceived Usefulness (PUS), Dissemination of Information (DI), Responsibility (RES), Liability (LIB), Translucency (TRN), Trust (TST), and Intention to Use (INT) were found to satisfy this criterion (Rasoolimanesh et al., 2017). Statistical analysis confirmed that the primary data supported all eleven hypotheses (H1 to H10).

Table 5. R^2 of the dependent variables

Construct	R Square (R^2)
Liability (LIB)	0.350
Intention to Use (INT)	0.226
Perceived Usefulness (PUS)	0.484
Dissemination of Information (DI)	0.595
Responsibility (RES)	0.380
Translucency (TRN)	0.361
Trust (TST)	0.599

*Table 6. Hypotheses-testing (significant at * $p \leq 0.01$)*

Hypotheses	Relationship	Path	t-Values	p-Values	Result
H1	PEUS -> DI	0.771	30.163	0.000	Accepted
H2	PEUS -> RES	0.616	10.795	0.000	Accepted
H3	PEUS -> LIB	0.592	10.892	0.000	Accepted
H4	PEUS -> TRN	0.601	12.083	0.000	Accepted
H5	DI -> TST	0.217	4.318	0.000	Accepted
H6	RES -> TST	-0.097	0.91	0.363	Rejected
H7	LIB -> TST	0.732	8.026	0.000	Accepted
H8	TRN -> TST	-0.009	0.14	0.889	Rejected
H9	PEUS -> PUS	0.696	21.816	0.000	Accepted
H10	TST -> INT	0.475	10.869	0.000	Accepted

The initial hypothesis demonstrates a connection between PEUS and DI, indicating that perceived ease of use significantly influences the dissemination of information about digital currency on social media; thereby supporting H1. The second hypothesis establishes the relationship between PEUS and RES, indicating that perceived ease of use positively influences citizen perception towards the government's digital currency initiative. This suggests that citizens believe the government will consider public suggestions and expectations for digital currency services, thereby accepting H2. The third hypothesis explores the association between PEUS and LIB, indicating that when individuals perceive the system as convenient and flexible, it fosters a belief among young people that the government will be accountable for its actions and decisions regarding the digital currency initiative. Consequently, H3 is accepted. Hypothesis four highlights the correlation between PEUS and TRN, revealing that when the system is easy to use without constraints, young people believe that the government's information, procedures, and policies regarding digital currency will be transparent to the nation's citizens. Thus, H4 is supported. The fifth hypothesis uncovers the relationship between DI and TST, indicating that when the government shares quality information about digital currency on social media, it generates trust among young people in the government's services and initiatives. Therefore, H5 can be accepted. The sixth hypothesis suggests the association between RES and TST, but the results show that the government's responsibility does not influence the trustworthiness of young people. Hence, H6 is rejected. The seventh hypothesis identifies the relationship between LIB and TST, revealing that the government's accountability for its decisions and actions cultivates trust among young people, prompting them to prefer the digital currency initiative. Therefore, H7 is supported. The next hypothesis, H8, discusses the relationship between TRN and TST, but the results indicate that the transparency of the government does not influence trust among young people regarding the digital currency initiative. Hence, H8 is rejected.H9 examines the relationship between PEUS and PUS, finding that perceived ease of use influences perceived usefulness. Thus, H9 is supported. Finally, the tenth hypothesis reveals the association between TST and INT, demonstrating that when the government builds trust among young people, they develop an intention to use the digital currency service. This suggests that young people trust the government in terms of information on social media, transparency, responsibility, and more, leading to their intention to use digital currency. Hence, H10 is supported. The research study employed the bootstrapping method to test the effects, using 5000 repeated samples at a 95 percent confidence level. The goodness of fit in PLS-SEM was assessed through the Standardised Root Mean Square Residual (SRMR) value, which predicts the model's fitness. The threshold limit for the SRMR value is 0.08. In the present study, the obtained SRMR value is 0.072, which is below the threshold level. Therefore, the developed model can be considered good.

Discussion and Conclusions

The primary aim of this study was to examine how young individuals' attitudes and behaviors regarding digital currency are influenced by social media and government initiatives, with a focus on their propensity to adopt it. The research findings offer valuable insights into the factors that impact the acceptance and uptake of digital currency among the youth. This study contributes significantly to the field of technology and digital services by being the first of its kind to explore the intention of young people in India to utilize digital currency. It utilizes a unique model to assess their acceptance of this initiative, making it a benchmark for future research on digital currency, particularly in countries with a sizable young population and high technology usage. Additionally, the study adopts the PEUS model as an independent construct to measure young individuals' intention to adopt digital currency, a methodology validated by previous studies. The results emphasize the significance of system flexibility, convenience, information dissemination, and responsibility in influencing acceptance. Confirmatory factor analysis and structural equation modeling using PLS-SEM were employed as the analytical approaches in this study. These methods have gained broad acceptance among academics, scholars, and students due to their accurate results and reliable reporting. Therefore, researchers can refer to this study when planning to write research articles using similar methodologies. Furthermore, the research findings highlight the substantial impact of government actions on young individuals' inclination to embrace digital currency. Government policies, regulations, and official endorsements play a crucial role in building trust and reliability in digital currencies. The study reveals that when the government demonstrates support and creates a favorable environment for acceptance, young people's intentions are significantly influenced, and their confidence in using digital currencies increases. As a result, policymakers should prioritize implementing measures that support and encourage youth engagement with digital currencies.

In conclusion, this study underscores the significant influence of social media and government initiatives on shaping young people's inclination to adopt digital currency. The results emphasize the value of social media platforms as tools for endorsing digital currencies and raising awareness among the youth. Additionally, government support, policies, and endorsements play a vital role in establishing trust and confidence in digital currencies, thereby influencing the willingness of young individuals to embrace them.

Theoretical and Managerial implications

The significance of social media in shaping the intentions of young individuals towards embracing digital currency is underscored by the research article. This finding expands the body of knowledge on technology adoption by highlighting the important role social media platforms play in helping young people accept and use digital currency. The study highlights the significance of government measures in influencing young people's intentions about the adoption of digital currency. The study deepens our understanding of how policy interventions might influence attitudes and behaviours towards developing financial technology by analysing the effects of governmental initiatives. By incorporating several constructs, including social media, governmental activities, and youth intention towards digital currency, the article adds to theoretical knowledge. This integration provides a thorough understanding of the elements that influence the adoption of digital money and lays the groundwork for future studies on technology adoption and innovation.

The findings suggest that in order to encourage the younger generation to accept digital currencies, organisations and policymakers must actively engage with social media platforms. They can efficiently disseminate information, respond to concerns, and establish trust with young people by creating a strong online presence and utilising social media platforms, which will encourage favourable attitudes towards the use of digital currency. To build an atmosphere that encourages the adoption of digital currencies, governmental organisations and regulatory bodies should work with technology firms and financial institutions. Policymakers can promote youth engagement while resolving regulatory and security issues through collaborations and efforts centred on user-friendly digital currency solutions.

In summary, the research report reveals important findings regarding the variables influencing young people's propensity to accept digital currency. It provides theoretical and practical implications that can influence future research and help with the creation of tactics to promote the use of digital money among the younger generation.

Limitations and Future Research

Due to potential sample bias and the study's exclusive focus on youngsters, the findings may not be applicable to all age groups or demographics. Due to response bias and social desirability bias, where participants may not always offer correct information or may alter their responses to fit to societal standards, the study's dependence on self-reported data obtained through surveys or interviews presents this risk.The study is constrained in its capacity to establish causal links and acquire insights into the changing nature of young people's opinions towards digital currency over time because it used a cross-sectional design and only collected data at one moment in time. Although the research emphasises how social media and government initiatives influence young people's attitudes towards digital currency, other important factors like education, financial literacy, and peer pressure are not adequately addressed, which restricts our ability to fully understand the perspectives of young people. One can look into the long-term changes in young people's attitudes towards digital money by performing longitudinal studies. This approach would provide a clearer picture of youth behaviour and intentions while also providing a deeper knowledge of how attitudes are formed and changed through time.

It would be good to compare different age groups and demographic divisions in order to gain more thorough research of the elements influencing young people's intentions about digital currency. This method would enable researchers to identify distinct generational and cultural influences by examining variations in attitudes and behaviours across various groups. Incorporating qualitative research techniques like in-depth interviews or focus groups would be beneficial to improve the results gained through quantitative procedures. Insightful observations about the underlying motives, experiences, and views of young people regarding digital currency would result from this combination. Researchers can discover subtle characteristics that may be missed by quantitative surveys by digging further into these qualitative features. The understanding of young people's intents towards digital currency would be improved by creating multidimensional frameworks that take a wider range of elements, such as education, financial literacy, peer influence, and cultural norms, into account. This all-encompassing strategy would offer a more holistic perspective of the issues influencing teenage adoption or resistance.

REFERENCES

Abd. Hamida, Razakb, Abu Bakarc. & Abdullah. (2016). The Effects Of Perceived Usefulness And Perceived Ease Of Use On Continuance Intention To Use E-Government. *7th International Economics & Business Management Conference, 35,* 644 – 649.

Adgaonkar, S. (2022). A Study on Advantages and Disadvantages of Digital Currency in India with Special Reference to Rupee. *International Journal of Research Publication and Reviews, 3*(11), 2092–2096.

Agur, I., Ari, A., & Dell'Ariccia, G. (2022). Designing central bank digital currencies. *Journal of Monetary Economics, 125,* 62–79. doi:10.1016/j.jmoneco.2021.05.002

Anthony, N., & Michel, N. (2022). Central Bank Digital Currency: Assessing the Risks and Dispelling the Myths. *Policy Analysis,* 941.

Anuradha, A., Shilpa, R., Thirupathi, M., Padmapriya, S., Supramaniam, G., Booshan, B., & Thangam, D. (2023). Importance of Sustainable Marketing Initiatives for Supporting the Sustainable Development Goals. In *Handbook of Research on Achieving Sustainable Development Goals With Sustainable Marketing* (pp. 149–169). IGI Global. doi:10.4018/978-1-6684-8681-8.ch008

Ayedh, A., Echchabi, A., Battour, M., & Omar, M. (2020). Malaysian Muslim investors' behaviour towards the blockchain-based Bitcoin cryptocurrency market. *Journal of Islamic Marketing, 12*(4), 690–704. doi:10.1108/JIMA-04-2019-0081

Brunnermeier, M. K., James, H., & Landau, J. P. (2019). The digitalization of money (No. w26300). National Bureau of Economic Research.

Chahal, J., & Rani, N. (2022). Exploring the acceptance for e-learning among higher education students in India: Combining technology acceptance model with external variables. *Journal of Computing in Higher Education, 34*(3), 844–867. doi:10.100712528-022-09327-0 PMID:35668837

Chen, L., & Aklikokou, A. K. (2020). Determinants of E-government Adoption: Testing the Mediating Effects of Perceived Usefulness and Perceived Ease of Use. *International Journal of Public Administration, 43*(10), 850–865. doi:10.1080/01900692.2019.1660989

Davis, F. D. (1989). Perceived usefulness, perceived ease of use, and user acceptance of information technology. *Management Information Systems Quarterly, 13*(3), 319–340. doi:10.2307/249008

Diamantopoulos, A., & Siguaw, J. A. (2006). Formative Versus Reflective Indicators in Organizational Measure Development: A Comparison and Empirical Illustration. *British Journal of Management*, *17*(4), 263–282. doi:10.1111/j.1467-8551.2006.00500.x

Farahat, A. (2012). Applying the Technology Acceptance Model to Online Learning in the Egyptian Universities. *Procedia: Social and Behavioral Sciences*, *64*, 95–104. doi:10.1016/j.sbspro.2012.11.012

Gainey, T. W., & Klaas, B. S. (2003). The outsourcing of training and development: Factors impacting client satisfaction. *Journal of Management*, *29*(2), 207–229. doi:10.1177/014920630302900205

Gefen, D., Karahanna, E., & Straub, D. W. (2003). Trust and TAM in online shopping: An integrated model. *Management Information Systems Quarterly*, *27*(1), 51–90. doi:10.2307/30036519

Global Statistics Report. (2023). *India Social Media Statistics 2023 | Most Used Top Platforms – The Global Statistics*. Author.

Goodell, G., Al-Nakib, H. D., & Tasca, P. (2021). A digital currency architecture for privacy and owner-custodianship. *Future Internet*, *13*(5), 130. doi:10.3390/fi13050130

Hair, J. F., Hult, G. T. M., Ringle, C. M., & Sarstedt, M. (2017). A Primer on Partial Least Squares Structural Equation Modeling (PLS-SEM) (2nd ed.). Sage Publications Inc.

Haque, & Shoaib. (2023). The digital currency in India: Challenges and prospects. *Bench Council Transactions on Benchmarks, Standards and Evaluations*, *3*, 10107.

Hartanto, D., Dalle, J., Akrim, A., & Anisah, H. U. (2021). Perceived effectiveness of e-governance as an underlying mechanism between good governance and public trust: A case of Indonesia. *Digital Policy. Regulation & Governance*, *23*(6), 598–616. doi:10.1108/DPRG-03-2021-0046

Hung, S.Y., Chen, K., & Yi-Kuan, S. (2020). The effect of communication and social motives on E-government services through social media groups. *Behaviour and Information Technology*, *39*(7). . do i:10.1080/0144929X.2019.1610907

Hyun, S. (2010). Predictors of Leadership quality and loyalty in the chain restaurant industry. *Cornell Hospitality Quarterly*, *51*(2), 251–267. Advance online publication. doi:10.1177/1938965510363264

Karumban, S., Sanyal, S., Laddunuri, M. M., Sivalinga, V. D., Shanmugam, V., Bose, V., . . . Murugan, S. P. (2023). Industrial Automation and Its Impact on Manufacturing Industries. In Revolutionizing Industrial Automation Through the Convergence of Artificial Intelligence and the Internet of Things (pp. 24-40). IGI Global.

Kaur. (2019). Digital currency and its implications in India. *Money Digital Currency*, 64-67.

Keister, T., & Monnet, C. (2022). Central bank digital currency: Stability and information. *Journal of Economic Dynamics & Control*, *142*, 104501. doi:10.1016/j.jedc.2022.104501

Khan, S., Umer, R., Umer, S., & Naqvi, S. (2021). Antecedents of trust in using social media for E-government services: An empirical study in Pakistan. *Technology in Society*, *64*, 101400. Advance online publication. doi:10.1016/j.techsoc.2020.101400

Kim, S.-B., & Kim, D.-Y. (2016). The impacts of corporate social responsibility, service quality, and transparency on relationship quality and customer loyalty in the hotel industry. *Asian Journal of Sustainability and Social Responsibility, 1*(1), 39–55. doi:10.118641180-016-0004-1

Kline, R. (2010). Principles And Practice Of Structural Equation Modeling. Guilford Press.

Kock, N., & Lynn, G. (2012). Lateral Collinearity and Misleading Results in Variance-Based SEM: An Illustration and Recommendations. *Journal of the Association for Information Systems, 13*(7), 546–580. doi:10.17705/1jais.00302

Kulkarni, A. (2022). *Public perception of the "Digital Rupee" in India*. National College of Ireland.

Kun Wiryanti & Fardinal. (2020). The Effect of Perceived Ease of Use on the Quality of Accounting Information Systems and its Impact on the Quality of Accounting Information. *Saudi Journal of Business and Management Studies*, 571-577.

Ma, Y. J., Gam, H. J., & Banning, J. (2017). Perceived ease of use and usefulness of sustainability labels on apparel products: Application of the technology acceptance model. *Fashion and Textiles, 4*(3), 2–20. doi:10.118640691-017-0093-1

Madnick, S. E., Wang, R. Y., Lee, Y. W., & Zhu, H. (2009). Overview and framework for data and information quality research. *Journal of Data and Information Quality, 1*(1), 1-22.

MarlanHutahaean, JavanisaEunike, & Silalahi. (2023). Do Social Media, Good Governance, and Public Trust Increase Citizens' e-Government Participation? Dual Approach of PLS-SEM and fsQCA. *Human Behavior and Emerging Technologies*, 1–19.

Marmora, P. (2022). Does monetary policy fuel bitcoin demand? Event-study evidence from emerging markets. *Journal of International Financial Markets, Institutions and Money, 77*, 101489. doi:10.1016/j.intfin.2021.101489

Medina, C., & Rufín, R. (2015). Transparency policy and students' satisfaction and trust. *Transforming Government, 9*(3), 309–323. doi:10.1108/TG-07-2014-0027

Murugan, S. P., Shivaprasad, G., Dhanalakshmi, A., Sriram, V. P., Rajput, K., Mahesh, B. N., & Kedla, S. (2023). The Impact of COVID-19 on the Indian Microfinance Industry and Its Sustainability. In *Transforming Economies Through Microfinance in Developing Nations* (pp. 160–188). IGI Global. doi:10.4018/978-1-6684-5647-7.ch009

Narula, S., Shiva, A., & Shahi, S. (2020). *What drives retail investors' investment decisions? Evidence from no mobile phone phobia (Nomophobia) and investor fear of missing out (I-FoMo)*. doi:10.31620/JCCC.06.20/02

Nichols, J., Biros, D., Sharda, R., & Shimp, U. (2012). The Emergence of Organizational Process Liability as a Future Direction for Research on Technology Acceptance. *International Journal of Social and Organizational Dynamics in IT, 2*(4), 1–13. doi:10.4018/ijsodit.2012100101

Park, J. Y., Perumal, S. V., Sanyal, S., Ah Nguyen, B., Ray, S., Krishnan, R., Narasimhaiah, R., & Thangam, D. (2022). Sustainable Marketing Strategies as an Essential Tool of Business. *American Journal of Economics and Sociology, 81*(2), 359–379. doi:10.1111/ajes.12459

Rasoolimanesh, S. M., Roldán, J. L., Jaafar, M., & Ramayah, T. (2017). Factors Influencing Residents' Perceptions toward Tourism Development: Differences across Rural and Urban World Heritage Sites. *Journal of Travel Research*, *56*(6), 760–775. doi:10.1177/0047287516662354

Riquelme, H. E., & Rios, R. E. (2010). The moderating effect of gender in the adoption of mobile banking. *International Journal of Bank Marketing*, *28*(5), 328–341. doi:10.1108/02652321011064872

Sabani, A. (2021). Investigating the influence of transparency on the adoption of e-Government in Indonesia. *Journal of Science and Technology Policy Management*, *12*(2), 236–255. doi:10.1108/JSTPM-03-2020-0046

Samuel, Onasanya, & Olumorin. (2018). Perceived usefulness, ease of use and adequacy of use of mobile technologies by Nigerian university lecturers. *International Journal of Education and Development Using Information and Communication Technology*, *14*(3), 5–16.

San Martín, S., & Camarero, C. (2009). How perceived risk affects online buying. *Online Information Review*, *33*(4), 629–654. doi:10.1108/14684520910985657

Sarstedt, M., Ringle, C. M., & Hair, J. F. (2021). Partial Least Squares Structural Equation Modeling. In *Handbook of Market Research* (pp. 1–47). Springer International Publishing. doi:10.1007/978-3-319-05542-8_15-2

Seth, S. (2021). *Central bank digital currency (CBDC)*. Investopedia. https://www.investopedia.com/terms/c/central-bank-digital-currency-cbdc.asp#citation-10

Shankar, A., & Datta, B. (2018). Factors affecting mobile payment adoption intention: An Indian perspective. *Global Business Review*, *19*(3, suppl), S72–S89. doi:10.1177/0972150918757870

Shanmugam, V., Asha, N., Samanvitha, C., Murthy, L. N., & Thangam, D. (2021). An analysis of bilateral trade between india and korea. *Journal of Contemporary Issues in Business and Government*, *27*(2).

Simona Sternad & SamoBobek. (2013). Impacts of TAM-based external factors on ERP acceptance. *International Conference on Project MANagement / HCIST 2013 - International Conference on Health and Social Care Information Systems and Technologies*, *9*, 33-42.

Sriram, V. P., Sanyal, S., Laddunuri, M. M., Subramanian, M., Bose, V., Booshan, B., . . . Thangam, D. (2023). Enhancing Cybersecurity Through Blockchain Technology. In Handbook of Research on Cybersecurity Issues and Challenges for Business and FinTech Applications (pp. 208-224). IGI Global.

Thangam, D., Arumugam, T., Velusamy, K., Subramanian, M., Ganesan, S. K., & Suryakumar, M. (2022). COVID-19 Pandemic and Its Brunt on Digital Transformation and Cybersecurity. In Cybersecurity Crisis Management and Lessons Learned From the COVID-19 Pandemic (pp. 15-42). IGI Global.

Thangam, D., & Chavadi, C. (2023). Impact of Digital Marketing Practices on Energy Consumption, Climate Change, and Sustainability. *Climate and Energy*, *39*(7), 11–19. doi:10.1002/gas.22329

Thangam, D., Malali, A. B., Subramanian, G., Mohan, S., & Park, J. Y. (2022). Internet of things: a smart technology for healthcare industries. In *Healthcare Systems and Health Informatics* (pp. 3–15). CRC Press.

Thangam, D., Malali, A. B., Subramanian, G., & Park, J. Y. (2022). Transforming Healthcare through Internet of Things. In *Cloud and Fog Computing Platforms for Internet of Things* (pp. 15–24). Chapman and Hall/CRC. doi:10.1201/9781003213888-2

Thangam, D., Malali, A. B., Subramaniyan, G., Mariappan, S., Mohan, S., & Park, J. Y. (2022). Relevance of Artificial Intelligence in Modern Healthcare. In *Integrating AI in IoT Analytics on the Cloud for Healthcare Applications* (pp. 67–88). IGI Global. doi:10.4018/978-1-7998-9132-1.ch005

Thangam, D., Malali, A. B., Subramaniyan, G., Mariappan, S., Mohan, S., & Park, J. Y. (2022). Relevance of Artificial Intelligence in Modern Healthcare. In *Integrating AI in IoT Analytics on the Cloud for Healthcare Applications* (pp. 67–88). IGI Global. doi:10.4018/978-1-7998-9132-1.ch005

Thangam, D., Vaidya, G. R., Subramanian, G., Velusamy, K., Selvi Govindarajan, K., & Park, J. Y. (2022). The Portrayal of Women's Empowerment in Select Indian Movies. *American Journal of Economics and Sociology*, *81*(1), 187–205. doi:10.1111/ajes.12451

Treiblmaier, H., & Sillaber, C. (2021). The impact of blockchain on e-commerce:a framework for salient research topics. *Electronic Commerce Research and Applications*, *48*, 101054. doi:10.1016/j.elerap.2021.101054

Truong, Y., & McColl, R. (2011). Intrinsic motivations, self-esteem, and luxury goods consumption. *Journal of Retailing and Consumer Services*, *18*(6), 555–561. doi:10.1016/j.jretconser.2011.08.004

Venkatesh, V., Thong, J. Y. L., & Xu, X. (2012). Consumer acceptance and use of information technology: Extending the unified theory of acceptance and use of technology. *Management Information Systems Quarterly*, *36*(1), 157–178. doi:10.2307/41410412

Waddock. (2004). Creating Corporate Accountability: Foundational Principles to Make Corporate Citizenship Real. *Journal of Business Ethics, 50*(4), 313-327.

Wüst, K., Kostiainen, K., Delius, N., & Capkun, S. (2022, November). Platypus: A Central Bank Digital Currency with Unlinkable Transactions and Privacy-Preserving Regulation. In *Proceedings of the 2022 ACM SIGSAC Conference on Computer and Communications Security* (pp. 2947-2960). 10.1145/3548606.3560617

Xie, J., Ye, L., Huang, W., & Ye, M. (2021). Understanding FinTech platform adoption: Impacts of perceived value and perceived risk. *Journal of Theoretical and Applied Electronic Commerce Research*, *16*(5), 1893–1911. doi:10.3390/jtaer16050106

Yi, G., Zainuddin, N. M. M., & Bt Abu Bakar, N. A. (2021). Conceptual model on internet banking acceptance in China with social network influence. *Int. J. Inf. Vis.*, *5*(2), 177–186. doi:10.30630/joiv.5.2.403

Youth in India. (2022). *4*th *issue*. Ministry of Statistics and Programme Implementation.

Zhou, L., Wang, W., Xu, J. D., Liu, T., & Gu, J. (2018, November). Perceived Information Transparency in B2C e-commerce: An Empirical Investigation. *Information & Management*, *55*(7), 912–927. Advance online publication. doi:10.1016/j.im.2018.04.005

Compilation of References

AAP. (2018). Scott Morrison tells students striking over climate change to be 'less activist'. *The Guardian.*

Abaido, G. M. (2020). Cyberbullying on social media platforms among university students in the United Arab Emirates. *International Journal of Adolescence and Youth*, 25(1), 407–420. doi:10.1080/02673843.2019.1669059

Abbas, A. F., Jusoh, A., Mas'od, A., Alsharif, A. H., & Ali, J. (2022). Bibliometrix analysis of information sharing in social media. In Cogent Business and Management (Vol. 9, Issue 1). doi:10.1080/23311975.2021.2016556

Abd. Hamida, Razakb, Abu Bakarc. & Abdullah. (2016). The Effects Of Perceived Usefulness And Perceived Ease Of Use On Continuance Intention To Use E-Government. *7th International Economics & Business Management Conference*, 35, 644 – 649.

Abidin, C. (2021). From "networked publics" to "refracted publics": A companion framework for researching "below the radar" studies. *Social Media + Society*, 7(1), 2056305120984458. doi:10.1177/2056305120984458

Abi-Jaoude, E., Naylor, K. T., & Pignatiello, A. (2020). Smartphones, social media use and youth mental health. *Canadian Medical Association Journal*, 192(6), E136–E141. doi:10.1503/cmaj.190434 PMID:32041697

Abu Elnasr, E. (2022). Social Media Use in E-Learning amid COVID 19 Pandemic: Indian Students' Perspective. *International Journal of Environmental Research and Public Health*, 19(9), 5380. doi:10.3390/ijerph19095380 PMID:35564771

Abu-Shanab, E., & Alsmadi, N. (2019, March). Blogs as an Effective Social Media Tool in Education. In *Society for Information Technology & Teacher Education International Conference* (pp. 367-373). Association for the Advancement of Computing in Education (AACE).

Adgaonkar, S. (2022). A Study on Advantages and Disadvantages of Digital Currency in India with Special Reference to Rupee. *International Journal of Research Publication and Reviews*, 3(11), 2092–2096.

Agboola, A. (2006). *Information and communication technology (ICT) in banking operations in Nigeria: An evaluation of recent experiences.* Academic Press.

Agnihotri, D., Kulshreshtha, K., & Tripathi, V. (2022). Emergence of social media as new normal during COVID-19 pandemic: A study on innovative complaint handling procedures in the context of banking industry. *International Journal of Innovation Science*, 14(3/4), 405–427. doi:10.1108/IJIS-10-2020-0199

Agur, I., Ari, A., & Dell'Ariccia, G. (2022). Designing central bank digital currencies. *Journal of Monetary Economics*, 125, 62–79. doi:10.1016/j.jmoneco.2021.05.002

Ahmad, M., & Khiyal, M. S. H. (2023). Assessment of land administration in Pakistan and the potential role of volunteered geographic information. In Handbook of Research on Driving Socioeconomic Development With Big Data. doi:10.4018/978-1-6684-5959-1.ch014

Ahmad, M., Khayal, M. S. H., & Tahir, A. (2022). Analysis of Factors Affecting Adoption of Volunteered Geographic Information in the Context of National Spatial Data Infrastructure. *ISPRS International Journal of Geo-Information*, *11*(2), 120. Advance online publication. doi:10.3390/ijgi11020120

Ahmad, T. (2019). Law and Policy Relating to Bank Fraud and its Prevention and Control. *Int'l JL Mgmt. & Human.*, *2*, 7.

Ahmed, S., & Kumar, D. (2019, March). The influence of Social media in Education system: The Case of Digital India. *International Journal of Research in Advent Technology*, (Special Issue), 175–179.

Aishwarya, S., & Millath, M.A. (2019) Effectiveness of online marketing and hedonism among university students in Singapore. *International Journal of Recent Technology and Engineering*, *8*(2), 727–734.

Akhmetzyanova, A. I. (2016). The Theoretical Analysis of the Phenomenon of Anticipation in Psychology. *International Journal of Environmental and Science Education*, *11*(7), 1559–1570.

Akhmetzyanova, A. I., Artemyeva, T. V., Nigmatullina, I. A., & Tvardovskaya, A. A. (2017). Anticipation in the Structure of Psychological Mechanisms of Deviance: Analytical Research. *Man in India*, *97*(14), 251–265.

Akimova, E., Korshunova, N., Fedorov, A., Shatayeva, O., & Shipkova, O. (2021). New challenges in changing times: the digital educational support for financial literacy education. *SHS Web of Conferences, 98*, 05020. 10.1051hsconf/20219805020

Alamri, M. M., Almaiah, M. A., & Al-Rahmi, W. M. (2020). Social media applications afecting students' academic performance: A model developed for sustainability in higher education. *Sustainability (Basel)*, *12*(16), 6471. doi:10.3390u12166471

Alawadhi, N. (2021). *India asks WhatsApp to withdraw new privacy policy, answer 14 questions*. Business Standard. https://www.business-standard.com/article/current-affairs/india-asks-WhatsApp-to-withdraw-new-privacy-policy-answer-14-questions-121011900741_1.html

Alawadhi, N. (n.d.). *Govt again asks WhatsApp to take back its contentious privacy policy update*. Business Standard. https://www.business-standard.com/article/technology/india-directs-WhatsApp-for-withdrawal-of-its-revised-privacy-policy-121051900594_1.html

Alawode, A. J., & Kaka, E. U. (2011). Information and communication technology (ICT) and banking industry. *Mediterranean Journal of Social Sciences*, *2*(4), 71–74.

Al-Azawei, A. (2019). What Drives Successful Social Media in Education and E-Learning? A Comparative Study on Facebook and Moodle. *Journal of Information Technology Education*, *18*, 18. doi:10.28945/4360

Alcaide Muñoz, L., Rodríguez Bolívar, M. P., & López Hernández, A. M. (2017). Transparency in governments: A meta-analytic review of incentives for digital versus hard-copy public financial disclosures. *American Review of Public Administration*, *47*(5), 550–573. doi:10.1177/0275074016629008

Al-Dmour, H., Masa'deh, R. E., Salman, A., Abuhashesh, M., & Al-Dmour, R. (2020). Influence of social media platforms on public health protection against the COVID-19 pandemic via the mediating effects of public health awareness and behavioral changes: Integrated model. *Journal of Medical Internet Research*, *22*(8), e19996. doi:10.2196/19996 PMID:32750004

Alguliyev, R., Aliguliyev, R., & Yusifov, F. (2018). Role of social networks in E-government: Risks and security threats. *Online Journal of Communication and Media Technologies*, *8*(4), 363–376.

Ali, A., & Imran, M. (2020). The Evolution of National Spatial Data Infrastructure in Pakistan-Implementation Challenges and the Way Forward. *International Journal of Spatial Data Infrastructures Research*, *15*(0).

Ali, A., Imran, M., Jabeen, M., Ali, Z., & Mahmood, S. A. (2021). Factors influencing integrated information management: Spatial data infrastructure in Pakistan. *Information Development*. Advance online publication. doi:10.1177/02666669211048483

Allam, A. A., AbuAli, A. N., Ghabban, F. M., Ameerbakhsh, O., Alfadli, I. M., & Alraddadi, A. S. (2021). Citizens satisfaction with E-Government mobile services and M-Health application during the COVID-19 pandemic in Al-Madinah Region. *Journal of Service Science and Management, 14*(6), 636–650. doi:10.4236/jssm.2021.146040

Alles, P., Rohanachandra, Y., Amarakoon, L., & Prathapan, S. (2021). Psychological distress, challenges and perceived needs among doctors and nurses during the COVID-19 pandemic, in a tertiary care hospital in Sri Lanka. *Sri Lanka Journal of Psychiatry, 12*(1), 4–10. doi:10.4038ljpsyc.v12i1.8279

Almeida, F., & Costa, O. (2023). Perspectives on financial literacy in undergraduate students. *Journal of Education for Business, 98*(1), 1–8. doi:10.1080/08832323.2021.2005513

Almeida, F., Santos, J. D., & Monteiro, J. A. (2020). The challenges and opportunities in the digitalization of companies in a post-COVID-19 World. *IEEE Engineering Management Review, 48*(3), 97–103. doi:10.1109/EMR.2020.3013206

Alston, M. (2020). *Research for social workers: An introduction to methods*. Routledge. doi:10.4324/9781003117094

Alter, C., Haynes, S., & Worland, J. 2019. Greta Thunberg: TIME's Person of the Year 2019. *Time Magazine*.

Amarullah, A. H., Runturambi, A. J. S., & Widiawan, B. (2021, June). Analyzing cyber crimes during Covid-19 time in Indonesia. In *2021 3rd International Conference on Computer Communication and the Internet (ICCCI)* (pp. 78-83). IEEE. 10.1109/ICCCI51764.2021.9486775

Ananda, F. (2022). Facilitate the Community, Disdukcapil Launches the Automated Dukcapil Pavilion Machine (ADM) in Jayapura City. *Tribunnews*. https://bit.ly/3NOAASM

Andreou, P. C., & Anyfantaki, S. (2021). Financial literacy and its influence on internet banking behavior. *European Management Journal, 39*(5), 658–674. doi:10.1016/j.emj.2020.12.001

Anggraeni. (2015). Implementation of E-Government at the District Level: A Case Study of Pelalawan District, Riau. *Jurnal Sistem Informasi, 7*(2). https://doi.org/ doi:10.36706/jsi.v7i2.2269

Anggraeny, C. (2013). Health Service Innovation in Improving Service Quality at the Jagir Health Center, Surabaya City. *Kebijakan dan Manajemen Publik, 1*(1), 85–93. http://journal.unair.ac.id/filerPDF/11%20Cindy_KMP%20V1%20N1%20Jan-April%202013.pdf. Accessed 05 April 2022.

Ani, P. (2023). *Worldwide Digital Population 2023*. Statista. https://www.statista.com/statistics/617136/digital-population-worldwide/

Anindita, B. (2016). Social Media and Education Sector: Enriching Relationship. *Commentary-4 Global Media Journal–Indian Edition Sponsored by the University of Calcutta, 7*(1). https://www.caluniv.ac.in/global-mdia-journal/COMMENT-2016-NOV/C4.pdf

Anisa, H. N. (2019). *Implementation of Three In One (3 In 1) Services in Population Administration Services of Karanganyar Regency*. Skripsi, Universitas Negeri Semarang. http://lib.unnes.ac.id/38869/1/3301415043.pdf

Ansari, J. A. N., & Khan, N. A. (2020). Exploring the role of social media in collaborative learning the new domain of learning. *Smart Learn. Environ., 7*(1), 9. doi:10.118640561-020-00118-7

Anthony, N., & Michel, N. (2022). Central Bank Digital Currency: Assessing the Risks and Dispelling the Myths. *Policy Analysis*, 941.

Anuradha, A., Shilpa, R., Thirupathi, M., Padmapriya, S., Supramaniam, G., Booshan, B., & Thangam, D. (2023). Importance of Sustainable Marketing Initiatives for Supporting the Sustainable Development Goals. In *Handbook of Research on Achieving Sustainable Development Goals With Sustainable Marketing* (pp. 149–169). IGI Global. doi:10.4018/978-1-6684-8681-8.ch008

Appel, G., Grewal, L., Hadi, R., & Stephen, A. T. (2020). The future of social media in marketing. *Journal of the Academy of Marketing Science, 48*(1), 79–95. doi:10.100711747-019-00695-1 PMID:32431463

Aragón, M. E., López-Monroy, A. P., González, L. C., & Montes-y-Gómez, M. (2020). *Attention to emotions: detecting mental disorders in social media.* Paper presented at the Text, Speech, and Dialogue: 23rd International Conference, TSD 2020, Brno, Czech Republic. 10.1007/978-3-030-58323-1_25

Aral, S., Dellarocas, C., & Godes, D. (2013). Introduction to the special issue social media and business transformation: A framework for research. *Information Systems Research, 24*(1), 3–13. doi:10.1287/isre.1120.0470

Argüelles, A. J., Cortés, H. D., Ramirez, O. E. P., & Bustamante, O. A. (2021). Technological Spotlights of Digital Transformation: Uses and Implications Under COVID-19 Conditions. In Information Technology Trends for a Global and Interdisciplinary Research Community (pp. 19-49). IGI Global.

Arora, N., Rana, M., & Prashar, S. (2023). How Does Social Media Impact Consumers' Sustainable Purchase Intention? *Review of Marketing Science.* doi:10.1515/roms-2022-0072

Arumugam, T., Latha Lavanya, B., Karthik, V., Velusamy, K., Kommuri, U. K., & Panneerselvam, D. (2022). Portraying Women in Advertisements: An Analogy Between Past and Present. *American Journal of Economics and Sociology, 81*(1), 207–223. doi:10.1111/ajes.12452

Arumugam, T., Sethu, S., Kalyani, V., Shahul Hameed, S., & Divakar, P. (2022). Representing Women Entrepreneurs in Tamil Movies. *American Journal of Economics and Sociology, 81*(1), 115–125. doi:10.1111/ajes.12446

Asghar, M. Z., Iqbal, A., Seitamaa-Hakkarainen, P., & Barbera, E. (2021). Breaching learners' social distancing through social media during the covid-19 pandemic. *International Journal of Environmental Research and Public Health, 18*(21), 11012. Advance online publication. doi:10.3390/ijerph182111012 PMID:34769534

Ashktorab, Z., Brown, C., Nandi, M., & Culotta, A. (2014). Tweedr: Mining twitter to inform disaster response. *ISCRAM 2014 Conference Proceedings - 11th International Conference on Information Systems for Crisis Response and Management.*

Askar, M., Aboutabl, A. E., & Galal, A. (2022). Utilising Social Media Data Analytics to Enhance Banking Services. *Intelligent Information Management, 14*(1), 1–14. doi:10.4236/iim.2022.141001

Aula, P. (2010). Social media, reputation risk and ambient publicity management. *Strategy and Leadership, 38*(6), 43–49. doi:10.1108/10878571011088069

Ayedh, A., Echchabi, A., Battour, M., & Omar, M. (2020). Malaysian Muslim investors' behaviour towards the blockchain-based Bitcoin cryptocurrency market. *Journal of Islamic Marketing, 12*(4), 690–704. doi:10.1108/JIMA-04-2019-0081

Azeez, N. P. A., & Akhtar, S. M. J. (2021). Digital financial literacy and its determinants: An empirical evidences from rural India. *South Asian Journal of Social Studies and Economics, 11*(2), 8–22. doi:10.9734ajsse/2021/v11i230279

Bacher-Hicks, A., Goodman, J., Green, J. G., & Holt, M. K. (2022). The COVID-19 pandemic disrupted both school bullying and cyberbullying. *American Economic Review: Insights, 4*(3), 353–370. doi:10.1257/aeri.20210456

Bagga, R. (2018). The National Cyber Security Policy of India 2013: An Analytical Study. *Indian JL & Just., 9*, 164.

Baier, A. L. (2019). The ethical implications of social media: Issues and recommendations for clinical practice. *Ethics & Behavior*, *29*(5), 341–351. doi:10.1080/10508422.2018.1516148

Balbi, G., & Magaudda, P. (2018). *A history of digital media: An intermedia and global perspective*. Routledge. doi:10.4324/9781315209630

Banday, M. T., & Mattoo, M. M. (2013). *Social media in E-governance: A study with special reference to India.*

Banisar, D., & Davies, S. (1991). Global Trends in Privacy Protection: An International Survey of Privacy, Data Protection, And Surveillance Laws and Developments. *The John Marshall Journal of Computer & Information Law*, 18.

Banks, S., Cai, T., De Jonge, E., Shears, J., Shum, M., Sobočan, A. M., Strom, K., Truell, R., Úriz, M. J., & Weinberg, M. (2020). Practising ethically during COVID-19: Social work challenges and responses. *International Social Work*, *63*(5), 569–583. doi:10.1177/0020872820949614

Bao, J., Lian, D., Zhang, F., & Yuan, N. J. (2016). Geo-social media data analytic for user modeling and location-based services. *SIGSPATIAL Special*, *7*(3), 11–18. Advance online publication. doi:10.1145/2876480.2876484

Barmuta, K. A., Akhmetshin, E. M., Andryushchenko, I. Y., Tagibova, A. A., Meshkova, G. V., & Zekiy, A. O. (2020). Problems of business processes transformation in the context of building digital economy. *Entrepreneurship and Sustainability Issues*, *8*(1), 945–959. doi:10.9770/jesi.2020.8.1(63)

Baron, R. M., & Kenny, D. A. (1986). The Moderator-Mediator Variable Distinction in Social Psychological Research. Conceptual, Strategic, and Statistical Considerations. *Journal of Personality and Social Psychology*, *51*(6), 1173–1182. doi:10.1037/0022-3514.51.6.1173 PMID:3806354

Barr, R., & Masser, I. (2019). Geographic Information: a resource, a commodity, an asset or an infrastructure? In Geographic Information Systems to Spatial Data Infrastructures (pp. 87–108). CRC Press.

Barrett-Maitland, N., & Lynch, J. (2020). Social media, ethics and the privacy paradox. *Security and privacy from a legal, ethical, and technical perspective, 49*.

Barsky, A. (2017). Ethics alive! The 2017 NASW code of ethics: What's new. *New Social Worker*.

Barsky, A. E. (2017). Social work practice and technology: Ethical issues and policy responses. *Journal of Technology in Human Services*, *35*(1), 8–19. doi:10.1080/15228835.2017.1277906

Basu, S., Marimuthu, Y., Sharma, N., Sharma, P., Gangadharan, N., & Santra, S. (2020). Attitude towards mobile learning among resident doctors involved in undergraduate medical education at a government medical college in Delhi, India. *Journal of Education and Health Promotion*, *9*(1), 321. Advance online publication. doi:10.4103/jehp.jehp_443_20 PMID:33426125

Bawre, S., & Kar, S. (2019). Social media and financial institutions in the Indian context. *International Journal of Economics and Business Research*, *18*(3), 343–355. doi:10.1504/IJEBR.2019.102734

Beaumont, E., Chester, P., & Rideout, H. (2017). Navigating ethical challenges in social media: Social work student and practitioner perspectives. *Australian Social Work*, *70*(2), 221–228. doi:10.1080/0312407X.2016.1274416

Bekmamedova, N., & Shanks, G. (2014, January). Social media analytics and business value: a theoretical framework and case study. In *2014 47th Hawaii international conference on system sciences* (pp. 3728-3737). IEEE. 10.1109/HICSS.2014.464

Benavides, L. M. C., Tamayo Arias, J. A., Arango Serna, M. D., Branch Bedoya, J. W., & Burgos, D. (2020). Digital transformation in higher education institutions: A systematic literature review. *Sensors (Basel)*, *20*(11), 3291. doi:10.339020113291 PMID:32526998

Bennet, A. (2015). *Social Media: Global Perspectives, Applications and Benefits and Dangers*. Novinka.

Bennett, N. J., Di Franco, A., Calò, A., Nethery, E., Niccolini, F., Milazzo, M., & Guidetti, P. (2019). Local support for conservation is associated with perceptions of good governance, social impacts, and ecological effectiveness. *Conservation Letters*, *12*(4), e12640. doi:10.1111/conl.12640

Bennett, W. L. (2012). The personalization of politics: Political identity, social media, and changing patterns of participation. *The Annals of the American Academy of Political and Social Science*, *644*(1), 20–39. doi:10.1177/0002716212451428

Bergmann, Z., & Ossewaarde, R. (2020). Youth climate activists meet environmental governance: Ageist depictions of the FFF movement and Greta Thunberg in German newspaper coverage. *Journal of Multicultural Discourses*, *15*(3), 267–290. doi:10.1080/17447143.2020.1745211

Berman, E. M., Bowman, J. S., West, J. P., & Van Wart, M. R. (2021). *Human resource management in public service: Paradoxes, processes, and problems*. CQ Press.

Berndsen, J. (2020). Greta Thunberg: the climate striking catalyst. *Diggit Magazine*. https://www.diggitmagazine.com/articles/greta-thunberg-climate-striking-catalyst

Berthet, V. (2022). The Impact of Cognitive Biases on Professionals' Decision-Making: A Review of Four Occupational Areas [Review]. *Frontiers in Psychology*, *12*, 802439. Advance online publication. doi:10.3389/fpsyg.2021.802439 PMID:35058862

Bertot, J. C., Jaeger, P. T., & Grimes, J. M. (2010). Using ICTs to create a culture of transparency: E-government and social media as openness and anti-corruption tools for societies. *Government Information Quarterly*, *27*(3), 264–271. doi:10.1016/j.giq.2010.03.001

Bertot, J. C., Jaeger, P. T., & Hansen, D. (2012). The impact of polices on government social media usage: Issues, challenges, and recommendations. *Government Information Quarterly*, *29*(1), 30–40. doi:10.1016/j.giq.2011.04.004

Bertot, J. C., Jaeger, P. T., Munson, S., & Glaisyer, T. (2010). Social media technology and government transparency. *Computer*, *43*(11), 53–59. Advance online publication. doi:10.1109/MC.2010.325

Best, P., Manktelow, R., & Taylor, B. (2014). Online communication, social media and adolescent wellbeing: A systematic narrative review. *Children and Youth Services Review*, *41*, 27–36. doi:10.1016/j.childyouth.2014.03.001

Bharucha, J. (2018). Exploring education-related use of social media: Business students perspectives in a changing India. *Education + Training*, *60*(2), 198–212. doi:10.1108/ET-07-2017-0105

Bican, P. M., & Brem, A. (2020). Digital business model, digital transformation, digital entrepreneurship: Is there a sustainable "digital"? *Sustainability (Basel)*, *12*(13), 5239. doi:10.3390u12135239

Boddy, J., & Dominelli, L. (2017). Social media and social work: The challenges of a new ethical space. *Australian Social Work*, *70*(2), 172–184. doi:10.1080/0312407X.2016.1224907

Boland-Prom, K. W. (2009). Results from a national study of social workers sanctioned by state licensing boards. *Social Work*, *54*(4), 351–360. doi:10.1093w/54.4.351 PMID:19780465

Bonanomi, M. M., Hall, D. M., Staub-French, S., Tucker, A., & Talamo, C. M. L. (2020). The impact of digital transformation on formal and informal organizational structures of large architecture and engineering firms. *Engineering, Construction, and Architectural Management, 27*(4), 872–892. doi:10.1108/ECAM-03-2019-0119

Bonini, T., Caliandro, A., & Massarelli, A. (2016). Understanding the value of networked publics in radio: Employing digital methods and social network analysis to understand the Twitter publics of two Italian national radio stations. *Information Communication and Society, 19*(1), 40–58. doi:10.1080/1369118X.2015.1093532

Booth, R. G., Strudwick, G., & Fraser, R. (2017, May). The transformative power of social media: Considerations for practice and emerging leaders. []. Sage CA: Los Angeles, CA: SAGE Publications.]. *Healthcare Management Forum, 30*(3), 138–141. doi:10.1177/0840470417693017 PMID:28929851

Borkar, K. D. M., Rodrigues, P. A., & Mascarenhas, A. A. S. (2022). A Study on Trend and Pattern of Beneficiaries of Prime Minister Employment Generation Scheme. *Webology, 19*(1), 2019–2027. Advance online publication. doi:10.14704/WEB/V19I1/WEB19136

Bose, A. (2016),"Social Media And Education Sector: Enriching Relationship"Global Media Journal – Indian Edition Sponsored by the University of Calcutta, 7.

Boulianne, S., Lalancette, M., & Ilkiw, D. (2020). "School strike 4 climate": Social media and the international youth protest on climate change. *Media and Communication, 8*(2), 208–218. doi:10.17645/mac.v8i2.2768

Boyd, D. (2010). Social network sites as networked publics: Affordances, dynamics, and implications. In *A networked self* (pp. 47–66). Routledge.

Brandes, L., Franck, E., & Nüesch, S. (2008). Local heroes and superstars: An empirical analysis of star attraction in German soccer. *Journal of Sports Economics, 9*(3), 266–286. doi:10.1177/1527002507302026

Bria, F. (2013). *Social media and their impact on organisations: building Firm Celebrity and organisational legitimacy through social media* [Doctoral dissertation, Imperial College London].

Brill, C. K. (2001). Looking at the social work profession through the eye of the NASW Code of Ethics. *Research on Social Work Practice, 11*(2), 223–234. doi:10.1177/104973150101100209

Broby, D. (2021). Financial technology and the future of banking. *Financial Innovation, 7*(1), 1–19. doi:10.118640854-021-00264-y

Brooks, L. 2021. COP26 protesters' anger and frustration tinged with optimism. *The Guardian.* https://www.theguardian.com/environment/2021/nov/03/cop26-protesters-anger-and-frustration-tinged-with-optimism

Brunnermeier, M. K., James, H., & Landau, J. P. (2019). The digitalization of money (No. w26300). National Bureau of Economic Research.

Bruns, A., & Highfield, T. (2015). Is Habermas on Twitter?: Social media and the public sphere. In The Routledge companion to social media and politics (pp. 56-73). Routledge.

Bryer, T. A., & Zavattaro, S. M. (2011). Social media and public administration: Theoretical dimensions and introduction to the symposium. *Administrative Theory & Praxis, 33*(3), 325-340.

Campagna, M., Floris, R., Massa, P., & Mura, S. (2018). Social media geographic information: The community perspective in planning knowledge. In *Environmental Information Systems* (Vol. 1). Concepts, Methodologies, Tools, and Applications. doi:10.4018/978-1-5225-7033-2.ch003

Campbell, M. (2020). Ecological disaster' develops in Slovakia as river contaminated by orange iron. *Euronews*. https://www.euronews.com/green/2022/05/23/ecological-disaster-develops-in-slovakia-as-river-is-contaminated-by-iron

Candra Sari, R., Rika Fatimah, P. L., Ilyana, S., & Dwi Hermawan, H. (2022). Augmented reality (AR)-based sharia financial literacy system (AR-SFLS): A new approach to virtual sharia financial socialization for young learners. *International Journal of Islamic and Middle Eastern Finance and Management, 15*(1), 48–65. doi:10.1108/IMEFM-11-2019-0484

Cao, G., Wang, S., Hwang, M., Padmanabhan, A., Zhang, Z., & Soltani, K. (2015). A scalable framework for spatiotemporal analysis of location-based social media data. *Computers, Environment and Urban Systems, 51*, 70–82. Advance online publication. doi:10.1016/j.compenvurbsys.2015.01.002

Carlo Bertot, J., Jaeger, P. T., & Grimes, J. M. (2012). Promoting transparency and accountability through ICTs, social media, and collaborative e-government. *Transforming government: people, process and policy, 6*(1), 78-91.

Carrington, D. (2018). Avoiding meat and diary is 'single biggest way' to reduce your impact on Earth. *The Guardian*. https://www.theguardian.com/environment/2018/may/31/avoiding-meat-and-dairy-is-single-biggest-way-to-reduce-your-impact-on-earth

Carroll, L. N., Au, A. P., Detwiler, L. T., Fu, T., Painter, I. S., & Abernethy, N. F. (2014). Visualization and analytics tools for infectious disease epidemiology: A systematic review. *Journal of Biomedical Informatics, 51*, 287–298. doi:10.1016/j.jbi.2014.04.006 PMID:24747356

Cassidy, W., Faucher, C., & Jackson, M. (2017). Adversity in University: Cyberbullying and Its Impacts on Students, Faculty and Administrators. *International Journal of Environmental Research and Public Health, 14*(8), 14. doi:10.3390/ijerph14080888 PMID:28786941

Castaldi, C. (2020). All the great things you can do with trademark data: Taking stock and looking ahead. *Strategic Organization, 18*(3), 472–484. doi:10.1177/1476127019847835

Castelnovo, W., Misuraca, G., & Savoldelli, A. (2016). Smart Cities Governance: The Need for a Holistic Approach to Assessing Urban Participatory Policy Making. *Social Science Computer Review, 34*(6), 724–739. Advance online publication. doi:10.1177/0894439315611103

Chadwick, A., & Dennis, J. (2017). Social Media, Professional Media and Mobilisation in Contemporary Britain: Explaining the Strengths and Weaknesses of the Citizens' Movement 38 Degrees. *Political Studies, 65*(1), 42–60. doi:10.1177/0032321716631350

Chadwick, A., Dennis, J. W., & Smith, A. P. (2016). Politics in the age of hybrid media: power, systems, and media logics. In A. Bruns, G. Enli, E. Skogerbø, A. Olof Larsson, & C. Christensen (Eds.), *The Routledge Companion to Social Media and Politics* (pp. 7–22). Routledge.

Chahal, J., & Rani, N. (2022). Exploring the acceptance for e-learning among higher education students in India: Combining technology acceptance model with external variables. *Journal of Computing in Higher Education, 34*(3), 844–867. doi:10.100712528-022-09327-0 PMID:35668837

Chan, C. (2016). A scoping review of social media use in social work practice. *Journal of Evidence-Informed Social Work, 13*(3), 263–276. doi:10.1080/23761407.2015.1052908 PMID:26176999

Chan, C. (2018). Analysing social networks for social work practice: A case study of the Facebook fan page of an online youth outreach project. *Children and Youth Services Review, 85*, 143–150. doi:10.1016/j.childyouth.2017.12.021

Chan, C., & Ngai, S. S. Y. (2019). Utilizing social media for social work: Insights from clients in online youth services. *Journal of Social Work Practice, 33*(2), 157–172. doi:10.1080/02650533.2018.1504286

Chandani, A., Divekar, R., Neeraja, B., Mehta, M., & Atiq, R. (2022, February). A Study to Analyze Use of Social Media by Private and Public Sector Banks in India. In *Achieving $5 Trillion Economy of India: Proceedings of 11th Annual International Research Conference of Symbiosis Institute of Management Studies* (pp. 135-152). Singapore: Springer Nature Singapore. 10.1007/978-981-16-7818-9_8

Chandradasa, M., & Kuruppuarachchi, K. A. L. A. (2020). Mental health impact of the COVID-19 pandemic. *Sri Lanka Journal of Medicine, 29*(2), 1. doi:10.4038ljm.v29i2.218

Chanias, S., Myers, M. D., & Hess, T. (2019). Digital transformation strategy making in pre-digital organizations: The case of a financial services provider. *The Journal of Strategic Information Systems, 28*(1), 17–33. doi:10.1016/j.jsis.2018.11.003

Chatterjee, S., & Kar, A. K. (2020). Why do small and medium enterprises use social media marketing and what is the impact: Empirical insights from India. *International Journal of Information Management, 53*, 102103. doi:10.1016/j.ijinfomgt.2020.102103

Chaturvedi, M. M., Gupta, M. P., & Bhattacharya, J. (2008). *Cyber security infrastructure in India: a study. Emerging Technologies in E-Government.* CSI Publication.

Chauhan, P., Sharma, P., Chauhan, R., & Jain, A. (2019). National eCommerce Policy: What India's new (Draft) eCommerce Policy outlines for Online Retailers and its Regulatory aspects. *International Journal of Drug Regulatory Affairs, 7*(3), 30–33. Advance online publication. doi:10.22270/ijdra.v7i3.335

Chavadi, C. (2021). Growth drivers, characteristics, preference and challenges faced by Fast Moving Consumer Goods-A study with reference to Bengaluru. *Turkish Online Journal of Qualitative Inquiry, 12*(7).

Chavadi, C. A., & Kokatnur, S. S. (2008). Consumer Expectation and Perception of Fast Food Outlets: An Empirical Study in Davangere. *ICFAI Journal of Services Marketing, 6*(2).

Chavadi, C. A., & Kokatnur, S. S. (2008). Consumer Expectation and Perception of Fast Food Outlets: An Empirical Study in Davangere. *ICFAI Journal Of Services Marketing, 6*(2).

Chavadi, C. A., & Kokatnur, S. S. (2009). Impact of Short-Term Promotional Ads on Food Retailing. *ICFAI Journal of Consumer Behavior, 4*(1).

Chavadi, C. A., Arul, M. J., & Sirothiya, M. (2020). Modelling the effects of creative advertisements on consumers: An empirical study. *Vision (Basel), 24*(3), 269–283. doi:10.1177/0972262920926074

Chavadi, C. A., Hiremath, C. V., & Hyderabad, R. L. (2014). Customer loyalty appraisal based on store characteristics: An alternative approach. *Indian Journal of Marketing, 44*(5), 18–29. doi:10.17010/ijom/2014/v44/i5/80375

Chavadi, C. A., & Kokatnur, S. S. (2009). RFID Adoption by Indian Retailers: An Exploratory Study. *The Icfai University Journal of Supply Chain Management, 6*(1), 60–77.

Chavadi, C. A., Menon, S. R., & Sirothiya, M. (2019). Measuring Service Quality Perceptions of Indian E-retailers: An Evaluative Study. *Metamorphosis, 18*(2), 92–102. doi:10.1177/0972622519886232

Chavadi, C. A., Menon, S. R., & Sirothiya, M. (2019). Modelling the Effects of Brand Placements in Movies: An Investigative Study of Event Type and Placement Type. *Vision (Basel), 23*(1), 31–43. doi:10.1177/0972262918821227

Chavadi, C. A., Vishwanatha, M. R., & Mubeen, S. (2018). Ghee with Glee: A Study of How Consumers Evaluate Product Packaging. *Metamorphosis, 17*(2), 100–110. doi:10.1177/0972622518817407

Chen, H. T., & Li, X. (2017). The contribution of mobile social media to social capital and psychological well-being: Examining the role of communicative use, friending and self-disclosure. *Computers in Human Behavior*, *75*, 958–965. doi:10.1016/j.chb.2017.06.011

Chen, J., & Wang, Y. (2021). Social media use for health purposes: Systematic review. *Journal of Medical Internet Research*, *23*(5), e17917. doi:10.2196/17917 PMID:33978589

Chen, L., & Aklikokou, A. K. (2020). Determinants of E-government Adoption: Testing the Mediating Effects of Perceived Usefulness and Perceived Ease of Use. *International Journal of Public Administration*, *43*(10), 850–865. doi:10.1080/01900692.2019.1660989

Chen, Q., Min, C., Zhang, W., Wang, G., Ma, X., & Evans, R. (2020). Unpacking the black box: How to promote citizen engagement through government social media during the COVID-19 crisis. *Computers in Human Behavior*, *110*, 106380. doi:10.1016/j.chb.2020.106380 PMID:32292239

Cheung, C. M., & Lee, M. K. (2010). A theoretical model of intentional social action in online social networks. *Decision Support Systems*, *49*(1), 24–30. doi:10.1016/j.dss.2009.12.006

Chikandiwa, S. T., Contogiannis, E., & Jembere, E. (2013). The adoption of social media marketing in South African banks. *European Business Review*, *25*(4), 365–381. doi:10.1108/EBR-02-2013-0013

Chuang, I. T., Benita, F., & Tunçer, B. (2022). Effects of urban park spatial characteristics on visitor density and diversity: A geolocated social media approach. *Landscape and Urban Planning*, *226*, 104514. Advance online publication. doi:10.1016/j.landurbplan.2022.104514

Chun, S. A., & Reyes, L. F. L. (2012). Social media in government. *Government Information Quarterly*, *29*(4), 441–445. doi:10.1016/j.giq.2012.07.003

Cilliers, L., & Chinyamurindi, W. (2020). Perceptions of cyber bullying in primary and secondary schools among student teachers in the Eastern Cape Province of South Africa. *The Electronic Journal on Information Systems in Developing Countries*, *86*(4), e12131. doi:10.1002/isd2.12131

Comer, M. J., & Bell, J. A. (2020). The Association of Social Work Boards. In Encyclopedia of Social Work. doi:10.1093/acrefore/9780199975839.013.1341

Connolly, K. (2019). Greta Thunberg in Twitter spat with German rail firm. *The Guardian*. https://www.theguardian.com/environment/2019/dec/15/greta-thunberg-in-twitter-spat-with-german-rail-firm

Corbyn, Z. (2011). Twitter to track dengue fever outbreaks in Brazil. *New Scientist*, *211*(2821), 18. Advance online publication. doi:10.1016/S0262-4079(11)61685-0

Cortés-Cediel, M. E., Cantador, I., & Bolívar, M. P. R. (2021). Analyzing Citizen Participation and Engagement in European Smart Cities. *Social Science Computer Review*, *39*(4), 592–626. Advance online publication. doi:10.1177/0894439319877478

Coşkun, M., & Ozturan, M. (2018). #europehappinessmap: A framework for multi-lingual sentiment analysis via social media big data (a Twitter case study). *Information (Basel)*, *9*(5), 102. Advance online publication. doi:10.3390/info9050102

Costa, P. F., Badolato, I. da S., Borba, R. L. R., & Strauch, J. C. M. (2019). Strategy for extraction of foursquare's social media geographic information through data mining. *Boletim de Ciências Geodésicas*, *25*(1), e2019005. Advance online publication. doi:10.15901982-21702019000100005

Couldry, N. (2009). Does 'the media' have a future? *European Journal of Communication*, *24*(4), 437–449. doi:10.1177/0267323109345604

Criado, J. I., Sandoval-Almazan, R., & Gil-Garcia, J. R. (2013). Government innovation through social media. *Government Information Quarterly*, *30*(4), 319–326. doi:10.1016/j.giq.2013.10.003

Croucher, S. M., Nguyen, T., & Rahmani, D. (2020). Prejudice toward Asian Americans in the COVID-19 pandemic: The effects of social media use in the United States. *Frontiers in Communication*, *5*, 39. doi:10.3389/fcomm.2020.00039

Crowe, S., Cresswell, K., Robertson, A., Huby, G., Avery, A., & Sheikh, A. (2011). The case study approach. *BMC Medical Research Methodology*, *11*(1), 100. doi:10.1186/1471-2288-11-100 PMID:21707982

Dabh, M. D. (2016). Geofencing: A Generic Approach to Real Time Location based Tracking System. *IRACST – International Journal of Computer Networks and Wireless Communications*, *6*(6).

Dadashzadeh, M. (2010). Social media in government: From eGovernment to eGovernance. [JBER]. *Journal of Business & Economics Research*, *8*(11). doi:10.19030/jber.v8i11.51

Dalmia, V. P. (2017). *Data protection laws in india—Everything you must know—Data protection—India*. Mondaq Ltd. https://www.mondaq.com/india/data-protection/655034/data-protection-laws-in-india---everything-you-must-know

Dave, P., Master, K., Makwana, P., Goel, P., & Ganatra, A. (2021). *Mental Health Analysis of Indians during Pandemic*. Paper presented at the Data Science and Computational Intelligence: Sixteenth International Conference on Information Processing, ICInPro 2021, Bengaluru, India. 10.1007/978-3-030-91244-4_23

Davis, F. D. (1989). Perceived usefulness, perceived ease of use, and user acceptance of information technology. *Management Information Systems Quarterly*, *13*(3), 319–340. doi:10.2307/249008

De Falco, C. C., Crescentini, N., & Ferracci, M. (2021). *The Spatial Dimension in Social Media Analysis*. doi:10.4018/978-1-7998-8473-6.ch029

De FalcoA.De FalcoC. C.FerracciM. (2022). Geo-Social Media and Socio-Territorial Distribution: A Study on the Italian Case. *Italian Sociological Review*, *12*(Special Issue 7). doi:10.13136/isr.v12i7S.577

Deep, V., & Sharma, P. (2018, December). Analysis and Impact of Cyber Security Threats in India using Mazarbot Case Study. In *2018 International Conference on Computational Techniques, Electronics and Mechanical Systems (CTEMS)* (pp. 499-503). IEEE.

Delello, J. A., McWhorter, R. R., & Camp, K. M. (2015). Using social media as a tool for learning: A multi-disciplinary study. In EdMedia+ Innovate Learning Online 2022 (Vol. 14, pp. 163-180). Association for the Advancement of Computing in Education (AACE).

Democracy Now. (2019). School Strike for Climate: Meet 15-Year-Old Activist Greta Thunberg, Who Inspired a Global Movement. *Democracy Now*. https://www.democracynow.org/2018/12/11/meet_the_15_year_old_swedish

Dery, K., Sebastian, I. M., & van der Meulen, N. (2017). The digital workplace is key to digital innovation. *MIS Quarterly Executive*, *16*(2).

Dewi, V. I. (2022). How do demographic and socioeconomic factors affect financial literacy and its variables? *Cogent Business & Management*, *9*(1), 2077640. Advance online publication. doi:10.1080/23311975.2022.2077640

Dhesinghraja, J., & Sendhilkumar, M. (2015). An Overview of Supply Chain Management on Apparel Order Process in Garment Industries, Bangalore. *Journal of Exclusive Management Science*, *4*.

Diamantopoulos, A., & Siguaw, J. A. (2006). Formative Versus Reflective Indicators in Organizational Measure Development: A Comparison and Empirical Illustration. *British Journal of Management*, *17*(4), 263–282. doi:10.1111/j.1467-8551.2006.00500.x

Diggelmann, O., & Cleis, M. N. (2014). How the right to privacy became a human right. *Human Rights Law Review*, *14*(3), 441–458. doi:10.1093/hrlr/ngu014

Dion, M., AbdelMalik, P., & Mawudeku, A. (2015). Big Data and the Global Public Health Intelligence Network (GPHIN). *Canada Communicable Disease Report*, *41*(9), 209–214. Advance online publication. doi:10.14745/ccdr. v41i09a02 PMID:29769954

Disdukcapil Kota Jayapura. (2020). *Dukcapil Prevent Corona*. https://bit.ly/3tM6uY6

Dixon, S. (2023). *Global Social Networks Ranked by Number of Users 2023*. Statista. https://www.statista.com/statistics/272014/global-social-networks-ranked-by-number-of-users/

Donovan, J., Rose, D., & Connolly, M. (2017). A crisis of identity: Social work theorising at a time of change. *British Journal of Social Work*, *47*(8), 2291–2307. doi:10.1093/bjsw/bcw180

Dr, M., & Ayisha Millath, A. C. (2019). Indian Tea production Overview and Price Analysis. *International Journal of Advanced Science and Technology*, *28*(19), 1253–1259.

Dr, M., & Ayisha Millath, D. S. N. (2019). Identifying Work-Family Conflict Among IT Employees of Infopark, Kochi, Kerala. *International Journal of Advanced Science and Technology*, *28*(19), 1164–1176.

Dr, M., & Ayisha Millath, R. K. R. (2019). A Study and Analysis on Sustainable Business Models for Indian Automotive Industry. *International Journal of Advanced Science and Technology*, *28*(19), 953–959.

Duan, H. K., Vasarhelyi, M. A., Codesso, M., & Alzamil, Z. (2023). Enhancing the government accounting information systems using social media information: An application of text mining and machine learning. *International Journal of Accounting Information Systems*, *48*, 100600. Advance online publication. doi:10.1016/j.accinf.2022.100600

Dukcapil.kemendagri.go.id. (2021). *Dukcapil Wins KIPP's Top Commendable Innovations, Reverses Problems with Innovation*. https://bit.ly/3mJbtF6

Dumitraşcu, V. (2015). Social activism: theories and methods. *Revista Universitară de Sociologie*, *11*(1), 84-94. https://www.ceeol.com/search/article-detail?id=716528

Duncan-Daston, R., Hunter-Sloan, M., & Fullmer, E. (2013). Considering the ethical implications of social media in social work education. *Ethics and Information Technology*, *15*(1), 35–43. doi:10.100710676-013-9312-7

Dutta, A. (2020). Impact of digital social media on Indian higher education: alternative approaches of online learning during COVID-19 pandemic crisis. *International journal of scientific and research publications*, *10*(5), 604-611.

Dwijayanti, N., Iqbal, M., & Zulfikar, M. (2022). The role of Islamic fintech P2PL in increasing inclusion and financial literacy of MSMEs. *Journal of Islamic Finance*, *11*(1), 94–101. https://journals.iium.edu.my/iiibf-journal/index.php/jif/article/view/638

Dwivedi, Y. K., Ismagilova, E., Hughes, D. L., Carlson, J., Filieri, R., Jacobson, J., Jain, V., Karjaluoto, H., Kefi, H., Krishen, A. S., Kumar, V., Rahman, M. M., Raman, R., Rauschnabel, P. A., Rowley, J., Salo, J., Tran, G. A., & Wang, Y. (2021). Setting the future of digital and social media marketing research: Perspectives and research propositions. *International Journal of Information Management*, *59*, 2021. doi:10.1016/j.ijinfomgt.2020.102168

Dye, T. D., Alcantara, L., Siddiqi, S., Barbosu, M., Sharma, S., Panko, T., & Pressman, E. (2020). Risk of COVID-19-related bullying, harassment and stigma among healthcare workers: An analytical cross-sectional global study. *BMJ Open*, *10*(12), e046620. doi:10.1136/bmjopen-2020-046620 PMID:33380488

Efendi, K., Tumija, T., Handayani, N., & Rifai, M. (2022). *Public Service Innovation Model in Sragen Regency*. Jurnal Media Birokrasi. doi:10.33701/jmb.v4i1.2327

El Hilali, W., & El Manouar, A. (2019, March). Towards a sustainable world through a SMART digital transformation. In *Proceedings of the 2nd International Conference on Networking, Information Systems & Security* (pp. 1-8). ACM. 10.1145/3320326.3320364

Elaraby, N., Bolock, A. E., Herbert, C., & Abdennadher, S. (2021). *Anxiety Detection During COVID-19 Using the character computing ontology*. Paper presented at the Highlights in Practical Applications of Agents, Multi-Agent Systems, and Social Good. The PAAMS Collection: International Workshops of PAAMS 2021, Salamanca, Spain. 10.1007/978-3-030-85710-3_1

Elbedour, S., Alqahtani, S., Rihan, I. E. S., Bawalsah, J. A., Booker-Ammah, B., & Turner, J. F. Jr. (2020). Cyberbullying: Roles of school psychologists and school counselors in addressing a pervasive social justice issue. *Children and Youth Services Review*, *109*, 104720. doi:10.1016/j.childyouth.2019.104720

El-Ebiary, Y. A. B., Bamansoor, S., Abu-Ulbeh, W., Amir, W. M., Saany, S. I. A., & Yusoff, M. H. (2020). A prognosis of Chinese E-governance. *IJETT*, *68*, 86–89. doi:10.14445/22315381/CATI1P215

Ellison, N. B., Gibbs, J. L., & Weber, M. S. (2015). The use of enterprise social network sites for knowledge sharing in distributed organizations: The role of organizational affordances. *The American Behavioral Scientist*, *59*(1), 103–123. doi:10.1177/0002764214540510

Enikolopov, R., Makarin, A., & Petrova, M. (2020). Social media and protest participation: Evidence from Russia. *Econometrica*, *88*(4), 1479–1514. doi:10.3982/ECTA14281

Estelami, H., & Florendo, J. (2021). The Role of Financial Literacy, Need for Cognition and Political Orientation on Consumers' Use of Social Media in Financial Decision Making. *Journal of Personal Finance*, *20*(2).

European Data Protection Supervisor. (2023, July 14). *Data protection*. European Union. https://edps.europa.eu/data-protection/data-protection_en

Eveland, W. P. Jr, & Dunwoody, S. (2000). Examining information processing on the World Wide Web using think aloud protocols. *Media Psychology*, *2*(3), 219–244. doi:10.1207/S1532785XMEP0203_2

Fagherazzi, G., Goetzinger, C., Rashid, M. A., Aguayo, G. A., & Huiart, L. (2020). Digital health strategies to fight COVID-19 worldwide: Challenges, recommendations, and a call for papers. *Journal of Medical Internet Research*, *22*(6), e19284. doi:10.2196/19284 PMID:32501804

Faisal, M., Chandramohan, S., Millath, M. A., & Karthick, A. V. (2019) Influence of Fashion Behavior on Store Choice among the Arts College Students in Sivganga District. *International Journal of Recent Technology and Engineering*, *8*(2), 672-676.

Faisal, M., Chandramohan, S., Millath, M. A., &Karthick, A. V. (2019). Influence of Fashion Behavior on Store Choice among the Arts College Students in Sivganga District. *International Journal of Recent Technology and Engineering*, *8*(2), 672-676.

Fang, L., Mishna, F., Zhang, V. F., Van Wert, M., & Bogo, M. (2014). Social media and social work education: Understanding and dealing with the new digital world. *Social Work in Health Care*, *53*(9), 800–814. doi:10.1080/00981389.2014.943455 PMID:25321930

Farahat, A. (2012). Applying the Technology Acceptance Model to Online Learning in the Egyptian Universities. *Procedia: Social and Behavioral Sciences*, *64*, 95–104. doi:10.1016/j.sbspro.2012.11.012

Fasnacht, D. (2018). Banking for the Next Generation, Management for Professionals. *Open Innovation Ecosystems*, 2(8), 231-243. doi:10.1007/978-3-319-76394-1_8

Fast, I., Sørensen, K., Brand, H., & Suggs, L. S. (2014). Social Media for Public Health: An Exploratory Policy Analysis. *European Journal of Public Health*, 25(1), 162–166. doi:10.1093/eurpub/cku080 PMID:24942532

Felt, M. (2016). Social media and the social sciences: How researchers employ Big Data analytics. *Big Data & Society*, 3(1), 2053951716645828. doi:10.1177/2053951716645828

Fenech, R., Baguant, P., & Ivanov, D. (2019). The changing role of human resource management in an era of digital transformation. *Journal of Management Information & Decision Sciences*, 22(2).

Fernandez, V., & Gallardo-Gallardo, E. (2021). Tackling the HR digitalization challenge: Key factors and barriers to HR analytics adoption. *Competitiveness Review*, 31(1), 162–187. doi:10.1108/CR-12-2019-0163

Financial, D., Consumer, S., & Series, I. (2010). Social Media in Financial Services. *Insight (American Society of Ophthalmic Registered Nurses)*.

Fletcher, G., & Griffiths, M. (2020). Digital transformation during a lockdown. *International Journal of Information Management*, 55, 102185. doi:10.1016/j.ijinfomgt.2020.102185 PMID:32836642

G. Thamaraiselvi (2019), A Gap Analysis on Awareness and Utilization of Social Media Banking – The New Line of Self Service Banking. (2019). *International Journal of Innovative Technology and Exploring Engineering*, 9, 456-459. doi:10.35940/ijitee.B1215.1292S219

Gainey, T. W., & Klaas, B. S. (2003). The outsourcing of training and development: Factors impacting client satisfaction. *Journal of Management*, 29(2), 207–229. doi:10.1177/014920630302900205

Gajendran, N. (2020). Web-sites and social media technologies as implements of E-Governance: A study of North East India. *Indian Journal of Science and Technology*, 13(31), 3188–3197. doi:10.17485/IJST/v13i31.1016

Gan. (2017). *Jayapura City Government Uses Innovation to Make it Easier for Residents to Obtain Resident Documents*. https://bit.ly/3zHmnTc

Gandy-Guedes, M. E., Vance, M. M., Bridgewater, E. A., Montgomery, T., & Taylor, K. (2016). Using Facebook as a tool for informal peer support: A case example. *Social Work Education*, 35(3), 323–332. doi:10.1080/02615479.2016.1154937

Gao, H., Barbier, G., & Goolsby, R. (2011). Harnessing the crowdsourcing power of social media for disaster relief. *IEEE Intelligent Systems*, 26(3), 10–14. Advance online publication. doi:10.1109/MIS.2011.52

Gao, Z., Wang, S., & Gu, J. (2020). Public participation in smart-city governance: A qualitative content analysis of public comments in urban China. *Sustainability (Basel)*, 12(20), 8605. Advance online publication. doi:10.3390u12208605

Garai-Fodor, M., Varga, J., & Csiszarik-Kocsir, A. (2022). Generation-specific perceptions of financial literacy and digital solutions. *2022 IEEE 20th Jubilee World Symposium on Applied Machine Intelligence and Informatics (SAMI)*. IEEE. 10.1109/SAMI54271.2022.9780717

Garcia-Rubio, C., Redondo, R. P. D., Campo, C., & Vilas, A. F. (2018). Using entropy of social media location data for the detection of crowd dynamics anomalies. *Electronics (Basel)*, 7(12), 380. Advance online publication. doi:10.3390/electronics7120380

Garg, P., Gupta, B., Dzever, S., Sivarajah, U., & Kumar, V. (2020). Examining the Relationship between Social Media Analytics Practices and Business Performance in the Indian Retail and IT Industries: The Mediation Role of Customer Engagement. *International Journal of Information Management, 52*, 102069. Advance online publication. doi:10.1016/j.ijinfomgt.2020.102069

Gefen, D., Karahanna, E., & Straub, D. W. (2003). Trust and TAM in online shopping: An integrated model. *Management Information Systems Quarterly, 27*(1), 51–90. doi:10.2307/30036519

George, A. L., & Bennett, A. (2005). *Case studies and theory development in the social sciences. 2005*. MIT Press.

Gerbaudo, P. (2012). *Tweets and the streets: Social media and contemporary activism*. Pluto Press. https://www.jstor.org/stable/j.ctt183pdzs

GhelaniD.HuaT. K.KoduruS. K. R. (2022). Cyber Security Threats, Vulnerabilities, and Security Solutions Models in Banking. Authorea Preprints. doi:10.22541/au.166385206.63311335/v1

Gideon, F., Lang, G., & Benbunan-Fich, R. (2010). the transformative Power of social Media on emergency and Crisis Management. *International Journal of Information Systems for Crisis Response and Management, 2*(1), 1–10. doi:10.4018/jiscrm.2010120401

Girard, A., Fallery, B., & Rodhain, F. (2014). Integration of social media in recruitment: a delphi study. In *Social Media in Human Resources Management* (Vol. 12, pp. 97–120). Emerald Group Publishing Limited. doi:10.1108/S1877-6361(2013)0000012009

Global Statistics Report. (2023). *India Social Media Statistics 2023 | Most Used Top Platforms – The Global Statistics*. Author.

Gohary, E. E. (2019). The impact of financial technology on facilitating e-government services in Egypt. *Journal of Distribution Science, 17*(5), 51–59. doi:10.15722/jds.17.5.201905.51

Goodchild, M. F. (2007). Citizens as sensors: The world of volunteered geography. GeoJournal. doi:10.100710708-007-9111-y

Goodell, G., Al-Nakib, H. D., & Tasca, P. (2021). A digital currency architecture for privacy and owner-custodianship. *Future Internet, 13*(5), 130. doi:10.3390/fi13050130

Gorwa, R. (2019). What is platform governance? *Information Communication and Society, 22*(6), 854–871. doi:10.1080/1369118X.2019.1573914

Govindasamy, K. A., & Palanichamy, N. (2021). *Depression detection using machine learning techniques on twitter data*. Paper presented at the 2021 5th international conference on intelligent computing and control systems (ICICCS). 10.1109/ICICCS51141.2021.9432203

Goyal, K., & Kumar, S. (2021). Financial literacy: A systematic review and bibliometric analysis. *International Journal of Consumer Studies, 45*(1), 80–105. doi:10.1111/ijcs.12605

Granier, B., & Kudo, H. (2016). How are citizens involved in smart cities? Analysing citizen participation in Japanese "smart Communities." *Information Polity, 21*(1), 61–76. Advance online publication. doi:10.3233/IP-150367

Greer, J. (2016). Resilience and personal effectiveness for social workers. *Resilience and Personal Effectiveness for Social Workers,* 1-184.

Griffith, J., & Leston-Bandeira, C. (2020). How are parliaments using new media to engage with citizens? In *The Impact of Legislatures* (pp. 380–397). Routledge. doi:10.4324/9781003033783-20

Gröbe, M., & Burghardt, D. (2020). Micro diagrams: Visualization of categorical point data from location-based social media. *Cartography and Geographic Information Science*, *47*(4), 305–320. Advance online publication. doi:10.1080/15230406.2020.1733438

Gruner, R. L., Power, D., & Bergey, P. K. (2013). Leveraging social media technology for business transformation: The case of corporate social communities. In *Social media in strategic management* (Vol. 11, pp. 27–42). Emerald Group Publishing Limited. doi:10.1108/S1877-6361(2013)0000011006

Guess, A. M., Lerner, M., Lyons, B., Montgomery, J. M., Nyhan, B., Reifler, J., & Sircar, N. (2020). A digital media literacy intervention increases discernment between mainstream and false news in the United States and India. *Proceedings of the National Academy of Sciences of the United States of America*, *117*(27), 15536–15545. doi:10.1073/pnas.1920498117 PMID:32571950

Gunawan, A., Sadri, M., Pulungan, D. R., & Koto, M. (2022). Study of phenomenon on consumption behavior of Medan City students during pandemic: Financial literacy on E-commerce. *Webology*, *19*(1), 2853–2872. doi:10.14704/WEB/V19I1/WEB19190

Gupta, S., & Yadav, A. (2017). The impact of electronic banking and information technology on the employees of banking sector. *Management and Labour Studies*, *42*(4), 379–387. doi:10.1177/2393957517736457

Guru Charan Sharma. (2021). The Digitalization of Education Through Social Media. *International Journal of Creative Research Thoughts, 9*(5). https://ijcrt.org/papers/IJCRT2105473.pdf

Gutiérrez, V., Amaxilatis, D., Mylonas, G., & Muñoz, L. (2018). Empowering Citizens Toward the Co-Creation of Sustainable Cities. *IEEE Internet of Things Journal*, *5*(2), 668–676. Advance online publication. doi:10.1109/JIOT.2017.2743783

Guzman, J. (2023). Social Media Statistics for Australia. *Melt Water.* https://www.meltwater.com/en/blog/social-media-statistics-australia

Hair, J. F., Hult, G. T. M., Ringle, C. M., & Sarstedt, M. (2017). A Primer on Partial Least Squares Structural Equation Modeling (PLS-SEM) (2nd ed.). Sage Publications Inc.

Hai, T. N., Van, Q. N., & Thi Tuyet, M. N. (2021). Digital transformation: Opportunities and challenges for leaders in the emerging countries in response to COVID-19 pandemic. *Emerging Science Journal*, *5*(1), 21–36. doi:10.28991/esj-2021-SPER-03

Hakala, F. P. (2021). *The Greta Effect on Global Environmental Governance: Testing the Applicability of Frame Theory.*

Halder, D., & Jaishankar, K. (2021). Cyber governance and data protection in India: A critical legal analysis. In *Routledge Companion to Global Cyber-Security Strategy* (pp. 337–348). Routledge. doi:10.4324/9780429399718-28

Hamstead, Z. A., Fisher, D., Ilieva, R. T., Wood, S. A., McPhearson, T., & Kremer, P. (2018). Geolocated social media as a rapid indicator of park visitation and equitable park access. *Computers, Environment and Urban Systems*, *72*, 38–50. Advance online publication. doi:10.1016/j.compenvurbsys.2018.01.007

Hanna, E., Ward, L. M., Seabrook, R. C., Jerald, M., Reed, L., Giaccardi, S., & Lippman, J. R. (2017). Contributions of social comparison and self-objectification in mediating associations between Facebook use and emergent adults' psychological well-being. *Cyberpsychology, Behavior, and Social Networking*, *20*(3), 172–179. doi:10.1089/cyber.2016.0247 PMID:28263683

Haque, & Shoaib. (2023). The digital currency in India: Challenges and prospects. *Bench Council Transactions on Benchmarks, Standards and Evaluations*, *3*, 10107.

Harrabin, R. (2019). Plant-based diet can fight climate change. *BBC News*. https://www.bbc.com/news/science-environment-49238749

Hartanto, D., Dalle, J., Akrim, A., & Anisah, H. U. (2021). Perceived effectiveness of e-governance as an underlying mechanism between good governance and public trust: A case of Indonesia. *Digital Policy. Regulation & Governance*, 23(6), 598–616. doi:10.1108/DPRG-03-2021-0046

Hasan, S., & Ukkusuri, S. V. (2014). Urban activity pattern classification using topic models from online geo-location data. *Transportation Research Part C, Emerging Technologies*, 44, 363–381. Advance online publication. doi:10.1016/j.trc.2014.04.003

Hasan, S., Ukkusuri, S. V., & Zhan, X. (2016). Understanding social influence in activity location choice and lifestyle patterns using geolocation data from social media. *Frontiers in ICT (Lausanne, Switzerland)*, 3. Advance online publication. doi:10.3389/fict.2016.00010

Haudi, H. (2023). The role of financial literacy, financial attitudes, and Family Financial Education on personal financial management and Locus of Control of university students. *International Journal of Social and Management Studies*, 4(2), 107–116. doi:10.5555/ijosmas.v4i2.289

Hecklau, F., Galeitzke, M., Flachs, S., & Kohl, H. (2016). Holistic approach for human resource management in Industry 4.0. *Procedia CIRP*, 54, 1–6. doi:10.1016/j.procir.2016.05.102

Hellman, R. (2011, October). The cloverleaves of social media challenges for e-governments. In *Proceedings of eChallenges e-2011 Conference* (pp. 1-8).

Hermansson, C., Jonsson, S., & Liu, L. (2022). The medium is the message: Learning channels, financial literacy, and stock market participation. *International Review of Financial Analysis*, 79(101996), 101996. doi:10.1016/j.irfa.2021.101996

He, W., Wu, H., Yan, G., Akula, V., & Shen, J. (2015). A novel social media competitive analytics framework with sentiment benchmarks. *Information & Management*, 52(7), 801–812. doi:10.1016/j.im.2015.04.006

Hidayati, N., Kartikowati, S., & Gimin, G. (2021). The influence of income level, financial literature, and social media use on teachers consumption behavior. *Journal of Educational Sciences*, 5(3), 479. doi:10.31258/jes.5.3.p.479-490

Himelein-Wachowiak, M., Giorgi, S., Devoto, A., Rahman, M., Ungar, L., Schwartz, H. A., Epstein, D. H., Leggio, L., & Curtis, B. (2021). Bots and misinformation spread on social media: Implications for COVID-19. In Journal of Medical Internet Research (Vol. 23, Issue 5). doi:10.2196/26933

Hinailiyas. (2021). *Right to privacy under article 21 and the related conflicts*. Legal Services India; Legal Services India. https://www.legalservicesindia.com/article/1630/Right-To-Privacy-Under-Article-21-and-the-Related-Conflicts.html

Hiremath, C. V., Chavadi, C. A., & Yatgiri, P. Y. (2013). Cloud Technology as an Alternative for Marketing Information System: An Empirical Study. *International Journal of Management. Research and Business Strategy, 2*(4).

Hiremath, C. V., Chavadi, C. A., &Yatgiri, P. Y. (2013). Cloud Technology as an Alternative for Marketing Information System: An Empirical Study. *International Journal of Management. Research and Business Strategy, 2*(4).

Hitchcock, L. I., & Young, J. A. (2016). Tweet, tweet!: Using live Twitter chats in social work education. *Social Work Education*, 35(4), 457–468. doi:10.1080/02615479.2015.1136273

Hoffmann, M., & Heft, A. (2020). "Here, There and Everywhere": Classifying Location Information in Social Media Data - Possibilities and Limitations. *Communication Methods and Measures*, 14(3), 184–203. Advance online publication. doi:10.1080/19312458.2019.1708282

Hofmann, S., Beverungen, D., Räckers, M., & Becker, J. (2013). What makes local governments' online communications successful? Insights from a multi-method analysis of Facebook. *Government Information Quarterly*, *30*(4), 387–396. doi:10.1016/j.giq.2013.05.013

Hosain, M. S. (2023). Integration of social media into HRM practices: A bibliometric overview. *PSU Research Review*, *7*(1), 51–72. doi:10.1108/PRR-12-2020-0039

Hswen, Y., Qin, Q., Brownstein, J. S., & Hawkins, J. B. (2019). Feasibility of using social media to monitor outdoor air pollution in London, England. *Preventive Medicine*, *121*, 86–93. Advance online publication. doi:10.1016/j.ypmed.2019.02.005 PMID:30742873

Huang, H., Yao, X. A., Krisp, J. M., & Jiang, B. (2021). Analytics of location-based big data for smart cities: Opportunities, challenges, and future directions. *Computers, Environment and Urban Systems*, *90*, 101712. Advance online publication. doi:10.1016/j.compenvurbsys.2021.101712

Hua, Y., & Feng, T. (2021). Geographic Information Systems. In J. Wang & F. Wu (Eds.), *Advances in Cartography and Geographic Information Engineering* (pp. 387–441). Springer Singapore. doi:10.1007/978-981-16-0614-4_11

Hudders, L., De Jans, S., & De Veirman, M. (2021). The commercialization of social media stars: A literature review and conceptual framework on the strategic use of social media influencers. *International Journal of Advertising*, *40*(3), 327–375. doi:10.1080/02650487.2020.1836925

Hung, S.Y., Chen, K., & Yi-Kuan, S. (2020). The effect of communication and social motives on E-government services through social media groups. *Behaviour and Information Technology*, *39*(7). . doi:10.1080/0144929X.2019.1610907

Hunt, A., & Specht, D. (2019). Crowdsourced mapping in crisis zones: Collaboration, organisation and impact. *Journal of International Humanitarian Action*, *4*(1), 1. Advance online publication. doi:10.118641018-018-0048-1

Hussain, H. (2019). Barriers and Drivers of using social media in e-goverance: A global case study. In *2019 IEEE International Symposium on Signal Processing and Information Technology (ISSPIT)* (pp. 1-6). IEEE. 10.1109/ISSPIT47144.2019.9001764

Hyland-Wood, B., Gardner, J., Leask, J., & Ecker, U. K. (2021). Toward effective government communication strategies in the era of COVID-19. *Humanities & Social Sciences Communications*, *8*(1), 30. doi:10.105741599-020-00701-w

Hyun, S. (2010). Predictors of Leadership quality and loyalty in the chain restaurant industry. *Cornell Hospitality Quarterly*, *51*(2), 251–267. Advance online publication. doi:10.1177/1938965510363264

Iivari, N., Sharma, S., & Ventä-Olkkonen, L. (2020). Digital transformation of everyday life–How COVID-19 pandemic transformed the basic education of the young generation and why information management research should care? *International Journal of Information Management*, *55*, 102183. doi:10.1016/j.ijinfomgt.2020.102183 PMID:32836640

Ilham, S. S. M. S. (2021). *E-Governance*. Deepublish.

India, P. R. S. (2021). *The personal data protection bill, 2019*. PRS Legislative Research. https://prsindia.org/billtrack/the-personal-data-protection-bill-2019

Ingale, K. K., & Paluri, R. A. (2022). Financial literacy and financial behaviour: A bibliometric analysis. *Review of Behavioral Finance*, *14*(1), 130–154. doi:10.1108/RBF-06-2020-0141

Islam, T., Mukhopadhyay, S. C., & Suryadevara, N. K. (2017). Smart Sensors and Internet of Things: A Postgraduate Paper. *IEEE Sensors Journal*, *17*(3), 577–584. Advance online publication. doi:10.1109/JSEN.2016.2630124

Ismagilova, E., Hughes, L., Rana, N. P., & Dwivedi, Y. K. (2020). Security, privacy and risks within smart cities: Literature review and development of a smart city interaction framework. *Information Systems Frontiers*, 1–22. PMID:32837262

Ivanov, S. (2019). Ultimate transformation: How will automation technologies disrupt the travel, tourism and hospitality industries? *Zeitschrift für Tourismuswissenschaft*, *11*(1), 25–43. doi:10.1515/tw-2019-0003

Jain, O., Gupta, M., Satam, S., & Panda, S. (2020). Has the COVID-19 pandemic affected the susceptibility to cyberbullying in India? *Computers in Human Behavior Reports*, *2*, 100029. doi:10.1016/j.chbr.2020.100029 PMID:34235292

Jannah, A. M., Murwatiningsih, M., & Oktarina, N. (2021). The effect of financial literacy, social media, and social environment towards the consumptive behavior of students at SMA Negeri Kabupaten Jepara. *The Journal of Economic Education*, *10*(1), 85–93. doi:10.15294/jeec.v9i2.43986

Jayapurakota.go.id. (2015). *Daku Papua, Special Data for Indigenous Papuans (OAP)*. https://bit.ly/3xMKlvg

Jayapurakota.go.id. (2016). *Nikcapil Kilat, Fast Execution and Obtaining of Marriage Certificate*. https://bit.ly/3twmjls

Jayapurakota.go.id. (2020). *Dukcapil Prevents Corona*. https://bit.ly/39uM1Qq

Jayasuriya, N., & Azam, F. (2018). The Impact of Social Media Marketing on Brand Equity: A Study of Fashion-Wear Retail in Sri Lanka. *International Review of Management and Marketing*, *7*(5), 178–183.

Jean-Baptiste, C. B. (2021). *Cyberbullying: The Digital World of Awareness and Emerging Concerns* [Doctoral dissertation]. Long Island University, CW Post Center.

Jeet, V. (2015). *The Growing Relevance of Social Media in Governance*. New Gen Soft. https://newgensoft.com/blog/the-growing-relevance-of-social-media-in-governance/

Jennifer Lund. (2023). How Customer Experience Drives Digital Transformation. Available at: https://www.superoffice.com/blog/digital-transformation/

Jennings, W., Stoker, G., Bunting, H., Valgarðsson, V. O., Gaskell, J., Devine, D., McKay, L., & Mills, M. C. (2021). Lack of trust, conspiracy beliefs, and social media use predict COVID-19 vaccine hesitancy. *Vaccines*, *9*(6), 593. doi:10.3390/vaccines9060593 PMID:34204971

Jing, F., Li, Z., Qiao, S., Zhang, J., Olatosi, B., & Li, X. (2023). Using geospatial social media data for infectious disease studies: a systematic review. In International Journal of Digital Earth (Vol. 16, Issue 1). doi:10.1080/17538947.2022.2161652

Jung, J., Petkanic, P., Nan, D., & Kim, J. H. (2020). When a girl awakened the world: A user and social message analysis of Greta Thunberg. *Sustainability (Basel)*, *12*(7), 2707. doi:10.3390u12072707

Jyoti, J., & Bhau, S. (2016). Empirical investigation of moderating and mediating variables in between transformational leadership and related outcomes: A study of higher education sector in North India. *International Journal of Educational Management*, *30*(6), 1123–1149. Advance online publication. doi:10.1108/IJEM-01-2015-0011

Kadam, A. B., & Atre, S. R. (2020). Negative impact of social media panic during the COVID-19 outbreak in India. *Journal of Travel Medicine*, *27*(3), taaa057. doi:10.1093/jtm/taaa057 PMID:32307545

Kakinuma, Y. (2022). Financial literacy and quality of life: A moderated mediation approach of fintech adoption and leisure. *International Journal of Social Economics*, *49*(12), 1713–1726. doi:10.1108/IJSE-10-2021-0633

Kalyani, V. (2017). Empowering Women Farmers Participation in Organic Agricultural Development. *International Journal of Multidisciplinary Educational Research*, *6*(2), 187.

Kalyani, V. (2017). Empowering Women Farmers Participation In Organic Agricultural Development. *International Journal of Multidisciplinary Educational Research*, *6*(2), 187.

Kalyani, V. (2018). Organic farming in Tamil Nadu: Status, Issues and Prospects. American International Journal of Research in Humanities. *Arts and Social Sciences*, *21*(1), 82–86.

Kalyani, V. (2020). *Perception of Certified Organic Farmers towards Organic Farming Practices in Pudukkottai District of TamilNadu (No. 4784)*. Easy Chair.

KalyaniV. (2021). A Study of Effect of Social Networking Sites on the Self-Esteem of Adolescent Girl Students Belonging to Urban Areas of Sivaganga District. Available at SSRN 3879915. doi:10.2139/ssrn.3879915

Kalyani, V. (2021). *Marketing Intelligence Practices on Fmcg Consumer Preferences and Buying Behaviour Pattern Using Social Network Analysis (No. 5857)*. EasyChair.

Kalyani, V. (2021). *Parental Involvement in Improving Children's Learning in Social Work Perspective (No. 5107)*. Easy Chair.

Kalyani, V. (2021). *The Employee Engagement on Human Resources Information System Practice Through E-Learning Training (No. 5856)*. EasyChair.

Kalyani, V. (2021c). *Parental Involvement in Improving Children's learning in Social Work Perspective (No. 5107)*. Easy Chair.

Kalyani, V. (2021d). *The Employee Engagement on Human Resources Information System Practice through E-Learning Training (No. 5856)*. Easy Chair.

Kalyani, V. (2023). Regression Analysis in R: A Comprehensive View for the Social Sciences. *Journal of the Royal Statistical Society. Series A, (Statistics in Society)*, qnad081. doi:10.1093/jrsssa/qnad081

Kalyani, V., Arumugam, T., & Surya Kumar, M. (2022). Women in Oppressive Societies as Portrayed in Kollywood Movies. *American Journal of Economics and Sociology*, *81*(1), 173–185. doi:10.1111/ajes.12450

Kandipi, H. D. (2021). *Jayapura City Government Collaborates with GrabExpress to send residence documents*. https://bit.ly/3NNSwwR

Kankanamge, N., Yigitcanlar, T., Goonetilleke, A., & Kamruzzaman, M. (2020). Determining disaster severity through social media analysis: Testing the methodology with South East Queensland Flood tweets. *International Journal of Disaster Risk Reduction*, *42*, 101360. Advance online publication. doi:10.1016/j.ijdrr.2019.101360

Kaplan, A. M., & Haenlein, M. (2010). Users of the world, unite! The challenges and opportunities of Social Media. Business Horizons, 53(1), 59-68. doi:10.1016/j.bushor.2009.09.003

Kaplan, A., & Haenlein, M. (2020). Rulers of the world, unite! The challenges and opportunities of artificial intelligence. *Business Horizons*, *63*(1), 37–50. doi:10.1016/j.bushor.2019.09.003

Kapoor, K. K., Tamilmani, K., Rana, N. P., Patil, P., Dwivedi, Y. K., & Nerur, S. (2018). Advances in Social Media Research: Past, Present and Future. *Information Systems Frontiers*, *20*(3), 531–558. doi:10.100710796-017-9810-y

Kapsoulis, N., Psychas, A., Palaiokrassas, G., Marinakis, A., Litke, A., & Varvarigou, T. (2020). Know your customer (KYC) implementation with smart contracts on a privacy-oriented decentralized architecture. *Future Internet*, *12*(2), 41. doi:10.3390/fi12020041

Karakiza, M. (2015). The impact of social media in the public sector. *Procedia: Social and Behavioral Sciences*, *175*, 384–392. doi:10.1016/j.sbspro.2015.01.1214

Karmakar, S., & Das, S. (2021). Understanding the rise of Twitter-based cyberbullying due to COVID-19 through comprehensive statistical evaluation. *Proceedings of the 54th Hawaii international conference on system sciences.* 10.24251/HICSS.2021.309

Karthick, A. V., & Millath, D. M. A. (2019). *Management of digital libraries for active learning environment: Trends and challenges.* Library Philosophy and Practice.

Karthick, A. V., Millath, D. M. A., & Thowseaf, S. (2018). Elucidating Water Supply, Demand and Contamination in Tamil Nadu. *Shanlax. International Journal of Management, 5*(3), 209–219.

Karthick, A. V., Millath, M. A., Karthik, R. R., & Faisal, M. (2019). Influence of social marketing on rain water harvesting practices for water recycling system. *International Journal of Recent Technology and Engineering, 8*(2), 654–661.

Karthik, R. R., Thowseaf, S., & Millath, M. A. (2018). Impact of demonetization and GST on stock price of automobile sector. *ZENITH International Journal of Multidisciplinary Research, 8*(11), 35–44.

Karumban, S., Sanyal, S., Laddunuri, M. M., Sivalinga, V. D., Shanmugam, V., Bose, V., & Murugan, S. P. (2023). Industrial Automation and Its Impact on Manufacturing Industries. In Revolutionizing Industrial Automation Through the Convergence of Artificial Intelligence and the Internet of Things (pp. 24-40). IGI Global.

Karumban, S., Sanyal, S., Laddunuri, M. M., Sivalinga, V. D., Shanmugam, V., Bose, V., . . . Murugan, S. P. (2023). Industrial Automation and Its Impact on Manufacturing Industries. In Revolutionizing Industrial Automation Through the Convergence of Artificial Intelligence and the Internet of Things (pp. 24-40). IGI Global.

Katongole, S. P., Yaro, P., & Bukuluki, P. (2021). *The impact of COVID-19 on mental health of frontline health workers in Ghana and Uganda Mental Health Effects of COVID-19.* Elsevier.

Katzenbach, C., & Ulbricht, L. (2019). Algorithmic governance. *Internet Policy Review, 8*(4), 1–18. doi:10.14763/2019.4.1424

Kaur. (2019). Digital currency and its implications in India. *Money Digital Currency*, 64-67.

Kaur, M., & Saini, M. (2023). Indian government initiatives on cyberbullying: A case study on cyberbullying in Indian higher education institutions. *Education and Information Technologies, 28*(1), 581–615. doi:10.100710639-022-11168-4 PMID:35814802

Kaushik, V., & Walsh, C. A. (2019). Pragmatism as a research paradigm and its implications for social work research. *Social Sciences (Basel, Switzerland), 8*(9), 255. doi:10.3390ocsci8090255

Kazemi, A., PaEmami, V. M., Abbaszadeh, A., & Pourzamani, J. (2013). Impact of brand identity on customer loyalty and word of mouth communications, considering mediating role of customer satisfaction and brand commitment (Case study: Customers of Mellat Bank in Kermanshah). *International Journal of Academic Research in Economics and Management Sciences, 2*(4), 1–14. doi:10.6007/IJAREMS/v2-i4/1

Kee, D. M. H., Al-Anesi, M. A. L., & Al-Anesi, S. A. L. (2022). Cyberbullying on Social Media under the Influence of COVID-19. *Global Business and Organizational Excellence, 41*(6), 11–22. doi:10.1002/joe.22175

Keister, T., & Monnet, C. (2022). Central bank digital currency: Stability and information. *Journal of Economic Dynamics & Control, 142*, 104501. doi:10.1016/j.jedc.2022.104501

Kethineni, S. (2020). Cybercrime in India: Laws, regulations, and enforcement mechanisms. The Palgrave Handbook of International Cybercrime and Cyberdeviance, 305-326.

Khairul, K., & Aulia Putri, R. (2022). *The correlation between the students' habit to watch English YouTube channel and their speaking skill.* ELECT. doi:10.37301/elect.v1i2.56

Khan, M. S., & Ahmad, Z. (2022). The effects of financial literacy and social media on financial behaviour. In Mixed Methods Perspectives on Communication and Social Media Research (pp. 144–164). doi:10.4324/9781003265887-12

Khan, G. F., Swar, B., & Lee, S. K. (2014). Social media risks and benefits: A public sector perspective. *Social Science Computer Review, 32*(5), 606–627. doi:10.1177/0894439314524701

Khan, M. N., Ashraf, M. A., Seinen, D., Khan, K. U., & Laar, R. A. (2021). Social Media for Knowledge Acquisition and Dissemination: The Impact of the COVID-19 Pandemic on Collaborative Learning Driven Social Media Adoption. *Frontiers in Psychology, 12*, 648253. doi:10.3389/fpsyg.2021.648253 PMID:34135814

Khan, N. A., & Khan, A. N. (2019). What followers are saying about transformational leaders fostering employee innovation via organisational learning, knowledge sharing and social media use in public organisations? *Government Information Quarterly, 36*(4), 101391. doi:10.1016/j.giq.2019.07.003

Khanna, A., & Arora, B. (2009). A study to investigate the reasons for bank frauds and the implementation of preventive security controls in Indian banking industry. *International Journal of Business Science and Applied Management, 4*(3), 1–21.

Khan, S., Umer, R., Umer, S., & Naqvi, S. (2021). Antecedents of trust in using social media for E-government services: An empirical study in Pakistan. *Technology in Society, 64*, 101400. Advance online publication. doi:10.1016/j.techsoc.2020.101400

Khurana, P. (2019). Digital Education: Impact of Social Media in Quality Higher Education, *An international peer-Reviewed open Access. Journal of Interdisciplinary Studies, 2*(1). https://www.gapinterdisciplinarities.org/res/articles/(372-375).pdf

Kietzmann, J. H., Hermkens, K., McCarthy, I. P., & Silvestre, B. S. (2011). Social media? Get serious! Understanding the functional building blocks of social media. *Business Horizons, 54*(3), 241–251. doi:10.1016/j.bushor.2011.01.005

Kimball, E., & Kim, J. (2013). Virtual boundaries: Ethical considerations for use of social media in social work. *Social Work, 58*(2), 185–188. doi:10.1093wwt005 PMID:23724583

Kim, J., & Lee, J. (2021). An analysis of spatial accessibility changes according to the attractiveness index of public libraries using social media data. *Sustainability (Basel), 13*(16), 9087. Advance online publication. doi:10.3390u13169087

Kim, S.-B., & Kim, D.-Y. (2016). The impacts of corporate social responsibility, service quality, and transparency on relationship quality and customer loyalty in the hotel industry. *Asian Journal of Sustainability and Social Responsibility, 1*(1), 39–55. doi:10.118641180-016-0004-1

Kim, Y., Wang, Y., & Oh, J. (2016). Digital Media Use and Social Engagement: How Social Media and Smartphone Use Influence Social Activities of College Students. *Cyberpsychology, Behavior, and Social Networking, 19*(4), 264–269. doi:10.1089/cyber.2015.0408 PMID:26991638

Kintonova, A., Vasyaev, A., & Shestak, V. (2021). Cyberbullying and cyber-mobbing in developing countries. *Information and Computer Security, 29*(3), 435–456. doi:10.1108/ICS-02-2020-0031

Kiran Jason Samuel. (2014). The Human Resources & Social Media Revolution. *Torry Harris.* https://www.torryharris.com/blog/the-human-resources-and-social-media-revolution

Kitchin, R. (2014b). The Data Revolution: Big Data, Open Data, Data Infrastructures & Their Consequences. In The Data Revolution: Big Data, Open Data, Data Infrastructures & Their Consequences. doi:10.4135/9781473909472

Kitchin, R. (2014a). Big Data, new epistemologies and paradigm shifts. *Big Data & Society, 1*(1). doi:10.1177/2053951714528481

Klein, T. (2022). A note on GameStop, short squeezes, and autodidactic herding: An evolution in financial literacy? *Finance Research Letters, 46*(102229), 102229. doi:10.1016/j.frl.2021.102229

Kline, R. (2010). Principles And Practice Of Structural Equation Modeling. Guilford Press.

Klinger, U., & Svensson, J. (2015). The emergence of network media logic in political communication: A theoretical approach. *New Media & Society, 17*(8), 1241–1257. doi:10.1177/1461444814522952

Kock, N., & Lynn, G. (2012). Lateral Collinearity and Misleading Results in Variance-Based SEM: An Illustration and Recommendations. *Journal of the Association for Information Systems, 13*(7), 546–580. doi:10.17705/1jais.00302

Koh, J. X., & Liew, T. M. (2022). How loneliness is talked about in social media during COVID-19 pandemic: Text mining of 4,492 Twitter feeds. *Journal of Psychiatric Research, 145*, 317–324. doi:10.1016/j.jpsychires.2020.11.015 PMID:33190839

Kompella, L. (2020). Socio-technical transitions and organizational responses: Insights from e-governance case studies. *Journal of Global Information Technology Management, 23*(2), 89–111. doi:10.1080/1097198X.2020.1752082

Koskelainen, T., Kalmi, P., Scornavacca, E., & Vartiainen, T. (2023). Financial literacy in the digital age – A research agenda. *The Journal of Consumer Affairs, 57*(1), 507–528. doi:10.1111/joca.12510

Kostanski, L. (2012). Crowd-Sourcing Geospatial Information for Government Gazetteers. *Tenth United Nations Conference on the Standardization of Geographical Names.*

Kristiawan, M., Suryani, I., Muntazir, M., Areli, A.J., Agustina, M., Kafarisa, R.F., Saputra, A.G., Diana, N., Agustina, E., Oktarina, R., & Hisri, T.B. (2018). *Educational Innovation.* Jawa Timur: WADE Publish.

Kuchciak, I., & Wiktorowicz, J. (2021). Empowering financial education by banks—Social media as a modern channel. *Journal of Risk and Financial Management, 14*(3), 118. doi:10.3390/jrfm14030118

Kulai, A., Sankhe, M., Anglekar, S., & Halbe, A. (2021). *Emotion analysis of Covid tweets using FastText supervised classifier model.* Paper presented at the 2021 International Conference on Communication information and Computing Technology (ICCICT). 10.1109/ICCICT50803.2021.9510156

Kulkarni, A. (2022). *Public perception of the "Digital Rupee" in India.* National College of Ireland.

Kumar, M. S., & Krishnan, D. S. G. (2020). *Perceived Usefulness (PU), Perceived Ease of Use (PEOU), and Behavioural Intension to Use (BIU): Mediating effect of Attitude toward Use (AU) with reference to Mobile wallet Acceptance and Adoption in Rural India.* Academic Press.

Kumari, S., & Jindal, P. (2021). The Impact of Social Media on Customer Satisfaction in the Indian Banking Industry. *Journal of Management Information and Decision Sciences, 24*, 1–15.

Kumari, S., Jindal, P., & Mittal, A. (2023). Employee Productivity: Exploring the Multidimensional Nature with Acculturation, Open Innovation, Social Media Networking and Employee Vitality in the Indian Banking Sector: An Analytical Approach. *International Journal of Professional Business Review, 8*(7), e02535–e02535. doi:10.26668/businessreview/2023.v8i7.2535

Kumar, K. S. V., & Devi, V. R. (2014). Social Media in Financial Services – A Theoretical Perspective. *Procedia Economics and Finance, 11*, 306–313. doi:10.1016/S2212-5671(14)00198-1

Kumar, P., Pillai, R., Kumar, N., & Tabash, M. I. (2023). The interplay of skills, digital financial literacy, capability, and autonomy in financial decision making and well-being. *Borsa Istanbul Review, 23*(1), 169–183. doi:10.1016/j.bir.2022.09.012

Kumar, S. (2018). An Assessment of Impact of GST on India's Online Retail Sector. *Economic Affairs*, *63*(4). Advance online publication. doi:10.30954/0424-2513.4.2018.16

Kumar, V. A., Pandey, K. K., & Punia, D. K. (2014). Cyber security threats in the power sector: Need for a domain specific regulatory framework in India. *Energy Policy*, *65*, 126–133. doi:10.1016/j.enpol.2013.10.025

Kun Wiryanti & Fardinal. (2020). The Effect of Perceived Ease of Use on the Quality of Accounting Information Systems and its Impact on the Quality of Accounting Information. *Saudi Journal of Business and Management Studies*, 571-577.

Kusumasari, B., & Alam, Q. (2012). Bridging the gaps: The role of local government capability and the management of a natural disaster in Bantul, Indonesia. *Natural Hazards*, *60*(2), 761–779. doi:10.100711069-011-0016-1

Kwan, J. S.-L., & Lim, K. H. (2021). *Tweetcovid: A system for analysing public sentiments and discussions about covid-19 via twitter activities*. Paper presented at the 26th International Conference on Intelligent User Interfaces-Companion. 10.1145/3397482.3450733

Lakshmikumaran, C. (2023, January 13). Digital Personal Data Protection Bill: What rights does it give individuals? *The Economic Times*. https://economictimes.indiatimes.com/wealth/legal/will/digital-personal-data-protection-bill-what-rights-does-it-give-individuals/articleshow/96535688.cms?from=mdr

Lallie, H. S., Shepherd, L. A., Nurse, J. R., Erola, A., Epiphaniou, G., Maple, C., & Bellekens, X. (2021). Cyber security in the age of COVID-19: A timeline and analysis of cyber-crime and cyber-attacks during the pandemic. *Computers & Security*, *105*, 102248. doi:10.1016/j.cose.2021.102248 PMID:36540648

Landsbergen, D. (2010, June). Government as part of the revolution: Using social media to achieve public goals. In *Proceedings of the 10th European conference on e-government* (pp. 243-250).

Lan, M., Liu, L., Hernandez, A., Liu, W., Zhou, H., & Wang, Z. (2019). The spillover effect of geotagged tweets as a measure of ambient population for theft crime. *Sustainability (Basel)*, *11*(23), 6748. Advance online publication. doi:10.3390u11236748

Lapaslhoknga. (2021). *Bureaucracy Reform*. https://bit.ly/3zAH6Z8

Lee, J. H. (2021). *Understanding Public Attitudes toward COVID-19 with Twitter*. Paper presented at the 2021 Systems and Information Engineering Design Symposium (SIEDS). 10.1109/SIEDS52267.2021.9483708

Lee-Geiller, S., & Lee, T. D. (2019). Using government websites to enhance democratic E-governance: A conceptual model for evaluation. *Government Information Quarterly*, *36*(2), 208–225. doi:10.1016/j.giq.2019.01.003

Lee, N. M., & VanDyke, M. S. (2015). Set it and forget it: The one-way use of social media by government agencies communicating science. *Science Communication*, *37*(4), 533–541. doi:10.1177/1075547015588600

Lee, S. C. (2020). Social work and social media: Organizing in the digital age. *Journal of Public Health Issues and Practices*, *4*(1), 1–6. doi:10.33790/jphip1100158

Lelisho, M. E., Pandey, D., Alemu, B. D., Pandey, B. K., & Tareke, S. A. (2023). The Negative Impact of Social Media during COVID-19 Pandemic. *Trends in Psychology*, *31*(1), 123–142. Advance online publication. doi:10.100743076-022-00192-5

Lenadora, D., Gamage, G., Haputhanthri, D., Meedeniya, D., & Perera, I. (2020). *Exploratory analysis of a social media network in Sri Lanka during the COVID-19 virus outbreak*. arXiv preprint arXiv:2006.07855.

Lessard, L. M., & Puhl, R. M. (2021). Adolescent academic worries amid COVID-19 and perspectives on pandemic-related changes in teacher and peer relations. *The School Psychologist*, *36*(5), 285–292. doi:10.1037pq0000443 PMID:34292037

Leviastuti, A., Santika, T. D., & Prasetyo, I. (2022). Empowering women through social media-based financial-literacy education program. *RSF Conference Series: Business, Management and Social Sciences, 2*(1), 88–95. doi:10.31098/bmss.v2i1.520

Liao, Q., Yuan, J., Dong, M., Yang, L., Fielding, R., & Lam, W. W. T. (2020). Public engagement and government responsiveness in the communications about COVID-19 during the early epidemic stage in China: Infodemiology study on social media data. *Journal of Medical Internet Research, 22*(5), e18796. doi:10.2196/18796 PMID:32412414

Li, F., Larimo, J., & Leonidou, L. C. (2021). Social media marketing strategy: Definition, conceptualization, taxonomy, validation, and future agenda. *Journal of the Academy of Marketing Science, 49*(1), 51–70. doi:10.100711747-020-00733-3

Linders, D. (2012). From e-government to we-government: Defining a typology for citizen coproduction in the age of social media. *Government Information Quarterly, 29*(4), 446–454. doi:10.1016/j.giq.2012.06.003

Lindqvist, E., & Östling, R. (2010). Political polarization and the size of government. *The American Political Science Review, 104*(3), 543–565. doi:10.1017/S0003055410000262

Lin, Y. (2022). Social media for collaborative planning: A typology of support functions and challenges. *Cities (London, England), 125*, 103641. Advance online publication. doi:10.1016/j.cities.2022.103641

Liu, L., Wang, R., Guan, W. W., Bao, S., Yu, H., Fu, X., & Liu, H. (2022). Assessing Reliability of Chinese Geotagged Social Media Data for Spatiotemporal Representation of Human Mobility. *ISPRS International Journal of Geo-Information, 11*(2), 145. Advance online publication. doi:10.3390/ijgi11020145

LotfianM.IngensandJ. (2021). Using geo geo-tagged flickr images to explore the correlation between land cover classes and the location of bird observations. *International Archives of the Photogrammetry, Remote Sensing and Spatial Information Sciences - ISPRS Archives, 43*(B4-2021). doi:10.5194/isprs-archives-XLIII-B4-2021-189-2021

Lu, G., Kubli, M., Moist, R., Zhang, X., Li, N., Gächter, I., & Fleck, M. (2022). Tough times, extraordinary care: A critical assessment of chatbot-based digital mental healthcare solutions for older persons to fight against pandemics like covid-19. *Proceedings of Sixth International Congress on Information and Communication Technology: ICICT 2021, 1*. 10.1007/978-981-16-2377-6_68

Luqman, D., Marpaung, F. H., Marpaung, M. C., Girsang, A. S., & Muhamad Isa, S. (2019). City Traffic Analysis Based on Facebook Data. *Proceeding - 2019 International Conference on ICT for Smart Society: Innovation and Transformation Toward Smart Region, ICISS 2019*. 10.1109/ICISS48059.2019.8969835

Lyons, A., & Kass-Hanna, J. (2021). A multidimensional approach to defining and measuring financial literacy in the digital age. SSRN *Electronic Journal*. doi:10.4324/9781003025221-7

Lyons, A. C., & Kass-Hanna, J. (2021). A methodological overview to defining and measuring "digital" financial literacy. *Financial Planning Review, 4*(2). doi:10.1002/cfp2.1113

Lyons, A. C., & Kass-Hanna, J. (2021). Financial inclusion, financial literacy and economically vulnerable populations in the middle east and north Africa. *Emerging Markets Finance & Trade, 57*(9), 2699–2738. doi:10.1080/1540496X.2019.1598370

Madnick, S. E., Wang, R. Y., Lee, Y. W., & Zhu, H. (2009). Overview and framework for data and information quality research. *Journal of Data and Information Quality, 1*(1), 1-22.

Madyatmadja, E. D., Nindito, H., & Pristinella, D. (2019, November). Citizen attitude: Potential impact of social media based government. In *Proceedings of the 2019 3rd International Conference on Education and E-Learning* (pp. 128-134). ACM. 10.1145/3371647.3371653

Magro, M. J. (2012). A review of social media use in e-government. *Administrative Sciences*, 2(2), 148–161. doi:10.3390/admsci2020148

Majid, R., & Nugraha, R. A. (2022). The CROWDFUNDING AND ISLAMIC SECURITIES: THE ROLE OF FINANCIAL LITERACY. *Journal of Islamic Monetary Economics and Finance*, 8(1), 89–112. doi:10.21098/jimf.v8i1.1420

Malhotra, P., & Singh, B. (2016). Presence of banking in social media: Indian evidence. *International Journal of Business Forecasting and Marketing Intelligence*, 2(2), 117 - 127. doi:10.1504/IJBFMI.2016.078149

MalhotraD. P. (2017). Impact of social networking sites on financial performance: A case study of Indian banks. Available at SSRN 2965888. doi:10.2139/ssrn.2965888

Mamgain, A., Joshi, U., & Chauhan, J. (2020). Impact of Social Media in Enhancing Agriculture Extension. *Agriculture and Food: E-Newsletter, 2*(9).

Manacorda, M., & Tesei, A. (2020). Liberation technology: Mobile phones and political mobilization in Africa. *Econometrica*, 88(2), 533–567. doi:10.3982/ECTA14392

Manickam, T., Vinayagamoorthi, G., Gopalakrishnan, S., Sudha, M., & Mathiraj, S. P. (2022). Customer Inclination on Mobile Wallets With Reference to Google-Pay and PayTM in Bengaluru City. [IJEBR]. *International Journal of E-Business Research*, 18(1), 1–16. doi:10.4018/IJEBR.293295

Manikandan, G., Murugaiah, S., Velusamy, K., Ramesh, A. B. K., Rathinavelu, S., Viswanathan, R., & Jageerkhan, M. N. (2022). Work Life Imbalance and Emotional Intelligence: A Major Role and Segment Among College Teachers. *International Journal of Professional Business Review*, 7(6), e0832. doi:10.26668/businessreview/2022.v7i6.832

Mansoor, M. (2021). Citizens' trust in government as a function of good governance and government agency's provision of quality information on social media during COVID-19. *Government Information Quarterly*, 38(4), 101597. doi:10.1016/j.giq.2021.101597 PMID:34642542

Manzira, F. M., & Bankole, F. (2018, October). Application of Social Media Analytics in the banking sector to drive growth and sustainability: A proposed integrated framework. In *2018 Open Innovations Conference (OI)* (pp. 223-233). IEEE. 10.1109/OI.2018.8535833

MarlanHutahaean, JavanisaEunike, & Silalahi. (2023). Do Social Media, Good Governance, and Public Trust Increase Citizens' e-Government Participation? Dual Approach of PLS-SEM and fsQCA. *Human Behavior and Emerging Technologies*, 1–19.

Marmora, P. (2022). Does monetary policy fuel bitcoin demand? Event-study evidence from emerging markets. *Journal of International Financial Markets, Institutions and Money*, 77, 101489. doi:10.1016/j.intfin.2021.101489

Marongwe, N., & Garidzirai, R. (2021). Together but Not Together: Challenges of Remote Learning for Students Amid the COVID-19 Pandemic in Rural South African Universities. *Research in Social Sciences and Technology*, 6(3), 213–226. Advance online publication. doi:10.46303/ressat.2021.39

Marson, S. M., DeAngelis, D., & Mittal, N. (2010). The Association of Social Work Boards' licensure examinations: A review of reliability and validity processes. *Research on Social Work Practice*, 20(1), 87–99. doi:10.1177/1049731509347858

Martí, P., Pérez del Hoyo, R., Nolasco-Cirugeda, A., Serrano-Estrada, L., & García-Mayor, C. (2021). The potential of location-based social networks for participatory urban planning. In Smart Cities and the un SDGs. doi:10.1016/B978-0-323-85151-0.00008-7

Mason, A. N., Narcum, J., & Mason, K. (2021). Social media marketing gains importance after Covid-19. *Cogent Business & Management*, 8(1), 1870797. doi:10.1080/23311975.2020.1870797

Mastley, C. P. (2017). Social Media and Information Behavior: A Citation Analysis of Current Research from 2008–2015. *The Serials Librarian*, *73*(3–4), 339–351. doi:10.1080/0361526X.2017.1356420

Matamoros-Fernández, A., & Farkas, J. (2021). Racism, hate speech, and social media: A systematic review and critique. *Television & New Media*, *22*(2), 205–224. doi:10.1177/1527476420982230

Mavenroad.com. (2019). Fridays for Future: The Social Media Impact of Greta Thunberg: How the young climate change activist is raising awareness within social media. *Maven Road*. https://mavenroad.com/fridaysforfuture-the-social-media-impact-of-greta-thunberg/

Ma, Y. J., Gam, H. J., & Banning, J. (2017). Perceived ease of use and usefulness of sustainability labels on apparel products: Application of the technology acceptance model. *Fashion and Textiles*, *4*(3), 2–20. doi:10.118640691-017-0093-1

McCombs, M., & Stroud, N. J. (2014). Psychology of agenda-setting effects: Mapping the paths of information processing. *Review of Communication Research*, *2*, 68–93. doi:10.12840/issn.2255-4165.2014.02.01.003

McFadden, P., Campbell, A., & Taylor, B. (2019). Corrigendum: This is a correction to: Resilience and Burnout in Child Protection Social Work: Individual and Organisational Themes from a Systematic Literature Review, The British Journal of Social Work, Volume 45, Issue 5, July 2015, Pages 1546–1563. *British Journal of Social Work*, *49*(2), 552–553. doi:10.1093/bjsw/bcw051

McKitrick, M. K., Schuurman, N., & Crooks, V. A. (2023). Collecting, analyzing, and visualizing location-based social media data: review of methods in GIS-social media analysis. In GeoJournal (Vol. 88, Issue 1). doi:10.100710708-022-10584-w

MCNAMARA, L. (2011). Social media: What role should it play in the courts? [Law Society of South Australia]. *Bulletin*, *33*(4), 22–23.

Medina, C., & Rufín, R. (2015). Transparency policy and students' satisfaction and trust. *Transforming Government*, *9*(3), 309–323. doi:10.1108/TG-07-2014-0027

Meijer, A., & Thaens, M. (2018). Urban Technological Innovation: Developing and Testing a Sociotechnical Framework for Studying Smart City Projects. *Urban Affairs Review*, *54*(2), 363–387. Advance online publication. doi:10.1177/1078087416670274

Meitriana, M. A., Yuliarmi, N. N., Utama, M. S., & Marhaeni, A. A. I. N. (2022). Social capital-based financial literacy to improve business performance: A narrative review. *International Journal on Social Science. Economics and Art*, *12*(2), 83–90. doi:10.35335/ijosea.v12i2.97

Menon, S. R., & Chavadi, C. A. (2022). A Research-based Approach to Identify the Health-conscious Consumers in India. *Metamorphosis*, *21*(2), 118–128. doi:10.1177/09726225221098783

Meoli, M., Rossi, A., & Vismara, S. (2022). Financial literacy and security-based crowdfunding. *Corporate Governance*, *30*(1), 27–54. doi:10.1111/corg.12355

Mergel, I., Edelmann, N., & Haug, N. (2019). Defining digital transformation: Results from expert interviews. *Government Information Quarterly*, *36*(4), 101385. doi:10.1016/j.giq.2019.06.002

Metcalfe, B. D., & Rees, C. J. (2005). Theorizing advances in international human resource development. *Human Resource Development International*, *8*(4), 449–465. doi:10.1080/13678860500354601

Meyer, J. P., Allen, N. J., & Smith, C. A. (1993). Commitment to organizations and occupations: Extension and test of a three-component conceptualization. *The Journal of Applied Psychology*, *78*(4), 538–551. doi:10.1037/0021-9010.78.4.538

Mhlanga, D. (2020). Industry 4.0 in finance: The impact of artificial intelligence (ai) on digital financial inclusion. *International Journal of Financial Studies, 8*(3), 45. doi:10.3390/ijfs8030045

Millath. (2019a). Indian Tea production Overview and Price Analysis. *International Journal of Advanced Science and Technology, 28*(19), 1253 - 1259.

Millath. (2019b). Identifying Work-Family Conflict Among IT Employees of Infopark, Kochi, Kerala. *International Journal of Advanced Science and Technology, 28*(19), 1164 - 1176.

Millath. (2019c). A Study and Analysis on Sustainable Business Models for Indian Automotive Industry. *International Journal of Advanced Science and Technology, 28*(19), 953 - 959.

Millath, M. A., & Thowseaf, S. (2016). Export performance of Special Economic Zones in India and its economic contribution. *International Journal of Innovative Research in Management Studies, 1*(10), 24–28.

Millath, M. A., & Thowseaf, S. (2017). An investigative study on stock performance of selected companies in food and beverage sector listed under BSE. *ZENITH International Journal of Business Economics & Management Research, 7*(4), 59–70.

Ministry of Home Affairs. (2019). *Pelayanan GISA Hadir di Kota Jayapura.* https://dukcapil.kemendagri.go.id/berita/baca/229/pelayanan-gisa-hadir-

Miranda, F. J., Chamorro, A., Rubio, S., & Morgado, V. (2013). Evaluation of social networks sites in the banking sector: An analysis of top 200 international banks. *Journal of Internet Banking and Commerce, 18*(2), 1–17.

Mishaal, D., & Abu-Shana, E. B. (2015). *The Effect of Using Social Media in Governments: Framework of Communication Success.* doi:10.15849/icit.2015.0069

Mishaal, D. A., & Abu-Shanab, E. A. (2017). Utilizing Facebook by the Arab World Governments. *International Journal of Public Administration in the Digital Age, 4*(3), 53–78. doi:10.4018/IJPADA.2017070105

Mishna, F., Bogo, M., Root, J., Sawyer, J. L., & Khoury-Kassabri, M. (2012). "It just crept in": The digital age and implications for social work practice. *Clinical Social Work Journal, 40*(3), 277–286. doi:10.100710615-012-0383-4

Misra, S., Cheng, L., Genevie, J., & Yuan, M. (2014). The iphone effect: The quality of in-person social interactions in the presence of mobile device. *Environment and Behavior*, 1–24.

Mogaji, E., Soetan, T. O., & Kieu, T. A. (2020). The implications of artificial intelligence on the digital marketing of financial services to vulnerable customers. *Australasian Marketing Journal, j-ausmj.*

Mohamed, S. M., Yehia, E., & Marie, M. (2022). Relationship between E-CRM, Service Quality, Customer Satisfaction, Trust, and Loyalty in banking Industry. *Future Computing and Informatics Journal, 7*(2), 51–74. doi:10.54623/fue.fcij.7.2.5

Mohd Padil, H., Kasim, E. S., Muda, S., Ismail, N., & Md Zin, N. (2022). Financial literacy and awareness of investment scams among university students. *Journal of Financial Crime, 29*(1), 355–367. doi:10.1108/JFC-01-2021-0012

Moleong, L. J. (2017). *Qualitative Research Methodology* (Revised Edition). Remaja Rosda Karya.

Moore, M. (2023). Fake accounts on social media, epistemic uncertainty and the need for an independent auditing of accounts. *Internet Policy Review, 12*(1).

Morgan, P. J. (2021). Fintech, financial literacy, and financial education. In The Routledge Handbook of Financial Literacy (pp. 239–258). doi:10.4324/9781003025221-21

Mossbridge, J., Tressoldi, P., & Utts, J. (2012). Predictive physiological anticipation preceding seemingly unpredictable stimuli: A meta-analysis. *Frontiers in Psychology*, *3*, 390. doi:10.3389/fpsyg.2012.00390 PMID:23109927

Mucan, B., & Özeltürkay, E. Y. (2014). Social Media Creates Competitive Advantages: How Turkish Banks Use This Power? A Content Analysis of Turkish Banks through their Webpages. *Procedia: Social and Behavioral Sciences*, *148*, 137–145. doi:10.1016/j.sbspro.2014.07.027

Mudasih, I., & Subroto, W. T. (2021). The effect of financial literacy, digital literacy, and entrepreneurial learning outcome on entrepreneur behavior of students at SMK Negeri 1 Surabaya. *Technium Soc. Sci. J.*, *15*, 303.

Mugilan, A., Kanmani, R., Deva Priya, M., Christy Jeba Malar, A., & Suganya, R. (2021). Smart Sentimental Analysis of the Impact of Social Media on COVID-19. *Micro-Electronics and Telecommunication Engineering: Proceedings of 4th ICMETE 2020*. 10.1007/978-981-33-4687-1_42

Mugisha, C. (2018). Social Work in a Digital Age: The Need to Integrate Social Media in Social Work Education in the UK. *Journal of Social Work Education and Practice*, *3*(4), 1–10.

Muhammad, R., Zhao, Y., & Liu, F. (2019). Spatiotemporal analysis to observe gender based check-in behavior by using social media big data: A case study of Guangzhou, China. *Sustainability (Basel)*, *11*(10), 2822. Advance online publication. doi:10.3390u11102822

Mullappallykayamkulath, M. A. (2022). Digital Financial Literacy and its Impact on the Financial Behaviour of Millennials: An Empirical Investigation. *International Journal of Financial Management*, *12*(3).

Muluk, K. (2008). *Knowledge Management: The Key to Success in Local Government Innovation*. Bayumedia Publishing.

Munna, A. S., & Khanam, R. (2021). Analysis of the value and advantages of financial literacy and digitalization to the individual. *International Journal of Asian Education*, *2*(2), 141–152. doi:10.46966/ijae.v2i2.80

Muñoz-Céspedes, E., Ibar-Alonso, R., & de Lorenzo Ros, S. (2021). Financial literacy and sustainable consumer behavior. *Sustainability (Basel)*, *13*(16), 9145. doi:10.3390u13169145

Murugan, S. P., Shivaprasad, G., Dhanalakshmi, A., Sriram, V. P., Rajput, K., Mahesh, B. N., & Kedla, S. (2023). The Impact of COVID-19 on the Indian Microfinance Industry and Its Sustainability. In *Transforming Economies Through Microfinance in Developing Nations* (pp. 160–188). IGI Global. doi:10.4018/978-1-6684-5647-7.ch009

Mustaffa, N., Mahmud, W. A. W., Ahmad, F., & Mahbob, M. H., & AbdRahim, M. H. (2013). Kebergantungan Internet danaktiviti online remajadiLembahKelang. JurnalKomunikasi. *Malaysian Journal of Communication*, *29*(1), 199–212.

Muttaqin, M. Z., Idris, U., & Ilham, I. (2021). The Challenge of Implementing the Neutrality of Civil Servants (Study of Symbolic Violence in Pilkada). *JWP*, *6*(1), 1–14. doi:10.24198/jwp.v6i1.32065

Nahar, A. I. M., Shahrul, S. N. S., Rozzani, N., & Saleh, S. K. (2022). Factors affecting financial literacy rate of millennial in Malaysia. *International Journal of Publication and Social Studies*, *7*(1), 1–11. doi:10.55493/5050.v7i1.4433

Naiem, R., Kaur, J., Mishra, S., & Saxena, A. (2022). Impact of COVID-19 Pandemic on Mental Health Using Machine Learning and Artificial Intelligence. *International Conference on Innovative Computing and Communications: Proceedings of ICICC 2021*, 1. 10.1007/978-981-16-2594-7_21

Nair, D.S., & Millath, M.A. (2019) Identifying family-work conflict among employees of the travancore cements limited, Kottayam, Kerala. *International Journal of Recent Technology and Engineering*, *8*(2), 718–726.

Nair, D. S., & Millath, M. A. (2018). An analytical study on the influence of gender on the reasons for opting flexible working hours among faculties of engineering colleges in Trivandrum District of Kerala. *ZENITH International Journal of Multidisciplinary Research*, *8*(12), 195–200.

Nandhini, B. S., & Sheeba, J. I. (2015, March). Cyberbullying detection and classification using information retrieval algorithm. In *Proceedings of the 2015 international conference on advanced research in computer science engineering & technology (ICARCSET 2015)* (pp. 1-5). 10.1145/2743065.2743085

Narula, S., Shiva, A., & Shahi, S. (2020). *What drives retail investors' investment decisions? Evidence from no mobile phone phobia (Nomophobia) and investor fear of missing out (I-FoMo)*. doi:10.31620/JCCC.06.20/02

Nasikhah, M. A. (2019). *Information Technology-Based Public Transportation Service Innovations*. Jurnal Inovasi Ilmu Sosial Dan Politik. doi:10.33474/jisop.v1i1.2670

Naslund, J. A., & Deng, D. (2021). Addressing mental health stigma in low-income and middle-income countries: A new frontier for digital mental health. *Ethics, Medicine, and Public Health*, *19*, 100719. doi:10.1016/j.jemep.2021.100719 PMID:35083375

Nekliudov, N. A., Blyuss, O., Cheung, K. Y., Petrou, L., Genuneit, J., Sushentsev, N., Levadnaya, A., Comberiati, P., Warner, J. O., Tudor-Williams, G., Teufel, M., Greenhawt, M., DunnGalvin, A., & Munblit, D. (2020). Excessive media consumption about COVID-19 is associated with increased state anxiety: Outcomes of a large online survey in Russia. *Journal of Medical Internet Research*, *22*(9), e20955. doi:10.2196/20955 PMID:32788143

Nguyen, Q. C., Kath, S., Meng, H. W., Li, D., Smith, K. R., VanDerslice, J. A., Wen, M., & Li, F. (2016). Leveraging geotagged Twitter data to examine neighborhood happiness, diet, and physical activity. *Applied Geography (Sevenoaks, England)*, *73*, 77–88. Advance online publication. doi:10.1016/j.apgeog.2016.06.003 PMID:28533568

Nichols, J., Biros, D., Sharda, R., & Shimp, U. (2012). The Emergence of Organizational Process Liability as a Future Direction for Research on Technology Acceptance. *International Journal of Social and Organizational Dynamics in IT*, *2*(4), 1–13. doi:10.4018/ijsodit.2012100101

NSDC. (2023). *Skilling India's Youth, Shaping India's Future*. NSDC. https://nsdcindia.org/sites/default/files/files/NSDC-Annual-Report-2019-20.pdf

Nugent, S. G. (2005). *If Socrates Had Email* [Commencement Speech]. https://www.kenyon.edu/x29475.xml

Nusakini.com. (2017). *Press HP Deed to Become Jayapura City*. https://bit.ly/39nZ6uY

Nyakurukwa, K., & Seetharam, Y. (2022). Household stock market participation in South Africa: The role of financial literacy and social interactions. *Review of Behavioral Finance*. doi:10.1108/RBF-03-2022-0083

Ogbe, M., & Lujala, P. (2021). Spatial crowdsourcing in natural resource revenue management. *Resources Policy*, *72*, 102082. Advance online publication. doi:10.1016/j.resourpol.2021.102082

Oginni, S. O., & Moitui, J. N. (2015). Social Media and Public Policy Process in Africa: Enhanced Policy Process in Digital Age. In *Consilience. Journal of Sustainable Development*, *14*(2).

Oh, S. H., Lee, S. Y., & Han, C. (2021). The effects of social media use on preventive behaviors during infectious disease outbreaks: The mediating role of self-relevant emotions and public risk perception. *Health Communication*, *36*(8), 972–981. doi:10.1080/10410236.2020.1724639 PMID:32064932

Olan, F., Jayawickrama, U., Arakpogun, E. O., Suklan, J., & Liu, S. (2022). Fake news on social media: The Impact on Society. *Information Systems Frontiers*, 1–16. doi:10.100710796-022-10242-z PMID:35068999

Olesen, T. (2022). Greta Thunberg's iconicity: Performance and co-performance in the social media ecology. *New Media & Society*, 24(6), 1325–1342. doi:10.1177/1461444820975416

Ombudsman.go.id. (2020). *Ombudsman Banten Holds Interactive Dialogue, Checks the Effectiveness and Innovation of Disdukcapil Administration Services*. https://bit.ly/3QfloQa

Ortiz-Ospina, E. (2019). The rise of social media. *Our world in data, 18*.

Osella, M., Ferro, E., & Pautasso, E. (2016). Toward a Methodological Approach to Assess Public Value in Smart Cities. In Public Administration and Information Technology (Vol. 11). doi:10.1007/978-3-319-17620-8_7

Owuor, I., & Hochmair, H. H. (2020). An overview of social media apps and their potential role in geospatial research. In ISPRS International Journal of Geo-Information (Vol. 9, Issue 9). doi:10.3390/ijgi9090526

Ozdemir, M., Sari, A. L., & Irwandi, I. (2021). The influence of motivation, Financial Literacy, and social media Financial Platforms on student investment interest. *Komitmen: Jurnal Ilmiah Manajemen, 2*(2), 68–82. doi:10.15575/jim.v2i2.14381

Palermo, S., Benedetti, F., Costa, T., & Amanzio, M. (2015). Pain anticipation: An activation likelihood estimation meta-analysis of brain imaging studies. *Human Brain Mapping, 36*(5), 1648–1661. doi:10.1002/hbm.22727 PMID:25529840

Pan, B., & Crotts, J. C. (2016). Theoretical models of social media, marketing implications, and future research directions. In Social Media in Travel, Tourism and Hospitality: Theory, Practice and Cases, pp. 73-85

Panggabean, T. T. N., & Saragih, A. (2020). Implementation Of State Civil Service (ASN) Management Through E-Government In The New Normal Era. *Civil Service, 14*(1), 93–103. https://jurnal.bkn.go.id/index.php/asn/article/view/265/200

Papacharissi, Z. (Ed.). (2010). *A networked self: Identity, community, and culture on social network sites*. Routledge. doi:10.4324/9780203876527

Papuatoday. (2018). *E-Waniambey App Promotes*. https://bit.ly/3zDD81I

Paquet, G. (1999). Governance Through Social Learning. Governance Through Social Learning. doi:10.26530/OAPEN_578818

Parise, S. (2007). Knowledge management and human resource development: An application in social network analysis methods. *Advances in Developing Human Resources, 9*(3), 359–383. doi:10.1177/1523422307304106

Parker, J. (2020). Social work practice: Assessment, planning, intervention and review. *Social Work Practice,* 1-264.

Park, J. Y., Perumal, S. V., Sanyal, S., Ah Nguyen, B., Ray, S., Krishnan, R., Narasimhaiah, R., & Thangam, D. (2022). Sustainable Marketing Strategies as an Essential Tool of Business. *American Journal of Economics and Sociology, 81*(2), 359–379. doi:10.1111/ajes.12459

Park, J., & Cho, K. (2009, September). Declining relational trust between government and publics, and potential prospects of social media in the government public relations. In *Proceedings of EGPA Conference 2009 The Public Service: Service Delivery in the Information Age*. ACM.

Park, M. J., Kang, D., Rho, J. J., & Lee, D. H. (2016). Policy role of social media in developing public trust: Twitter communication with government leaders. *Public Management Review, 18*(9), 1265–1288. doi:10.1080/14719037.2015.1066418

Parusheva, S. (2017). Social Media Banking Models: A case study of a practical implementation in banking sector. *Икономически изследвания*, (3), 125-141.

Parycek, P., & Viale, G. (2017). Drivers of smart governance: Towards to evidence-based policy-making. *ACM International Conference Proceeding Series, Part F128275*. 10.1145/3085228.3085255

Patel, P. K., & Mallappa, V. K. H. (2022). *Predictive Factors for Farmers' Knowledge of Social Media for Sustainable Agricultural Development*. Indian Journal of Extension Education. doi:10.48165/IJEE.2022.58412

Patwardhan, P., & Ramaprasad, J. (2005, May). Internet dependency relations and online activity exposure, involvement and satisfaction: A study of American and Indian internet users. In *Annual convention of the International Communication Association* (Vol. 13). Academic Press.

Paul, S., & Das, S. (2023). Investigating information dissemination and citizen engagement through government social media during the COVID-19 crisis. *Online Information Review, 47*(2), 316–332. doi:10.1108/OIR-06-2021-0307

Pejić Bach, M., Krstić, Ž., Seljan, S., & Turulja, L. (2019). Text mining for big data analysis in financial sector: A literature review. *Sustainability (Basel), 11*(5), 1277. doi:10.3390u11051277

Pereira, G. V., Parycek, P., Falco, E., & Kleinhans, R. (2018). Smart governance in the context of smart cities: A literature review. In Information Polity (Vol. 23, Issue 2). doi:10.3233/IP-170067

Pfister, P., & Lehmann, C. (2023). Measuring the Success of Digital Transformation in German SMEs. *Journal of Small Business Strategy, 33*(1), 1–19. doi:10.53703/001c.39679

Picazo-Vela, S., Fernández-Haddad, M., & Luna-Reyes, L. F. (2016). Opening the black box: Developing strategies to use social media in government. *Government Information Quarterly, 33*(4), 693–704. doi:10.1016/j.giq.2016.08.004

Piocuda, J. E., Smyers, J. O., Knyshev, E., Harris, R. J., & Rai, M. (2015). Trends of internationalization and collaboration in US psychology journals 1950–2010. *Archives of Scientific Psychology, 3*(1), 82–92. doi:10.1037/arc0000020

Potgieter, L. M., & Naidoo, R. (2017). Factors explaining user loyalty in a social media-based brand community. *S.A. Journal of Information Management, 19.* . doi:10.4102/sajim.v19i1.744

Pradheep, T., Sheeba, J. I., Yogeshwaran, T., & Pradeep Devaneyan, S. (2017, December). Automatic Multi Model Cyber Bullying Detection from Social Networks. *Proceedings of the International Conference on Intelligent Computing Systems.* 10.2139srn.3123710

Prakoso, S. G., Timorria, I. F., & Murtyantoro, A. P. (2021, November). Social media interconnection between people: Greta Thunberg's influence on the climate movement. [). IOP Publishing.]. *IOP Conference Series. Earth and Environmental Science, 905*(1), 012136. doi:10.1088/1755-1315/905/1/012136

Praveen, S., Ittamalla, R., & Deepak, G. (2021). Analysing Indian general public's perspective on anxiety, stress and trauma during Covid-19-a machine learning study of 840,000 tweets. *Diabetes & Metabolic Syndrome, 15*(3), 667–671. doi:10.1016/j.dsx.2021.03.016 PMID:33813239

Prensky, M. (2001). Digital Natives, Digital Immigrants: Do They Really Think Differently? *On the Horizon, 9*(6), 1–8. doi:10.1108/10748120110424843

Privacy International. (2017, October 23). *What is privacy?* Privacy International. https://privacyinternational.org/explainer/56/what-privacy

Priyono, A., Moin, A., & Putri, V. N. A. O. (2020). Identifying digital transformation paths in the business model of SMEs during the COVID-19 pandemic. *Journal of Open Innovation, 6*(4), 104. doi:10.3390/joitmc6040104

Przybylski, A. K., & Weinstein, N. (2013). Can you connect with me now? How the presence of mobile communication technology influences face-to- face conversation quality. *Journal of Social and Personal Relationships, 30*(3), 237–246. doi:10.1177/0265407512453827

Przybylski, A. K., & Weinstein, N. (2019). Investigating the motivational and psychosocial dynamics of dys-regulated gaming: Evidence from a preregistered cohort study. *Clinical Psychological Science, 7*(6), 1257–1265. doi:10.1177/2167702619859341

Pucihar, A. (2020). The digital transformation journey: Content analysis of Electronic Markets articles and Bled eConference proceedings from 2012 to 2019. *Electronic Markets, 30*(1), 29–37. doi:10.100712525-020-00406-7

Purwanti, T., & Suharyadi, R. (2018). Implementation of Government Policy on Population Administration (Study of the Study on the Population Service System in Sindang Beliti Ilir District, Rejang Lebong Regency). *MIMBAR : Jurnal Penelitian Sosial Dan Politik, 7*(1), 59–67. doi:10.32663/jpsp.v7i1.425

Putri, A. M., Damayanti, S. M., & Rahadi, R. A. (2022). DIGITAL FINANCIAL LITERACY IN INDONESIA: A LITERATURE REVIEW. *Central Asia & the Caucasus (14046091), 23*(1).

Putri, L. D. M., & Mutiarin, D. (2018). *The effectiveness of public policy innovations; Its influence on the quality of public services in Indonesia.* Jurnal Ilmu Pemerintahan.

Qian, T., Chen, J., Li, A., Wang, J., & Shen, D. (2020). Evaluating spatial accessibility to general hospitals with navigation and social media location data: A case study in Nanjing. *International Journal of Environmental Research and Public Health, 17*(8), 2752. Advance online publication. doi:10.3390/ijerph17082752 PMID:32316229

Rachman, F. H. (2020). *Twitter sentiment analysis of Covid-19 using term weighting TF-IDF and logistic regression.* Paper presented at the 2020 6th Information Technology International Seminar (ITIS).

Radford, A. (2019). Jeremy Clarkson says Greta Thunberg is an 'idiot' who has killed the car show. *SBS.* https://www.sbs.com.au/news/article/jeremy-clarkson-says-greta-thunberg-is-an-idiot-who-has-killed-the-car-show/1857ddhh5

Radwan, M. (2022). The Role of Social Media in Government Communication during Covid-19 Pandemic: The Case of KSA. *Journal of Social Sciences, 10*, 368–383.

Rahim, N., Ismail, N., & Karmawan, K. (2022). Financial literacy and financial behaviour: An overview of key drivers. *Proceedings of the 1st International Conference on Social, Science, and Technology, ICSST 2021*, Tangerang, Indonesia. 10.4108/eai.25-11-2021.2319348

Rajeswari, V., & Millath, A. (2003). Brand Preference towards Water Purifier-A Study. *Indian Journal of Marketing, 13*, 9–15.

Ramah. (2017). *Jayapura City Dispendukcapil will take part in South Korea's education and training.* https://bit.ly/3O98QrI

Rana, R., & Singhal, R. (2015). Chi-square test and its application in hypothesis testing. *Journal of the Practice of Cardiovascular Sciences*, 69–71.

Rasoolimanesh, S. M., Roldán, J. L., Jaafar, M., & Ramayah, T. (2017). Factors Influencing Residents' Perceptions toward Tourism Development: Differences across Rural and Urban World Heritage Sites. *Journal of Travel Research, 56*(6), 760–775. doi:10.1177/0047287516662354

Ravalier, J., & Boichat, C. (2018). *UK social workers: Working conditions and wellbeing.* Bath Spa University.

Razmerita, L., Kirchner, K., & Nielsen, P. (2016). What factors influence knowledge sharing in organizations? A social dilemma perspective of social media communication. *Journal of Knowledge Management*, *20*(6), 1225–1246. doi:10.1108/JKM-03-2016-0112

Reamer, F. G. (2013). Social work in a digital age: Ethical and risk management challenges. *Social Work*, *58*(2), 163–172. doi:10.1093wwt003 PMID:23724579

Reeve, J. (2016). A grand theory of motivation: Why not? *Motivation and Emotion*, *40*(1), 31–35. doi:10.100711031-015-9538-2

Reinartz, W., Wiegand, N., & Imschloss, M. (2019). The impact of digital transformation on the retailing value chain. *International Journal of Research in Marketing*, *36*(3), 350–366. doi:10.1016/j.ijresmar.2018.12.002

Ricciardelli, L. A., Nackerud, L., Quinn, A. E., Sewell, M., & Casiano, B. (2020). Social media use, attitudes, and knowledge among social work students: Ethical implications for the social work profession. *Social Sciences & Humanities Open*, *2*(1), 100008. doi:10.1016/j.ssaho.2019.100008

Ridho, W. F. (2022). Comparison of social media as a platform for financial literacy source. *Jurnal Aplikasi Manajemen Dan Bisnis*, *3*, 1–14. doi:10.5281/ZENODO.7260311

Riquelme, H. E., & Rios, R. E. (2010). The moderating effect of gender in the adoption of mobile banking. *International Journal of Bank Marketing*, *28*(5), 328–341. doi:10.1108/02652321011064872

Rizon, R., Anastasia, N., & Evelyn, E. (2021). The influence of demography, social media, risk attitude, and overconfidence on the financial literacy of users social media in Surabaya. [IJFIS]. *International Journal of Financial and Investment Studies*, *2*(1), 10–19. doi:10.9744/ijfis.2.1.10-19

Rizwan, M., Wan, W., & Gwiazdzinski, L. (2020). Visualization, spatiotemporal patterns, and directional analysis of urban activities using geolocation data extracted from LBSN. *ISPRS International Journal of Geo-Information*, *9*(2), 137. Advance online publication. doi:10.3390/ijgi9020137

Roberts, J. A., & David, M. E. (2020). The social media party: Fear of missing out (FoMO), social media intensity, connection, and well-being. *International Journal of Human-Computer Interaction*, *36*(4), 386–392. doi:10.1080/10447318.2019.1646517

Rodriguez-Rivas, M. E., Varela, J. J., González, C., & Chuecas, M. J. (2022). The role of family support and conflict in cyberbullying and subjective well-being among Chilean adolescents during the Covid-19 period. *Heliyon*, *8*(4), e09243. doi:10.1016/j.heliyon.2022.e09243 PMID:35445156

Rodzalan, S. A., Arif, H., & Noor, N. N. M. (2021). Formal Generalization of Cyber Bullying: A Review Study. *Annals of the Romanian Society for Cell Biology*, 3105–3117.

Rootman, C., & Cupp, N. (2016). The impact of social media on customer satisfaction and retention in the banking industry: Views of clients and managers. *Journal of Chemical Information and Modeling*, 281–298.

Rotich, K. J. (2015). History, evolution and development of human resource management: A contemporary perspective. *Global Journal of Human Resource Management*, *3*(3), 58–73.

Roy, K. C., Cebrian, M., & Hasan, S. (2019). Quantifying human mobility resilience to extreme events using geo-located social media data. *EPJ Data Science*, *8*(1), 18. Advance online publication. doi:10.1140/epjds13688-019-0196-6

Ruhlandt, R. W. S. (2018). The governance of smart cities: A systematic literature review. *Cities (London, England)*, *81*, 1–23. Advance online publication. doi:10.1016/j.cities.2018.02.014

Rusmiyati. (2020). Public Service Innovation at the One Stop Integrated Service Office 19 in the Autonomous Region of Depok City, West Java Province. *Jurnal Ilmiah Adminstrasi Pemerintah Daerah, 12*(1), 19–25. https://doi.org/ doi:10.33701/jiapd.v12i1.1341

Rutledge, J. (2015). Economics as Energy Framework: Complexity, Turbulence, Financial Crises, and Protectionism. *Review of Financial Economics, 25*(1), 10–18. doi:10.1016/j.rfe.2015.02.003

S, M., & Millath M, A. (2019). Talent Management an Emerging Trend for Employee Effectiveness in Corporate Hospitals. *International Journal of Recent Technology and Engineering, 8*(4S5), 69–71

S, M., & Millath, A. (2019). Talent Management an Emerging Trend for Employee Effectiveness in Corporate Hospitals. *International Journal of Recent Technology and Engineering, 8*(4S5), 69–71

Sabani, A. (2021). Investigating the influence of transparency on the adoption of e-Government in Indonesia. *Journal of Science and Technology Policy Management, 12*(2), 236–255. doi:10.1108/JSTPM-03-2020-0046

Sabaruddin, R. A., & Saee, S. (2021). *Malay Tweets: Discovering Mental Health Situation during COVID-19 Pandemic in Malaysia.* Paper presented at the 2021 IEEE 19th Student Conference on Research and Development (SCOReD). 10.1109/SCOReD53546.2021.9652759

Sachs, M., & Parycek, P. (2010). Open government-information flow in Web 2.0. *Euro. J. ePractice, 9,* 1-70.

Sahoo, N. (2020). *Mounting majoritarianism and political polarization in India.* Political Polarization in South and Southeast Asia.

Saifullina, N. A., & Akhmetzyanova, A. I. (2018). Anticipation of Individuals with Communication Disabilities: Problem Current State Review. *HELIX, 8*(1), 2506–2511. doi:10.29042/2018-2506-2511

Saija, L., & Pappalardo, G. (2022). An Argument for Action Research-Inspired Participatory Mapping. *Journal of Planning Education and Research, 42*(3), 375–385. Advance online publication. doi:10.1177/0739456X18817090

Salam, R. (2021). Changes and Innovations in Public Services in the New Normal Era of the Covid-19 Pandemic. *Journal of Public Administration and Government, 3*(1), 28–36. https://doi.org/ doi:10.22487/jpag.v3i1.138

Saldanha, T. (2019). *Why digital transformations fail: The surprising disciplines of how to take off and stay ahead.* Berrett-Koehler Publishers.

Samuel, Onasanya, & Olumorin. (2018). Perceived usefulness, ease of use and adequacy of use of mobile technologies by Nigerian university lecturers. *International Journal of Education and Development Using Information and Communication Technology, 14*(3), 5–16.

Samuel, J., Rahman, M. M., Ali, G. M. N., Samuel, Y., Pelaez, A., Chong, P. H. J., & Yakubov, M. (2020). Feeling positive about reopening? New normal scenarios from COVID-19 US reopen sentiment analytics. *IEEE Access : Practical Innovations, Open Solutions, 8,* 142173–142190. doi:10.1109/ACCESS.2020.3013933 PMID:34786280

San Martín, S., & Camarero, C. (2009). How perceived risk affects online buying. *Online Information Review, 33*(4), 629–654. doi:10.1108/14684520910985657

Sandoval-Almazan, R., & Valle-Cruz, D. (2021). Social Media Use in Government Health Agencies: The COVID-19 Impact. *Information Polity, 26*(4), 459–475. doi:10.3233/IP-210326

Sanyal, S., Kalimuthu, M., Arumugam, T., Aruna, R., Balaji, J., Savarimuthu, A., & Patil, S. (2023). Internet of Things and Its Relevance to Digital Marketing. In *Opportunities and Challenges of Industrial IoT in 5G and 6G Networks* (pp. 138–154). IGI Global. doi:10.4018/978-1-7998-9266-3.ch007

Saraladevi, E., Chandramohan, S., & Millath, M.A. (2019). Online shopping behavior pattern among school children. *International Journal of Recent Technology and Engineering, 8*(2), 695–699.

Sarigianni, C., Thalmann, S., & Manhart, M. (2016, January). Protecting knowledge in the financial sector: An analysis of knowledge risks arising from social media. In *2016 49th Hawaii International Conference on System Sciences (HICSS)* (pp. 4031-4040). IEEE.

Sarstedt, M., Ringle, C. M., & Hair, J. F. (2021). Partial Least Squares Structural Equation Modeling. In *Handbook of Market Research* (pp. 1–47). Springer International Publishing. doi:10.1007/978-3-319-05542-8_15-2

Sathe, G. (2021). *WhatsApp Is Still Sharing a Lot of Your Data.* Gadgets 360. https://www.gadgets360.com/apps/opinion/WhatsApp-new-privacy-policy-sharing-data-with-facebook-2353796

Sawalha, S., Al-Jamal, M., & Abu-Shanab, E. (2019). The influence of utilising Facebook on e-government adoption. *Electronic Government, an International Journal, 15*(1), 1-20.

Sawhney, A., & Ahuja, V. (2022). Drivers of Social Media Content Marketing in the Banking Sector. In Research Anthology on Social Media Advertising and Building Consumer Relationships, 12(3), pages 54-72. doi:10.4018/978-1-6684-6287-4.ch023

Sawhney, A., & Ahuja, V. (2022). Drivers of social media content marketing in the banking sector: A literature review. *Research Anthology on Social Media Advertising and Building Consumer Relationships*, 396-418.

Sawhney, A., Ahuja, V., & Sharma, P. (2022). *Role of Social Media in the Indian Banking Sector.* Multidisciplinary Perspectives Towards Building a Digitally Competent Society., doi:10.4018/978-1-6684-5274-5.ch002

Schnader, J. (2019). The Implementation of Artificial Intelligence in Hard and Soft Counterterrorism Efforts on Social Media. *Santa Clara High-Technology Law Journal, 36*, 42.

Scholl, H. J., & Scholl, M. C. (2014). Smart Governance: A Roadmap for Research and Practice. *IConference 2014 Proceedings.*

Schulz, A., Ortmann, J., & Probst, F. (2012). Getting user-generated content structured: Overcoming information overload in emergency management. *2012 IEEE Global Humanitarian Technology Conference*, 143–148. 10.1109/GHTC.2012.31

Sedera, D., Tan, C. W., & Xu, D. (2022). Digital business transformation in innovation and entrepreneurship. *Information & Management, 59*(3), 103620. doi:10.1016/j.im.2022.103620

See, L., Mooney, P., Foody, G., Bastin, L., Comber, A., Estima, J., Fritz, S., Kerle, N., Jiang, B., Laakso, M., Liu, H. Y., Milèinski, G., Nikšieč, M., Painho, M., Podör, A., Olteanu-Raimond, A. M. R., & Rutzinger, M. (2016). Crowdsourcing, citizen science or volunteered geographic information? The current state of crowdsourced geographic information. *ISPRS International Journal of Geo-Information, 5*(5), 55. Advance online publication. doi:10.3390/ijgi5050055

Seldal, M. M. N., & Nyhus, E. K. (2022). Financial vulnerability, financial literacy, and the use of digital payment technologies. *Journal of Consumer Policy, 45*(2), 281–306. doi:10.100710603-022-09512-9 PMID:35283545

Selvia, G., Rahmayanti, D., Afandy, C., & Zoraya, I. (2021). *The effect of financial knowledge, financial behavior and financial inclusion on financial well-being.* Proceedings of the 3rd Beehive International Social Innovation Conference, BISIC 2020, Bengkulu, Indonesia. 10.4108/eai.3-10-2020.2306600

Seth, S. (2021). *Central bank digital currency (CBDC).* Investopedia. https://www.investopedia.com/terms/c/central-bank-digital-currency-cbdc.asp#citation-10

Setiawan, M., Effendi, N., Santoso, T., Dewi, V. I., & Sapulette, M. S. (2022). Digital financial literacy, current behavior of saving and spending and its future foresight. *Economics of Innovation and New Technology*, *31*(4), 320–338. doi:10.1080/10438599.2020.1799142

SFLC.IN. (2017, October 24). *Right to privacy under udhr and iccpr*. Privacy Bytes; Privacy Bytes. https://privacy.sflc.in/universal/

Shah, Khan, I., & Sadiqa, M. (2015). Impact of Service Quality on Customer Satisfaction of Banking Sector Employees: a Study of Lahore, Punjab. *Vidyabharati International Interdisciplinary Research Journal*.

Shaher, M. A. A., & Radwan, A. F. (2022). The Role of Social Media in Government Communication during Covid-19 Pandemic: The Case of KSA. *Journal of Emergency Management and Disaster Communications*, *3*(02), 131–150. doi:10.1142/S2689980922500099

Shah, R. (2019). Cyber Crimes In India: Trends And Prevention. *International Journal of Research and Analytical Reviews*, *6*(1).

Shankar, A., & Datta, B. (2018). Factors affecting mobile payment adoption intention: An Indian perspective. *Global Business Review*, *19*(3, suppl), S72–S89. doi:10.1177/0972150918757870

Shanmugam, V., Asha, N., Samanvitha, C., Murthy, L. N., & Thangam, D. (2021). An analysis of bilateral trade between india and korea. *Journal of Contemporary Issues in Business and Government*, *27*(2).

Sharma, B., & Kataria, G. (2022). Surge in Cybercrime against Children in India amid the Pandemic. *Int'l JL Mgmt. & Human.*, *5*, 1279.

Sharma, P., & Pandher, J. S. (2018). Quality of teachers in technical higher education institutions in India. Higher Education. *Skills and Work-Based Learning*, *8*(4), 511–526. Advance online publication. doi:10.1108/HESWBL-10-2017-0080

Shvaher, O. A., Degtyarev, S. I., & Polyakova, L. G. (2021). The effect of social media on financial literacy. *International Journal of Media and Information Literacy*, *6*(1), 211–218. doi:10.13187/ijmil.2021.1.211

Siddiqui, S., & Singh, T. (2016). Social media its impact with positive and negative aspects. *International journal of computer applications technology and research*, *5*(2), 71-75.

Signorini, A., Segre, A. M., & Polgreen, P. M. (2011). The use of Twitter to track levels of disease activity and public concern in the US during the influenza A H1N1 pandemic. *PLoS One*, *6*(5), e19467. doi:10.1371/journal.pone.0019467 PMID:21573238

Silva, P., Tavares, A. F., Silva, T., & Lameiras, M. (2019). The good, the bad and the ugly: Three faces of social media usage by local governments. *Government Information Quarterly*, *36*(3), 469–479. Advance online publication. doi:10.1016/j.giq.2019.05.006

Simangunsong, E., & Handoko, R. (2020). The role of social media in Indonesia for business transformation strategy. *International Research Journal of Business Studies*, *13*(1), 99–112. doi:10.21632/irjbs.13.1.99-112

Simona Sternad & SamoBobek. (2013). Impacts of TAM-based external factors on ERP acceptance. *International Conference on Project MANagement / HCIST 2013 - International Conference on Health and Social Care Information Systems and Technologies*, *9*, 33-42.

Simonofski, A., Fink, J., & Burnay, C. (2021). Supporting policy-making with social media and e-participation platforms data: A policy analytics framework. *Government Information Quarterly*, *38*(3), 101590. Advance online publication. doi:10.1016/j.giq.2021.101590

Sinclair, A. J., Peirson-Smith, T. J., & Boerchers, M. (2017). Environmental assessments in the Internet age: The role of e-governance and social media in creating platforms for meaningful participation. *Impact Assessment and Project Appraisal*, *35*(2), 148–157. doi:10.1080/14615517.2016.1251697

Singh, J. (2021). *WhatsApp Privacy Policy Update: What Happens When You Don't Accept?* Gadgets 360. https://www.gadgets360.com/apps/news/WhatsApp-privacy-policy-update-changes-what-happens-if-you-dont-agree-details-facebook-data-2376020

Singh, N., Chakraborty, A., Biswas, S. B., & Majumdar, M. (2020). Impact of social media in banking sector under triangular neutrosophic arena using MCGDM technique. *Neutrosophic Sets and Systems, 35*, 153-176.

Singh, S. R. (2021, January 18). Don't use WhatsApp if you don't like it: Delhi HC. *The Hindu*. https://www.thehindu.com/news/national/dont-use-whatsapp-if-you-dont-like-it-delhi-hc/article33599671.ece

Singh, A. N., Picot, A., Kranz, J., Gupta, M. P., & Ojha, A. (2013). Information security management (ism) practices: Lessons from select cases from India and Germany. *Global Journal of Flexible Systems Managment*, *14*(4), 225–239. doi:10.100740171-013-0047-4

Singh, S. (2020). *Department for Promotion of Industry and Internal Trade Ministry of Commerce and Industry Government of India Consolidated FDI Policy (Effective from October 15, 2020)*. Department for Promotion of Industry and Internal Trade Ministry of Commerce and Industry Government of India.

Sinha, R. (2018). *Committee Reports: Report Summary on A Free and Fair Digital Economy*, PRS Legislative Research. https://prsindia.org/policy/report-summaries/free-and-fair-digital-economy

Sirothiya, M., & Chavadi, C. (2020). Compressed biogas (cbg) as an alternative and sustainable energy source in India: Case study on implementation frameworks and challenges. *Invertis Journal of Renewable Energy*, *10*(2), 49–64. doi:10.5958/2454-7611.2020.00007.7

Sirothiya, M., & Chavadi, C. (2020). Evaluating marketing strategies ofcompressed biogas (CBG) companies in India using decision tree analysis. *IIMS Journal of Management Science*, *11*(3), 219–237. doi:10.5958/0976-173X.2020.00012.0

Sirothiya, M., & Chavadi, C. (2020). Role of compressed biogas to assess the effects of perceived value on customer satisfaction and customer loyalty. *BIMTECH Bus. Perspect*, *1*, 70–89.

Sitinjak, E., Meidityawati, B., Ichwan, R., Onggosandojo, N., & Aryani, P. (2018). Enhancing Urban Resilience through Technology and Social Media: Case Study of Urban Jakarta. *Procedia Engineering*, *212*, 222–229. Advance online publication. doi:10.1016/j.proeng.2018.01.029

Sivarajah, U., Irani, Z., Gupta, S., & Mahroof, K. (2020). Role of big data and social media analytics for business to business sustainability: A participatory web context. *Industrial Marketing Management*, *86*, 163–179. doi:10.1016/j.indmarman.2019.04.005

Sobaci, M. Z. (2016). Social media and local governments: An overview. Social media and local governments. *Theory into Practice*, 3–21.

Song, C., & Lee, J. (2013, June). Can social media restore citizen trust in government? In *Public Management Research Conference*, Madison, Wisconsin.

Song, C., & Lee, J. (2016). Citizens' use of social media in government, perceived transparency, and trust in government. *Public Performance & Management Review*, *39*(2), 430–453. doi:10.1080/15309576.2015.1108798

Soomro, T. R., & Hussain, M. (2019). Social Media-Related Cybercrimes and Techniques for Their Prevention. *Appl. Comput. Syst.*, *24*(1), 9–17. doi:10.2478/acss-2019-0002

Sriram, V. P., Sanyal, S., Laddunuri, M. M., Subramanian, M., Bose, V., Booshan, B., & Thangam, D. (2023). Enhancing Cybersecurity Through Blockchain Technology. In Handbook of Research on Cybersecurity Issues and Challenges for Business and FinTech Applications (pp. 208-224). IGI Global.

Sriram, V. P., Sanyal, S., Laddunuri, M. M., Subramanian, M., Bose, V., Booshan, B., . . . Thangam, D. (2023). Enhancing Cybersecurity Through Blockchain Technology. In Handbook of Research on Cybersecurity Issues and Challenges for Business and FinTech Applications (pp. 208-224). IGI Global.

Sriram, V. P., Sanyal, S., Laddunuri, M. M., Subramanian, M., Bose, V., Booshan, B., & Thangam, D. (2023). Enhancing Cybersecurity Through Blockchain Technology. In *Handbook of Research on Cybersecurity Issues and Challenges for Business and FinTech Applications* (pp. 208–224). IGI Global.

Srivastava, M. (2013). Social Media and Its Use by the Government. *Journal of Public Administration and Governance*, *3*(2), 161–172. doi:10.5296/jpag.v3i2.3978

Srivastava, S. (2012). Pessimistic side of information & communication technology: Cyber bullying and legislature laws. *International Journal of Advances in Computer Science and Technology*, *1*(1).

Sriyono, H., Sugiarto, G. B., Dearelsa, D., Anisyah, F., & Nur, A. (n.d.). *Peran Mbkm Dalam Peningkatan Kinerja Umkm Melalui Literasi Keuangan Dan Digital Marketing Di Desa Ketanireng Kecamatan Prigen Kabupaten Pasuruan*. PSSH. https://pssh.umsida.ac.id/index.php/pssh/article/download/301/233

Stamati, T., Papadopoulos, T., & Anagnostopoulos, D. (2015). Social media for openness and accountability in the public sector: Cases in the greek context. *Government Information Quarterly*, *32*(1), 12–29. Advance online publication. doi:10.1016/j.giq.2014.11.004

Stefanidis, A., Crooks, A., & Radzikowski, J. (2013). Harvesting ambient geospatial information from social media feeds. *GeoJournal*, *78*(2), 319–338. Advance online publication. doi:10.100710708-011-9438-2

Stevens, J.C. (2010). *Homeland Security*. Webeucracy: The Collaborative Revolution)

Stoker, G. (1998). Governance as theory: Five propositions. *International Social Science Journal*, *50*(155), 17–28. Advance online publication. doi:10.1111/1468-2451.00106

Suchocka, L., Yarasheva, A., Medvedeva, E., Aleksandrova, O., Alikperova, N., & Kroshilin, S. (2022). Modern media space and financial literacy of young people. *Humanities and Social Sciences Quarterly*, *29*(1), 61–71. doi:10.7862/rz.2022.hss.05

Sudhahar, M., & Fernandez, N. N. (2016). A Study on Effectiveness of Social Networking Sites in Advertising with Special Reference to Erode District-Tamilnadu (India). *International Journal of Management and Social Sciences*, *4*(9), 509–518.

Sukarmin. (2020). *Public Service Innovation Through Population Administration for Persons with Disabilities (Inclusive Administration) at the Population and Civil Registry Office of Bulukumba Regency*. Skripsi, Universitas Muhammadiyah Makassar. https://digilibadmin.unismuh.ac.id/upload/12604-Full_Text.pdf

Tagaymuratovna, P. D. (2022). Cyberbullying as a socio-psychological problem and legal ways to solve it abroad. *EPRA International Journal of Research and Development*, *7*(2), 28–31.

Talwar Thakore & Associates. (2022). *Data Protected India*. Linklaters. https://www.linklaters.com/en/insights/data-protected/data-protected---india

Tanwar, S., Paul, T., Singh, K., Joshi, M., & Rana, A. (2020, June). Classification and imapct of cyber threats in India: a review. In *2020 8th International Conference on Reliability, Infocom Technologies and Optimization (Trends and Future Directions) (ICRITO)* (pp. 129-135). IEEE. 10.1109/ICRITO48877.2020.9198024

Ted.com. (2019). *Why you should be a climate activist.* TED. https://www.ted.com/talks/luisa_neubauer_why_you_should_be_a_climate_activist

Teng, X., Wu, Z., & Yang, F. (2022). Research on the Relationship between Digital Transformation and Performance of SMEs. *Sustainability (Basel), 14*(10), 6012. doi:10.3390u14106012

Teraspapua. (2020). *Merlan Uloli, Create Innovations That Will Bear Rewards.* https://bit.ly/3mILoG0

Teraspapua. (2022). *Make Services Easy for the Community, Jayapura City Government Places ADM Machines at Saga Mall Abepura.* https://bit.ly/3Ql8Cjh

Thakur, K., Hayajneh, T., & Tseng, J. (2019). Cyber security in social media: Challenges and the way forward. *IT Professional, 21*(2), 41–49. doi:10.1109/MITP.2018.2881373

Thangam, D., Arumugam, T., Velusamy, K., Subramanian, M., Ganesan, S. K., & Suryakumar, M. (2022). COVID-19 Pandemic and Its Brunt on Digital Transformation and Cybersecurity. In Cybersecurity Crisis Management and Lessons Learned From the COVID-19 Pandemic (pp. 15-42). IGI Global.

Thangam, D., Malali, A. B., Subramaniyan, S. G., Mariappan, S., Mohan, S., & Park, J. Y. (2021). Blockchain Technology and Its Brunt on Digital Marketing. In Blockchain Technology and Applications for Digital Marketing (pp. 1-15). IGI Global. doi:10.4018/978-1-7998-8081-3.ch001

Thangam, D., & Chavadi, C. (2023). Impact of Digital Marketing Practices on Energy Consumption, Climate Change, and Sustainability. *Climate and Energy, 39*(7), 11–19. doi:10.1002/gas.22329

Thangam, D., Malali, A. B., Subramanian, G., Mohan, S., & Park, J. Y. (2022). Internet of things: a smart technology for healthcare industries. In *Healthcare Systems and Health Informatics* (pp. 3–15). CRC Press.

Thangam, D., Malali, A. B., Subramanian, G., & Park, J. Y. (2022). Transforming Healthcare through Internet of Things. In *Cloud and Fog Computing Platforms for Internet of Things* (pp. 15–24). Chapman and Hall/CRC. doi:10.1201/9781003213888-2

Thangam, D., Malali, A. B., Subramaniyan, G., Mariappan, S., Mohan, S., & Park, J. Y. (2022). Relevance of Artificial Intelligence in Modern Healthcare. In *Integrating AI in IoT Analytics on the Cloud for Healthcare Applications* (pp. 67–88). IGI Global. doi:10.4018/978-1-7998-9132-1.ch005

Thangam, D., Vaidya, G. R., Subramanian, G., Velusamy, K., Selvi Govindarajan, K., & Park, J. Y. (2022). The Portrayal of Women's Empowerment in Select Indian Movies. *American Journal of Economics and Sociology, 81*(1), 187–205. doi:10.1111/ajes.12451

Thawab, M. A., Thowseaf, S., Millath, M. A., & Ali, K. M. (2019) Reconnoitering the Impact of Economic Variables on Fruit Pulp Export from Tamil Nadu. *International Journal of Recent Technology and Engineering, 8*(4), 58-65.

The Enterprisers Project. (2023). *what is digital transformation?* The Enterprisers. https://enterprisersproject.com/what-is-digital-transformation

The Indian Express. (2022). 'You and me are a team': When Barack Obama met a 16-year-old climate change activist. *The Indian Express.* https://indianexpress.com/article/trending/trending-globally/barack-obama-met-environmentalist-greta-thunberg-6005450/

Theguardian.com. (2019). The Swedish 15-year-old who's cutting class to fight the climate crisis. *The Guardian.* https://www.theguardian.com/science/2018/sep/01/swedish-15-year-old-cutting-class-to-fight-the-climate-crisis

Theindianexpress.com. (2020). Greta Thunberg recycles Donald Trump's tweet to her in 2019, tells him to 'chill'. *The Indian Express.* https://indianexpress.com/article/trending/trending-globally/greta-thunberg-recycles-trump-old-mockery-tweet-as-he-tries-to-stop-vote-count-6976467/

Thesocialflame.com. (2022). Greta Thunberg on Instagram. *The Social Flame.* https://thesocialflame.com/en/influencer/gretathunberg

Thirupathi, M, V. B., Kolur, V. P. ,Sriram, D. N. K. M, S., B. & P., S. K. (2022). *A Meta-Appraisal on UTAUT Model towards Accessibility and Adaptability of Digital Mobile Wallet Usage in India.* 2022 International Conference on Innovative Computing, Intelligent Communication and Smart Electrical Systems (ICSES), Chennai, India. . doi:10.1109/ICSES55317.2022.9914089

Thirupathi, M., Vinayagamoorthi, G., &Mathiraj, S. P. (2019). Effect Of cashless payment methods: A case study perspective analysis. *International Journal of scientific & technology research, 8*(8), 394-397.

Thirupathi, M., & Gopalakrishnan, D. S. (2019). Impact of E-Media Among College Students. *Journal of Emerging Technologies and Innovative Research, 6*(5), 185–192.

Thirupathi, M., Vinayagamoorthi, G., Gopalakrishnan, S., Sriram, V. P., & Kavitha, S. (2019). Accessibility and Adaptability of Emerging Technology among Mobile Wallet Customer using TAM model. *Journal of Contemporary Issues in Business and Government, 27*(2), 2411–2435.

Thomas, A., & Gupta, V. (2021). Social capital theory, social exchange theory, social cognitive theory, financial literacy, and the role of knowledge sharing as a moderator in enhancing financial well-being: From bibliometric analysis to a conceptual framework model. *Frontiers in Psychology, 12,* 664638. doi:10.3389/fpsyg.2021.664638 PMID:34093360

Thornton-Rice, A., & Moran, N. (2022). The invisible frontier: Practitioner perspectives on the privacy implications of utilising social media in mental health social work practice. *British Journal of Social Work, 52*(4), 2271–2290. doi:10.1093/bjsw/bcab184

Thowseaf, S., Millath, M. A., & Ali, K. M. Aftermath Effect Of GST On Consumer Purchasing Power. *Resturamt Business, 118*(5), 122-131.

Thowseaf, M. A. S., & Millath, M. A. (2016). A study on GST implementation and its impact on Indian industrial sectors and export. *International Journal of Management Research and Social Science, 3*(2), 27–30.

Thowseaf, S., & Millath, M. A. (2016). An analysis on Indian Forex for examining investment and trade option. *International Journal of Advanced Research in Management and Social Sciences, 5*(9), 47–54.

Thowseaf, S., & Millath, M. A. (2016). Factors Influencing Export - A Conceptual Analysis. *International Journal of Management, 7*(2), 150–158.

Thowseaf, S., & Millath, M. A. (2017). Delineation on Demonetization Impact on Indian Economy. *International Journal of Innovative Knowledge Concepts, 5,* 7.

Thunberg, G. (2020). *Greta Thunberg. Climate Change 'as Urgent'as Coronavirus.* Justin Rowalt BBC Interview.

Toivonen, T., Heikinheimo, V., Fink, C., Hausmann, A., Hiippala, T., Järv, O., Tenkanen, H., & Di Minin, E. (2019). Social media data for conservation science: A methodological overview. In Biological Conservation (Vol. 233). doi:10.1016/j.biocon.2019.01.023

Torous, J., Bucci, S., Bell, I. H., Kessing, L. V., Faurholt-Jepsen, M., Whelan, P., Carvalho, A. F., Keshavan, M., Linardon, J., & Firth, J. (2021). The growing field of digital psychiatry: Current evidence and the future of apps, social media, chatbots, and virtual reality. *World Psychiatry; Official Journal of the World Psychiatric Association (WPA)*, *20*(3), 318–335. doi:10.1002/wps.20883 PMID:34505369

Treiblmaier, H., & Sillaber, C. (2021). The impact of blockchain on e-commerce:a framework for salient research topics. *Electronic Commerce Research and Applications*, *48*, 101054. doi:10.1016/j.elerap.2021.101054

Tripathi, S. (2021). Determinants of Digital, Transformation in the Post-Covid-19 Business World. IJRDO-. *Journal of Business and Management*, *7*(6), 75–81.

Tripathy, M. R., & Kaur, T. (2012). Perceptions of employees on information checks by employers using social networking sites in IT sector. *Management and Labour Studies*, *37*(4), 345–358. doi:10.1177/0258042X13484866

Truong, Y., & McColl, R. (2011). Intrinsic motivations, self-esteem, and luxury goods consumption. *Journal of Retailing and Consumer Services*, *18*(6), 555–561. doi:10.1016/j.jretconser.2011.08.004

Tsai, M. H., & Wang, Y. (2021). Analyzing twitter data to evaluate people's attitudes towards public health policies and events in the era of covid-19. *International Journal of Environmental Research and Public Health*, *18*(12), 6272. Advance online publication. doi:10.3390/ijerph18126272 PMID:34200576

Turner, D. (2016). 'Only connect': Unifying the social in social work and social media. *Journal of Social Work Practice*, *30*(3), 313–327. doi:10.1080/02650533.2016.1215977

Turner, D., Bennison, G., Megele, C., & Fenge, L. A. (2016). Social work and social media: Best friends or natural enemies? *Social Work Education*, *35*(3), 241–244. doi:10.1080/02615479.2016.1164283

Turner, F. J. (Ed.). (2017). *Social work treatment: Interlocking theoretical approaches*. Oxford University Press.

Twumasi, M. A., Jiang, Y., Ding, Z., Wang, P., & Abgenyo, W. (2022). The mediating role of access to financial services in the effect of financial literacy on household income: The case of rural Ghana. *SAGE Open*, *12*(1), 215824402210799. doi:10.1177/21582440221079921

Udovita, P. V. M. V. D. (2020). Conceptual review on dimensions of digital transformation in modern era. *International Journal of Scientific and Research Publications*, *10*(2), 520–529. doi:10.29322/IJSRP.10.02.2020.p9873

Ulas, D. (2019). Digital transformation process and SMEs. *Procedia Computer Science*, *158*, 662–671. doi:10.1016/j.procs.2019.09.101

Ullah, W., & Haidery, K. (2019). Analyzing the Spatiotemporal Patterns in Green Spaces for Urban Studies Using Location-Based Social Media Data. *ISPRS International Journal of Geo-Information*, *8*(11), 506. Advance online publication. doi:10.3390/ijgi8110506

Uma Ganesh. (2022). *Need of the hour: Social media an absolute must for banks*. Available at: https://www.financialexpress.com/industry/banking-finance/need-of-the-hour-social-media-an-absolute-must-for-banks/2416559/

United Nations. (1948). *Universal declaration of human rights*. United Nations. https://www.un.org/en/about-us/universal-declaration-of-human-rights

Uppal, R. K. (2008). Information Technology Changing Performance of Banking Industry-Emerging Challenges and New Potentials. *Gyan Management Journal*, *2*(1), 76–99.

Urbach, N., Drews, P., & Ross, J. (2017). Digital business transformation and the changing role of the IT function. *MIS Quarterly Executive*, *16*(2), 1–4.

Vakeel, K. A., & Panigrahi, P. K. (2018). Social media usage in E-government: Mediating role of government participation. *Journal of Global Information Management, 26*(1), 1–19. Advance online publication. doi:10.4018/JGIM.2018010101

Van Nguyen, H., Ha, G. H., Nguyen, D. N., Doan, A. H., & Phan, H. T. (2022). Understanding financial literacy and associated factors among adult population in a low-middle income country. *Heliyon, 8*(6), e09638. doi:10.1016/j.heliyon.2022.e09638 PMID:35677404

Vandana Ahuja. (2020). *The 7 Functional Benefits of social media for the banking industry.* Available at: https://customerthink.com/the-7-functional-benefits-of-social-media-for-the-banking-industry/

Venigalla, A. S. M., Chimalakonda, S., & Vagavolu, D. (2020). *Mood of India during Covid-19-an interactive web portal based on emotion analysis of Twitter data.* Paper presented at the Conference companion publication of the 2020 on computer supported cooperative work and social computing. 10.1145/3406865.3418567

Venkatesh, V., Thong, J. Y. L., & Xu, X. (2012). Consumer acceptance and use of information technology: Extending the unified theory of acceptance and use of technology. *Management Information Systems Quarterly, 36*(1), 157–178. doi:10.2307/41410412

Ventola, C. L. (2014). Social media and health care professionals: Benefits, risks, and best practices. *P&T, 39*(7), 491. PMID:25083128

Verhoef, P. C., Broekhuizen, T., Bart, Y., Bhattacharya, A., Dong, J. Q., Fabian, N., & Haenlein, M. (2021). Digital transformation: A multidisciplinary reflection and research agenda. *Journal of Business Research, 122*, 889–901. doi:10.1016/j.jbusres.2019.09.022

Vial, G. (2019). Understanding digital transformation: A review and a research agenda. *The Journal of Strategic Information Systems, 28*(2), 118–144. doi:10.1016/j.jsis.2019.01.003

Videovice.com. (2019). Make the World Greta Again. *Vice.* https://video.vice.com/en_us/video/vice-make-the-world-greta-again/5ca5f6cbbe40770ec567d7b7

Vinayamoorthi, G., & Thirupathi, M. (2020). Consumer's Adoption of Digital Wallets With Special Reference to Bangalore City. *Shanlax International Journal of Management, 8*(2), 108–113. doi:10.34293/management.v8i2.3429

Viviani, M., Crocamo, C., Mazzola, M., Bartoli, F., Carrà, G., & Pasi, G. (2021). Assessing vulnerability to psychological distress during the COVID-19 pandemic through the analysis of microblogging content. *Future Generation Computer Systems, 125*, 446–459. doi:10.1016/j.future.2021.06.044 PMID:34934256

Voomets, K., Riitsalu, L., & Siibak, A. (2021). Improving financial literacy via social media: The case of Kogumispäevik. *Eesti Haridusteaduste Ajakiri =. Estonian Journal of Education, 9*(2), 127–154. doi:10.12697/eha.2021.9.2.06

Voorberg, W. H., Bekkers, V. J. J. M., & Tummers, L. G. (2015). A Systematic Review of Co-Creation and Co-Production: Embarking on the social innovation journey. *Public Management Review, 17*(9), 1333–1357. Advance online publication. doi:10.1080/14719037.2014.930505

Voshel, E. H., & Wesala, A. (2015). Social media & social work ethics: Determining best practices in an ambiguous reality. *Journal of Social Work Values and Ethics, 12*(1), 67–76.

Vrontis, D., Christofi, M., Pereira, V., Tarba, S., Makrides, A., & Trichina, E. (2022). Artificial intelligence, robotics, advanced technologies and human resource management: A systematic review. *International Journal of Human Resource Management, 33*(6), 1237–1266. doi:10.1080/09585192.2020.1871398

Vrontis, D., Makrides, A., Christofi, M., & Thrassou, A. (2021). Social media influencer marketing: A systematic review, integrative framework and future research agenda. *International Journal of Consumer Studies*, *45*(4), 617–644. doi:10.1111/ijcs.12647

Waddock. (2004). Creating Corporate Accountability: Foundational Principles to Make Corporate Citizenship Real. *Journal of Business Ethics, 50*(4), 313-327.

Wagner, S. H., & Gilbert, M. C. (2018). Social work educators' evaluations of regulatory boards. *The Right for the Elderly to Commit Suicide*, *15*(2), 81.

Wahi, A. K., Medury, Y., & Misra, R. K. (2014). Social Media: The Core of Enterprise 2.0. [July.]. *International Journal of Service Science, Management, Engineering, and Technology*, *5*(3), 1–15. doi:10.4018/ijssmet.2014070101

Wang, H., Xiong, L., Guo, J., Lu, M., & Meng, Q. (2023). Predicting the antecedents of discontinuous usage intention of mobile government social media during public health emergencies. *International Journal of Disaster Risk Reduction*, *87*, 103582. Advance online publication. doi:10.1016/j.ijdrr.2023.103582

Waring, R. L., & Buchanan, F. R. (2010). Social networking web sites: The legal and ethical aspects of pre-employment screening and employee surveillance. *Journal of Human Resources Education*, *4*(2), 14–23.

Warner, K. S., & Wäger, M. (2019). Building dynamic capabilities for digital transformation: An ongoing process of strategic renewal. *Long Range Planning*, *52*(3), 326–349. doi:10.1016/j.lrp.2018.12.001

Webster, C. W. R., & Leleux, C. (2018). Smart governance: Opportunities for technologically-mediated citizen co-production. *Information Polity*, *23*(1), 95–110. Advance online publication. doi:10.3233/IP-170065

Weiner, B. (2012). *An attributional theory of motivation and emotion*. Springer Science & Business Media.

Wen. (2021). *Innovative, ADM Machine in Jayapura City Government Simplifies Administrative Affairs*. https://bit.ly/3MMtH2T

Westwood, J. (2014). *Social work and social media: An introduction to applying social work principles to social media*.

Wicks, R. H. (2013). Media information processing. In *Psychology of entertainment* (pp. 103–120). Routledge.

Widyastuti, M., & Hermanto, Y. B. (2022). The effect of financial literacy and social media on micro capital through financial technology in the creative industry sector in East Java. *Cogent Economics & Finance*, *10*(1), 2087647. doi:10.1080/23322039.2022.2087647

Wijayanti, N., & Kartawinata, B. R. (2022). Effect of financial literacy, financial confidence, external locus of control, on personal finance management (object of study on East Java students). *Budapest International Research and Critics Institute-Journal (BIRCI-Journal)*, *5*(4), 30106–30114. doi:10.33258/birci.v5i4.7171

Wike, R., Silver, L., Fetterolf, J., Huang, C., Austin, S., Clancy, L., & Gubbala, S. (2022). *Social media seen as mostly good for democracy across many nations, but US is a major outlier*. Pew Research Center's Global Attitudes Project.

Willke, H. (2007). *Smart governance: governing the global knowledge society*. Campus Verlag.

Willoughby, M. (2019). A review of the risks associated with children and young people's social media use and the implications for social work practice. *Journal of Social Work Practice*, *33*(2), 127–140. doi:10.1080/02650533.2018.1460587

Wiryanto, W. (2019). Replication of the Population Administration Service Innovation Model in Indonesia. *INOBIS: Jurnal Inovasi Bisnis Dan Manajemen Indonesia*, *3*(1), 27–40. doi:10.31842/jurnal-inobis.v3i1.118

Woodcock, J., & Johnson, M. R. (2019). Live streamers on Twitch. tv as social media influencers: Chances and challenges for strategic communication. *International Journal of Strategic Communication, 13*(4), 321–335. doi:10.1080/1553118X.2019.1630412

Wulan, R. R., & Mustam, M. (2017). Improving Service Quality in the Context of Bureaucratic Reform in the Land Office of Semarang City. *Journal of Public Policy and Management Review, 6*(3), 1–20. doi:10.14710/jppmr.v6i3.16740

Wüst, K., Kostiainen, K., Delius, N., & Capkun, S. (2022, November). Platypus: A Central Bank Digital Currency with Unlinkable Transactions and Privacy-Preserving Regulation. In *Proceedings of the 2022 ACM SIGSAC Conference on Computer and Communications Security* (pp. 2947-2960). 10.1145/3548606.3560617

Xie, J., Ye, L., Huang, W., & Ye, M. (2021). Understanding FinTech platform adoption: Impacts of perceived value and perceived risk. *Journal of Theoretical and Applied Electronic Commerce Research, 16*(5), 1893–1911. doi:10.3390/jtaer16050106

Yadav, R. K., Bagga, T., & Johar, S. (2020). E–governance impact on ease of doing business in India. *PalArch's Journal of Archaeology of Egypt/Egyptology, 17*(7), 6188-6203.

Yang, C., Xiao, M., Ding, X., Tian, W., Zhai, Y., Chen, J., Liu, L., & Ye, X. (2019). Exploring human mobility patterns using geo-tagged social media data at the group level. In Journal of Spatial Science (Vol. 64, Issue 2). doi:10.1080/14498596.2017.1421487

Yang, D., Qu, B., & Cudre-Mauroux, P. (2021). Location-Centric Social Media Analytics: Challenges and Opportunities for Smart Cities. *IEEE Intelligent Systems, 36*(5), 3–10. Advance online publication. doi:10.1109/MIS.2020.3009438

Yanto, H., Ismail, N., Kiswanto, K., Rahim, N. M., & Baroroh, N. (2021). The roles of peers and social media in building financial literacy among the millennial generation: A case of indonesian economics and business students. *Cogent Social Sciences, 7*(1), 1947579. doi:10.1080/23311886.2021.1947579

Yanto, H., Kiswanto, Baroroh, N., Hajawiyah, A., & Rahim, N. M. (2022). The roles of entrepreneurial skills, financial literacy, and digital literacy in maintaining MSMEs during the COVID-19 pandemic. *Asian Economic and Financial Review, 12*(7), 504–517. doi:10.55493/5002.v12i7.4535

Yanuar, R. M. (2019). Public Service Innovation (Case Study: Public Safety Center (PSC) 119 Bantul Regency as Health and Emergency Services). *Jurnal Ilmu Pemerintahan, 04*(0274), 20. doi:10.31629/kemudi.v4i1.1335

Yarchi, M., Baden, C., & Kligler-Vilenchik, N. (2021). Political polarization on the digital sphere: A cross-platform, over-time analysis of interactional, positional, and affective polarization on social media. *Political Communication, 38*(1-2), 98–139. doi:10.1080/10584609.2020.1785067

Ye, X., & Andris, C. (2021). Spatial social networks in geographic information science. In International Journal of Geographical Information Science (Vol. 35, Issue 12). doi:10.1080/13658816.2021.2001722

Yellow, S. M. R. (2020). *Social Media Report.* Yellow. https://www.yellow.com.au/social-media-report/ accessed on August 12, 2023.

Yi, G., Zainuddin, N. M. M., & Bt Abu Bakar, N. A. (2021). Conceptual model on internet banking acceptance in China with social network influence. *Int. J. Inf. Vis., 5*(2), 177–186. doi:10.30630/joiv.5.2.403

Yin, H., Yang, S., & Li, J. (2020). *Detecting topic and sentiment dynamics due to COVID-19 pandemic using social media.* Paper presented at the Advanced Data Mining and Applications: 16th International Conference, ADMA 2020, Foshan, China. 10.1007/978-3-030-65390-3_46

Yin, R. K. (2005). *Case study research, design and method.* London: Sage Publications Ltd. https://www.firstpost.com/tech/news-analysis

Yin, R. K. (2009). Case study research, design and method. London: Sage Publications Ltd.

Ying, F., Dartey, S., Ahakwa, I., Odai, L. A., Bright, D., & Amoabeng, S. M. (2021). Ascertaining the perceived risks and benefits of social media usage on the behavioural intent of employees: study of the banking sectors in Ga-West municipality: mediating role of user satisfaction. *International Research Journal of Advanced Engineering and Science,* *6*(1), 109–116.

Young, J. C., Arthur, R., Spruce, M., & Williams, H. T. P. (2021). Social sensing of heatwaves. *Sensors (Basel), 21*(11), 3717. Advance online publication. doi:10.339021113717 PMID:34073608

Youth in India. (2022). *4ᵗʰ issue.* Ministry of Statistics and Programme Implementation.

Yuan, Y. P., Dwivedi, Y. K., Tan, G. W. H., Cham, T. H., Ooi, K. B., Aw, E. C. X., & Currie, W. (2023). Government digital transformation: Understanding the role of government social media. *Government Information Quarterly, 40*(1), 101775. doi:10.1016/j.giq.2022.101775

Yusriadi, Y. (2018). *Change Management in Bureaucratic Reform Towards Information Technology (IT).* Jurnal Mitra Manajemen. doi:10.52160/ejmm.v2i2.39

Zaitul, Z., & Ilona, D. (2022). Is financial literacy associated with SME sustainability during COVID-19? *KnE Social Sciences,* 100–115. doi:10.18502/kss.v7i6.10613

Zeng, D., Chen, H., Lusch, R., & Li, S. H. (2010). Social media analytics and intelligence. *IEEE Intelligent Systems, 25*(6), 13–16. doi:10.1109/MIS.2010.151

Zhang, S., Zhen, F., Wang, B., Li, Z., & Qin, X. (2022). Coupling Social Media and Agent-Based Modelling: A Novel Approach for Supporting Smart Tourism Planning. *Journal of Urban Technology, 29*(2), 79–97. Advance online publication. doi:10.1080/10630732.2020.1847987

Zhang, X., Yang, Y., Zhang, Y., & Zhang, Z. (2020). Designing tourist experiences amidst air pollution: A spatial analytical approach using social media. *Annals of Tourism Research, 84,* 102999. Advance online publication. doi:10.1016/j.annals.2020.102999

Zhao, B., & Sui, D. Z. (2017). True lies in geospatial big data: Detecting location spoofing in social media. *Annals of GIS, 23*(1), 1–14. Advance online publication. doi:10.1080/19475683.2017.1280536

Zhao, J., & Li, T. (2021). Social capital, financial literacy, and rural household entrepreneurship: A mediating effect analysis. *Frontiers in Psychology, 12,* 724605. doi:10.3389/fpsyg.2021.724605 PMID:34512479

Zhou, L., Wang, W., Xu, J. D., Liu, T., & Gu, J. (2018, November). Perceived Information Transparency in B2C e-commerce: An Empirical Investigation. *Information & Management, 55*(7), 912–927. Advance online publication. doi:10.1016/j.im.2018.04.005

Zhu, L., Yu, T., Liu, Y., & Zhou, L. (2020). Analyses on the Spatial Distribution Characteristics of Urban Rental Housing Supply and Demand Hotspots Based on Social Media Data. *2020 5th IEEE International Conference on Big Data Analytics, ICBDA 2020.* 10.1109/ICBDA49040.2020.9101317

Zhuravskaya, E., Petrova, M., & Enikolopov, R. (2020). Political effects of the internet and social media. *Annual Review of Economics*, *12*(1), 415–438. doi:10.1146/annurev-economics-081919-050239

Zhu, T., & Xiao, J. J. (2022). Consumer financial education and risky financial asset holding in China. *International Journal of Consumer Studies*, *46*(1), 56–74. doi:10.1111/ijcs.12643

Ziyadin, S., Suieubayeva, S., & Utegenova, A. (2020). Digital transformation in business. In Digital Age: Chances, Challenges and Future 7 (pp. 408-415). Springer International Publishing. doi:10.1007/978-3-030-27015-5_49

Zook, M., Graham, M., Shelton, T., & Gorman, S. (2010). Volunteered Geographic Information and Crowdsourcing Disaster Relief: A Case Study of the Haitian Earthquake. *World Medical & Health Policy*, *2*(2), 6–32. doi:10.2202/1948-4682.1069

Zul. (2021). *Jayapura City Government Makes It Easy for People to Print Population Documents*. https://bit.ly/3OaBvwr

About the Contributors

Chandan Chavadi is the Dean & Professor of the Presidency Business School, Presidency College, Bengaluru. A PhD from Karnatak University, Dharwad, and an MBA (Mktg.) He holds a primary degree in B.E. (E&C). He has two years of corporate experience before his moving to academics. He has been in academics for the last 21 years. He has 32 papers & 2 book reviews to his credit, published in reputed journals and magazines such as ABDC-C journals, Web of Science, Scopus, UGC Care list and other indexed journals. Under Google scholar indices, he has total citations of 90, h-index of 6 & i10-index of 4. His paper has been accepted for publication in the IIM –A Vikalpa. Five of his research papers were recently published in the IIM Kozhikode Society And Management Review journal, IIM-Shillong Journal of Management Science, Business Perspective & Research journal of K J Somaiya Institute of Management, the MDI journal "Vision", and IIM-Lucknow journal "Metamorphosis". He is the recipient of Labdhi Bhandari Best Paper Award for the 7th IIM-A International Marketing Conference held on 11th to 13th Jan 2017. He is a recognized PhD Guide in Management for Bangalore City University.

* * *

Munir Ahmad is a Ph.D. in Computer Science with over 23 years of extensive experience in spatial data development, management, processing, visualization, and quality control. He has dedicated expertise in open data, crowdsourced data, volunteered geographic information, and spatial data infrastructure. A seasoned professional with extensive knowledge in the field, he has served as a trainer for the latest spatial technologies. With a passion for research and over 25 publications in the same field, he obtained his Ph.D. degree in Computer Science from Preston University Pakistan, in 2022. He is committed to advancing the industry and sharing knowledge through his expertise and experience. #SpatialData #GIS #GeoTech.

Ganesh B. is Academic Director, Am Maxwell International Institute for Education and Research, Karnataka, India.

Seenivasan B. is serving as Assistant Professor of Commerce in Sacred Heart College, Tirupattur from 2012-13. He is serving in the field of higher education from the year 2004 (19 Years of experience). He completed under graduation in commerce in Sacred Heart College with Fr. Panambara Medal, M.Com and M.Phil in Commerce in Loyola College Chennai with Gold Medals. He also cleared the UGC-NET in 2010 and completed doctorate in Commerce in the field of ATMs and Debit Card payments. He is focused on research with more than 15 publications at International level and National level. He is renowned for expertise in Income Tax and Marketing.

Macherla Bhagyalakshmi is working as Assistant professor, Department of Professional Studies, Christ University, Bangalore and she is having 25 years of teaching and research experience. She has published research papers in Scopus, UGC approved and leading National and International journals, presented papers in various International and national conferences.

David Winster Praveenraj D. is a Faculty, Management Consultant, Soft Skills Trainer and a Motivational Speaker. He is into conduct of Management Development Programmes, Personality Development & Personal Effectiveness Programmes for executives at various levels. He is rendering consultancy services in Drafting & Implementation of Standard Operating Procedures, Design of Performance Management Systems, Drafting HR policies, Competency Mapping, Implementation of Quality Circles, arriving at Management Policies, Market Research, Advertising and Branding for varied industries out of which a major contribution is for the RMG Industry. Dr.David has a flair for adopting novel teaching methodologies and experiential learning toolsin delivery of courses and the various programmes he conducts.

Kavitha Desai is a Professor in the Department of Professional Studies, CHRIST (Deemed to be University), Bangalore. Her research interests mainly includes Supply Chain Management, Digital Financial Literacy, Organizational Culture etc. She obtained PhD in Commerce from Sri Venkateswara University, Tirupathi. She has more than 20 years of research, teaching and administrative experience and has published several research papers in journals of national and international repute with 71 citations and h index of 4. Having guided 7 PhD. scholars, she has also been associated with research and consultancy projects in the area of Commerce and Management. She has presented research papers at several International and National Conferences. She is on the boards of reputed academic institutions and has organised several national and international conferences and workshops.

Joel Jebadurai Devapitchai is currently working as Assistant Professor in Department of MBA, St. Joseph's College of Engineering, OMR, Chennai. He is having 6 years of experience in teaching and 4 years in research. He has undertaken the Major Research Project sponsored by Indian Council of Social sciences Research, New Delhi, India. He has published various research articles in various national and international journals.

Sudha E. is working as an Assistant Professor in CHRIST (Deemed to be University), Bangalore Yeshwanthpur campus. She holds Finance from Vellalar College for Women, Erode Affiliated to Bharathiar University Coimbatore. Her research title is based on An Analytical Evaluation on Green Accounting and Disclosure Practices of Selected Indian Companies. She clinched UGC-NET in Commerce during 2019 and qualified module 1 of Executive Level in ICSI. She completed M.Com from Salem Sowdeswari College and MBA from Bharathidasan University. She was graduated from Periyar University, Salem. She uprights in academic writing, and has excellent interpersonal and communication skills. She is an active researcher and published 2 articles in Scopus indexed Journal, 6 articles under UGC CARE listed journals and Presented 16 research papers in National and International conferences. In recent times, she has published a book on "Financial Accounting". She demonstrates her strength in Costing, Accounting, Finance and Taxation.

Manoj G. is currently working as Assistant Professor in Department of Management Studies, VelTech Rangarajan Dr. Sagunthala R&D Institute of Science and Technology (Deemed to be University), Avadi, Chennai. He has more than 8 years 5 months of teaching experience with specialization in HR and Marketing. He Holds a B.Sc., M.B.A., M. Phil., and Ph.D. in Management from Bharathidasan University, Trichy. He has published several articles including in many Scopus Indexed Journals, Web of Science, UGC Care Journals and has presented papers in many National and International Conferences. He has authored and Published Seven Books (Human Resource Management, Marketing Management, International Business Management, Management accounting, Research Methodology, Strategic Management, Entrepreneurship Development) with ISBN. He is an Editorial Board member of VITP Journal. He has Published a patent titled "Device to track Tax Lien". He also holds membership in various Professional Bodies. He has attended many Seminars, FDP and Workshops. He has been honored by the Puducherry Research Institute of Management, Education and Science organization with the "Young Achiever Award" for the year 2021 in recognition and appreciation for his outstanding contributions. He has occupied many responsible positions and has also served as the Head of the Department and has actively contributed towards placement of students.

Vinayagamoorthi G. is an Assistant Professor of Commerce at Alagappa University at Karaikudi. He is guiding 4 Ph.D. scholars and M.Phil scholars, He is having 54 citations and 3 h-Index, and he has published several research papers in Scopus, UGC approved and leading International journals, and presented papers in national and international conferences. His areas of expertise are Business, General Management.

Sathis Kumar Ganesan (popularly known as Professor GSK)'s philosophy of life is "Be the Cause of Changes" that transform the generations. Dr Sathis Kumar envisioned to serve the society towards sustainability in terms of social, economic and philosophical ideologies through sharing knowledge by learning, researching, teaching and outreach activities. Professor GSK has more than 15 years of academic understanding and evidence-based research observations in economics, society, public policy, and sustainability. His subject area of expertise and practice are Macro Economic Analysis, Business Environment and Entrepreneurship in Emerging Economies, Sustainability, Evidence-based Research Intelligence, and Application of Artificial Intelligence, Big Data and Business Analytics for Public Policy Making. At present, Professor GSK serves as a Chief Policy Researcher, at Centre for Excellence in Policy Research and Insights, Chennai. Earlier, he served as Chief Learning Officer at Dr. GSK's Social Lab, Bangalore; Associate Professor at Presidency University, Bengaluru, Karnataka; Assistant Professor at Great Lakes Institute of Management, Chennai, The Gandhigram Rural Institute – Deemed University, Dindigul, and Alagappa University, Karaikudi; and Project Associate at Indian Institute of Technology-Madras (IIT-M), Chennai, Tamil Nadu. He is also a seasoned entrepreneur with two successful learning attempts in EdTech startups – one of that was experimented with his own business management students. Professor GSK is also serving as honorary consultant for the non-government organizations working for society and sustainability, specifically new generation early start-ups and Community Based Organizations.

Vimala Govindaraju is working as University Lecturer from Faculty of Language and Communication, University Malaysia Sarawak, Malaysia.

Ilham, M.Si, is a permanent lecturer at the Public Administration Study Program, Faculty of Social and Political Sciences (FISIP) Cenderawasih University Jayapura. Books ever written, including; one of the authors of the anthology "Observing Technological Readiness in the Campus System" and the first author of a book entitled "Pandemi in Mother Earth: Literature Study of Handling the Covid-19 Pandemic in Indonesia" published by Syiah Kuala University Press, as well as the author of the book "E-Governance" which published on deepublish, is also one of the authors of a book entitled "Women's Forest: Local Wisdom of the Tobati-Enggros People in Caring for Mangrove Forest Ecosystems in the Youtefa Bay Area, Jayapura City, Papua".

U. A. Piumi Ishanka obtained her Master's degree and Ph.D. in 2015 and 2018 respectively from the Graduate School of Engineering, Nagaoka University of Technology, Japan. She worked as a Software Engineer for two years and joined Sabaragamuwa University of Sri Lanka in 2011. Currently, she is serving as a senior lecturer attached to the Faculty of Computing. Her research interests include Intelligent System Applications and Soft Computing.

Ashok J. is currently working as Professor in CHRIST (Deemed to be University) Bangalore in School of Business & Management. He is a doctorate in Human Resource Management. He has over 25 years of exposure to Teaching, Research and Industry. He has developed, designed and delivered many Management Development Programmes for senior and middle level managers. He has published several research papers in National & International Journal of repute and presented many papers in conferences. So far, he has successfully guided 8 PhD scholars.

Sudarvel J. is Assistant Professor, Department of Management, Karpagam Academy of Higher Education, Coimbatore, India.

Logasakthi Kandasamy is currently associated with Universal Business School, Universal AI University, designated as an Associate Professor -HR. His research work broadly covers in the area of OB-HRM and social sciences. Research work of Dr.Logasakthi has been published in various titles such as Emotional Intelligence, Stress Management, Pedagogical design and Sustainable Learning Outcome. The published papers in the reputed journals were indexed in Scopus, ABDC & SCI. Basically, he is a NLP Trainer who offered more than hundred training programmes to the Corporate and Teaching fraternity in the name of Management Development Program, Executive Development Program.

Ravishankar Krishnan has more than 13 years of wide-ranging experience in teaching, research, administration and industrial relations. He has worked in Veltech and other reputed institutions. He holds a Master's Degree in Management Studies from Periyar Institute of Management Studies and a Ph.D. from Anna University, Guindy, Chennai. His teaching and research are in the field of Logistics, Supply Chain, Human Resources, and Sustainability. He has published and indexed more than 10 research articles in Scopus and ABDC (B Category). Also, more than 25 research articles in various peer-reviewed journals. He actively participated and presented various papers in National and International level seminars/conferences. He has worked on an AICTE funded research project on "Eradication of Plastic Bags'' and handled a major funded project as a Project Director from ICSSR on "Impact of Digital Media and E-learning Solutions on Contemporary Management Education". He has cleared UGC-NET and TN-SET exams.

Banujan Kuhaneswaran received his Bachelor of Science degree in 2019 with the Second Class Upper Division from Sabaragamuwa University of Sri Lanka. He is currently attached to the Department of Computing and Information Systems as a Lecturer in Computer Science. His research interests include Data Mining, Knowledge Management, Ontology Modeling, Business Process Simulation.

Devaraja Nayaka M.'s work experience includes 9 years in Academics. He has been teaching Corporate Governance, International Business, Research interests include Corporate Governance, Corporate Financial Reporting.

Maruthamuthu M. is an Assistant Professor (T) in the Department of Business Administration, Government Arts and Science College, Kadayanallur, Tamilnadu, India. The author has completed Ph.D. from Periyar University, Salem, Tamilnadu and has Marketing Management as one of the interesting field in Management. He has many publications and is presently workings on many papers. His other areas of specialization include Entrepreneurship, HRM, Service Marketing and etc. Number of scholars are doing their research under his supervision and served as Internal Examiner for some scholars in his previous workplace. He have teaching and research experience more than 7 years on the same.

Sudha M. is working as Associate professor of Department of Management Studies in Acharya Institute of Graduate Studies in Bangalore, which is NAAC Re-accredited A grade college and she is having more than 17 years teaching and research experience. She is having published several research papers in Scopus, UGC approved and leading international journals and presented papers in national and international conferences.

Mariyappan M. S. R. is Dean School of Management, Veltech Rangarajan Dr Sagunthala R&D Institute of Science and Technology, Chennai.

Thirupathi Manickam, M.Com, M.Phil, B.Ed, TN-SET, KSET, Ph.D., is presently working as an Assistant professor in the Department of Professional Studies at Christ University, Bangalore. It is one of the leading institution in Bangalore, Karnataka, and the institution is Accreditated by NIRF, NBA and NAAC Accredited university. He has more than 7 years of teaching and Research experience. He has 44 citations and 3 h-Index. He has published 22 research papers in Scopus, Web of Science, UGC-CARE, and UGC-approved and leading International journals and 11 presented papers in national and international conferences. He has also participated in over 40 seminars, conferences, FDP & workshops at the National and International Levels. His areas of expertise are Financial Accounting, Corporate Accounting, Financial Management, Management Accounting, Taxation, Digital Marketing and Technology Management.

Haritha Muniraju is having 13years of teaching and research experience in commerce and management at various institutions. She also performed various administrative roles and responsibilities such as Program Coordinator, Examination in charge and IQAC Coordinator. She has authored 12 books in commerce and management and committee member for various research associations.

Satheesh Pandian Murugan is presently working as Assistant Professor in the Department of Economics and Centre for Research in Economics, Arumugam Pillai Seethai Ammal College, Tiruppattur, Sivaganga (Dt), Tamil Nadu, India. He is having Nine years of teaching experience along with the M.A., M.Phil., Ph.D., qualifications. He has earned his Ph.D from the Madurai Kamarajar University. He has published more than 10 research papers in his credit both in National and International level. His areas of research interests are Agricultural and Industrial Economics.

M. Zaenul Muttaqin, M.Si, is a lecturer at the Public Administration Study Program, Faculty of Social and Political Sciences (FISIP) Cenderawasih University Jayapura. His interests and expertise are public policy, communication and policy advocacy, human resource management.

Yosephina Ohoiwutun is head of the Postgraduate Masters of Public Administration Study Program at Cenderawasih University and a member of the Indonesian Association for Public Administration (IAPA) Central Leadership Council (DPP). Her interests and expertise are public policy, human resource management, and public service management.

Hridhya P. is working in Christ Univeristy as an Assistant Professor, specialised in the areas of finance, financial literacy, and investment decisions.

Elantheraiyan Perumal is an academician having 11years of experience in teaching, Industry research and administrative task and presently working as an Assistant Professor in School of Management Vel Tech Rangarajan Dr. Sagunthala R & D Institute of Science and Technology Avadi, Chennai- Tamil Nadu. Graduated in Physics from A.M. Jain College University of Madras (2006) and MBA (HR & Marketing) from Madha Engineering College Anna University Chennai (2008). Obtained PhD in Management from Bharathiar University Coimbatore in 2018.Research interests are Organisational Behaviour, Emotional Intelligence, Competency Mapping, Organic farming, Opinion Mining Supply Chain Management and other areas of General Management and also guided more than 80 MBA, BBA, BCOM projects. Published 17 research papers in various Scopus Indexed International journals &National Journals. Organized a series of National Conference and Management Meet every year and member of MISTE. Organized several National Seminars and workshops for the benefit of students in igniting their business and entrepreneurial spirit. Started as an HR in Telecom sector in 2008.Made a career shift and chose academics in 2009 due to passion for teaching and affinity towards students community development . Had gone as a resource person for various academic oriented programs and given career guidance to students of various domain. Interested in nurturing students potentialities and making them a healthy psychological being. Has a keen interest towards agriculture and farmers especially in organic farming sector. Envisages a better environment, economy and welfare of the farmers who are the back bone of our nation and economy, but still underrated compared to others. Has a desire to turn students into Agropreneurs for the betterment of the society and nation.

Hariharan R., MSc (F&CA), M.Phil., MBA, Ph.D., is currently working as Assistant Professor in School of Business and Management, CHRIST (Deemed to be University), Yeshwanthpur campus, Bangalore. He has 8 years of teaching and 11 years of research experience. He holds PhD degree in Finance (Banking Technology) from Department of Banking Technology, Pondicherry Central University, Puducherry. He has published almost 35 research papers include in Scopus, Web of science, Thomas Returners, UGC care list and peer viewed Journals. He has authored 10 books and 8 chapters in edited volume books in International and National publishers. He also holds 2 copy rights from Indian Copyright office, India and Filed one Patent in India Patent office. He has done his certification from Microsoft on Certified Business Management Specialist, module (finance & warehouse) and NSE on Financial Markets in AMFI (Mutual Fund Advisor) module of NCFM. He has been resource person and delivered guest lecturer for MBA Schools and Universities on topic of Data Analysis using Excel and other statistical software. His area of interest is Finance, Banking, Enterprise Resource Planning, Analytics, Information Technology and Statistical Packages.

Sankar Ganesh R. is Associate Professor, Department of Management Studies, Vel Tech Rangarajan Dr. Sagunthala R&D Institute of Science and Technology, Chennai, India.

Velmurugan R. is Professor in Commerce, Karpagam Academy of Higher Education, Coimbatore, India.

Baranihdharan S. is specialized in Finance Economics and Econometrics and Having 5 years research experience, 2 years of Industrial experience and 6 years of teaching experience. He has Published 5 patent, 37 research articles in international and national journal which are indexed in Scopus, WoS, Proquest, ABDC, etc.

Thandayuthapani S. has more than 8 years of teaching experience with specialization in Finance and Marketing. He has worked in VelTech and reputed Institutions. He holds a B.Com., MBA., M. Phil., and Ph.D. in Management from Periyar University, Salem. He has published several articles including in many Scopus Indexed Journals, Web of Science, UGC Care Journals and has presented papers in many National and International Conferences. He has authored and Published one Book (Financial Management) with ISBN. He also holds membership in various Professional Bodies. He has attended many Seminars, FDP and Workshops. He has occupied many responsible positions and has also served as the Head of the Department and has actively contributed towards coordinating the students for various programmes.

Gopalakrishnan Subramaniyan is Head, Research and Development Cell, Project Director [ICSSR] & Associate Professor, Department of Commerce & Management, Acharya Institute of Graduate Studies, Bangalore. He has completed a Major Research Project on "Solid Waste Management" funded by ICSSR (Indian Council of Social Sciences Research). Has 25 years of experience including 12 years of industry and 13 years of teaching Management and Commerce subjects. He has International experience of 1 year working in Nigeria as an Assistant Professor, University of UYO, Nigeria. Published more than 30 articles in refereed journals with 58 citations, h-INDEX -3 and i10 INDEX – 1. He is also the Editor and Reviewer for Elsevier and other Journals.

Madhusudanan Sundaresan is Assistant Professor, PG Department of Social Work, Dwaraka Doss Goverdhan Doss Vaishnav College, Arumbakkam, Chennai.

Vince Tebay is a lecturer at the State Administration Science Faculty of Social and Political Sciences (FISIP), Cenderawasih University Jayapura. Her interests and expertise are the study of organizational behavior, public service management, and gender-based public policy.

Ravi V. has 15 years of teaching experience in Accounting and Finance subjects at various affiliated colleges at different capacities. The research areas are accounts, finance and social issues. Two international certification on conference and FDP has been attended during 2017-19 at Asia pacific and Cyberjaya University, Malaysia, also published research papers in various national and international journals along with one patent publication on Impact of insurance company's contribution towards the growth of SMEs.

Index

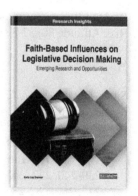

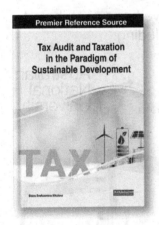

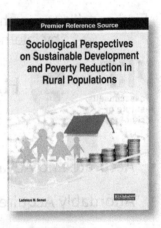

Printed in the United States
by Baker & Taylor Publisher Services

Printed in the United States
by Baker & Taylor Publisher Services